MUNDO)real

MEDIA edition

Teacher's Edition

1

CAMBRIDGE
UNIVERSITY PRESS

Edi
numen

© Editorial Edinumen, 2016

Authors:
Eduardo Aparicio, María Carmen Cabeza, Francisca Fernández, Patricia Fontanals,
Luisa Galán, Amelia Guerrero, Emilio José Marín, Celia Meana, Liliana Pereyra and Francisco Fidel Riva.
Coordination Team: Celia Meana.

ISBN - Teacher's Edition: 978-110-7473294

First published 2016
20 19 18 17 16 15 14 13 12 11 10 9 8 7 6 5 4

Printed in the Mexico by Editorial Impresora Apolo, S.A. de C.V.

Editorial Coordination:
Mar Menéndez

Cover Design:
Juanjo López

Design and Layout:
Juanjo López, Antonio Arias and Carlos Yllana

Cambridge University Press
32 Avenue of the Americas
New York, NY 10013

Editorial Edinumen
José Celestino Mutis, 4. 28028 Madrid. España
Telephone: (34) 91 308 51 42
Fax: (34) 91 319 93 09
e-mail: edinumen@edinumen.es
www.edinumen.es

TABLE OF CONTENTS

INTRODUCTION TO THE PROGRAM

STUDENT BOOK

APPENDIX

PROGRAM AT A GLANCE

Mundo Real Media Edition is a four-level Spanish language program designed for high school students that uses lively and compelling content, images, and video to teach the language that learners need to succeed in and outside the classroom.

Each level of *Mundo Real Media Edition* provides a complete curriculum of instruction for one year of high school Spanish.

 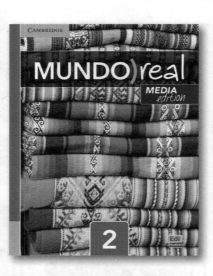  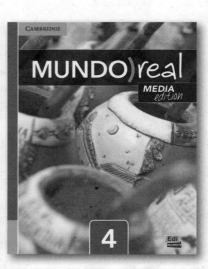

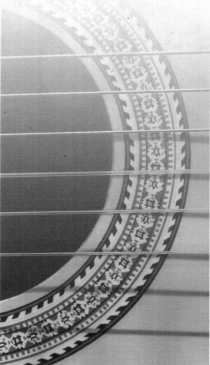   

Mundo Real Media Edition offers a communicative approach that focuses on functional, real-life language. The program's guided and manageable content encourages students to begin speaking the language immediately. With real-life themes, high-interest content, and natural speech, *Mundo Real* teaches the language relevant to students' lives.

Student Book

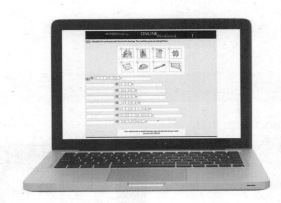

Online Workbook

Teacher's Edition

eBooks

Digital Master Guide

Cuaderno para hispanohablantes

ELEteca, **Cambridge / Edinumen's educational platform** (**https://cambridgespanish.edinumen.es**), offers **additional material** for teachers and students which expands and complements all three levels of the program.

STUDENT RESOURCES

STUDENT'S BOOK

Mundo Real Media Edition uses lively and compelling content, images, and video to teach real-world language. The student book's experiential format encourages the development of strong communicative skills, which will increase your comfort level in real-world settings.

EBOOK

Mundo Real Media Edition eBooks are fully interactive and fully integrated with the Learning Management System ELEteca. Integrated audio and a seamless connection to online video content, as well as online and offline modes for Mac, PC, iOS, and Android, make using your eBook simple.

ONLINE WORKBOOK

The *Mundo Real Media Edition* online workbook features a wide variety of activity types and exercises, and includes embedded video, a video note-taking feature, and speech recognition technology.

CUADERNO PARA HISPANOHABLANTES

The *Mundo Real Media Edition* Cuaderno para hispanohablantes is written exclusively for native speakers who have grown up speaking conversational Spanish, and includes sophisticated activities and lessons that expand on the Student's Book.

Mundo Real Media Edition features a wealth of digital resources designed to supplement and enhance the Student's Book. All are available in the rich, interactive world of *Mundo Real Media Edition* ELEteca—in one place, with one password.

Interactive Activities

Online Workbook and eBook Integration

The *Mundo Real Media Edition* Online Workbook and eBook are accessible through ELEteca, so you can access all of your digital resources in one place, using one password.

Gamification

"La Pasantía", a game that allows you to engage with the Spanish language in a fun context, as you compete to win a spot on the staff of a Spanish newspaper.

Mundo Real Media Edition contains a wealth of video content, which:
- highlights both the unit theme and the culture of the Spanish-speaking world
- clarifies difficult grammar points and language skills
- models authentic language and a wide variety of accents and dialects

¡Acción!

Mundo Real Media Edition features a brand new narrative video series that aligns with each chapter of the Student's Book, modeling and synthesizing the communicative skills of the text.

Video segments are connected but episodic, and set in and around a Latin American university. Real-life situations and activities –navigating a new city, shopping, playing and watching sports– model relevant language in context, building a student's ability to communicate outside the classroom.

Voces Latinas

Cultural video segments expand upon the cultural sections of the text, inviting students to explore the traditions and histories of different areas of the Spanish-speaking world.

Grammar Tutorials

These short clips can be used to introduce new grammar concepts, or to reinforce and review difficult skills. Explanations and examples are all in Spanish, encouraging critical thinking in the target language.

Casa del Español

These street interviews model the target grammar and vocabulary skills in an authentic and engaging context, and feature a wide range of language varieties and dialects.

ELETECA FOR TEACHERS

The **ELEteca** is an online learning management platform that provides additional teaching options with the following technology resources:

DIGITAL MASTER GUIDE

The Digital Master Guide is a Digital Teacher's Edition including related resources that allows teachers to access and use the materials dynamically anywhere, using any kind of device (iPad and Android tablets, PC and Apple computers), or in the classroom with a computer and an interactive whiteboard to engage students.

IMPORTANT: To download and install the Digital Master Guide, the teacher should first enter and register in ELEteca and follow the instructions to complete the process.

Assessments

A comprehensive bank of downloadable, editable assessments.

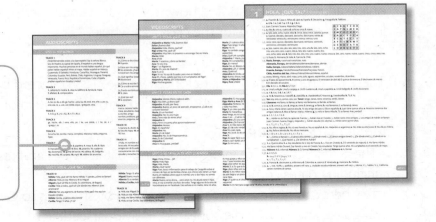

Appendix and extra resources

Downloadable documents with all the material needed to get the best experience from the course: audioscripts, videoscripts for *¡Acción!* Section, Workbook answer keys and audioscripts, User's Guide for the cooperative activities suggested for students on ELEteca.

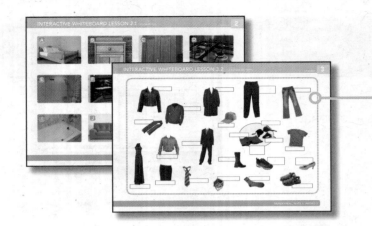

Interactive Whiteboard Lessons

The Interactive Whiteboard Lessons are additional resources which are downloadable from ELEteca and inter-referenced throughout the Teacher's Guide, that provide additional opportunities for teachers to present new material and for students to practice in a dynamic way.

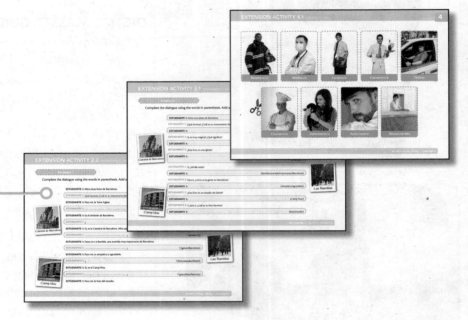

Extension Activities (Photocopiable)

The Extension Activities are downloadable from ELEteca and can be printed and distributed to students for classroom group activities that enhance learning.

ELETECA DATA MANAGEMENT SYSTEM

ELEteca collects data for the teachers to help adapt their pedagogical approach, gathering information on student use of the online activities and tests and how well students have performed on these. Teachers can use ELEteca to generate reports on individual students and for the class as a whole.

Class Reports

These reports summarize data for the whole class collected by ELEteca, based on individual student responses, allowing teachers to make decisions about student grouping and inform further review, revision, practice, and instruction.

Individual Student Reports

• These reports provide information on what activities and tests an individual student has completed and their scores, including dates completed.
• Teachers can retrieve the tests completed by students to gain further insight into a student's level of command of the language and provide personalized, individual feedback.

ACTIVATING YOUR DIGITAL INSTRUCTOR ACCESS

ELEteca is the Learning Management System that accompanies your *Mundo Real Media Edition* Student's Book.

To activate your ELEteca resources visit **https://cambridgespanish.edinumen.es**, and follow the instructions to create an account and activate your access code.

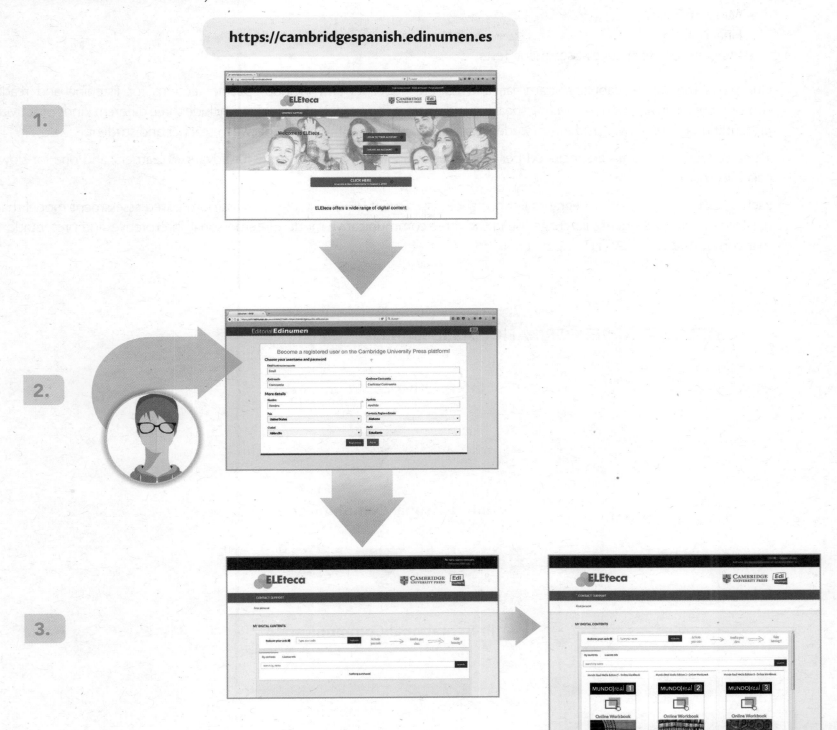

https://cambridgespanish.edinumen.es

1.

2.

3.

The *MundoReal Media Edition* testing program offers comprehensive means for evaluating student performance.

The Assessment Program Components include:

- Comprehensive ready-made test for each unit
- Additional Test Bank questions for customized assessment
- Midterm Exam
- Final Exam
- Integrated Performance Assessment Tests

Unit Tests measure vocabulary, grammar, and culture concepts and include specific sections for listening and reading comprehension, in addition to covering speaking and writing. The modules for speaking include three different kinds of activities: presentational, interactive (student-to-student) and communicative interaction between teacher and student.

Three editable Test Banks are included per unit: one for on-level assessment, one for advanced learners, and one for slower-paced learners.

Each unit also contains one Integrated Performance Assessment (IPA) Test. IPA is a classroom-based assessment model that is used for evaluating student's language use in the three communicative modes (interpersonal, interpretive, and presentational) that correspond to the ACTFL standards.

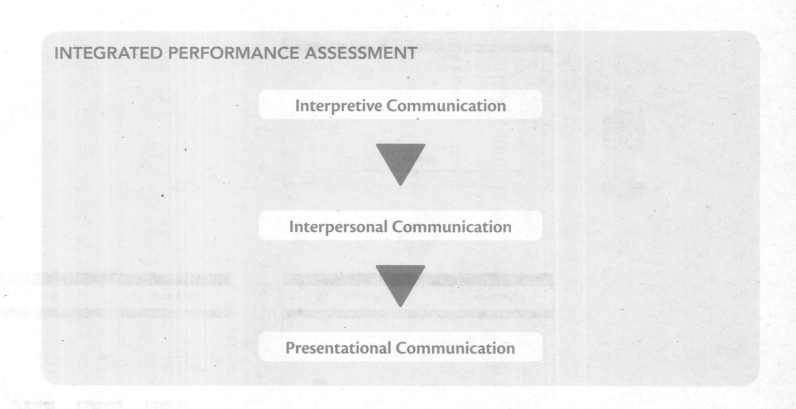

INTEGRATED PERFORMANCE ASSESSMENT

Interpretive Communication

Interpersonal Communication

Presentational Communication

UNIT OPENER

Objectives for the Unit Opener

This section provides a quick summary of objectives for the unit opener and how it connects the unit's learning outcomes.

Objectives for the Unit

The unit's learning objectives are an organizational tool for both the teacher and the student. Teachers can use them to preview what students will learn, and they serve as a way to assess whether students have mastered the main ideas and skills.

Unit Resources at a Glance

All of the teacher's resources available for the unit are listed here for quick reference.

Instructional Strategies

These provide specific recommendations to the teacher for presenting and teaching the material to students.

Common Core Standards

A correlation to the four strands of the Common Core Standards is provided in the Unit Opener, listing which activities in each section of the unit correspond to each of these strands.

Core Resources

This lists the specific instructional resources *Mundo Real Media Edition* provides for each section of the unit.

Objectives for the Lessons

Each section starts with a list of learning objectives that teachers can use as an organizational tool. Teachers can use them to preview what students will learn in this section, and they serve as a way to assess whether students have mastered the main ideas and skills.

Answers

An answer key is provided immediately below the activities for quick reference and to facilitate feedback to students.

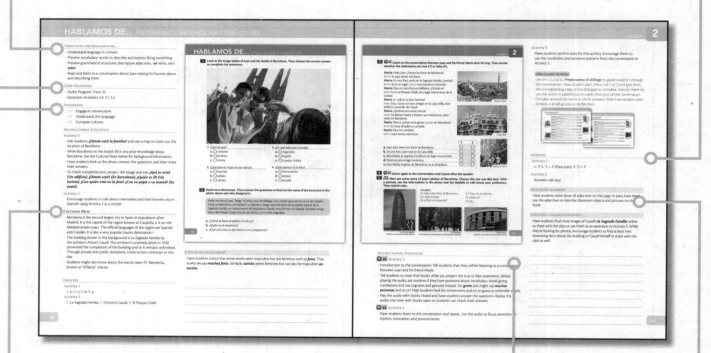

Cultural Notes

These notes provide support for the teacher, with additional cultural information to share with students, bringing Hispanic culture alive for students and motivating them to learn.

Extensions and Alternative Activities

These supplementary activities allow teachers to give students more practice, if needed.

Activity-Specific Instructional Strategies

These instructional strategies provide specific recommendations to the teacher for teaching the unit content and for guiding students on how to carry out specific activities.

Standards for Learning Languages

This lists the ACTFL Standards for Learning Languages covered in this section.

UNIT STRUCTURE

Each unit of *Mundo Real Media Edition* follows a consistent, clear sequence of instruction.

UNIT SECTION	PEDAGOGICAL PURPOSE
UNIDAD	**UNIT OPENER** • This is a visual introduction to the unit theme. Each unit focuses on a different real-world content area. • Discussion questions act as a springboard for students to begin using the language immediately, creatively adapting language they have learned previously to respond to new situations.
HABLAMOS DE...	**PREVIEWING LANGUAGE AND STRUCTURES** • A sample dialog, featuring engaging images related to the unit theme, previews important structures and vocabulary from the unit. • These dialogs immediately engage students in the language, improving their listening and reading comprehension skills.
COMUNICA	**COMMUNICATIVE FUNCTIONS** • Develops speaking skills and oral interaction using communicative structures and activities.
¡ACCIÓN!	**INTEGRATED LANGUAGE VIDEO** • Built around a video segment following the lives of students in Spain. This authentic language input not only strengthens comprehension and listening skills, but also acts as a model for speaking. • Before, during, and after viewing activities provide a structured approach to viewing the video. The video contextualizes the content of the unit in a familiar scenario.
PALABRA POR PALABRA	**LANGUAGE AND VOCABULARY** • Introduces high-frequency vocabulary, which is practiced and expanded throughout the unit.
GRAMÁTICA	**GRAMMAR IN CONTEXT** • Presents three to four grammar points in each unit. • *Gramática* allows students to examine and practice specific grammar points and language functions from the unit while enabling them to sharpen their listening and speaking skills. • Accessible and contextualized grammar charts and presentations provide students with added clarity.
DESTREZAS	**COMMUNICATIVE SKILLS** • Integrates key language skills (listening, reading comprehension, oral and written expression). • Provides guided strategies and activities related to the unit theme to further student comprehension and learning.
PRONUNCIACIÓN	**PRONUNCIATION** • Activities focus on the high-priority features of phonetics, stress, and intonation, to help students improve overall speech.
SABOR HISPANO	**CULTURE IN CONTEXT** • Presents different aspects of Hispanic cultures using images, maps, and other cultural realia to provide students a window into the Hispanic world.
RELATO	**COMPREHENSIVE PRACTICE** • Brings the unit's content together through a fictional text and encourages students to build their reading and listening comprehension skills.
EVALUACIÓN	**SELF-ASSESSMENT** • A built-in self-assessment for students to assess their knowledge of the content covered in each unit.
EN RESUMEN: VOCABULARIO/ GRAMÁTICA	**UNIT REVIEW** • A one-page glossary of the unit vocabulary and a one-page summary of grammar structures covered in each unit for easy reference and review. • Teacher's Edition models for students how to review vocabulary and grammar and provides instructional strategies to help students develop learning and studying skills.
AHORA COMPRUEBA	**CUMMULATIVE REVIEW** • A built-in cumulative self-assessment every two units for students to assess their knowledge of the content covered in the previous units. • Teachers can assign point value to each activity as a way for students to self-assess. If students achieve less than 80% on each activity, teachers can direct them to En resumen in the previous units for unit sections to review.

STUDENT RESOURCES

 Pair icon: indicates that the activity is designed to be done by students working in pairs.

 Group icon: indicates that the activity is designed to be done by students working in small groups or as a whole class.

 xx **Audio icon:** indicates recorded material either as part of an activity or a reading text.

 Language icon: provides additional language and grammar support in presentations and activities.

 Regional variation icon: provides examples of regional variations in the language.

 Recycling icon: provides a reminder of previously taught material that students will need to use in an activity.

EXPLORE A UNIT

A dynamic image provides a visual introduction to the unit theme. Each unit theme focuses on a different real-world content area.

A discussion question acts as a springboard for students to begin using the language immediately, creatively adapting language they have learned previously to respond to new situations.

UNIDAD

7 ¡CUÁNTAS COSAS!

- ¿Cómo es tu habitación?
- ¿Qué cosas tienes en tu habitación?
- ¿Te gusta tener una habitación ordenada o no es importante para ti?

Le encantan la música y la tecnología

196

In this unit, you will learn to:

- Describe objects and their uses
- Make comparisons
- Point out things
- Talk about larger quantities (100–999)
- Avoid repetition

Using
- *Para qué* and *para*
- Comparatives
- Demonstrative pronouns
- Direct object pronouns

Cultural Connections
- Share information about gift-giving and holidays in Hispanic countries, and compare cultural similarities

SABOR HISPANO
¡Viva el Carnaval!
- Bolivia, Ecuador y Perú

¡ACCIÓN!

197

Each unit of *Mundo Real Media Edition* contains eleven focused sections:

Hablamos de...	Destrezas / Pronunciación
Comunica	Sabor hispano
¡Acción!	Relato
Palabra por palabra	Evaluación
Gramática	En resumen

HABLAMOS DE..., a sample dialogue featuring engaging images related to the unit theme, previews important structures and vocabulary from the unit. These dialogues immediately engage students in the language, improving their listening and reading comprehension skills.

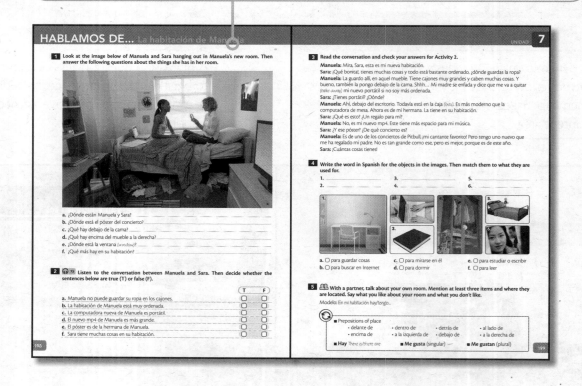

COMUNICA develops speaking skills and oral interaction using communicative structures and activities.

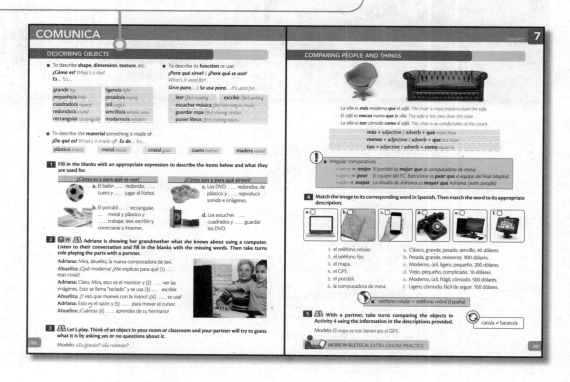

¡ACCIÓN! is built around a video segment following the lives of students in Spain. This authentic language input not only strengthens comprehension and listening skills, but also acts as a model for speaking.

Before, during, and after viewing activities provide a structured approach to viewing the video. The video contextualizes the content of the unit in a familiar scenario.

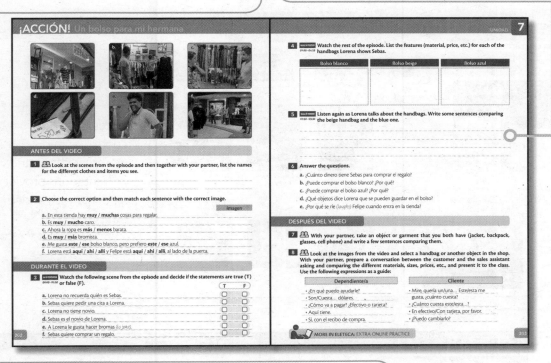

PALABRA POR PALABRA introduces high-frequency vocabulary, which is practiced and expanded throughout the unit.

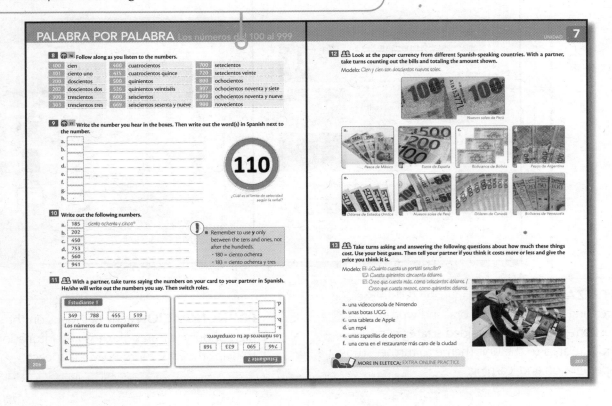

GRAMÁTICA presents three to four grammar points in each unit. **Gramática** allows students to examine and practice specific grammar points and language functions from the unit while enabling them to sharpen their listening and speaking skills.

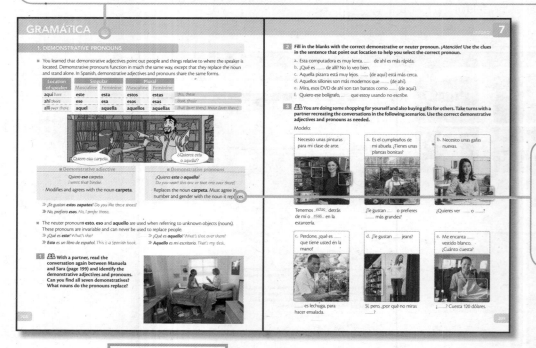

Accessible and contextualized grammar charts and presentations provide students with added clarity.

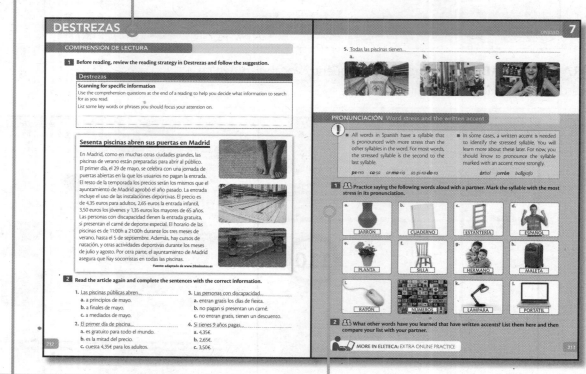

DESTREZAS integrates key language skills —listening and reading comprehension, oral and written expression— and provides guided strategies and activities related to the unit theme to further student comprehension and learning.

PRONUNCIACIÓN activities focus on the high-priority features of stress and intonation, to help students improve overall speech.

SABOR HISPANO presents different aspects of Hispanic cultures using images, maps, and other cultural realia to provide students with a window into the Hispanic world.

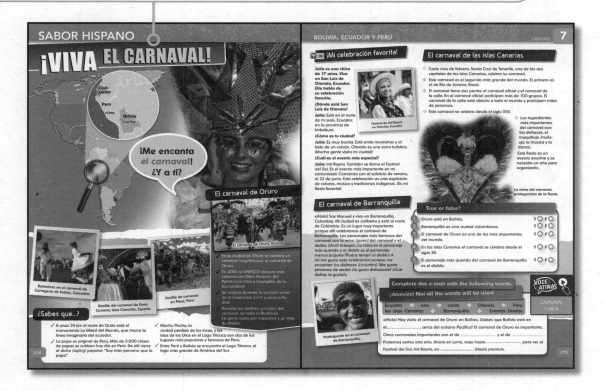

RELATO brings the unit's content together through a fictional text and encourages students to build their reading and listening comprehension skills.

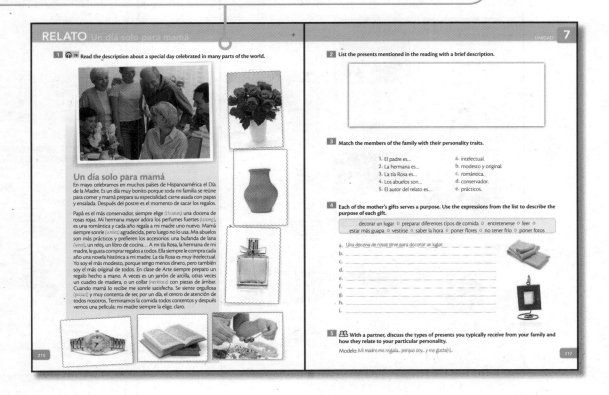

EVALUACIÓN is an integrated review for students to assess their knowledge of the content covered in each unit.

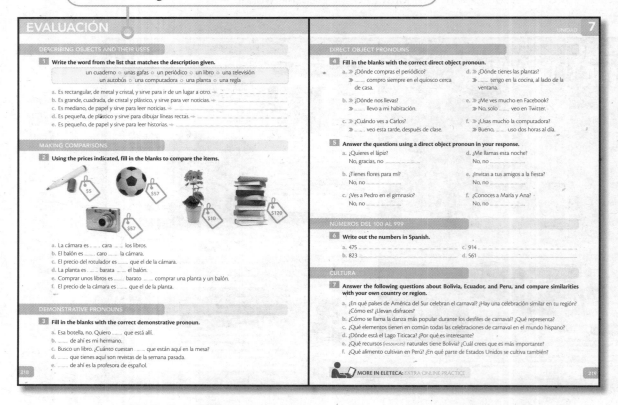

EN RESUMEN contains a glossary of the vocabulary and grammar structures covered in each unit for easy reference and review.

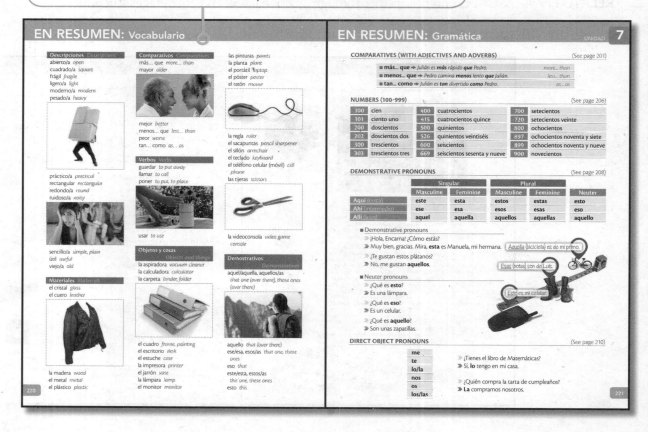

ACKNOWLEDGMENTS

The authors and publisher would like to thank the following teachers for their insight and comments during the development of *Mundo Real Media Edition*. The experience and intuition of these educators was crucial in the development of this course.

Jeremy Aldrich - Harrisonburg City Public Schools (VA), **Susan Allen** - Eastern High School (NJ), **Marilu Alvarado** - Academia Margarita Muniz (MA), **Jose M. Aviña** - Sunset High School (TX), **Vicki S. Baggia** - Phillips Exeter Academy (NH), **David Barkley** - George C. Marshall High School (VA), **Vanda Baughman** - Cascade High School (OR), **Emily A. Berry** - Irvington Preparatory Academy (IN), **Candace Blatt** - Kokomo High School (IN), **Pilar Blazey** - Wilson High School (WA), **Patricia Boyarizo** - Ragsdale High School (NC), **Sonia Brandon** - Fork Union Military Academy (VA), **Ariel Bueno** - Lake Ridge High School (TX), **Maria L. Cabra** - Ronald W. Reagan / Doral Senior High School (FL), **Lilian M. Castillo de Hutchinson** - The Loomis Chaffee School (CT), **John S. Coco** - Cocalico School District (CO), **Pamela Conte** - Nordonia Hills City Schools (OH), **Rita Morales Cooley** - The Madeira School (VA), **Deb Dargay** - Bloomington Jefferson High School (MN), **Jesús López Díez** - Dana Hall School (MA), **Maria Elena Downes** - NYOS Charter School (NY), **Marsha Dragonetti** - Latin School of Chicago (IL), **Yvonne Easaw** - Richland School District Two (SC), **Cristina Escotto** - Fredericksburg Academy (VA), **Margaret K. Esten** - South Portland High School (OR), **Calvin Feehan** - Redwood High School (CA), **Scott L. Fisher** - McGavock High School (TN), **Mary Jo Flood** - Royal High School (CA), **Alejandra Fonseca** - Wyandanch Memorial High School (NY), **William Frank** - Pinkerton Academy (NH), **Coleen Garcia** - La Serna High School (CA), **Ramón García-Tamaran** - Bloomington High School South (IN), **Angela Giffin** - Stevens High School (SD), **Jeanne Gilbert** - The Hawbridge School (NC), **Robert Giosh** - The Latin School of Chicago (IL), **Xiomara Gonzalez** - Barbara Goleman Senior High School (FL), **Adriana Gonzalez-Novello** - Trinity School (NY), **Catherine A. Haney** - Loudoun County Public Schools (VA), **Ana Hermoso** - The Hotchkiss School (CT), **Wilson R. Hernández** - Hightstown High School (NJ), **Lesley Hinson** - Churchill High School (TX), **Efila Jzar-Simpson** - Ben Davis University High School (IN), **Anne Karakash, M.A.** - Franklin Academy (NC), **Nora L. Kinney** - Montini Catholic High School (IL), **Ivonete Kinson-Blackwelder** - North Pole High School (AK), **Heather Kissel** - TechBoston Academy (MA), **Dr. Jean Robert Lainé** - Putnam City Public Schools (OK), **William A. Leheny** - Garces Memorial High School (CA), **Jacqueline Liebold** - Groton Dunstable Regional High School (MA), **Patricio Lopez** - Harborfields High School (NY), **Adrianna Madril** - Martin Luther High School (CA), **Amanda Mancilla** - Union County Public Schools (NC), **Alice Nan Mannix** - Brown County High School (IN), **Nilma M. Martin Antonetti** - Richard Montgomery High School (MD), **Amanda Marvin** - The Barstow School (MO), **Rubenm Mascarenas** - Teacher Summit High School (TX), **Maritza Massopust** - Adelson Educational Campus (NV), **Justin Vanlee McClain** - Bishop McNamara High School (MD), **Marcelina McCool** - West Philadelphia High School (PA), **Darcie McGee** - Minnesota Online High School (MN), **Jennifer Mitchell** - The Hun School of Princeton (NJ), **Kathleen Monks** - Holley Central School (NY), **Yolanda Montague** - Stuarts Draft High School (VA), **Weston Moody** - Manhattan-Ogden School (NY), **Sydney Munson** - All Saints' Episcopal School (TX), **Sergio Navarro** - Redondo Union High School (CA), **Carmen Neale** - Watkinson School (CT), **Valerie Neri** - Park Center Senior High - International Baccalaureate World School (MN), **Andrew Noelle** - Central Magnet School (TN), **Marie G. Nuzzi** - Garden City High School (NY), **Santa Olmedo** - Foothill High School (CA), **Joseph A. Parodi** - Marianapolis Preparatory School (CT), **Olga A. Pietrantonio** - Blaine High School (WA), **Tim Pillsbury** - Trinity-Pawling School (NY), **Viviana Planine** - Newton South High School (MA), **Sofia Catalina Pollock** - John Champe High School (VA), **Andrew Poolman** - The Haverford School (PA), **Gregory Prais** - Detroit Catholic Central High School (MI), **Ashleigh Marsh Prendable** - Montgomery County Public Schools (MD), **Cecilia Remeta** - Palos Verdes High School (CA), **Mary Beth Ricci** - Olathe South High School (OK), **Gimara Richards, M.A.T.** - Stonewall Jackson High School (VA), **Myra M. Rios, M.A.** - Lower Merion High School (PA), **Alison Robinson** - Fort Worth Country Day School (TX), **Norman Sargen** - Agnes Irwin School (PA), **David M. Sawyer** - The Covenant School (VA), **Carl A. Seese** - Twin Lakes High School (IN), **Rosana Serna** - Seven Lakes High School (TX), **Bertha Sevilla** - Notre Dame Academy (CA), **Jonathan L. Sirois** - Tabor Academy (MA), **Ellen J. Spitalli** - Naperville Central High School (IL), **Maribel Squibb** - Sharyland High School (TX), **Tamara Tamez** - Nimitz High School (TX), **Yamila Tamny** - River Ridge High School (FL), **Susan Tawney** - Ragsdale High School (NC), **Candida Thompson** - Academy of Richmond County (GA), **Lisa Todd** - Colorado Academy (CO), **Delia Topping** - Central Magnet School (TN), **Yari Torres** - Douglass High School (TN), **Rachel Torrie** - Woodinville High School (WA), **Rosanna Tucci** - Miami Beach Senior High (FL), **Karen Twyford** - Highland High School (IL), **Maria Vazquez** - Mother Seton Regional High School (NJ), **Janice Ventresco** - Avon High School (OH), **Barbara A. Volkman** - Lanphier High School (IL), **Michelle Warner** - East Muskingum Schools (OH), **Rhonda L. Wells** - DeKalb County School District (GA), **Rand Wiseman** - Gig Harbor High School (WA).

PROFESSIONAL ORGANIZATIONS AND RESOURCES

These organizations provide a wealth of teaching resources with online materials, conferences, and workshops.

American Association of Teachers of Spanish and Portuguese (AATSP)

AATSP's mission is to promote the study and teaching of the Spanish and Portuguese languages and their corresponding literatures and cultures at all levels of education.

http://www.aatsp.org/

The American Council on the Teaching of Foreign Languages (ACTFL)

ACTFL is an individual membership organization of more than 12,000 language educators and administrators, dedicated to the improvement and expansion of the teaching and learning of all languages at all levels of instruction.

www.actfl.org

In addition, ACTFL provides an "Alignment of the National Standards for Learning Languages with the Common Core Standards" at the following URL:

http://www.actfl.org/news/reports/alignment-the-national-standards-learning-languages-the-common-core-state-standards

Center for Applied Linguistics (CAL)

Language acquisition experts at the Center for Applied Linguistics focus on language education at all levels of instruction. They conduct language research, professional development for language teachers, information collection and dissemination, and program evaluation.

www.cal.org

National Capital Language Resource Center

NCLRC is a joint project of Georgetown University, The George Washington University, and the Center for Applied Linguistics. NCLRC is located in Washington, DC, and is one of fifteen nonprofit Language Resource Centers funded by the U.S. Department of Education.

http://www.nclrc.org

Partnership for 21st Century Skills (P21)

P21's mission is "To serve as a catalyst to position 21st century readiness at the center of US K12 education by building collaborative partnerships among education, business, community and government leaders." P21's focus includes the learning of foreign languages in K–12.

http://www.p21.org

Regional Foreign Language Conferences and Teacher Organizations

- The Central States Conference on the Teaching of Foreign Languages (CSCTFL)
  http://www.csctfl.org/
- The Greater Washington Association of Teachers of Foreign Languages http://www.gwatfl.org/
- Southern Conference on Language Teaching
  http://scolt.webnode.com/
- Southwest Conference on Language Teaching
  http://www.swcolt.org/
- Northeast Conference on the Teaching of Foreign Languages
  http://alpha.dickinson.edu/prorg/nectfl/index.html
- Pacific Northwest Council for Languages (PNCFL)
  http://www.pncfl.org

BIBLIOGRAPHICAL REFERENCES

Teaching Methods

Gattegno, C. (1976). *The Common Sense of Teaching Foreign Languages.* New York: Educational Solutions.

Holt, D. (1993). *Cooperative Learning: A Response to Linguistic and Cultural Diversity.* McHenry, IL, and Washington, DC: Delta Systems and Center for Applied Linguistics.

Johnson, K. (1982). *Communicative Syllabus Design and Methodology.* Oxford: Pergamon.

Krashen, S.D. (1981). *Second Language Acquisition and Second Language Learning.* Oxford: Pergamon.

Krashen, S.D., & Terrell, T.D. (1983). *The Natural Approach: Language Acquisition in the Classroom.* Englewood Cliffs, NJ: Prentice Hall.

Larsen-Freeman, D. (2000). *Techniques and Principles in Language Teaching* (2nd ed.). Oxford: Oxford University Press.

Littlewood, W. (1982). *Communicative Language Teaching: An Introduction.* Cambridge: Cambridge University Press.

Littlewood, W. (1992). *Teaching Oral Communication: A Methodological Framework.* Oxford: Blackwell.

Lozanov, G. (1978). *Suggestology and Outlines of Suggestopedy.* New York: Gordon and Breach.

Lozanov, G., & Gateva, E. (1988). *The Foreign Language Teacher's Suggestopedic Manual.* New York: Gordon and Breach.

National Standards in Foreign Language Education Project (1999, 2006). *Standards for Foreign Language Learning in the 21st Century (SFFLL)* (2nd & 3rd edns.). Lawrence, KS: Allen Press.

Nunan, D. (1999). Second Language Teaching and Learning. Boston: Heinle & Heinle.

Richards, J. C., & Rodgers, T.S. (2001). *Approaches and Methods in Language Teaching.* (2nd ed.). Cambridge: Cambridge University Press.

Stern, H.H. (1983). *Fundamental Concepts of Language Teaching.* Oxford: Oxford University Press.

Access for All Students / Differentiated Instruction

Downey, D.M. (1992, April). *Accommodating the foreign language learning disabled student.* Paper presented at the Foreign Language and Learning Disabilities Conference, The American University, Washington, DC.

Ganschow, L., Myer, B.J., & Roeger, K. (1989). Foreign language policies and procedures for students with specific learning disabilities. *Learning Disabilities Focus,* 5(1), 50-58.

Ganschow, L. and Schneider, E. (2006). *Assisting Students With Foreign Language Learning Difficulties in School. From Perspectives on Language and Literacy, Special Edition 2006.* Baltimore, MD: International Dyslexia Association.

Gardner, Howard E. (1993). *Multiple Intelligences: The Theory in Practice.* New York: Basic Books.

Teaching Spanish to Spanish Heritage Speakers

American Association of Teachers of Spanish and Portuguese. (2000). Volume I. *Spanish for native speakers: AATSP Professional Development Series Handbook for Teachers K-16. A handbook for teachers.* Fort Worth, TX: Harcourt College Publishers.

Jim Cummins "Beyond Curricular Scripts and Instructional Techniques: Implementing Classroom Interactions that Foster Power, Identity, Imagination, and Intellect Among Bilingual Students." NABE conference. Philadelphia, PA. March 2002.

Poey, Delia and Virgil Suárez. (1992) *Iguana Dreams.* New York, Harper Collins. Samaniego et al. (2002).

Webb, J.B., & Miller, B.L. (Eds.) (2000). *Teaching Heritage Language Learners: Voices from the Classroom.* Yonkers, NY: American Council on the Teaching of Foreign Languages.

Additional Bibliographical References

For additional reading suggestions and teaching materials, visit the following sites.

- **CAL Resource Guides Online**
  http://www.cal.org/resources/archive/rgos/methods.html
- **NCLRC Teaching Materials for Spanish**
  http://nclrc.org/teaching_materials/materials_by_language/spanish.html
- **Resource Publications from AATSP**
  http://www.aatsp.org/?page=RESOURCPUB

Estados Unidos

Phoenix

Dallas

El Paso

Tijuana   Mexicali

Houston

Chihuahua

Monterrey

Mazatlán

MÉXICO

Colima   México D. F.

Veracruz

Acapulco

GUATEMALA

MÉXICO, CENTROAMÉRICA Y CARIBE

EL SALVADOR

HONDURAS

Atlanta

CUBA

Miami

Bahamas

La Habana

Cienfuegos

Camagüey

Guantánamo

Mérida

Santiago de Cuba

Haití

REPÚBLICA DOMINICANA

PUERTO RICO

Santo Domingo

San Juan

La Romana

Ponce

Belice

San Pedro Sula

Ciudad de Guatemala

Tegucigalpa

NICARAGUA

agua

San Salvador

León

Managua

Granada

San José

COSTA RICA

Puntarenas

Panamá

Colón

PANAMÁ

Caracas

Barranquilla

Medellín

Bogotá

Cali

Islas Galápagos

Quito

Iquitos

Brasil

Trujillo

Lima

Cuzco

Arequipa

La Paz

Santa Cruz

Sucre

VENEZUELA

COLOMBIA

BOLIVIA

ECUADOR

Asunción

PARAGUAY

Córdoba

Rosario

PERÚ

Santiago de Chile

Buenos Aires

Montevideo

Bahía Blanca

URUGUAY

Comodoro Rivadavia

TE32

CHILE

Río Gallegos

Punta Arenas

ARGENTINA

SUDAMÉRICA Y ESPAÑA

La Coruña
Bilbao
Francia
Barcelona
Madrid ⊙
Portugal
Valencia
Sevilla

ESPAÑA

País	Capital
Argentina	Buenos Aires
Más información en: Unidad 8	
Bolivia	La Paz
Más información en: Unidad 7	
Chile	Santiago de Chile
Más información en: Unidad 8	
Colombia	Bogotá
Más información en: Unidad 5	
Costa Rica	San José
Más información en: Unidad 4	
Cuba	La Habana
Más información en: Unidad 6	
Ecuador	Quito
Más información en: Unidad 7	
El Salvador	San Salvador
Más información en: Unidad 4	
España	Madrid
Más información en: Unidad 2	
Guatemala	Ciudad de Guatemala
Más información en: Unidad 4	

País	Capital
Honduras	Tegucigalpa
Más información en: Unidad 4	
México	México D.F.
Más información en: Unidad 3	
Nicaragua	Managua
Más información en: Unidad 4	
Panamá	Panamá
Más información en: Unidad 5	
Paraguay	Asunción
Más información en: Unidad 8	
Perú	Lima
Más información en: Unidad 7	
Puerto rico	San Juan
Más información en: Unidad 6	
Rep. Dominicana	Santo Domingo
Más información en: Unidad 6	
Uruguay	Montevideo
Más información en: Unidad 8	
Venezuela	Caracas
Más información en: Unidad 5	

CULTURE PHOTOS

Argentina *Glaciar Perito Moreno (Perito Moreno Glacier). Located in the Glacier National Park in Patagonia, Argentina, it is a place of spectacular beauty and great glaciological and geomorphic interest.

Bolivia Salar de Uyuni. Situated in the southwest of Bolivia, it is the largest continuous salt flat in the world, covering an area of 10,582 km2 (4,085 square miles) and holds one of the biggest deposits of lithium in the world.

Chile Desierto de Atacama (Atacama Desert). Situated in the Norte Grande in Chile, it is the most arid desert on the planet and covers an area of approximately 105,000km2. It is considered to be one of the best places in the world for observing the skies and studying astronomy.

Colombia *Cartagena de Indias.** Located on the shores of the Caribbean Sea, the city was founded in 1533. It holds such historic sites as the San Felipe Castle, the Palace of the Inquisition, the Clock Tower, the city walls and the Colonial streets.

Costa Rica Río Celeste. Flowing through the Tenorio Volcano National Park, this river is famous for its sky blue color, an optical effect produced by the high concentration of aluminum silicates in its waters. According to a local legend, the river is this color because "when God finished painting the heavens, He washed his brushes in the waters of this river."

Cuba *La Habana (Havana). Havana is the capital of the Republic of Cuba and its largest city, main port and cultural and economic center. Founded in 1519, the historic center is famed for its decadent beauty and atmosphere.

Ecuador *Islas Galápagos (The Galapagos Islands). An archipelago in the Pacific Ocean, located 972 km off the coast of Ecuador. Apart from being a World Heritage Site, UNESCO declared the Galapagos Islands to be a Biosphere Reserve in 1985. The islands are the natural habitat of several species in danger of extinction, among them, the giant tortoises.

El Salvador El volcán Izalco (The Izalco Volcano). "Place in the dark sands" in the Nahuatl language, it is the youngest of the volcanoes in El Salvador and one of the youngest in the continent. The volcano erupted continuously for almost 200 years and the flames could be seen from the ocean – hence its nickname: *Lighthouse of the Pacific*.

España *La Alhambra (The Alhambra). Situated in Granada, in the south of Spain, it is an elaborate complex of palaces and fortress where the sultans of the Moorish Kingdom of Granada lived during the XIIIth – XVth centuries. The interior decoration is striking, in andalusi style, and the palace stands in an incomparable natural setting.

Guatemala *Tikal.** Situated in the region of Petén, in what is today Guatemala, in the Tikal National Park, it is one of the largest archaeological sites and urban centers of the pre-Columbian Maya civilization.

Honduras *Ruinas de Copán (Copán Ruins). An archaeological site located in the west of Honduras. It is famous for its magnificent Maya ruins, considered now to be the Paris of the Central American Maya world.

México *Pirámide de Kukulkán (Kukulkán Pyramid). A pre-Hispanic building located in the Yucatan Peninsula, built in the XIIth century AD by the Mayas in the ancient city of Chichén Itzá. The Temple of Kukulkán shows the profound knowledge of mathematics, geometry, acoustics and astronomy of the Mayas.

Nicaragua Granada. Situated between Xalteva and Lake Nicaragua, it was founded in 1524 by the Spanish conquistador, Francisco Hernández de Córdoba. It is also known as *La Gran Sultana* because of its Andalusian Moorish appearance. The Colonial architecture of its historic center, as well as the surrounding natural setting, make it the main tourist destination in Nicaragua.

Panamá El canal de Panamá (The Panama Canal). It is an inter-oceanic channel between the Caribbean Sea and the Pacific Ocean, which cuts across the isthmus of Panama at its narrowest point. It opened in 1914 and had the effect of shortening maritime communications in distance and time between remote places of the world. The United States, China, Chile, Japan and South Korea are the five principal users of the canal.

Paraguay *Ruinas jesuíticas (Jesuit Ruins). The Jesuit missions formed a group of thirty missionary settlements founded in the XVIIth century by the Company of Jesus among the Guaraní Indians, for the purpose of evangelizing them. These missions saved more than 100,000 Indians from slavery. At present all that is left are the imposing ruins of these villages, such as Jesús, Trinidad and Santa Rosa.

Perú *Machu Picchu.** A religious sanctuary and vacation residence of the Inca emperor Pachacútec, in the middle of the XVth century, it lies between the mountains of Machu Picchu and Huayna Picchu in the south of Peru. Machu Picchu is considered a masterpiece of both architecture and engineering. The site was recently declared one of the seven wonders of the modern-day world.

Puerto Rico *Castillo de San Felipe del Morro (San Felipe del Morro Castle). A Spanish fortification built at the northern end of San Juan, Puerto Rico, in the XVIth century. Its purpose was to protect Puerto Rico and the Bay of San Juan from any invasion that might turn the fort into an enemy base from which to invade and attack other Spanish towns and ships.

República Dominicana Isla Saona (Saona Island). Situated in the south east of the Dominican Republic, it forms part of the Este National Park and is one of the largest of its islands. Its endless beaches of fine white sand are lined with coconut palms. Here, numerous species of birds and marine animals live. The island is protected officially and therefore there are no buildings on its shores.

Uruguay Punta del Este. It is a peninsular city situated on the southern end of Uruguay and one of the most important spa cities in Latin America. *Los Dedos, La Mano, Monumento al ahogado* or *Hombre emergiendo a la vida* are famous sculptures on the Brava Beach, which has become one of the best-known places in Uruguay.

Venezuela *Parque Nacional de Canaima (Canaima National Park). Situated in the state of Bolívar, Venezuela, it stretches over 30,000 km2 as far as the border with Guyana and Brazil. Because of its size it is considered to be the sixth largest national park in the world. Almost 65% of the park is taken up with rock mesetas called *tepuyes*, a unique biological environment, of great interest to geologists. The steep cliffs and waterfalls are spectacular sights.

* All these places have been declared World Heritage Sites by UNESCO. **World Heritage Site** is the title granted by UNESCO (United Nations Educational, Scientific and Cultural Organization) to specific places on the planet (forests, mountains, lakes, caves, deserts, buildings, architectural complexes, cultural routes, cultural panoramas or cities) which have been proposed and confirmed for inclusion on this list. The aim of the program is to catalog, preserve and publicize places of exceptional cultural or natural interest for the common heritage of mankind.

UNESCO was founded on November 16, 1945, with the purpose of contributing to peace and safety in the world through education, science, culture and communications.

WHY STUDY SPANISH

WHY SPANISH?

Learning to communicate in Spanish can help you achieve a more vibrant and prosperous future, especially in today's globalizing world. As of 2014, **more than 450 million people speak Spanish** as a native language, making Spanish is the second most common native language in the world. According to a study by the Instituto Cervantes, **45 million people in the United States** speak Spanish as a first or second language. That's a Spanish-speaking community the size of the whole country of Spain!

Spanish is the most-spoken language in the Western Hemisphere, and the official language of the European Union, making it an important language for international business. By learning Spanish, you'll be joining 20 million other students worldwide who are learning to speak Spanish. You'll also be gaining a valuable professional skill on an increasingly bilingual continent. **¡Bienvenidos!**

WHY COMMUNICATIVE EXPERIENTIAL LEARNING?

Mechanical learning doesn't work.

How did you learn to ride a bike? Did you sit in a chair while someone explained the fundamentals of bike riding to you, or did you go outside and give it a try yourself? Did you get better by memorizing a set of expert techniques, or did you suffer a few skinned knees until you improved?

If you're like most people, you learned by doing —and we don't think learning a language should be any different. When you learn out-of-context grammar and vocabulary skills, or complete exercises designed to perfect isolated language functions, it can be difficult to combine these skills when you want to express something new, or understand something that you've never heard before. Even more importantly, this kind of instruction can make us forget that Spanish is a living language that is spoken creatively and individually by people all over the world.

We need to feel, experience and reflect in order to learn.

When we learn by doing —by following our own initiative and self-direction— we associate the things we learn with specific feelings and experiences, which helps us comprehend and retain new language. Activities that connect with our emotions awaken our curiosity, and help us remember what we've learned years later.

Communicative Experiential Learning is self-directed, and constructed according to the unique styles and needs of each individual. Differences in learning style and speed are allowed for and embraced in the experiential classroom.

Learning is more rewarding as part of a community.

Communicative Experiential Learning also creates a supportive peer environment, in which learners are truly part of a classroom community. Learning by doing naturally encourages cooperative learning strategies, and rewards an open exchange of ideas and experiences.

Spanish is a vital, living language —which can be surprisingly easy to forget when you're conjugating endless strings of AR verbs! Communicative Experiential Learning reminds us that the purpose of language is to connect with ourselves and with our communities, both locally and globally.

MUNDO)real

MEDIA edition

Student Book

1

Cover Photograph:

Guitarra española. *"La guitarra clásica o española es uno de los instrumentos más universales que existen y factor fundamental para que el flamenco y el tango hayan sido nombrados Patrimonio Inmaterial de la Humanidad. La guitarra surge a raíz del contacto entre las culturas cristiana y musulmana, y ha ido evolucionando y enriqueciéndose a lo largo de los siglos con las aportaciones de otras culturas. Este instrumento, en sus distintas variedades, está presente en todos los ritmos latinos y ha supuesto un punto de unión de los diferentes pueblos hispanos".* David Isa.

Miguel, ¿Se queda como está o cambio el pie de imprenta?

© Editorial Edinumen, 2016

Authors:
Eduardo Aparicio, Cecilia Bembibre, María Carmen Cabeza, Noemí Cámara, Francisca Fernández, Patricia Fontanals, Luisa Galán, Amelia Guerrero, Emilio José Marín, Celia Meana, Liliana Pereyra and Francisco Fidel Riva.
Coordination Team: David Isa, Celia Meana and Nazaret Puente.

ISBN - Student Book: 978-1-107-10986-5

First published 2016
20 19 18 17 16 15 14 13 12 11 10 9 8 7 6 5 4 3 2 1

Printed in the United States of America

Editorial Coordination:
Mar Menéndez

Cover Design:
Juanjo López

Design and Layout:
Juanjo López, Analia García, Sara Serrano, Carlos Casado
Antonio Arias, Carlos Yllana and Lucila Bembibre

Illustrations:
Carlos Casado

Photos:
See page 270

Cambridge University Press
32 Avenue of the Americas
New York, NY 10013

Editorial Edinumen
José Celestino Mutis, 4. 28028 Madrid. España
Telephone: (34) 91 308 51 42
Fax: (34) 91 319 93 09
e-mail: edinumen@edinumen.es
www.edinumen.es

SCOPE AND SEQUENCE

 Pair icon: indicates that the activity is designed to be done by students working in pairs.

 Group icon: indicates that the activity is designed to be done by students working in small groups or as a whole class.

 xx **Audio icon:** indicates recorded material either as part of an activity or a reading text.

Language icon: provides additional language and grammar support in presentations and for activities.

 Regional variation icon: provides examples of regional variations in the language.

Recycling icon: provides a reminder of previously taught material that students will need to use in an activity.

ACKNOWLEDGMENTS

The authors and publisher would like to thank the following teachers for their insight and comments during the development of *Mundo Real Media Edition*. The experience and intuition of these educators was crucial in the development of this course.

Jeremy Aldrich - Harrisonburg City Public Schools (VA), **Susan Allen** - Eastern High School (NJ), **Marilu Alvarado** - Academia Margarita Muniz (MA), **Jose M. Aviña** - Sunset High School (TX), **Vicki S. Baggia** - Phillips Exeter Academy (NH), **David Barkley** - George C. Marshall High School (VA), **Vanda Baughman** - Cascade High School (OR), **Emily A. Berry** - Irvington Preparatory Academy (IN), **Candace Blatt** - Kokomo High School (IN), **Pilar Blazey** - Wilson High School (WA), **Patricia Boyarizo** - Ragsdale High School (NC), **Sonia Brandon** - Fork Union Military Academy (VA), **Ariel Bueno** - Lake Ridge High School (TX), **Maria L. Cabra** - Ronald W. Reagan / Doral Senior High School (FL), **Lilian M. Castillo de Hutchinson** - The Loomis Chaffee School (CT), **John S. Coco** - Cocalico School District (CO), **Pamela Conte** - Nordonia Hills City Schools (OH), **Rita Morales Cooley** - The Madeira School (VA), **Deb Dargay** - Bloomington Jefferson High School (MN), **Jesús López Díez** - Dana Hall School (MA), **Maria Elena Downes** - NYOS Charter School (NY), **Marsha Dragonetti** - Latin School of Chicago (IL), **Yvonne Easaw** - Richland School District Two (SC), **Cristina Escotto** - Fredericksburg Academy (VA), **Margaret K. Esten** - South Portland High School (OR), **Calvin Feehan** - Redwood High School (CA), **Scott L. Fisher** - McGavock High School (TN), **Mary Jo Flood** - Royal High School (CA), **Alejandra Fonseca** - Wyandanch Memorial High School (NY), **William Frank** - Pinkerton Academy (NH), **Coleen Garcia** - La Serna High School (CA), **Ramón García-Tamaran** - Bloomington High School South (IN), **Angela Giffin** - Stevens High School (SD), **Jeanne Gilbert** - The Hawbridge School (NC), **Robert Giosh** - The Latin School of Chicago (IL), **Xiomara Gonzalez** - Barbara Goleman Senior High School (FL), **Adriana Gonzalez-Novello** - Trinity School (NY), **Catherine A. Haney** - Loudoun County Public Schools (VA), **Ana Hermoso** - The Hotchkiss School (CT), **Wilson R. Hernández** - Hightstown High School (NJ), **Lesley Hinson** - Churchill High School (TX), **Efila Jzar-Simpson** - Ben Davis University High School (IN), **Anne Karakash, M.A.** - Franklin Academy (NC), **Nora L. Kinney** - Montini Catholic High School (IL), **Ivonete Kinson-Blackwelder** - North Pole High School (AK), **Heather Kissel** - TechBoston Academy (MA), **Dr. Jean Robert Lainé** - Putnam City Public Schools (OK), **William A. Leheny** - Garces Memorial High School (CA), **Jacqueline Liebold** - Groton Dunstable Regional High School (MA), **Patricio Lopez** - Harborfields High School (NY), **Adrianna Madril** - Martin Luther High School (CA), **Amanda Mancilla** - Union County Public Schools (NC), **Alice Nan Mannix** - Brown County High School (IN), **Nilma M. Martin Antonetti** - Richard Montgomery High School (MD), **Amanda Marvin** - The Barstow School (MO), **Rubenm Mascarenas** - Teacher Summit High School (TX), **Maritza Massopust** - Adelson Educational Campus (NV), **Justin Vanlee McClain** - Bishop McNamara High School (MD), **Marcelina McCool** - West Philadelphia High School (PA), **Darcie McGee** - Minnesota Online High School (MN), **Jennifer Mitchell** - The Hun School of Princeton (NJ), **Kathleen Monks** - Holley Central School (NY), **Yolanda Montague** - Stuarts Draft High School (VA), **Weston Moody** - Manhattan-Ogden School (NY), **Sydney Munson** - All Saints' Episcopal School (TX), **Sergio Navarro** - Redondo Union High School (CA), **Carmen Neale** - Watkinson School (CT), **Valerie Neri** - Park Center Senior High - International Baccalaureate World School (MN), **Andrew Noelle** - Central Magnet School (TN), **Marie G. Nuzzi** - Garden City High School (NY), **Santa Olmedo** - Foothill High School (CA), **Joseph A. Parodi** - Marianapolis Preparatory School (CT), **Olga A. Pietrantonio** - Blaine High School (WA), **Tim Pillsbury** - Trinity-Pawling School (NY), **Viviana Planine** - Newton South High School (MA), **Sofia Catalina Pollock** - John Champe High School (VA), **Andrew Poolman** - The Haverford School (PA), **Gregory Prais** - Detroit Catholic Central High School (MI), **Ashleigh Marsh Prendable** - Montgomery County Public Schools (MD), **Cecilia Remeta** - Palos Verdes High School (CA), **Mary Beth Ricci** - Olathe South High School (OK), **Gimara Richards, M.A.T.** - Stonewall Jackson High School (VA), **Myra M. Rios, M.A.** - Lower Merion High School (PA), **Alison Robinson** - Fort Worth Country Day School (TX), **Norman Sargen** - Agnes Irwin School (PA), **David M. Sawyer** - The Covenant School (VA), **Carl A. Seese** - Twin Lakes High School (IN), **Rosana Serna** - Seven Lakes High School (TX), **Bertha Sevilla** - Notre Dame Academy (CA), **Jonathan L. Sirois** - Tabor Academy (MA), **Ellen J. Spitalli** - Naperville Central High School (IL), **Maribel Squibb** - Sharyland High School (TX), **Tamara Tamez** - Nimitz High School (TX), **Yamila Tamny** - River Ridge High School (FL), **Susan Tawney** - Ragsdale High School (NC), **Candida Thompson** - Academy of Richmond County (GA), **Lisa Todd** - Colorado Academy (CO), **Delia Topping** - Central Magnet School (TN), **Yari Torres** - Douglass High School (TN), **Rachel Torrie** - Woodinville High School (WA), **Rosanna Tucci** - Miami Beach Senior High (FL), **Karen Twyford** - Highland High School (IL), **Maria Vazquez** - Mother Seton Regional High School (NJ), **Janice Ventresco** - Avon High School (OH), **Barbara A. Volkman** - Lanphier High School (IL), **Michelle Warner** - East Muskingum Schools (OH), **Rhonda L. Wells** - DeKalb County School District (GA), **Rand Wiseman** - Gig Harbor High School (WA).

ACTIVATING ELETECA

HOW TO ACCESS ELETECA

ELEteca is the Learning Management System that accompanies your *Mundo Real Media Edition* Student's Book.

To activate your ELEteca resources visit **https://cambridgespanish.edinumen.es**, and follow the instructions to create an account and activate your access code.

https://cambridgespanish.edinumen.es

1.

2.

3.

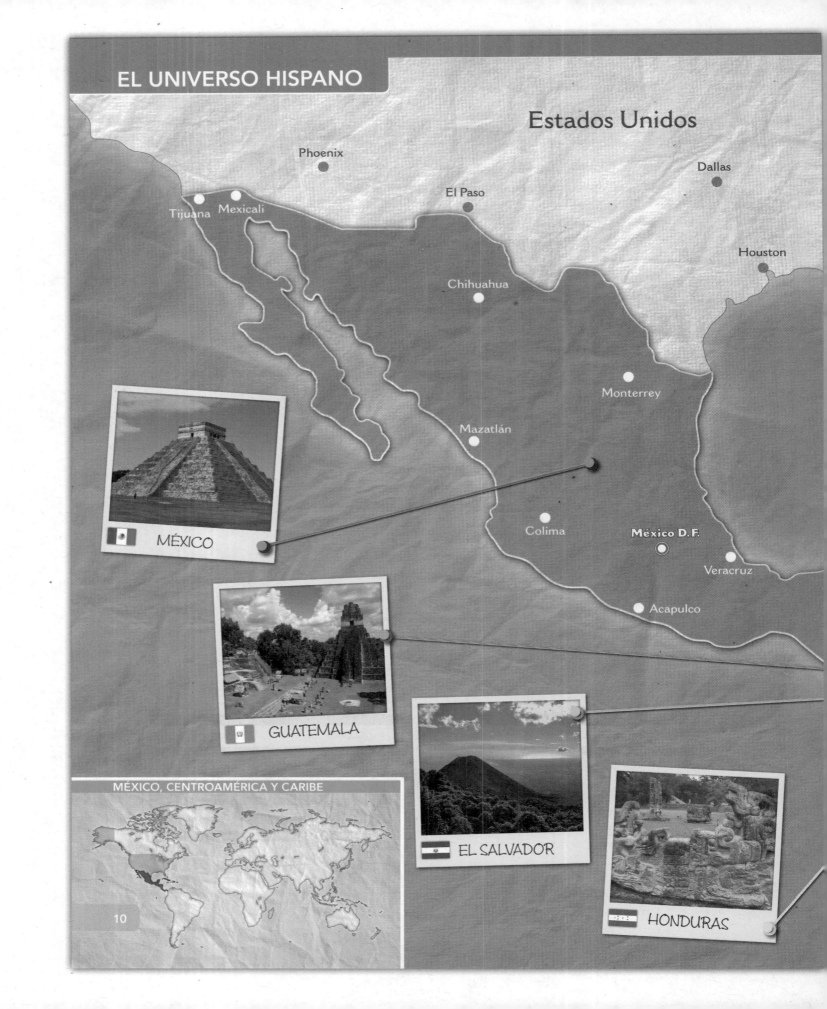

Estados Unidos

Phoenix

Dallas

El Paso

Houston

Tijuana   Mexicali

Chihuahua

Monterrey

Mazatlán

MÉXICO

Colima

México D. F.

Veracruz

Acapulco

GUATEMALA

MÉXICO, CENTROAMÉRICA Y CARIBE

EL SALVADOR

10

HONDURAS

Atlanta

REPÚBLICA DOMINICANA

CUBA

Miami

PUERTO RICO

Bahamas

La Habana

Mérida

Cienfuegos

Camagüey

Guantánamo

Santiago de Cuba

Haití

Santo Domingo

San Juan

La Romana

Ponce

Belice

San Pedro Sula

Ciudad de Guatemala

Tegucigalpa

NICARAGUA

COSTA RICA

Antigua

San Salvador

León

Managua

Granada

San José

Puntarenas

Panamá

Colón

PANAMÁ

VENEZUELA

COLOMBIA

PARAGUAY

URUGUAY

ECUADOR

PERÚ

BOLIVIA

CHILE

ARGENTINA

Caracas

Barranquilla

Medellín

Bogotá

Cali

Islas Galápagos

Quito

Iquitos

Trujillo

Brasil

Lima

Cuzco

Arequipa

La Paz

Santa Cruz

Sucre

Asunción

Córdoba

Rosario

Santiago de Chile

Buenos Aires

Montevideo

Bahía Blanca

Comodoro Rivadavia

Río Gallegos

Punta Arenas

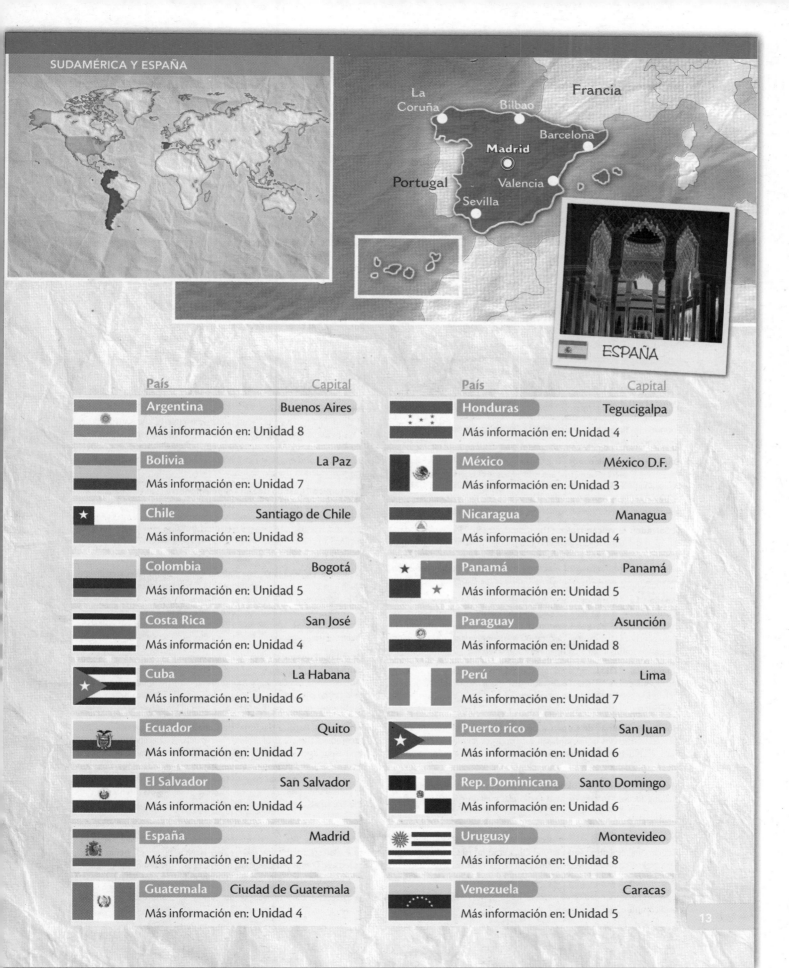

La Coruña

Francia

Bilbao

Barcelona

Madrid

Portugal

Valencia

Sevilla

ESPAÑA

País	Capital
Argentina	Buenos Aires
Más información en: Unidad 8	
Bolivia	La Paz
Más información en: Unidad 7	
Chile	Santiago de Chile
Más información en: Unidad 8	
Colombia	Bogotá
Más información en: Unidad 5	
Costa Rica	San José
Más información en: Unidad 4	
Cuba	La Habana
Más información en: Unidad 6	
Ecuador	Quito
Más información en: Unidad 7	
El Salvador	San Salvador
Más información en: Unidad 4	
España	Madrid
Más información en: Unidad 2	
Guatemala	Ciudad de Guatemala
Más información en: Unidad 4	

País	Capital
Honduras	Tegucigalpa
Más información en: Unidad 4	
México	México D.F.
Más información en: Unidad 3	
Nicaragua	Managua
Más información en: Unidad 4	
Panamá	Panamá
Más información en: Unidad 5	
Paraguay	Asunción
Más información en: Unidad 8	
Perú	Lima
Más información en: Unidad 7	
Puerto rico	San Juan
Más información en: Unidad 6	
Rep. Dominicana	Santo Domingo
Más información en: Unidad 6	
Uruguay	Montevideo
Más información en: Unidad 8	
Venezuela	Caracas
Más información en: Unidad 5	

CULTURE PHOTOS

Argentina *Glaciar Perito Moreno** (Perito Moreno Glacier). Located in the Glacier National Park in Patagonia, Argentina, it is a place of spectacular beauty and great glaciological and geomorphic interest.

Bolivia Salar de Uyuni. Situated in the southwest of Bolivia, it is the largest continuous salt flat in the world, covering an area of 10,582 km2 (4,085 square miles) and holds one of the biggest deposits of lithium in the world.

Chile Desierto de Atacama (Atacama Desert). Situated in the Norte Grande in Chile, it is the most arid desert on the planet and covers an area of approximately 105,000km2. It is considered to be one of the best places in the world for observing the skies and studying astronomy.

Colombia *Cartagena de Indias. Located on the shores of the Caribbean Sea, the city was founded in 1533. It holds such historic sites as the San Felipe Castle, the Palace of the Inquisition, the Clock Tower, the city walls and the Colonial streets.

Costa Rica Río Celeste. Flowing through the Tenorio Volcano National Park, this river is famous for its sky blue color, an optical effect produced by the high concentration of aluminum silicates in its waters. According to a local legend, the river is this color because "when God finished painting the heavens, He washed his brushes in the waters of this river."

Cuba *La Habana (Havana). Havana is the capital of the Republic of Cuba and its largest city, main port and cultural and economic center. Founded in 1519, the historic center is famed for its decadent beauty and atmosphere.

Ecuador *Islas Galápagos (The Galapagos Islands). An archipelago in the Pacific Ocean, located 972 km off the coast of Ecuador. Apart from being a World Heritage Site, UNESCO declared the Galapagos Islands to be a Biosphere Reserve in 1985. The islands are the natural habitat of several species in danger of extinction, among them, the giant tortoises.

El Salvador El volcán Izalco (The Izalco Volcano). "Place in the dark sands" in the Nahuatl language, it is the youngest of the volcanoes in El Salvador and one of the youngest in the continent. The volcano erupted continuously for almost 200 years and the flames could be seen from the ocean – hence its nickname: *Lighthouse of the Pacific*.

España *La Alhambra (The Alhambra). Situated in Granada, in the south of Spain, it is an elaborate complex of palaces and fortress where the sultans of the Moorish Kingdom of Granada lived during the XIIIth – XVth centuries. The interior decoration is striking, in andalusi style, and the palace stands in an incomparable natural setting.

Guatemala *Tikal. Situated in the region of Petén, in what is today Guatemala, in the Tikal National Park, it is one of the largest archaeological sites and urban centers of the pre-Columbian Maya civilization.

Honduras *Ruinas de Copán (Copán Ruins). An archaeological site located in the west of Honduras. It is famous for its magnificent Maya ruins, considered now to be the Paris of the Central American Maya world.

México *Pirámide de Kukulkán (Kukulkán Pyramid). A pre-Hispanic building located in the Yucatan Peninsula, built in the XIIth century AD by the Mayas in the ancient city of Chichén Itzá. The Temple of Kukulkán shows the profound knowledge of mathematics, geometry, acoustics and astronomy of the Mayas.

Nicaragua Granada. Situated between Xalteva and Lake Nicaragua, it was founded in 1524 by the Spanish conquistador, Francisco Hernández de Córdoba. It is also known as *La Gran Sultana* because of its Andalusian Moorish appearance. The Colonial architecture of its historic center, as well as the surrounding natural setting, make it the main tourist destination in Nicaragua.

Panamá El canal de Panamá (The Panama Canal). It is an inter-oceanic channel between the Caribbean Sea and the Pacific Ocean, which cuts across the isthmus of Panama at its narrowest point. It opened in 1914 and had the effect of shortening maritime communications in distance and time between remote places of the world. The United States, China, Chile, Japan and South Korea are the five principal users of the canal.

Paraguay *Ruinas jesuíticas (Jesuit Ruins). The Jesuit missions formed a group of thirty missionary settlements founded in the XVIIth century by the Company of Jesus among the Guaraní Indians, for the purpose of evangelizing them. These missions saved more than 100,000 Indians from slavery. At present all that is left are the imposing ruins of these villages, such as Jesús, Trinidad and Santa Rosa.

Perú *Machu Picchu. A religious sanctuary and vacation residence of the Inca emperor Pachacútec, in the middle of the XVth century, it lies between the mountains of Machu Picchu and Huayna Picchu in the south of Peru. Machu Picchu is considered a masterpiece of both architecture and engineering. The site was recently declared one of the seven wonders of the modern-day world.

Puerto Rico *Castillo de San Felipe del Morro (San Felipe del Morro Castle). A Spanish fortification built at the northern end of San Juan, Puerto Rico, in the XVIth century. Its purpose was to protect Puerto Rico and the Bay of San Juan from any invasion that might turn the fort into an enemy base from which to invade and attack other Spanish towns and ships.

República Dominicana Isla Salona (Saona Island). Situated in the south east of the Dominican Republic, it forms part of the Este National Park and is one of the largest of its islands. Its endless beaches of fine white sand are lined with coconut palms. Here, numerous species of birds and marine animals live. The island is protected officially and therefore there are no buildings on its shores.

Uruguay Punta del Este. It is a peninsular city situated on the southern end of Uruguay and one of the most important spa cities in Latin America. *Los Dedos, La Mano, Monumento al ahogado* or *Hombre emergiendo a la vida* are famous sculptures on the Brava Beach, which has become one of the best-known places in Uruguay.

Venezuela *Parque Nacional de Canaima (Canaima National Park). Situated in the state of Bolívar, Venezuela, it stretches over 30,000 km2 as far as the border with Guyana and Brazil. Because of its size it is considered to be the sixth largest national park in the world. Almost 65% of the park is taken up with rock mesetas called *tepuyes*, a unique biological environment, of great interest to geologists. The steep cliffs and waterfalls are spectacular sights.

* All these places have been declared World Heritage Sites by UNESCO. **World Heritage Site** is the title granted by UNESCO (United Nations Educational, Scientific and Cultural Organization) to specific places on the planet (forests, mountains, lakes, caves, deserts, buildings, architectural complexes, cultural routes, cultural panoramas or cities) which have been proposed and confirmed for inclusion on this list. The aim of the program is to catalog, preserve and publicize places of exceptional cultural or natural interest for the common heritage of mankind.

UNESCO was founded on November 16, 1945, with the purpose of contributing to peace and safety in the world through education, science, culture and communications.

WHY SPANISH?

Learning to communicate in Spanish can help you achieve a more vibrant and prosperous future, especially in today's globalizing world. As of 2014, **more than 450 million people speak Spanish** as a native language, making Spanish is the second most common native language in the world. And according to a study by the Instituto Cervantes, **45 million people in the United States** speak Spanish as a first or second language. That's a Spanish-speaking community the size of the whole country of Spain!

Spanish is the most-spoken language in the Western Hemisphere, and the official language of the European Union, making it an important language for international business. By learning Spanish, you'll be joining 20 million other students worldwide who are learning to speak Spanish. You'll also be gaining a valuable professional skill on an increasingly bilingual continent. ¡Bienvenidos!

WHY COMMUNICATIVE EXPERIENTIAL LEARNING?

Mechanical learning doesn't work.

How did you learn to ride a bike? Did you sit in a chair while someone explained the fundamentals of bike riding to you, or did you go outside and give it a try yourself? Did you get better by memorizing a set of expert techniques, or did you suffer a few skinned knees until you improved?

If you're like most people, you learned by doing —and we don't think learning a language should be any different. When you learn out-of-context grammar and vocabulary skills, or complete exercises designed to perfect isolated language functions, it can be difficult to combine these skills when you want to express something new, or understand something that you've never heard before. Even more importantly, this kind of instruction can make us forget that Spanish is a living language that is spoken creatively and individually by people all over the world.

We need to feel, experience and reflect in order to learn.

When we learn by doing —by following our own initiative and self-direction— we associate the things we learn with specific feelings and experiences, which helps us comprehend and retain new language. Activities that connect with our emotions awaken our curiosity, and help us remember what we've learned years later.

Communicative Experiential Learning is self-directed, and constructed according to the unique styles and needs of each individual. Differences in learning style and speed are allowed for and embraced in the experiential classroom.

Learning is more rewarding as part of a community.

Communicative Experiential Learning also creates a supportive peer environment, in which learners are truly part of a classroom community. Learning by doing naturally encourages cooperative learning strategies, and rewards an open exchange of ideas and experiences.

Spanish is a vital, living language —which can be surprisingly easy to forget when you're conjugating endless strings of AR verbs! Communicative Experiential Learning reminds us that the purpose of language is to connect with ourselves and with our communities, both locally and globally.

STUDENT RESOURCES

STUDENT'S BOOK

Mundo Real Media Edition uses lively and compelling content, images, and video to teach real-world language. The student book's experiential format encourages the development of strong communicative skills, which will increase your comfort level in real-world settings.

EBOOK

Mundo Real Media Edition eBooks are fully interactive and fully integrated with the Learning Management System ELEteca. Integrated audio and a seamless connection to online video content, as well as online and offline modes for Mac, PC, iOS, and Android, make using your eBook simple.

ONLINE WORBOOK

The *Mundo Real Media Edition* online workbook features a wide variety of activity types and exercises, and includes mbedded video, a video note-taking feature, and speech recognition technology.

CUADERNO PARA HISPANOHABLANTES

The *Mundo Real Media Edition* Cuaderno para hispanohablantes is written exclusively for native speakers who have grown up speaking conversational Spanish, and includes sophisticated activities and lessons that expand on the Student's Book.

ELETECA

Mundo Real Media Edition features a wealth of digital resources designed to supplement and enhance the Student's Book. All are available in the rich, interactive world of *Mundo Real Media Edition* ELEteca—in one place, with one password.

Interactive Activities

Audio and Video

- **¡Acción!** Narrative video that complements the student book.

- **Voces Latinas** Cultural clips to introduce the Spanish-speaking world.

- **Grammar Tutorials** Short grammar presentations to reinforce tricky skills.

- **Casa del Español** Street interviews that model authentic language.

Gamification

"La Pasantía", a game that allows you to engage with the Spanish language in a fun context, as you compete to win a spot on the staff of a Spanish newspaper.

Online Workbook and eBook Integration

The *Mundo Real Media Edition* Online Workbook and eBook are accessible through ELEteca, so you can access all of your digital resources in one place, using one password.

OBJECTIVES FOR UNIT OPENER

- Introduce unit theme: **Así somos** about people and objects in the classroom
- Culture: Learn about Spanish and its presence around the world

STANDARDS

1.2. Understand the language

2.1. Practices and perspectives

INSTRUCTIONAL STRATEGIES

This preliminary unit is designed to make student's exposure to the language classroom a successful, enjoyable experience and to set them at ease with the language learning process. The unit provides students with high-frequency vocabulary and useful strategies for learning Spanish. Encourage students to discover similarities between languages and access prior knowledge they may have acquired along the way. This unit also introduces students to the Hispanic world and Spanish-speaking countries.

Talk about Spanish in the U.S. and around the world.

Have students look at the photograph. Read the caption aloud: **¡Bienvenidos a la clase de español!** Ask students what they think it means in English. Use gestures to help access meaning.

Use the photograph to preview unit vocabulary, including common school vocabulary: **estudiante**, **escuela**, **maestro** or **profesor**.

Ask the introductory question: **¿Hablas español?** and related questions about the image: **¿Cuántos estudiantes hay? ¿Cuántos maestros hay? ¿Hablan español o inglés? Y tú, ¿hablas inglés?**

Ask questions to help students share any words they may already know in Spanish. Students may know a few simple words like **hola**, **sí**, **no**, **mi casa**, **gracias**, **español**, **un poquito**, **uno**, **dos**, **tres**. Acknowledge and value any prior knowledge of Spanish they may already have. Help them realize that they all know some Spanish.

UNIDAD

0 ASÍ SOMOS

¡Bienvenidos a la clase de español!

⟫ ¿Hablas español?

18

INTRODUCING HERITAGE SPEAKERS

Explain that many young people in the U.S. are heritage speakers of Spanish. These are students who have learned some Spanish at home from their families.

Find out if there are any heritage speakers in the classroom. Invite them to introduce themselves and tell how much Spanish they know and who they learned it from. Encourage them to share what they can do well in Spanish and what they want to improve on. For instance, some may understand spoken Spanish, but not feel comfortable speaking it.

Establish a spirit of mutual respect and appreciation for all heritage speakers regardless of proficiency level, as well as for monolingual English speakers who are new to Spanish. Encourage all students to learn from each other and to help each other.

ADDITIONAL UNIT RESOURCES

Interactive Whiteboard Lessons (IWB)	Audio
IWB: 0.1	🎧 1 to 11

In this unit, you will learn to:

- Recognize words in Spanish that are related to English
- Identify objects and people in a classroom
- Ask what something means
- Ask how to say something in Spanish
- Ask someone to repeat or explain
- Spell in Spanish

Using

- Cognates
- Spanish alphabet
- Classroom expressions
- Punctuation for questions and exclamations

Cultural Connections

- Connect information about Spanish and the Spanish-Speaking world, and compare cultural similarities

SABOR HISPANO

- Yo hablo español, ¿y tú?
- Nuestros países

Gran Via

Metro

19

INTRODUCTION TO LEARNING OUTCOMES

The unit learning objectives are an organizational tool for you and your students. Encourage students to read the learning outcomes before starting the unit and when they prepare for a test

LEARNING OUTCOMES

- Recognize words in Spanish that are related to English (cognates)
- Identify objects and people in a classroom
- Ask what something means
- Ask how to say something in Spanish
- Ask someone to repeat or explain
- Spell in Spanish
- Connect information about Spanish and the Spanish-speaking world, and compare cultural similarities.

NOTE

The structure of this unit differs from regular units in length and organization. The intention is to situate students in the classroom setting and provide them with the tools to jumpstart their learning.

Students will learn basic greetings and introductions in Unidad 1. Switch between the two units depending on the level and eagerness of your students.

CULTURAL NOTE (FOR IMAGES)

A Quechua Indian woman from the Andes region of Peru • Mayan masks carved from wood • Traditional Mexican tamales (steamed corn husks filled with meat, cheese, vegetables and spices in a doughy center) • Three young ladies from Buenos Aires, Argentina • Mariachi band • Metro stop in downtown Madrid, Spain • Colorful houses in La Boca neighborhood in Buenos Aires, Argentina where tango originated • Traditional windmills of La Mancha, Spain, famous for the setting of one of the world's most celebrated novels, *Don Quijote de La Mancha*.

NOTE

Common Core State Standards (CCSS)

The four strands of the *Common Core State Standards for English Language Arts (ELA) and Literacy in History / Social Studies, Science, and Technical Subjects* are represented in the National Standards for Learning Languages by the Communication standards: Interpersonal, Interpretive, and Presentational. The three modes of communication align with the goals in Reading, Writing, Speaking, and Listening by emphasizing the purpose behind the communication.

THREE MODES OF COMMUNICATION: UNIT 0

	INTERPERSONAL	INTERPRETIVE	PRESENTATIONAL
LOS PAÍSES DEL MUNDO HISPANO		1, 2, 3	3
EN ESPAÑOL	2, 3	1, 2, 3	4
EL ALFABETO ESPAÑOL	6	1, 2, 3, 4, 5	
EN LA CLASE DE ESPAÑOL	6, 7	1, 2, 3, 4, 5, 6	7
CULTURA		SABOR HISPANO	

LOS PAÍSES DEL MUNDO HISPANO

OBJECTIVES FOR LOS PAÍSES DEL MUNDO HISPANO

- Understand language in context
- Preview vocabulary: names of Spanish-speaking countries
- Preview grammatical structures: the verbs *ser*, *estar*, *hablar*
- Read and listen to a recording of a teacher introducing herself

CORE RESOURCES

- Audio Program: Track 1
- Interactive Whiteboard Lesson: IWB 0.1

STANDARDS

1.1	Engage in conversation
1.2	Understand the language
4.2	Compare cultures

INSTRUCTIONAL STRATEGIES

Activity 1

- Model how to pronounce the name of each country in Spanish. Encourage students to draw conclusions about differences in pronunciation in English and Spanish and to share what they understand about the sounds of letters in Spanish.
- Use IWB 0.1, **Los países del mundo hispano** to point out the location of these countries and other place names such as the surrounding oceans and seas.

- Avoid providing direct translations at this point. Help students with meaning by pointing to the map and using other gestures.
- Invite students to share what they know about these countries.

ANSWERS

Activity 1

True statements are: a, c, d.

SLOWER-PACED LEARNERS

Give students enough opportunity to practice the pronunciation of the Spanish-speaking countries, particularly those that are spelled the same as in English.

PRE-AP LEARNERS

Ask students to identify differences in spelling: Perú, Peru; México, Mexico; Panamá, Panama. Help students understand how the accent mark affects the pronunciation.

HERITAGE LANGUAGE LEARNERS

If there are any heritage students in the classroom, invite them to share where their family is from and if they have ever visited that country.

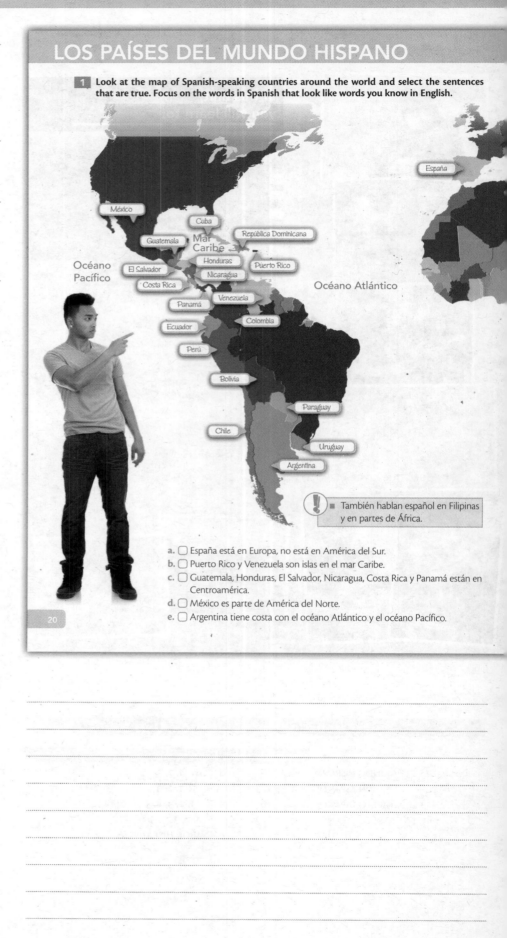

LOS PAÍSES DEL MUNDO HISPANO

1 Look at the map of Spanish-speaking countries around the world and select the sentences that are true. Focus on the words in Spanish that look like words you know in English.

España

México

Cuba

República Dominicana

Guatemala · Mar Caribe

Honduras · Puerto Rico

Océano Pacífico · El Salvador · Nicaragua

Costa Rica

Venezuela · Océano Atlántico

Panamá

Colombia

Ecuador

Perú

Bolivia

Paraguay

Chile

Uruguay

Argentina

> ! ■ También hablan español en Filipinas y en partes de África.

a. ☐ España está en Europa, no está en América del Sur.
b. ☐ Puerto Rico y Venezuela son islas en el mar Caribe.
c. ☐ Guatemala, Honduras, El Salvador, Nicaragua, Costa Rica y Panamá están en Centroamérica.
d. ☐ México es parte de América del Norte.
e. ☐ Argentina tiene costa con el océano Atlántico y el océano Pacífico.

20

2 🎧 **¹** **Follow along as you listen to the teacher welcome her students to Spanish class. Then indicate if the statements that follow are true (T) or false (F).**

¡Hola! Bienvenidos todos a la clase español. Soy la señora Blanco. Soy de Madrid, la capital de España. El español es una lengua importante. Muchas personas en el mundo hablan español. ¿En qué países hablan español? Miren el mapa. Hablan español en México, Guatemala, El Salvador, Honduras, Costa Rica, Nicaragua, Panamá, Colombia, Ecuador, Perú, Bolivia, Chile, Argentina, Uruguay, Paraguay, Venezuela, Puerto Rico, República Dominicana, Cuba y España.

¿Hablan español en Estados Unidos?

	T	F
1. According to the teacher, Spanish is an important language.	☐	☐
2. She says that people in Guatemala, Paraguay, and Brazil speak Spanish.	☐	☐
3. The teacher is from Spain.	☐	☐
4. Her name is Mrs. Blanco.	☐	☐
5. Madrid is the capital of Spain.	☐	☐
6. At the end, she states that people in the United States speak Spanish.	☐	☐

3 **Identify each country below and include any information you know about the country.**

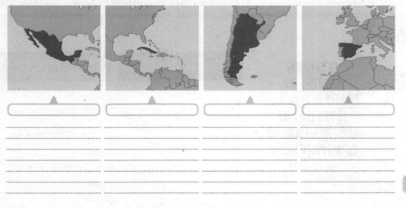

INSTRUCTIONAL STRATEGIES

🎧 **1** **Activity 2**

Use the audio to focus students' attention on rhythm, intonation, and pronunciation. Have students respond chorally as needed.

Activity 3

Invite students to work on their own, using the information that has already been shared in the class in Activity 1. Call on students to share what they know about these countries. Provide language support by repeating basic information in Spanish to help students get accustomed to hearing Spanish.

ANSWERS

Activity 2

1. T; 2. F; 3. T; 4. T; 5. T; 6. F.

Activity 3

Answers will vary and should reflect information about Mexico, Cuba, Argentina, and Spain.

SLOWER-PACED LEARNERS

Have students listen to the audio more than once before having them answer the questions.

PRE-AP LEARNERS

For Activity 2, ask students to correct the information in the false statements. Invite them to try to do it in Spanish using simple strategies such as placing "no" in front of the verb: **No hablan español en Brasil.**

HERITAGE LANGUAGE LEARNERS

For Activity 2, invite students to read the text aloud to their classmates, if needed.

For Activity 3, call on students to share the information they know about the highlighted countries to help their peers get accustomed to hearing different Spanish accents. Encourage them to share memories or impressions of the people and culture.

OBJECTIVES FOR EN ESPAÑOL

- Present common cognates
- Provide practice to recognize and identify cognates in Spanish
- Use vocabulary to refer to everyday objects

CORE RESOURCES

- Audio Program: Track 2

STANDARDS

1.2 Understand the language
4.1 Evaluate similarities and differences in language

INSTRUCTIONAL STRATEGIES

🎧 2 Activity 1

- With books closed, have students listen to the audio.
- Ask if they recognize any words. Encourage them to share any similarities they notice between the words they have heard and words they know in English.
- Explain that English and Spanish share many words that are similar and that, although they sound different, some can still be recognizable. Tell them that these words are called cognates.
- Have students look at the words in the book. Help them notice differences and similarities in how those words are spelled in English and invite them to share what they notice. For instance, they might notice that most words in Spanish have an additional vowel at the end compared to their English counterpart, such as: *music* / *música*, *class* / *clase*, *telephone* / *teléfono*, *map* / *mapa*, *alphabet* / *alfabeto*. Help them conclude that most words in Spanish end in a vowel.
- Play the audio again and have them complete the activity individually by matching the words to the images below.

ANSWERS

Activity 1

1. g; **2.** b; **3.** f; **4.** c; **5.** d; **6.** e; **7.** h; **8.** a.

Activity 2

Answers will vary and should reflect identification of English / Spanish cognates and familiar words such as: *menú*, *burritos*, *tacos*, *nachos*, *sopas*, *ensaladas*, *hamburguesas*, *sándwich*, *café*.

Unfamiliar words: *carnes*, *pollo*, *trucha* (*trout*), *onces* (snack served between lunch and dinner in Colombia, similar to English tea).

SLOWER-PACED LEARNERS

Invite students to say the names of cities in California, Arizona, New Mexico and Texas. Choose those that are cognates (i.e., **San Francisco**, **Los Ángeles**, **Nogales**, **Santa Fe**, **San Antonio**).

ADVANCED LEARNERS

Challenge students to think of other names they may know in Spanish for foods and encourage them to pronounce them correctly in Spanish.

HERITAGE LANGUAGE LEARNERS

Invite students to share any words they use for the objects in Activity 1 that are different. Have students write the words and then read them aloud in Spanish.

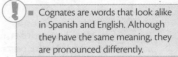

EN ESPAÑOL

1 🎧 2 Listen to the following words in Spanish and see how many you understand. Then match the word to the appropriate image below. Use your knowledge of cognates to help you.

1. cafetería .... ☐
2. música .... ☐
3. clase .... ☐
4. teléfono .... ☐
5. familia .... ☐
6. mapa .... ☐
7. alfabeto .... ☐
8. computadora .... ☐

> **!** ■ Cognates are words that look alike in Spanish and English. Although they have the same meaning, they are pronounced differently.

a.

b.

c.

d.

e.

f.

g.

h.

ABCDEF GHIJKL MNÑOPQ RSTUV WXYZ

2 👥 Look at the following menu posted outside a restaurant in Cartagena, Colombia. With a partner, make a list of the words you recognize. Then try guessing at some of the unfamiliar words.

DESAYUNOS
MENÚ DEL DÍA
BURRITOS-TACOS-NACHOS
SOPAS-ENSALADAS
HAMBURGUESAS-SANDWICH
CARNES-POLLO-TRUCHA
ONCES-CAFÉ

Familiar words	Unfamiliar words and their possible meaning

3 🔲 With a partner, look at the following signs and try to determine what each one is saying. Concentrate on the words you recognize and use the visuals to guess at unfamiliar words. Compare your answers with those of another pair.

a.

b.

c.

d.

e.

f.

4 Create your own sign using the expressions above and present it to the class.

INSTRUCTIONAL STRATEGIES

Activity 3

- As you review answers with students, ask them to identify the word in Spanish: *¿Cómo se dice "park" en español?*
- Give examples of word families: *peligro*, **peligroso**. Ask students if they have ever seen signs with *peligro* (they can often be seen in public buildings to indicate slippery floors or by construction sites).
- Ask students to find the two opposites: *entrada* / **salida**.

Activity 4

Provide vocabulary as needed while encouraging students to make use of the words presented so far.

ANSWERS

Activity 3

Answers will vary.

Activity 4

Answers will vary.

SLOWER-PACED LEARNERS

Ask students to write down 20 words that they have learned so far. Have them compare lists with a partner.

ADVANCED LEARNERS

Have students create a memory game using all the words from the unit so far. Assign one partner to collect the words and the other to collect the images (clip art, hand-drawn, etc.).

HERITAGE LANGUAGE LEARNERS

Pair students with advanced learners and ask them to build a memory game by collecting all the words seen so far in this unit and combining them with pictures. Invite them to expand vocabulary with other cognates they may know.

OBJECTIVES FOR EL ALFABETO ESPAÑOL

• Recognize letters in Spanish

CORE RESOURCES

• Audio Program: Tracks 3, 4, 5

STANDARDS

4.1   Compare languages

INSTRUCTIONAL STRATEGIES

🎧 3 **Activity 1**

• Students listen to the recording of the alphabet in Spanish and repeat. Replay, if needed.

• Write letters at random on the board and have students tell you what they are in Spanish.

• Go back to Activity 1 on page 22 and ask students to spell those words out, *(c-l-a-s-e)*.

CULTURAL NOTE

• Prior to the publication of *Nueva Ortografía de la Real Academia Española* in 1999, the Spanish alphabet included two more letters: *ch*, and *ll*. Older dictionaries will have separate sections for those letters after *c* and *l*, respectively, and older books with an index in the back will alphabetize terms based on that earlier system.

• Some Spanish speakers will still refer to diagraphs *ch* and *ll* as the letter *che*, and the letter *elle*. *Be* is the name of the letter *b* in Spain. In other countries it is also called *be grande* or *be larga*. The letter *v* is also called *ve corta*.

• If time allows, ask students to look up **Real Academia Española** online, learn about its history, and use the free online dictionary. Help them understand that one of the main functions of the Academia is to maintain a dictionary of the language and to publish a grammar of Spanish used as a standard reference in all Spanish-speaking countries.

🎧 4 **Activity 2**

Audioscript

1. be; 2. ge; 3. jota; 4. erre; 5. jota; 6. equis; 7. ce; 8. pe.

🎧 5 **Activity 3**

Audioscript

a. ge, hache, efe; b. eme, eñe, pe; c. ka, doble ve/doble uve, ce; d. be, de, e; e. i griega/ye, i, te.

ANSWERS

Activity 2

1. b; 2. g; 3. j; 4. r; 5. j; 6. x; 7. c; 8. p.

Activity 3

a. J; b. N; c. G; d. V; e. L.

EL ALFABETO ESPAÑOL

1 🎧 3 Listen and repeat the letters in Spanish.

2 🎧 4 Listen to the letters in Spanish and select the correct option.

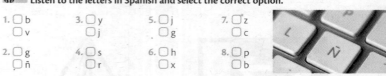

1. ◯ b   3. ◯ y   5. ◯ j   7. ◯ z
   ◯ v   ◯ j   ◯ g   ◯ c

2. ◯ g   4. ◯ s   6. ◯ h   8. ◯ p
   ◯ ñ   ◯ r   ◯ x   ◯ b

3 🎧 5 Listen and select the letter in each group that is not mentioned.

4 Write the name of the letters to spell out the following Hispanic countries. Then write the name of the country on the map.

a.
(V) (E) (N) (E) (Z) (U) (E) (L) (A)
uve   e   ene   e   zeta   u   e   ele   a

b.
(U) (R) (U) (G) (U) (A) (Y)
_____

c.
(E) (C) (U) (A) (D) (O) (R)
_____

d.
(P) (A) (R) (A) (G) (U) (A) (Y)
_____

e.
(H) (O) (N) (D) (U) (R) (A) (S)
_____

Map labels:
México, Cuba, República Dominicana, Puerto Rico, Guatemala, El Salvador, Nicaragua, Costa Rica, Panamá, Colombia, Perú, Brasil, Bolivia, Chile, Argentina

5 Write out the names of the following countries where Spanish is spoken.

a. Pe - a - ene - a - eme - a ➡ ....
b. E - ese - pe - a - eñe - a ➡ ....
c. Eme - e - equis - i - ce - o ➡ ....
d. Be - o - ele - i - uve - i - a ➡ ....
e. A - erre - ge - e - ene - te - i - ene - a ➡ ....
f. Che - i - ele - e ➡ ....

6 👥 Write out the letters of your name in Spanish in the name. Then, in groups of three or four, take turns spelling your name out to each other.

HOLA
mi nombre es

Modelo: E1: Hola, mi nombre es "ese – te – e – uve – e".
E2: Hola, Steve.

INSTRUCTIONAL STRATEGIES

Activity 4

Students write out the name of each letter for the country names provided. They should also locate the country on the map and write the name in the space provided.

Activity 5

To review answers, have students spell out the letters then say the country. Spell out the names of other countries to see who can guess it first. Have students spell out classroom items in Spanish for the class to guess.

Activity 6

Do this as a whole class activity to begin introducing students to each other.

ANSWERS

Activity 4

a. Model provided.

b. U, erre, u, ge, u, a, i griega.

c. E, ce, u, a, de, o, erre.

d. Pe, a, erre, a, ge, u, a, i griega.

e. Hache, o, ene, de, u, erre, a, ese.

Activity 5

a. Panamá; **b.** España; **c.** México; **d.** Bolivia; **e.** Argentina; **f.** Chile.

Activity 6

Answers will vary.

SLOWER-PACED LEARNERS

Provide students with a list of words covered in this unit (i.e., names of countries, cognates) and have them play hangman taking turns.

ADVANCED LEARNERS

Have students play "scattergories" using the letters of the alphabet as categories. All words are valid, but cognates count double.

HERITAGE LANGUAGE LEARNERS

Ask students to write a list with words that have *b/v* and *g/j*. Then, ask them to dictate those words to each other.

EN LA CLASE DE ESPAÑOL

OBJECTIVES FOR EN LA CLASE DE ESPAÑOL

- Learn classroom expressions
- Learn names for common classroom objects

CORE RESOURCES

- Audio Program: Tracks 6, 7, 8

STANDARDS

- 1.1   Engage in conversation
- 1.2   Understand the language
- 4.1   Compare languages

INSTRUCTIONAL STRATEGIES

🎧 6 Activity 1

- Have students complete the activity on their own.
- Play "Hangman" with students, using the following target expression: INSTRUCCIONES DE CLASE.
- First, draw 20 blanks (13 - 2 - 5) on the board for that expression. Then ask students to call out vowels or consonants and fill in all the blanks as the students call out the letters found in the expression. List separately all letters called out but not found in the expression, so that students can keep track.
- Once all the blanks are filled, read the expression to them. Explain that INSTRUCCIONES DE CLASE are classroom commands or instructions. Tell students that in this activity and the next one, they will learn some classroom commands.
- Proceed to teach each classroom command using gestures and facial expressions.

Activity 2

- Have students complete this activity individually.

ANSWERS

Activity 2

a. escucha; b. escribe; c. pregunta; d. fíjate; e. relaciona; f. habla; g. lee.

SLOWER-PACED LEARNERS

Have students create flashcards for common classroom phrases and then use them to play charades.

ADVANCED LEARNERS

Invite students to play charades using the classroom phrases.

HERITAGE LANGUAGE LEARNERS

Invite students to write other phrases that might be heard in a typical classroom and share them with the rest of the class. Asking students to write first will help them focus from the very start on the importance of correct spelling.

EN LA CLASE DE ESPAÑOL

1 🎧 6 Look at the drawings as you listen to the words commonly used to give instructions in class.

escucha | lee | escribe
marca | completa | relaciona
habla | pregunta | fíjate

2 Indicate what word from the list above is most likely associated with each of the images below.

a. ....   b. ....   c. ....

d. ....   e. ....   f. ....   g. ....

3 🎧 **7** **Look at the drawing of the classroom and listen to the words for the people and objects you see.**

1. la profesora	6. el lápiz	11. el cuaderno	16. la mochila
2. el estudiante	7. el marcador	12. el diccionario	17. la carpeta
3. la papelera	8. el borrador	13. la goma de borrar	18. el mp4
4. la mesa	9. el libro	14. la tableta	19. el tablero de anuncios
5. la silla	10. el pizarrón	15. el bolígrafo	20. la puerta

4 **Identify the items in the following backpacks.**

🎧 **7** Activity 3

- Have students listen to the audio and repeat.
- Invite students to identify objects in the classroom by their letters, using an "I Spy" type of format, saying "Veo, veo", for example:

➤ Veo, veo.

Ɔ ¿Qué ves?

➤ Una cosa que empieza por la letra eme.

Ɔ ¿Qué letras tiene?

➤ Tiene una eme y una ese.

Ɔ Mesa.

Use gestures to act out **Veo, veo** (hand over eyes) and **¿Qué letras tiene?** (holding up fingers), etc.

Extension

Have students work in pairs. Each student chooses three words from the list. Then one tells the other the three words for him or her to locate the object in the picture.

Activity 4

Extension

After reviewing answers, ask students to share contents of their own backpacks with the class. Provide additional vocabulary as needed.

ANSWERS

Activity 4

1. mochila; **2.** libro; **3.** bolígrafo; **4.** goma de borrar; **5.** lápiz; **6.** cuaderno; **7.** mp4.

SLOWER-PACED LEARNERS

Students who need extra practice can write down the spelling of each of these objects and practice with each other.

PRE-AP LEARNERS

Have students count the total number of classroom objects shared by their peers in Activity 4.

HERITAGE LANGUAGE LEARNERS

Ask students to write alternative names for the classroom objects they may know of (i.e., **lapicero**, **pluma**, **bolsa**, **pizarra**). Point out that their words are valid, but that you may choose to use other choices in class.

INSTRUCTIONAL STRATEGIES

🎧 **8** Activity 5

- Have students listen to the audio and write down the words they understand or recognize.
- Then have them listen to the audio again while following the written conversation.
- Once students have understood the entire audio, ask similar questions to those they have heard.
- Point out the use of question marks and exclamation points in Spanish. Model intonation for questions.

Activity 6

- Have students complete this activity individually. Then have them check their responses with a partner. This will provide an opportunity for self-learning, as well as oral interaction.
- Go over the correct answers with the whole class.

ANSWERS

Activity 6

a. significa / escribe / Está; **b.** se escribe / repetir; **c.** se dice / Puede escribirlo; **d.** significa / escribe.

Activity 7

Answers will vary and should reflect vocabulary and expressions learned.

SLOWER-PACED LEARNERS

For Activity 7, ask students to practice orally with each other first, and then submit one of the conversations in writing.

ADVANCED LEARNERS

For Activity 6, have students substitute new words in the first conversation to practice vocabulary with each other. For example, **¿Qué significa papelera?**

HERITAGE LANGUAGE LEARNERS

Pair students with a non-heritage language learners for Activity 7. Have the other students use their partner to ask about additional words.

EN LA CLASE DE ESPAÑOL

5 🎧 **8** Listen to some examples of questions you might use in Spanish class with your teacher.

Para comunicarte con tu profesor/profesora:

» **¿Cómo se dice** *blackboard* **en español?** *How do you say* blackboard *in Spanish?*
» Pizarrón.

» Estos son mis amigos, Luis y Pablo. *These are my friends, Luis and Pablo.*
» No entiendo. **¿Puede repetir,** por favor? *I don't understand.* **Can you repeat, please?**
» Estos son mis amigos, Luis y Pablo.

» **¿Qué significa "pizarrón"?** *What does* "pizarrón" *mean?*
» *Blackboard.*

» ¿Cómo se escribe "cuaderno" en español? *How do you spell* "cuaderno" *in Spanish?*
» Ce - u - a - de - e - erre - ene - o.

» ¿Puede escribirlo en el pizarrón? *Can you write it on the board?*
» Sí, claro. *Yes, of course.*

» ¿Está bien así? *Is this right?*
» Sí, está bien. *Yes, it's fine.*

■ In Spanish, question marks and exclamation points are placed before and after the sentence. Notice that at the beginning they are written upside down.
  » *¿Está bien así?*
  » *¡Perfecto!*

6 👥 **Fill in the blanks to complete the following conversations. Then practice them aloud with a partner.**

a. » ¿Qué .... "carpeta"?
» "Carpeta" es *folder* en inglés.
» ¿Cómo se ....?
» Ce - a - erre - pe - e - te - a.
» ¿.................. bien así?
» Sí, está bien.

b. » ¿Cómo .... "papelera" en español?
» Pe - a - pe - e - ele - e - erre - a.
» ¿Puede ...., por favor?
» Pe - a - pe - e - ele - e - erre - a.

c. » ¿Cómo .... *backpack* en español?
» Mochila.
» ¿.................. en el pizarrón?
» Sí, claro.

d. » ¿Qué .... "libro"?
» "Libro" es *book* en inglés.
» ¿Cómo se ....?
» Ele - i - be - erre - o.

7 👥 **With a partner, create your own conversations using the expressions above and the vocabulary from Activity 3.**

DESTREZAS

UNIDAD 0

In this section of every unit, you will practice three of the four communication skills: reading, writing, and speaking. Specific strategies are presented to guide you as you complete the activities. Use the strategies in **Destrezas** to become a better learner.

COMPRENSIÓN DE VOCABULARIO

In the beginning, learning Spanish is all about learning vocabulary and expressions. Learning vocabulary is the first step to begin communicating in Spanish. Review the learning strategies in **Destrezas** and follow the suggestions to help you learn new vocabulary.

Destrezas

Making visual flashcards

In addition to making traditional flashcards with Spanish on one side and English on the other, try creating visual flashcards. Draw a picture of a word or action on one side of a card and the Spanish word on the other. Be sure to include the article before each noun. You don't have to be a great artist, as you are the only one that needs to know what the drawing represents. Use them to quiz yourself or have others use the cards to quiz you.

1 Create visual flashcards for the following words from the unit.

el bolígrafo	el marcador
el borrador	la mesa
la carpeta	la mochila
el cuaderno	la papelera
el diccionario	la silla
la goma de borrar	el tablero de anuncios
el lápiz	la tableta

2 Exchange flashcards with a partner and quiz each other on the new vocabulary words. *¡Atención!* Each of you should be responding to your own cards.

PRONUNCIACIÓN The Spanish vowels

In Spanish, each vowel has only one sound and is pronounced the same way in almost every case.

Vowel	Sounds like	Examples
a	*a* in f*a*ther, but shorter	*marca, carpeta, habla*
e	*e* in th*e*y, but shorter	*mesa, estudiante, clase*
i	*i* in mach*i*ne, but shorter	*sí, escribe, amigo*
o	*o* in z*o*ne, but shorter	*nombre, profesora, goma*
u	*u* in r*u*le, but shorter	*anuncio, pregunta, escucha*

1 🎧 9 Listen and repeat after the speaker.

2 🎧 10 List the words you hear in the appropriate column according to their vowel sound.

a	e	i	o	u

29

OBJECTIVES FOR DESTREZAS

• Strategies for learning new vocabulary

STANDARDS

1.2   Understand the language

INSTRUCTIONAL STRATEGIES

Activity 1

Make sure students read the **Destrezas** box before proceeding to do the activity.

OBJECTIVES FOR PRONUNCIACIÓN

• Practice correct pronunciation of Spanish vowels

CORE RESOURCES

• Audio Program: Tracks 9, 10

STANDARDS

1.2   Understand the language
4.1   Compare languages

INSTRUCTIONAL STRATEGIES

🎧 9 **Activity 1**

Introduce the five vowels with sample words and books closed. Ask students to sound out the words as you write them on the board: ***marca***, ***mesa***, ***amigo***, ***profesora***, ***maestra***, ***pregunta***. Write these words on the board and pronounce them. Ask students to draw conclusions about the sounds of the vowels in English. Help them realize that, unlike English, the five vowels in Spanish have a fairly consistent sound in all Spanish words.

Audioscript

marca, carpeta, habla; mesa, estudiante, clase; sí, escribe, amigo; nombre, profesora, goma; anuncio, pregunta, escucha.

🎧 10 **Activity 2**

Point out that they will be listening to a series of words they may not know, but that most of them are cognates. Tell students to focus only on the vowel sounds and not worry about meaning. Repeat the audio to allow students a second opportunity to listen to the words or instruct students to write the number of the word they hear in the appropriate column.

Audioscript

1. banana; **2.** dividir; **3.** tú; **4.** color; **5.** insistir; **6.** depender; **7.** planta; **8.** foto; **9.** mapa; **10.** excelente; **11.** lente; **12.** un; **13.** honor; **14.** sí; **15.** bus.

ANSWERS

Activity 1

Students listen and repeat.

Activity 2

a. 1, 7, 9; **e.** 6, 10, 11; **i.** 2, 5, 14; **o.** 4, 8, 13; **u.** 3, 12, 15.

SLOWER-PACED LEARNERS

For Activity 2, pause the audio between words for students. Then play it again so students can check their answers.

HERITAGE LANGUAGE LEARNERS

Use the audio as a dictation and have students write down the words they hear. Have students check their spelling with a partner.

OBJECTIVES FOR SABOR HISPANO

- Learn about Spanish-speaking countries in Latin America and Spain
- Learn how many people speak Spanish around the world
- Learn quick facts about Spanish speakers in the U.S.

CORE RESOURCES

- Audio Program: Track 11

STANDARDS

1.2   Understand the language
2.1   Practices and perspectives
4.1   Compare cultures

INSTRUCTIONAL STRATEGIES

- Introduce the topic by asking students what they know about Spanish around the world.
- Talk about the map. Ask: **Where are the majority of the Spanish-speaking countries located? How did the Spanish language spread to the Americas?** (Exploration by individuals such as Cristóbal Colón, Ponce de León, Hernán Cortés, etc.). **Which country is further north, Ecuador or Bolivia? Which countries are islands?** and so on.
- Elicit from students what they already know about the countries featured in the photographs: Mexico, Puerto Rico, Costa Rica, Argentina. Read the captions aloud.
- Bring other images to class (or project them on a whiteboard) and have students guess in which country they may have been taken. Use these pictures to have a conversation about stereotypes and cultures.
- Alternatively, ask students to bring a picture that does not fit their views of a given country. Have students discuss their pictures with each other.

SLOWER-PACED LEARNERS

Read the passage in Spanish together with students. You have to read it more than once to encourage students that struggle with reading.

ADVANCED LEARNERS

Have students prepare a short presentation about a Spanish-speaking country of their choice. They should add: a fact that everybody relates to that country, a fact that nobody would relate to that country and 2-3 pictures that reflect the (geographical, cultural, historical...) diversity of that country.

HERITAGE LANGUAGE LEARNERS

Ask students to bring pictures from their countries (their own pictures or from the Internet). Students should bring both stereotypical and non-stereotypical pictures so they can talk about stereotypes and how they affect the perceptions we have of other countries.

SABOR HISPANO

YO HABLO ESPAÑOL, ¿Y TÚ?

El español es la segunda lengua más hablada en el mundo. Se habla en casi toda América Latina y España. Se habla en Filipinas y en algunas partes de África. ¡Apréndelo!

Catedral Metropolitana en el Zócalo de la capital mexicana, México D.F.

Playa Flamenco en la Isla de Culebra, Puerto Rico

Machu Picchu en Perú

Bosque tropical en Costa Rica

Barrio de La Boca en Buenos Aires, Argentina

¿Sabes que....? (Do you know that...?)

- ✓ Spanish is the second most widely spoken language in the world. (Mandarin is first and English is third).
- ✓ Spanish is the third language with the highest number of Internet users (8% of the total number of users).
- ✓ Another name for Spanish is Castilian (castellano), named after the region in Spain where it originated.
- ✓ The letter ñ only exists in Spanish.

NUESTROS PAÍSES

Select the correct option to complete each sentence.

1. Spanish is the **first / second** most widely spoken language in the world.
2. The letter **q / ñ** is unique to Spanish.
3. The majority of students in the United States study **Spanish / Japanese**.
4. **Many / Not many** people speak Spanish.
5. Another name for Spanish is **Castilian / European Spanish**.
6. Spanish is the **second / third** language with the highest number of Internet users.

España
- Madrid
- Barcelona
- Valencia
- Sevilla

Molinos de viento
en Castilla, España

🎧 11 **Underline the cognates and other words you recognize in the following text.**

«Hola, mi nombre es Sofía y soy estudiante. Estudio inglés en la escuela. Mi escuela es grande y tengo muchos amigos. Mis amigos son de Ecuador, México y Perú. Uso la computadora para comunicarme con mis amigos. También uso la computadora para estudiar y escuchar música. Y tú, ¿estudias español en clase?».

Quick facts!

Fuentes: Universidad de Lyon, *Top Languages in Global Information Production Study*, Academia de la Lengua Española, Informe 2012 Instituto Cervantes.

✓ In the United States, Spanish is the second most widely spoken language.
✓ Spanish is the second most studied language among students in the United States.

✓ According to a study from the University of Lyon, France, Spanish speakers can pronounce 7.8 syllables per second. (Only Japanese has a higher number of syllables per second).

31

INSTRUCTIONAL STRATEGIES

- Elicit what students know about Spanish as a spoken and written language, its music, and its literature. Do they know any Spanish-language writers or musicians?
- Ask them if they have ever been to any of the countries featured here or any other Spanish-speaking country. Encourage them to share their experiences.
- Have students complete the first activity on this page and compare answers.

🎧 11 Play the audio while students follow. Have them identify the cognates while you record them on the board. Practice pronunciation. Replay the audio with books closed and have students signal with thumbs up or raised hands each time they hear one of the cognates.
- Ask: **¿Cómo es tu escuela? ¿Es grande o pequeña? ¿Tienes amigos de México, Ecuador, etc.? ¿De dónde son tus amigos? ¿Usas la computadora para estudiar o escuchar música?** and so on. Accept one word answers at this stage.

ANSWERS

Select the correct option...

1. second; 2. ñ; 3. Spanish; 4. Many; 5. Castilian; 6. third.

Cognates

Answers will vary and should reflect cognates, such as **estudiante, inglés, escuela, computadora, comunicarme, estudiar, música**.

SLOWER-PACED LEARNERS

Use the audio to focus students' attention on rhythm, intonation, and pronunciation. Have students respond chorally as needed.

PRE-AP LEARNERS

Provide students with a picture of a person, and a list of characteristics, and have them write a similar description. Have students present their introduction to the class.

HERITAGE LANGUAGE LEARNERS

Have students record themselves with their smartphones for a minute. Have them count how many words per second they are able to pronounce.

OBJECTIVES FOR EN RESUMEN: VOCABULARIO

- Review unit vocabulary and expressions
- Practice communicative skills

STANDARDS

1.2 Understand the language

1.3 Present information

INSTRUCTIONAL STRATEGIES

- Model how to use the vocabulary list to review new words and expressions learned in this unit.
- Use simple materials, such as index cards or self-adhesive notes.
- Self-adhesive notes can be used for writing nouns from the vocabulary list on them, then using them to place the correct labels on objects in the classroom or pictures in the book.
- Index cards can be used as flash cards with the Spanish term on one side and the English term on the other, or a picture or drawing.
- Students can work in pairs or groups, using the self-adhesive notes and index cards as they would the cards of a board game to help each other practice the unit vocabulary.
- Encourage students to write labels or captions for the photos on this page. Remind them to use the vocabulary and expressions they have learned in this unit.

EN RESUMEN: Vocabulario

INSTRUCCIONES EN LA CLASE *Instructions for class* (See page 26)

 completa *complete*
 escribe *write*
 escucha *listen*
 fíjate *look at*
 habla *speak*

 lee *read*
 marca *mark*
 pregunta *ask*
 relaciona *match*

EN LA CLASE DE ESPAÑOL *In Spanish class* (See page 27)

 el bolígrafo *pen*
 el borrador *eraser*
 la carpeta *folder*
 el cuaderno *notebook*

 el diccionario *dictionary*
 el estudiante *student (male)*
 la estudiante *student (female)*
la goma de borrar *pencil eraser*

 el lápiz *pencil*
 el marcador *marker*
 la mesa *table, desk*
 la mochila *backpack*

EN RESUMEN: Gramática

el mp4 *mp4*

la papelera
wastepaper basket

el pizarrón *blackboard*

el profesor *teacher (male)*

la profesora *teacher
(female)*

la puerta *door*

la silla *chair*

el tablero
de anuncios
bulletin board

la tableta
tablet

PARA COMUNICARTE CON TU PROFESOR/PROFESORA *To communicate with your teacher*   (See page 28)

¿Cómo se dice… en español? *How do you say… in Spanish?*
¿Cómo se escribe… en español? *How do you spell… in Spanish?*
¿Está bien así? *Is this right?*
Hola, mi nombre es… *Hi, my name is…*
No entiendo. *I don't understand.*
¿Puede escribirlo en el pizarrón? *Can you write it on the blackboard?*
¿Puede repetir, por favor? *Can you repeat, please?*
¿Qué significa…? *What does… mean?*
Sí, claro. *Yes, of course.*
Sí, está bien. *Yes, it's fine.*

OTRAS PALABRAS Y EXPRESIONES ÚTILES *Other useful words and expressions*

bienvenidos *welcome*
está/están *is/are located*
el mundo hispano *Hispanic world*
los países *countries*

33

OBJECTIVES FOR EN RESUMEN: GRAMÁTICA

- Review unit grammar
- Practice communicative skills

STANDARDS

1.2   Understand the language
1.3   Present information

INSTRUCTIONAL STRATEGIES

- Ask them which activities they found easy and which they found challenging.
- Encourage them to repeat any activities they found particularly challenging.

SLOWER-PACED LEARNERS

Help students organize the review by sections so they can better absorb the information. Pair them with a student who is more confident with the vocabulary to review together.

ADVANCED LEARNERS

Have students create 4 review questions to share as part of a whole class review.

HERITAGE LANGUAGE LEARNERS

Have students create an original conversation using as many words and expressions from the unit as possible.

OBJECTIVES FOR UNIT OPENER

- Introduce unit theme: **Hola, ¿Qué tal?** about greetings, introductions, and responding to basic questions
- Culture: Learn about Spanish-speakers in the U.S.

STANDARDS

- 1.2   Understand the language
- 2.1   Practices and perspectives

INSTRUCTIONAL STRATEGIES

Introduce unit theme and objectives: Talk about Hispanic communities in the U.S. Have students look at the image. Read the caption aloud: **Los muchachos son buenos amigos.** Clasp your hands together to demonstrate **buenos amigos**.

Ask questions to help students recycle content from the previous unit. For instance, encourage them to use expressions they have learned to ask about meaning, such as: **¿Cómo se dice "table" en español? ¿Cómo se escribe en español? ¿Qué significa "amigos"?**

Use the image to preview unit vocabulary, including common greetings: **Buenos días** and **¿Qué tal?** Help students access meaning by making frequent use of gestures or visuals.

Ask the introductory questions:

- **¿Son profesores o estudiantes?**
- **¿Están en clase o en un restaurante?**
- **¿Cómo se dice "friends" en español?**

Ask related questions: **¿Cuántas muchachas hay? ¡Hay una, dos, tres?** (while holding up fingers to clarify). **¿Cuántos muchachos hay?** Ask some *yes/no* questions.

ANSWERS

Answers will vary. Possible answers might include the following.

- Son estudiantes.
- Están en un restaurante.
- En español, "friends" es "amigos".

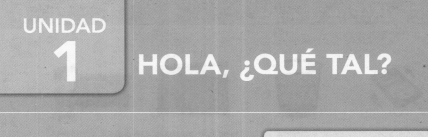

UNIDAD 1

HOLA, ¿QUÉ TAL?

>> ¿Son profesores o estudiantes?
>> ¿Están en clase o en un restaurante?
>> ¿Cómo se dice "friends" en español?

34

Los muchachos son buenos amigos.

ADDITIONAL UNIT RESOURCES

Extension Activities (EA) (Photocopiable)	Interactive Whiteboard Lessons (IWB)	Audio	Video	Online ELEteca
EA: 1.1, 1.2	IWB: 1.1, 1.2	12 to 22	Diálogo 1	EXTENSIÓN DIGITAL

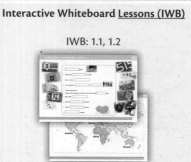

In this unit, you will learn to:

 Say hello, good-bye, and make introductions

Give your age and say where you are from

Ask others about themselves

Identify some common professions

Express dates and phone numbers

Using

- Subject pronouns and the verb *ser*
- Verbs *tener* and *llamar(se)*
- Definite and indefinite articles

Cultural Connections

- Share information about the Spanish language and Hispanic communities in the United States, and compare cultural similarities

SABOR HISPANO

Hispanos en Estados Unidos
- Estados Unidos

¡ACCIÓN!

35

INTRODUCTION TO LEARNING OUTCOMES

The unit's learning objectives are an organizational tool for you and your students. Use them to preview what students will learn, and they serve as a way for you to assess whether your students have mastered the main ideas and skills. Encourage your students to read the learning outcomes both before starting the unit and when they prepare for a test.

LEARNING OUTCOMES

- Use appropriate greetings
- Share basic information, such as name, age, and address
- Ask others for basic information, such as name, age, and address
- Identify some common professions
- Express dates and phone numbers

INSTRUCTIONAL STRATEGIES

- Use the unit opener to introduce students to a preview of the vocabulary and the cultural topics for this unit.
- Have students look at the images on this page and relate them to the objectives listed.
- Invite students to read the topic for **Sabor hispano** and preview that section in the unit.
- Introduce the video series in **¡Acción!** and ask students to predict what they think the episode will be about.
- Encourage students to use the images to practice interpersonal and interpretive communication skills. Ask questions such as: **¿Qué ven en estas fotos? ¿Qué fotos son interesantes?**
- Have students work in pairs to talk about the images using the questions you have modeled. Then have volunteers present to the class what they understand this unit to be about.

NOTE

Common Core State Standards (CCSS)

The four strands of the *Common Core State Standards for English Language Arts (ELA) and Literacy in History / Social Studies, Science, and Technical Subjects* are represented in the National Standards for Learning Languages by the Communication standards: Interpersonal, Interpretive, and Presentational. The three modes of communication align with the goals in Reading, Writing, Speaking, and Listening by emphasizing the purpose behind the communication.

THREE MODES OF COMMUNICATION: UNIT 1			
	INTERPERSONAL	INTERPRETIVE	PRESENTATIONAL
HABLAMOS DE...	6	1, 2, 4, 5	5, 7
COMUNICA	2, 4	1, 3	2
¡ACCIÓN!	2	1, 3, 4, 5	6
PALABRA POR PALABRA	4, 5, 6, 7, 10, 12	2, 3, 4, 7, 10, 11	8
GRAMÁTICA	6, 10	1, 2, 3, 4, 5, 6, 8, 9	7, 10
CULTURA		SABOR HISPANO	
RELATO	3, 4, 5	1, 2, 5	5

OBJECTIVES FOR HABLAMOS DE...

- Understand language in context
- Preview vocabulary: greetings, introductions, and adjectives to indicate national origin
- Preview grammatical structures: the verbs **ser**, **tener**, **llamarse**
- Read and listen to a conversation about friends meeting for the first time, introducing themselves, and sharing basic information

CORE RESOURCES

- Audio Program: Tracks 12, 13, 14

STANDARDS

1.1   Engage in conversation

1.2   Understand the language

4.2   Compare cultures

INSTRUCTIONAL STRATEGIES

Activity 1

- Encourage students to look at the image and describe what they see: **¿Qué ven?** Help students access meaning of unfamiliar words such as: **compañeros**, **vacaciones**, **biblioteca** by giving examples in Spanish: **Esteban es un compañero de clase. ¿Eres compañero/a de clase de Esteban?** and so on.

🎧 12 Activity 2

- Introduction to the conversation. Tell students to close their books. Explain that it is the first day of classes and the students in Activity 1 have just introduced themselves to each other.
- Check for previous knowledge by asking students what they think the characters will say (in English) in their introductions. Before playing the audio, clarify that students should focus on information that they need to answer the *true/false* questions.
- Play the audio two times. During the first time, ask students to listen to Alberto and Cecilia and, during the second time, to Miguel and Nélida. Finally, have students open the book and review the conversation. Observe, provide support and correct students as needed.

🎧 12 Activity 3

Use the audio to focus students' attention on rhythm, intonation, and pronunciation. Have students respond chorally as needed.

ANSWERS

Activity 1

1. b; 2. a; 3. c; 4. c.

Activity 2

a. F (es argentino); b. T; c. T; d. F (Cecilia es de Bogotá); e. F (Cecilia tiene 14 años y Nélida tiene 15 años).

HABLAMOS DE... Los compañeros de clase

1 Look at the image below of students studying together in the library. Then choose the correct answer to complete the sentences.

1. La imagen representa...
   - **a.** ☐ una foto de familia.
   - **b.** ☐ una foto de compañeros de clase.
   - **c.** ☐ una foto de vacaciones.

2. Los muchachos están...
   - **a.** ☐ en la biblioteca.
   - **b.** ☐ en un parque.
   - **c.** ☐ en la cafetería.

3. En la imagen...
   - **a.** ☐ hay 4 muchachos.
   - **b.** ☐ hay 1 muchacho y 3 muchachas.
   - **c.** ☐ hay 2 muchachos y 3 muchachas.

4. Los muchachos tienen en la mano *(hand)*...
   - **a.** ☐ mochilas y libros.
   - **b.** ☐ carpetas y cuadernos.
   - **c.** ☐ bolígrafos y lápices.

2 🎧 12 Follow along as you listen to a conversation between students meeting for the first time. Then indicate whether each sentence is true (T) or false (F).

Nélida: Hola, ¿qué tal? Me llamo Nélida. Y ustedes, ¿cómo se llaman?
Alberto: Hola, yo soy Alberto y él es Miguel.
Miguel: ¿Qué tal? Ella es Cecilia. Es colombiana, de Bogotá.
Cecilia: Hola a todos, ¿qué tal? ¿De dónde eres, Alberto? ¿Eres americano?
Alberto: No, soy argentino, de Buenos Aires, pero vivo aquí en Estados Unidos.
Nélida: Cecilia, ¿cuántos años tienes?
Cecilia: Tengo 14 años. ¿Y tú?
Nélida: Tengo 15 años.
Miguel: Bueno, muchachos, vamos a clase. ¡Hasta luego!
Alberto: Sí, es verdad, ¡hasta luego!
Nélida y Cecilia: ¡Adiós!

	T	F
a. Alberto es español.	☐	☐
b. Cecilia tiene 14 años.	☐	☐
c. Cecilia es colombiana.	☐	☐
d. Miguel es de Bogotá.	☐	☐
e. Nélida y Cecilia tienen 14 años.	☐	☐

36 **3** 🎧 12 Listen again to the conversation and repeat after the speaker.

SLOWER-PACED LEARNERS

Write phrases from the conversation on the board and ask students *either/or* questions help them identify who said it. For example, **Tengo 14 años. ¿Es Cecilia o Nélida?**

HERITAGE LANGUAGE LEARNERS

For Activity 1, have students describe what other objects they see in the image and what they think the students are doing. Have them write their own captions for the scene.

4 🎧 **13** Listen to Miguel, Nélida, Cecilia, and Alberto talk about where they are from. Then fill in the missing words in the sentences below.

   a. Miguel es de Los Ángeles, él es ....

   b. Alberto es de Buenos Aires, él es ....

   c. Nélida es de Madrid, ella es ....

   d. Cecilia es de Bogotá, ella es ....

5 🎧 **14** 👥 Follow along as you listen to the conversations below. What is the difference between them? Then, in groups of three, practice the conversations aloud with each of you taking a part.

a.

b.

Víctor: ¡Hola, Susana! ¿Qué tal estás?
Susana: Bien. Mira, este es Antonio, un amigo de clase.
Víctor: Hola, Antonio.
Antonio: ¡Hola! ¿Qué tal?

Jesús: Buenos días, Leonor. ¿Cómo está usted?
Leonor: Muy bien, gracias. Mire, le presento al señor Fernández.
Sr. Fernández: Encantado.
Jesús: Encantado.

> ⚠ ■ The following abbreviations are used for a person's title:
> señor ➡ Sr.   señora ➡ Sra.   señorita ➡ Srta.

6 👥 Read the following expressions and decide whether they would most likely be used in formal (F) or informal (I) situations. Then write what you think the expressions mean. Compare your answers with a partner.

	F	I	What do you think it means?
a. Hola, ¿qué tal?	☐	☐	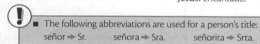
b. Buenos días, ¿cómo está?	☐	☐	
c. Encantado.	☐	☐	

7 👥 In groups of three, take turns introducing each other in formal and informal situations using the conversations above as a model. *¡Atención!* Be sure to substitute your own information.

37

UNIDAD 1

INSTRUCTIONAL STRATEGIES

🎧 **13** Activity 4

Use the audio to focus students' attention on rhythm, intonation, and pronunciation. Have students respond chorally as needed.

Audioscript

   a. Hola, soy Miguel. Soy americano, de Los Ángeles.

   b. Hola, yo soy Alberto. Soy de Buenos Aires, Argentina.

   c. Hola, me llamo Nélida. Soy española, de Madrid.

   d. Hola, yo soy Cecilia. Soy colombiana, de Bogotá.

🎧 **14** Activity 5

Use the audio to focus students' attention on rhythm, intonation, and pronunciation. Have students respond chorally as needed.

CULTURAL NOTE

Point out that formal address is used with people you do not know (or have not been introduced to) and with older people as a sign of respect.

Activity 7

Have students work in groups for this activity. Encourage them to use the vocabulary and sentence patterns from the conversations they have heard in the audio activities.

ANSWERS

Activity 4

   a. americano; **b.** argentino; **c.** española; **d.** colombiana.

Activity 6

   a. Informal; **b.** Formal; **c.** Formal.

SLOWER-PACED LEARNERS

Encourage students for Activity 1 to use learning strategies from the previous unit such as how to infer meaning from cognates: ***parque***, ***vacaciones***, ***cafetería***...

ADVANCED LEARNERS

For Activity 4, have students think about the use of "americano/a" to refer to people from the United States. How do you think people from Latin America may feel about that?

HERITAGE LANGUAGE LEARNERS

For Activity 6, have students share other ways to greet they know. Ask them whether they are formal or informal, and how they decide when to use one or the other.

COMUNICA COMMUNICATIVE FUNCTIONS

OBJECTIVES FOR COMUNICA

- Present the communicative functions of the unit:
  – Greetings, introductions, and saying good-bye
  – Asking and giving information about yourself
- Practice formal and informal ways of introducing oneself

CORE RESOURCES

- Extension Activities: EA 1.1
- Audio Program: Track 15
- Interactive Online Materials - ELEteca

STANDARDS

1.1   Engage in conversation
1.2   Understand the language

INSTRUCTIONAL STRATEGIES FOR GREETINGS, INTRODUCTIONS, AND SAYING GOOD-BYE

- Discuss formal vs. informal language with students: **When do we use formal language? When do we use informal language? When is it appropriate to use one or the other?** Elicit from them what they know about formal and informal language in English and Spanish.
- Point out that in Spanish we use the pronoun **tú** and its verb forms to address someone informally, such as friends and family members, while we use the pronoun **usted** and its verb forms to address people formally, such as teachers and strangers.

Alternative Activity

Use EA 1.1, **Puzle de saludos, presentaciones y despedidas,** to introduce the expressions. Have students separate into groups of four. Give each group a set of cut-up sections of chart and have them reconstruct the expressions.

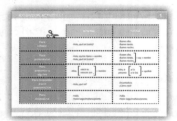

Activity 1

- Ask questions: **¿Quiénes son? ¿Dónde están? ¿Qué hacen? ¿Qué relación crees que tienen entre ellos?**
- As you go along, keep track of student responses by writing them on the board.

Activity 2

Remind students that they can also use **Hola, mi nombre es...** when introducing themselves.

GRAMMAR NOTE

Remind students that the verb endings for **tú** and **usted** are different: **¿Cómo estás?** is for informal **tú** and **¿Cómo está?** is for formal **usted**.

COMUNICA

GREETINGS, INTRODUCTIONS, AND SAYING GOOD-BYE

Informal	Formal
■ Para saludar *To say hello*	
Hola, ¿qué tal? *Hi, what's up?*	Buenos días / tardes. *Good morning/afternoon.*
Hola, ¿qué tal estás? *Hi, how are you doing?*	Buenas noches. *Good evening, Good night.*
■ Para presentarse *To introduce yourself*	
Hola, soy... *Hi, I'm...*	Buenos días,
Hola, me llamo... *Hi, my name is...*	Buenas tardes/noches, | soy...
■ Para presentar a alguien *To introduce someone*	
Mira, este es Dan. *Hey, this is...*	Mire, le presento al Sr. Pérez.
Mira, esta es Jenny. *Hey, this is...*	*Look, I'd like to introduce you to Mr. Pérez.*
Mira, estos son Dan y Bill. *Hey, these are...*	Mire, le presento a la Sra. Díaz.
Mira, estas son Jenny y Ana. *Hey, these are...*	*Look, I'd like to introduce you to Mrs. Díaz.*
■ Para responder a una presentación *To respond to an introduction*	
Hola, ¿qué tal? *Hi, what's up?*	Encantado. *Delighted (said by a male).*
	Encantada. *Delighted (said by a female).*
	¿Cómo está? *How do you do?*
■ Para despedirse *To say good-bye*	
Adiós. *Good-bye.*	
Hasta luego / mañana / pronto. *See you later/tomorrow/soon.*	

1 Look at the drawings below. Then read the conversations and match them to the appropriate drawing.

a. ○   b. ○   c. ○   d. ○

1. » Buenos días, Sra. Gómez, ¿cómo está?
   » Bien, Carlitos.

2. » Hola, ¿cómo te llamas?
   » Yo me llamo Marta. ¿Y tú?
   » Yo soy Daniel. ¿Qué tal?

3. » Hola, papá, este es mi amigo Alberto.
   » Encantado.
   » Hola.

4. » ¡Adiós, chicos!
   » ¡Hasta mañana, profesor!

2 👥 Walk around the classroom and introduce yourself informally to three classmates. Then introduce yourself to three different classmates using formal expressions.

ANSWERS

Activity 1

1. a; 2. d; 3. c; 4. b.

SLOWER-PACED LEARNERS

Help students distinguish between formal and informal language by asking them to list people they know who they would address with formal language. Then have them do the same for informal address.

ASKING AND GIVING INFORMATION ABOUT YOURSELF

» **¿Cómo te llamas?** *What's your name?*
» **Me llamo Francisca García Mejías.**
  My name is Francisca García Mejías.

» **¿De dónde eres?** *Where are you from?*
» **Soy de México. / Soy mexicana.**
  I'm from Mexico. / I'm Mexican.

» **¿Cuántos años tienes?** *How old are you?*
» **Tengo 15 años.** *I'm 15 years old.*

» **¿Dónde vives?** *Where do you live?*
» **Vivo en Puebla. / Vivo en la calle Reina.**
  I live in Puebla. / I live on Reina Street.

» **¿Qué haces?** *What do you do?*
» **Soy estudiante.** *I'm a student.*

■ People in Spanish-speaking countries often use two last names. In the case of Francisca García Mejías, García is Francisca's father's last name and Mejías is her mother's. In this way, both sides of the family are represented.

■ Other jobs or professions

For males	For females		For males	For females	
profesor	profesora	*teacher*	cantante	cantante	*singer*
médico	médica	*doctor*	futbolista	futbolista	*soccer player*
enfermero	enfermera	*nurse*	tenista	tenista	*tennis player*
bibliotecario	bibliotecaria	*librarian*	actor	actriz	*actor/actress*

3 🎧 15 👥 **Listen to the following conversations and fill in the missing words. Then practice the conversation with a partner.**

1. En el médico

Médica: ¿Cómo te llamas?
Carlos: Me llamo Carlos.
Médica: ¿Cuántos años ....?
Carlos: Tengo 5 ....

2. En la biblioteca

Sra. Díaz: ¿Cómo te llamas?
Rosalía: Me .... Rosalía Castro Gómez.
Sra. Díaz: ¿........ vives?
Rosalía: Vivo en la calle Molina.

3. En la calle

Miguel: ¿De dónde ....?
Beatriz: Soy puertorriqueña.
Miguel: ¿Y .... haces?
Beatriz: ....profesora.

4 👥 **With a partner, take turns introducing yourself as one of the people in the images. Give your name, age, where you are from, and what you do. Use your imagination and the cues in the images to help you create your profile.**

MORE IN ELETECA: EXTRA ONLINE PRACTICE

39

OBJECTIVES FOR COMUNICA

• Present the communicative functions of the unit:
  – Asking and giving information about yourself and others
  – Learn common professions in Spanish

CORE RESOURCES

• Extension Activities: EA 1.2
• Audio Program: Track 15

STANDARDS

1.1   Engage in conversation
1.2   Understand the language
1.3   Present information
4.1   Compare languages

INSTRUCTIONAL STRATEGIES FOR ASKING AND GIVING INFORMATION ABOUT YOURSELF

• Write the following professions in separate columns on the board or project the table from the book: **profesor / profesora**; **medico / médica**; **enfermero / enfermera**. Ask students to point out the differences between the two sets of nouns and what they refer to. Remind them that nouns in Spanish are either feminine or masculine. Help them notice the endings.

• Help students understand the concepts of cognates vs. false cognates. For instance, Spanish **actor** means *actor*, but **médico** means "doctor" not "medic".

• Review other nouns from the list and write them on the board. Help students notice the professions that change ending for masculine and feminine and those that do not, such as **cantante** and nouns ending in **–ista**: **futbolista, tenista**. Remind students that the article will change with these professions to indicate male or female: **el futobolista/la futbolista**; **el cantante/la cantante**.

🎧 15 **Activity 3**

Before playing the audio, have students read the conversations and try to fill in the missing words. Then play the audio.

Extension

Assign pairs of students a conversation to memorize and then present to the class.

Activity 4

Extension

Use EA 1.2, **Personajes famosos**, so students can practice in third person. Separate students into groups of four and give each student a card (A, B, C, D) with a famous celebrity. Have students ask each other questions to guess who the person is.

ANSWERS

Activity 3

1. tienes / años; **2.** llamo / Dónde; **3.** eres / qué / Soy.

ADVANCED LEARNERS

Have students research two or three famous Hispanics in the fields of sports, medicine, and the arts. Have them write an introduction for each one saying who they are, where they are from, and where they currently live.

OBJECTIVES FOR ¡ACCIÓN!

- Provide students with a structured approach to viewing the video
- Contextualize the content of the unit in a familiar scenario

CORE RESOURCES

- Unit Video 1 - Saludos y mochilas
- Online Materials - ELEteca

STANDARDS

1.1 Interpersonal communication

1.2 Interpretive communication

2.1 Culture: Practices and perspectives

INSTRUCTIONAL STRATEGIES

Previewing: Antes del video

- Introduce the episode and read the title aloud. Give students the names of the characters in the images: (1) **Esta es Lorena,** (2) **Estos son Eli, Juanjo y Alfonso**. Encourage them to look carefully at the images so that they can become familiar with the characters.
- Point to the different characters and ask students: **¿Es una muchacha o un muchacho? ¿Es Eli o Lorena? ¿Cómo se llaman los dos muchachos? ¿Son estudiantes o profesores? ¿Qué tiene Eli en la mano?**
- Tell students to think again about the title and ask them what they think this video will be about.

Activity 1

Have students complete Activity 1 individually and share their ideas with the class.

Activity 2

Then have students work in pairs to complete Activity 2. Call on students to share their answers while you record them on the board.

Activity 3

Encourage students to use expression from **Comunica** to get them started.

Viewing: Durante el video

- ▶ Point out to students that they will not necessarily understand every word in the segment.
- Remind them to listen actively and to pay attention to facial expressions, gestures, and body language.
- Play the entire episode without pauses and ask students what they understood.
- Then play it again pausing to allow students to complete the Activities 4 and 5. Use the printed time codes as a guide

ANSWERS

Activity 1

Informal.

Activity 2

a. Hola, ¿qué tal? / Hola, ¿qué tal estás?; **b.** Soy / Me llamo; **c.** Mira, este es / esta es; **d.** Hola, ¿qué tal? / Encantado / Encantada; **e.** Adiós / Hasta luego/mañana/pronto; ¿Cuál es tu número de telefono?; **g.** ¿De dónde eres?; **h.** ¿Cuántos años tienes?; **i.** ¿Cómo te llamas?

Activity 3

Answers will vary. Possible answers: **a.** ¿Cómo te llamas?; **b.** Mira, estos son Juanjo y Alfonso; **c.** Me llamo Juanjo; **d.** Encantada; **e.** ¿Cuál es tu número de teléfono?; **f.** Hasta luego.

¡ACCIÓN! Saludos y mochilas

1. 2. 3.
4. 5. 6.

ANTES DEL VIDEO

1 👥 Look at the people in Images 2 and 4 and describe what they are doing. Are these situations formal or informal?

2 👥 With a partner, list the expressions you would use in Spanish in the following situations.

- **a.** Para saludar: ....
- **b.** Para presentarse: ....
- **c.** Para presentar a alguien: ....
- **d.** Para responder a la presentación: ....
- **e.** Para despedirse: ....
- **f.** Para preguntar el número de teléfono: ....
- **g.** Para preguntar la nacionalidad: ....
- **h.** Para preguntar la edad: ....
- **i.** Para preguntar el nombre: ....

3 Write a sentence or caption for each of the images.

	Frase		Frase
Imagen 1		Imagen 4	
Imagen 2		Imagen 5	
Imagen 3		Imagen 6	

DURANTE EL VIDEO

4 ⊟ Watch the following scene and identify the objects from the list below mentioned in the conversation.
01:23 - 01:50

> libros o lápiz o cuadernos o bolígrafos o tableta o carpetas
> marcador o goma de borrar o diccionario

40

Activity 4

4. libros, bolígrafos, carpetas, diccionario.

SLOWER-PACED LEARNERS

Frequently, students just stop listening as soon as they hear the first word they don't understand. Encourage students from the onset not to adopt this bad habit. Point out that they will be surprised to see how much they really are able to understand when reaching beyond the words and focusing on the action, gestures, and expressions.

ADVANCED LEARNERS

For Activity 3, have students work in pairs and encourage them to use their imagination and sense of humor to create original captions using the words and expressions they have learned so far. Record the best ones on the board to set the bar for the level of expectations you have for them.

DURANTE EL VIDEO

5 🔊 **Listen again to the conversation between Lorena and Eli and fill in the missing words.**
02:09 - 02:50

Lorena: ¿(a) .... estudiante?
Eli: Sí. Voy a la universidad. (b) .... también. Somos (c) ....
Lorena: Por cierto, mi nombre es Lorena.
Eli: Hola, Lorena. ¡Encantada! Yo (d) .... Eli.
Lorena: ¡Encantada, Eli!
Eli: ¿(e) .... eres, Lorena?

Lorena: (f) .... de Venezuela. Estoy aquí por trabajo. Es mi primera semana en la ciudad. ¡Y mi primer día de trabajo en esta tienda!
Eli: ¡(g) .... a la ciudad!
Lorena: ¡Gracias! ¿Ustedes son de (h) .... ?
Eli: Yo soy (i) .... Vivo aquí con mis padres desde agosto de 2010.

6 **Complete the sentences with the nationality and country of each person.**

a. Lorena es ...., es de ....
b. Eli es ...., es de ....
c. Alfonso es ...., es de ....
d. Juanjo es ...., es de ....

7 **Watch the whole episode and indicate whether the following statements are true (T) or false (F).**

	T	F
a. Eli y sus amigos viven en la ciudad.	☐	☐
b. Lorena no tiene amigos en la ciudad.	☐	☐
c. Lorena trabaja los fines de semana.	☐	☐
d. Es el mes de septiembre.	☐	☐
e. En la tienda no hay mochilas.	☐	☐

DESPUÉS DEL VIDEO

8 👥 **In groups of three, create a similar situation. Assign each member a role to play (A, B, or C). Then, prepare a conversation in which Students A and B are friends and Student C is new to the school. Include the following words.**

bienvenido/a ○ encantado/a ○ compañeros/as ○ fin de semana ○ ustedes ○ soy ○ aquí

9 👥 **Present your conversation to the class.**

 **MORE IN ELETECA:** EXTRA ONLINE PRACTICE

41

OBJECTIVES FOR LOS NÚMEROS DEL 0 AL 31

- Present the vocabulary needed to practice the communicative and grammatical functions for the unit: Numbers 0 through 31
- Identify words for numbers 0–31 in Spanish
- Use numbers to share personal information, such as age and phone number

CORE RESOURCES

- Audio Program: Tracks 16, 17
- Interactive Whiteboard Lesson: IWB 1.1
- Interactive Online Materials - ELEteca

STANDARDS

1.1	Engage in conversation
1.2	Understand the language
1.3	Present information

INSTRUCTIONAL STRATEGIES

🎧 16 Activity 1

- Before listening to the audio, assign a number from 0 to 31 to each student. Have students read out their number in order.
- Then call out numbers at random and ask the student with each of those numbers to raise his or her hand or to stand. Then listen to the audio.

🎧 17 Activity 2

Audioscript

28, 14, 11, 25, 15, 13, 9.

Activity 3

Help students pronounce correctly the numbers projected on the screen.

Alternative Activity

Use IWB 1.1, *Los números*, to do a number matching activity.

ANSWERS

Activity 2

28, 14, 11, 25, 15, 13, 9.

Activity 3

a. treinta; **b.** siete; **c.** ocho; **d.** diez; **e.** veintiséis; **f.** veintidós.

Activity 4

1. diez; **2.** siete; **3.** quince; **4.** cuatro; **5.** veinte; **6.** cinco; **7.** catorce; **8.** ocho; **9.** once. The secret number is ***dieciocho***.

PALABRA POR PALABRA Los números del 0 al 31

1 🎧 16 **Listen and repeat the numbers in Spanish.**

0	cero	8	ocho	16	dieciséis	24	veinticuatro
1	uno	9	nueve	17	diecisiete	25	veinticinco
2	dos	10	diez	18	dieciocho	26	veintiséis
3	tres	11	once	19	diecinueve	27	veintisiete
4	cuatro	12	doce	20	veinte	28	veintiocho
5	cinco	13	trece	21	veintiuno	29	veintinueve
6	seis	14	catorce	22	veintidós	30	treinta
7	siete	15	quince	23	veintitrés	31	treinta y uno

2 🎧 17 **Listen to the numbers and select the ones you hear.**

☐ 3   ☐ 2   ☐ 16   ☐ 7   ☐ 12   ☐ 11   ☐ 25

☐ 15   ☐ 9   ☐ 14   ☐ 28   ☐ 18   ☐ 13   ☐ 20

3 **Write out the numbers for the following math problems.**

a. 6 x 5 = ...   **d.** 20 ÷ 2 = ...

b. 3 + 4 = ...   **e.** 7 + 15 + 4 = ...

c. 15 – 7 = ...   **f.** 11 x 2 = ...

4 👥 **Write the numbers to the following math problems to complete the puzzle and uncover the secret number. Check your answers with a partner.**

1. Cinco más cinco.   **4.** Dos más dos.   **7.** Siete por dos.

2. Veintiuno entre tres.   **5.** Diecinueve más uno.   **8.** Doce menos cuatro.

3. Tres por cinco.   **6.** Quince entre tres.   **9.** Diez más uno.

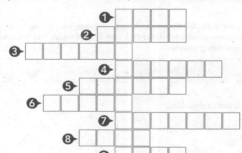

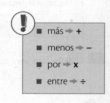

- más ➡ +
- menos ➡ –
- por ➡ x
- entre ➡ ÷

ADVANCED LEARNERS

Bingo. Ask students to create a 5x5 table and insert different numbers from 0-30 in each cell. Ask students to take turns calling out numbers.

HERITAGE LANGUAGE LEARNERS

Bingo. Have students write the numbers that have been called out on the blackboard. Remind students that numbers up to thirty should be written as one word. Combinations such as ***diez y siete*** and ***veinte y dos*** are not correct.

UNIDAD **1**

UNIDAD **1**

5 Read the **Modelo** aloud taking parts with a partner. Then ask and exchange telephone numbers with three other classmates. ¡**Atención!** It is not necessary to give your real number.

Modelo:

¿Cuál es tu número de teléfono?

Es el 659 241 487

6 **Let's play.** Think of a number from 1 to 31. Your partner will try to guess that number in Spanish. Use a thumbs up or down signal to indicate a higher or lower number. Then switch roles and play again.

7 Look at the following people. Write out the number for the age you think they are. Then, with a partner, take turns asking each other to see if you agree. Use the Modelo provided.

Tomás tiene .... años.   Paco tiene .... años.   Teresa tiene .... años.   Marcos tiene .... años.

Modelo: E1: ¿Cuántos años tiene...?
E2: Tiene... años.
E1: Sí, es verdad. / No, creo que tiene... años.

8 Introduce yourself to three classmates. Greet them and ask each one's name and age. Then introduce them to the class.

To ask someone's age	To introduce someone
¿**Cuántos años tienes?**	**Este es** Mike./**Esta es** Melissa.

43

INSTRUCTIONAL STRATEGIES

Activity 5

- Now that students have learned the numbers in Spanish, this is a good opportunity to learn how to ask someone for his or her phone number as well as give out one's phone number to someone.
- Read the model aloud, then have them practice in pairs.
- Remind students that they can make up phone numbers if they wish.

Activity 7

Read the **Modelo** aloud, then have them practice with a partner.

ANSWERS

Activity 7

Answers will vary, but approximate ages are: Tomás, 10; Paco, 16; Teresa, 20; and Marcos 7.

SLOWER-PACED LEARNERS

For Activity 6, have students break down the numbers into smaller chunks. For example, have them start with numbers between 1 and 15, then move increase by five or practice with numbers 16 to 31.

ADVANCED LEARNERS

Challenge students to create math problems in Spanish whose sum does not exceed 31. Compete to see who can use the most numbers without repeating. Then have students read aloud for the class to solve.

HERITAGE LANGUAGE LEARNERS

Ask students to share ways in which they state telephone numbers in the country where their family is from. For example, in Spain, people will often give their number by tens instead of using single digits.

OBJECTIVES FOR LOS MESES DEL AÑO Y LA FECHA

- Present the vocabulary needed to practice the communicative and grammatical functions for the unit: months of the year
- Ask and provide dates in Spanish
- Identify common dates in a year

CORE RESOURCES

- Audio Program: Track 18

STANDARDS

1.1 Engage in conversation
1.2 Understand the language
1.3 Present information
4.2 Compare cultures

INSTRUCTIONAL STRATEGIES

🎧 18 Activity 9

- After playing the audio, write the numbers 1 through 12 on the board and model how to say the name of the month for each, such as **enero** for 1 and **febrero** for 2.
- Point to any of the twelve numbers at random and ask students to say the month corresponding to that number, based on your modeling.

CULTURE NOTE

Día de San Valentín is also known as **Día del amor y la amistad** and **Día de los enamorados**. **Navidad** can also be referred to as **(las) Pascuas** in Spain and other countries. In fact, **Santa Claus** is referred to as **Viejito Pascuero** in Chile. **Septiembre** is often written as **setiembre**, although the formal register prefers **septiembre**.

NOTE

Point out that Spanish-speakers will often omit the definite article and verb when giving today's date: **Es (el) cuatro de junio.**

Activity 11

Lionel Messi: Argentine soccer player who plays for F.C. Barcelona. **Mario López:** American TV host and actor of Mexican descent. He has appeared in several TV series and films. **Alejandro Bedoya:** American soccer player who plays for French club Nantes of Colombian descent. **Zoe Saldaña:** American dancer and actress of Dominican and Puerto Rican descent. **Enrique Iglesias:** Spanish singer and songwriter, son of Julio Iglesias and Isabel Preysler. **Sofía Vergara:** Colombian actress, comedian and model. Ariadna **Thalia** Sodi Miranda: Mexican songwriter, actress and singer.

Consider playing songs by the singers, showing short videoclips or goals by the soccer players to students in class.

Extension

After students complete the activity, distribute previously prepared index cards to serve as identity cards. On each index card, write a fictitious name or someone from history. Distribute the cards to students and have them work in pairs to ask each other questions about the name of the person and their birthday.

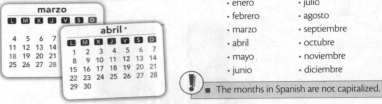

PALABRA POR PALABRA Los meses del año y la fecha

9 🎧 **18** Listen to the names of the months in Spanish and repeat.

marzo
L	M	X	J	V	S	D
4	5	6	7			
11	12	13	14			
18	19	20	21			
25	26	27	28			

abril
L	M	X	J	V	S	D
1	2	3	4	5	6	7
8	9	10	11	12	13	14
15	16	17	18	19	20	21
22	23	24	25	26	27	28
29	30					

- enero
- febrero
- marzo
- abril
- mayo
- junio
- julio
- agosto
- septiembre
- octubre
- noviembre
- diciembre

❗ ■ The months in Spanish are not capitalized.

≫ *¿Qué día es hoy? What's today's date?*
≫ *Es el 4 de junio. It's June 4th.*

≫ *¿Cuándo es tu cumpleaños? When is your birthday?*
≫ *Es el 11 de mayo. It's May 11th.*

10 👥 **Answer the following questions by writing out the correct date. Then compare your answers with a partner.**

1. ¿Cuándo es el Día de la Independencia de Estados Unidos?
2. ¿Cuándo es el Día de San Valentín?
3. ¿Cuándo es Navidad *(Christmas)*?
4. ¿Cuándo es el último *(last)* día del año?
5. ¿Cuándo es el primer *(first)* día del año?
6. ¿Qué día es hoy?

11 👥 **In pairs, take turns asking each other for the missing names and birthdays of the famous people on each of your cards. Do you know who they are? Then use the astrological chart to give their sign.**

Modelo: E1: Su cumpleaños es el 24 de junio. ¿Quién es? E2: ¿Cuándo es el cumpleaños de Lionel Messi?
E2: Es **Lionel Messi**. Es Cáncer. E1: Es el **24 de junio**. Es Cáncer.

Estudiante 1
Nombre	Cumpleaños
1.	24 de junio
2.	el 10 de octubre
3. Alejandro Bedoya	el 29 de abril
4. Zoe Saldaña	el 19 de junio
5. Enrique Iglesias	
6.	el 10 de julio
7. Thalía	el 26 de agosto

Estudiante 2
Nombre	Cumpleaños
1. Lionel Messi	el 24 de junio
2. Mario López	el 10 de octubre
3.	el 29 de abril
4. Zoe Saldaña	
5. Enrique Iglesias	el 8 de mayo
6. Sofía Vergara	el 10 de julio
7.	el 26 de agosto

Acuario	Tauro	Leo	Escorpión
20 de enero - 19 de febrero	20 de abril - 20 de mayo	23 de julio - 22 de agosto	23 de octubre - 21 de noviembre
Piscis	**Géminis**	**Virgo**	**Sagitario**
20 de febrero - 20 de marzo	21 de mayo - 21 de junio	23 de agosto - 21 de septiembre	22 de noviembre - 21 de diciembre
Aries	**Cáncer**	**Libra**	**Capricornio**
21 de marzo - 19 de abril	22 de junio - 22 de julio	22 de septiembre - 22 de octubre	22 de diciembre - 19 de enero

12 👥 **In groups of four, take turns guessing each other's birthday. Start with the month, then the day and see who guesses the complete date first. Use a thumbs up or down signal to indicate a higher or lower month or date.**

Modelo: ¿Es en...? ¿Es el... de...?

ANSWERS

Activity 10

1. el 4 de julio; **2.** el 14 de febrero; **3.** el 25 de diciembre; **4.** el 31 de diciembre; **5.** el 1 de enero; **6.** Answer should reflect today's date.

Activity 11

1. hoy; **2.** 25 de septiembre; **3.** 25 de septiembre; **4.** el 14 de febrero.

Los países y las nacionalidades

13 Look at the maps of different parts of the world. Write the names of the countries from the list in the appropriate spots on the maps.

> Cuba ○ España ○ China ○ Francia ○ India ○ Italia
> Puerto Rico ○ República Dominicana ○ México ○ Japón

14 With a partner, fill in the missing nationalities in Spanish. Use the clues already provided in the chart to help you with the forms.

> ■ Nationalities in Spanish are not capitalized. They also vary in form when referring to a man (*hombre*) or a woman (*mujer*). Do you see a pattern in the way they are formed?

País	Hombre	Mujer
Cuba	cubano	
China		china
México		mexicana
Italia	italiano	
India	indio	india
Puerto Rico	puertorriqueño	
República Dominicana	dominicano	
Francia	francés	
Japón		japonesa
España		española
Ecuador		ecuatoriana
Perú	peruano	
Chile	chileno	

15 🎧 19 Listen to Olga introduce her friends Daniel and Susie. Then choose the correct nationality for each of them.

a. Daniel es... ☐ español. **b.** Susie es... ☐ india. **c.** Olga es... ☐ cubana.
☐ francés. ☐ china. ☐ italiana.
☐ dominicano. ☐ japonesa. ☐ puertorriqueña.

MORE IN ELETECA: EXTRA ONLINE PRACTICE

45

OBJECTIVES FOR LOS PAÍSES Y LAS NACIONALIDADES

• Present the communicative functions of the unit: Countries and nationalities

CORE RESOURCES

• Audio Program: Track 19
• Interactive Whiteboard Lesson: IWB 1.2

STANDARDS

1.1 Engage in conversation
1.2 Understand the language
1.3 Present information
4.2 Compare languages

INSTRUCTIONAL STRATEGIES

Activity 13

Pre-teach the terms *país* (country) and *nacionalidad* (nationality), and provide examples: *País: México; Nacionalidad: mexicano/a.*

Alternative Activity

Project IWB 1.2, *Los países*, and ask students to identify the countries they recognize on the map. Write the names of the countries mentioned on the board in Spanish.

🎧 19 **Activity 15**

Play the audio for students to pick out the nationality of each person.

Audioscript

Olga: Hola, Susie.

Susie: Hola, ¿qué tal?

Olga: Muy bien. Mira, este es Daniel, mi amigo de Francia.

Susie: ¡Hola, Daniel! Yo soy china. ¿Qué tal en la clase de español?

Daniel: Muy bien. Mi amiga cubana, Olga, es mi guía…

ANSWERS

Activity 13

First map: Puerto Rico, México, Cuba, República Dominicana. **Second map:** Francia, Italia, España. **Third map:** China, Japón, India.

Activity 14

Cuba: cubana; **China:** chino; **México:** mexicano; **Italia:** italiana; **Puerto Rico:** puertorriqueña; **República Dominicana:** dominicana; **Francia:** francesa; **Japón:** japonés; **España:** español; **Ecuador:** ecuatoriano; **Perú:** peruana; **Chile:** chilena.

Activity 15

a. francés; **b.** china; **c.** cubana.

HERITAGE LANGUAGE LEARNERS

Using the maps at the start of the book, have students list the nationalities of as many Spanish-speaking countries as they can in Spanish. Call on several students to say them out loud while another student writes them on the board.

OBJECTIVES FOR GRAMÁTICA 1

• Present the grammatical structures needed to practice the communicative functions of the unit: Definite and indefinite articles
• Use articles to identify specific people, places, and things

CORE RESOURCES

• Interactive Online Materials - ELEteca

STANDARDS

1.1   Engage in conversation
1.2   Understand the language
4.1   Compare languages

INSTRUCTIONAL STRATEGIES

1. Definite and Indefinite Articles

• Write the following words on the board: **el libro**, **los libros**; **la silla**, **las sillas**. Then write the English translation under each: *the book, the books; the chair, the chairs.*
• Ask students what they notice about the various forms of the article *the* in Spanish. Elicit prior knowledge regarding what they know about masculine and feminine nouns in Spanish and if they see any patterns, such as masculine nouns ending in **–o** and feminine nouns ending in **–a**.
• Have students open the book and walk them through the explanations given for definite and indefinite articles.

Activity 1

• Make sure students understand that all nouns in Spanish, including inanimate objects, have a gender, such as **el libro** and **la silla**.
• Provide additional support for nouns that do not follow this general rule, such as **el lápiz**, **el profesor**, **la/el estudiante**.

Activity 2

• Make sure students understand that all definite and indefinite articles must agree with the noun not only in gender, but in number as well. Remind them that if the noun is singular, the article will be singular and if the noun is plural, the article must be plural.
• Additional practice: Hold up a dictionary for example and ask: **¿Qué es?** to elicit, **Es un diccionario**. Continue with **¿De quién es? Es el diccionario de la profesora**. And so on with other classroom objects.

ANSWERS

Activity 1

a. un/el; **b.** una/la; **c.** un/el; **d.** una/la; **e.** un/el; **f.** un/el; **g.** una/la; **h.** un/el.

Activity 2

a. unas/las; **b.** unos/los; **c.** unas/las; **d.** unos/los; **e.** unas/las; **f.** unos/los.

SLOWER-PACED LEARNERS

Provide a model for Activity 1 to help students get started. Use *either/ or* questions to choose the correct article and gender. Do the same with Activity 2.

GRAMÁTICA

1. DEFINITE AND INDEFINITE ARTICLES

■ In Spanish, there are four definite articles that correspond to the English *the*.

	Masculine	Feminine
Singular	**el libro** *the book*	**la silla** *the chair*
Plural	**los libros** *the books*	**las sillas** *the chairs*

■ In both Spanish and English, the definite article is used to identify and talk about specific people, places, or things we know.

El pizarrón es negro. The blackboard is black.   *La profesora es de Perú. The teacher is from Peru.*
Los estudiantes son americanos. The students are American.

■ There are four indefinite articles in Spanish that correspond to the English *a*, *an*, and *some*.

	Masculine	Feminine
Singular	**un** cuaderno *a notebook*	**una** mochila *a backpack*
Plural	**unos** cuadernos *some notebooks*	**unas** mochilas *some backpacks*

■ The indefinite article is used to talk about nonspecific people, places, or things.
Eduardo es un amigo. Eduardo is a friend.
San Antonio es una ciudad bonita. San Antonio is a pretty city.
Necesito unos marcadores. I need some markers.

■ In Spanish, definite and indefinite articles match nouns in number (singular / plural) and gender (masculine / feminine). Most nouns ending in **–o** are masculine and most ending in **–a** are feminine.

1 Write the indefinite and definite articles for the following people and things.

a. ...... / ...... lápiz
b. ...... / ...... profesora
c. ...... / ...... estudiante
d. ...... / ...... carpeta
e. ...... / ...... profesor
f. ...... / ...... bolígrafo
g. ...... / ...... estudiante
h. ...... / ...... diccionario

2 Write the plural forms of indefinite and definite articles for these objects.

a. .... / .... sillas
b. .... / .... cuadernos
c. .... / .... papeleras
d. .... / .... libros
e. .... / .... mochilas
f. .... / .... teléfonos

2. SUBJECT PRONOUNS AND THE VERB *SER*

- Subject pronouns refer to people and often come before the verb to show who is doing the action or is being described. The chart below lists the subject pronouns in Spanish with their meaning in English.

yo *I*		**nosotros/nosotras** *we*	
tú *you (informal)*		**vosotros/vosotras** *you (plural, Spain)*	
usted *you (formal)*		**ustedes** *you (plural)*	
él *he*		**ellos** *they (all males or mixed)*	
ella *she*		**ellas** *they (all females)*	

- Both **tú** and **usted** are used when speaking directly to someone. Use **tú** when that person is a friend. Use **usted** when speaking to someone in a formal situation or to show respect.

- Use **ustedes** when speaking to a group of people. Your teacher, for example, will address the class as **ustedes**. The English equivalent would be *you all*.

- Use **nosotras** and **ellas** when referring to a group of all females.

- **Vosotros/vosotras** is used in Spain.

¿De dónde son ustedes?

- You have already been using the forms of the verb **ser** to make introductions and say where you and others are from. Here are all the forms of **ser** with the subject pronouns and meaning in English.

SER *(to be)*			
yo	**soy** *I am*	nosotros/as	**somos** *we are*
tú	**eres** *you are*	vosotros/as	**sois** *you are (plural, Spain)*
usted	**es** *you are (formal)*	ustedes	**son** *you are (plural)*
él	**es** *he is*	ellos	**son** *they (all males or mixed)*
ella	**es** *she is*	ellas	**son** *they (all females)*

- Spanish speakers often omit the subject pronouns when using **yo**, **tú**, **nosotros/as**, and **vosotros/as** since the verb ending already carries that information.

   Yo soy *de Madrid.* ➡ **Soy** *de Madrid.* (The form **soy** can only apply to **yo**)

   Tú eres *de Santiago.* ➡ **Eres** *de Santiago.* (The form **eres** can only apply to **tú**)

- **Usted**, **él** and **ella** use the same form of the verb: **es**.

- **Ustedes**, **ellos** and **ellas** use the same form: **son**.

OBJECTIVES FOR GRAMÁTICA 2

- Present the grammatical structures needed to practice the communicative functions of the unit: Subject pronouns and the verb **ser**

- Talk about where people are from

STANDARDS

1.1	Engage in conversation
1.2	Understand the language
4.1	Compare languages

INSTRUCTIONAL STRATEGIES

2. Subject Pronouns and the Verb *SER*

- Walk students through the explanations on this page. Help them compare the English verb *to be* and the Spanish verb *ser*.

- Make sure students understand that, like English, the conjugation for **ser** in Spanish has unique forms for practically each person. However, point out that **usted/él/ella** share the same form: **es**. The same is true for **ustedes/ellos/ellas**: **son**. Compare this to English *they are* and *you are*.

- The **vosotros** form will be presented in all verb charts but will not be actively practiced. Add these forms to your classroom practice or to any of the exercises in this program if you so wish.

SLOWER-PACED LEARNERS

Remind students that **ser** is not used to express age, as seen on page 39: **Tengo 16 años**.

HERITAGE LANGUAGE LEARNERS

Ask students to explain how they address different members of their extended family, i.e., how would they say "How are you?" to them. You can use this opportunity to talk about the **vos** form, which is used in most of Latin America in different ways. Countries where the **voseo** is most common include Argentina, Uruguay, and Costa Rica.

GRAMÁTICA GRAMMAR IN CONTEXT

INSTRUCTIONAL STRATEGIES

Activity 3

Remind students that any subject added to **yo** will result in the **nosotros** form of the verb.

Activity 4

Call on students to role-play the conversations with a partner once you have reviewed the answers.

Activity 5

Expand on student answers by asking: **¿Quién es Penélope Cruz? ¿De dónde son tus amigos? ¿Son de California también? ¿De dónde es Shakira? ¿Son buenos jugadores de tenis?** and so on.

ANSWERS

Activity 3

a. ella; b. ellas; c. él; d. ellos; e. nosotros; f. nosotros.

Activity 4

¿De dónde es usted?; ¿De dónde son ustedes?; ¿De dónde eres?; ¿De dónde eres?

Activity 5

a. es; b. son; c. soy; d. somos; e. eres; f. es; g. son; h. es.

Activity 6

Este es Daniel. Es profesor de inglés en España. Es de Estados Unidos. Es muy inteligente.

¡Hola a todos! Yo soy Claudia. Soy estudiante en la escuela secundaria. También soy futbolista, pero ¡no profesional! Y tú, ¿de dónde eres?

Next page

¡Hola! Nosotros somos amigos. Somos americanos pero somos de todas partes. Diego es de Colombia. Jennifer es de Chicago. Tomás y Elena son de México. Y ustedes, ¿de dónde son?

Dolores y Pablo no son estudiantes. Ellos son enfermeros en un hospital importante. Dolores es peruana y Pablo es americano.

SLOWER-PACED LEARNERS

Provide guided practice before having students complete Activity 6. Do the first paragraph together and then to help students understand the changes that need to be made, change Daniel's name to Juana and say, **Esta es Juana**, and continue together from there. Change the name one more time to Daniel and Pedro, **Estos son Daniel y Pedro**, and so on.

ADVANCED LEARNERS AND HERITAGE LANGUAGE LEARNERS

Look for additional information about the celebrities mentioned on this page (Penélope Cruz, Shakira, Rafael Nadal and David Ferrer) and prepare a description including the following information: full name, birthdate, age, astrological sign, profession, and nacionality.

GRAMÁTICA

3 Choose the subject pronoun from the list below that you would use to talk about the following people.

> él ○ ella ○ ellos ○ ellas ○ nosotros

Modelo: Carlos → él

a. María → ....

b. María y Clara → ....

c. Juan → ....

d. María y Juan → ....

e. María, Juan y yo → ....

f. Tú y yo → ....

4 Look at the following people and select the correct question you would use to ask where each one is from. ¡*Atención!* One question will be used more than once.

> ¿De dónde eres? ○ ¿De dónde es usted? ○ ¿De dónde son ustedes?

5 Choose the correct form of *ser* from the options.

a. Penélope Cruz **soy** / **es** / **eres** actriz.

b. Los profesores **son** / **somos** / **soy** interesantes.

c. Yo **eres** / **es** / **soy** estudiante.

d. Mis amigos y yo **son** / **somos** / **eres** de California.

e. Y tú, ¿**eres** / **es** / **son** italiano?

f. Shakira **son** / **somos** / **es** cantante.

g. Rafael Nadal y David Ferrer **somos** / **eres** / **son** tenistas.

h. Sr. Ramos, ¿**es** / **son** / **somos** usted bibliotecario?

6 Complete the sentences with the correct form of *ser* to describe the following people. Then check your answers with a partner.

Este .... Daniel. .... profesor de inglés en España. .... de Estados Unidos. .... muy inteligente.

¡Hola a todos! Yo .... Claudia. .... estudiante en la escuela secundaria. También .... futbolista, pero ¡no profesional! Y tú, ¿de dónde ....?

! Additional vocabulary: también → *also* pero → *but*

48

¡Hola! Nosotros .... amigos. .... americanos pero .... de todas partes. Diego .... de Colombia. Jennifer .... de Chicago. Tomás y Elena .... de México. Y ustedes, ¿de dónde ....?

Dolores y Pablo no .... estudiantes. Ellos .... enfermeros en un hospital importante. Dolores .... peruana y Pablo .... americano.

7 👥 **Write a similar description about yourself. Then read it aloud to a classmate. What do you have in common?**

Modelo: E1: Nosotros somos...
E2: No somos...

> ⚠️ To say that something is not true for you, use **no** before the verb.
> *Yo no soy de Bogotá. I'm not from Bogota.*

3. PRESENT TENSE OF *LLAMAR(SE)* AND *TENER*

■ You have been using the expression **me llamo** to tell someone your name. The expression comes from the verb **llamar(se)**.

LLAMAR(SE) *(to be called)*			
yo	me llamo *I am called*	nosotros/as	nos llamamos *we are called*
tú	te llamas *you are called*	vosotros/as	os llamáis *you are (plural, Spain) called*
usted	se llama *you are called (formal)*	ustedes	se llaman *you are (plural) called*
él	se llama *he is called*	ellos	se llaman *they are called*
ella	se llama *she is called*	ellas	se llaman *they are called*

■ The verb **llamar(se)** literally means to be called and <u>not</u> *my name is*. Its meaning in English may sound strange to you, but it is absolutely clear to all Spanish speakers.

> ¿Cómo **te llamas**? *What's your name? / What are you called?*
> **Me llamo** Alberto. *My name is Alberto. / I'm called Alberto.*

> ¿Cómo **se llama** el profesor? *What's the teacher's name? / What is the teacher called?*
> **Se llama** Sr. Estévez. *His name is Mr. Estévez. / He's called Mr. Estévez.*

OBJECTIVES FOR GRAMÁTICA 3

- Present the grammatical structures needed to practice the communicative functions of the unit: The verbs **llamar(se)** and **tener**
- Ask someone's age and give one's name

STANDARDS

1.1 Engage in conversation
1.2 Understand the language
4.1 Compare languages

INSTRUCTIONAL STRATEGIES

3. Present Tense of *LLAMAR(SE)* and *TENER*

- Walk students through the explanations on this page. Help them compare expressions in English to ask someone's name and provide one's name.
- Alert students to the fact that **Me llamo Alberto** is the common expression for giving one's name, but that it does not translate literally to *My name is Alberto*. The construction in Spanish is closer to *I am called* or *They call me Alberto*.

SLOWER-PACED LEARNERS

Give each student one card with the names of two classmates. Have one student choose one name and say: **Yo no me llamo Owen**, **me llamo Danie**l. **Él se llama Owen**. The student mentioned by the first student is the next one to do the activity.

PRE-AP LEARNERS

Have students choose a partner (consider adding heritage learners as well). When called on, the students will have to introduce themselves: **Nos llamamos Owen y Ben**.

HERITAGE LANGUAGE LEARNERS

Ask students to talk to their classmates about Spanish names in their families: last names, frequent middle names, whether parents and children have the same names or not, etc.

INSTRUCTIONAL STRATEGIES

The Verb TENER

Walk students through the explanations in the book.

CULTURAL NOTE

- Enrique Iglesias is a pop singer. He was born in Madrid and is the son of Julio Iglesias.
- Pitbull is a Cuban American rap singer. He was born in Miami.

Activity 8

Circulate around the room to ensure that students are including the reflexive pronouns in their responses.

Activity 9

Once you have reviewed the answers, have a student ask one of the questions posed and then call on a classmate to give the correct answer.

Activity 10

Have students present in small groups to ensure everyone has a chance. Check on students and ask questions to check comprehension. **¿Es verdad que tienes 14 años?**

ANSWERS

Activity 8

a. se llama; b. se llama; c. nos llamamos; d. te llamas; e. se llaman; f. me llamo.

Activity 9

a. te llamas ➡ Me llamo; b. tienen ➡ Tienen; c. tiene ➡ tengo; d. se llama ➡ Se llama; e. tiene ➡ Tiene; f. se llaman ➡ Nos llamamos.

SLOWER-PACED LEARNERS

Give students cards with 2-3 numbers. Have one student choose one number and say: **Yo no tengo XX años, tengo XX años**. Repeat.

ADVANCED LEARNERS

Have students use the contents of their backpacks for extra practice with **tener**: **Tengo una mochila. Tengo un bolígrafo.**

HERITAGE LANGUAGE LEARNERS

Point out to students that in Spanish, the definite article is sometimes used in front of titles such as **Sr., Sra., Srta.** Have them check the pages in this unit and write down examples with and without the article.

GRAMÁTICA

■ You have also been using the expression **tengo... años** to tell someone your age. This expression comes from the verb **tener**.

TENER... AÑOS (to be... years old)			
yo	tengo... años *I am... years old*	nosotros/as tenemos... años *we are... years old*	
tú	tienes... años *you are... years old*	vosotros/as tenéis... años *you are... years old (plural, Spain)*	
usted	tiene... años *you are (for.)... years old*	ustedes	tienen... años *you are... years old (plural)*
él	tiene... años *he is... years old*	ellos	tienen... años *they are... years old*
ella	tiene... años *she is... years old*	ellas	tienen... años *they are... years old*

■ Without **años**, the verb **tener** by itself means *to have*.
Yo **tengo** una computadora. *I have a computer.*
Los estudiantes **tienen** mochilas. *The students have backpacks.*

8 Write the correct form of the verb *llamar(se)* in the following sentences. ¡*Atención!* Be sure to use the complete expression made up of two words.

a. Ella .... Paquita.
b. Mi amigo .... Raúl.
c. Nosotras .... Susana y Luisa.
d. Tú .... Nacho, como *(like)* mi amigo.
e. Los cantantes .... Enrique Iglesias y Pitbull.
f. Yo no .... Celia.

9 Choose the correct form of the question and answer from the options.

Pregunta *(Question)*	Respuesta *(Answer)*
1. ¿Cómo **te llamas / se llaman**?	a. **Me llamo / Se llama** Isabel.
2. ¿Cuántos años **tienen / tengo** los estudiantes?	b. **Tienen / Tengo** 15 años.
3. ¿**Tienes / Tiene** usted teléfono celular?	c. Sí, **tengo / tenemos** teléfono celular.
4. ¿Cómo **me llamo / se llama** la bibliotecaria?	d. **Te llamas / Se llama** Sra. Menéndez.
5. ¿Cuántos años **tengo / tiene** Luis?	e. **Tiene / Tienes** 13 años.
6. ¿Cómo **se llaman / nos llamamos** ustedes?	f. **Nos llamamos / Se llaman** Ana y Ricardo.

10 Prepare some questions to interview a classmate about his/her name, age, origin/nationality, what he/she does, and what's in his/her backpack. Use the chart below to help you prepare your questions in Spanish. After the interview, introduce your classmate to the class using all the information you collected about him/her.

	Pregunta en español	
name?	....	Modelo: Este/Esta es...
age?	....	
origin?	....	
do?	....	
backpack?	....	

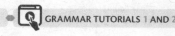
MORE IN ELETECA: EXTRA ONLINE PRACTICE ● GRAMMAR TUTORIALS 1 AND 2

50

DESTREZAS

COMPRENSIÓN DE LECTURA

1 Read about the people in the images. Before reading, review the reading strategy in Destrezas and answer the questions.

Destrezas

Before you start to read, search for clues in the image to help you understand unfamiliar words.
- *Who appears in the image?*
- *What are they wearing or doing?*

a.

b.

c.

María es chilena. Es enfermera y vive en Madrid.

Manuel tiene 14 años. Vive en Italia, pero es español. Es estudiante.

Carmen es profesora. Es de México y tiene 28 años.

2 Read the passages again and choose the correct answer below.

1. María es... y vive en...
- **a.** profesora ... Francia.
- **b.** enfermera ... España.
- **c.** médica ... Portugal.

2. Manuel tiene... y es de...
- **a.** catorce años ... España.
- **b.** once años ... México.
- **c.** catorce años... Italia.

3. Carmen es... y es...
- **a.** chilena ... policía.
- **b.** italiana ... estudiante.
- **c.** mexicana ... profesora.

PRONUNCIACIÓN The sounds of *ch* and *ñ*

1 🎧 **20** Listen to the sounds of *ch* and *ñ* in the words below. Then listen again and repeat after the speaker.

1. mu**cha**cho, mu**cha**cha, co**che**, dicio**cho**, escu**char**
2. **niño**, espa**ñol**, ense**ñar**, ma**ña**na, compa**ñero**

- The **ch** sequence in Spanish produce a single sound similar to the *ch* sound in English: *Chile*, *church*.
- The **ñ** exists only in the Spanish alphabet. The sound is similar to the *ny* in *canyon*.

2 👥 Underline the *ch* and *ñ* in the sentences below. Then take turns with a partner reading the sentences aloud.

a.

b.

c.

El muchacho escucha música en el coche.

Los niños españoles comen chocolate.

La muchacha española dice: "Hasta mañana".

 MORE IN ELETECA: EXTRA ONLINE PRACTICE

51

OBJECTIVES FOR SABOR HISPANO

- Learn about people of Hispanic origin in the U.S.
- Learn about Spanish and its influences on U.S. culture and in U.S. communities
- Connect new information to what you already know about Spanish

CORE RESOURCES

- Audio Program: Track 21

STANDARDS

1.2	Understand the language
2.1	Practices and perspectives
4.1	Compare cultures

INSTRUCTIONAL STRATEGIES

- Introduce the topic by asking students what they know about people of Hispanic origin in the U.S. and Spanish-language TV in the U.S.
- Talk about the images and the map. Elicit what students already know about people of Hispanic origin in the U.S. Share what you know about these people in the U.S.
- Read the captions together and ask questions to check comprehension.
- Ask students to identify which of the points in **¿Sabes que...?** surprised and/or interested them most.

CULTURAL NOTE

In Mexico, Cinco de Mayo is known as the "Día de la Batalla de Puebla" (Battle of Puebla Day). Though it is an important day historically, it is not a big national celebration in Mexico itself. It marks the victory of the Mexican army near the city of Puebla against the invading French forces in 1862. It is not Mexico's Independence Day, which is celebrated on September 16. However, Cinco de Mayo is celebrated throughout the U.S. as Mexican Pride Day, taking on new meaning. People who are not Mexican also join in to celebrate Mexican heritage and culture in the U.S. and other parts of the world on this day.

CULTURAL NOTE

U.S. groups from Latin American or Spanish descent refer to themselves with different names. **Hispano** or **Latino** are usually considered synonyms, although some groups may prefer one or the other. Some groups from specific countries uses more precise names such as **mexicanoamericano**, **puertorriqueño**, **cubanoamericano**. **Chicano** is usually employed for Mexican-Americans, particularly those living in California, Arizona, New Mexico and Texas.

CULTURAL NOTE

When reading **Un día sin hispanos** remind students that a high percentage of the Latino population in the U.S. is documented. Some people have prejudices towards Latinos. You may want to ask students to share those stereotypes with each other. Ask them to think about what groups (ethnic, religious, social, etc.) they identify with, and how they would feel if they were judged by the characteristics shared by only a small percentage of that group's members.

SABOR HISPANO

HISPANOS EN EE.UU.

¡Aquí hablamos español también!

Estados Unidos
- San Francisco
- Albuquerque · Toledo
- Los Ángeles · Tucson
- · San Antonio
- · Miami

Nombres de ciudades en EE.U con origen español

MISSION SAN MIGUEL ARCÁNGEL

- ✓ Florida, New México y Louisiana tienen pasado español.
- ✓ Otros territorios tienen pasado mexicano como Sasabe y Tucson, Arizona.
- ✓ Muchos lugares en EE.UU. tienen nombres en español: California, Florida, Arizona, Nevada, Montana, Colorado... ¿Qué otros nombres de estados tienen origen español?

Una joven familia mexicana prepara Halloween.

Madre e hija celebran la Navidad.

Celebraciones del Cinco de Mayo en las calles de Montpellier, Vermont, EE.UU.

¿Sabes que...?

- ✓ Los hispanos en EE.UU. representan un 16,9*% de la población del país.
- ✓ Los hispanos o latinos vienen de América Latina o España.
- ✓ Los hispanos en EE.UU. son la comunidad hispanohablante más grande del mundo, después de México.
- ✓ Se habla español en EE.UU. desde (since) el año 1565.
- ✓ La palabra *hispano* se usa en EE.UU. desde 1970.
- ✓ En 1988, Ronald Reagan proclama el Mes Nacional de la Herencia Hispana, que se celebra todos los años del 15 de septiembre al 15 de octubre.

52

*In Spanish, the comma is used in place of the decimal point and vice versa, so the number 16,9 is equal to 16.9 in English.

ESTADOS UNIDOS UNIDAD **1**

🎧 21 ¡Famosos y en español!

Muchos famosos que viven en EE.UU. son hispanos o de origen hispano. También hay muchos famosos que hablan español: Will Smith, Gwyneth Paltrow, Viggo Mortensen y otros.
¿Sabes qué famosos son hispanos o de origen hispano? ¡Marca las casillas!

Demi Lovato tiene ascendencia mexicana y española.

- ○ Alexis Bledel
- ○ Nick Jonas
- ○ Selena Gómez
- ○ Taylor Lautner
- ○ Demi Lovato
- ○ Bruno Mars
- ○ Justin Bieber
- ○ Enrique Iglesias
- ○ Wilmer Valderrama
- ○ Penélope Cruz
- ○ Victoria Justice
- ○ Miley Cyrus

Un día sin hispanos

Juan Martínez trabaja en una fábrica de conservas (canned food). Él habla de un día importante en su vida.

«Son las seis de la mañana. Camino al centro de mi ciudad. Hoy es un día importante. Las personas indocumentadas de origen hispano protestamos: trabajamos aquí y somos parte de la comunidad. Hay mucha gente. Todos queremos vivir aquí con la documentación necesaria. Los hispanos sí somos importantes».

Protestas de marzo de 2006

Fuentes: Univisión, Pew Research, Nielsen, The Associated Press, MayDay, RedOrbit, American Civil Liberties Union, CNN, Census Bureau.

Univisión, ¿la cadena más popular?

- ❖ Univisión es la cadena (channel) de televisión más grande de EE.UU.
- ❖ Univisión emite desde (since) 1962.
- ❖ Los programas más populares son las telenovelas.
- ❖ Muchos programas y telenovelas son producciones de canales mexicanos como Televisa y El Canal de las Estrellas.
- ❖ Univisión tiene una media (average) de 1,81* millones de espectadores (viewers) de entre 18 y 49 años, más que las cadenas en inglés.
- ❖ Fusión es una nueva cadena de Univisión. Es para jóvenes latinos educados en español e inglés.

Un grupo de amigos ven un partido de fútbol.

Here is a list of more U.S. city names in Spanish. Can you match the name in Spanish to its meaning in English?

1. Dos Palos, California
2. Boca Raton, Florida
3. Amarillo, Texas
4. Mesa Vista, California
5. Casa Grande, Arizona
6. Buena Vista, Florida
7. Pueblo, Colorado

- a. town
- b. two sticks
- c. good view
- d. rat's mouth
- e. big house
- f. table view
- g. yellow

VOCES LATINAS ▶
HISPANOS INFLUYENTES EN EE.UU.

Complete the sentences using the words listed below.

mexicanas ✳ telenovelas ✳ popular ✳ 16,9% ✳ protestas

1. Los hispanos son un _____ de la población de EE.UU.
2. Univisión es la cadena más _____ de EE.UU.
3. Los programas más populares de Univisión son las _____ .
4. Muchos programas de Univisión son producciones _____ .
5. En el movimiento 'Un día sin hispanos' hay muchas _____ .

53

- An audio recording accompanies each text. Vary between silent reading, reading aloud, and playing the audio.
- Elicit what students know about famous people of Hispanic origin in the U.S.
- Ask them if they have ever watched Spanish-language TV. Encourage them to describe the type of programming they have seen.
- Have students complete the activities on this page and compare their answers.

ANSWERS

¡Famosos y en español!

Alexis Bledel (of Argentinian descent), Selena Gómez (father is of Mexican descent), Demi Lovato (of Mexican descent), Bruno Mars (of Puerto Rican and Filipino descent), Enrique Iglesias (Spanish), Wilmer Valderrama (of Colombian and Venezuelan descent), Penélope Cruz (Spanish), Victoria Justice (mother is of Puerto Rican descent).

U.S. city names in Spanish

1. b; 2. d; 3. g; 4. f; 5. e; 6. c; 7. a.

Sentence completions

1. 16,9%; 2. popular; 3. telenovelas; 4. mexicanas; 5. protestas.

SLOWER-PACED LEARNERS

Have students brainstorm some TV series that feature Latino actors and/or include Latino characters. Encourage students to think of athletes, politicians, scientists, entrepreneurs of Latino descent as well.

ADVANCED LEARNERS AND HERITAGE LANGUAGE LEARNERS

Ask students to look for information about Latinos that are not so popular as Shakira, Jennifer López or Thalía. Suggest names such as Sonia Sotomayor, Marco Rubio and Susana Martínez.

HERITAGE LANGUAGE LEARNERS

Ask students to think about who they consider to be a Latino role model and explain what it is about the person that merits such a distinction. Ask students to describe the qualities they would expect to a role model to embody.

OBJECTIVES FOR RELATO

- Revisit unit themes, grammar, vocabulary, and culture in a new context
- Improve reading comprehension skills

CORE RESOURCES

- Audio Program: Track 22

STANDARDS

- 1.1   Engage in conversation
- 1.2   Understand the language
- 1.3   Present information
- 2.1   Practices and perspectives

INSTRUCTIONAL STRATEGIES

Activity 1

The purpose of this activity is to review the nationalities taught in this unit. Students complete this activity individually or in pairs.

🎧 22 Activity 2

- You may choose to play the audio and have students follow along in their books or you may want to call on students to read aloud.
- As part of a second reading, have students underline the nationalities and numbers that appear in the reading.
- Ask students: **¿Cuál de los personajes que aparecen es Guillermo?** Have students explain why they chose him and not one of the others.

ANSWERS

Activity 1

a. dominicano, dominicana, República Dominicana; b. mexicano, mexicana, México; c. chino, china, China; d. indio, india, India; e. colombiano, colombiana, Colombia.

SLOWER-PACED LEARNERS

Explain the meaning of some words and expressions included in the reading that may be confusing, such as **quiere**, **perro**, **comprendernos**, **palabras**, **hasta luego**. Heritage and Pre-AP learners may help here.

ADVANCED LEARNERS AND HERITAGE LANGUAGE LEARNERS

Encourage students to pick out some of the differences in punctuation between Spanish and English. For instance, the use of a colon instead of a comma in the salutation of the letter, and no comma before **y** in a series **(Bo, Óscar, Asmita y yo)**.

RELATO El club de español de la escuela

1 Fill in the missing information in the chart below.

	Masculino	Femenino	País
a.			República Dominicana
b.		mexicana	
c.			China
d.		india	
e.	colombiano		

2 🎧 22 Guillermo was elected President of the Spanish Club at his school. Read the e-mail he sent to his friend Michael telling him about the other Spanish Club officers.

> Asunto: El club del español
>
> De: Guillermo   Para: Michael
>
> Hola, Michael:
>
> ¿Qué tal? Mira, esta es una foto del club de español en la escuela.
>
> El Sr. Pérez es el consejero (*advisor*) del club y también es profesor de español. Es colombiano y habla perfectamente inglés y español. En el comité ejecutivo somos cuatro estudiantes: Bo, Óscar, Asmita y yo.
>
> Bo tiene quince años y es chino. Habla un poco de español pero comprende mucho. Todos los días habla con sus amigos por teléfono. Quiere ser médico y trabajar en un hospital.
>
> Óscar es estudiante. Es dominicano y tiene diecisiete años. Habla mucho en clase y siempre escucha música en su mp4. Tiene un perro, se llama Chato. Tiene muchas fotos de Chato en su teléfono.
>
> Asmita es india. Tiene catorce años y es estudiante. Asmita habla muy bien español, pero a veces dice palabras en inglés.
>
> En el club solo hablamos en español y es un poco difícil comprendernos, pero es muy divertido.
>
> Hasta luego,
>
> Guillermo

54

3 **With a partner, identify the person matching each description below. *¡Atención!* Guillermo is also included in the descriptions.**

	Bo	Óscar	Asmita	El Sr. Pérez	Guillermo
a. Tiene un perro.	☐	☐	☐	☐	☐
b. Es de China.	☐	☐	☐	☐	☐
c. Tiene 16 años.	☐	☐	☐	☐	☐
d. Es india.	☐	☐	☐	☐	☐
e. Es dominicano.	☐	☐	☐	☐	☐
f. Tiene 15 años.	☐	☐	☐	☐	☐
g. Habla español perfectamente.	☐	☐	☐	☐	☐
h. Es mexicano.	☐	☐	☐	☐	☐
i. Tiene 14 años.	☐	☐	☐	☐	☐
j. Es de Colombia.	☐	☐	☐	☐	☐

4 **Take turns asking each other the following questions about Guillermo's e-mail.**

a. ¿Quién tiene quince años?

b. ¿Cómo se llama la chica india?

c. ¿Qué hace el Sr. Pérez?

d. ¿Cómo se llama el chico que tiene diecisiete años?

e. ¿De dónde es Bo?

f. ¿Cuántos años tiene Asmita?

g. ¿Cómo se llama el perro de Óscar?

5 **Put these words in the correct order to make logical sentences. Then, with a partner, write an appropriate question for each response.**

a. llamo / Asmita / me		¿ ?
b. tengo / años / diecisiete		¿ ?
c. se / Chato / llama / el perro		¿ ?
d. el Sr. Pérez / es / colombiano		¿ ?
e. el profesor / la clase / de / es		¿ ?

Note

Remind students that information about Guillermo is also included in Activity 3 and that they should be able to determine which descriptions refer to him (by process of elimination).

Answers

Activity 3

a. Óscar; b. Bo; c. Guillermo; d. Asmita; e. Óscar; f. Bo; g. el Sr. Pérez; h. Guillermo; i. Asmita; j. el Sr. Pérez.

Activity 4

a. Bo; b. Asmita; c. Es profesor; d. Óscar; e. China; f. Catorce; g. Chato.

Activity 5

a. Me llamo Asmital, ¿Cómo te llamas?; b. Tengo diecisiete años, ¿Cuántos años tienes?; c. El perro se llama Chato, ¿Cómo se llama el perro?; d. El Sr. Pérez es colombiano, ¿De dónde es el Sr. Pérez?; e. Es el profesor de la clase, ¿Qué hace el Sr. Pérez?

Slower-paced Learners

Students may be confused by what question words to use in Activity 5. Help students answer the questions (or ask more advanced students to help them) Then for extra practice, have them write similar questions using the same questions words .

Advanced Learners and Heritage Language Learners

Pair advanced learners and heritage language learners with slower-paced learners so they can help students with unknown words and their pronunciation. They can read aloud the questions.

OBJECTIVES FOR EVALUACIÓN

- Review grammar, vocabulary and culture from the unit
- Monitor student progress

CORE RESOURCES

- Interactive Online Materials - ELEteca

STANDARDS

1.2	Understand the language
1.3	Present information
2.1	Practices and perspectives
4.1	Compare cultures

INSTRUCTIONAL STRATEGIES

- Activities can be completed individually and then reviewed with the class.
- Extend by asking students if they agree with the answer given and then writing it on the board. Provide explanations as needed.
- You may wish to assign point values to each activity as a way for students to monitor their progress.
- If students achieve less than 80% on each activity, direct them to **En resumen** for page numbers to review.

ANSWERS

Activity 1

a. ¿Cómo te llamas? Me llamo Emilio.
b. ¿Cuántos años tienes? Tengo dieciocho años.
c. ¿De dónde eres? Soy argentino.
d. ¿Cuál es tu número de teléfono? No tengo teléfono.
e. ¿Qué haces? Soy estudiante.

Activity 2

a. español / española; b. dominicano / dominicana; c. mexicano / mexicana; d. indio / india; e. francés / francesa; f. cubano / cubana.

Activity 3

a. uno; b. ocho; c. veinte; d. tres; e. doce; f. cuatro; g. cinco; h. nueve; i. dieciocho.

Activity 4

a. Quince de junio; b. Treinta de noviembre; c. Trece de marzo; d. Veinticuatro de enero.

EVALUACIÓN

ASKING AND GIVING INFORMATION

1 Fill in the blanks with a word from the list to form logical questions and answers.

> soy ○ qué ○ tienes ○ cómo ○ dieciocho ○ tengo ○ dónde ○ cuál ○ soy ○ llamo

a. » ¿.................... te llamas? » Me .... Emilio.
b. » ¿Cuántos años ....? » Tengo .... años.
c. » ¿De .... eres? » .... argentino.
d. » ¿.................... es tu número de teléfono? » No .... teléfono.
e. » ¿.................... haces? » .... estudiante.

PAÍSES Y NACIONALIDADES

2 Write the correct nationality for the following countries. Include both male and female forms.

a. España .... / ....
b. República Dominicana .... / ....
c. México .... / ....
d. India .... / ....
e. Francia .... / ....
f. Cuba .... / ....

NÚMEROS DE 0 A 31

3 Write out the following numbers.

a.	1	d.	3	g.	5
b.	8	e.	12	h.	9
c.	20	f.	4	i.	18

LOS MESES DEL AÑO Y LA FECHA

4 Rewrite the following dates in Spanish.

a. June 15 ....
b. November 30 ....
c. March 13 ....
d. January 24 ....

5 Match the image to the corresponding month of the year.

a. ☐ diciembre
b. ☐ agosto
c. ☐ marzo
d. ☐ febrero

DEFINITE AND INDEFINITE ARTICLES

6 Write the correct indefinite article.

a. .... bolígrafo
b. .... consola

c. .... sillas
d. .... enfermeros

7 Write the correct definite article.

a. .... números
b. .... país

c. .... mesas
d. .... consola

PRESENT TENSE OF *SER, TENER* AND *LLAMAR(SE)*

8 Complete each sentence with the correct form of *ser, tener* or *llamar(se)*. ¡Atención! Use the subject pronouns to help you with the form.

a. Ella .... María y yo me llamo Adrián.
b. Ellos .... dieciséis años.
c. Nosotros .... españoles.

d. Él .... estudiante de español.
e. ¿ .... ustedes de Puerto Rico?
f. David y yo .... trece años.
g. Ellos .... Juan y Adrián.

CULTURA

9 Answer the following questions about Hispanics in the United States and in your community.

a. ¿Cómo se llama el estado donde vives? ¿Es de origen español? ¿Tiene algún significado (*meaning*) especial?
b. ¿Qué es Univisión y por qué es importante? ¿Tienes Univisión en tu región?
c. ¿Qué fiesta mexicana celebran muchos americanos?
d. ¿Qué actor americano habla español?
e. ¿Quién es Demi Lovato? ¿Cuál es su ascendencia (*ancestry*)? ¿Tienes ascendencia hispana?

 MORE IN ELETECA: EXTRA ONLINE PRACTICE

CULTURAL NOTE

Image b. features a scene from **Carnaval** which takes place in February.

ANSWERS

Activity 5

a. agosto; b. febrero; c. marzo; d. diciembre.

Activity 6

a. un; b. una; c. unas; d. unos.

Activity 7

a. los; b. el; c. las; d. la.

Activity 8

a. se llama; b. tienen; c. somos; d. es; e. Son; f. tenemos; g. se llaman.

Activity 9

a. Answers will vary; b. Es la cadena de television más grande de EE. UU.; c. La fiesta del Cinco de Mayo; d. Will Smith; e. Es americana con ascendencia mexicana y española.

OBJECTIVES FOR EN RESUMEN: VOCABULARIO

• Review unit vocabulary and expressions
• Practice communicative skills

STANDARDS

1.2 Understand the language
1.3 Present information

INSTRUCTIONAL STRATEGIES

• Model how to use the vocabulary list to review new words and expressions learned in this unit.
• Use simple materials, such as index cards or self-adhesive notes.
• Self-adhesive notes can be used for writing nouns from the vocabulary list on them, then using them to place the correct labels on objects in the classroom or pictures in the book.
• Index cards can be used as flash cards with the Spanish term on one side and the English term on the other, or a picture or drawing.
• Students can work in pairs or groups, using the self-adhesive notes and index cards as they would the cards of a board game to help each other practice the unit vocabulary.
• Encourage students to write labels or captions for the images on this page. Remind them to use the vocabulary and expressions they have learned in this unit.

EN RESUMEN: Vocabulario

Saludos *Greetings*

Buenos días. *Good morning.*
Buenas tardes. *Good afternoon.*
Buenas noches. *Good evening/night.*
¿Qué tal? *What's up?*
¿Qué tal estás? *How are you doing?*

Presentaciones *Introductions*

Mire, le presento a (al)... *Look, I'd like to introduce you to...*
Mira, este/esta es... *Hey, this is...*
Mira, estos/estas son... *Hey, these are...*
Encantado/a. *Delighted.*
¿Cómo estás? *How do you do? (informal)*

Despedidas *Saying good-bye*

Adiós. *Good-bye.*
Hasta luego. *See you later.*
Hasta pronto. *See you soon.*

Pedir información *Asking questions*

¿Cómo te llamas? *What's your name?*
¿Cuántos años tienes? *How old are you?*
¿De dónde eres? *Where are you from?*
¿Dónde vives? *Where do you live?*
¿Qué haces? *What do you do?*

Profesiones *Professions*

actor / actriz *actor / actress*
bibliotecario / bibliotecaria *librarian*
cantante *singer*

enfermero / enfermera *nurse*
futbolista *soccer player*
médico / médica *doctor*
profesor / profesora *teacher*
tenista *tennis player*

Nacionalidades *Nationalities*

chino/a *Chinese*
cubano/a *Cuban*
chileno/a *Chilean*
dominicano/a *Dominican*
ecuatoriano/a *Ecuadorian*
español / española *Spanish*

francés / francesa *French*
indio/a *Indian*
italiano/a *Italian*
japonés / japonesa *Japanese*
mexicano/a *Mexican*
peruano/a *Peruvian*
puertorriqueño/a *Puerto Rican*

Artículos *Articles*

el / la / los / las *the*
un / una *a, an*
unos / unas *some, a few*

Pronombres de sujeto *Subject pronouns*

yo *I*
tú *you (informal)*
usted *you (formal)*
él *he*
ella *she*
nosotros/as *we*
vosotros/as *you (plural, Spain)*
ustedes *you, you all (plural)*
ellos *they (males or mixed)*
ellas *they (females)*

Verbos *Verbs*

llamar(se) *to be called*
ser *to be*
tener *to have*
tener... años *to be... years old*

Palabras y expresiones útiles *Useful words and expressions*

el amigo / la amiga *friend*
¿Cuándo es tu cumpleaños? *When is your birthday?*

pero *but*
perro *dog*

¿Qué día es hoy? *What's today's date?*
Señor (Sr.) *Mr.*
Señora (Sra.) *Mrs.*
Señorita (Srta.) *Miss./Ms.*
también *also*

EN RESUMEN: Gramática

NUMBERS 0-31

(See page 42)

0	cero	8	ocho	16	dieciséis	24	veinticuatro
1	uno	9	nueve	17	diecisiete	25	veinticinco
2	dos	10	diez	18	dieciocho	26	veintiséis
3	tres	11	once	19	diecinueve	27	veintisiete
4	cuatro	12	doce	20	veinte	28	veintiocho
5	cinco	13	trece	21	veintiuno	29	veintinueve
6	seis	14	catorce	22	veintidós	30	treinta
7	siete	15	quince	23	veintitrés	31	treinta y uno

ARTICLES

(See page 46)

	Indefinite articles		Definite articles	
	Masculine	Feminine	Masculine	Feminine
Singular	un	una	el	la
Plural	unos	unas	los	las

SUBJECT PRONOUNS

(See page 47)

Singular	Plural
yo	nosotros/nosotras
tú	vosotros/vosotras
usted/él/ella	ustedes/ellos/ellas

PRESENT TENSE

(See page 49)

	LLAMAR(SE)	SER	TENER
yo	me llamo	soy	tengo
tú	te llamas	eres	tienes
usted/él/ella	se llama	es	tiene
nosotros/as	nos llamamos	somos	tenemos
vosotros/as	os llamáis	sois	tenéis
ustedes/ellos/ellas	se llaman	son	tienen

OBJECTIVES FOR EN RESUMEN: GRAMÁTICA

- Review unit grammar
- Practice communicative skills

STANDARDS

| 1.2 | Understand the language |
| 1.3 | Present information |

INSTRUCTIONAL STRATEGIES

- Model how to review grammar.
- Ask if they can remember additional examples for each grammar topic
- Model how to find and go back to the appropriate page in the unit to review any grammar topic they may need help with.
- Invite students to review the grammar activities they completed in this unit.
- Ask them what grammar activities they found easy and which they found challenging. Encourage them to repeat any activities they found particularly challenging.
- Create groups of students with mixed abilities (some who have mastered the unit grammar, and some who have not), and have them review and practice the grammar activities with each other.

OBJECTIVES FOR UNIT OPENER

- Introduce unit theme: **Estás en tu casa** about home, people, and things
- Culture: Learn about homes in Hispanic countries

STANDARDS

1.2 Understand the language

2.1 Practices and perspectives

INSTRUCTIONAL STRATEGIES

- Introduce unit theme and objectives: Talk about the home, and the places we like. Have students look at the photograph. Read the caption aloud: **El muchacho estudia en la cocina**.
- Ask questions to recycle content from previous unit. Point to items such as the pen and the chair and ask students **¿Qué es esto? (un bolígrafo, una mesa)**.
- Use the photograph to preview unit vocabulary, such as: **estudiar**. Help students access meaning by making frequent use of gestures or visuals.
- Ask the introductory questions.
  - **¿Cuántos años tiene el muchacho?**
  - **¿Está en casa o en clase?**
  - **Y tú ¿estás en casa o en clase?**
- Ask related questions: **¿Qúe usa para estudiar? ¿Usa lápiz o bolígrafo? ¿Escribe en el libro o en el cuaderno?** Ask some *yes/no* questions: **¿Está en la mesa? ¿Está solo o con un amigo?**

ANSWERS

Answers will vary. Possible answers might include the following:

- El muchacho tiene 14 años.
- El muchacho no está en la clase. Está en su casa.
- Estoy en la escuela.

ADVANCED LEARNERS

Ask some volunteers to stand up and describe the boy in the picture in a short paragraph using expressions learned in Unit 1: **El muchacho tiene 14 años. Es americano. Es cáncer. El cumpleaños del muchacho es el...** Have other students answer questions based on the description provided by his fellow student.

UNIDAD
2
ESTÁS EN TU CASA

》》 ¿Cuántos años tiene el muchacho?
》》 ¿Está en casa o en clase?
》》 Y tú, ¿estás en casa o en clase?

60

El muchacho estudia en la cocina.

ADDITIONAL UNIT RESOURCES

Extension Activities (EA) (Photocopiable)	**Interactive Whiteboard Lessons (IWB)**	**Audio**	**Video**	**Online ELEteca**
EA: 2.1, 2.2, 2.3	IWB: 2.1.	23 to 33	Diálogo 2	

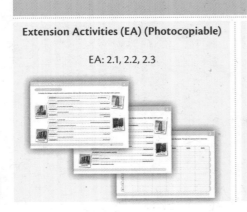

In this unit, you will learn to:

- Express opinions and preferences
- Describe people, places, and things
- Talk about your home
- Talk about activities
- Say where you and others are

Using

- Descriptive adjectives
- -ar verbs
- Verb *estar*
- Numbers to 101

Cultural Connections

- Share information about homes in Hispanic countries, and compare cultural similarities

SABOR HISPANO

Vivir en España
- España

¡ACCIÓN!

61

LEARNING OUTCOMES

- Express opinions and preferences
- Describe people, places, and things
- Talk about your home
- Talk about activities
- Say where you and others are from

INSTRUCTIONAL STRATEGIES

- Use the unit opener to introduce a preview of the vocabulary and the cultural topics for this unit.
- Have students look at the images on this page and relate them to the objectives listed. Ask questions such as: *¿Qué ven en estas fotos? ¿Qué fotos son interesantes?*
- Invite students to read the topic for **Sabor hispano** and preview that section in the unit.
- Ask students to predict what they think the episode for **¡Acción!** will be about.
- Have students work in pairs to talk about the images using the questions you have modeled. Then have volunteers present to the class what they understand this unit to be about.

HERITAGE LANGUAGE LEARNERS

Provide more introductory information related to **Sabor hispano**. Show students a short video clip about Spain and/or pictures, for instance, from http://www.spain.info/. Ask students what they know about Spain and whether they have been there.

THREE MODES OF COMMUNICATION: UNIT 2			
	INTERPERSONAL	INTERPRETIVE	PRESENTATIONAL
HABLAMOS DE...	5	1, 2, 3	
COMUNICA	2, 5	1, 4	2, 3
¡ACCIÓN!	5	1, 2, 3, 4	
PALABRA POR PALABRA	3, 4, 6, 10, 13, 14	2, 5, 7, 8, 9, 12	6, 10, 14
GRAMÁTICA	8, 10	1, 2, 3, 4, 5, 6, 7, 9	7, 8, 10
DESTREZAS		1, 3	2
CULTURA		SABOR HISPANO	
RELATO	4, 5	1, 2, 3	5, 6

OBJECTIVES FOR HABLAMOS DE...

- Understand language in context
- Preview vocabulary: words to describe and express liking something
- Preview grammatical structures: descriptive adjectives, -*ar* verbs, verb *estar*
- Read and listen to a conversation about Juan visiting his favorite places and describing them

CORE RESOURCES

- Audio Program: Track 23
- Extension Activities: EA 2.1, 2.2

STANDARDS

1.1 Engage in conversation
1.2 Understand the language
4.2 Compare cultures

INSTRUCTIONAL STRATEGIES

Activity 1

- Ask students: **¿Dónde está la familia?** and use a map to point out the location of Barcelona.
- Write Barcelona on the board. Elicit any prior knowledge about Barcelona. See the Cultural Note below for background information.
- Have students look at the photo, answer the questions, and then share their answers.
- To check comprehension, project the image and ask: **¿Qué es esto? (Un edificio)**; **¿Dónde está? (En Barcelona)**; **¿Quién es él? (Un turista)**; **¿Con quién está en la foto? ¿Con su papá o su mamá? (Su papá)**.

Activity 2

Encourage students to talk about themselves and their favorite city in Spanish using Activity 2 as a model.

CULTURAL NOTE

- Barcelona is the second largest city in Spain in population, after Madrid. It is the capital of the region known as Cataluña. It is on the Mediterranean coast. The official languages of the region are Spanish and Catalán. It is also a very popular tourist destination.
- The building shown in the background is *La Sagrada Familia* by the architect Antoni Gaudí. The architect's untimely death in 1926 prevented the completion of the building and so it remains unfinished. Through private and public donations, construction continues to this day.
- Students might also know about the soccer team FC Barcelona., known as "el Barça" /barsa/.

ANSWERS

Activity 1

1. c; **2.** c; **3.** b; **4.** a.

Activity 2

1. La Sagrada Familia; **2.** (Antoni) Gaudí; **3.** El Parque Güell.

HABLAMOS DE... Una ciudad española

1 Look at the image below of Juan and his family in Barcelona. Then choose the correct answer to complete the sentences.

1. ¿Qué es Juan?
- **a.** ☐ cantante
- **b.** ☐ profesor
- **c.** ☐ turista

2. ¿Qué tiene la mujer en las manos?
- **a.** ☐ mochila
- **b.** ☐ tableta
- **c.** ☐ cámara

3. ¿En qué país está la familia?
- **a.** ☐ Argentina
- **b.** ☐ España
- **c.** ☐ Estados Unidos

4. ¿Qué aparece en la foto?
- **a.** ☐ monumento
- **b.** ☐ parque
- **c.** ☐ escuela

2 Read more about Juan. Then answer the questions to find out the name of the structure in the photo above and who designed it.

Hola, me llamo Juan. Tengo 14 años y soy de Málaga, una ciudad que está en el sur de España. Estoy en Barcelona, mi ciudad (*city*) favorita. Tengo muchas fotos de la ciudad. Esta es de la Sagrada Familia, un monumento del arquitecto Gaudí, muy famoso en España. También tengo fotos del Parque Güell, otra de sus obras (*works*) más originales.

a. ¿Cómo se llama el edificio (*building*)?
b. ¿Quién es el arquitecto?
c. ¿Qué otra obra es del mismo (*same*) arquitecto?

SLOWER-PACED LEARNERS

Have students notice that some words seem masculine but are feminine, such as **fotos**. That is why we say **muchas fotos**. Similarly, **turista** seems feminine but can also be masculine: **un turista**.

3 🎧 23 **Listen to the conversation between Juan and his friend María after his trip. Then decide whether the statements are true (T) or false (F).**

María: Hola, Juan. ¿Tienes las fotos de Barcelona?
Juan: Sí, aquí tienes mis fotos.
María: En esta foto, estás en la Sagrada Familia, ¿verdad?
Juan: Sí, es un lugar (place) muy bonito y conocido.
María: Para mí, esta foto es bellísima. ¿Dónde es?
Juan: Es en el Parque Güell, otro lugar importante de la ciudad.
María: ¿Y cuál es tu foto favorita?
Juan: Esta. Estoy con dos amigos en la Casa Milà, otro edificio conocido de Gaudí.
María: ¿Quiénes son estos chicos?
Juan: Se llaman Karen y Mateo, son mexicanos, pero viven en Barcelona.
María: Para ti, ¿cómo es la gente (people) en Barcelona?
Juan: Es muy simpática y amable.
María: Para mí, también.
Juan: Aquí tienes más fotos.

Parque Güell

Casa Milà

	T	F
a. Juan solo tiene tres fotos de Barcelona.	☐	☐
b. En una foto, Juan está en la Casa Milà.	☐	☐
c. Para María, la Sagrada Familia es un lugar muy bonito.	☐	☐
d. Karen es una amiga mexicana.	☐	☐
e. Para María, la gente de Barcelona no es simpática.	☐	☐

Mateo y Karen

4 🎧 23 **Listen again to the conversation and repeat after the speaker.**

5 👥 **Here are some more of Juan's photos of Barcelona. Choose the one you like best. With a partner, use the information in the photo and the Modelo to talk about your preference. Then switch roles.**

Modelo:
E1: Mira estas fotos de Barcelona.
E2: ¡Qué bonitas!
E1: ¿Cuál es tu favorita?

E2: Para mí, es esta de...
E1: ¿Qué es?
E2: Es...

La Torre Agbar.
Edificio símbolo de Barcelona

La Rambla.
Avenida muy importante en Barcelona, España

Camp Nou.
Estadio de fútbol del FC Barcelona

63

Activity 5

Have students work in pairs for this activity. Encourage them to use the vocabulary and sentence patterns from the conversation in Activity 3.

Alternative Activity

Use EA 2.1 and 2.2 **Preparamos el diálogo** to guide students through the conversation. Have student pairs select role 1 or 2 and give them the corresponding copy of the dialogue to complete. Instruct them to use the words in parenthesis to create their part of the conversation. Circulate around the room to check answers. Then have student pairs present in small groups or to the class.

ANSWERS

Activity 3

a. T; **b.** T; **c.** F (Para Juan); **d.** T; **e.** F.

Activity 5

Answers will vary.

ADVANCED LEARNERS

Have students write down all adjectives on this page. In pairs, have them use the adjectives to describe classroom objects and pictures on the book.

HERITAGE LANGUAGE LEARNERS

Have students find more images of Gaudí's **la Sagrada Familia** online to share with the class or use them as an extension to Activity 5. While they're looking for photos, encourage students to find at least two interesting facts about the building or Gaudí himself to share with the class as well.

INSTRUCTIONAL STRATEGIES

🎧 23 **Activity 3**

- Introduction to the conversation: Tell students that they will be listening to a conversation between Juan and his friend María.

- Tell students to close their books while you project the true or false statements. Before playing the audio, ask students if they have questions about vocabulary. Avoid giving translations and use cognates and gestures instead. For **gente** you might say **muchas personas** and so on. Help students look for connections and try to guess at unfamiliar words.

- Play the audio with books closed and have students answer the questions. Replay the audio, this time with books open so students can check their answers.

🎧 23 **Activity 4**

Have students listen to the conversation and repeat. Use the audio to focus attention on rhythm, intonation, and pronunciation.

OBJECTIVES FOR COMUNICA

- Present communicative functions of the unit:
  - Talking about preferences
  - Talking about school subjects and sports
- Practice using adjectives that describe a preference, such as **favorito/a**

CORE RESOURCES

- Interactive Online Materials - ELEteca

STANDARDS

1.1   Engage in conversation

1.2   Understand the language

INSTRUCTIONAL STRATEGIES FOR TALKING ABOUT PREFERENCES

Activity 1

Present the adjective **favorito/a** and model how to ask someone about his or her favorite sport, animal, or food: **¿Cuál es tu deporte favorito? ¿Cuál es tu animal favorito? ¿Cuál es tu comida favorita?**

> #### Alternative Activity
>
> - Review new vocabulary first. With books closed, set up the following sentences and have students guess at the missing letters.
>
>   España es un P _ _ S; El gato es un A _ _ _ _ L; La literatura es una A _ _ _ _ _ _ _ _ A; an so on.
>
> - Then have students complete the activity. To check answers, have students take turns asking each other about their preferences: **¿Cuál es tu animal favorito?**

Activity 2

- Introduce students to the names of school subjects. Point out that the words for school subjects are cognates, very similar to English, and can be easily decoded: **Arte, Biología, Ciencias, Español, Historia, Matemáticas, Deportes**.
- Review the school subjects and sports in the boxes and encourage students to guess at their meaning.
- For additional practice, have students meet in groups and collect the data about their favorite subject or sports, as in a survey, then present the results to the rest of the class.

GRAMMAR NOTE

- Remind students that the adjective **favorito/a** must match the gender of the noun, and that most masculine nouns end in **–o** and most feminine nouns end in **–a**.
- Point out that the nouns **animal**, **país**, and **deporte** are masculine nouns.

ANSWERS

Activity 1

a. animal; **b.** asignatura; **c.** deporte; **d.** comida; **e.** número; **f.** país.

Activity 2

Answers will vary.

COMUNICA

TALKING ABOUT PREFERENCES

Para preguntar	Para responder
¿Cuál es tu deporte favorito?	(Mi deporte favorito es) el tenis.
¿Cuál es tu animal favorito?	(Mi animal favorito es) el gato (*cat*).
¿Cuál es tu comida (*food*) favorita?	(Mi comida favorita es) el queso.

1 Look at María's favorite things and fill in the blanks with the appropriate word from the list.

> país o animal o deporte o asignatura o número o comida

a. Mi .... favorito es el perro.

b. Mi .... favorita es Matemáticas.

c. Mi .... favorito es el baloncesto.

d. Mi .... favorita es el queso.

e. Mi .... favorito es el quince.

f. Mi .... favorito es México.

2 With a partner, take turns asking each other about your favorite things and record your partner's answers in the survey chart below.

Modelo: ¿Cuál es tu... favorito/a?

❗	❗
■ Here are some of the **subjects** you study in school. Can you tell what they are? • Arte • Español • Música • Biología • Historia • Educación Física • Ciencias • Matemáticas • Geografía ■ Otras asignaturas / materias (*other subjects*): • Artes y letras (*arts and humanities*) • Computación (*computer science*)	■ **Deportes** (*sports*) • el baloncesto / el básquetbol • el béisbol • el fútbol • el fútbol americano • el golf • el tenis • el vóleibol

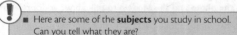

Encuesta sobre gustos

■ número	■ asignatura	■ animal
■ comida	■ deporte	■ país

SLOWER-PACED LEARNERS

As an extension to Activity 2, play Pictionary to practice the school subjects and charades to practice the sports. Call on volunteers to draw the subjects or act out the sports you give to them. The rest of the class guesses the answers. Set time limits. Consider dividing the class into teams to create a competition.

ADVANCED LEARNERS AND HERITAGE LANGUAGE LEARNERS

Encourage more advanced students to add names of sports or school subjects that they may know of and are not included on this page. Ask them other questions such as **¿Cuál es el deporte favorito de los argentinos? ¿De los españoles? ¿De los cubanos?**

EXPRESSING OPINIONS

Para mí, *For me,*		
Para ti, *For you,*		
Para usted, *For you (formal),*		fantástico *fantastic.*
Para él/ella, *For him/her,*		genial *great.*
Para nosotros/as, *For us,*	**el español es**	fácil *easy.*
Para vosotros/as, *For you (pl. Spain),*	Spanish is	divertido *fun.*
Para ustedes, *For you (all),*		interesante *interesting.*
Para ellos/ellas, *For them,*		importante *important.*
		aburrido *boring.*
		difícil *difficult.*

En mi opinión, *In my opinion,...*

Pienso / Creo / Opino que... *I think / I believe / My opinion is that...*

Showing agreement and disagreement with someone's opinion

?	**✓**		**✗**	
¿Y para ti?	Para mí, también.	*For me too.*	Para mí, no.	*Not for me.*
¿Verdad?	Sí, es verdad.	*Yes, that's true.*	No, no es verdad.	*No, that's not true.*
¿Qué crees?	Creo que sí.	*I believe so.*	Creo que no.	*I don't believe so.*

3 🎧 24 👥 **Listen to the following conversations. Then take turns role playing with a partner.**

  a. Mateo: Para mí, Colombia es un país muy bonito. ¿Y para ti?
    Belén: Para mí, también.

  b. Jesús: Para mí, el fútbol americano es fantástico. ¿Y para ustedes?
    María y Daniel: Para nosotros, no.

  c. Pedro: Para ti, el español es un idioma muy fácil, ¿verdad?
    Jorge: Sí, es verdad.

4 🎧 25 **Listen to María and Juan as they are interviewed about their preferences. Decide if they agree or disagree about the following.**

	✓	✗
a. La gente de Barcelona es abierta.		
b. El fútbol es un deporte divertido.		
c. El inglés es una lengua difícil.		
d. Una ciudad pequeña es aburrida.		
e. Es interesante leer *(to read)* todos los días.		

5 👥 **Take turns expressing your preferences and asking your partner for his / her opinion about the following topics: *el fútbol, la comida china, la música rap, la clase de Ciencias.***

  Modelo: Para mí / Creo que / En mi opinión, el fútbol es.

 MORE IN ELETECA: EXTRA ONLINE PRACTICE

OBJECTIVES FOR COMUNICA

- Present the communicative functions of the unit:
  - Expressing opinions
  - Practice using adjectives to express an opinion

CORE RESOURCES

- Extension Activities: EA 2.3
- Audio Program: Tracks 24, 25

STANDARDS

  1.1 Engage in conversation
  1.2 Understand the language
  1.3 Present information
  4.1 Compare languages

INSTRUCTIONAL STRATEGIES FOR EXPRESSING OPINIONS

- Write on the board: ***Para mí, el español es fantástico. Para mí, la música es fantástica.*** Ask students to point out the differences between the two sentences and what they refer to. Review other adjectives from the list and write them on the board. Place a smiley face next to the positive ones, such as ***fantástico*** and a sad face next to the negative ones, such as ***aburrido.***
- Model expressions to show agreement: ***Para mí, también. Sí, es verdad. Creo que sí.*** Then model expressions to show disagreement: ***Para mí, no. No, no es verdad. Creo que no.*** Have students repeat these sentences after you and point out the differences between the two sets of sentences.
- Review other pronouns from the chart, such as ***ti, usted, él/ella, nosotros, ustedes, ellos/ellas.***

🎧 24 **Activity 3**

Tell students to pay attention to the opinions expressed in the dialogue, and whether people are agreeing or disagreeing. Then have students take turns role-playing with a partner.

🎧 25 **Activity 4**

Help students understand that they are listening for whether María and Juan agree with each other or not.

See audioscript on page APP5.

Activity 5

Distribute a copy of EA 2.3, ***Nuestras opiniones.*** Ask students to first write their opinions. Then have students ask each other using the language structures learned: ***Para mí, la playa es divertida, ¿y para ti?*** The goal is to have students draw conclusions about what they agree on.

NOTE

Playa is new vocabulary. Describe it or show images of it to help explain that it means *beach.*

ANSWERS

Activity 4

  a. Agree; **b.** Disagree; **c.** Disagree; **d.** Agree; **e.** Disagree.

SLOWER-PACED LEARNERS

Before students speak on their own in Activity 5, elicit examples of adjectives and other descriptions that relate to the list of items. Write the words on the board in the form of a chart so students can refer to them when expressing their own opinions about the different topics.

OBJECTIVES FOR ¡ACCIÓN!

- Provide students with a structured approach to viewing the video
- Contextualize the content of the unit in a familiar scenario

CORE RESOURCES

- Unit Video 2 - Unos muebles ho-rri-bles
- Online Materials - ELEteca

STANDARDS

- 1.1 Interpersonal communication
- 1.2 Interpretive communication
- 2.1 Culture: Practices and perspectives

INSTRUCTIONAL STRATEGIES

Previewing: Antes del video

Activity 1

- Focus students' attention on the title of the video and the images. Check their comprehension of **muebles** by pointing out details in the images and classroom that are examples of furniture. Elicit words that have been already been presented, such as **silla** and **mesa**.
- Ask students to think about why **horribles** has been broken up in the title. Encourage them to make predictions about how this will relate to the video.
- Put students into pairs to talk about their rooms, and remind them to take notes. Call on a few volunteers to report back on their partners' rooms.

Activity 2

- Have students work individually first. Then put them into pairs to compare their answers. Direct them to the vocabulary summary on page 84 to check their answers.

Activity 3

- Remind students to use their knowledge of cognates and context clues to eliminar options and help them arrive at the correct answers.
- Take a class poll to see which answers were the most popular. Then call on volunteers to explain their answers. Encourage correction among classmates, if necessary.

Viewing: Durante el video

Activity 4

- Play the video, reminding students to listen for the words in Activity 2.
- After going over the answers to Activity 2, pose a question to the class to check their general comprehension of the video, such as **¿Cuál es el problema con los muebles?** or **¿Cuál es el conflicto entre Juanjo y Alfonso?** Help them along as needed by asking related *yes/no* questions or providing sentence stems that they can complete, such as **Juanjo cree que los muebles son…**

Activity 5

- Remind them of the verb **medir** presented in Activity 3. Replay or pause this section of the video as needed.

ANSWERS

Activity 2

mesilla, lámpara, estantería, libro, cama.

Activity 3

b, c.

¡ACCIÓN! Unos muebles ho-rri-bles

1. 2. 3.
4. 5. 6.

ANTES DEL VIDEO

1 👥 Take turns describing your room to your partner. Talk about the furniture and other objects in your room and what they look like. Take notes.

2 Look at the list below and indicate the words for the objects that appear in Image 2.

- ◯ mesa
- ◯ silla
- ◯ muebles
- ◯ lámpara
- ◯ estantería
- ◯ habitación
- ◯ cama
- ◯ puerta
- ◯ televisión
- ◯ alfombra
- ◯ armario
- ◯ libro
- ◯ mesilla
- ◯ espejo
- ◯ sofá
- ◯ computadora

3 Look at Image 1. Do you know the name in Spanish for this tool and its use? Make your best guess and choose from the options provided.

Es…	Se usa para…
a. un termómetro.	**a.** pesar los alimentos.
b. un metro.	**b.** medir la temperatura.
c. un peso.	**c.** medir los objetos.

DURANTE EL VIDEO

4 List the words from Activity 2 that are mentioned in the episode.

5 🎬 00:48 - 01:30 Juanjo and Alfonso are arranging their room so that everything fits. Watch again while Juanjo measures the table and listen for the expression he uses to give the measurements. Write what he says.

Activity 4

mesa, cama, mesilla, estantería, puerta, armario, muebles, habitación, libro, sofá.

Activity 5

La mesa mide… cincuenta y siete centímetros.

SLOWER-PACED LEARNERS

As an alternate approach to Activity 1, have students draw pictures of their rooms first. They can use their pictures to show and talk to their partners about their rooms. Later on in the lesson, after more vocabulary has been presented, have students label their pictures.

HERITAGE LANGUAGE LEARNERS

After watching the video the first time, elicit and confirm the characters' names. Then ask students to think about and respond to these questions in pairs: **¿Quién menciona Drácula en el video y por qué? ¿Quién cambia de opinion en el video? ¿Por qué?**

6 🎬 01:30 - 03:15 **Watch the next segment and listen closely to the adjectives Juanjo and Alfonso use to talk about their things. Check off the adjectives you hear. ¡Atención! Pay careful attention to number and gender.**

- ☐ blanca
- ☐ azul
- ☐ negros
- ☐ feos
- ☐ guapos
- ☐ grande
- ☐ antiguos
- ☐ baratos
- ☐ bonito
- ☐ pequeña
- ☐ terribles
- ☐ verdes
- ☐ modernos
- ☐ favoritos
- ☐ amarillo

7 **Watch the entire episode from beginning to end and write the expressions the characters use to ask and give their opinion.**

	Pedir opinión	Expresar opinión
1		
2		
3		

8 **Look at Images 4, 5, and 6 of the characters in the episode. Write who appears in each image and their opinion about the furniture using the expressions in Activity 7.**

Imagen 4: ....–...

Imagen 5: ....–...

Imagen 6: ....–...

9 👥 **Write what you think about their furniture and share your opinion with several of your classmates.**

DESPUÉS DEL VIDEO

10 👥 **With a partner, measure the following objects in class. One of you will measure while the other records in Spanish. Create your own tool for measuring if you don't have a measuring tape!**

a. mesa: .... **b.** silla: .... **c.** puerta: .... **d.** libro: ....

11 **Write a sentence using the adjectives you checked off in Activity 6. ¡Atención! Be sure to use the correct object or person to match number and gender of the adjective.**

Modelo: La mesa del profesor es blanca.

12 👥 **Read five of the sentences you wrote in Activity 11 and ask your partner for his/her opinion using the expressions from the video. Be sure your partner responds using similar expressions.**

Modelo: E1: La mesa del profesor es blanca, ¿verdad?
E2: Para mí, no es blanca, es beige...

13 👥 **Describe your room once more to your partner. This time, include new words and expressions you learned in the episode as needed.**

💻 **MORE IN ELETECA:** EXTRA ONLINE PRACTICE

67

---

adjectives that describe opinions, not facts. For example, sentence about size and color don't usually reflect opinions.

- Take a class poll to find out who agrees most with each character from the video.

Post-viewing: Después del video

Activity 10

- If a ruler or measuring tape isn't available, model how students can use other tools (such as their fingers, feet, or folders) to measure objects and how to describe those measurements.
- Have pairs compare answers to see if they agree. Ask follow-up questions, such as **¿Es grande? ¿Es pequeño/a?**

Activity 11

- Model another sample sentence to remind students how the gender and number of the adjectives should change. Elicit the changes from the class and write the sentence on the board.
- Have students swap papers with a partner and correct each other's sentences. Monitor their work and go over any particularly challenging sentences or recurring errors as a class.

Activity 12

- Refer students back to the expressions for showing agreement and disagreement with someone's opinion on page 65 for more support.

Activity 13

- As an extension or alternative approach to this activity, have students describe another room from their home or school.
- Encourage students to make a list of the objects that their partners mention and ask follow-up questions about other pieces of furniture and details about them. You may want to model how to use **¿Hay...?** to ask if something is there: **¿Hay un espejo en tu habitación? ¿Hay una mesilla? ¿De qué color es?**

ANSWERS

Activity 6

blanca, azul, feos, modernos, antiguos, baratos, grande, pequeña.

Activity 7

¿te gustan?, ¿verdad?, ¿Qué opinas tú?, yo creo que, en mi opinión, para mí.

Activity 8

Imagen 4: Alfonso – Opina que los muebles son de estilo clásico y elegante; **Imagen 5:** Juanjo – Cree que los muebles son horribles; **Imagen 6:** Eli – Para Eli los muebles son un poco antiguos.

SLOWER-PACED LEARNERS

You may want to allow students to work with a partner to complete Activity 8.

ADVANCED LEARNERS

If students finish writing their sentences in Activity 11 before the rest of the class, challenge them to write sentences using other words from Activity 6 that were not checked off.

HERITAGE LANGUAGE LEARNERS

Have students write a summary of the video in their own words using the images on page 66 to help them. Tell them to be sure to include the characters, the conflict, and the resolution.

INSTRUCTIONAL STRATEGIES

Activity 6

When going over the answers, challenge students to link the adjectives to the objects described in the video.

Activity 7

Play the video, pausing as desired to focus students' attention and give them time to write the questions and phrases.

Activity 8

- Tell students to use the list of adjectives in Activity 6 and them expressions in Activity 7 to help them formulate the sentences about each character's opinion.
- Call on volunteers to share their answers, guiding any corrections that may be needed.

Activity 9

- Remind them to use full sentences to write their opinions. Remind them to choose

OBJECTIVES FOR LOS COLORES

- Present the vocabulary needed to practice the communicative and grammatical functions for the unit: colors
- Identify the main colors in Spanish
- Talk about objects of different colors

CORE RESOURCES

- Audio Program: 26
- Interactive Online Materials - ELEteca

STANDARDS

1.1   Engage in conversation
1.2   Understand the language
1.3   Present information

INSTRUCTIONAL STRATEGIES

🎧 26 Activity 1

Have students use the color spots in the book to identify colors in Spanish, then listen to the audio. Help students pronounce the **j** in **anaranjado** and **rojo**. Invite students to describe objects in the room by their color, such as: **El lápiz es amarillo**.

Activity 2

- To prepare for this activity, start by talking about the American flag. Say: **Los colores de la bandera americana son rojo, blanco y azul**.
- Tell students that the flags in this activity are all from different Spanish-speaking countries. Have them write down the colors for each of the flags and try to name the countries they represent.

Activity 3

Circulate around the room to ensure students are responding with the correct forms of the adjectives.

ANSWERS

Activity 2

1. Argentina: azul y blanco; **2.** Perú: rojo y blanco; **3.** Colombia: amarillo, azul, rojo; **4.** España: rojo y amarillo; **5.** Bolivia: rojo, amarillo, verde; **6.** Chile: azul, blanco, rojo.

Activity 3

1. El gato es gris y pequeño; El perro es marrón y grande. **2.** La catedral es roja y amarilla; Es antigua; Es grande. **5.** Las sillas son rojas; Son grandes; La mesa es blanca. **4.** La mochila es gris; el balón es blanco y negro; los libros son rojos.

PALABRA POR PALABRA Los colores

1 🎧 **26** Listen to the names for the colors in Spanish.

→ rojo   ⇒ blanco   → amarillo   → marrón   → anaranjado

→ azul   → negro   → verde   → gris

- marrón = color café, castaño
- anaranjado = naranja
- rojo = colorado

2 Write the colors for each of the flags below. Can you name any of the countries they represent?

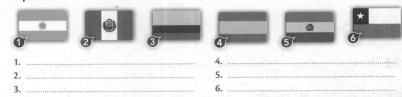

1. ....
2. ....
3. ....
4. ....
5. ....
6. ....

3 👥 Take turns asking each other about the images. Use the question cues provided. ¡Atención! Remember to use the correct form of the adjectives.

1. ¿De qué color es el gato? ¿Es grande o pequeño? ¿De qué color es el perro? ¿Es grande o pequeño?

2. ¿De qué color es la catedral de Granada en Nicaragua? ¿Es moderna o antigua? ¿Es grande o pequeña?

3. ¿De qué color son las sillas? ¿Son grandes o pequeñas? ¿De qué color es la mesa?

4. ¿De qué color es/son...?

!
- Colors in Spanish agree in number and gender with the noun.
La mesa es amarill**a**.
Los cuadern**os** son amarill**os**.

SLOWER-PACED LEARNERS

As an extension to Activity 1, have students identify classroom objects that are **amarillos**, **rojos**, **azules**, **anaranjados**, etc.

ADVANCED LEARNERS

Have students follow up with the information provided by the slower-paced learners in Activity 1 and say a sentence: **La mochila de David es azul. El cuaderno de Melissa es rojo.**

HERITAGE LANGUAGE LEARNERS

After reviewing the flags in Activity 2, have students look for other flags from Spanish-speaking countries. Have them play a game with the whole class, which has to guess how the flag is and what country it belongs to. You may need to add the words **arriba**, **abajo**, **medio**, **izquierda**, and **derecha**.

La casa

4 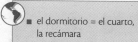 **Look at the names of the rooms in a house and practice saying them aloud with a partner. Then take turns asking each other about the color of each room.**

Modelo:
E1: ¿De qué color es...?
E2: Es...

a. ¿De qué color es el dormitorio?

b. ¿De qué color es el salón?

c. ¿De qué color es la cocina?

d. ¿De qué color es el cuarto de baño?

La cocina

El dormitorio

El cuarto de baño

El salón

- el dormitorio = el cuarto, la recámara
- el salón = la sala, la sala de estar
- el cuarto de baño = el baño

5 🎧 **27** **Listen to Elena talk about her favorite rooms and colors. Then match the room to the correct color.**

1. el salón	**a.** verde
2. la clase	**b.** amarillo
3. la cocina	**c.** blanco
4. el dormitorio	**d.** anaranjada

6 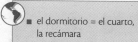 **With a partner, take turns asking and talking about the rooms in your house. Ask about colors and his/her preferences. Use the questions and expressions you learned in Comunica.**

Modelo:

¿Cuál es tu habitación favorita en casa?

Para mí, es la cocina.

¿De qué color es?

Es blanca.

69

OBJECTIVES FOR LA CASA

- Present the vocabulary needed to practice the communicative and grammatical functions for the unit: rooms in the house
- Identify the main rooms in a house
- Talk about rooms in a house

CORE RESOURCES

- Audio Program: Track 27

STANDARDS

1.1	Engage in conversation
1.2	Understand the language
1.3	Present information

INSTRUCTIONAL STRATEGIES

Activity 4

- Help students pronounce the names of the various rooms in the house: **la cocina**, **el dormitorio**, **el cuarto de baño**, **el salón**. Have students practice saying the names of rooms first. Then have them work in pairs to say what color each room is, such as: **La cocina es roja, blanca y gris.** Remind students to pay attention to the gender of each noun and make the colors agree in gender with the noun.
- Point out the language variations between regions and include any other words you may know.

🎧 **27** **Activity 5**

Play audio and review answers by having students respond in full sentences. **El salón es verde** and so on.

Audioscript

Para mí, la cocina es mi lugar favorito de la casa. Mi cocina es muy grande y de color anaranjado. Es un color que no me gusta mucho. Yo prefiero el color blanco, como mi salón, porque es un color más tranquilo y relajado. Aunque el amarillo es un color que da mala suerte en España, mi dormitorio es de este color. No tengo problemas. Un color que no me gusta es el verde, como el color de mi clase.

Activity 6

Model the conversation with a student. Call on student pairs to present to the class.

ANSWERS

Activity 4

a. El dormitorio es azul; **b.** El salón es anaranjado y blanco; **c.** La cocina es roja y gris; **d.** El cuarto de baño es verde y blanco.

Activity 5

1. c; **2.** a; **3.** d; **4.** b.

Activity 6

Answers will vary.

ADVANCED LEARNERS

As an extension to Activity 6, have students ask each other about their favorite sports teams and describe the colors of their uniforms / jerseys.

- Present the vocabulary needed to practice the communicative and grammatical functions for the unit: furniture and household items
- Identify pieces of furniture and household items
- Describe the furniture in a room

CORE RESOURCES

- Audio Program: Track 28
- Interactive Whiteboard Lessons: IWB 2.1

STANDARDS

1.1 Engage in conversation
1.2 Understand the language
1.3 Present information
4.2 Compare cultures

INSTRUCTIONAL STRATEGIES

Activity 7

This activity asks students to guess at unfamiliar words using some of the strategies presented so far, such as cognates and language in context. With a partner, students interpret what furniture and household items these words refer to.

28 Activity 8

Alternative Activity

Use IWB 2.1, *Los muebles*, to teach the vocabulary related to furniture. Say the name for one of the pieces of furniture or household items pictured and ask students to point to the correct one.

Activity 9

Remind students of the different language variations used to describe these rooms, which are presented on the previous page. To elicit correct responses, ask them where each item would normally be found: **¿Dónde está normalmente la mesa?**

Activity 10

- Project the image of the room. Review the **Modelo**, pointing to the objects as you go. Draw some of your own examples on the board.
- Call on students to describe their partner's room according to what they drew.

ANSWERS

Activity 8

a. la cama; **b.** la mesilla; **c.** el armario; **d.** la estufa; **e.** la ducha; **f.** el horno; **g.** el lavabo; **h.** la mesa; **i.** la bañera; **j.** el sofá; **k.** el espejo y la cómoda; **l.** la estantería.

Activity 9

La cocina: la estufa, el horno, la mesa; **El dormitorio:** la cama, la mesilla, el armario; **El cuarto de baño:** el lavabo, la ducha, la bañera, el espejo; **El salón:** el sofá, la estantería, la mesa.

PALABRA POR PALABRA Los muebles

7 Look at the list of words for furniture in Spanish and practice saying them aloud with a partner. Can you guess their meaning?

- el armario
- la ducha
- la estufa
- la mesa
- la cama
- el espejo y la cómoda
- el horno
- la mesilla
- la bañera
- la estantería
- el lavabo
- el sofá

8 28 Listen and write the words you hear under each image. Use the list above.

a. la | b. la | c. el armario | d. la
e. la | f. el horno | g. el | h. la mesa
i. la bañera | j. el | k. el y la | l. la estantería

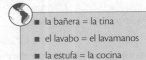

- la bañera = la tina
- el lavabo = el lavamanos
- la estufa = la cocina

9 Write the names of the furniture and household items in the appropriate column below.

La cocina	El dormitorio	El cuarto de baño	El salón

10 Describe your room and the furniture in it to your partner. Include the color and size of the items. Your partner will try to recreate it on a separate piece of paper.

Modelo: Tengo un dormitorio muy bonito. Tengo una cama azul. Tengo dos mesillas y una silla anaranjada.

ADVANCED LEARNERS

Have students write sentences about each of the images in Activity 8. They can describe their size, color, style, or location, or they can give their opinions about them. Have them share their sentences with a partner.

Los números del 32 al 101

11 🎧 **29** Listen and repeat the numbers after the speaker.

32	treinta y dos	65	sesenta y cinco	98	noventa y ocho
40	cuarenta	70	setenta	99	noventa y nueve
43	cuarenta y tres	76	setenta y seis	100	cien
50	cincuenta	80	ochenta	101	ciento uno
54	cincuenta y cuatro	87	ochenta y siete		
60	sesenta	90	noventa		

- Use **y** after the number 30. *Veintinueve, treinta, treinta y uno...*
- Use **cien** for one hundred (100) and **ciento** for numbers higher than one hundred. *Cien, ciento uno, ciento dos...*

12 🎧 **30** Write out the numbers you hear. Use the list above to help you.

a. ....
b. ....
c. ....
d. ....
e. ....
f. ....

13 👥 Take turns with a partner asking and giving prices for the furniture and items at the yard sale below.

Estudiante 1:
1. la cómoda azul
2. la silla blanca
3. el espejo pequeño

Estudiante 2:
1. la silla anaranjada
2. la mesilla blanca
3. la cómoda amarilla

$89 $98 $45 $39 $31 $75

- To talk about prices, use the following expressions:
  - **¿Cuánto cuesta** la mochila?
    How much is the backpack?
  - **Cuesta** treinta dólares.
    It costs thirty dollars.

14 👥 You are looking for some inexpensive furniture for your room. With a budget of $100 to spend, ask your partner how much two items would cost at the yard sale. Negotiate to get the price you want.

Modelo: E1: ¿Cuánto cuestan la silla blanca y el armario azul?
E2: Cuestan ciento cuarenta y tres dólares.
E1: Solo tengo cien dólares.
E2: Lo siento (Sorry). / Está bien. Trato hecho (It's a deal).

 MORE IN ELETECA: EXTRA ONLINE PRACTICE

71

🎧 **30** Activity 12
Audioscript

noventa y siete; treinta y ocho; cuarenta y cinco; ciento uno; sesenta y cuatro; setenta y nueve.

Activity 13

- Project the image and review the prices of the items. Practice with: **¿Cuánto cuesta?**
- Point out that **uno** before masculine nouns changes to **un** as in **treinta y un dólares**, **treinta y un libros**, and so on.
- If necessary, explain the difference between **el armario** and **la cómoda**. **El armario tiene puertas.**

Activity 14

- Act out the **Modelo** with a student. Use gestures and emotion to demonstrate the meaning of **Lo siento** and **Trato hecho**.
- Call on student pairs to present to the class.

ANSWERS

Activity 12

a. 97; **b.** 38; **c.** 45; **d.** 101; **e.** 64; **f.** 79.

Activity 13

Estudiante 1
1. el armario azul: noventa y ocho dólares.
2. la silla blanca: cuarenta y cinco dólares.
3. el espejo pequeño: treinta y nueve dólares.

Estudiante 2
1. la silla anaranjada: setenta y cinco dólares.
2. la mesilla blanca: treinta y un dólares.
3. el armario amarillo: ochenta y nueve dólares.

Activity 14

Answers will vary but should reflect use of expressions modeled to negotiate prices.

SLOWER-PACED LEARNERS

Play bingo with a multi-level class. Have all students write a 5x5 table and insert different numbers from 31-100 in each cell. Slower-paced students listen and focus on correctly identifying the numbers to complete their charts.

ADVANCED LEARNERS

While playing bingo, advanced learners take turns calling out numbers for additional speaking practice. Remind them to pronounce the words clearly so their classmates can correctly identify them.

HERITAGE LANGUAGE LEARNERS

While playing bingo, heritage language learners take turns writing out the numbers on the board after they've been called, focusing on the correct spelling of the numbers.

OBJECTIVES FOR LOS NÚMEROS DEL 32 AL 101

- Present the vocabulary needed to practice the communicative and grammatical functions for the unit: numbers 32 to 101
- Talk about prices and furniture

CORE RESOURCES

- Audio Program: Tracks 29, 30

INSTRUCTIONAL STRATEGIES

🎧 **29** Activity 11

- Play the audio and then practice additional numbers by holding up fingers on one or both hands first for tens and then for ones. Call on students to do the same to practice.
- Review the use of **y** with numbers after thirty.

GRAMÁTICA GRAMMAR IN CONTEXT

OBJECTIVES FOR GRAMÁTICA 1

- Present the grammatical structures needed to practice the communicative functions of the unit: gender, number, and agreement of nouns and adjectives
- Describe how things are using adjectives that agree in gender and number with the noun they qualify

CORE RESOURCES

- Interactive Online Materials - ELEteca

STANDARDS

- 1.1   Engage in conversation
- 1.2   Understand the language
- 4.1   Compare languages

INSTRUCTIONAL STRATEGIES

1. Gender, Number, and Agreement of Nouns and Adjectives

- Ask students about the gender of nouns in Spanish and compare that to English. Students should understand by now that all nouns in Spanish, including inanimate objects, have a gender, such as **el libro** and **la silla**.
- Elicit prior knowledge regarding what students know about masculine and feminine nouns in Spanish. Ask them if they know any rules about the gender of nouns and have them give examples, such as most masculine nouns ending in **–o** and most feminine nouns ending in **–a**.
- Elicit prior knowledge about adjectives in Spanish and how, unlike English, they agree in gender and number with the nouns they qualify. Ask students to provide examples they may already know.

Activity 1

Teach or review any vocabulary students may not recognize.

Activity 2

Help students recognize that some adjectives in Spanish do not change in gender, and use the same form with both feminine and masculine nouns, such as **grande** and **azul**.

Plurals of Nouns and Adjectives

After the previous activity, ask students to combine the nouns from the first exercise with the adjectives from the second exercise. Invite them to pair other nouns and adjectives they have learned to practice gender and number agreement in Spanish.

ANSWERS

Activity 1

a. F; b. M; c. F; d. M; e. M; f., F; g. M; h. M.

Activity 2

a. horrible; b. divertida; c. pequeña; d. buena; e. interesante; f. genial.

GRAMÁTICA

1. GENDER, NUMBER, AND AGREEMENT OF NOUNS AND ADJECTIVES

NOUNS

- In Spanish, words that name a person, place or thing (nouns) are grouped into two genders: masculine and feminine. All nouns (both persons and objects) fall into one of these groups. Most nouns that end in **–o** are masculine, and most nouns that end in **–a** are feminine.

El bolígra**fo** (masc.) the pen
La cámara (fem.) the camera

> ! **Exceptions**
> **el** problema, **el** día, **el** mapa, **el** diploma
> **la** mano, **la** radio

1   Indicate whether the following nouns are masculine or feminine.

	M F		M F		M F		M F
a. familia	☐ ☐	c. chica	☐ ☐	e. niño	☐ ☐	g. bolígrafo	☐ ☐
b. libro	☐ ☐	d. queso	☐ ☐	f. pizarra	☐ ☐	h. mapa	☐ ☐

ADJECTIVES

- Adjectives are words that describe nouns. The adjective must agree in gender (masculine or feminine) and number (singular or plural) with the noun it modifies. Look at the chart below to see how adjectives change to show agreement with feminine nouns.

	Masculine	Feminine
Adjectives that end in **–o** change to **–a**:	bonit**o**	bonit**a**
Adjectives that end in **–e**, no change:	grande	grande
Adjectives that end in a consonant, no change:	azul	azul
Nationalites that end in a consonant, add **–a**:	español	español**a**

2   Write the feminine forms of the following adjectives.

a. horrible ➡ ....
b. divertido ➡ ....
c. pequeño ➡ ....

d. bueno ➡ ....
e. interesante ➡ ....
f. genial ➡ ....

PLURALS OF NOUNS AND ADJECTIVES

- Look at the chart below to see how plurals are formed for both nouns and adjectives.

	Nouns	Adjectives
Words that end in a vowel, add **–s**	mesa / mes**as**	grande / grande**s**
Words that end in a consonant, add **–es**[1]	actor / actor**es**	azul / azul**es**

[1] Words that end in a **–z**, change **–z** to **–ces**: lápiz/lápices.

3 Write the plural forms of the following nouns.

a. hombre ➡ ....
b. borrador ➡ ....
c. marcador ➡ ....
d. carpeta ➡ ....
e. libro ➡ ....
f. pez ➡ ....

Los lápices de colores

AGREEMENT

■ In Spanish, articles and adjectives must agree in number and gender with the nouns they modify.

Masculine	Feminine
el carro bonito y azul	la silla bonita y azul
los carros bonitos y azules	las sillas bonitas y azules

4 Complete the following adjectives to show agreement with the noun.

a. El chico es guapo. / La chica es guap........
b. La gata es bonita. / El gato es bonit........
c. Los carros son grandes. / El carro es grand........
d. La mochila es azul. / Las mochilas son azul........

2. PRESENT TENSE OF –AR VERBS

■ Spanish has three groups of verbs which are characterized by the ending of the infinitive. The largest group of Spanish infinitives end in **–ar**. You will learn about the other two groups in Unidad 3. First look at the following infinitives in Spanish and their meaning in English.

Spanish Infinitive	English Infinitive	Spanish Infinitive	English Infinitive
amar	to love	escuchar	to listen to
bailar	to dance	estudiar	to study
caminar	to walk	hablar	to speak
cantar	to sing	pasear	to go for a walk
comprar	to buy	trabajar	to work
descansar	to rest	viajar	to travel

Activity 3

- If students have difficulty adding the correct plural ending to Spanish nouns, point out the following rules:

– Nouns ending in a vowel add **–s**.

– Nouns ending in **–z** make the plural by changing the **–z** to **–ces**. Point out the caption: **Los lápices de colores** and ask students for the singular form of pencil.

– Nouns ending in any other consonant add **–es**. Students may have difficulty remembering and applying this last rule. Remind them that, unlike English, Spanish cannot add just **–s** to a final consonant, rather it adds **–es**, as in **marcador / marcadores**, **español / españoles**, **papel / papeles**.

OBJECTIVES FOR GRAMÁTICA 2

- Present the grammatical structures needed to practice the communicative functions of the unit: Present tense of verbs ending in **–ar**
- Talk about actions in the present

CORE RESOURCES

- Audio Program: 31

STANDARDS

1.1	Engage in conversation
1.2	Understand the language
4.1	Compare languages

INSTRUCTIONAL STRATEGIES

2. Present Tense of –AR Verbs

Some students might have difficulty understanding the grammatical term *infinitive*. Explain that an infinitive is the basic form of a verb, without a specific ending that would tie it to a particular subject or tense. Help students compare Spanish and English verb conjugation. When conjugating most verbs in English, only the third person singular (*he/she/it*) has a special ending, as in *I walk* vs. *he/she/it walks*. In Spanish, the verb ending will also change for first person (*yo, nosotros/as*), second person (*tú, vosotros/as, ustedes*), and third person (*usted/él/ella, ustedes/ellos/ellas*). The verb **to be** in English has more variations for the different subjects, which is more similar to the way verbs are conjugated in Spanish.

ANSWERS

Activity 3

a. hombres; b. borradores; c. marcadores; d. carpetas; e. libros; f. peces.

Activity 4

a. La chica es guapa; b. El gato es bonito; c. El carro es grande; d. Las mochilas son azules.

ADVANCED LEARNERS

Challenge students to think of other nouns or adjectives that follow each of the spelling rules explained for plural in Activity 3. Create a competition. Put students in pairs to create a list of words for each category in a set amount of time. When time is up, have students compare their lists with another pair. Each pair receives a point for those words that the other team doesn't have. The team with the most points wins.

HERITAGE LANGUAGE LEARNERS

Have students write other **-ar** verbs. Collect lists and select regular verbs.

INSTRUCTIONAL STRATEGIES

🎧 **31** **Activity 5**

Audioscript

1. hablamos; 2. caminan; 3. escuchas; 4. bailo; 5. hablo; 6. camina; 7. bailamos; 8. escuchan.

Extension

After students complete the activity, divide the class into six groups. Each group will be one of six persons: **yo, tú, él/ella, nosotros, ustedes, ellos/ellas**. As you call out the verbs **hablar, caminar, escuchar** and **bailar**, each group will say the correct present verb form for its person.

Activity 6

CULTURAL NOTE

Flamenco is a type of music from Andalucía in southern Spain. Since 2010, UNESCO designated flamenco as Intangible Cultural Heritage.

Activity 7

Set up the activity by asking students to focus on the image first and come up with questions they might ask to find out more about the girl and boy. For example: **¿De dónde es? ¿Qué estudia? ¿Qué música escucha? ¿Qué hacen los fines de semana?** Record them on the board to be answered after students complete the activity.

Extension

Have students write a similar paragraph about themselves and a good friend.

Activity 8

Call on students to share information about themselves. Then ask student pairs to present what they had in common.

ANSWERS

Activity 5

1. nosotros; 2. ustedes/ellos/ellas; 3. tú; 4. yo; 5. yo; 6. usted/él/ella/usted; 7. nosotros; 8. ustedes/ellos/ellas.

Activity 6

a. hablo; b. escuchas; c. baila; d. caminamos; e. cantan; f., estudian.

Activity 7

se llama (llamarse); estudia (estudiar); Habla (hablar); Toca (tocar); canta (cantar); escucha (escuchar); se llama (llamarse); Estudia (estudiar); viaja (viajar); pasean (pasear); visitan (visitar).

Activity 8

a. hablo; b. escucho; c. se llama; d. estudia; e. paseamos.

HERITAGE LANGUAGE LEARNERS

Have students read aloud Activity 7 to the class. Encourage them to find videos of **flamenco** dancers and images of **el parque del Retiro** in Spain that they can post to an online forum for the class.

GRAMÁTICA

■ In Spanish, we use a formula to conjugate verbs, that is, to show who is doing the action. To form the present tense of verbs ending in **–ar**, drop the **–ar** ending from the infinitive, and add the appropriate ending as shown in the chart below.

Subject pronouns	Infinitive HABLAR	Endings for –ar verbs		
yo	habl	–o	hablo	*I speak*
tú	habl	–as	hablas	*you (informal) speak*
usted				*you (formal) speak*
él	habl	–a	habla	*he speaks*
ella				*she speaks*
nosotros/as	habl	–amos	hablamos	*we speak*
vosotros/as	habl	–áis	habláis	*you (plural, Spain) speak*
ustedes				*you (plural) speak*
ellos	habl	–an	hablan	*they speak*
ellas				

5 🎧 **31** **Listen to the verb forms and choose the correct subject pronoun for each verb.**

1. nosotros ....   3. ....   5. ....   7. ....
2. ....   4. ....   6. ....   8. ....

6 **Write the correct form of the infinitive in parenthesis.**

a. Yo (hablar) .... perfectamente el inglés.
b. ¿Tú (escuchar) .... música española?
c. Marta (bailar) .... flamenco.
d. Carlos y yo (caminar) .... por el parque.
e. Ustedes (cantar) .... muy bien.
f. Ellos (estudiar) .... en el instituto.

7 **Read the following text about Juan and underline all the –ar verb forms. Then identify the infinitive that each conjugated verb comes from.**

Este muchacho se llama Juan, no es de aquí. Es español y estudia francés. Habla inglés muy bien. Toca la guitarra en un grupo y canta. También escucha todo tipo de música en su mp4. Su mejor amiga se llama María. Estudia en Madrid, pero viaja mucho. Ahora está en Italia. Ellos siempre pasean por el parque del Retiro los fines de semana y visitan otras ciudades.

8 👥 **Complete the following sentences to describe what you and others do. Use the correct form of the verb. You can choose an option in parenthesis or use one of your own. Then share your answers with a partner. What do you have in common?**

a. En casa, yo (hablar) .... (mucho / español / inglés /...).
b. Yo (escuchar) .... música en (mi mp4 / mi computadora / mi teléfono celular /...).
c. Mi amigo (llamarse) .... (Bart / Paco / Jack /...).
d. Él (estudiar) .... (Matemáticas / Español / Biología /...).
e. Mi amigo y yo (pasear) .... por (el parque / la ciudad / la calle /...).

3. THE VERB *ESTAR*

- The verb **estar** also ends in **–ar**, but it is considered irregular because it does not follow the same formula as regular **–ar** verbs. Look at the forms below.

ESTAR			
yo	**estoy**	nosotros/as	**estamos**
tú	**estás**	vosotros/as	**estáis**
usted/él/ella	**está**	ustedes/ellos/ellas	**están**

- The verb **estar** is used to express where someone or something is located.
  *Yo **estoy en** clase. I'm in class.*   *Juan **está en** Barcelona. Juan is in Barcelona.*

- It is also used to express how you and others are feeling.
  ¿Cómo estás? How are you?   *Estoy bien. I'm fine.*   *Estoy contento. I'm happy.*

- Here are some adjectives that describe how someone is feeling.

bien *well*	**contento/a** *happy*	**enfermo/a** *sick*	**triste** *sad*

*Hoy estoy muy **contento** porque empiezan las vacaciones.*
I'm very happy today because it's the start of vacation.
*María está **enferma**. Tiene gripe. María is sick. She has the flu.*

9 Match the people to the correct form of the verb *estar* to complete the sentences.

1. Alberto
2. Me llamo Dani y
3. Los estudiantes
4. Luisa y tú
5. Tú

a. estás contenta.
b. están en España.
c. están tristes.
d. estoy en Internet.
e. está en la biblioteca.

10 👥 With a partner, take turns asking each other where the people in the photos are and how they are feeling. Use *Dónde está(n)* and *Cómo está(n)* in your questions. ¡Atención! Be sure to use the correct form of the adjective when describing these people.

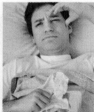
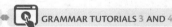

MORE IN ELETECA: EXTRA ONLINE PRACTICE ● GRAMMAR TUTORIALS 3 AND 4

OBJECTIVES FOR GRAMÁTICA 3

- Present the grammatical structures needed to practice the communicative functions of the unit: Present tense of **estar**
- Talk about where people are and how they are feeling

INSTRUCTIONAL STRATEGIES

3. The Verb ESTAR

Guide students through the presentation. Review adjectives to describe feelings using gestures and visuals.

Activity 9

Check comprehension by asking individual students similar questions about how they and others are feeling and where they are. Ask: **Y tú, ¿estás contento o triste? ¿Dónde está tu papá / mamá? ¿En casa o en el trabajo?** and so on.

Activity 10

Ask the class to come up with names for the people in the images. Ask students what form of the verb they should use in each case.

ANSWERS

Activity 9

1. e; **2.** d; **3.** b/c; **4.** b/c; **5.** a.

Activity 10

Answers will vary but should reflect correct form of the verb **estar** and unit vocabulary.

SLOWER-PACED LEARNERS

Students may not remember the nouns needed for the places in Activity 10. You can write a few locations on the board from which they will have to choose: **clase**, **biblioteca**, **cocina**, **sala**, **hospital**, **parque**, **cuarto de baño**, etc.

ADVANCED LEARNERS

As an extension to Activity 10, have students make up two extra situations for this activity and ask them to describe them to their peers. Students draw the situation on their notebooks or on the board.

OBJECTIVES FOR DESTREZAS

- Listing furniture and household objects to improve vocabulary
- Labeling as a learning strategy to remember vocabulary

STANDARDS

1.2   Understand the language

1.3   Present information

INSTRUCTIONAL STRATEGIES

Activities 1 and 2

- Review the strategy with students to make sure they understand.
- Do not preview or pre-teach the vocabulary for this section, as it is intended to simulate a test. Set a time limit for students to complete these tasks, approximately 15 minutes.

SLOWER-PACED LEARNERS

For additional practice, ask students to bring a picture of their bedrooms (or any bedroom) and describe them to the class.

ADVANCED LEARNERS

Ask students to bring a picture of their bedrooms (or any bedroom) and have them compare their pictures with the one in Activity 1.

HERITAGE LANGUAGE LEARNERS

After other students have presented pictures and descriptions of their rooms, have heritage language learners identify which of the described bedrooms dissimilar to their own rooms.

DESTREZAS

COMPRENSIÓN DE VOCABULARIO

1 **Look at the drawing of Miguel's room. Then review the strategy in Destrezas and follow the suggestion.**

Destrezas

Label and practice words

Label the words you know in Spanish for the furniture and objects in the drawing. Then practice saying them aloud. This will help you prepare for the questions that follow.

2 **Look at the items you have labeled in the drawing and write a description for each one as in the Modelo.**

Modelo: La silla es azul y negra.

3 Choose the correct answer to complete each sentence.

1. El dormitorio es…
  a. una habitación.
  b. un mueble.
  c. un sofá.

2. .... música en la computadora.
  a. Estoy
  b. Hablo
  c. Escucho

3. La cama es…
  a. rojo.
  b. roja.
  c. rojas.

4. La … es marrón.
  a. estantería
  b. lámpara
  c. silla

5. Los bolígrafos están en…
  a. la mesa.
  b. la mesilla.
  c. la estantería.

6. Los libros .... son cuatro.
  a. verdes
  b. verdos
  c. verdas

7. .... mí, el dormitorio es grande.
  a. Por
  b. Para
  c. A

8. En el dormitorio, nosotros .... bien.
  a. estudio
  b. estudiáis
  c. estudiamos

PRONUNCIACIÓN The sounds of *h, ll, y*

1 Read about the sounds these letter make. Then, with a partner, practice reading aloud the sentences that follow.

Vowel	Sounds like	Examples
h	The letter **h** in Spanish is silent.	• *Hablo inglés.* • *Hola amigos.* • *Ahora son las tres de la tarde.* • *La enfermera está en el hospital.*
ll	When used together **ll** makes the sound of the *y* in *yet*.	• *¿Cómo te llamas?* • *¿Cómo se llama usted?* • *Tengo una mesilla amarilla.* • *Vivo en la calle Villanueva.*
y	The letter **y** in Spanish is similar to the sound of **ll** or the English *y* in *yet*. When it stands alone to mean *and* or when it comes at the end of a word, **y** is pronounced like *ee* in the English *see*.	• *Yolanda tiene treinta **y** dos años.* • *Hoy es el treinta **y** uno de mayo.* • *Maya **y** yo somos amigos.* • *Estoy bien, ¿**y** tú?*

 **MORE IN ELETECA:** EXTRA ONLINE PRACTICE

Activity 3

• Tell students to complete the sentences based on the image in Activity 1. Set a time limit of about three minutes.
• Put students into pairs to compare answers. Call on volunteers to write the complete sentences on the board and confirm the answers as a class.

ANSWERS

Activity 3

  1. a; **2.** c; **3.** b; **4.** a; **5.** a; **6.** a; **7.** b; **8.** c.

OBJECTIVES FOR PRONUNCIACIÓN

• Practice correct pronunciation: silent h and /y/

CORE RESOURCES

• Interactive Online Materials - ELEteca

STANDARDS

  1.2   Understand the language
  4.1   Compare languages

INSTRUCTIONAL STRATEGIES

Activity 1

  Introduce the sounds with sample words and books closed. Ask students to spell out the words as you write them on the board.

ANSWERS

Activity 1

  Students practice pronunciation with a partner.

SLOWER-PACED LEARNERS

Elicit more examples of the words from each of the three categories in Activity 1 and write them on the board. Put students in pairs to practice the words orally with a partner. Then challenge them to say the words again, this time in aa sentence. They can write the sentences together first and then take turns reading them aloud to each other.

ADVANCED LEARNERS

Say more words from each of the three categories in Activity 1 aloud, one at a time. Students listen and write them down. When you finish reading your list, put students into pairs to practice saying and spelling the words aloud and to compare and correct their answers. Go over any discrepancies as a class.

HERITAGE LANGUAGE LEARNERS

Challenge students to write individual sentences that use all three vowel sounds in them. Have students compare sentences in small groups and check each other's spelling.

OBJECTIVES FOR SABOR HISPANO

- Learn about a country: Spain
- Learn about different types of housing in Hispanic countries
- Compare housing in Hispanic countries with housing in the U.S.

CORE RESOURCES

- Audio Program: 32

STANDARDS

1.2 Understand the language

2.1 Practices and perspectives

4.1 Compare cultures

INSTRUCTIONAL STRATEGIES

- Introduce the topic by asking students what they know about Spain, its people, and the types of homes they live in.
- Talk about the images and the map. Elicit what they already know about Spain. Share what you know about Spain with students.
- Read the captions together and ask questions to check comprehension. Point out the Spanish *patio* and make students aware that English borrowed the word *patio* from Spanish. However, traditionally in Spanish, a *patio* refers to a big courtyard.
- Ask students to identify which of the points in **¿Sabes que..?** surprises and/or interests them most.
- Describe the meaning of these words for housing in Spanish. Please note that these definitions apply mostly to Spain and may have different meanings or not be known in other countries:
  - *estudio* ➡ a studio or one-room apartment. These are common in the bigger cities, like Madrid and Barcelona: *Tiene solo una habitación. La cocina, el dormitorio y el salón-comedor están todos en la misma habitación. Pero el cuarto de baño está en una habitación aparte. ¡Claro! También hay más estudios en las ciudades grandes como Madrid y Barcelona.*
  - *apartamento* ➡ a one-bedroom apartment: *Tiene un dormitorio.*
  - *piso* ➡ an apartment with more than one bedroom: *Tiene más de un dormitorio y es más grande que un apartamento.*
  - *adosado* ➡ a townhome, usually with two stories, that shares a common wall with the house next door: *Tiene dos pisos pero comparte pared con la casa de al lado* (use gestures to explain *two floors and one wall*).
  - *chalé* ➡ stand-alone single-family home: *Una casa independiente para una sola familia.*

HERITAGE LANGUAGE LEARNERS

Put students into small groups to come up with a list of other words related to housing that they may know: *rancho*, *estancia*, *departamento*, *mansión*, *villa*, *finca*, *cabaña*, *cabina*, *casona*, *ático*, etc. Have them number or reorder the words by size and share their lists with the class.

SABOR HISPANO

VIVIR EN ESPAÑA

¡Ven a Europa y visita España!

España
Madrid · Barcelona · Valencia · Sevilla

La vida en este país europeo es muy interesante...

El patio de una casa española

Pisos tradicionales en el centro de Madrid

Un chalet en Marbella

Apartamentos modernos en Barcelona

- ✓ En España hay muchos tipos de viviendas (*housing*). Por ejemplo: pisos o apartamentos, chalets (casa con jardín) y casas tradicionales con un gran patio.
- ✓ El 78% de la gente española vive en ciudades. El 22% vive en zonas rurales.
- ✓ Para los españoles, es importante ser el propietario (*owner*) de su casa. El 80% de ellos prefiere comprar una casa antes que alquilar (*rent*).

¿Sabes que...?

- ✓ En España viven más de 47 millones de personas.
- ✓ Las dos ciudades españolas más importantes son Madrid, la capital, y Barcelona.
- ✓ España es el lugar más popular del mundo para ir de vacaciones: ¡58 millones de turistas la visitan cada año!
- ✓ Además del cumpleaños, algunos (*some*) españoles celebran el día de su santo (*saint's day*), según la tradición católica. Por ejemplo, si te llamas Juan, celebras tu santo el 24 de junio.
- ✓ España es uno de los países con más energía renovable (*renewable*) de Europa. ¡Es un país «verde»!

78

ESPAÑA

🎧 32 Una casa famosa

«¡Hola! Mi nombre es Lidia y soy de Barcelona. Me encanta vivir en mi ciudad: es bonita, cosmopolita y moderna. Yo vivo en un piso en el centro: es viejo, pero la decoración y los muebles son modernos.

Mi edificio favorito en Barcelona es la Casa Milà, o La Pedrera. Está en el Paseo de Gracia, número 92. Es un famoso edificio del arquitecto Antonio Gaudí, inspirado en la naturaleza *(nature)*. Me gustan mucho los balcones de la casa porque son originales. También me encanta la azotea *(roof terrace)*: allí hay muchas columnas y una vista *(view)* bonita de la ciudad. En La Pedrera viven varias familias... ¡Qué suerte tienen!».

La Pedrera, en Barcelona, y su azotea

El pueblo más bonito

El pueblo *(town)* de Priego de Córdoba está en Andalucía, una región en el sur de España. Según *(According to)* una encuesta del periódico ABC, es el pueblo más bonito de España.

Es un lugar con mucha historia y sitios interesantes. Por ejemplo, la calle Real es una calle pequeña, de piedra *(cobblestones)*, con casas de color blanco. En primavera *(spring)*, la gente decora sus casas con plantas y flores.

Una calle con plantas en Priego de Córdoba

Fuentes: abc.es, Banco Mundial, fotocasa.es, *El País*, Ministerio de Industria, Energía y Turismo, Europapress, INJUVE.

Vivir en familia

❖ En España, muchos jóvenes españoles menores de *(younger than)* 30 años viven con sus padres *(parents)*. Solo el 20% es independiente.

❖ Los motivos son una combinación de tradición y economía. La familia es muy importante en la cultura española, pero, además, muchos jóvenes no tienen trabajo y no pueden alquilar una casa.

❖ Los jóvenes españoles dicen *(say)* que la familia y los amigos son las cosas más importantes en su vida.

❖ Vivir con los padres hasta los 30 años también es normal en muchos países latinoamericanos.

La familia es muy importante para los jóvenes españoles.

Decide if the information in the sentence is true (T), false (F) or the information was not presented (N/P).

1	La azotea está en la parte de arriba de un edificio.	T ○ F ○ N/P ○
2	Es normal vivir con la familia a los 40 años.	T ○ F ○ N/P ○
3	Lidia vive en un piso viejo.	T ○ F ○ N/P ○
4	La Pedrera está en Barcelona.	T ○ F ○ N/P ○
5	La calle Real de Priego es una calle principal muy larga.	T ○ F ○ N/P ○

VOCES LATINAS
VIVIR EN ESPAÑA

Match each question with the correct answer.

1	¿Qué tipo de viviendas hay en España?	a	Porque es una tradición y por motivos económicos.
2	¿Cuántos turistas visitan España cada año?	b	De color blanco.
3	¿Por qué muchos jóvenes viven con sus padres?	c	Hay pisos o apartamentos, casas y chalets.
4	¿Dónde está La Pedrera?	d	Más de 58 millones.
5	¿De qué color son las casas de la calle Real de Priego?	e	En el Paseo de Gracia, en Barcelona.

79

INSTRUCTIONAL STRATEGIES

🎧 32

- An audio recording accompanies each text on this page. Vary between silent reading, reading aloud, and playing the audio.
- Write two big labels on the board: ***Pueblo*** and ***Ciudad***. Ask students to list towns or cities that can be listed under each of those two labels. Then ask them to meet in groups of 4 or 5 and discuss how towns and cities are alike and different. Remind them of some of the descriptive words they have learned in this unit, such as ***pequeño*** / ***grande***, ***tranquilo*** / ***dinámica***, ***aburrido*** / ***divertida***.
- Identify and explain any vocabulary from the reading students may find difficult to understand.
- Have students complete the activities at the bottom of this page and compare their answers with others.

ANSWERS

True or False

1. T; 2. F; 3. T; 4. T; 5. N/P.

Matching

1. c; 2. d; 3. a; 4. e; 5. b.

CULTURAL NOTE

Spain is divided in 17 ***Autonomías*** and 2 ***Ciudades autónomas*** (Ceuta and Melilla): Andalucía, Aragón, Principado de Asturias, Islas Baleares, Canarias, Cantabria, Castilla-La Mancha, Castilla y León, Cataluña, Comunidad Valenciana, Extremadura, Galicia, La Rioja, Comunidad de Madrid, Comunidad Foral de Navarra, País Vasco, Región de Murcia. There are several Autonomías that have additional official languages, such as in Cataluña (Catalán, Aranés), Comunidad Valenciana (Valenciano), Islas Baleares (Catalán), País Vasco (Euskera) and Galicia (Gallego). Spain is a Parlamentary or Constitutional Monarchy. Most people are Catholic but Spain is not a confessional state.

SLOWER-PACED LEARNERS

Have students find or complete a map of Spain, labeling its 17 ***Autonomías*** and 2 ***Ciudades autónomas.***

ADVANCED LEARNERS

Using ***Una casa famosa*** as a model, have students write a description about where their live and a famous building or location that's nearby. Have students present their descriptions to the class, ideally with visual support. Alternatively, you may choose to have students record their paragraphs outside of class and post them to a class website, where they can listen to and post comments on each other's material.

OBJECTIVES FOR RELATO

- Revisit unit themes, grammar, vocabulary, and culture in a new context
- Improve reading comprehension skills

CORE RESOURCES

Audio Program: 33

STANDARDS

1.1 Engage in conversation
1.2 Understand the language
1.3 Present information
2.1 Practices and perspectives

INSTRUCTIONAL STRATEGIES

Activity 1

The purpose of this activity is to review the present tense of *–ar* verbs taught in this unit while introducing some verbs that will appear in the reading. Students complete this activity individually or in pairs.

🎧 33 Activity 2

- Before students read the text, tell them that Raquel is a young teen from Spain. The reading explains a "problem" she is having in a very simple way. Tell students that they are allowed to look up words they might not know.
- Suggest that students read the text through once to get the gist and then fill in the blanks during a second reading. They can work in pairs and use the images as visual cues. Remind them that the pictures are not in the same order as the blanks they need to fill in the text.

Extension

Once students have completed the activity, ask them to read sections aloud to work on their pronunciation and intonation. Follow up with a discussion, encouraging students to express their opinion about Raquel and whether she has a real problem or not. Ask students what problems people their age face and what solutions they can think of.

CULTURAL NOTE

- Shakira is an internationally known star from Colombia.
- Raquel is from Sevilla, located in Andalucía, in southern Spain.
- Black as the color that the teacher probably likes is based on the cultural value attached to black as a sad or boring color.
- The yellow color of the sofa refers to the fact that in Spain, yellow is considered bad luck.

ANSWERS

Activity 1

a. bailar; **b.** hablar; **c.** amar; **d.** escuchar; **e.** preguntar; **f.** descansar; **g.** cantar; **h.** estar; **i.** comprar; **j.** tener.

Activity 2

1. escucho; **2.** edificio; **3.** dormitorio; **4.** profesora; **5.** negro; **6.** mp4; **7.** salón; **8.** cocina.

SLOWER-PACED LEARNERS

Give students time to put captions or vocabulary notes next to the images before they read the text in Activity 2. Invite them to share these with a partner and elicit more ideas and related language before they begin reading to help them prepare.

RELATO Los problemas de Raquel

1 Write the infinitive in Spanish for the verbs below.

a. bailo → ....
b. habla → ....
c. estoy → ....
d. escuchan → ....
e. pregunta → ....
f. descansas → ....
g. cantamos → ....
h. estamos → ....
i. compran → ....
j. tengo → ....

2 🎧 33 Read the text below about Raquel and the problems she is having at home and at school. As you read, fill in the blanks with the word for one of the images below that fits the context. *¡Atención!* The images are not in the order in which they will appear in the reading.

Los problemas de Raquel

Para mí, la música es lo más importante. Yo (1) .... música todos los días en mi casa. En mi opinión, Shakira es la mejor cantante y me gusta bailar con su música. Compro todas las canciones nuevas de mis cantantes favoritos y bailo y canto en mi dormitorio. Vivo en un (2) .... de apartamentos en Barcelona y mi vecino (*neighbor*) habla con mi madre: "¡Señora, Raquel hace mucho ruido (*noise*)! ¡Baila por las noches y es imposible descansar!". Mi madre escucha atentamente y luego habla conmigo: "¡Raquel, prohibido bailar en tu (3) .... !". Pienso que mi vecino es horrible. Seguro que el color preferido de mi vecino es el negro.

¡Pero tengo 14 años! ¡Solo estoy contenta cuando bailo y canto con la música!

En la escuela, la (4) .... me pregunta: "Raquel, ¿de dónde es Cristobal Colón?", pero yo escucho mi mp4 y no respondo a la pregunta. La profesora habla con mi madre: "Raquel escucha todo el día el mp4 en clase". Seguro que el color preferido de mi profesora es el (5) .... también.

No puedo (*can't*) escuchar el (6) .... en clase porque la profesora habla con mi madre.

No puedo bailar en el (7) .... porque mi vecino es antipático y habla con mi madre.

No puedo bailar en la (8) .... porque es pequeña y mi madre está ahí.

¡Tengo muchos problemas!

HERITAGE LANGUAGE LEARNERS

After completing Activity 2, challenge students to retell the story in their own words using only the images to prompt them.

3 Indicate whether each sentence is true (T) or false (F).

	T	F
a. Raquel es española.	☐	☐
b. Raquel tiene 15 años.	☐	☐
c. El color preferido de la profesora de Raquel es el rojo.	☐	☐
d. El salón de Raquel es blanco.	☐	☐
e. La cocina de Raquel es pequeña.	☐	☐
f. Raquel escucha a la profesora.	☐	☐

4 Select the questions for Estudiante 1 or Estudiante 2 and write out your answers. Then ask your partner the same questions to check your answers. Your partner will do the same with his/her questions.

Question words

- **cómo** ➡ *¿Cómo te llamas?*
- **cuál** ➡ *¿Cuál es tu color favorito?*
- **cuánto** ➡ *¿Cuánto cuesta?*
- **cuántos** ➡ *¿Cuántos años tienes?*

- **de dónde** ➡ *¿De dónde eres?*
- **dónde** ➡ *¿Dónde vives?*
- **por qué** ➡ *¿Por qué estás triste?* (why)
- **qué** ➡ *¿Qué haces?*

Estudiante 1

a. ¿De dónde es Raquel?
b. ¿Cuántos años tiene?
c. ¿Quién es la cantante favorita de Raquel?

Estudiante 2

a. ¿Qué hace Raquel todos los días?
b. ¿Por qué cree que su vecino es antipático?
c. ¿Por qué la profesora habla con su madre?

5 Read the following conversations and write the names of the person who probably said them. Then take turns role playing.

» .... ¡Prohibido bailar en la casa!
» ....pero mamá... Necesito bailar.
» .... ¡Basta de ruidos! ¡Esto es horrible!
» ....pero señor García. Usted no es moderno...
» .... ¡Voy ahora mismo a hablar con tu madre!

6 Make a list of the things you can't do at home or in class. Use the expression *No puedo* + infinitive.

No puedo ver la televisión porque mis padres protestan............................
....
....
....
....

81

Activity 6

For this writing exercise, first ask students to think about things that they are not allowed and make a list. Then ask them to write about the items on their list as a first-person narrative.

(Extension)

After students complete this activity, invite them to create a classroom poster listing what is allowed and what is not allowed, using these headings: ***Está prohibido*** and ***Está permitido***. Students can write what is allowed and not allowed on sticky notes and post them under the correct heading. For example: ***No podemos comer en clase. Podemos hablar en español.***

ANSWERS

Activity 3

a. T; b. F; c. F; d. T; e. T; f. F.

Activity 4

Estudiante 1

a. Raquel es de Sevilla; b. Tiene 14 años; c. Shakira.

Estudiante 2

a. Canta y baila; b. Porque no le permite bailar; c. Porque escucha todo el día el mp4.

Activity 5

La madre de Raquel: ¡Prohibido bailar en la terraza!; **Raquel:** ...pero mamá... Necesito bailar; **El vecino:** ¡Basta de ruidos! ¡Esto es horrible!; **Raquel:** ...pero señor García. Usted no es moderno...; **El vecino / la profesora:** ¡Voy ahora mismo a hablar con tu madre!

Activity 6

Answers will vary but should reflect proper use of the expression ***No puedo*** + ***infinitive***.

SLOWER-PACED LEARNERS

Have students write a longer dialogue using the input from Activity 5. Have them act it out.

ADVANCED LEARNERS

Have students write a letter to a friend about their problems. Encourage them to use what they wrote for Activity 6. Remind students that not all problems need to be real.

INSTRUCTIONAL STRATEGIES

Activity 3

- Have students answer the questions individually. Encourage them to find and circle or underline the related information in the text.
- Go over the answers, prompting students to correct the false sentences.

Activity 4

Have students work in pairs with each one first answering his/her own set of questions individually. Then students ask each other to check answers.

Activity 5

- During the role-play, encourage students to use the appropriate tone for the mother and Raquel.
- Call on student pairs to present to the class.

OBJECTIVES FOR EVALUACIÓN

- Review grammar, vocabulary and culture from the unit
- Complete self-assessment

CORE RESOURCES

- Interactive Online Materials - ELEteca

STANDARDS

- 1.2 Understand the language
- 1.3 Present information
- 2.1 Practices and perspectives
- 4.1 Compare cultures

INSTRUCTIONAL STRATEGIES

- Activities can be completed individually and then reviewed with the class. Vary by asking students if they agree with the answer given and then writing it on the board. Provide explanations as needed.
- You may wish to assign point values to each activity as a way for students to monitor their progress.
- Direct students to the indicated review pages in **En resumen** if they make more than one or two mistakes in any one section.

ANSWERS

Activity 1

1. Para mí, el sofá es un mueble fantástico. Para mí, también; **2.** Shakira es mi cantante favorita. Creo que Julieta Venegas canta mejor; **3.** Creo que la cocina es el lugar importante de la casa. No es verdad. El dormitorio es mi favorito; **4.** Para mí, el rojo es mi color favorito. Para mí, el color azul.

Activity 2

a. el salón; **b.** el baño; **c.** el dormitorio; **d.** la cocina.

Activity 3

a. blanca; **b.** negra; **c.** dormitorio; **d.** baño.

Activity 4

a. lavabo (porque no es una parte de la casa); **b.** estufa (porque no está en el baño); **c.** grande (porque no es un color).

Activity 5

a. treinta y dos; **b.** veinticinco; **c.** cincuenta y ocho; **d.** cuarenta y ocho; **e.** ochenta y nueve; **f.** noventa y uno.

EVALUACIÓN

EXPRESSING PREFERENCES AND OPINIONS

1 Match the first two columns to express preferences. Then choose a statement from the last column to express an opinion about the preference.

1. Para mí, el sofá
2. Shakira
3. Creo que la cocina
4. Para mí, el rojo

a. es mi cantante favorita.
b. es mi color favorito.
c. es el lugar importante de la casa.
d. es un mueble fantástico.

- No es verdad. El dormitorio es mi favorito.
- Para mí, también.
- Creo que Julieta Venegas canta mejor.
- Para mí, el color azul.

LA CASA, LOS MUEBLES Y LOS COLORES

2 Look at the images below and write the name in Spanish of the room it represents.

3 Use the images above to answer the following questions.

a. ¿De qué color es la cama? ➡ ....
b. ¿De qué color es la mesa del salón? ➡ ....
c. ¿Cómo se llama la habitación donde está la cama? ➡ ....
d. ¿Cómo se llama la habitación donde está la ducha? ➡ ....

4 Select the word that does not belong in the series.

a. dormitorio / salón / lavabo / cocina / terraza ➡ ....
b. estufa / ducha / bañera / lavabo / espejo ➡ ....
c. negro / amarillo / verde / grande / azul ➡ ....

LOS NÚMEROS

5 Fill in the missing words to complete the numbers in Spanish.

a. 32 ➡ treinta y ....
b. 25 ➡ .... cinco.
c. 58 ➡ .... y ocho.
d. 48 ➡ cuarenta y ....
e. 89 ➡ ochenta y ....
f. 91 ➡ .... y uno.

GENDER, NUMBER, AND AGREEMENT OF NOUNS AND ADJECTIVES

6 Choose the correct response from the options.

a. El armario es **blanca / blanco**.

b. **El / Los** espejo es muy grande.

c. El dormitorio de Carmen es **rojo / roja**.

d. **La / El** sofá está en el salón.

e. La cocina es **verde / verdes**.

f. El cuarto de baño es **pequeño / pequeños**.

g. **El / La** salón tiene muebles **modernos / modernas**.

h. ¿Cuál es tu color **favorito / favorita**?

i. El baño es **grande / grandes**.

PRESENT TENSE OF –AR VERBS AND ESTAR

7 List the verbs under the correct subject pronoun according to the form.

hablas ∘ escucho ∘ camina ∘ compran ∘ visitas ∘ terminamos ∘ bailo ∘ me llamo

yo	tú	usted/él/ella	nosotros/as	ustedes/ellos/ellas

8 Fill in the blanks with the correct form of the verb in parenthesis.

a. Pedro (bailar) .... muy bien.

b. Paola y Marta (comprar) .... mochilas rojas.

c. Yo (escuchar) .... la radio por la noche.

d. Valencia (estar) .... en España.

e. Ustedes (visitar) .... a su antiguo profesor.

f. Tú (hablar) .... mucho.

g. Lucía (estar) .... en la escuela.

h. Nosotros (estar) .... contentos.

CULTURA

9 Answer the following questions about Spain and compare similarities with your own country or region.

a. ¿Qué es La Pedrera? ¿De quién es? ¿Cuál es el edificio más (most) espectacular de tu ciudad o región?

b. ¿Qué dicen (say) los jóvenes españoles de su familia y amigos? ¿Es verdad para ti también?

c. ¿Qué tipo de viviendas hay en España? ¿En qué tipo de casa vives tú?

d. ¿Qué celebran los españoles además de (in addition to) su cumpleaños? ¿Qué celebras tú?

e. ¿Por qué es España un país "verde"? ¿Piensas que tu país o región es "verde"?

 **MORE IN ELETECA:** EXTRA ONLINE PRACTICE

83

ANSWERS

Activity 6

a. blanco; b. El; c. rojo; d. El; e. verde; f. pequeño; g. El, modernos; h. favorito; i. grande.

Activity 7

yo: escucho, bailo, me llamo;

tú: hablas, visitas;

usted/él/ella: camina;

nosotros/as: terminamos;

ustedes/ellos/ellas: compran.

Activity 8

a. baila; b. compran; c. escucho; d. está; e. visitan; f. hablas; g. está; h. estamos.

Activity 9

Answers will vary.

a. Es un famoso edificio en Barcelona. Es del arquitecto Gaudí.

b. Dicen que la familia y los amigos son las cosas más importantes en su vida.

c. Hay pisos, apartamentos, chalets y casas tradicionales.

d. Celebran el día de su santo.

e. Porque usa energía renovable.

OBJECTIVES FOR EN RESUMEN: VOCABULARIO

- Review unit vocabulary and expressions
- Practice communicative skills

STANDARDS

1.2 Understand the language

1.3 Present information

INSTRUCTIONAL STRATEGIES

- Encourage students to use self-adhesive notes to place on correct objects in their house.
- Index cards can be used as flash cards with the Spanish term on one side and the English term on the other, or a picture or drawing.
- Students can work in pairs or groups, using vocabulary flashcards as they would the cards of a board game to help each other practice the unit vocabulary.
- Encourage students to write labels or captions for the photos on this page. Remind them to use the vocabulary and expressions they have learned in this unit.
- Challenge students to write sentences that use two or three vocabulary items together. Model how they can combine nouns, verbs, and adjectives to make such sentences: **Descanso en mi clase de Geografía porque es aburrida. Paseo por el parque cada mañana cuando camino a la escuela,** etc.

EN RESUMEN: Vocabulario

Los lugares *Places*
la ciudad *city*

el edificio *building*
la escuela *school*
el parque *park*

Los deportes *Sports*
el baloncesto / el básquetbol *basketball*
el béisbol *baseball*
el fútbol *soccer*
el fútbol americano *football*
el golf *golf*
el tenis *tennis*
el vóleibol *volleyball*

Las asignaturas *School subjects*
Arte *art*
Artes y letras *arts and humanities*
Biología *biology*
Ciencias *science*
Computación *computer science*
Educación Física *physical education*
Español *Spanish*
Geografía *geography*
Historia *history*
Matemáticas *math*
Música *music*

Descripciones *Descriptions*
aburrido/a *boring*
bonito/a *beautiful, pretty*
difícil *difficult*
divertido/a *funny*
fácil *easy*
fantástico/a *fantastic*
favorito/a *favorite*
genial *great*
grande *big*
guapo/a *handsome / pretty*
importante *important*
interesante *interesting*

pequeño/a *small*
simpático/a *likeable*

Los colores *Colors*
amarillo *yellow*

anaranjado / naranja *orange*
azul *blue*
blanco *white*
gris *grey*
marrón *brown*
negro *black*
rojo *red*
verde *green*

La casa y los muebles *House and furniture*
el armario *closet*
la bañera *bathtub*
la cama *bed*
la cómoda *chest of drawers*
la cocina *kitchen*
el cuarto de baño *bathroom*
el dormitorio *bedroom*

la ducha *shower*
el espejo *mirror*
la estantería *shelf*
la estufa *stove*
la habitación *room*
el horno *oven*
el lavabo *sink*
la mesa *table*
la mesilla *bedside table*
el sofá *sofa*
el salón *living room*

Verbos Verbs
amar *to love*
bailar *to dance*
caminar *to walk*
cantar *to sing*
comprar *to buy*
descansar *to rest*
escuchar *to listen*
estar *to be*
estar bien *to be fine*
estar contento/a *to be happy*

estar enfermo/a *to be sick*
estar triste *to be sad*
estudiar *to study*
hablar *to speak*
pasear *to stroll*
trabajar *to work*
viajar *to travel*

Interrogativos *Questions words*
cómo *how*
cuál *which one*
cuánto *how much*
cuántos *how many*
de dónde *from where*
dónde *where*
por qué *why*
qué *what*

Palabras y expresiones útiles *Useful words and expressions*
Creo que... *I believe that...*
¿Cuánto cuesta? *How much does it cost?*
En mi opinion... *In my opinion...*
Lo siento. *I'm sorry.*
Para mí, ti, él... *For me, you, him,...*
Pienso que... *I think that...*
el animal *animal*
la cámara *camera*
la comida *food, meal*
el gato *cat*

84

EN RESUMEN: Gramática

GENDER, NUMBER, AND AGREEMENT OF NOUNS AND ADJECTIVES

(See page 72)

Singular	
Masculine	Feminine
–o	–a
el bolígrafo	la cámara

Plural		
Masculine/Feminine		
Termina en vocal: +s	Termina en consonante: +es	Termina en z: +ces
Ends in a vowel: +s	*Ends in a consonant: +es*	*End in a z: -ces*
mesa / mesas	actor / actores	lápiz / lápices

Feminine forms of adjectives

- Adjectives that end in –o change to –a: *blanco* / *blanca*.
- Adjectives that end in –e, no change: *elegante*.
- Adjectives that end in a consonant, no change: *fácil*.
- Nationalites that end in a consonant, add –a: *francés* / *francesa*.

Plural forms of nouns and adjectives

- Words that end in a vowel, add –s: *moreno* / *morenos*.
- Words that end in a consonant, add –es: *joven* / *jóvenes*.

AGREEMENT

(See page 73)

Singular			
Masculine	Feminine	Masculine/Feminine	
–o	–a	–e	–consonante
el carro bonito	la silla bonita	el carro grande	el carro azul
		la silla grande	la silla azul

Plural			
los carros bonitos	las sillas bonitas	los carros grandes	los carros azules
		las sillas grandes	las sillas azules

PRESENT TENSE OF -AR VERBS AND ESTAR

(See pages 73-75)

	HABLAR	ESTAR (irregular)
yo	hablo	estoy
tú	hablas	estás
usted/él/ella	habla	está
nosotros/as	hablamos	estamos
vosotros/as	habláis	estáis
ustedes/ellos/ellas	hablan	están

85

OBJECTIVES FOR EN RESUMEN: GRAMÁTICA

- Review unit grammar
- Practice communicative skills

STANDARDS

- 1.2 Understand the language
- 1.3 Present information

INSTRUCTIONAL STRATEGIES

- Model how to review grammar.
- Have them review the Learning Outcomes in the unit opener to assess whether they feel they have mastered the main ideas and skills.
- Ask them if they can remember additional examples for each grammar topic.
- Model how to find and go back to the appropriate page in the unit to review any grammar topic they may need help with.
- Invite students to review the grammar activities they completed in this unit.
- Ask them what grammar activities they found easy and which they found challenging. Encourage them to repeat any activities they found particularly challenging.
- Call on a volunteer to come to the front of the room. Say a noun aloud and have the student add a logical adjective that agrees with the noun in gender and number. Continue to provide nouns, one after the other. The student stays in front of the room as long as he or she provides a correct response. Set a time limit, and have someone in class keep track of the time. Have another student keep track of how many correct replies the volunteer says. When time is up, invite another volunteer to the front of the room to see if he or she can provide more correct replies in the given time.
- Encourage students to take the online test in ELEteca to determine which aspects of the unit they need to study and review the most.

OBJECTIVES FOR AHORA COMPRUEBA

- Review grammar, vocabulary and culture from the last two units
- Complete self-assessment

CORE RESOURCES

- Audio Program: Track 34

STANDARDS

1.2   Understand the language
1.3   Present information
2.1   Practices and perspectives
4.1   Compare cultures

INSTRUCTIONAL STRATEGIES

- Activities can be completed individually or in pairs and then reviewed with the class.
- You may wish to assign point values to each activity as a way for students to monitor their progress. If students achieve less than 80% on each activity, direct them to **En resumen** in the previous two units for page numbers to review.

Activity 1

Have students fill in the blanks with the correct word from the word bank.

🎧 **34 Activity 2**

Students complete the activity after listening to the interview with José Sol. Students may need to listen to the audio more than once.

See audioscript on page APP5.

Activity 3

Students decide where José's answers should go in the interview on the next page.

ANSWERS

Activity 1

Me llamo José Sol. Soy cantante, canto canciones románticas y divertidas. Pienso que mis canciones son fantásticas. Para mí, cantar es genial. Soy español, de Toledo. Tengo veinte años. Tengo dos guitarras, una negra y una azul. La guitarra azul es mi favorita.

Activity 2

a. La canción de los colores; b. Toledo; c. En Madrid; d. Muy grande; e. Cuatro; f. En el salón.

Activity 3

7, 5, 2, 3, 1, 4, 6.

---

1 José Sol is a "famous" singer. Fill in the blanks with words from the list to learn more about him.

> divertidas ○ para ○ cantante ○ tengo ○ soy
> ○ negra ○ es ○ llamo ○ tengo ○ favorita

Me .... José Sol. Soy ...., canto canciones románticas y .... Pienso que mis canciones son fantásticas. .... mí, cantar .... genial. .... español, de Toledo. .... veinte años. .... dos guitarras, una .... y una azul. La guitarra azul es mi ....

2 🎧 **34** Listen to an interview with José Sol on the radio. Then answer the questions.

a. ¿Cuál es su canción favorita?
b. ¿Cuál es su ciudad favorita?
c. ¿Dónde vive ahora José?
d. ¿Cómo es su casa?
e. ¿Cuántas habitaciones tiene?
f. ¿Dónde escribe sus canciones?

a. ....
b. ....
c. ....
d. ....
e. ....
f. ....

3 Read José Sol's answers to the reporter's questions and decide where the answers should go in the interview on the next page. Write the correct numbers on the blanks.

Respuestas de José Sol

1. No, no, ahora vivo en Madrid, en una casa muy grande, con cuatro dormitorios, dos cocinas, tres cuartos de baño y un salón.
2. Mi canción favorita es *La canción de los colores*. Es mi nueva canción.
3. Pienso que Madrid es genial, pero para mí, Toledo es mi ciudad favorita. Yo soy de Toledo y me gusta cantar allí.
4. Creo que el salón. En el salón escribo mis canciones.
5. Igualmente.
6. Gracias a vosotros, adiós.
7. Hola, buenos días.

Periodista: Tenemos con nosotros al famoso cantante José Sol. Buenos días, José.

José Sol: 7

Periodista: Encantado de conocerte, es un placer para mí.

José Sol: ....

Periodista: De todas tus canciones, ¿cuál es tu canción favorita?

José Sol: ....

Periodista: Has cantado en muchas ciudades. Pero, ¿cuál es tu ciudad favorita?

José Sol: ....

Periodista: ¿Dónde vives? ¿En Toledo?

José Sol: ....

Periodista: Increíble. ¿Cuál es tu habitación favorita?

José Sol: ....

Periodista: Muchas gracias por la entrevista y hasta pronto.

José Sol: ....

4 With a partner, prepare a similar interview between a "famous" singer and a reporter. Use the interview with José Sol as a model.

5 José Sol sings in all these countries, represented here with their flags. Write the colors of each flag.

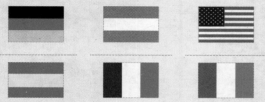

6 Here is an excerpt from one of José Sol's songs, *La canción de los colores*. Fill in the missing words using the images to complete the song.

La .... es verde, el .... es verde.
Oh, oh, oh
La .... es roja, el .... es rojo.
Oh, oh, oh
El .... es azul, la .... es azul.
Oh, oh, oh.

87

INSTRUCTIONAL STRATEGIES

Activity 4

Students work with a partner to prepare a similar dialogue. One student plays a famous singer while the other student plays the interviewer.

Activity 5

This is to review colors by looking at the flags of several countries. Before students start to work on this activity, ask if they know any of the countries that these flags represent.

Activity 6

Students complete the song with the correct vocabulary. The target vocabulary words are provided in the images. Pay close attention to the use of the articles taught (*el* and *la*) and how a change in the gender of the noun will have an impact on the ending for the colors (*rojo* vs. *roja*).

ANSWERS

Activity 4

Answers will vary and should reflect the previous paragraph as a model.

Activity 5

Flags are: Alemania, Argentina, Estados Unidos, España, Francia, Italia.
Alemania: negro, rojo y amarillo; **Argentina:** azul y blanco; **Estados Unidos:** rojo, azul y blanco; **España:** rojo y amarillo; **Francia:** azul, blanco y rojo; **Italia:** verde, blanco y rojo.

Activity 6

La **cama/habitación** es verde, el **baño** es verde.

Oh, oh, oh.

La **mesa** es roja, el **sofá** es rojo.

Oh, oh, oh.

El **salón** es azul, la **cocina** es azul.

Oh, oh, oh.

SLOWER-PACED LEARNERS

Have students make a list of the learning objectives noted in the opening spreads of the two previous units. Tell them to ask themselves: How well can I do this: very well, well, or not well? Then pair students who can't do an objective well with another student who can; that way, they can teach each other what they know and help each other review.

ADVANCED LEARNERS

For those students who have a good handle on the vocabulary, grammar, and cultural content of the units, encourage them to focus on the development of their listening, speaking, reading, and writing skills prior to quizzes and tests. Challenge them to spend thirty minutes a night for four nights before the assessment focusing on one of each of the four skills each night. In addition to redoing the skills-based activities within the units, encourage them to seek new, related (and fun) material online to help them practice.

HERITAGE LANGUAGE LEARNERS

For students who already have a base of the language, challenge them to put themselves in the position of the teacher prior to assessments. How would they teach a non-native speaker the content of the previous two units? Have them develop worksheets, activities, games, presentations, and lesson plans that could be used to teach other students the material. By putting students in this new role, they will enhance their own knowledge and become masters of the content.

OBJECTIVES FOR UNIT OPENER

- Introduce unit theme: **Mi familia** about people, clothing, and family activities
- Culture: Learn about Hispanic families and celebrations

STANDARDS

1.2   Understand the language

2.1   Practices and perspectives

INSTRUCTIONAL STRATEGIES

- Introduce unit theme and objectives: Talk about families, personalities, and things they do together. Have students look at the image. Read the caption aloud: **La familia celebra la fiesta de los quince años en San Miguel de Allende, México.** Ask: **¿Cuántos años tiene la muchacha? ¿Es una celebración formal o informal?**
- Ask questions to help students recycle content from previous unit. For instance, encourage them to use expressions to ask about meaning, such as: **¿De qué color es el vestido de la muchacha?** (indicate dress by pointing or gesturing), **¿De dónde es la familia? ¿Qué crees que hacen los invitados en la fiesta? ¿Bailan? ¿Qué más?** (escuchan música, hablan, etc.)
- Use the image to preview unit vocabulary, including clothing: **La muchacha y su madre llevan vestidos elegantes. El padre lleva un traje formal. ¿De qué color es?** Help students access meaning by making frequent use of gestures or visuals.
- Ask the introductory questions.
  - **¿Cómo celebras tu cumpleaños?**
  - **¿Tienes una fiesta de cumpleaños en casa?**
  - **¿Invitas a tus amigos y familia?**
- Ask related questions: **¿A cuántas personas invitas a tu fiesta? ¿Tienes una familia grande o pequeña? ¿Recibes muchos regalos?**

SLOWER-PACED LEARNERS

When eliciting information about the opening image, write key words and/or sample responses on the board. Have students underline or highlight key words from the caption on page 88: **familia, fiesta, quince años**, and **México**. If you're having students answer the target questions in pairs, partner slower-paced students with faster-paced students.

UNIDAD
3
¡MI FAMILIA ES MUY SIMPÁTICA!

≫ ¿Cómo celebras tu cumpleaños?
≫ ¿Tienes una fiesta de cumpleaños en casa?
≫ ¿Invitas a tus amigos y familia?

La familia celebra la fiesta de los quince años en San Miguel de Allende, México.

88

ADDITIONAL UNIT RESOURCES

Extension Activities (EA) (Photocopiable)	**Interactive Whiteboard Lessons (IWB)**	**Audio**	**Video**	**Online ELEteca**
EA: 3.1, 3.2, 3.3, 3.4	IWB: 3.1, 3.2	35 to 44	Diálogo 2	EXTENSIÓN DIGITAL

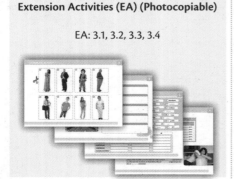
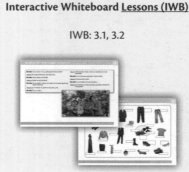
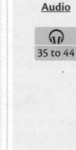

In this unit, you will learn to:

- [ ] Describe family members
- [ ] Describe physical characteristics
- [ ] Describe personality traits and physical conditions
- [ ] Ask and say what people are like
- [ ] Express possession
- [ ] Talk about clothes

Using

- *-er* and *-ir* verbs
- Possessive adjectives
- Demonstrative adjectives

Cultural Connections

- Connect information about Hispanic families and celebrations, and compare cultural similarities

SABOR HISPANO

La familia mexicana
- México

¡ACCIÓN!

89

LEARNING OUTCOMES

- Describe family members
- Describe physical characteristics
- Describe personality traits and physical conditions
- Ask and say what people are like
- Express possession
- Talk about clothes

INSTRUCTIONAL STRATEGIES

- Use the unit opener to preview the vocabulary and the cultural topics for this unit.
- Have students look at the images on this page and relate them to the objectives listed. Elicit examples of possessive adjectives and demonstrative adjectives in English to help them make the connections. Ask questions such as: *¿Qué ven en estas fotos? ¿Qué fotos son interesantes?*
- Invite students to read the topic for **Sabor hispano** and preview that section in the unit. *¿Qué crees que hace la familia en la foto? ¿Qué hacen el hombre y la mujer de la foto? ¿Cómo están? ¿Contentos o tristes?*
- Ask students to predict what they think the episode for **¡Acción!** will be about. *¿Quiénes aparecen en la imagen? ¿Dónde están?*
- Have students work in pairs to talk about the images using the questions you have modeled. Then have volunteers present to the class what they understand this unit to be about.

ADVANCED LEARNERS

Have students research a country besides Mexico that has **la Fiesta de los quince años**. Encourage them to identify a few key similarities or differences between the traditions.

HERITAGE LANGUAGE LEARNERS

Encourage students to share their own experiences with or cultural knowledge of **la Fiesta de los quince años**. Have students interview any friends or relatives from Spanish-speaking countries to find out about their experiences and report back to the class. Invite them to bring in photos or videos from the celebrations.

THREE MODES OF COMMUNICATION: UNIT 3			
	INTERPERSONAL	INTERPRETIVE	PRESENTATIONAL
HABLAMOS DE...	6	1, 2, 4, 5	6
COMUNICA	1, 3, 5	2, 4	3
¡ACCIÓN!	1	2, 3, 4, 5	1
PALABRA POR PALABRA	5, 6, 9, 10, 11	2, 3, 4, 8	9, 10, 11
GRAMÁTICA	3, 9	1, 2, 4, 5, 6, 7, 8	3, 6, 9
DESTREZAS		1, 2, 3	
CULTURA		SABOR HISPANO	
RELATO	6	1, 2, 3, 4, 5	7

OBJECTIVES FOR HABLAMOS DE...

- Understand language in context
- Preview vocabulary: family, physical characteristics, personality traits
- Preview grammatical structures: possessive adjectives and demonstrative adjectives
- Read and listen to a conversation about Nicolás and his family

CORE RESOURCES

- Audio Program: 35
- Interactive Whiteboard Lesson: IWB 3.1

STANDARDS

1.1 Engage in conversation
1.2 Understand the language
4.2 Compare cultures

INSTRUCTIONAL STRATEGIES

Activity 1

- Project the IWB 3.1 **Trabajamos con el diálogo,** and ask students: **¿Cuántas personas hay en la familia?** Indicate **un padre, una madre, dos hijos.** Point to the two boys: **Ellos son hermanos.** Ask: **¿Dónde está la familia? (en el parque, en el jardín); ¿Cómo están? (contentos).**
- Have students look at the photo and answer the questions, then share their answers.
- To check comprehension, project the image and ask: **¿Quién es él? (Nicolás); ¿Con quién está en la foto? ¿Con sus padres o sus abuelos? (Sus padres); ¿Cuántos años creen que tiene Nicolás? ¿Y su hermano?**

🎧 35 Activity 2

Introduction to the conversation: Tell students that they will be listening to a conversation between Nicolás and his friend María. Have students review the statements before they listen. Answer any questions students may have about the vocabulary.

Alternative Activity

Project IWB 3.1, **Trabajamos con el diálogo**, and have students put the conversation in a logical order without using their books. Play the audio and have student pairs check and compare order. Play the audio once more. Finally, read the conversation together from the text to confirm the correct order, then have students complete the activity.

ANSWERS

Activity 1

a, b, d, f, g.

Activity 2

a. F; b. F; c. T; d. T; e. F.

HABLAMOS DE... La familia de Nicolás

1 Look at the image of Nicolás and his family and select the sentences that are true.

a. ○ Esta es la familia de Nicolás.
b. ○ Aparecen cuatro personas.
c. ○ Puedes ver una chica joven y un chico joven.
d. ○ Puedes ver un chico joven y un niño.
e. ○ El niño tiene más de catorce años.
f. ○ El niño tiene menos de catorce años.
g. ○ El señor y la señora son los padres de Nicolás.
h. ○ El señor y la señora son los abuelos de Nicolás.

2 🎧 35 Listen to the following conversation and indicate if the statements are true (T) or false (F).

Nicolás: Mira, María, mi familia.
María: ¿Quién es ese hombre?
Nicolás: Es mi padre. Y ella es mi madre. Es morena, igual que todos nosotros.
María: Sí, es verdad. Tu padre es muy alto, ¿no?
Nicolás: Sí, y es calvo...
María: ¿Tu hermano es este que lleva pantalón marrón? Es muy guapo.
Nicolás: Sí, y también es muy simpático.
María: ¿Cuántos años tiene?
Nicolás: Es mi hermano pequeño. Tiene 8 años.
María: Tiene el pelo rizado como tú. Ustedes son muy parecidos.
Nicolás: Sí, es cierto. Y tú, ¿cuántos hermanos tienes?
María: No tengo hermanos. Soy hija única.

	T	F
a. La madre de Nicolás es rubia.	○	○
b. El padre de Nicolás es bajo.	○	○
c. El hermano de Nicolás es muy guapo y simpático.	○	○
d. El hermano de Nicolás es pequeño y tiene el pelo rizado.	○	○
e. María tiene un hermano mayor.	○	○

SLOWER-PACED LEARNERS

After Activity 2, have students add labels to the photo in Activity 1: **padre (alto, calvo), madre (morena), hermano (guapo, simpático, pelo rizado, 8 años).**

ADVANCED LEARNERS

If you don't do IWB 3.1 as a class, give copies of it to these students to do before or while listening to the audio from Activity 2. As an extension activity, give students similar photos to the ones from Activity 1 or invite them to use their own family photos. Have them write a dialogue like the one in Activity 2 based on the new picture.

3 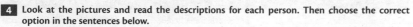 🎧 35 **Listen to the conversation again and repeat.**

4 **Look at the pictures and read the descriptions for each person. Then choose the correct option in the sentences below.**

Es rubia, tiene los ojos azules y el pelo largo y liso. Es antipática.

Es alta y morena. Tiene el pelo largo y rizado. Lleva un vestido rojo.

Es pelirrojo y muy divertido. Tiene el pelo corto y rizado. Es joven. Tiene diez años.

Es morena y simpática. Tiene el pelo corto.

Es mayor, es gordo y tiene el pelo blanco. Lleva una camisa verde.

Es calvo. No lleva barba. Tiene los ojos verdes. Lleva gafas y una camisa roja.

a. Mi hermano **lleva** / **es** una camisa azul.
b. Mi hermana es **morena** / **rojo** y tiene el pelo **rizado** / **joven**.
c. Mi padre no tiene pelo. **Es calvo** / **Tiene el pelo liso**.
d. Ese señor tiene setenta años. Es **mayor** / **joven**.
e. Mi madre es **divertido** / **simpática**.

5 👥 **Work with a partner and take turns describing each other using the expressions above.**

Modelo:

Mi compañero es moreno y tiene el pelo corto. Lleva una camisa verde. No tiene barba.

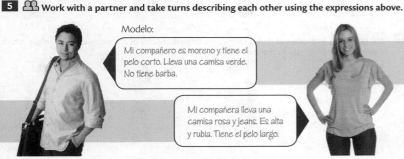

Mi compañera lleva una camisa rosa y jeans. Es alta y rubia. Tiene el pelo largo.

91

INSTRUCTIONAL STRATEGIES

🎧 **35 Activity 3**

Use the audio to focus students' attention on rhythm, intonation, and pronunciation. You may have students respond chorally as many times as needed.

Activity 4

- Find out what students may already know about describing physical characteristics before they begin the activity. Tell them to look at the people in the photos and ask them: *¿Cómo son las personas de las fotos? ¿Son similares o diferentes? ¿Qué diferencias hay entre ellas?* Have students read each description aloud with a partner.
- After you review the answers, ask students to match the statements with the people above. *¿Quién es la muchacha de la primera foto? (la hermana); ¿Cómo lo sabes? ¿Qué más sabes de ella?* and so on. Clarify the meaning of *sabes*. At this point, the term is for reception only.

Activity 5

- Review the **Modelo** with students and encourage them to provide additional descriptions. To review, call on a student to describe another student for the class to guess who it is.
- Do this activity in small groups or as a written assignment.

ANSWERS

Activity 4

a. lleva; b. morena, rizado; c. Es calvo; d. mayor; e. simpática.

SLOWER-PACED LEARNERS

To help students digest the new vocabulary presented in Activity 4, create a chart categorizing the different words: hair color (*rubio/a, moreno/a, pelirrojo/a, pelo blanco*), hairstyle (*pelo largo, pelo corto, pelo liso, pelo rizado, calvo*), etc.

HERITAGE LANGUAGE LEARNERS

Invite students to make a video in which their family members introduce themselves to the class in Spanish. They can say their names, where they're from, their age, their relationship to the student, and a brief description of themselves. Play the students' videos for the class or post them on a class website.

OBJECTIVES FOR COMUNICA

- Present the communicative functions of the unit: Describing physical characteristics
- Practice adjectives with **ser**, **tener**, and **llevar**

CORE RESOURCES

- Extension Activities: EA 3.1
- Audio Program: 36
- Interactive Online Materials - ELEteca

STANDARDS

1.1 Engage in conversation
1.2 Understand the language

INSTRUCTIONAL STRATEGIES FOR DESCRIBING PHYSICAL CHARACTERISTICS

- Present adjectives and list them under the appropriate category on the board: **ser**, **tener**, **llevar**. Whenever possible, group words in opposites (**gordo** / **delgado**, **alto** / **bajo**, and so on) as you present them.
- Use visuals and gestures to present **gafas**, **bigote**, **barba**, and so on.

GRAMMAR NOTE

- The opposite of **joven** can also be **viejo**. The expression **mayor** or **persona mayor** is preferred as it is considered to be more respectful.
- With **el pelo**, use **tener** to describe a person's natural or customary hair color. Use **llevar** to describe hair color that is temporary, and the same for **bigote**, **barba**, and **gafas**.

Activity 1

For additional practice, have student pairs describe another classmate to their partner to guess who it is.

🎧 36 **Activity 2**

Before you play the audio, ask questions about the people in the images. **¿Quién lleva jeans? ¿Quién tiene el pelo largo?** and so on.

See audioscript on page APP6.

Activity 3

- Tell students they must provide three descriptions before their classmates can reply. You may want to increase the level of competition by using the Alternative Activity below.

Alternative Activity

Use EA 3.1 ¿Quién es quién? to play a guessing game. In pairs, one student describes a person on the sheet and the other guesses who it is. Students may also give each person a name to facilitate communication.

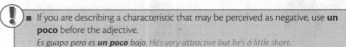

COMUNICA

DESCRIBING PHYSICAL CHARACTERISTICS

¿Cómo es?		
Es...	**Tiene los ojos...**	**Tiene / Lleva el pelo** (hair)...
fuerte *strong*	oscuros *dark*	rubio/a *blond*
delgado/a-gordo/a *thin/overweight*	claros *light*	moreno/a *dark brown*
alto/a-bajo/a *tall/short*	grandes *big*	castaño/a *light brown*
feo/a *unattractive*	pequeños *little*	pelirrojo/a *red*
guapo/a *attractive*	azules *blue*	liso *straight*
joven *young*	verdes *green*	rizado *curly*
mayor *old*	negros *black*	largo *long*
calvo *bald*	marrones *brown*	corto *short*

Tiene la boca/la nariz...	Lleva	
grande *big*	bigote *mustache*	gafas *glasses*
pequeña *small*	barba *beard*	una camisa blanca *a white shirt*

❗ ■ If you are describing a characteristic that may be perceived as negative, use **un poco** before the adjective.
*Es guapo pero es **un poco** bajo. He's very attractive but he's a little short.*

1 👥 In pairs, describe a mutual friend or another student in class. Use the following expressions to talk about his/her characteristics: *Es..., Tiene el pelo..., Tiene los ojos...*

Modelo: E1: ¿Cómo es Mary?
E2: Tiene el pelo negro, los ojos...

2 🎧 36 Listen to the descriptions and identify the person being described.

a.   b.   c.   d.

3 👥 Let's play. In groups of three, take turns describing one of the people below to see which of you guesses correctly in the shortest amount of time.

a.   b.   c.   d.

ANSWERS

Activity 2

a. Ana; **b.** Ricardo; **c.** Pedro; **d.** José.

SLOWER-PACED LEARNERS

Before students listen to Activity 2, have them jot down key words from the presentation next to each photo so they know which words to listen for. (You may have them work in pairs with Advanced or Heritage Language Learners to do this).

ADVANCED LEARNERS

As an extension to Activity 3, have students create an identity for one of the people in the photos and write a paragraph about him or her.

DESCRIBING PERSONALITY TRAITS AND PHYSICAL CONDITIONS

- Use the verb **ser** to describe a person's characteristics.
  *Nuria **es** inteligente. Nuria is intelligent.*
  *Marta **es** una chica muy amable. Marta is a very nice girl.*

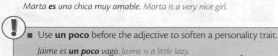

(!) ■ Use **un poco** before the adjective to soften a personality trait.
  *Jaime es **un poco** vago. Jaime is a little lazy.*

SER	TENER
soy	tengo
eres	tienes
es	tiene
somos	tenemos
sois	tenéis
son	tienen

- Use **tener** to describe a person's physical condition.
  *Nicolás **tiene** calor. Nicolás is warm.*

- Here is a list of adjectives and expressions that describe personality traits and physical conditions:

SER
simpático/a ≠ antipático/a *likeable ≠ disagreeable*
divertido/a ≠ aburrido/a *fun ≠ boring*
trabajador/a ≠ vago/a *hard-working ≠ lazy*
abierto/a ≠ tímido/a *outgoing ≠ shy*
amable ≠ maleducado/a *polite ≠ rude*
hablador/a *talkative*
inteligente *intelligent*

TENER
Tener hambre *to be hungry*
Tener sed *to be thirsty*
Tener calor *to be warm*
Tener frío *to be cold*
Tener sueño *to be sleepy*

4 🎧 37 👥 **Listen to the conversations and fill in the missing words. Then practice the conversations with a partner.**

a. **Nuria:** Mi amiga Marta tiene ....
   Luis: ¿Por qué?
   Nuria: Porque no lleva ....

b. **Alberto:** El profesor de Lengua es muy ....
   Luis: Sí, es verdad, y también es muy .... en clase.

c. **Juanjo:** Mi novia es divertida, ..., inteligente...
   Carlos: ¿No tiene defectos?
   Juanjo: Bueno, sí, es un poco ....

Marta

5 👥 **With a partner, take turns describing what your friend is like.**

Modelo: E1: ¿Cómo es tu amigo?
        E2: Es...

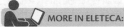 **MORE IN ELETECA:** EXTRA ONLINE PRACTICE

OBJECTIVES FOR COMUNICA

- Present the communicative functions of the unit: Describing personality traits and physical states
- Practice adjectives with **ser** and expressions with **tener**
- Recycle the forms of **ser** and **tener**

CORE RESOURCES

- Audio Program: 37

STANDARDS

1.1   Engage in conversation
1.2   Understand the language
1.3   Present information
4.1   Compare languages

INSTRUCTIONAL STRATEGIES FOR DESCRIBING PERSONALITY TRAITS AND PHYSICAL CONDITIONS

- Write the following sentences: ***Nuria es inteligente*** and ***Nicolás tiene calor***. Ask students to point out the differences between the two sentences and what they are describing. Students should be able to tell that the first sentence describes a characteristic and the second is about a person's state or condition.
- Have students focus on the grammatical structures used in each sentence and describe how each one is constructed (**ser** + adjective vs. **tener** + noun).
- Review the explanations with students. Emphasize masculine and feminine adjective endings, as well as adjectives that do not change for gender.

🎧 **37** Activity 4

- Have students read each conversation silently to themselves and fill in the missing words. Then have students compare their answers with a classmate.
- Play the audio to confirm answers. Explain the words **abrigo** and **defectos** which are new.

Audioscript

a. **Nuria:** Mi amiga Marta tiene frío.
   Luis: ¿Por qué?
   Nuria: Porque no lleva abrigo.

b. **Alberto:** El profesor de Lengua es muy amable.
   Luis: Sí, es verdad, y también es muy divertido en clase.

c. **Juanjo:** Mi novia es divertida, trabajadora, inteligente...
   Carlos: ¿No tiene defectos?
   Juanjo: Bueno, sí, es un poco habladora.

Activity 5

[Alternative Activity]

Have students write out the descriptions. Collect them, and read aloud for the class.

ANSWERS

Activity 4

a. frío / abrigo; **b.** amable / divertido; **c.** trabajadora / habladora

---

HERITAGE LANGUAGE LEARNERS

Have students research and find a photo of a celebrity or important figure from a Spanish-speaking country and write a description of him or her using five or more words from the presentation. Invite them to present the photos and descriptions, post them online, or display them around the room.

OBJECTIVES FOR ¡ACCIÓN!

• Provide students with a structured approach to viewing the video
• Contextualize the content of the unit in a familiar scenario

CORE RESOURCES

• Unit Video 3 - La chica más guapa del mundo
• Online Materials - ELEteca

STANDARDS

1.1   Interpersonal communication
1.2   Interpretive communication
2.1   Culture: Practices and perspectives

INSTRUCTIONAL STRATEGIES

Previewing: Antes del video

Have students look at the images from the video. Ask: *¿Tienes fotos de tu familia en tu casa, en tu celular, en tu cartera? ¿De quiénes son?* Focus their attention on the second image: *¿Hablas con tus amigos sobre la ropa? ¿Cuándo? ¿Escuchas sus opiniones?*

Activity 1

• Put students in pairs to answer the questions. Remind them to look closely at the images and use whatever context clues are available to them, including the title of the video, to help them make the best guesses.
• Review the answers as a class. Ask students to explain their answers and model how to use process of elimination strategies to help them determine the best answers.

Viewing: Durante el video

Activity 2

• This is a two-part activity. Students will check their answers from Activity 1 and then order the sentences in Activity 2 based on what they see and hear in the video.
• Give students time to read the sentences in Activity 2 before you play the video.

ANSWERS

Activity 1

1. b; **2.** a; **3.** c; **4.** c; **5.** c; **6.** b.

Activity 2

1. d; **2.** a; **3.** f; **4.** h; **5.** b; **6.** g; **7.** c; **8.** e.

SLOWER-PACED LEARNERS

Consider giving students the first and last statements in Activity 2 to limit the amount of information they have to listen for during the first viewing.

ADVANCED LEARNERS

Have students compare their answers for Activity 2 with a partner. While doing so, encourage them to add more detailed information related to each of the sentences based on what they can remember from the video.

¡ACCIÓN! La chica más guapa del mundo

1.   2.   3.

4.   5.   6.

ANTES DEL VIDEO

1 👥 Look at the scenes from the episode and then with a partner, choose the best description for each one.

Imagen 1. Las muchachas hablan de…
   a. la boda de la tía de Eli.
   b. la graduación de la tía de Eli.
   c. el cumpleaños de la tía de Eli.

Imagen 2. Eli y Lorena hablan de ropa en…
   a. la habitación de Eli.
   b. en una tienda.
   c. en un mercado.

Imagen 3. Es una foto de…
   a. Eli de pequeña con su padre.
   b. el tío de Eli con su primo Felipe.
   c. el padre de Eli con su hermano Sebas.

Imagen 4. Eli describe a…
   a. su tío.
   b. su madre y a su tía.
   c. su madre.

Imagen 5. Felipe habla con…
   a. su primo Sebas de un partido de futbol.
   b. su amigo Sebas de sus problemas.
   c. su amigo Sebas de las muchachas.

Imagen 6. Sebas…
   a. llama a Felipe para quedar.
   b. describe a Lorena, la amiga de Eli.
   c. está triste porque Felipe no contesta al teléfono.

DURANTE EL VIDEO

2 Watch the complete episode and check your answers to Activity 1. Then number the statements in the correct order.

a. ☐ Eli describe las fotos de su familia antes de entrar al dormitorio.

b. ☐ Sebas espía a las muchachas y comenta por celular a su amigo Felipe que Lorena, la nueva amiga de Eli, es muy linda.

c. ☐ Las muchachas creen que la pregunta de Sebastián es divertida.

d. ☐ Lorena llega a casa de Eli y comenta qué bonita es.

e. ☐ Lorena escoge (*chooses*) un vestido para una posible cita con Sebas.

f. ☐ Eli dice que está muy preocupada porque tiene que elegir ropa para una cita.

g. ☐ Sebas decide entrar al dormitorio y preguntar a Lorena si tiene novio para demostrar que no es tímido.

h. ☐ Lorena y Eli hablan de la ropa ideal para una cita y Eli muestra sus prendas.

3 Watch the episode again and match the characters to what they are thinking.

Lorena Eli  Sebastián Felipe

Pensamientos:............ Pensamientos:............ Pensamientos:............ Pensamientos:............

a. Todas las amigas de Eli son guapas.

b. Para la primera cita es muy importante llevar falda, ¡siempre falda!

c. ¿Qué me pongo para mi cita?

d. ¿Qué ropa lleva Lorena? ¿Cómo es?

e. Esa falda es muy corta.

f. ¿Tiene novio Lorena?

g. No soy tímido.

h. ¡Mi hermano solo piensa en chicas!

i. Esta familia vive en una casa muy bonita.

j. Lorena es totalmente diferente a las otras amigas de Eli.

k. Su hermano es muy divertido.

l. Seguro que su apartamento es muy bonito.

DESPUÉS DEL VIDEO

4 Answer the following questions.

a. ¿Qué personajes hacen descripciones físicas?

b. ¿A quién describen?

c. ¿Cómo los describen?

5 👥 Think back to the different items of clothing that appear in the episode and identify the items that did not.

> pantalones ○ zapatos ○ bañador ○ falda ○ camisa ○ zapatillas ○ bufanda ○ jersey
> pijama ○ abrigo ○ vestido ○ camiseta ○ gorro ○ botas ○ chaqueta ○ pantalones cortos

6 👥 In groups of three or four, create a similar conversation and present it to the class. Describe where you are, the occasion and the clothes needed.

 MORE IN ELETECA: EXTRA ONLINE PRACTICE

95

INSTRUCTIONAL STRATEGIES

Activity 3

• Before playing the video again, have students read the sentences and try to match the thoughts with the characters based on what they remember.

• Play the video a second time for students to complete the activity.

Post-viewing: Después del video

Activity 4

• Have students write their responses individually based on what they can remember.

• Then allow students to compare their answers with a partner and add more details to their own responses.

Activity 5

Point out that they have been asked to focus on what items were not in the video. Suggest that they cross out the items that they saw.

Activity 6

• As a class, brainstorm a list of locations, occasions, and clothes they might use in their conversations.

• To help students organize their ideas, encourage them to create an outline or timeline of events for the conversation. Remind them to think about the purpose or goal of the conversation (***Necesito algo para llevar a un partido de fútbol...***), add a problem or conflict (***...pero no tengo nada del color rojo del equipo***), and end with a resolution (***Puedes llevar esta camisa roja de mi hermano***).

• Have them use their notes to write the conversations. Remind them to create a speaking part for each member of the group. Encourage them to practice the conversation, using gestures and props to make their presentations more dynamic.

ANSWERS

Activity 3

Lorena: b, e, i, k. **Eli:** c, h, l. **Sebastián:** g, j. **Felipe:** a, d, f.

Activity 4

a. Eli, Lorena y Sebas; **b.** Eli describe a su madre, a su tía, a su padre. Lorena describe a Eli de pequeña y a la tía de Eli. Sebas describe a Lorena; **c.** Eli dice que ella ahora tiene el pelo liso, su padre está casi calvo y tiene el pelo blanco, su madre lleva gafas y lleva el pelo mas largo. Lorena dice que Eli tiene el pelo muy rizado y su tía es muy alta y delgada. Sebas dice que Lorena tiene el pelo liso y castaño, tiene los ojos grandes y marrones, lleva pantalones cortos de color blanco y una blusa de flores de color azul.

Activity 5

bañador, zapatillas, bufanda, jersey, pijama, abrigo, gorro, botas, chaqueta.

SLOWER-PACED LEARNERS

Allow students to answer the questions in Activity 4 with a partner so they can share and help remind each other of the various details from the video.

HERITAGE LANGUAGE LEARNERS

Put students into groups of four, assigning each one a character from the video. Using the sequence of events in Activity 2 and the characters' thoughts in Activity 3, have students reenact the main events in the video using their own words. They can change roles for additional practice.

OBJECTIVES FOR LA FAMILIA

- Present the vocabulary needed to practice the communicative and grammatical functions of the unit: Family and family relationships
- Identify family members

CORE RESOURCES

- Audio Program: 38, 39
- Extension Activities: EA 3.2
- Interactive Online Materials - ELEteca

STANDARDS

- 1.1 Engage in conversation
- 1.2 Understand the language
- 1.3 Present information
- 4.2 Compare cultures

INSTRUCTIONAL STRATEGIES

🎧 38 Activity 1

- Bring in a photo of you with your own family or project an image from the Internet of a famous family to see how much background knowledge students have on the topic. Ask students: *¿A quién conocen en la foto? ¿Qué relación hay entre las personas?*
- Introduce the expression, *se parece a*, for additional practice: *Jaime se parece a Daniela*.
- Play the audio as students follow along in their books. Review the regional variations in the box.

Activity 2

- To check comprehension, have students prepare questions about the relationships in Jaime's family and ask each other. For example: *¿Quién es Rosa? Rosa es la mujer de Francisco, la madre de Jaime, Carmen y Daniela*, and so on.
- Use EA 3.2, *Una familia muy especial*, to review family members. Have students complete as many descriptions as possible about each of the members of the Simpson family in the boxes provided. Modelo: *Homer es el padre de Bart. Es el...* and so on. Students should keep these sheets to add to them later. See Alternative Activity 5.

ANSWERS

Activity 2

a. esposo; b. padre; c. hermana; d. hijos; e. abuelos; f. esposa g. tía; h. primos; i. nietos; j. sobrinos.

PALABRA POR PALABRA La familia

1 🎧 38 Look at the drawing of Jaime's family. Follow along as you listen to the description of who everyone is.

- España:
  - la esposa = la mujer
  - la mamá = la madre
  - el esposo = el marido
  - el papá = el padre

La familia de Jaime no es muy grande. Su papá se llama Francisco Arnal y su mamá, Rosa Sabater. Francisco y Rosa son esposo y esposa. Tienen tres hijos: la mayor es Carmen que tiene 16 años, Jaime, su hermano, tiene 12 años, y Daniela, la hermana pequeña, tiene 8 años. El padre de Francisco se llama Juan, y su madre, Ester. Juan y Ester son los abuelos de Carmen, Jaime y Daniela. Jaime y sus hermanos son los nietos de Juan y Ester y los sobrinos de Pilar, su tía, la hermana de Francisco. Pilar está casada con Pablo y tienen dos hijos: María y Luis. María y Luis son los primos de Jaime y de sus hermanas.

2 Complete the sentences using the information from the reading.

a. Francisco es el .... de Rosa.
b. El .... de Jaime se llama Francisco.
c. Daniela es la .... de Jaime.
d. Francisco y Rosa tienen tres ....
e. Los .... de Jaime se llaman Juan y Ester.
f. Rosa es la .... de Francisco.
g. Pilar es la .... de Carmen.
h. María y Luis son .... de Daniela.
i. Juan y Ester tienen cinco ....
j. Pilar tiene tres ....

Instead of having students prepare own their questions as suggested in Activity 2, consider providing a list of prepared questions and perhaps a mix of possible answers.

After doing Activity 1, have students create a family tree of Jaime's family. In addition to having students ask and answer questions about Jaime's family as suggested after Activity 2, you can have students write two true statements and one false statement about Jaime's family. Then they can share them with a partner and identify and correct the false statements.

3 🎧 39 **Listen to Paula talk about her family and identify Paula's relationship to the following people.**

a. Julia ➡ ....
c. Pepe ➡ ....
b. Sara ➡ ....
d. Antonio ➡ ....

4 **Choose the correct option to complete the sentences so that they apply to you.**

1. Yo soy .... de mis abuelos.
a. el nieto   b. la nieta.

2. Yo soy .... de mi hermana.
a. la hermana   b. el hermano

3. Yo soy .... de mis tíos.
a. el sobrino   b. la sobrina

4. Yo soy ....de mis padres.
a. el hijo   b. la hija

5. Yo soy .... de mis primos.
a. la prima   b. el primo

5 👥 **Take turns asking your partner about the following members of his/her family.**

┌─────────────────────────────┐
│ tíos ○ hermanos menores   │
│ ○ abuelos ○ un primo favorito │
└─────────────────────────────┘

Modelo: E1: ¿Tienes hermanos?
E2: Sí, tengo un hermano.
E1: ¿Cómo se llama?
E2: Mi hermano se llama Jeff.

6 👥 **Let's play. Give a definition in Spanish describing family relationships. Your partners will identify the relative you are referring to.**

La madre de mi madre...

Es la abuela.

97

INSTRUCTIONAL STRATEGIES

🎧 **39 Activity 3**

Audioscript

Hola, me llamo Paula y tengo 12 años. Vivo en Valencia con mis padres y mis hermanos. Tengo dos hermanos; Julia, mi hermana mayor y Carlos, mi hermano pequeño. Mis padres se llaman Manuel y Sara. El hermano de mi padre, mi tío Antonio vive también cerca de nuestra casa y es muy divertido. Mis abuelos, Pepe y Carmen, viven en Madrid, pero en verano vienen a vernos a Valencia.

Activity 4

The purpose of this activity is for students to get accustomed to using the correct gender of nouns when talking about themselves. Call on several students to read all the sentences aloud as they relate to the individual student. Have students turn to a classmate and take turns reading the sentences to each other. Listen for the correct word choice from students.

Activity 5

• In addition to giving family names and relationships, have students describe physical characteristics and personality traits.
• Before starting the activity, have students draw their own family trees. Students can also create their partner's family tree based on the description they hear. Afterwards, they compare to see if they are accurate.

Alternative Activity

Use EA 3.2, *Una familia muy especial* for additional practice. Have students complete each box with a description of each member of the Simpson family including physical and character traits. This can be assigned as classwork or homework.

Activity 6

This activity can be done in small groups or as a whole class activity.

ANSWERS

Activity 3

a. hermana; b. madre; c. abuelo; d. tío.

Activity 4

Answers will be either all masculine or all feminine forms of the nouns.

Activities 5 and 6

Answers will vary.

HERITAGE LANGUAGE LEARNERS

Have students find a photo of a family from a Spanish language TV show. Have students write five sentences about the relationships between the characters.

PALABRA POR PALABRA LANGUAGE AND VOCABULARY

OBJECTIVES FOR LA ROPA

- Present the vocabulary needed to practice the communicative and grammatical functions for the unit: Articles of clothing
- Talk about what people are wearing

CORE RESOURCES

- Audio Program: 40
- Interactive Whiteboard Lesson: IWB 3.2

STANDARDS

1.1	Engage in conversation
1.2	Understand the language
1.3	Present information
4.2	Compare cultures

INSTRUCTIONAL STRATEGIES

🎧 40 **Activity 7**

- To determine students' previous knowledge, call on a volunteer to come to the front of the class and ask the class to describe what he/she is wearing. Repeat with other volunteers as needed.
- Play the audio as students follow along.
- Use IWB 3.2, **La tienda de ropa**, to fill in the correct words for each article of clothing.

SLOWER-PACED LEARNERS

Have students cut out pictures of each item from magazines and use the pictures to create vocabulary flash cards.

ADVANCED LEARNERS

As an extension to Activity 7, have students use the words in context by making sentences with each item. They can do this in writing or by taking turns speaking with a partner.

HERITAGE LANGUAGE LEARNERS

Have students search Spanish magazines and/or websites of stores in Spanish-speaking countries to find advertisements and sales for each item of clothing. Have them create a collection of clippings or printouts with the key words circled or highlighted.

PALABRA POR PALABRA La ropa

7 🎧 40 **Follow along as you listen to the words for different articles of clothing.**

gorra — suéter — jeans — chaqueta — pantalones — zapato de tacón — bufanda — abrigo — cinturón — camisa — bota — falda — traje — corbata — tenis — vestido — sandalias — calcetín — camiseta

- el calcetín = la media (muchos países)
- la chaqueta = la cazadora (España), la chamarra (México, Centroamérica)
- la falda = la saya, la pollera (Sudamérica)
- los jeans = los vaqueros (España), los mahones (Puerto Rico), la pitusa (Cuba)
- el suéter = el jersey (España)
- el tenis = la zapatilla de deporte

8 Complete the sentences to describe what Santiago and Noelia are wearing according to the drawings.

Santiago lleva una .... amarilla, una .... negra, una .... de rayas y un .... verde. Su .... es marrón y sus .... son anaranjados.

Noelia lleva unas .... y un .... de color marrón. Lleva también una .... de flores y una .... de color rosa.

9 Describe to your partner what he/she is wearing today.

10 Tell your partners what you usually wear in the following situations.

a. Cuando tengo frío…
b. Cuando tengo una fiesta elegante…
c. Cuando estoy con mis amigos…
d. En julio y agosto…

11 Answer the following questions and then share your responses with a partner.

a. ¿Qué tres prendas de vestir usas a diario?

b. ¿Cuáles son las tres prendas de vestir que te gusta comprar?

c. Describe alguna ropa nueva que tienes.

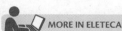 **MORE IN ELETECA:** EXTRA ONLINE PRACTICE

99

INSTRUCTIONAL STRATEGIES

Activity 8

Explain the difference between *jersey* and *camiseta*. A jersey is heavier than a *camiseta* which is a t-shirt. You may also want to point out that the *sandalias* that Noelia is wearing are actually *chanclas* or *flip-flops*.

Alternative activity

Have students describe what the people in Jaime's family on page 96 are wearing.

Activity 9

Alternative activity

• Have students describe to a partner what other classmates are wearing. The winner is the one who guesses the correct person with the least number of clues.
• Include additional clothes vocabulary as needed.

Activity 10

Have students report back to the class what they learned about their partner.

Activity 11

• Review the questions first with students. Provide examples as needed for comprehension.
• You may wish to assign this as a written activity.

ANSWERS

Activity 8

Santiago: gorra, camiseta, camisa, pantalón, cinturón, zapatillas de deporte.
Noelia: sandalias, cinturón, falda, camiseta.

Activities 9 to 11

Answers will vary and should reflect vocabulary and expressions taught.

ADVANCED LEARNERS

For additional practice, provide students with more scenarios in Activity 10: *Cuando voy a la playa…, Cuando hago deporte…, Cuando salgo de comer a un restaurante…, Cuando voy al teatro…,* etc. Give them access to bilingual dictionaries to look for any clothing items they wish to say that haven't been presented in Activity 7.

HERITAGE LANGUAGE LEARNERS

Have students write responses to the three questions in Activity 11 about a friend or family member that they know very well. Have them share their answers with a partner, and encourage them to check each other's spelling and mark any necessary corrections.

OBJECTIVES FOR GRAMÁTICA 1

- Present the grammatical structures needed to practice the communicative functions of the unit: Present tense of regular **–er** and **–ir** verbs
- Describe what your family does

CORE RESOURCES

- Extension Activities: EA 3.3
- Interactive Online Materials - ELEteca

STANDARDS

1.1	Engage in conversation
1.2	Understand the language
4.1	Compare languages

INSTRUCTIONAL STRATEGIES

1. Present Tense of –ER and –IR Verbs

- Before you introduce the forms, ask students to recall the conjugation of regular **–ar** verbs with examples.
- Ask students about conjugations in English and explain that in Spanish there are three different types of conjugations, **–ar** (which they already learned) **–er** and **–ir**.
- Present the endings and meanings of the verbs.
- Use EA 3.3, **El presente de indicativo**, to provide students with examples of other **–er** and **–ir** conjugated verbs along with a review of **–ar** verbs. First have students match the action on the left with the correct verb. In this way, students are introduced to the forms and meanings of **–er** and **–ir** verbs. Then have students complete the chart with the correct verb endings for each conjugation.

Activity 1

- Introduce the activity by asking students: **¿Tienen hermanos? ¿Cuántos? ¿Se parecen físicamente a ti? ¿Qué tienen en común? ¿Discuten?**, etc.
- Point out that **discutir** is a false cognate and that it means to argue, debate, not discuss.

  ### Extension

  Have students write a similar description about themselves, their siblings, and how they all get along. Students share their paragraphs with a partner to see what they have in common.

Activity 2

- Elicit possible conclusions to the first sentence. Call on volunteers to write possible full sentences for the first prompt on the board. Have students work individually to complete the rest of the sentences.
- Have students read their sentences aloud to a partner. Review the correct verb conjugations as a class.

GRAMÁTICA

1. PRESENT TENSE OF –ER AND –IR VERBS

■ You have already learned the forms of verbs in Spanish end in **–ar**. There are two other groups of regular verbs, whose infinitives end in **–er** and **–ir**. To create the present tense forms of **–er** and **–ir** verbs, drop the endings from the infinitives, then add the verb endings as shown in the chart. Do **–er** and **–ir** verbs share the same endings?

	COMER (to eat)	VIVIR (to live)
yo	como	vivo
tú	comes	vives
usted/él/ella	come	vive
nosotros/as	comemos	vivimos
vosotros/as	coméis	vivís
ustedes/ellos/ellas	comen	viven

*Yo **como** con mi familia. I eat with my family.*
*Mi familia **vive** en Buenos Aires. My family lives in Buenos Aires.*

! **Ver** is irregular in the **yo** form only:

VER
veo
ves
ve
vemos
veis
ven

■ Here are some useful **–er** and **–ir** verbs:

–ER		–IR	
aprender *to learn*		**abrir** *to open*	
beber *to drink*		**asistir** *to attend*	
leer *to read*		**discutir** *to argue*	
ver *to see*		**escribir** *to write*	

1 Read the following text and fill in the blanks with the correct form of the verbs.

Enrique y Marta son hermanos, (vivir) .... juntos, pero son muy diferentes. Él siempre (comer) .... pasta y ella ensalada. Él (beber) .... café y ella té. Los dos (leer) .... novelas, pero él (leer) .... novelas de aventuras y ella novelas de amor. Marta (aprender) .... italiano y Enrique, inglés. Los amigos de Enrique y Marta siempre (escribir) .... correos electrónicos para comunicarse con ellos. Marta (abrir) .... los correos todos los días, pero Enrique no. Son diferentes, pero nunca (discutir) ....

2 Complete the following sentences with the correct form of the verbs and add a logical ending.

a. Mi familia y yo (vivir) ....
b. Normalmente yo (comer) ....
c. Mi prima Julia (vivir) ....
d. En un restaurante, nosotros (comer) ....

ANSWERS

Activity 1

viven; come; bebe; leen; lee; aprende; escriben; abre; discuten.

Activity 2

Answers will vary. Verb forms include.
a. vivimos; **b.** como; **c.** vive; **d.** comemos.

SLOWER-PACED LEARNERS

Provide possible logical endings for the sentences in Activity 2 so they can focus on the verb conjugations.

ADVANCED LEARNERS

Challenge students to write negative sentences and questions using the same prompts and verbs in Activity 2.

3 👥 **Take turns asking each other when you do the following activities.**

Modelo: *cuándo / comer / en restaurante*

¿Cuándo comes en un restaurante?

Como en un restaurante los domingos.

a. cuándo / **comer** / con tus padres
b. a qué hora / **asistir** / a clase
c. cuándo / **ver** / la televisión
d. cuándo / **leer** / libros
e. a qué hora / **abrir** / los correos electrónicos

2. POSSESSIVE ADJECTIVES

■ Possessive adjectives tell you *whose* object or person is being referred to (*my car, his book, her mother,* etc.). In Spanish, possessive adjectives agree in number with the nouns that follow them. Here are the possessive adjectives in Spanish:

	Singular		Plural	
	Masculine	Feminine	Masculine	Feminine
my	**mi** carro	**mi** casa	**mis** carros	**mis** casas
your	**tu** carro	**tu** casa	**tus** carros	**tus** casas
his/her/your (for.)	**su** carro	**su** casa	**sus** carros	**sus** casas
our	**nuestro** carro	**nuestra** casa	**nuestros** carros	**nuestras** casas
your (pl. Spain)	**vuestro** carro	**vuestra** casa	**vuestros** carros	**vuestras** casas
their/your (pl.)	**su** carro	**su** casa	**sus** carros	**sus** casas

Mi *carro es grande. My car is big.*

Marisa tiene dos gatos. **Sus** *gatos son negros. Marisa has two cats. Her cats are black.*

■ Possesive adjectives must agree in number (singular/plural) with the noun they modify. In addition to agreeing in number, **nuestro** and **vuestro** must also agree in gender.
Nuestro *tío es divertido. Our uncle is fun.*   **Nuestra** *tía es rubia. Our aunt is blond.*

4 👥 **Choose the correct option in each sentence. Then, with a partner, say who the people or objects belong to.**

a. **Mi / Nuestros / Mis** hermanas son altas.
b. **Su / Sus / Nuestro** padres están alegres.
c. **Mi / Tu / Tus** abuelos son muy mayores.
d. **Tus / Sus / Su** habitación es pequeña.
e. **Mis / Nuestros / Tu** amigas son muy simpáticas.
f. **Mi / Nuestro / Sus** hijas estudian en Francia.

5 **Complete each sentence with an appropriate possessive adjective.**

a. (yo) .... amigo aprende portugués.
b. (ellos) .... perro se llama Lupo.
c. (nosotros) .... padres son médicos.
d. (tú) .... camisa es muy bonita.
e. (ustedes) .... casa es muy grande.
f. (ella) .... primos viven cerca.

101

Activity 3

• Confirm that students know which verb forms should be used in the questions (*tú*) and the responses (*yo*).
• Encourage students to take notes about their partners' answers. Have each students interview two classmates. Ask students to report back on their classmates' responses, making comparisons between them.

OBJECTIVES FOR GRAMÁTICA 2

• Present grammatical structures needed to practice communicative functions of the chapter: Possessive adjectives
• Talk about your family and friends

CORE RESOURCES

• Extension Activities: EA 3.4

STANDARDS

1.1   Engage in conversation
1.2   Understand the language
4.1   Compare languages

INSTRUCTIONAL STRATEGIES

2. Possessive Adjectives

• Go over the forms of possessive adjectives in the chart, then have students fill in the missing forms in chart in EA 3.4, **Los adjetivos posesivos**.
• Review any vocabulary in Activity 2 that students may have difficulty understanding. Then have students fill in the blanks. Point out that the text is written from both Nicolás and Daniel's point of view.

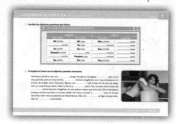

ANSWERS EA 3.4

Activity 2

mi / Nuestro / Nuestros / su / su / mi / su / nuestras / nuestra.

Activity 4

Extension

Have students rewrite the sentences changing them from singular to plural or vice versa.

Activity 5

Alternative activity

Ask students to identify other categories of words in the text such as verbs, family vocabulary, etc.

ANSWERS

Activity 4

a. Mis; **b.** Sus; **c.** Tus; **d.** Su; **e.** Mis; **f.** Sus.

Activity 5

a. Mi; **b.** Su; **c.** Nuestros; **d.** Tu; **e.** Su; **f.** Sus.

HERITAGE LANGUAGE LEARNERS

Working with a partner, have students write three questions and answers that use possessive adjectives: 1) *tu/mi*, 2) *su/su*, and 3) *vuestro/nuestro*. Have each pair present the questions and answers aloud to the class.

INSTRUCTIONAL STRATEGIES

Activity 6

- Ask questions to check comprehension and practice using the third person pronouns *su* and *sus*. Ask: *¿Quiénes son Javier y Marisa? (sus padres), ¿Quién es Dani? (su hermano), ¿Cómo es Ana? (inteligente y alegre)* and so on. Explain the meaning of *travieso*.
- This activity can be turned into a written assignment. Have students use the text as a model to write about their own (or imagined) families.

  #### Extension

  Have students underline other structures in the text such as verbs, family vocabulary, and descriptive adjectives from the unit.

ANSWERS

Activity 6

Nuestros, Nuestro, Nuestra, Mi, mi, mi, sus, tu.

OBJECTIVES FOR GRAMÁTICA 3

- Present the grammatical structures needed to practice the communicative functions of the unit: Demonstrative adjectives
- Pointing out people and things

STANDARDS

1.1　Engage in conversation

1.2　Understand the language

4.1　Compare languages

INSTRUCTIONAL STRATEGIES

3. Demonstrative Adjectives

- Introduce the concept by pointing out objects in the classroom and asking students about them. Combine *este*, *ese*, *aquel* with *aquí*, *ahí* and *allí* to familiarize students with the forms and uses of demonstratives.
- Ask: *Carlos, ¿me puedes traer aquel libro de allí* (gesturing over there); *María, ¿es esa de ahí tu carpeta? ¿De quién es este bolígrafo que hay aquí?*
- Present the information in the chart and go over the explanations.

GRAMMAR NOTE

Point out that in some countries Spanish speakers use *acá* in place of *aquí* and *allá* in place of *allí*.

SLOWER-PACED LEARNERS

Have students take turns reading the text in Activity 6 aloud to a partner for additional speaking and pronunciation practice.

HERITAGE LANGUAGE LEARNERS

Using the text in Activity 6 as a model, have students write similar paragraphs about their own families.

GRAMÁTICA

6　**Underline the possessive adjectives in the following text.**

> Tengo dos hermanos: Dani y Ana. Nuestros padres se llaman Javier y Marisa. Vivimos en Sevilla. Nuestro padre es alto y delgado y nuestra madre es rubia. Mi hermano Dani tiene 11 años y mi hermana Ana tiene casi seis. Ana es muy inteligente y alegre. Dani es muy divertido y un poco vago en el colegio. La hermana de mi padre tiene dos hijos gemelos. Está muy cansada porque sus hijos son un poco traviesos. ¿Cómo es tu familia?

3. DEMONSTRATIVE ADJECTIVES

- Demonstrative adjectives point out people and objects and indicate how far away these people or objects are from the speaker. For example, for people or objects that are:

  1. close to the speaker, use **este**;

  2. at an intermediate distance or between the speaker and the listener, use **ese**;

  3. far away from both, use **aquel**.

Location of speaker	Singular Masculine	Singular Feminine	Plural Masculine	Plural Feminine	
aquí *here*	**este**	**esta**	**estos**	**estas**	*this, these*
ahí *there*	**ese**	**esa**	**esos**	**esas**	*that, those*
allí *over there*	**aquel**	**aquella**	**aquellos**	**aquellas**	*that (over there), those (over there)*

- As with other adjectives, demonstratives agree in gender and number with the nouns that follow. **este** zapato *this shoe* / **estos** zapatos *these shoes*

- These forms can also be used as pronouns, but must still agree in number and gender with the noun(s) they are replacing. Read the examples below.

> Este es mi amigo Manuel. Es muy simpático.

This is my friend Manuel. He is very nice.

> Ese es mi abuelo. ¡Es muy divertido!

That's my grandfather. He's a lot of fun!

UNIDAD **3**

Aquellos son mis amigos.
Son un poco tímidos.

***Those** are my friends.*
They are a little shy.

7 **Change the sentences from singular to plural or vice versa.**

a. Esa mujer está muy nerviosa....................
b. Estos muchachos son un poco habladores. ....
c. Aquel hombre tiene los ojos azules. ....
d. Aquellas señoras son muy mayores. ....

8 **Complete the following sentences using a demonstrative adjective.**

a. .... camisetas de aquí son muy baratas, pero .... camisas de allí son más bonitas.
b. .... zapatos que tienes en la mano son muy bonitos, ¿verdad?
c. ¡Qué horror! .... música que ponen aquí es muy mala.
d. Y .... muchachas de allí, ¿de qué clase son?
e. .... muchacho de ahí, el que está sentado en la mesa, es mi compañero.

9 👥 **With a partner, take turns creating sentences for what the people in the images might say. Use demonstrative adjectives.**

Modelo: *Pienso que este suéter es muy bonito para ti.*

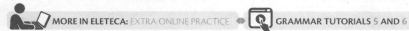 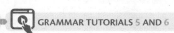

💻 **MORE IN ELETECA:** EXTRA ONLINE PRACTICE ◀ 🔲 **GRAMMAR TUTORIALS** 5 AND 6   103

INSTRUCTIONAL STRATEGIES

Activity 7

(**Extension**)

Have students change the words in the sentences from masculine to feminine and vice versa.

Activity 8

After students complete the activity, they switch papers with a partner and have him/her correct the activity. Student pairs should discuss the errors they found to arrive at the correct responses.

Activity 9

- To set up the activity, ask students about the people in the images, their relationship and what they are doing. Ask: *En la primera imagen, ¿dónde están las personas? ¿Son esposos, hermanos o amigos? ¿De qué color es la camisa?* and so on.
- Students can also create speech bubbles for the people in the images and then act out the scene. Encourage students to be creative and use as much vocabulary as possible.

ANSWERS

Activity 7

a. Esas mujeres están muy nerviosas; **b.** Este muchacho es un poco hablador; **c.** Aquellos hombres tienen los ojos azules; **d.** Aquella señora es muy mayor.

Activity 8

a. Estas, aquellas; **b.** Esos; **c.** Esta; **d.** aquellas; **e.** Ese.

ADVANCED LEARNERS

Have students work with a partner to create and present an extended conversation for one of the scenarios in Activity 9.

HERITAGE LANGUAGE LEARNERS

Have students choose an article from a Spanish language newspaper or website about a topic that interests them and write one or two sentences about its main idea. Then have them scan the article for examples of present tense –*er* and –*ir* verbs, possessive adjectives, and demonstrative adjectives, marking each group of words a different way, for example, by circling, underlining, or highlighting them.

OBJECTIVES FOR DESTREZAS

- Listing and identifying descriptive words to improve reading comprehension
- Making a chart to organize and improve writing skills

STANDARDS

1.2   Understand the language
1.3   Present information

INSTRUCTIONAL STRATEGIES

Comprensión de Lectura

Activity 1

Review the strategy with students to make sure they understand. Point out that it is a two-step process. In the first step, they should just list the adjectives and then decide whether each one refers to a physical or personality trait.

Extension

Have students write a paragraph similar to the one in Activity 2 and create a set of multiple-choice questions. Have them exchange readings with a partner and complete the activity. Also have them list and identify the descriptive words from the parapraphs and note whether they are personality or physical traits. In this way, students practice both reading and writing skills.

Activity 2

- Simulate a testing environment. Have students work individually and silently to answer the questions. Set a time limit for them to answer the questions.
- When time is up, review the answers as a class. Consider projecting the email and inviting students to come up and point out where they found their answers.

ANSWERS

Activity 2

1. a; 2. c; 3. b; 4. d; 5. b; 6. c.

SLOWER-PACED LEARNERS

To simplify Activity 2, you may choose to remove one or two of the answer choices.

ADVANCED LEARNERS

Have students write comprehension questions about the email to ask and answer with a partner, such as **¿Cuál es el apellido de David?**

HERITAGE LANGUAGE LEARNERS

Have students write an email like the one in Activity 1 and send it to a Spanish-speaking friend or relative. Have them invite their friends or relatives to write back in Spanish. Encourage them to share those responses with the class.

DESTREZAS

COMPRENSIÓN DE LECTURA

1 David has written an e-mail to his friend Marie. Before reading the e-mail, review the strategy in Destrezas and complete the list.

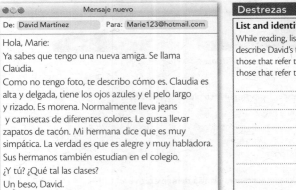

Mensaje nuevo

De: David Martínez   Para: Marie123@hotmail.com

Hola, Marie:
Ya sabes que tengo una nueva amiga. Se llama Claudia.
Como no tengo foto, te describo cómo es. Claudia es alta y delgada, tiene los ojos azules y el pelo largo y rizado. Es morena. Normalmente lleva jeans y camisetas de diferentes colores. Le gusta llevar zapatos de tacón. Mi hermana dice que es muy simpática. La verdad es que es alegre y muy habladora. Sus hermanos también estudian en el colegio.
¿Y tú? ¿Qué tal las clases?
Un beso, David.

Destrezas

List and identify descriptive words
While reading, list the words used to describe David's friend. Then identify those that refer to personality traits and those that refer to a physical aspect.

..............................(personality/physical)
..............................(personality/physical)
..............................(personality/physical)
..............................(personality/physical)
..............................(personality/physical)
..............................(personality/physical)

2 Read the e-mail again and select the correct completion for the sentences below.

1. David escribe un correo sobre...
   a. su nueva amiga.
   b. la amiga nueva de su hermana.
   c. su nuevo amigo de colegio.
   d. su nuevo amigo.

2. Claudia es...
   a. alta y guapa.
   b. baja y delgada.
   c. alta y delgada.
   d. baja y guapa.

3. Claudia tiene el pelo...
   a. rubio y largo.
   b. moreno y rizado.
   c. moreno y corto.
   d. rubio y corto.

4. Claudia lleva...
   a. vestido y zapatos de tacón.
   b. falda y zapatillas deportivas.
   c. pantalón y camisa.
   d. pantalón y camiseta.

5. Claudia es...
   a. triste, habladora y simpática.
   b. simpática, alegre y habladora.
   c. simpática, inteligente y alegre.
   d. habladora, amable y simpática.

6. Claudia tiene...
   a. una hermana.
   b. dos hermanos.
   c. hermanos.
   d. un hermano.

EXPRESIÓN E INTERACCIÓN ESCRITAS

3 Look at the following images. Select one and imagine that the person is a member of your family. Before you begin to write about this person, read the strategy in Destrezas and complete the chart.

Destrezas

Make a chart showing information about the family member. This will help you write your description.

a.

b.

c.

d.

Categoría	Detalles
relación	
descripción física	
personalidad	
ropa que lleva	
estado físico	

4 Write a description of this person using the notes you prepared.

Modelo: Este/Esta es mi..

....

PRONUNCIACIÓN The sounds of *k* and *s*

1 🎧 41 Listen to the pronunciation of the following words.

El sonido /k/	El sonido /s/
c + a → **calvo**	c + e → **cero**
c + o → **corto**	c + i → **cinco**
c + u → **curso**	z + a → **rizado**
qu + e → **pequeño**	z + o → **zorro**
qu + i → **tranquilo**	z + u → **zurdo**

2 👥 Read the following syllables aloud to your partner.

za-	co-	que-
ce-	cu-	zo-
qui-	ci-	ca-
zu-		

3 🎧 42 Write the words you hear under the corresponding image.

a.

b.

c.

d.

e.   f.

MORE IN ELETECA: EXTRA ONLINE PRACTICE

Expresión e Interacción Escritas

Activities 2 and 3

- Review the strategy with students to make sure they understand
- Allow students 25 minutes to prepare and write their paragraph.

  Extension

  - Group students according to the person they described and have them compare their paragraphs to see if they are in agreement.
  - Assign descriptions of two other people for students to complete for homework.
  - In the next class, have students exchange their new paragraphs and complete charts like the one in Activity 3 based on their partners' descriptions.

OBJECTIVES FOR PRONUNCIACIÓN

- Practice correct pronunciation: /k/ and /ɵ/

CORE RESOURCES

- Audio Program: 41, 42
- Interactive Online Materials - ELEteca

STANDARDS

1.2   Understand the language

4.1   Compare languages

INSTRUCTIONAL STRATEGIES

🎧 41 Activity 1

- Introduce the sounds with sample words and books closed. Ask students to spell out the words as you write them on the board. Remind them that they may not recognize all of the words.
- Play the audio and correct any errors on the board.

Audioscript

Calvo, corto, curso, pequeño, tranquilo, cero, cinco, rizado, zorro, zurdo.

Activity 2

Circulate to monitor student pronunciation.

🎧 42 Activity 3

Pause audio to allow students time to write the words correctly.

Audioscript

Cielo, zapatos, rizado, boca, querer, cine.

ANSWERS

Activity 3

a. cielo; **b.** zapatos, **c.** rizado; **d.** boca; **e.** querer; **f.** cine.

SLOWER-PACED LEARNERS

Give students a couple of details to help get them started with **Expresión e interacción escritas** Activity 3, or assign them a picture and have them work with a partner to complete the chart in preparation for the writing.

OBJECTIVES FOR SABOR HISPANO

- Learn about a country: Mexico
- Learn about Mexican families, celebrations, and traditions
- Compare celebrations with those in the United States

CORE RESOURCES

- Audio program: 43

STANDARDS

1.2	Understand the language
2.1	Practices and perspectives
4.1	Compare cultures

INSTRUCTIONAL STRATEGIES

- Introduce the topic by asking students what they know about Mexico and Mexican traditions.
- Talk about the images and the map. Share what you know about Mexico with students.
- Read the captions together and ask questions to check comprehension. Point out the name for tortilla chips in Spanish: **totopos**.
- Ask students to identify which of the points in **¿Sabes que...?** they find most surprising.

CULTURAL NOTE

Mexican Coke, or MexiCoke, has become increasingly popular and is now widely distributed in the US. It is sold in classically shaped glass bottles with labels painted directly on them, as opposed to the American Coke which is sold in plastic bottles with removable labels wrapped around them. Coca-Cola says that MexiCoke is made with cane sugar, not high fructose corn syrup like the US brand. In taste tests, MexiCoke has been described as more natural tasting and a little spicy, closer to the flavor of root beer. Consider conducting a taste test with your class to get their own impressions.

HERITAGE LANGUAGE LEARNERS

Have students compare and contrast facts about their families and traditions to those presented about Mexico.

SABOR HISPANO

LA FAMILIA MEXICANA

¡Bienvenidos a México!

México

Guadalajara • Ciudad de México

Oaxaca •

La familia es importante en la cultura mexicana

Palenque, antigua ciudad maya en Chiapas

Danza tradicional mexicana

Totopos con salsa, un plato típico

- ✓ En una comida familiar es normal ver a mucha gente: los abuelos, los tíos, los papás, los primos, los hijos, los nietos...
- ✓ En México, muchos hogares (homes) son familiares (90,5%) y el 97,3% vive en familia.
- ✓ El 70,9% del núcleo de una familia mexicana moderna está formado por los papás y los hijos.

¿Sabes que...?

- ✓ México D. F., la capital del país, es la ciudad más poblada de América del Norte: tiene casi 9 millones de personas... ¡Aquí hay más personas que en Nueva York!
- ✓ La palabra México es azteca. Significa «el ombligo (bellybutton) de la luna».
- ✓ México es el país con más taxis del mundo: solo en la capital hay más de... ¡250.000!
- ✓ México es el país que consume más productos de cola del mundo.
- ✓ También es el país con más museos: tiene 1.168... ¡Ándale!

Fuentes: INEGI, México, CIA Worlddata, Embajada de México en los EE. UU.

106

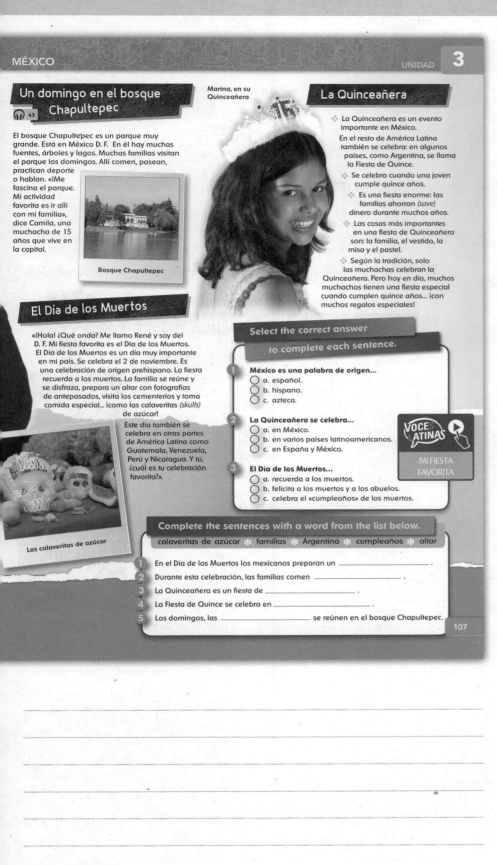

MÉXICO

Un domingo en el bosque Chapultepec

🎧 43

El bosque Chapultepec es un parque muy grande. Está en México D. F. En él hay muchas fuentes, árboles y lagos. Muchas familias visitan el parque los domingos. Allí comen, pasean, practican deporte o hablan. «¡Me fascina el parque. Mi actividad favorita es ir allí con mi familia», dice Camila, una muchacha de 15 años que vive en la capital.

Bosque Chapultepec

Marina, en su Quinceañera

La Quinceañera

❖ La Quinceañera es un evento importante en México.
En el resto de América Latina también se celebra: en algunos países, como Argentina, se llama la Fiesta de Quince.

❖ Se celebra cuando una joven cumple quince años.

❖ Es una fiesta enorme: las familias ahorran (save) dinero durante muchos años.

❖ Las cosas más importantes en una fiesta de Quinceañera son: la familia, el vestido, la misa y el pastel.

❖ Según la tradición, solo las muchachas celebran la Quinceañera. Pero hoy en día, muchos muchachos tienen una fiesta especial cuando cumplen quince años... ¡con muchos regalos especiales!

El Día de los Muertos

«¡Hola! ¿Qué onda? Me llamo René y soy del D. F. Mi fiesta favorita es el Día de los Muertos. El Día de los Muertos es un día muy importante en mi país. Se celebra el 2 de noviembre. Es una celebración de origen prehispano. La fiesta recuerda a los muertos. La familia se reúne y se disfraza, prepara un altar con fotografías de antepasados, visita los cementerios y toma comida especial... ¡como las calaveritas (skulls) de azúcar!

Este día también se celebra en otras partes de América Latina como Guatemala, Venezuela, Perú y Nicaragua. Y tú, ¿cuál es tu celebración favorita?».

Las calaveritas de azúcar

Select the correct answer to complete each sentence.

1 México es una palabra de origen...
○ a. español.
○ b. hispano.
○ c. azteca.

2 La Quinceañera se celebra...
○ a. en México.
○ b. en varios países latinoamericanos.
○ c. en España y México.

3 El Día de los Muertos...
○ a. recuerda a los muertos.
○ b. felicita a los muertos y a los abuelos.
○ c. celebra el «cumpleaños» de los muertos.

VOCES LATINAS ▶
MI FIESTA FAVORITA

Complete the sentences with a word from the list below.

calaveritas de azúcar ✳ familias ✳ Argentina ✳ cumpleaños ✳ altar

1 En el Día de los Muertos los mexicanos preparan un _____ .
2 Durante esta celebración, las familias comen _____ .
3 La Quinceañera es un fiesta de _____ .
4 La Fiesta de Quince se celebra en _____ .
5 Los domingos, las _____ se reúnen en el bosque Chapultepec.

107

INSTRUCTIONAL STRATEGIES

🎧 43

- An audio recording accompanies each text on this page. Play the audio or have students read. Then ask students questions to check comprehension and compare what they learned about Mexico and Mexican culture to their own experiences.
- Identify and explain any vocabulary from the reading students may find difficult to understand.

Un domingo en el bosque Chapultepec

Ask: *¿Qué parques grandes hay en tu ciudad? ¿Qué hacen allí las personas? ¿Es un lugar para familias? Explica.*

La Quinceañera

Ask: *¿Dónde se celebra? ¿Hay alguna celebración similar en tu cultura? ¿Cómo es?*

CULTURAL NOTE

In most **fiestas de quince**, it is customary for the father to dance the waltz with his daughter as the first dance. It is also common for the girls to perform a choreographed dance with her friends, as they usually do in Ecuador. In Argentina, Peru, Paraguay, and Uruguay, girls may also have **la ceremonia de las velas**, also known as **la ceremonia del árbol de la vida**. During the ceremony, 15 candles are lit. Each one symbolizes a year of life that is being left behind and relates to a special person, memory, or experience in the girl's life.

El Día de Muertos

Ask: *¿Es un día triste o alegre para los mexicanos? ¿Cómo lo sabes?* (Ask students to provide examples). *¿Hay alguna fiesta similar en tu cultura? ¿Cuál es tu celebración favorita?*

- Have students complete the activities at the bottom of this page and compare their answers with other students.

ANSWERS

Answer selections
   1. c; **2.** b; **3.** a.

Sentence completions
   1. altar; **2.** calaveritas de azúcar; **3.** cumpleaños; **4.** Argentina; **5.** familias.

SLOWER-PACED LEARNERS

Have slower-paced learners work with a partner to answer the questions. Encourage them to find and underline or highlight the answers in the text.

ADVANCED LEARNERS

Using the paragraph about Bosque Chapultepec as a model, have students research another park from a Spanish-speaking country and write a paragraph about it.

OBJECTIVES FOR RELATO

• Revisit unit themes, grammar, vocabulary, and culture in a new context
• Improve reading comprehension skills

CORE RESOURCES

• Audio Program: 44

STANDARDS

1.1 Engage in conversation
1.2 Understand the language
1.3 Present information
2.1 Practices and perspectives

INSTRUCTIONAL STRATEGIES

Activity 1

Have students complete the family tree with the vocabulary they learned to identify family members.

🎧 44 Activity 2

• Before students begin to read, introduce the topic by asking: **¿Se reúnen con sus familias para cenar o comer en sus fiestas tradicionales? ¿Qué otras tradiciones tienen?**

• Tell students that now they are going to read a text about a typical Christmas celebration: **las Navidades** from the perspective of a young person from Spain.

• To check students' comprehension, ask: **¿Dónde se reúne la familia del relato? ¿Qué problema tiene la madre del protagonista?**

SLOWER-PACED LEARNERS

Provide an answer bank for the family tree in Activity 1 or direct students to page 112 for a complete list of family members from the unit.

ADVANCED LEARNERS

Have students make a family tree about their own families, adding names, ages, where they live, and two descriptors of each person.

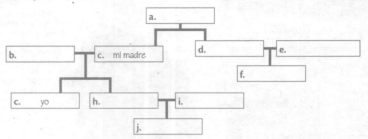

RELATO La cena de Nochebuena

1 Complete the following family tree with the correct vocabulary words to show family relationships.

```
                    a.
         ┌──────────┴──────────┐
    ┌────┴────┬──────┐      ┌───┴───┐
    b.      c. mi madre    d.      e.
                                   │
                                   f.
    ┌────────┬────────┐
    c.  yo   h.       i.
             │
             j.
```

2 🎧 44 Read the following text about a Spanish family getting together to celebrate a traditional Christmas Eve.

La cena de Nochebuena

Todos los años el mismo problema. Mi madre no sabe cómo organizar a la familia en la mesa. En total, somos nueve. Siempre es un desastre porque todos somos muy diferentes.

La abuela Julia, muy nerviosa y habladora, lleva siempre una falda y una camisa amarillas. Odia los teléfonos móviles, los vaqueros y el pelo largo en los hombres.

El tío Pepe, con corbata y traje negros, es muy pesimista y habla muy poco. Su mujer, Carmen, siempre habla por el móvil.

La prima Maribel es muy alegre pero bastante supersticiosa. Es actriz y no soporta el color amarillo. Lleva pantalones y vestidos de colores excepto el amarillo, claro…

Mi hermana Sara es muy tranquila e inteligente pero un poco tímida, siempre con sus vaqueros viejos y una camiseta donde está escrito: "Prohibido hablar por el móvil, gracias". Óscar, el novio de Sara, lleva el pelo largo y rizado. No habla mucho.

Mi padre es muy hablador, optimista y sociable, pero sus ojos no soportan los colores claros ni los muy oscuros.

Mi pobre mamá, que es muy buena, no sabe qué hacer ni dónde sentarnos para evitar conflictos.

■ En España, el color amarillo da mala suerte entre la gente del teatro. ¿Y en tu país?

ANSWERS

Activity 1

```
                    a. mis abuelos
         ┌──────────┴──────────────┐
    ┌────┴─────┬──────────┐    ┌────┴─────┐
  b. mi padre  c. mi madre   d. mi tía   e. mi tío
                                   │
                              f. mi primo/a
    ┌──────────┬──────────────────┐
  c. yo     h. mi hermano   i. la mujer de mi hermano/el marido de mi hermana
                   │
            j. mi sobrino/a
```

3 👥 With a partner, complete the descriptions with the information presented about the people in the reading.

a. La abuela Julia ➡ ....

b. El tío Pepe ➡ ....

c. La tía Carmen ➡ ....

d. La prima Maribel ➡ ....

e. Sara ➡ ....

f. Óscar ➡ ....

g. Papá ➡ ....

h. Mamá ➡ ....

4 Underline the words in the text that describe people. List them according to the categories below.

Descripción física	Descripción de carácter

5 The verbs *ser*, *tener*, and *llevar* are generally used to describe. Indicate the descriptive words in the list below that go with the verbs in the chart. ¡Atención! Some words can be used with both *tener* and *llevar*.

tíos ○ pelo largo ○ camisa ○ ojos marrones ○ delgado ○ nervioso ○ vaqueros ○ pesimista ○ jersey ○ alegre ○ piernas largas ○ tímida ○ camiseta ○ sociable ○ pelo rizado

ser	tener	llevar

6 👥 With a partner, arrange the seating chart below for this family's dinner.

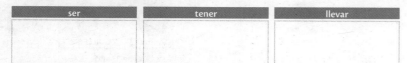

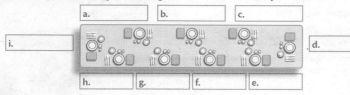

a. _____ b. _____ c. _____

i. _____   d. _____

h. _____ g. _____ f. _____ e. _____

7 👥 Tell the class about your own family celebration or tradition.

Modelo: En mi familia, nosotros...

109

INSTRUCTIONAL STRATEGIES

Activity 3

Call on individual students to share descriptions. Have other students add any missing information.

Activity 4

Remind students that what people are wearing is part of their physical description.

Activity 5

Write three adjectives on the board that describe you. Ask students if they agree and have them provide the correct verb for each characteristic. Once students have completed the descriptions, ask them to group the words in the correct category.

Activity 6

Have students arrange the table seating so that everyone has **una cena en paz**.

Activity 7

Alternative Activity

Encourage students to also describe what their family members are like, their personalities, and characteristics. Ask: **¿Cuántos son? ¿Qué comen? ¿Dónde se reúnen? ¿Quiénes se llevan mejor o peor? ¿Se visten de alguna manera especial?**

ANSWERS

Activity 3

La abuela Julia: es muy habladora, nerviosa, odia los teléfonos móviles, los vaqueros y el pelo largo en los hombres; **El tío Pepe:** es muy pesimista y habla muy poco; **La tía Carmen:** siempre habla por el móvil; **La prima Maribel:** es muy alegre, bastante supersticiosa, es actriz, no soporta el color amarillo; **Sara:** es muy tranquila, inteligente y un poco tímida; **Óscar:** no habla mucho; **Papá:** es muy hablador, optimista y sociable, sus ojos no soportan los colores claros ni los muy oscuros; **Mamá:** es muy buena.

Activity 4

Descripción física: lleva falda y camisa amarillas; lleva corbata y traje negros; lleva pantalones y vestidos de colores; lleva vaqueros viejos y camiseta.

Descripción de carácter: es muy nerviosa y habladora; es muy pesimista y habla muy poco; habla mucho (por el móvil); es muy alegre y bastante supersticiosa; es muy tranquila, inteligente y un poco tímida; , no habla mucho; es muy hablador, optimista y sociable; es muy buena.

Activity 5

Ser: delgado, nervioso, pesimista, alegre, tímida, sociable; **Tener:** pelo largo, ojos marrones, piernas largas, pelo rizado; **Llevar:** camisa, vaqueros, jersey, camiseta. (El *pelo largo* y el *pelo rizado* can also go with the verb *llevar*).

Activity 6

There are various seating arrangements possible. The objective is for students to negotiate where guests should sit and be able to explain why.

HERITAGE LANGUAGE LEARNERS

Have students research *Nochebuena* in Spain and report back on two or more common traditions for the holiday. Have them compare and contrast those traditions with those of their own family.

OBJECTIVES FOR EVALUACIÓN

- Review grammar, vocabulary and culture from the unit
- Complete self-assessment

CORE RESOURCES

- Interactive Online Materials - ELEteca

STANDARDS

- 1.2   Understand the language
- 1.3   Present information
- 2.1   Practices and perspectives
- 4.1   Compare cultures

INSTRUCTIONAL STRATEGIES

- Activities can be completed individually and then reviewed with the class. Vary by asking students if they agree with the answer given and then writing it on the board. Provide explanations as needed.
- You may wish to assign point values to each activity as a way for students to monitor their progress.
- Direct students to the indicated review pages in **En resumen** if they make more than one or two mistakes in any one section.

ANSWERS

Activity 1

guapa, largo, liso, castaño, pequeña / grande, grandes, azules, rubio, grande / pequeña, simpáticos, habladora, divertida, alegre, maleducado.

Activity 2

a. primo; **b.** abuelos; **c.** padres; **d.** hermana; **e.** hermano; **f.** tía; **g.** tío.

Activity 3

a. bufanda; **b.** falda; **c.** zapatillas; **d.** camiseta.

EVALUACIÓN

DESCRIBING PHYSICAL CHARACTERISTICS AND PERSONALITY TRAITS

1 David has written an e-mail to his friend Marie to tell her about his new friend. Read the e-mail and fill in the blanks with the correct word from the list below.

> habladora ○ alegre ○ liso ○ guapa ○ pequeña ○ divertida ○ azules ○ rubio
> grande ○ simpáticos ○ grandes ○ castaño ○ largo ○ maleducado

Mi amiga María es muy .... Lleva el pelo .... y .... de color .... Lleva gafas. Tiene la nariz .... y los ojos .... y .... Su hermano no se parece a ella porque es ...., tiene la nariz ...., los ojos oscuros y no lleva gafas. Los dos son muy .... María es muy .... y .... pero también es tímida. Su hermano es abierto y muy .... A veces es un poco irresponsable y ....

LA FAMILIA

2 Look at Guillermo's family and complete the sentences below to identify the family relationships.

a. Jacobo tiene 3 años. Es su ....
b. Carlos y Ana son sus ....
c. José y Carolina son sus ....
d. Adriana tiene 9 años. Es su ....
e. Carlitos tiene 13 años. Es su .... mayor.
f. La madre de Jacobo, es su ....
g. El padre de Jacobo se llama Juan. Es su ....

LA ROPA

3 Complete the sentences with the correct word according to the images on the right.

a. ¿Esta .... es de lana?
b. La .... de tu amiga es un poco corta.
c. Esas .... son muy cómodas.
d. No tenemos .... para hacer deporte.

PRESENT TENSE OF -ER AND -IR VERBS

4 Match the verbs to their subjects.

1. escribes
2. viven
3. comemos
4. tengo
5. aprende

a. nosotros
b. ustedes
c. yo
d. tú
e. ella

DEMONSTRATIVE ADJECTIVES

5 Complete the sentences with the correct demonstrative adjective.

a. .... camisa de ahí es como la camisa de mi padre.
b. .... profesor de allí que lleva barba es americano.
c. .... chicos de la última fila son de mi clase.
d. Tiene una falda azul como .... chaqueta que tú llevas.

POSSESSIVE ADJECTIVES

6 Select the correct option in each sentence.

a. **Mi / Nuestros / Mis** amigas son muy divertidas.
b. **Tu / Tus / Sus** casa está cerca del instituto.
c. **Mi / Nuestros / Tu** profesores son muy amables.
d. **Su / Sus / Nuestro** padres son altos.
e. **Su / Mis / Nuestras** amigas son muy simpáticas.
f. **Tu / Mis / Nuestras** compañeros están de excursión.

CULTURA

7 Answer the following questions about Mexico and compare similaties with your own country or region.

a. ¿Cómo es el bosque Chapultepec? ¿Qué tiene? ¿Cómo se llama un lugar similar en tu país o región?
b. ¿Qué hace la gente en México el Día de los Muertos? ¿Celebras algo similar por esas fechas?
c. Nombra cinco cosas importantes de la fiesta de la Quinceañera. ¿Hay una fiesta similar en tu cultura?
d. ¿En qué otros lugares se celebra la fiesta de la Quinceañera?
e. ¿Cuántos miembros tiene una familia mexicana hoy en día? ¿Cuántas personas hay en tu familia?

 **MORE IN ELETECA:** EXTRA ONLINE PRACTICE

ANSWERS

Activity 4

1. d; 2. b; 3. a; 4. c; 5. e.

Activity 5

a. Esa; b. Aquel; c. Aquellos / Esos; d. esta.

Activity 6

a. Mis; b. Tu; c. Nuestros; d. Sus; e. Mis / Nuestras; f. Mis.

Activity 7

a. Es un bosque muy grande y hay muchas fuentes, árboles y lagos;
b. La familia se reúne, se disfraza, prepara un altar con fotografías de antepasados, visita los cementerios y toma comida especial;
c. La familia, el vestido, la misa, el pastel, los regalos; d. En el resto de América Latina, Argentina, por ejemplo; e. Los papás y los hijos.

OBJECTIVES FOR EN RESUMEN: VOCABULARIO

- Review unit vocabulary and expressions
- Practice communicative skills

STANDARDS

1.2 Understand the language
1.3 Present information

INSTRUCTIONAL STRATEGIES

- Encourage students to use self-adhesive notes to place on correct objects in their house.
- Index cards can be used as flash cards with the Spanish term on one side and the English term on the other, or a picture or drawing.
- Students can work in pairs or groups, using vocabulary flashcards as they would the cards of a board game to help each other practice the unit vocabulary.
- Encourage students to write labels or captions for the photos on this page. Remind them to use the vocabulary and expressions they have learned in this unit.
- Put students in groups and hand out catalogs of different clothing stores. Either have them race to find and label as many items in Spanish as they can, or create a scavenger hunt for each group based on the known contents of each magazine, for example, **¿De qué color es la corbata en la página 14?**
- Play a game of charades using some for some of the verbs and personality traits that have been presented.
- Play a game of pictionary using the articles of clothing, physical descriptions, and parts of the body that have been presented.

EN RESUMEN: Vocabulario

La familia *Family*
la abuela *grandmother*
el abuelo *grandfather*
los abuelos *grandparents*

el esposo *husband*
la esposa *wife*
la hermana *sister*
el hermano *brother*
los hermanos *siblings*
la hija *daughter*
el hijo *son*
los hijos *children*
la madre *mother*
la nieta *granddaughter*
el nieto *grandson*
los nietos *grandchildren*
el padre *father*
los padres *parents*
el primo/a *cousin*
la sobrina *niece*
el sobrino *nephew*
la tía *aunt*
el tío *uncle*

La ropa *Clothes*
el abrigo *coat*
la bota *boot*
la bufanda *scarf*
el calcetín *sock*
la camisa *shirt*
la camiseta *t-shirt*
la chaqueta *jacket*
el cinturón *belt*
la corbata *tie*
la falda *skirt*

las gafas *glasses*

la gorra *baseball cap*
los jeans *jeans*
los pantalones *pants*
las sandalias *sandals*
el suéter *sweater*
los tenis *sneakers*
el traje *suit*
el vestido *dress*
los zapatos de tacón *high-heeled shoes*

Las descripciones *Descriptions*
abierto/a *outgoing*
aburrido/a *boring*
amable *polite*
antipático/a *disagreeable*
alto/a *tall*
azules *blue*
bajo/a *short*
barba *beard*
bigote *mustache*
calvo *bald*
castaño/a *light brown*
claros *light*
corto *short*
delgado/a *thin*
divertido/a *fun*
feo/a *unattractive*
fuerte *strong*
gordo/a *overweight*
grandes *big*
guapo/a *attractive*
hablador/a *talkative*
inteligente *intelligent*
joven *young*
largo *long*
liso *straight*
maleducado/a *rude*
mayor *old*
marrones *brown*
moreno/a *dark brown*
negros *black*
oscuros *dark*

pelirrojo/a *red hair*
pequeña *small*
pequeños *little*
rizado *curly*
rubio/a *blonde*

tímido/a *shy*
trabajador/a *hard-working*
una camisa blanca *a white shirt*
vago/a *lazy*
verdes *green*

Verbos *Verbs*
abrir *to open*
aprender *to learn*
asistir *to attend*
beber *to drink*
comer *to eat*
discutir *to argue*
escribir *to write*
leer *to read*
llevar *to wear*
tener... años *to be... years old*
tener calor *to be warm*
tener frío *to be cold*
tener hambre *to be hungry*
tener sed *to be thirsty*
tener sueño *to be sleepy*
tener *to have*
ver *to see*
vivir *to live*

Palabras y expresiones útiles *Useful words and expressions*
ahí *there*
allí *over there*
aquí *here*
la boca *mouth*
la nariz *nose*
los ojos *eyes*
un poco *a little*

112

EN RESUMEN: Gramática

PRESENT TENSE OF -ER AND -IR VERBS
(See page 100)

	COMER (to eat)	VIVIR (to live)
yo	como	vivo
tú	comes	vives
usted/él/ella	come	vive
nosotros/as	comemos	vivimos
vosotros/as	coméis	vivís
ustedes/ellos/ellas	comen	viven

POSSESSIVE ADJECTIVES
(See page 101)

Singular			Plural	
Masculine	Feminine		Masculine	Feminine
mi carro	**mi** casa		**mis** carros	**mis** casas
tu carro	**tu** casa		**tus** carros	**tus** casas
su carro	**su** casa		**sus** carros	**sus** casas
nuestro carro	**nuestra** casa		**nuestros** carros	**nuestras** casas
vuestro carro	**vuestra** casa		**vuestros** carros	**vuestras** casas
su carro	**su** casa		**sus** carros	**sus** casas

DEMONSTRATIVE ADJECTIVES
(See page 102)

Location of speaker	Singular		Plural	
	Masculine	Feminine	Masculine	Feminine
aquí	**este**	**esta**	**estos**	**estas**
ahí	**ese**	**esa**	**esos**	**esas**
allí	**aquel**	**aquella**	**aquellos**	**aquellas**

aquí   **ahí**   **allí**

113

OBJECTIVES FOR EN RESUMEN: GRAMÁTICA

- Review unit grammar
- Practice communicative skills

STANDARDS

1.2 Understand the language
1.3 Present information

INSTRUCTIONAL STRATEGIES

- Model how to review grammar.
- Have them review the Learning Outcomes in the unit opener to assess whether they feel they have mastered the main ideas and skills.
- Ask them if they can remember additional examples for each grammar topic.
- Remind students to go back to the appropriate page in the unit to review any grammar topic they may need help with.
- Invite students to redo some of the grammar activities they completed in this unit.
- Ask them what grammar activities they found easy and which they found challenging. Encourage them to repeat any activities they found particularly challenging.
- Have students role-play conversations based on each of the pictures on the page. They may write their conversations first and then present them to the class. Encourage them to be creative.

OBJECTIVES FOR UNIT OPENER

- Introduce unit theme: **Todos los días lo mismo** about daily routines and everyday activities
- Culture: Learn about daily life in Hispanic countries

STANDARDS

1.2 Understand the language
2.1 Practices and perspectives

INSTRUCTIONAL STRATEGIES

- Introduce unit theme and objectives: Talk about daily and weekly activities. Have students look at the photograph. Read the caption aloud: **Este muchacho tiene hambre por la mañana.**
- Ask questions to recycle content from previous unit. For instance: **¿Cómo tiene el pelo? ¿Cuántos años tiene el muchacho? ¿Qué ropa lleva?**
- Use the photograph to preview unit vocabulary, such as: **desayuno.** Help students access meaning by making frequent use of gestures or visuals.
- Ask the introductory questions
  - **¿Cómo es el muchacho?**
  - **¿Dónde está?**
  - **¿Qué hace?**
  - **Y tú, ¿tienes hambre por la mañana?**
- Ask related questions: **¿Qué come?** Ask some yes/no questions: **¿Lleva gafas? ¿Tiene los ojos azules?**

ANSWERS

Answers will vary. Possible answers might include the following.
- El muchacho es simpático. Tiene el pelo castaño.
- El muchacho está en su casa. Está en la cocina.
- El muchacho come / desayuna.

SLOWER-PACED LEARNERS

Brainstorm different food items that people eat for breakfast, lunch and dinner, and write them on the board.

ADVANCED LEARNERS

Put students into pairs to interview each other about their breakfast routines, asking questions about when, where, what, and with whom they each. Have them report back to the class compare their habits.

HERITAGE LANGUAGE LEARNERS

Have students talk about their meal traditions and those of their families. If students have been to Spanish-speaking countries ask them about what they ate there. Encourage students to remember the names of food and dishes in Spanish

UNIDAD 4
TODOS LOS DÍAS LO MISMO

Este muchacho tiene hambre por la mañana.

>> ¿Cómo es el muchacho? ¿Dónde está? ¿Qué hace?

>> Y tú, ¿tienes hambre por la mañana?

114

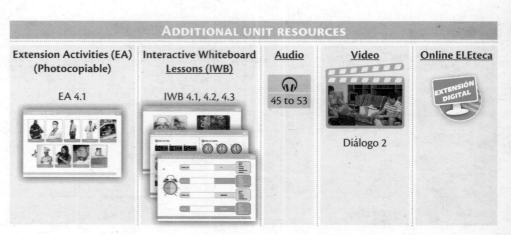

ADDITIONAL UNIT RESOURCES

Extension Activities (EA) (Photocopiable)	Interactive Whiteboard Lessons (IWB)	Audio	Video	Online ELEteca
EA 4.1	IWB 4.1, 4.2, 4.3	45 to 53	Diálogo 2	EXTENSIÓN DIGITAL

In this unit, you will learn to:

- Ask and give the day and time
- Describe daily routines and everyday activities
- Talk about professions
- Make plans

Using

- Stem-changing verbs *e>ie*, *o>ue*, and *e>i*
- Present tense of *hacer* and *salir*
- Reflexive verbs

Cultural Connections

- Share information about daily life in Hispanic countries, and compare cultural similarities

SABOR HISPANO

El puente entre las Américas

- El Salvador, Guatemala, Honduras, Nicaragua y Costa Rica

¡ACCIÓN!

115

LEARNING OUTCOMES

- Ask and give the day and time
- Describe daily routines and everyday activities
- Talk about professions
- Make plans

INSTRUCTIONAL STRATEGIES

- Use the unit opener to preview the vocabulary and cultural topics for this unit.
- Have students look at the images on this page and relate them to the objectives listed. Ask questions such as: **¿Qué ven en estas fotos? ¿Qué hacen las personas? ¿Qué profesión tiene la mujer?**
- Invite students to read the topic for **Sabor hispano** and preview that section in the unit. Ask questions such as: **¿Es un edificio o un templo? ¿Es una montaña o un volcán?**
- Ask students to predict what they think the episode for **¡Acción!** will be about. Ask: **¿Con quién habla María?**
- Have students work in pairs to talk about the images using the questions you have modeled. Then have volunteers present to the class what they understand this unit to be about.

SLOWER-PACED LEARNERS

Encourage students to recycle and retrieve vocabulary, including verbs, from previous units. Ask them to describe the pictures using colors, adjectives, **ser / estar**, and regular verbs.

ADVANCED LEARNERS

Ask students to prepare questions about the pictures using question words seen in previous units.

HERITAGE LANGUAGE LEARNERS

Have students share what they know about the countries listed in **Sabor hispano**. Ask: **¿Conoces El Salvador? ¿Conoces salvadoreños? ¿Qué comen? ¿Cuál es la capital de Costa Rica? ¿Cómo se llaman las personas de Nicaragua? ¿Y de Honduras?**, etc.

THREE MODES OF COMMUNICATION: UNIT 4			
	INTERPERSONAL	INTERPRETIVE	PRESENTATIONAL
HABLAMOS DE...	6	1, 2, 4, 5	6
COMUNICA	2, 5	1, 3, 4	5
¡ACCIÓN!	1, 2	3, 4, 5, 7	1, 6
PALABRA POR PALABRA	2, 4, 5, 6, 9, 10	3, 5, 7, 8	5, 10, 11
GRAMÁTICA	1, 3, 5	2, 4, 6, 8	3, 5, 7, 9
DESTREZAS		1, 2	2
CULTURA		SABOR HISPANO	
RELATO	3, 5	1, 2	4

OBJECTIVES FOR HABLAMOS DE...

- Understand language in context
- Preview vocabulary: making plans, expressions of time, days of the week, and professions
- Preview grammatical structures: Irregular verbs; present tense of *hacer*, *venir*, *salir*.
- Read and listen to a conversation about Daniel making plans with his friends.

CORE RESOURCES

- Audio Program: 45
- Interactive White Board Lessons: IWB 4.1, 4.2

STANDARDS

- 1.1 Engage in conversation
- 1.2 Understand the language
- 4.2 Compare cultures

INSTRUCTIONAL STRATEGIES

Activity 1

- Ask students to describe what the people in the photograph are wearing. Then have them choose the best text for the image.
- After reviewing answers, call on students to read the sentences in the other texts that did not correspond to the image.

🎧 45 Activity 2

- Before reading the conversation, project IWB 4.1, *Todos los días*. Write the following on the board: *Todos los días me levanto a las 6*. *Todos los días hago deporte.* Use gestures and facial expressions to show getting up in the morning and doing sports. Point to each activity and say, *Todos los días*, as a cue for students to respond with the activity depicted, *me levanto*, *hago deporte* and so on.

- Have students quickly review the dialogue before they listen.
- Have students listen to the conversation and answer the questions.

GRAMMAR NOTE

The verbs *despertarse* and *levantarse* are introduced here as lexical items. Reflexive verbs will be presented in the grammar section. For now, help students understand the meaning as needed: **"Se despierta" significa abrir los ojos. "Se levanta" es salir de la cama.**

ANSWERS

Activity 1

Texto 2

Activity 2

a. El padre de Lucía; b. Lucía; c. Andrés; d. Andrés; e. La madre de Candela; f. Daniel.

HABLAMOS DE... Los planes

1 Look at the image below of getting together to make plans. Then choose the text that best describes the image.

Texto 1
En la fotografía puedes ver a dos muchachos y a una muchacha que lleva gafas. La muchacha de gafas lleva una camiseta verde. En la imagen aparece una muchacha rubia, una morena y dos muchachos morenos.

Texto 2
En la fotografía aparecen dos muchachas, una rubia y una morena. Los dos muchachos son castaños. Las dos muchachas y los dos muchachos llevan chaquetas y el muchacho de gafas lleva una camiseta verde.

Texto 3
La fotografía representa a unos amigos. Las dos muchachas llevan bufanda. Aparecen dos muchachas morenas y dos muchachos rubios. El muchacho de gafas lleva barba.

2 🎧 45 **Listen to the conversation. Then write the name of the person described in each of the statements below.**

Daniel: ¿Qué les parece si hacemos un poco de deporte?
Lucía: Yo tengo mucho sueño. Me levanto todos los días a las 7 de la mañana.
Andrés: Yo no puedo ir. Los miércoles salgo a cenar con mis padres y me acuesto muy tarde.
Candela: ¿Y a qué hora estudias?
Andrés: Por las mañanas, me visto muy rápido y estudio un poco.
Daniel: Yo, en cambio, me despierto a las 9 y llego siempre tarde a la escuela.
Lucía: Chicos… Parecemos cuatro abuelos. Mi padre, que es médico, trabaja todo el día y siempre hace alguna actividad con nosotros.
Candela: Es verdad. Mi madre es profesora y siempre hace mucho deporte.
Daniel: Entonces, ¿por qué no quedamos mañana?
Lucía: Perfecto. ¿Quedamos a las 4?
Daniel: Vale. ¿Dónde quedamos?
Candela: Podemos quedar en la puerta de la escuela.
Andrés: Estupendo. Entonces… quedamos a las 4 en la puerta.

a. Es médico. .....El padre de Lucía.....
b. Se despierta siempre muy temprano. ....
c. Sale a cenar con sus padres todos los miércoles. ....
d. Estudia por la mañana. ....
e. Es profesora. ....
f. Llega tarde a la escuela. ....

116

SLOWER-PACED LEARNERS

For additional oral practice, have students practice the conversation in Activity 2 in small groups.

ADVANCED LEARNERS

Have students listen to the conversation in Activity 2 with their books closed. Before playing this audio, pose these questions to get them to focus on the main ideas: **¿De qué hablan los muchachos? ¿Qué deciden?**

HERITAGE LANGUAGE LEARNERS

Focusing just on the image in Activity 1, have students write possible lines of dialogue or thought bubbles for each of the people in it, anticipating what they might hear in Activity 2.

3 **45 Listen again to the conversation and repeat after the speaker.**

! ■ The verb **quedar** is used to arrange a time or place to meet with friends.
  ¿A qué hora **quedamos***? At what time should we meet?*
  Quedamos *a las cuatro. Let's meet at four.*
  ¿Dónde **quedamos***? Where should we meet?*
  Podemos **quedar** *en el parque. We can meet at the park.*

4 **Match the image to the correct description.**

1. ◯ Se levanta a las siete y veinticinco.
2. ◯ Estudia en la escuela hasta las dos.
3. ◯ Come a las dos y media de la tarde.
4. ◯ Hace deporte a las cinco.
5. ◯ Ve la televisión a las ocho.
6. ◯ Se acuesta a las diez y media.

5 **Look at the times below and write what the person in Activity 4 does at that time.**

a. 8:00 de la noche.....................
b. 7:25 de la mañana..................
c. 5:00 de la tarde.....................
d. Hasta las 2:00 de la tarde.......
e. 2:30 de la tarde.......................
f. 10:30 de la noche...................

6 **With a partner, take turns asking each other what you do at the following times.**
Modelo:

¿Qué haces a las 10 de la mañana?

Estudio en la biblioteca.

1. 9:00 de la mañana
2. 12:00 de la tarde
3. 4:00 de la tarde
4. 9:00 de la noche

Unas actividades:
• caminar a
• comer
• descansar
• escuchar
• estudiar
• hablar con
• pasear por
• ver

117

INSTRUCTIONAL STRATEGIES

 45 Activity 3
• Review the verb **quedar** and have students listen for its use as they listen to the conversation and repeat after the speaker.
• Use the audio to focus students' attention on rhythm, intonation, and pronunciation.

Alternative Activity
  Divide the class into four groups and assign a role from the conversation to each group. Each group will repeat that person's lines.

Activity 4
  Use IWB 4.2, **Los relojes** to pre-teach basic vocabulary about the times presented in the activity. Have students match the time to the correct clock.

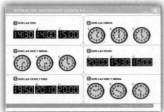

ANSWERS: FOR IWB 4.2
  1. reloj B; **2.** reloj A; **3.** reloj B; **4.** reloj C; **5.** reloj A; **6.** reloj C.
• Then have students complete Activity 4.

Activity 5
  Call on students to review answers in complete sentences: **A las ocho de la noche ve la televisión.**

Activity 6
• Review the activities in the recycling box and go over the times in the activity together.
• Circulate around the room as student pairs ask each other.

ANSWERS
Activity 4
  1. c; **2.** e; **3.** f; **4.** a; **5.** b; **6.** d.

Activity 5
  a. Ve la televisión; **b.** Se levanta; **c.** Hace deporte; **d.** Estudia; **e.** Come; **f.** Se acuesta.

Activity 6
  Answers will vary, but should include some of the vocabulary from the dialogue related to daily activities.

ADVANCED LEARNERS

At the end of the lesson, write some activities that students usually do on the board. Ask them to write down the times they do those activities. Then take a class poll. Have a student ask:
¿Cuántos ven la televisión a las 8? ¿A las 9?, etc.
¿Cuántos se levantan a las 6? ¿A las 7?, etc.
¿Cuántos hacen deporte a las 8 de la tarde? and so on.
Then put students into pairs to ask each other at least one follow-up question related to each activity.

OBJECTIVES FOR COMUNICA

• Present the communicative functions of the unit:
 – Talk about every day activities
 – Talk about different times of the day
• Practice using numbers to tell time

CORE RESOURCES

• Interactive Online Materials - ELEteca

STANDARDS

1.1 Engage in conversation
1.2 Understand the language

INSTRUCTIONAL STRATEGIES FOR TALKING ABOUT EVERYDAY ACTIVITIES

Walk students through the explanations on this page to learn time expressions, such as: **Todos los días**, **Por la mañana...**, **Por la tarde...**, **Por la noche**.

Activity 1

Project the image and call on students to recount Carmen's day, first by reading through the sentences in order, then using the images only. Provide cues as needed to help students go through the images.

Activity 2

• Have students answer the questions on their own.
• Then have students work in pairs to ask and respond to the questions in this activity. Circulate around the room to check that students are on task and responding correctly.

ANSWERS

Activity 1

1. e; **2.** a; **3.** d; **4.** f; **5.** b; **6.** c.

Activity 2

Answers will vary, but should reflect proper use of the time expressions taught.

SLOWER-PACED LEARNERS

For additional practice, have students add or change the time expressions in the sentences in Activity 1 and practice saying them with a partner.

ADVANCED LEARNERS

Tell students to add two more questions to the list in Activity 2 and ask them to their partners.

COMUNICA

TALKING ABOUT EVERYDAY ACTIVITIES

■ **Todos los días...**
Everyday...

...**me levanto** a las ocho. *...I get up at eight o'clock.*
...**desayuno**. *...I have breakfast.*
...**como** en casa. *...I eat (lunch) at home.*
...**ceno** con mis padres. *...I have dinner with my parents.*

■ **Por la mañana...**
In the morning...

...**me ducho** antes de desayunar. *...I shower before having breakfast.*
...**desayuno** en casa. *...I have breakfast at home.*
...**hago** la cama. *...I make my bed.*
...**estudio** en la escuela. *...I study at school.*

■ **Por la tarde...**
In the afternoon...

...**hago** deporte. *...I play sports.*
...**hago** la tarea. *...I do my homework.*

■ **Por la noche...**
At night...

...**ceno**. *...I have dinner.*
...**me acuesto** tarde. *...I go to bed late.*

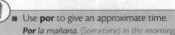 ■ Use **por** to give an approximate time. ***Por** la mañana. (Sometime) In the morning.*

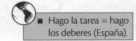 ■ Hago la tarea = hago los deberes (España).

1 Look at what Carmen does every day. Then, match the actions listed below to the correct images.

   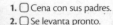

1. ☐ Cena con sus padres.
2. ☐ Se levanta pronto.
3. ☐ Hace la tarea.
4. ☐ Se acuesta a las 10:00 de la noche.
5. ☐ Se viste.
6. ☐ Estudia en la escuela.

2 Answer the following questions. Then, with a partner, take turns asking each other.

a. ¿Haces la tarea todos los días? ....
b. ¿Dónde estudias: en casa, en la biblioteca...? ....
c. ¿Dónde comes: en casa, en la escuela...? ....
d. ¿Con quién cenas: con tus padres, con tus amigos...? ....

118

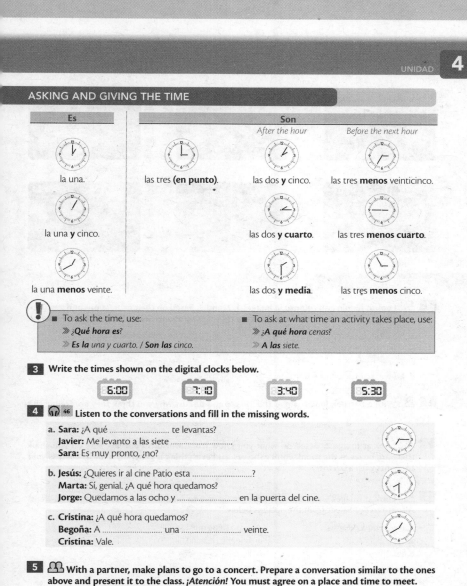

ASKING AND GIVING THE TIME

Es	Son	
	After the hour	*Before the next hour*
la una.	las tres **(en punto)**.	
	las dos **y** cinco.	las tres **menos** veinticinco.
la una **y** cinco.	las dos **y cuarto**.	las tres **menos cuarto**.
la una **menos** veinte.	las dos **y media**.	las tres **menos** cinco.

> (!) ■ To ask the time, use:
> » **¿Qué hora es?**
> » **Es la** una y cuarto. / **Son las** cinco.
>
> ■ To ask at what time an activity takes place, use:
> » **¿A qué hora** cenas?
> » **A las** siete.

3 Write the times shown on the digital clocks below.

> `6:00` `7:10` `3:40` `5:30`

4 🎧 46 Listen to the conversations and fill in the missing words.

a. Sara: ¿A qué .... te levantas?
Javier: Me levanto a las siete ....
Sara: Es muy pronto, ¿no?

b. Jesús: ¿Quieres ir al cine Patio esta ....?
Marta: Sí, genial. ¿A qué hora quedamos?
Jorge: Quedamos a las ocho y .... en la puerta del cine.

c. Cristina: ¿A qué hora quedamos?
Begoña: A .... una .... veinte.
Cristina: Vale.

5 With a partner, make plans to go to a concert. Prepare a conversation similar to the ones above and present it to the class. ¡Atención! You must agree on a place and time to meet.

Modelo: E1: ¿Quieres ir al concierto de José Sol?
E2: Vale. ¿A qué hora quedamos?

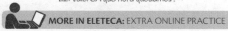 **MORE IN ELETECA:** EXTRA ONLINE PRACTICE

119

INSTRUCTIONAL STRATEGIES FOR ASKING AND GIVING THE TIME

- Walk students through the explanations on this page. Write the following on the board: **¿Qué hora es? Son** _____. Explain that these expressions are used to ask and tell time in Spanish.
- Use the sentence stems from IWB 4.3, **Preguntar y decir la hora** to show various times on a clock with moveable hands or use the one in the projection. Indicate times on the clock as you say them. For example, **Son las once y cinco / diez / cuarto / veinte / veinticinco / media**. Help students understand the meaning of the various expressions used to tell time in Spanish.

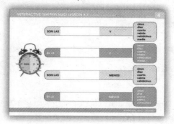

Activity 3

Have students check their answers with a partner.

🎧 46 **Activity 4**

See audioscript on page APP7.

Activity 5

Review the **Modelo** with students and ask them for ways they might continue the conversation to agree on a place and time to meet. Expand to include where they should meet.

ANSWERS

Activity 3

Son las seis; Son las siete y diez; Son las cuatro menos veinte; Son las cinco y media.

Activity 4

a. hora, y cuarto; **b.** noche, media; **c.** la, menos.

ADVANCED LEARNERS

Have students write their school schedule and talk with each other using expressions, such as **A las 10:00 tengo Matemáticas. A las 11:30 tengo Literatura**, etc.

HERITAGE LANGUAGE LEARNERS

Ask students whether their families or Latino friends do daily activities at different times. If they have been to Spanish-speaking countries encourage them to share what they know about daily routines in the Spanish-speaking world.

OBJECTIVES FOR COMUNICA

- Present the communicative functions of the unit:
  – Asking and giving time
  – Talking about activities done at different times of the day

CORE RESOURCES

- Audio Program: Track 46
- Interactive Whiteboard Lesson: IWB 4.3

STANDARDS

1.1 Engage in conversation
1.2 Understand the language
1.3 Present information
4.1 Compare languages

OBJECTIVES FOR ¡ACCIÓN!

- Provide students with a structured approach to viewing the video
- Contextualize the content of the unit in a familiar scenario

CORE RESOURCES

- Unit Video 4 – Problemas de horarios
- Online Materials - ELEteca

STANDARDS

1.1   Interpersonal communication
1.2   Interpretive communication
2.1   Culture: Practices and perspectives

INSTRUCTIONAL STRATEGIES

Previewing: Antes del video

Activity 1

Read the title of the video and direct students' attention to the images. Tell students to use all of the context clues available to them to make educated guesses.

Activity 2

- Elicit different expressions that they can use to express opinions (*Para mí, En mi opinión, Pienso / Creo / Opino que...*) and show agreement (*Para mí, también. / Sí, es verdad. / Creo que sí.*) or disagreement (*Para mí, no. / No, no es verdad. / Creo que no.*).
- Put students in pairs to discuss their ideas.

Activity 3

- Ask follow-up questions: *¿Hay habitaciones desordenadas en tu casa? ¿Cuáles son? ¿Por qué están desordenadas?*

Activity 4

- Have students answer the questions individually.
- Take a class poll to confirm the correct answers.

ANSWERS

Activity 1

a. No están contentos; e. Hablan de los horarios de clase.

Activity 4

a. un lápiz; b. escribir algo importante

¡ACCIÓN! Problemas de horarios

1.   2.   3.
4.   5.   6.

ANTES DEL VIDEO

1 Look at Juanjo and Alfonso in Images 1, 2, and 3. Based on their expressions and gestures, how do you think they are feeling? What are they talking about? Select from the options below.

a. No están contentos.
b. Hablan de una fiesta.
c. Tienen hambre.
d. Llaman por teléfono a sus amigos.
e. Hablan de los horarios de clase.
f. Hablan de los videojuegos.
g. Están enfermos.

2 With a partner, look again at the images and discuss why you think they are feeling this way.

3 Look at Image 2. Based on what you know from previous episodes, why do you think there are boxes in the room, empty shelves, and everything is generally a mess? Discuss your thoughts with a partner.

4 Look at Images 5 and 6. What does Juanjo give to Alfonso? What do you think he wants Alfonso to do? Select from the options below.

Juanjo le da a Alfonso...	Alfonso tiene que...
a. un papel.	a. borrar su horario.
b. un lápiz.	b. llamar a los amigos.
c. su teléfono celular.	c. escribir algo importante.
d. una goma de borrar.	d. hacer la tarea.

120

DURANTE EL VIDEO

5 Match the days and times to the correct activities for each of the boys.

Actividades de Juanjo

1. Lunes, martes y jueves a las 10:00h
2. Miércoles y viernes a las 7:00h de la mañana
3. Los martes por la tarde
4. Todos los lunes por la tarde

a. queda con unos amigos.
b. va al gimnasio.
c. se levanta.
d. empieza las clases.

Actividades de Alfonso

1. De lunes a viernes a las 8:30h
2. Todos los días a las 7:00h de la mañana
3. Todas las tardes

a. se levanta.
b. empiezan sus clases.
c. estudia y hace las tareas.

6 Select the correct profession from the list below for Juanjo's mother and Alfonso's father. Then write the times they usually get up for work.

bombero ○ enfermera ○ mecánico ○ profesor ○ cocinera ○ veterinario

Madre de Juanjo:............................ Padre de Alfonso:............................

7 Select the statements that apply to the episode.

a. ☐ Tienen muchas cajas en la habitación porque acaban de mudarse.
b. ☐ Comparten habitación.
c. ☐ Tienen muchas cosas del supermercado.
d. ☐ Los muchachos no están contentos con sus horarios.
e. ☐ Están tristes porque tienen poco tiempo libre.
f. ☐ Juanjo decide que no puede hacer las tareas de la casa por las tardes.

g. ☐ Alfonso tiene un padre mecánico.
h. ☐ La madre de Juanjo trabaja en un restaurante.
i. ☐ El plan de Juanjo es no hacer ninguna tarea de la casa.
j. ☐ Alfonso sale todas las noches.
k. ☐ Le da un lápiz a Alfonso para escribir las tareas de la casa que tiene que hacer.
l. ☐ Alfonso cree que algunas actividades de Juanjo son cómicas.

DESPUÉS DEL VIDEO

8 👥 Create a schedule of activities you have from Monday to Friday. Then in groups of three, find a time when you are all free to play basketball.

9 👥 In the episode, Juanjo tries to avoid doing his share of the chores. What chores do you do at home? Write a few sentences about what you do and when. Use verbs like *limpiar* (to clean), *lavar* (to wash), and *ordenar* (to straighten up).

 MORE IN ELETECA: EXTRA ONLINE PRACTICE

121

- After reviewing the answers, ask students to share their comments and impressions of the video and identify their favorite parts: *¿Qué opinas del video? ¿Cuál es tu parte favorita? ¿Cómo son tus horarios, buenos o malos? ¿Por qué? ¿Tienes tiempo libre? ¿Cuándo?*

Post-viewing: Después del video

Activity 8

- You may want to give students the option of changing the free-time activity to one that may suit their interests better than playing basketball.
- If a group is struggling to get started, suggest that begin by having each member state when he or she has free time. Suggest that someone in the group take notes on everyone's availability. Then have them should refer to the notes to determine the best time to get together.
- As an added challenge, combine two groups to see if they can find time to play a basketball game against each other (or do some other activity together).

Activity 9

- Elicit examples of chores from the class and write the verb phrases on the board. Call on a volunteer to write a sample sentence on the board using one of the phrases.

ANSWERS

Activity 5

Actividades de Juanjo: **1.** d; **2.** c; **3.** b; **4.** a.
Actividades de Alfonso: **1.** b; **2.** a; **3.** c.

Activity 6

Madre de Juanjo: enfermera; se levanta a las cinco y media de la mañana
Padre de Alfonso: mecánico; se levanta a las seis de la mañana

Activity 7

a, b, d, e, f, g, i, k, l

ADVANCED LEARNERS

Convert Activity 9 into a **Find someone who...** class mingling activity. Have students make a list of five different household chores and when they are done. Then have them survey the class until the find someone in the class who does the chore at the time they specified:

A: Ben, ¿lavas los platos por las noches?
B: No, no los lavo. Mi padre los lava cada noche.
A: Carla, ¿lavas los platos por las noches?
C: Sí, lavo los platos cada noche después de la cena.

HERITAGE LANGUAGE LEARNERS

Have students compare and contrast their own schedules to those of Juanjo and Alfonso in the video. Encourage them to write at least five sentences identifying similarities or differences.

INSTRUCTIONAL STRATEGIES

Viewing: Durante el video

Activity 5

- Before playing the video, give students time to read the phrases. Go over the instructions. Refer back to the images and confirm which character is Juanjo and which is Alfonso.
- Play the video. Go over the answers as a class.

Activities 6 and 7

- Go over the instructions to both activities before playing the video a second time. Invite students to mark any answers they remember. If they're not sure, suggest that they mark the material lightly or write notes nearby. This will help focus their viewing of the video for the second time.

OBJECTIVES FOR LOS DÍAS DE LA SEMANA

- Present the vocabulary needed to practice the communicative and grammatical functions for the unit: days of the week and schedules
- Identify days of the week in Spanish
- Talk about events during the week

CORE RESOURCES

- Audio Program: Track 47
- Interactive Online Materials - ELEteca

STANDARDS

1.1 Engage in conversation
1.2 Understand the language
1.3 Present information
3.2 Acquire information
4.1 Compare languages

INSTRUCTIONAL STRATEGIES

🎧 47 Activity 1

- After listening to the audio and repeating the days of the week, write the days on the board and have students repeat. Then erase everything but the first letter of each day of the week and use them as prompts, asking students to say the days of the week.
- Review the sample sentences and point out the use of the definite articles, plural forms, and how to state the day.
- You can also introduce additional vocabulary: **hoy**, **ayer**, and **mañana**.

Activity 2

Model the activity a few times with students to get them started.

Activity 3

- Write two sentences on the board: **El martes voy al cine. Los martes voy al cine**.
- Tell students that the first sentence states that you are going to the movies this coming Tuesday while the second sentence states a weekly habit of going to the movies every Tuesday.

GRAMMAR NOTE

- Point out that the days of the week in Spanish end in **–s**, except **sábado** and **domingo**.
- Therefore, the plural for **lunes**, **martes**, **miércoles**, **jueves**, **viernes** is the same as the singular, for example: **el martes** and **los martes**.

Activity 4

To vary, have students ask you about your own schedule during the week.

ANSWERS

Activity 3

a. los lunes; b. los martes; c. los miércoles; d. los jueves; e. los viernes; f. los sábados; g. los domingos; h. los fines de semana.

HERITAGE LANGUAGE LEARNERS

Encourage students to add extra information about what they are doing at each of the times in Activity 4 as well.

PALABRA POR PALABRA Los días de la semana

1 🎧 47 Listen to the days of the week and repeat after the speaker.

marzo

lunes	martes	miércoles	jueves	viernes	sábado	domingo
1	2	3	4	5	6	7
8	9	10	11	12	13	14
15	16	17	18	19	20	21
22	23	24	25	26	27	28
29	30	31				

- Most calendars in Spanish begin with Monday, not Sunday.
- The days of the week, like the months, are written in lower-case.
- Use the definite article, **el**, before the days of the week to say *on Monday, on Tuesday...* *Mi cumpleaños es **el lunes**. My birthday is on Monday.*
- In the plural, the days of the week express the idea of doing something regularly. *Tengo clase de música **los sábados**. I have music lessons on Saturdays.*
- The definite article, **el**, is not used when stating what day of the week it is. *Hoy es **domingo**. Today is Sunday.*
- Use **el fin de semana** to express weekend in Spanish. ***Los fines de semana** estudio en casa. On weekends, I study at home.*

2 👥 Using the calendar above, practice saying a date to your partner. He/She will respond with the day of the week.

Modelo: E1: ¿Qué día de la semana es el 4 de marzo?
E2: Es jueves.

3 Write the plural forms of the days of the week.

a. el lunes _los lunes_   c. el miércoles _____   e. el viernes _____   g. el domingo _____
b. el martes _____   d. el jueves _____   f. el sábado _los sábados_   h. el fin de semana _____

4 👥 With a partner, ask each other where you are at the following days and time during the week.

Modelo:
E1: ¿Dónde estás los lunes a las 8 de la mañana?
E2: Estoy en casa.

a. los viernes a las 4 de la tarde   d. los sábados por la noche
b. los sábados a las 10 de la mañana   e. los martes a las 12 de la tarde
c. los domingos por la mañana   f. los jueves a las 11 de la mañana

5 Read the conversation between Anabel and her friend, Olga. Then complete the chart below with Olga's activities.

Anabel   Olga

Olga, ¿cuándo estudias español?

¿Cuándo ves televisión?

¿Cuándo navegas por Internet?

¿Cuándo tienes clase de baile?

Los martes y los jueves por la mañana.

Normalmente los sábados por la tarde.

Por la tarde, todos los días.

Por la tarde, los lunes y miércoles.

navegar por Internet ○ estudiar español ○ tener clase de baile ○ ver televisión

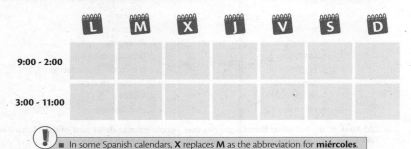

	L	M	X	J	V	S	D
9:00 - 2:00							
3:00 - 11:00							

(!) ■ In some Spanish calendars, **X** replaces **M** as the abbreviation for **miércoles**. Why do you think this is?

6 Answer the following questions. Then tell your partner when you do these things.

Modelo: Estudio español los martes antes de clase, ¿y tú?

a. ¿Cuándo estudias español?
b. ¿Cuándo navegas por Internet?
c. ¿Cuándo ves televisión?
d. ¿Cuándo tienes clase de baile (música, karate, religión…)?

123

INSTRUCTIONAL STRATEGIES

Activity 5

- Ask students what they think Anabel and Olga are talking about. Have them read the dialogue and confirm their predictions.
- Call on students to role-play the conversation to make sure students understand the content.
- Then have students to complete the chart showing Olga's activities for the week.

CULTURAL NOTE

Review the note about calendars and ask students to draw their own conclusions. Explain that the X is used to avoid confusing **miércoles** with **martes** as they both begin with **m**.

Activity 6

To vary from the question and answer format, have student pairs present to the class.

ANSWERS

Activity 5

Lunes: Navega por Internet por la tarde. Tiene clases de baile por la tarde. **Martes:** Estudia español por la mañana. Navega por Internet por la tarde. **Miércoles:** Navega por Internet por la tarde. Tiene clases de baile por la tarde. **Jueves:** Estudia español por la mañana. Navega por Internet por la tarde. **Viernes:** Navega por Internet por la tarde. **Sábado:** Ve la televisión por la tarde. Navega por Internet por la tarde. **Domingo:** Navega por Internet por lá tarde.

Activity 6

Answers will vary and should reflect the vocabulary and expressions taught.

SLOWER-PACED LEARNERS

Once the sentences have been corrected, have the slower-paced learners students write them on the board or type them on the computer.

ADVANCED LEARNERS

Students guess which activity is not true from the ones provided by the heritage language learners. Have them find out information to correct the false statement.

HERITAGE LANGUAGE LEARNERS

Have students write four activities that they usually do on different days and times of the week: **Los lunes me levanto a las 10:00.** One of those activities should be untrue.

OBJECTIVES FOR LAS PROFESIONES

- Present the vocabulary needed to practice the communicative and grammatical functions for the unit: jobs and occupations
- Talk about what people do

CORE RESOURCES

- Extension Activities: EA 4.1
- Audio Program: 48

STANDARDS

1.1   Engage in conversation
1.2   Understand the language
1.3   Present information
3.2   Acquire information
4.2   Compare cultures

INSTRUCTIONAL STRATEGIES

🎧 48 Activity 7

- Allow students time to fill in the spaces using the professions in the word bank. Remind students to use the correct gender.
- Play the audio to confirm.

Audioscript

1. Hola, me llamo Adela. Soy profesora y trabajo en una escuela; 2. Buenos días. Yo soy Antonio. Trabajo en un taller, porque soy mecánico; 3. Me llamo Elisa, soy enfermera y trabajo en un hospital; 4. Hola a todos. Mi nombre es David. Soy bombero y trabajo en Barcelona; 5. Me encantan los animales. Soy veterinaria y trabajo en la Clínica Mascotas; 6. Hola, ¿qué tal? Soy Carlos, el cocinero de los famosos y me encanta mi trabajo.

Activity 8

- Introduce the activity by asking students to describe where the people in Activity 7 probably work.
- Circulate around the room to check that students are on task and responding correctly.

Activity 9

- Review the list of activities and the expression **tiene que** + **infinitive**, presented on the next page.
- Point out regional differences for certain words as presented in the box. Add any other vocabulary you would like your students to know.
- Have students complete the activity in pairs.

ANSWERS

Activity 7

a. profesora; b. mecánico; c. enfermera; d. bombero; e. veterinaria; f. cocinero.

Activity 8

1. e; 2. c; 3. h; 4. b; 5. d; 6. f; 7. a; 8. g.

Activity 9

Contestar el teléfono: el/la recepcionista; **Cuidar a los enfermos:** el/la médico/a; **Cuidar a los animales:** el/la veterinario/a; **Crear programas en la computadora:** el/la informático/a; **Hacer películas:** el actor/la actriz; **Servir cafés, refrescos...:** el/la mesero/a; **Preparar comidas:** el/la cocinero/a; **Reparar carros:** el/la mecánico/a; **Dar clases:** el profesor/la profesora.

PALABRA POR PALABRA Las profesiones

7 🎧 48 Fill in the blanks under each image with the appropriate profession from the list. *¡Atención!* Remember to use the correct form of the noun to show agreement with the person in the image. Then listen to the audio to check your answers.

bombero/a ○ enfermero/a ○ profesor/profesora ○ cocinero/a ○ mecánico/a ○ veterinario/a

a. P☐☐☐☐☐☐☐☐   b. M☐☐☐☐☐☐☐   c. E☐☐☐☐☐☐☐☐

d. B☐☐☐☐☐☐   e. V☐☐☐☐☐☐☐☐☐☐   f. C☐☐☐☐☐☐☐

8 👥 Match the following professions to the location where the job mostly takes place. Then with a partner, read your answers aloud.

¿Dónde trabaja el/la...?

1. bombero/a
2. médico/a
3. mesero/a
4. cocinero/a
5. veterinario/a
6. actor/actriz
7. recepcionista
8. informático/a

trabaja (works) en

a. el hotel
b. la cocina
c. el hospital
d. la clínica veterinaria
e. la estación de bomberos
f. el teatro, en el cine...
g. la oficina
h. el restaurante

9 👥 Look at the following list of activities that people have to do as part of their jobs. Then take turns with a partner asking each other who has to do each activity.

- apagar fuegos *to put out fires*
- contestar el teléfono *to answer the phone*
- cuidar a los enfermos, a los animales *to take care of patients, animals*
- crear programas en la computadora *to create programs on the computer*
- hacer películas *to make movies*
- servir cafés, refrescos... *to serve coffee, soft drinks*
- preparar comidas *to prepare food*
- reparar carros *to repair cars*
- dar clases *to teach class*

Modelo: E1: ¿Quién tiene que apagar fuegos?
E2: El bombero o la bombera.

🌎 ■ la computadora = el ordenador (España) el computador
■ el carro = el coche (España)
■ el/la mesero/a = el/la camarero/a (España)

SLOWER-PACED LEARNERS

Working with a partner, have students write two lists: one with the names of the professions, and one with the verbs that explain what those professionals do based on the information from Activity 9. Have them write each item on an index or small piece of paper. Then have them turn the cards face-down and play a game of memory in which they try to find the cards that match: **médico / cuidar a los enfermos; bombero / apagar fuegos**; etc.

- Use the expression **tener + que** to talk about the things you and others have to do.
Tengo que hacer deporte. I have to play sports.
Tienes que trabajar. You have to work.
Tenemos que estudiar. We have to study.

¡Atención! Note that only the verb **tener** is conjugated.

10 Choose two of the following professions and role play with a partner. Take turns asking each other about your jobs. Use the following questions.

Modelo: E1: ¿A qué te dedicas?
E2: Soy médico.
E1: ¿Dónde trabajas?
E2: Trabajo en el hospital.
E1: ¿Qué tienes que hacer?
E2: Tengo que cuidar a los pacientes.

- ¿A qué te dedicas? ➡ ¿En qué trabajas? ➡ ¿Qué haces? (job-related)

11 In groups of three or four, take turns acting out a profession for your classmates to guess.

MORE IN ELETECA: EXTRA ONLINE PRACTICE

125

INSTRUCTIONAL STRATEGIES

Activity 10
- Role-play the **Modelo** with another student. Practice using both expressions: **¿A qué te dedicas?** and **¿Qué haces?**
- Check to make sure students understand the expression **tener que**.

Activity 11
- Use EA 4.1, **Las profesiones** to help students role-play these professions. They can work in groups of three or four. Distribute one profession to each student for them to act out that profession. Their partners have to guess what it is.

ANSWERS

Activity 10
Answers will vary but should reflect vocabulary for professions.

SLOWER-PACED LEARNERS
Before speaking in Activity 10, allow students to write captions or jot down notes next to the images to help them prepare for their conversations. Remind them not to read from their notes, but they may glance at them to help them remember words or phrases.

ADVANCED LEARNERS
Have students talk about their families and what they do for a living. Encourage them to use the vocabulary from unit 3.

HERITAGE LANGUAGE LEARNERS
Have students write about what they want to do for a living following this model: *Mi profesión ideal es ___ porque... Los ___ trabajan todos los días en ___ ;* etc.

OBJECTIVES FOR GRAMÁTICA 1

OBJECTIVES FOR GRAMÁTICA 1

- Present the grammatical structures needed to practice the communicative functions of the unit: Stem-changing verbs *e ➡ ie*, *o ➡ ue*, and *e ➡ i*
- Learn to conjugate verbs with stem changes

CORE MATERIALS

- Interactive Online Materials - ELEteca

STANDARDS

1.1 Engage in conversation
1.2 Understand the language
1.3 Present information
4.1 Compare languages

INSTRUCTIONAL STRATEGIES

1. Stem-changing Verbs *E ➡ IE*, *O ➡ UE*, and *E ➡ I*

- Walk students through the grammatical explanation in the book. Then provide practice by saying one of the verbs and a subject pronoun, asking students to say the correct verb form. For instance, say: *Dormir, él*. Students should answer: *él duerme*.
- Ask the following questions, which provide additional practice with these stem-changing verbs: *¿A qué hora empieza la clase de Educación Física? ¿A qué hora vuelves a casa? ¿Cuántas horas duermes por la noche? ¿A qué hora cierran las tiendas en tu barrio?*

CULTURAL NOTE

In Spain, *comer* is used to talk about eating lunch, not *almorzar*.

SLOWER-PACED LEARNERS

Play a dice game to practice stem-changing verb conjugations. Announce a stem-changing verb. Working with a partner, have students take turns rolling the dice and conjugating the verb based on the numbers they roll. Each number represents a different from of the verb: 1 means *yo*; 2 means *tú*; 3 means *usted/él/ella*, and so on. After a few minutes, continue play with another verb.

ADVANCED LEARNERS

Follow the same rules for the dice game explained for slower-paced learners. Pose the added challenge of having students make a sentence with the conjugated verb before switching turns with their partners.

HERITAGE LANGUAGE LEARNERS

Follow the same rules of the dice game explained for slower-paced learners. Pose the added challenge of having students ask a question to their partners using that form of the verb. Their partners must respond with a coherent answer before their take their turn rolling the dice.

GRAMÁTICA

1. STEM-CHANGING VERBS *E ➡ IE*, *O ➡ UE*, AND *E ➡ I*

- In Spanish, some verbs have an irregular stem in the present tense. The vowel in the last syllable of the stem changes from **e ➡ ie**, **o ➡ ue**, and **e ➡ i** in all forms except **nosotros/as** and **vosotros/as**. Look at the verb charts below to see examples of these types of verbs.
- **E ➡ IE**. The **e** in emp**e**zar changes to **ie** in all forms but **nosotros/as** and **vosotros/as**.

EMPEZAR *(to start, begin)*			
yo	empiezo	nosotros/as	empezamos
tú	empiezas	vosotros/as	empezáis
usted/él/ella	empieza	ustedes/ellos/ellas	empiezan

*Mis clases **empiezan** a las 8. My classes start at 8.*
*¿A qué hora **empiezas** la tarea? What time do you begin your homework?*

- Other verbs that stem change from **e ➡ ie**:

cerrar *to close*	La tienda **cierra** a las 10. *The store closes at 10.*
entender *to understand*	Ustedes **entienden** español. *You (all) understand Spanish.*
pensar *to think*	Yo **pienso** que es verdad. *I think it's true.*
preferir *to prefer*	Tú **prefieres** el color azul. *You prefer the color blue.*
querer *to want (to do something)*	Los estudiantes **quieren** descansar. *The students want to rest.*

- **O ➡ UE**. The **o** in v**o**lver changes to **ue** in all forms but **nosotros/as** and **vosotros/as**.

VOLVER *(to return)*			
yo	vuelvo	nosotros/as	volvemos
tú	vuelves	vosotros/as	volvéis
usted/él/ella	vuelve	ustedes/ellos/ellas	vuelven

*Yo **vuelvo** a casa a las 4. I return home at 4.*   *Mi padre **vuelve** a casa a las 6. My father returns home at 6.*

- Other verbs that stem change from **o ➡ ue**:

almorzar *to have lunch*	Yo **almuerzo** a las 12. *I have lunch at 12.*
dormir *to sleep*	Los estudiantes **duermen** mucho. *The students sleep a lot.*
poder *to be able to, can*	Nosotros **podemos** quedar a las 5. *We can meet up at 5.*

- **E ➡ I**. The **e** in s**e**rvir changes to **i** in all forms but **nosotros/as** and **vosotros/as**.

SERVIR *(to serve)*			
yo	sirvo	nosotros/as	servimos
tú	sirves	vosotros/as	servís
usted/él/ella	sirve	ustedes/ellos/ellas	sirven

≫ *¿Qué **sirven** en la cafetería? What do they serve in the cafeteria?*
≫ ***Sirven** pizza. They serve pizza.*

- Other verbs that stem change from **e ➡ i**:

pedir *to ask for, to order*	**Pido** pizza por teléfono. *I order pizza on the phone.*
repetir *to repeat*	La profesora **repite** la tarea. *The teacher repeats the homework.*

126

1 👥 **Ask your partner about his/her preferences.**

Modelo: E1: ¿Qué prefieres, un café o un refresco?
E2: Prefiero un refresco.

a. Matemáticas o Historia
b. el fútbol o el fútbol americano
c. un sofá o una silla
d. una casa o un apartamento
e. estudiar en casa o estudiar en la biblioteca
f. comer en McDonald's o comer en Taco Bell

2 👥 **Describe what the following people do using each of the verbs in parenthesis. Then take turns reading your sentences aloud to your partner.**

Modelo: Mi padre (volver a casa a las 3, almorzar en casa) ➡ Mi padre vuelve a casa a las 3. Almuerza en casa.

a. tú (empezar temprano, dormir poco por la mañana, pedir agua para beber)
b. nosotros (entender la tarea, almorzar en la cafetería, volver a casa a las 3)
c. Maribel (querer vivir en la ciudad, poder tener un perro en casa, preferir viajar en coche)
d. los estudiantes (poder bailar en su clase, repetir después de la profesora, cerrar los libros)

3 👥 **Using the sentences in Activity 2, tell your partner whether you do the same things. If you don't do the activity, add *no* before the verb.**

Modelo: Yo vuelvo a casa a las 3. No almuerzo en casa.

2. VERBS *HACER* AND *SALIR*

■ Some verbs in Spanish are irregular only in the **yo** form.

	HACER (to do, to make)	SALIR (to go out, to leave)
yo	hago	salgo
tú	haces	sales
usted/él/ella	hace	sale
nosotros/as	hacemos	salimos
vosotros/as	hacéis	salís
ustedes/ellos/ellas	hacen	salen

Yo **salgo** con mis amigos los sábados. *I go out with my friends on Saturdays.*
¿Cuándo **sales** con tus amigos? *When do you go out with your friends?*
Yo **hago** la cama todos los días. *I make my bed every day.*

Activity 1

Make sure students understand that this activity provides practice with the stem-changing verb **preferir**. If needed, remind them that the stem change is **e ➡ ie**, as in **prefieres** and **prefiero**.

Activity 2

- If needed, remind students that the stem changes in the verbs are as follows: **e ➡ ie, o ➡ ue**, and **e ➡ i**, as in **repetir / repite**, **entender / entiendo**, **querer / quiere**, **poder / pueden**.
- Review orally to help students get accustomed to the sounds and forms of these verbs.

Activity 3

Encourage students to take notes on their partners' differences so they can report back to the class or to another classmate for additional speaking practice.

OBJECTIVES FOR GRAMÁTICA 2

- Present the grammatical structures needed to practice the communicative functions of the unit: the verbs **hacer** and **salir**

INSTRUCTIONAL STRATEGIES

2. The verbs *HACER* and *SALIR*

Elicit from students what they already know about conjugating **hacer** and **salir** in the present. Ask them to think about what they already know about conjugating **−er** and **−ir** verbs. Help them realize that **hacer** and **salir** are only irregular in the first person: **hago, salgo**.

ANSWERS

Activity 1

Answers will vary and should reflect proper conjugation of **preferir** with stem change.

Activity 2

a. Tú empiezas temprano. Duermes poco por la mañana. Pides agua para beber.
b. Nosotros entendemos la tarea. Almorzamos en la cafetería. Volvemos a casa a las 3.
c. Maribel quiere vivir en la ciudad. Puede tener un perro en casa. Prefiere viajar en coche.
d. Los estudiantes pueden bailar en su clase. Repiten después de la profesora. Cierran los libros.

Activity 3

Answers will vary.

SLOWER-PACED LEARNERS

Help students create flashcards to memorize verb forms. They can use a card for each form and include a sentence that helps them remember the meaning of the verb in context.

ADVANCED LEARNERS AND HERITAGE LANGUAGE LEARNERS

Irregular verbs contest: Have students write a short text using as many irregular verbs as possible. The one who uses the most irregular verbs, wins.

Activity 4

First review with students which verb would apply in each image.

Activity 5

Have students report back to the class.

Activity 4

a. sale; b. hacemos; c. salen; d. salgo; e. hace; f. hacen.

Activity 5

a. Sales; b. Haces; c. Sales; d. Haces; e. Sales; f. Haces.

OBJECTIVES FOR GRAMÁTICA 3

Present the grammatical structures needed to practice the communicative functions of the unit: Reflexive verbs

INSTRUCTIONAL STRATEGIES

3. Reflexive Verbs

- Point out to students that reflexive verbs in Spanish are very common. Many of these verbs refer to actions related to our own personal care, such as washing one's hands, brushing one's teeth, getting ourselves up.
- Share with students that some of the most common reflexive verbs in Spanish are: *acostarse* (to lie down), *levantarse* (to get up), *ducharse* (to shower), *sentarse* (to sit), *vestirse* (to get dressed).
- Point out that a reflexive verb will always be indicated with *se* at the end of the infinitive. This will remind students to use a reflexive pronoun when conjugating this verb.

SLOWER-PACED LEARNERS

Encourage students to identify which verbs are reflexive and which are not by using some pictures of daily activities and asking: What do you "do" to yourself? *Lavarse, ducharse, afeitarse, peinarse*, etc. What do you "do" to something else? *Estudiar algo, cocinar algo, ver la televisión*, etc.

HERITAGE LANGUAGE LEARNERS

Tell students to ask follow-up questions to each of the questions in Activity 5. Then have them write a paragraph summarizing their partners' responses.

GRAMÁTICA

4 Fill in the blanks with the correct form of *hacer* or *salir* to describe what the following people do.

Patricia .... con sus amigos.

Nosotros .... la cena todas las noches.

Los niños .... corriendo de la escuela.

Yo .... con mi perro a pasear.

Roberto .... la tarea en su computadora.

El padre y el hijo .... la cama.

5 Take turns asking your partner if he/she does the activities shown in the images above. Use the correct form of *hacer* or *salir* in the questions below.

a. ¿..................... con tus amigos?
b. ¿..................... la cama?
c. ¿..................... con tu perro a pasear?
d. ¿..................... la tarea en tu computadora?
e. ¿..................... corriendo de la escuela?
f. ¿..................... la cena todas las noches?

3. REFLEXIVE VERBS

- A reflexive verb requires a reflexive pronoun (**me, te, se, nos, os, se**) that refers the action of the verb back to the person doing the action, the subject. In Spanish, reflexive verbs are often verbs used to describe actions related to personal care and daily routines. That is, actions that you do for yourself.

  Yo **me ducho**. *I shower (myself)*.

  Yo **me levanto**. *I get up (physically, by myself)*.

UNIDAD 4

■ Reflexive verbs in Spanish have regular **–ar**, **–er** or **–ir** endings. Some verbs will have a stem change. Look at the forms of the following reflexive verbs.

| | (e→ie) | (o→ue) | (e→i) |
	LEVANTARSE *to get up*	**DESPERTARSE** *to wake up*	**ACOSTARSE** *to go to bed*	**VESTIRSE** *to get dressed*
yo	me levanto	me desp**ie**rto	me ac**ue**sto	me v**i**sto
tú	te levantas	te desp**ie**rtas	te ac**ue**stas	te v**i**stes
usted/él/ella	se levanta	se desp**ie**rta	se ac**ue**sta	se v**i**ste
nosotros/as	nos levantamos	nos despertamos	nos acostamos	nos vestimos
vosotros/as	os levantáis	os despertáis	os acostáis	os vestís
ustedes/ellos/ellas	se levantan	se desp**ie**rtan	se ac**ue**stan	se v**i**sten

*Mi madre **se acuesta** a las 12. My mother goes to bed at 12.*
***Me visto** antes de desayunar. I get dressed before having breakfast.*
***Nos despertamos** tarde. We wake up late.*

■ Otros verbos reflexivos:
• ducharse *to shower*
• bañarse *to take a bath*

6 Fill in the blank with the correct reflexive pronoun. **¡Atención!** Remember that the reflexive pronoun and the form of the verb refer to the same subject (or person).

a. ¿A qué hora .... despiertan?

b. ¿A qué hora .... levantas?

c. ¿A qué hora .... acostamos?

d. ¿A qué hora .... ducha tu hermana?

7 Write out the answers to the questions above. **¡Atención!** Remember to conjugate the infinitives and use the correct reflexive pronouns.

a. Yo / levantarse / a las 8:00 ....

b. Mi hermana / ducharse / a las 7:30 ....

c. María y tú / despertarse / a las 8:30 ....

d. Nosotros / acostarse / a las 10:30 ....

8 Fill in the blanks with the verb that applies to the action shown in the corresponding image. **¡Atención!** Not all the actions shown are reflexive.

Todos los días, yo (a) .... pronto, a las 8:30. Desayuno y (b) .... Después, (c) .... Por la tarde, hago deporte con mis amigos. A las 10:30 (d) ...., pero siempre (e) .... un poco antes de dormirme.

9 Prepare a similar description about your day. Then take turns with a partner asking each other about what you do and when.

Modelo: E1: *¿A qué hora te levantas?* E2: *Me levanto a las siete.* E1: *¿Qué haces después?*

MORE IN ELETECA: EXTRA ONLINE PRACTICE ➞ **GRAMMAR TUTORIALS** 7 AND 8   129

Point out the verbs that change stem and review them with extra attention.

Activity 6

This activity asks students to provide the reflexive pronoun to help them understand that the pronoun and verb form work together.

Activity 7

Make sure that students are using the reflexive pronoun along with the verb forms.

Activity 8

Depending on how well your class seems to be grasping the concept, review the images ahead of time and have students identify the ones that show a reflexive action.

Extension

As a writing assignment, have students prepare a similar description about a typical day in their own lives.

Activity 9

Allow students some time to prepare their descriptions before working with a partner.

ANSWERS

Activity 6

a. se; **b.** te; **c.** nos; **d.** se.

Activity 7

a. Yo me levanto a las ocho; **b.** Mi hermana se ducha a las siete y media; **c.** María y tú se despiertan a las ocho y media; **d.** Nosotros nos acostamos a las diez y media.

Activity 8

a. me levanto; **b.** me ducho; **c.** desayuno; **d.** me acuesto; **e.** leo.

Activity 9

Answers will vary but should follow the model provided.

SLOWER-PACED LEARNERS

Help students create flashcards to memorize reflexive verb forms. They can use a card for each form and include a sentence that helps them remember the meaning of the verb in context.

ADVANCED LEARNERS

Reflexive verbs contest: Have students write a short text describing their daily routines using as many reflexive verbs as possible. The one who uses the most reflexive verbs, wins.

HERITAGE LANGUAGE LEARNERS

Have students interview a Spanish-speaking familiar member or friend about his or her routine and write a summary of it to share with the class.

OBJECTIVES FOR DESTREZAS

- Listen to specific information about daily activities to improve listening comprehension
- Writing as a learning strategy to remember vocabulary

CORE MATERIALS

- Audio Program: Track 49

STANDARDS

- 1.2 Understand the language
- 1.3 Present information

INSTRUCTIONAL STRATEGIES

Comprensión Auditiva

Activity 1

- Point out to students that listening for specific information is an important skill that will help them improve their listening comprehension.
- Review the strategy and guide them through the topics as needed.
- Remind them to listen for key terms that will help them answer the questions.

🎧 49 Activity 2

Audioscript

1. Hola, me llamo Juan. Soy estudiante de 1.º de la ESO. Mis clases empiezan a las nueve, por eso yo me levanto todos los días a las ocho; 2. En esta fotografía estamos mi madre, mi hermana y yo. Mi madre lleva unos zapatos rosas y mi hermana, rojos; 3. Hola, me llamo Marta y soy profesora de este instituto. Los estudiantes estudian inglés por la tarde y español, por la mañana; 4. Yo también soy profesor. Normalmente quedo con mis estudiantes para practicar español. El mejor día es el domingo, pero no puedo. Así que voy a quedar con ellos el martes.

INSTRUCTIONAL STRATEGIES

Expresión e Interacción Escritas

Activity 1

- Point out that organizing their ideas first is a good skill for effective writing.
- Explain that the **Destrezas** chart is organized into three topics and each topic has questions to help them come up with information they will use in their writing. Have them complete the chart in Activity 1 before they proceed to do the writing in Activity 2.

ANSWERS

Activity 2

1. b; 2. c; 3. a; 4. b.

ADVANCED LEARNERS

To further exploit the audio in Activity 2, have students listen again and take notes on other details that they notice. Then ask questions about segment to check their comprehension or have them formulate their own questions to ask a partner. For example: 1. *¿A qué hora empiezan las clases de Juan?* 2. *¿Qué muestra la persona que habla?* 3. *¿Cómo se llama la profesora?* 4. *¿Cuál es su profesión?*

DESTREZAS

COMPRENSIÓN AUDITIVA

1 You will listen to four separate audio recordings. Before playing the audio, review the listening strategy in Destrezas and follow the suggestion.

Destrezas
Listen for specific information
To listen efficiently, focus on the information you need in order to obtain the correct answer. Before listening to each segment, read the options. Then jot down or circle the specific information you need to listen for to help you select the correct answer. What information should you focus on in item...?

1. ....   3. ....

2. ....   4. ....

2 🎧 49 Listen to each short segment and then choose the best option based on the information you heard.

1. **a.** Juan se levanta todos los días a las 7.
   b. Juan se levanta todos los días a las 8.
   c. Juan se levanta todos los días a las 9.

2. **a.** Mi madre lleva unos zapatos rojos.
   b. Mi hermana lleva unos zapatos rosas.
   c. Mi hermana lleva unos zapatos rojos.

3. **a.** Estudian español por la mañana.
   b. Estudian inglés por la mañana en el colegio.
   c. Estudian inglés por la mañana en el instituto.

4. **a.** El profesor quiere quedar con sus amigos el lunes.
   b. El profesor quiere quedar con sus estudiantes el martes.
   c. El profesor quiere quedar el domingo por la tarde con sus estudiantes.

EXPRESIÓN E INTERACCIÓN ESCRITAS

1 In this section, you will be writing an e-mail to a friend describing what you do on a typical day. Before you begin to write, review the writing strategy in Destrezas and follow the suggestion.

Destrezas		
Create an activity chart		
Make a chart listing information about your day. This will help you organize your description.		
Topic	**Questions**	**Personal information**
Schedule	What time do you get up?	
	What is your morning routine?	
	What time do classes start?	
Activities	What do you normally do?	
	When and where do you do these activities?	
Free time activities	What do you do with your friends?	

2 Write an e-mail to your friend using the notes you prepared. Include all the necessary information for your e-mail.

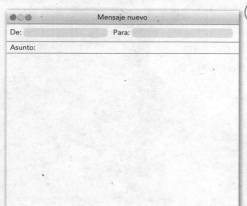

| Mensaje nuevo |
| De: Para: |
| Asunto: |

! ■ Use the following information to write an e-mail:
- De *From*
- Para *To*
- Asunto *Subject*
- Querido/a *Dear*
- Chao/Adiós/Hasta luego *[closing]*

PRONUNCIACIÓN The sounds of *b* and *v*

1 🎧 **50** Listen to the following words and repeat after the speaker.
1. **B**arcelona, sa**b**er, **b**i**b**lioteca, **b**olí**g**rafo, **bu**eno.
2. **Va**lencia, **ve**inte, **vi**vir, **vo**sotros, **vu**estro.

! ■ In Spanish, the letters **b** and **v** have the same sound, as the *b* in *boy*.

2 📖 Fill in the blanks with *b* or *v* to complete the spelling of these words you already know. Then practice saying them aloud with a partner.

a. be....er
b. vi....ir
c. e....aluación
d. escri....es
e. vol....emos
f. ....iblioteca
g. ha....lar
h. ....einte
i. ....ien
j. ....erde

3 Look at Daniel's after-school activities. Fill in the blanks with *b* or *v* to complete his schedule.

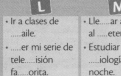

L	M	X	J	V
• Ir a clases de ....aile.	• Lle....ar al perro al ....eterinario.	• Partido de ....aloncesto.	• Tra....ajar unas horas en la ....i....lioteca.	• Jugar al fút....ol.
• ....er mi serie de tele....isión fa....orita.	• Estudiar ....iología por la noche.	• Escri....ir un correo a Tomás.	• Ir al cine con Ja....ier.	• Na....egar por Internet.

MORE IN ELETECA: EXTRA ONLINE PRACTICE

131

STANDARDS
1.2 Understand the language
3.2 Acquire information
4.1 Compare languages

INSTRUCTIONAL STRATEGIES

🎧 **50** Activity 1

Introduce the sounds with sample words and books closed. Ask students to spell out the words as you write them on the board: **Barcelona, bueno; veinte, vivir.** Point out that in Spanish the letters **b** and **v** have the exact same sound. In initial position, they both sound like the English *b* in *boy*. Help them realize that between vowels, the sound of the *b* in Spanish is much softer, and the lips do not fully close, but it is never like the sound of the **v**.

Audioscript
1. Barcelona, saber, biblioteca, bolígrafo, bueno.
2. Valencia, veinte, vivir, vosotros, vuestro.

Activity 2

Circulate around the room, provided help as needed.

Activity 3

After filling in the blanks, put students in pairs to check their answer..

ANSWERS

Activity 2
a. beber; **b.** vivir; **c.** evaluación; **d.** escribes; **e.** volvemos; **f.** biblioteca; **g.** hablar; **h.** veinte; **i.** bien; **j.** verde.

Activity 3
L: Ir a clases de baile. Ver mi serie de televisión favorita.
M: Llevar el perro al veterinario. Estudiar biología por la noche.
X: Partido de baloncesto. Escribir un correo a Tomás.
J: Trabajar unas horas en la biblioteca. Ir al cine con Javier.
V: Jugar al fútbol. Navegar por Internet.

SLOWER-PACED LEARNERS

Have students make lists of more words that have the letters **b** and **v**. Give them access to a dictionary or encourage them to flip through the vocabulary summaries at the end of each unit for more examples. Then have them swap lists with a partner and practice saying the words aloud.

ADVANCED LEARNERS

Have students personalize the information in Activity 3 to talk about their own after-school activities with a partner. If the information doesn't follow their own routines, tell them to use **no** in the sentences and then change the details to make the information true for them.

HERITAGE LANGUAGE LEARNERS

Challenge students to come up with their own tongue-twisters, **trabalenguas**, making sentences that use as many words with the letters **b** and **v** as possible. Then have them share their sentences in small groups. They should listen and write down the sentences their classmates say.

Activity 2

After students have written their emails, have them swap papers and check that all of the elements of the email have been included. Then have them proofread the emails and fix any spelling, vocabulary, or grammar mistakes that they notice.

ANSWERS

Activity 2
Answers will vary but should reflect organization of chart from Activity 1.

OBJECTIVES FOR PRONUNCIACIÓN
• Practice correct pronunciation of /b/ and /v/

CORE RESOURCES
• Audio Program: 50
• Interactive Online Materials - ELEteca

OBJECTIVES FOR SABOR HISPANO

- Learn about a region: Central America
- Learn about Central America's cultural heritage and ecological diversity
- Compare the landscape and cultural heritage of Central America with that of the U.S.

CORE RESOURCES

- Audio Program: Track 51

STANDARDS

2.1 Practices and perspectives
2.2 Products and perspectives
3.2 Acquire information
4.1 Compare cultures
5.2 Using language for personal enjoyment and enrichment

INSTRUCTIONAL STRATEGIES

- Introduce the topic by asking students what they know about Central America, its people, its history, and its landscape.
- Have students look at the map. What countries of Central America are they familiar with? Do they know anyone from a Central American country?
- Talk about the images and the map. Elicit what they already know about Central America. Share what you know about the region with students.
- Read the captions together and ask questions to check comprehension.
- Ask students to identify which of the points in **¿Sabes que...?** they find most surprising. Have students research additional information about: *el Juego de Pelota*, *Reef Pro El Salvador*, *la ruta Panamericana*, *la flor y fauna de la región*, and so on..

CULTURAL NOTE

Point out that Central America can be translated as Centroamérica or América Central. Remind students that Panamá is also part of Central America but will be covered later in the book. There is a non-Spanish-speaking country in the region, Belize (Belice in Spanish). Have students guess what language is spoken in Belice (it's official language is English, but Belizean Creole and Spanish are also spoken there). Brainstorm with students about the reasons why these countries appear in this chapter: in addition to their location, what cultural, historical and political traits do they share? Pictures included here will help them guess some answers: languages, traditions, political problems, etc.

SLOWER-PACED LEARNERS

Have students find out more information about **la ruta Panamericana** including where it begins, where it ends, and what countries it passes through. Have them draw the route on a map and add images of the route as it appears in different locations.

SABOR HISPANO

EL PUENTE ENTRE LAS AMÉRICAS

¡Adoro la naturaleza!

Guatemala
Guatemala
El Salvador
San Salvador
Honduras
Tegucigalpa
Nicaragua
Managua
Costa Rica
San José

Esta región de América Central tiene muchas sorpresas

Rana de ojos rojos

La catedral de San Salvador, en El Salvador

El volcán San Cristóbal, en Nicaragua

La fiesta de Santo Tomás, en Guatemala

✓ América Central tiene una historia muy rica, con herencia de las culturas maya y olmeca, española y africana.

✓ En América Central vive el 7% de las plantas y animales del planeta. Allí puedes ver jaguares, tortugas gigantes y monos araña *(spider monkeys)*.

✓ Además de español, en estos países se hablan varias lenguas indígenas

¿Sabes que...?

✓ La ruta *(highway)* Panamericana cruza América Central y llega hasta Sudamérica. Tiene 48.000 kilómetros... ies una de las rutas más largas del mundo!

✓ En la región hay más de 70 volcanes y 30 de ellos están activos. En Nicaragua hay 19 volcanes activos.

✓ En la fiesta de Santo Tomás, en Guatemala, hay una increíble competición de acrobacia.

✓ El concurso de surf, Reef Pro El Salvador, se celebra todos los años en Punta Roca. Es uno de los mejores lugares para hacer surf en la costa del Pacífico.

✓ El Juego de Pelota es un deporte de la civilización maya. En Guatemala hay más de 300 campos de juego que datan de 1400 a.C. *(B.C.)*.

132

EL SALVADOR, GUATEMALA, HONDURAS, NICARAGUA Y COSTA RICA

UNIDAD **4**

🎧 51 Un día «pura vida»

Mi nombre es Ana y soy de Costa Rica. Es el país más feliz del mundo, según el *Happy Planet Index*, porque la gente está contenta, vive una larga vida y respeta la naturaleza.

Aquí tenemos una frase típica: «pura vida». Significa que es importante disfrutar (*enjoy*) cada día. Normalmente, me levanto temprano y desayuno un café. Después, voy a la escuela. Las clases son interesantes y me gusta charlar con mis amigos.

Por la tarde, voy a la playa y hago surf. Dos veces por semana, voy a un santuario (*sanctuary*) de animales, donde soy voluntaria. Vivir en Costa Rica es increíble. ¡Pura vida!

La vida es relajada en el país más feliz del mundo

Las maras y la educación

Las maras son pandillas (*gangs*) de jóvenes violentos. Son un problema en varios países de América Central.

La violencia de las maras afecta a la educación, porque los profesores y los estudiantes tienen miedo (*are afraid*) de ir a clase.

En El Salvador, el gobierno tiene desde 2012 un pacto con las maras para terminar con la violencia. Honduras, donde 5.000 jóvenes son parte de alguna mara, quiere un pacto similar.

Un integrante de la mara Salvatrucha, de Honduras

Fuentes: BBC Mundo, Happy Planet Index, Instituto Cervantes.

El mundo maya y la tecnología

❖ En América Central se hablan varias lenguas indígenas. Guatemala es el país con más diversidad: ¡hay 21 idiomas, además del español!

❖ Más de 3 millones de personas hablan maya.

❖ Hay muchos proyectos que combinan la lengua maya y la tecnología. Por ejemplo, un traductor de Microsoft y una versión del navegador (*browser*) Firefox están en este idioma.

❖ El maya también se habla en México. Una nueva telenovela, *Baktún*, se emite en Internet en 2013. Es en maya, con subtítulos en español.

La pirámide de Tikal es parte de la historia maya de Guatemala.

Select the correct answer to complete each sentence.

1 En la fiesta de Santo Tomás
- ⃝ a. hay violencia.
- ⃝ b. hay un juego de pelota.
- ⃝ c. hay una competición de acrobacia.

2 La pirámide de Tikal
- ⃝ a. está en Guatemala.
- ⃝ b. está en Nicaragua.
- ⃝ c. está en Costa Rica.

3 Baktún es
- ⃝ a. una tradición maya.
- ⃝ b. una fiesta popular.
- ⃝ c. una nueva telenovela.

 VOCES LATINAS

VIVIR EN BUENOS AIRES

Link the two parts of the sentence.

1	En América Central vive...	a	un deporte de los antiguos mayas.
2	En la región hay...	b	la educación.
3	La pelota es...	c	disfrutar de cada día.
4	La frase «pura vida» significa...	d	30 volcanes activos.
5	La violencia de las maras afecta...	e	el 7% de las plantas y animales del planeta.

133

INSTRUCTIONAL STRATEGIES

🎧 51

- An audio recording accompanies each text on this page. Play the audio or have students read aloud. Then ask students questions to check comprehension and compare what they learned about Central America and its culture to their own experiences.
- Identify and explain any vocabulary words from the reading students may find difficult to understand.

Un día «pura vida»

Ask: **¿Creen que es importante respetar la naturaleza para tener una vida feliz? ¿Qué expresiones típicas usamos aquí para hablar de la vida?**

El mundo maya

You may want share examples of the spoken language by accessing video sites on the Internet for students to compare Mayan and Spanish. It is also interesting to point out similarities between Mayan and Egyptian pyramids. Encourage students to learn more about their histories.

Las maras y la educación

- Ask: **¿Existe este problema en Estados Unidos?** You may want to relate **las maras** to **acoso** (bullying) and the campaigns by schools and government to put an end to bullying.
- Direct students' attention to the photo. Have them discuss tattoos and how they feel about them. Some questions include: Do you know people who have tattoos? Why are the reasons people get tattoos? What happens when a tattoo identifies you with a specific group? What happens with tattoos when you get older?
- Have students complete the activities at the bottom of this page and compare their answers with others in the class.

ANSWERS

Answer selection

1. c; 2. a; 3. c.

Link the two parts of the sentence

1. e; 2. d; 3. a; 4. c; 5. b.

ADVANCED LEARNERS

Have students find an interesting image of each country highlighted here: El Salvador, Guatemala, Honduras, Nicaragua, and Costa Rica. The image should connect to the country's history, culture, politics, or natural environment in some way. Have them write a caption or brief description of each photo, making such a connection, and create a poster with all of them. Display the posters around the room.

HERITAGE LANGUAGE LEARNERS

If you have heritage learners from Central American descent, have them share pictures, traditions, foods, etc., from their countries. Other students may look for information about how much it costs and how long it takes to get to these countries. Discuss implications for Central American families who live in the US and want to visit their friends or families in their countries of origin.

OBJECTIVES FOR RELATO

• Revisit unit themes, grammar, vocabulary, and culture in a new context
• Improve reading comprehension skills

CORE RESOURCES

• Audio Program: Track 52

STANDARDS

1.1   Engage in conversation
1.2   Understand the language
1.3   Present information
2.1   Practices and perspectives
5.3   Using language for personal enjoyment and enrichment

INSTRUCTIONAL STRATEGIES

Activity 1

The purpose of this activity is to review some of the vocabulary from the unit while introducing some nouns that will appear in the reading. Students complete this activity individually or in pairs.

🎧 52 Activity 2

• Before students read the text, tell them that this is a text about the weekly routine of a modern family in a Spanish-speaking country.
• Play the audio while students read along. Then have students read the questions and go back to the text to find the information needed to answer.

Extension

Once students have completed the activity, ask them to read sections aloud to work on their pronunciation and intonation. Follow up with a discussion, encouraging students to express their opinion about the weekly routine of this family and how similar or different it is from their own weekly routine.

CULTURAL NOTE

• **Arroz con pollo** is a traditional dish from Spain known in all Spanish-speaking countries. It is particularly popular in Colombia, Cuba, Costa Rica, Nicaragua, Venezuela, Panama, Peru, and Puerto Rico.
• Explain that, in Spain, lunch usually takes place between 1:30 and 3:00, and dinner is from 9:00 to 10:30. Families with young children often have dinner earlier so the children can go to bed sooner. Restaurants will start serving dinner at 9:30. Tourists are reminded that restaurants may be empty or closed if they try to have an earlier dinner out.

ANSWERS

Activity 1

a. 5; b. 6; c. 2; d. 1; e. 4; f. 3.

Activity 2 (next page)

a. No; b. No; c. Sí; d. Sí; e. No.

RELATO El día a día de muchos hispanos

1 Match the images to the activity described.

a. ○ visitar a la familia
b. ○ ir al cine
c. ○ limpiar la casa
d. ○ hacer la compra
e. ○ arroz con pollo
f. ○ tostada con mantequilla y mermelada

2 🎧 52 Read the following description of the typical day-to-day of many Hispanics in the Spanish-speaking world. Then select *sí* or *no* based on what you learned from the reading section.

El día a día de muchos hispanos

La gente que visita nuestros países siempre dice que los horarios son diferentes al resto del mundo y que todo se hace más tarde.

Durante la semana no desayunamos mucho, solo café con leche o jugo de naranja, y salimos corriendo, mis padres al trabajo y mi hermana y yo a la escuela. Comemos normalmente de dos a tres de la tarde: papá en un restaurante cerca de la oficina, mamá en la cafetería de la empresa y yo en la escuela. No dormimos la siesta, porque también hacemos cosas por la tarde: ellos trabajan y yo voy a clases de guitarra. La cena en mi familia es a las ocho de la noche. Nos acostamos tarde, a las doce.

Los fines de semana son más relajados. El sábado por la mañana hacemos la compra y limpiamos la casa; por la tarde, quedamos con amigos, cenamos fuera o tomamos algo en una terraza. Los domingos nos levantamos mucho más tarde, desayunamos chocolate con pan dulce o tostadas con mantequilla y mermelada. Visitamos a la familia y comemos juntos. Ese día mis padres preparan una buena comida, como arroz con pollo o carne asada (grilled meat). Por la tarde, paseamos por el parque o vemos una película en el cine. Y descansamos para empezar la semana con energía. Este es el día a día de mi familia, ¿y el de la tuya?

134

HERITAGE LANGUAGE LEARNERS

Invite students to compare and contrast their knowledge and experience of daily routines in Spanish-speaking countries with the information in Activity 2 orally in class. Then have them write a description of that daily routine. Encourage them to talk to family members and friends to find out more detailed and accurate information for their writing.

Left Page

	Sí	No
a. Normalmente desayunan muy fuerte.	☐	☐
b. Durante la semana comemos en casa.	☐	☐
c. El fin de semana limpiamos la casa y hacemos la compra.	☐	☐
d. Los domingos vemos a la familia.	☐	☐
e. Nos acostamos muy temprano todos los días.	☐	☐

3 With a partner, list the activities that are typically done during the week and on weekends according to the reading.

De lunes a viernes	Los fines de semana

4 Write about what people typically do in your country or region during the day. Share your answers with the class.

El sábado por la mañana ....

Por la tarde ....

El domingo por la mañana ....

Por la noche ....

5 With a partner, take turns asking each other about your routines. Then record your partner's answers in the chart below.

a. ¿Qué haces el sábado por la mañana?
b. ¿Qué haces el sábado por la tarde?
c. ¿Qué haces el domingo por la mañana?
d. ¿Qué haces el domingo por la tarde?
e. ¿Qué haces durante la semana por las tardes?

lunes	martes	miércoles	jueves	viernes	sábado	domingo

135

INSTRUCTIONAL STRATEGIES

Activity 3

- Have students work in pairs to look for the information in the reading.
- They exchange answers with other students, or have the whole class go over the answers.

Activity 4

- An individual writing exercise to share with the whole class. Have volunteers read what they wrote to the whole class.
- Have a discussion about what is similar or different in terms of daily routines among different families.

Right Page

Activity 5

Have students work in pairs.

Alternative Activity

- Set up this activity as a round robin by having students pass information from a classmate in front to one behind them and so on to practice with different conjugations.
- Set up two rows of students facing each other and have students ask each other with one row moving to the right for a new partner. Circulate around the room taking notes to correct later on the board.

ANSWERS

Activity 3

Answers will vary. Possible answers given.

De lunes a viernes: No desayunan mucho. Van a trabajar y a la escuela. Normalmente comen fuera, cerca del centro de trabajo y en el instituto. Por las tardes, el protagonista toca la guitarra (Hacen alguna actividad). Cenan en casa, toda la familia junta a las diez. Se acuestan a las doce o a la una.

Los fines de semana: El sábado por la mañana hacen la compra y limpian la casa. Por la tarde, quedan con amigos, cenan fuera y toman algo en una terraza. Los domingos se levantan tarde y desayunan chocolate con churros o tostadas con mantequilla y mermelada. Visitan a la familia, comen juntos. Por la tarde pasean por el parque o ven una película en el cine.

Activity 4

Answers will vary and should reflect the unit vocabulary and expressions about daily and weekly activities.

Activity 5

Answers will vary and should reflect the information collected from their classmates.

SLOWER-PACED LEARNERS

After taking notes on their partners' responses in Activity 5, have students compare their charts with their partners and circle the similarities. Have them write sentences about them: **Mi amigo y yo vemos la televisión los miércoles por la tarde.**

ADVANCED LEARNERS

After completing Activity 5, have students think about which day of the week is their favorite and why. Then have them write a paragraph explaining their choice. Remind them that they can provide reasons why the other days are *not* their favorite to help justify their answers.

EVALUACIÓN SELF-ASSESSMENT

OBJECTIVES FOR EVALUACIÓN

- Review grammar, vocabulary and culture from the unit
- Complete self-assessment

CORE RESOURCES

- Interactive Online Materials - ELEteca

STANDARDS

- 1.2 Understand the language
- 2.1 Practices and perspectives
- 4.1 Compare cultures

INSTRUCTIONAL STRATEGIES

- Activities can be completed individually and then reviewed with the class. Vary by asking students if they agree with the answer given and then writing it on the board. Provide explanations as needed.
- You may wish to assign point values to each activity as a way for students to monitor their progress.
- Direct students to the indicated review pages in **En resumen** if they make more than one or two mistakes in any one section.

ANSWERS

Activity 1

a. Son las doce y veinticinco; **b.** Es la una menos cuarto; **c.** Son las seis y media; **d.** Son las cinco menos dos minutos; **e.** Son las ocho y diez; **f.** Son las diez y cuarto.

Activity 2

a. escuchar música; **b.** levantarse; **c.** limpiar la casa; **d.** comer; **e.** acostarse; **f.** quedar con amigos; **g.** navegar por Internet; **h.** hacer la compra; **i.** ver una película.

EVALUACIÓN

TELLING TIME

1 Look at the clocks and write out the time in Spanish.

a. _____
b. _____
c. _____
d. _____
e. _____
f. _____

EVERYDAY ACTIVITIES

2 Write the activity below its corresponding image.

> levantarse ○ comer ○ acostarse ○ quedar con amigos ○ escuchar música
> navegar por Internet ○ hacer la compra ○ ver una película ○ limpiar la casa

3 **Complete the description with an expression from the list below.**

> quedo ○ una tostada con mermelada y mantequilla a las 8:00h ○ me ducho ○ me acuesto

Me levanto a las 8:00 de la mañana todos los días, y (a) .... antes de ir a la escuela. Desayuno (b) .... Por la tarde estudio un poco y toco la guitarra. Cenamos toda la familia (c) .... y después veo un poco la tele en el salón. (d) .... a las 11:30 de la noche, porque ya tengo mucho sueño. El sábado por la tarde (e) .... con mis amigos y vemos una película en el cine.

STEM-CHANGING VERBS AND THE VERBS *HACER* AND *SALIR*

4 **Complete the sentences with the correct form of the verb in parenthesis.**
   a. Las clases (empezar) .... a las 9:00 de la mañana.
   b. Muchos españoles (querer) .... ver una película el fin de semana.
   c. María (dormir) .... ocho horas diarias.
   d. Raquel (pedir) .... un café al camarero.
   e. Tú y yo (querer) .... aprender español.
   f. ¿Tú (poder) .... hacer una paella?
   g. ¿Qué (hacer) .... con tus amigos?
   h. Nosotros (salir) .... los fines de semana.

REFLEXIVE VERBS

5 **Complete the sentences with the correct form of the verbs in parenthesis.**

   a. (Levantarse, yo) .... a las 8:00 de la mañana.
   b. (Vestirse, tú) .... antes de desayunar.
   c. (Ducharse, ella) .... por las mañanas.
   d. (Acostarse, ellos) .... muy tarde el sábado.

CULTURA

6 **Answer the following questions about Centroamérica and compare similarities with your own country or region.**

   a. ¿En qué país usan la expresión "pura vida"? ¿Qué expresión es popular en tu ciudad o región?
   b. ¿En qué lengua ofrece Firefox una versión de su navegador?
   c. ¿Qué lugares históricos y culturales puedes visitar en esta región? ¿Hay lugares similares en tu ciudad o región? Explícalo.
   d. ¿Qué deporte es muy popular?
   e. ¿Qué intentan controlar los gobiernos de El Salvador y Honduras? ¿Existe este problema en tu ciudad o región?

 **MORE IN ELETECA:** EXTRA ONLINE PRACTICE

137

Activity 3

   a. me ducho; **b.** una tostada con mermelada y mantequilla; **c.** a las 8; **d.** Me acuesto; **e.** quedo.

Activity 4

   a. empiezan; **b.** quieren; **c.** duerme; **d.** pide; **e.** queremos; **f.** puedes; **g.** haces; **h.** salimos.

Activity 5

   a. Yo me levanto; **b.** Tú te vistes; **c.** Ella se ducha; **d.** Ellos se acuestan.

Activity 6

   a. En Costa Rica; **b.** En maya; **c.** la catedral de San Salvador, el volcán San Cristóbal en Nicaragua, la fiesta de Santo Tomás en Guatemala, las pirámides de Tikal, and so on; **d.** El surf; **e.** La violencia y las maras.

EN RESUMEN UNIT REVIEW

OBJECTIVES FOR EN RESUMEN: VOCABULARIO

- Review unit vocabulary and expressions
- Practice communicative skills

STANDARDS

- 1.2 Understand the language
- 1.3 Present information

INSTRUCTIONAL STRATEGIES

- Encourage students to use self-adhesive notes to place on correct objects in their house.
- Index cards can be used as flash cards with the Spanish term on one side and the English term on the other, or a picture or drawing.
- Students work in pairs or groups, using vocabulary flashcards as they would the cards of a board game to help each other practice unit vocabulary.
- Encourage students to write labels or captions for the photos on this page. Remind them to use the vocabulary and expressions they have learned in this unit.

EN RESUMEN: Vocabulario

Las profesiones *Professions*
bombero/a *firefighter*
cocinero/a *cook*
informático/a *computer technician*
mecánico/a *mechanic*

médico/a *doctor*
mesero/a *waiter/waitress*
recepcionista *receptionist*

veterinario/a *veterinarian*

Decir la hora *Telling time*
¿A qué hora...? *At what time...?*
de la mañana *a.m.*
de la noche *p.m.*
de la tarde *p.m.*
en punto *sharp*
Es la una. *It's one o'clock.*
menos cuarto *quarter to*
¿Qué hora es? *What time is it?*

Son las dos. *It's two o'clock.*
y cuarto *quarter past/after (the hour)*
y media *half past (the hour)*

Expresiones de tiempo *Time expressions*
fin de semana *weekend*
por la mañana *in the morning*
por la noche *at night*

por la tarde *in the afternoon*
todos los días *every day*

Los días de la semana *Days of the week*
lunes *Monday*
martes *Tuesday*
miércoles *Wednesday*
jueves *Thursday*
viernes *Friday*
sábado *Saturday*
domingo *Sunday*

Verbos *Verbs*
acostarse (o>ue) *to go to bed*
almorzar (o>ue) *to have lunch*

cenar *to have dinner*
cerrar (e>ie) *to close*
desayunar *to have breakfast*

despertarse (e>ie) *to wake up*
dormir (o>ue) *to sleep*
ducharse *to shower*
empezar (e>ie) *to start, begin*
entender (e>ie) *to understand*

hacer deporte *to play sports*

hacer la tarea *to do homework*

hacer *to do, to make*
levantarse *to get up*
navegar por Internet *to go on the Internet*
pedir (e>i) *to ask for, to order*
pensar (e>ie) *to think*

poder (o>ue) *to be able, can*
preferir (e>ie) *to prefer*
quedar *to meet up with someone*
querer (e>ie) *to want (to do something)*
repetir (e>i) *to repeat*
salir *to go out, to leave*
servir (e>i) *to serve*
tener que *to have to (do something)*
vestirse (e>i) *to get dressed*

volver (o>ue) *to return*

138

EN RESUMEN: Gramática

UNIDAD 4

STEM-CHANGING VERBS (See page 126)

	ENTENDER e→ie	VOLVER o→ue	PEDIR e→i
yo	entiendo	vuelvo	pido
tú	entiendes	vuelves	pides
usted/él/ella	entiende	vuelve	pide
nosotros/as	entendemos	volvemos	pedimos
vosotros/as	entendéis	volvéis	pedís
ustedes/ellos/ellas	entienden	vuelven	piden

THE VERBS HACER AND SALIR (See page 127)

	HACER	SALIR
yo	hago	salgo
tú	haces	sales
usted/él/ella	hace	sale
nosotros/as	hacemos	salimos
vosotros/as	hacéis	salís
ustedes/ellos/ellas	hacen	salen

REFLEXIVE VERBS (See page 128)

	LEVANTARSE
yo	me levanto
tú	te levantas
usted/él/ella	se levanta
nosotros/as	nos levantamos
vosotros/as	os levantáis
ustedes/ellos/ellas	se levantan

139

Objectives for En resumen: Gramática
- Review unit grammar
- Practice communicative skills

Standards
- 1.2 Understand the language
- 1.3 Present information

Instructional Strategies
- Model how to review grammar.
- Have them review the Learning Outcomes in the unit opener to assess whether they feel they have mastered the main ideas and skills.
- Ask them if they can remember additional examples for each grammar topic
- Model how to find and go back to the appropriate page in the unit to review any grammar topic they may need help with.
- Invite students to review the grammar activities they completed in this unit.
- Ask them what grammar activities they found easy and which they found challenging. Encourage them to repeat any activities they found particularly challenging.
- Encourage students to take the online test in ELEteca to determine which aspects of the unit they need to study and review the most.

AHORA COMPRUEBA

OBJECTIVES FOR AHORA COMPRUEBA

- Review and recycle grammar, vocabulary and culture from the last two units
- Complete self-assessment

CORE RESOURCES

- Audio Program: Track 53

STANDARDS

1.2   Understand the language

1.3   Present information

2.1   Practices and perspectives

4.1   Compare cultures

INSTRUCTIONAL STRATEGIES

- Activities can be completed individually or in pairs and then reviewed with the class.
- When reviewing answers in class, expand by asking students if they agree with the answers given and then writing the correct answer on the board.
- You may wish to assign point values to each activity as a way for students to monitor their progress. If students achieve less than 80% on each activity, direct them to **En resumen** in the previous two units for page numbers to review.

Activity 1

After completing this activity, students compare their answers with a partner.

🎧 53 Activity 2

- Ask: **¿Quién creen que es Elena?** Students will confirm their answer when they listen to the audio.
- Play the audio the first time for students to answer individually. Then play it second time so students can compare their answers. Go over the correct answers with the whole class.

Audioscript

Hola, me llamo Elena, y os presento a mis amigos de la escuela: Julián es el muchacho de pelo corto, liso y rubio que lleva una camiseta a rayas. Está detrás del sofá. Santiago tiene pelo corto también, pero es moreno, lleva jeans y una camiseta azul, es muy alto. Beatriz es muy guapa y simpática, tiene el pelo largo, liso y es morena; tiene los ojos azules. Es hermana de Santiago. Javier es el más hablador de todos, tiene el pelo rizado y es muy moreno, sus ojos son marrones. Marta es su novia y mi mejor amiga, tiene un pelo precioso, largo y rojo; sus ojos son verdes. Y yo estoy sentada en el centro. Soy rubia, tengo el pelo rizado y muy largo, mis ojos son azules, llevo gafas pero solo para estudiar.

ANSWERS

Activity 1

1. Es rubio y lleva una camisa de rayas; **2.** Es moreno y lleva una camiseta verde; **3.** Es rubia y lleva jeans claros; **4.** Es morena; **5.** Es moreno y lleva una camiseta azul; **6.** Es pelirroja y lleva una blusa azul.

Activity 2

a. Beatriz: 4; **b.** Elena: 3; **c.** Javier: 5; **d.** Julián: 1; **e.** Marta: 6; **f.** Santiago: 2.

AHORA COMPRUEBA

1 Describe the people in the photo. Include a physical description of each person and what he/she is wearing.

1. ....

2. ....

3. ....

4. ....

5. ....

6. ....

2 🎧 53 Listen to Elena describe her friends. Then match the name to the correct image of the person based on the description you hear.

a. Beatriz:	➡	....
b. Elena:	➡	....
c. Javier:	➡	....
d. Julián:	➡	....
e. Marta:	➡	....
f. Santiago:	➡	....

REPASO UNIDADES 3 Y 4

REPASO
3-4

3 Read about Beatriz as she describes a typical day for her. Fill in the blanks with the correct form of the verb in parenthesis.

De lunes a viernes (levantarse) ....1......... a las 8 porque mi clase (empezar) ....2......... a las nueve. (Ducharse) ....3......... rápido, (desayunar) ....4......... leche con cereales y (correr) ....5......... a la escuela para no llegar tarde. (Comer) ....6......... a las dos con mi familia, mi madre es profesora de Matemáticas y llega a casa para comer con mi hermano y conmigo. Mi padre llega más tarde porque es médico y su día es más largo. Por la tarde (quedar) ....7......... con Marta y (estudiar) ....8......... juntas. (Hacer) ....9......... deporte los martes y jueves, los lunes y miércoles toco el piano. (Acostarse) ....10......... a las once y (leer) ....11......... un poco hasta las 12. ¡El fin de semana es mucho mejor! (Quedar) ....12......... con mis amigos y jugamos videojuegos o (salir) ....13......... y (ver) ....14......... una película en el cine.

4 Read the text again and answer the following questions about Beatriz's day.

a. ¿A qué hora se levanta Beatriz? ➡ _____
b. ¿Dónde come y con quién? ➡ _____
c. ¿Qué hace por las tardes de lunes a viernes? ➡ _____
d. ¿Cuándo queda con sus amigos? ➡ _____
e. ¿Qué hace antes de dormir? ➡ _____
f. ¿Cuáles son las profesiones de sus padres? ➡ _____

5 Complete the schedule below with the activities you typically do during the week.

	L	M	X	J	V	S	D
Mañana							
Tarde							

6 Look at the list of people in Beatriz's family and complete her family tree.

Carmen Solís Sevilla
Manuel Sánchez Román
Beatriz Sánchez Coronado
Carlos Sánchez Coronado
Ángeles Román López
Lucía Coronado Solís
Francisco Sánchez Márquez
Alberto Coronado Martín

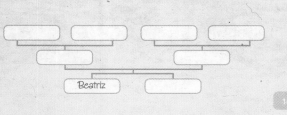

141

Activity 5

This is a free-writing activity and each student will complete it according to his or her day. Project the blank schedule and do with the whole class with each student filling their own agenda for the week. Once students have completed this individually, they write five questions to ask a partner about what they normally do. Each student must respond according to the information they wrote down on their schedule. Then partners trade schedules to show each other how close they were in understanding each other's schedule.

Activity 6

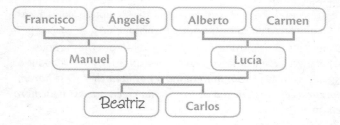

SLOWER-PACED LEARNERS

Have students make a list of the learning objectives noted in the opening spreads of the two previous units. Tell them to ask themselves: How well can I do this: very well, well, or not well? Then pair less confident students with stronger students so that they can help each other review.

ADVANCED LEARNERS

For those students who have a good handle on the vocabulary, grammar, and cultural content of the units, encourage them to focus on the development of their listening, speaking, reading, and writing skills prior to quizzes and tests. In addition to redoing the skills-based activities within the units, encourage them to seek new, related (and fun) material online to help them practice.

HERITAGE LANGUAGE LEARNERS

For students who already have a base of the language, challenge them to put themselves in the position of the teacher prior to assessments. How would they teach a non-native speaker the content of the previous two units? Have them develop worksheets, activities, games, presentations, and lesson plans that could be used to teach other students the material. By putting students in this new role, they will enhance their own knowledge and become masters of the content.

Activity 3

1. me levanto; 2. empieza; 3. Me ducho; 4. desayuno; 5. corro; 6. Como; 7. quedo; 8. estudiamos; 9. Hago; 10. Me acuesto; 11. leo; 12. Quedo; 13. salimos; 14. vemos.

Activity 4

a. Se levanta a las ocho de la mañana porque va a la escuela.

b. Come con su madre y su hermano en su casa.

c. Queda con Marta y estudian juntas, martes y jueves hace deporte y lunes y miércoles toca el piano.

d. Queda con sus amigos el fin de semana.

e. Lee un poco.

f. Su madre es profesora de Matemáticas y su padre es medico.

OBJECTIVES FOR UNIT OPENER

- Introduce unit theme: *¿Te gusta?* about foods we like and leisure activities
- Culture: Learn about traditional foods in Hispanic countries

STANDARDS

- 1.2 Understand the language
- 2.1 Practices and perspectives

INSTRUCTIONAL STRATEGIES

- Introduce unit theme and objectives: Talking about foods they like.
- Have students look at the photograph. Read the caption aloud: *Esta familia almuerza en su restaurante favorito.*
- Ask questions to help students recycle content from the previous unit. For instance, encourage them to use expressions to talk about the image, such as: *¿Es por la mañana o por la noche? ¿Qué hacen, almorzar o cenar? ¿Qué día de la semana creen que es? ¿Qué hora creen que es?*
- Use the photograph to preview unit vocabulary, including: *el arroz*, *el tomate*, *las verduras*. Help students access meaning by making frequent use of gestures or visuals.
- Ask the introductory questions.
  - *¿Comes en restaurantes con tu familia?*
  - *¿Prefieres la comida de restaurantes o la comida de casa?*
  - *¿Qué pides en tu restaurante favorito?*
- Ask related questions: *¿Qué ven en la mesa? ¿Cuántas personas vemos en esta familia?* Have students identify the family members. *¿Creen que celebran algún evento en especial?*

SLOWER-PACED LEARNERS

Encourage students to recycle and retrieve vocabulary, including verbs, and structures (mainly, the present tense) from previous units. Ask them to describe the pictures using colors, adjectives, *ser / estar*, and regular verbs. Use *yes/no* questions first and then progress to open-ended questions.

UNIDAD

5

¿TE GUSTA?

⋙ ¿Comes en restaurantes con tu familia?

⋙ ¿Prefieres la comida de restaurantes o la comida de casa?

⋙ ¿Qué pides en tu restaurante favorito?

Esta familia almuerza en su restaurante favorito.

142

ADDITIONAL UNIT RESOURCES

Extension Activities (EA) (Photocopiable)	Interactive Whiteboard **Lessons** (IWB)	Audio	Video	Online ELEteca
EA: 5.1, 5.2	IWB: 5.1	54 to 61	Diálogo 5	

In this unit, you will learn to:

- ☐ Talk about what you do in your free time
- ☐ Describe likes and dislikes
- ☐ Express agreement and disagreement
- ☐ Order in a restaurant
- ☐ Explain what part of the body hurts
- ☐ Describe how you are feeling

Using
- *Gustar* and similar verbs
- *Ser* and *estar*
- *También* and *tampoco*
- *Doler* and the parts of the body

Cultural Connections
- Share information about traditional foods in Hispanic countries, and compare cultural similarities

SABOR HISPANO
- ¡A comer, bailar y gozar!
- Panamá, Colombia y Venezuela

¡ACCIÓN!

143

LEARNING OUTCOMES

- Talk about what you do in your free time
- Describe likes and dislikes
- Express agreement and disagreement
- Order in a restaurant
- Explain what part of the body hurts
- Describe how you are feeling

UNIT PREVIEW

- Use the unit opener to introduce students to a preview of the vocabulary and the cultural topics for this unit.
- Encourage students to use the images to practice interpersonal and interpretive communication skills. Ask questions such as: **¿Qué ven en estas fotos? ¿Qué profesión está representada? (cocinero).**
- Have students look at the images on this page and relate them to the objectives listed.
- Invite students to read the topic for **Sabor hispano** and preview that section in the unit. Point out the image and ask students if they have ever heard of *arepas*. Explain that they are very popular in many regions of South America and that they will learn more about them.
- Introduce the video series in **¡Acción!** and ask students to predict what they think the episode will be about.
- If time allows, have students work in pairs to talk about the images using the questions you have modeled. Then have volunteers present to the class what they understand this unit to be about.

ADVANCED LEARNERS

Ask students to prepare questions about the pictures using question words seen in previous units. Invite them to ask these questions to the class.

HERITAGE LANGUAGE LEARNERS

Have students share what their families eat or what they have seen other Hispanic families eat. Other students can ask them questions, for example: **¿Tu familia come frijoles? ¿Tus amigos hispanos toman jugos de frutas?**

THREE MODES OF COMMUNICATION: UNIT 5			
	INTERPERSONAL	INTERPRETIVE	PRESENTATIONAL
HABLAMOS DE...	5	1, 2, 3, 4	5
COMUNICA	4, 7	1, 2, 3, 5, 6	4, 7
¡ACCIÓN!	1	1, 2, 3, 4	1
PALABRA POR PALABRA	2, 10, 11	1, 4, 7, 8, 9	2, 3, 5, 6, 10
GRAMÁTICA	2, 3, 4, 5, 9, 12	1, 7, 8, 10	3, 6, 11
DESTREZAS		1, 2, 3, 4	
CULTURA		SABOR HISPANO	
RELATO	5	1, 2, 3, 4	5, 6

OBJECTIVES FOR HABLAMOS DE...

- Preview vocabulary: after-school and free time activities
- Preview grammatical structures: **estar**, **gustar**, **doler**
- Read and listen to a conversation among school friends deciding what to do in their free time
- Understand language in context

CORE RESOURCES

- Audio Program: 54

STANDARDS

1.1   Engage in conversation

1.2   Understand the language

1.3   Present information

4.1   Compare languages

INSTRUCTIONAL STRATEGIES

Activity 1

Warm-up: Before opening the book, invite students to brainstorm around the idea of **La escuela y el tiempo libre**. Have students work in pairs and give them 3–5 minutes to brainstorm as many terms as they can. They write their ideas in two columns. Then elicit from the whole class what ideas they brainstormed and write them on the board. If needed, help them by providing the following terms. For **la escuela**: **estudiante**, **estudiar**, **clase**, **exámenes**, **aprender**. For **tiempo libre**: **deportes**, **videojuegos**, **jugar**, **fútbol**, **domingo**.

🎧 54 Activity 2

- Introduction to the conversation: Tell students to close their books. Explain that they will listen to a dialogue among friends about activities at school and outside of school.
- Check for prior knowledge by asking students what they think the characters will say.
- Before listening to the audio, clarify that students should focus on information that they need to answer the *true/false* questions.
- Play the audio twice. During the first time, ask students to listen to what these friends are saying about school. During the second time, they should listen to what these friends are planning on doing and who is agreeing with whom.
- Use the audio to focus students' attention on rhythm, intonation, and pronunciation. Have students respond chorally as needed.
- Finally, have students open the book and review the dialogue. Observe, provide support and correct students as needed.
- Have students answer the questions based on the audio and the photo in Activity 1.

ANSWERS

Activity 1

a. estudiantes; **b.** las 9 menos diez o las ocho y cincuenta; **c.** tomar un examen; **d.** tienen 14 o 15 años.

HABLAMOS DE... El tiempo libre

1 Look at the image below of students studying before going to class. Then complete the sentences according to the image.

a. La imagen representa a unos ....

b. En el reloj de la fotografía son ....

c. Los amigos estudian antes de ....

d. Los cuatro muchachos .... años.

2 🎧 54 Listen to the conversation. Then decide whether the following statements are true (T) or false (F).

Quique: ¿Qué tal, muchachos? ¿Qué tal llevan el examen?

Germán: Yo no muy bien, estoy un poco preocupado.

Carmen: Pero si tú estudias mucho, ¡seguro que te sale bien! ¿A que sí, Noelia?

Noelia: Pues claro. Yo creo que va a ser bastante fácil. Además, esta tarde ya no tenemos que estudiar.

Quique: Es verdad. ¿Qué quieren hacer? ¡Ah!, podemos jugar a videojuegos. Me encantan los videojuegos.

Germán: Es que estoy cansado de jugar siempre con los videojuegos.

Carmen: Vale, ¿y qué tal si hacemos deporte?

Germán: No sé, es que me duele (*hurts*) la pierna por el partido de fútbol del domingo.

Noelia: Podemos ir a comer algo. Germán, tú siempre tienes hambre, ¿no?

Germán: Vale, pero no quiero ir a un restaurante con mucha gente, que seguro que tenemos que esperar (*wait*) mucho para sentarnos (*to sit*) y estoy de mal humor.

Quique: ¿Qué? ¡Pero si siempre estás contento!

Carmen: Chévere, pues más tarde decidimos. Después del examen seguro que estás más contento.

Germán: Es verdad, chicos. ¿Vemos una película? Me gusta la nueva de ciencia ficción.

Quique: A mí también.

Carmen: Sí, de acuerdo.

144

SLOWER-PACED LEARNERS

For additional oral practice, put students into small groups to practice the conversation in Activity 2.

ADVANCED LEARNERS

After completing the sentences in Activity 1, challenge students to ask partners three additional questions about it. For example, they can ask questions related to their physical descriptions or other objects in the image.

	T	F
a. De lunes a viernes los chicos quedan en la puerta de la escuela a las nueve de la mañana.	☐	☐
b. Mañana no hay escuela.	☐	☐
c. Quique está de mal humor.	☐	☐
d. Noelia piensa que el examen va a ser bastante fácil.	☐	☐
e. Carmen y Quique están de acuerdo con Germán.	☐	☐

3 **Answer the following questions about the conversation.**

a. ¿Cuántos planes proponen (suggest) los amigos para hacer esta tarde? ....

b. ¿Qué plan deciden hacer finalmente? ....

c. ¿A quién le duele la pierna? ....

d. ¿Por qué Germán no quiere ir a comer? ....

e. ¿Por qué no quiere jugar a videojuegos? ....

4 **Match the caption to the image.**

1. ☐ A María y a Graciela les gusta el campo y montar en bici. Ahora están cansadas.

2. ☐ A Miguel le encanta chatear con sus amigos de Argentina. Es muy abierto.

3. ☐ A Andrés le gusta hacer fotos, también le gustan los perros. Es muy simpático.

4. ☐ A Paloma le encanta ir de compras y comprar zapatos. Está muy contenta.

5 👥 **With a partner, take turns saying which of the following activities you like to do in your free time.**

- chatear con amigos
- ir de compras y comprar…
- escuchar música en mi mp4
- jugar a videojuegos
- hacer deporte
- montar en bici
- hacer fotos
- ver una película

Modelo:

Me gusta ir de compras y comprar botas.

145

INSTRUCTIONAL STRATEGIES

Activity 3

- As a warm-up, ask students if they have similar conversations before school about what they are going to do later. Ask: *¿Es difícil decidir lo que quieren hacer? ¿Tienen ustedes muchas opciones? ¿Qué posibilidades mencionan los muchachos en su conversación?*

- Pre-teach **doler** using gestures: *Me duele la mano*, *me duele el estómago*, and so on.

- Have students work in pairs if you find they are having difficulty understanding the conversation.

Activity 4

- Have students recall the plans mentioned in the conversation while you list them on the board. Tell students that the images represent other free-time activities and have them complete the activity. If necessary, explain that **bici** is short for **bicicleta**.

- Review and add the new activities to the list on the board.

Activity 5

Introduce the activity talking about what you like to do. Write some sample sentences on the board: **En mi tiempo libre, me gusta hacer fotos.** Point out to students the expression: **me gusta + infinitive**.

ANSWERS

Activity 2

Answers will vary.

a. F (Students will notice from photo in Activity 1 that the friends meet at 8:50, not 9); **b.** Likely T (Students may infer that the dialogue happens on a Friday and that, based on their plans, this does not seem to be a school night); **c.** F; **d.** T; **e.** T.

Activity 3

a. Proponen cuatro planes: videojuegos, deporte, ir a un restaurante, ver una película; **b.** Ver una película; **c.** A Germán le duele la pierna; **d.** No quiere esperar. Está de mal humor; **e.** Está cansado de jugar siempre con los videojuegos.

Activity 4

1. c; **2.** d; **3.** a; **4.** b.

Activity 5

Answers will vary and should reflect the vocabulary and expressions modeled.

SLOWER-PACED LEARNERS

After Activity 5, have students practice and compare sentences with **gustar** and sentences in the simple present tense so they can make connections with their preferences and habits: **Me gusta chatear por la noche con mis amigos / Yo chateo por la noche con mis amigos. Me gusta ver películas / Yo veo películas por la noche.**

ADVANCED LEARNERS

Ask students to prepare questions for the class so all of them can have extra practice with **gustar** sentences: **¿Qué te gusta hacer por la mañana? ¿Qué te gusta hacer con tus amigos? ¿Dónde te gusta comer?**

HERITAGE LANGUAGE LEARNERS

While slower-paced learners have extra practice with **gustar**, have heritage language learners discuss how their own activities are different from the ones presented on this page. Ask them to write a short paragraph.

OBJECTIVES FOR COMUNICA

- Present the communicative functions of the unit:
  – Using the verb **ser** to describe personality traits and characteristics
  – Using the verb **estar** to describe moods
- Practice describing personality traits and moods

CORE RESOURCES

- Extension Activities: EA 5.1
- Audio Program: 55
- Interactive Online Materials - ELEteca

STANDARDS

1.1	Engage in conversation	1.3	Present information
1.2	Understand the language	4.1	Compare languages

INSTRUCTIONAL STRATEGIES

- Introduce new adjectives by having students first turn to page 144 and look for the following words: **preocupado**, **cansado**, **de mal humor**, **contento**, **abierto**, **simpatico**. Then ask students to categorize them according to whether they describe moods or characteristics. Ask which ones refer to a temporary condition and which describe a permanent quality.
- Point out that in Spanish **estar** is used to describe a person's mood or feelings at a particular moment while **ser** is used to describe personality traits and characteristics. **Ser** with **tranquilo** describes a characteristic, a calm, relaxed person, while **estar tranquilo** refers to a momentary feeling, often as a result of another action or situation. **Está tranquilo después de recibir la nota del examen**.

Activity 1

Review the answers as a class.

 55 Activity 2

Review the expressions **¿Qué te pasa?** and **venga** (come on, let's go). Point out that **venga** is used mostly in Spain. In other countries, **ándale** is more commonly used. Have students fill in the blanks before they listen to the audio.

Extension

Use EA 5.1, **¿Qué tal estás?**, as a follow-up to provide additional practice with **estar**. Possible answers include: 1. ¿Qué te pasa?; 2. nerviosa; 3. tranquila; 4. simpática; 5. de mal humor; 6. dar un paseo.

Activity 3

Go over the answers as a class, encouraging students to explain their decisions about the use of **ser** or **estar**.

Activity 4

Model a conversation with a volunteer. After students write their conversations, call on a few pairs to present their conversations to the class.

COMUNICA

ESTAR

- Use **estar** to describe a person's mood or feelings at a particular moment.
  *Germán **está** preocupado por el examen. Germán is (feeling) worried about the test.*

- Adjectives commonly used with **estar**:

tranquilo/a *(feeling) relaxed*	**de buen/mal humor** *in a good/bad mood*
preocupado/a *(feeling) worried*	**bien, perfecto** *(feeling) fine*
alegre, contento/a *(feeling) happy*	**cansado/a** *(feeling) tired*
triste *(feeling) sad*	**enfadado/a** *(feeling) angry*

 Use **ser** to describe personality traits and characteristics with:
- **tranquilo/a** *quiet*
- **inteligente** *intelligent*
- **simpático/a** *likeable*
- **antipático/a** *disagreeable*
- **alegre, divertido/a** *fun, lively*
- **aburrido/a** *boring*

1 Using *estar* and the expressions above, describe the mood indicated by the following emoticons. Check your answers with a partner.

a. ...Está triste...   b.   c.   d.   e.

2 🎧 55 Listen to the conversation and fill in the blanks with the missing words.
Carlos: ¿Qué te pasa, Rafael? Hoy no .... muy ....
Rafael: Bueno, es que .... un poco ....
Carlos: ¡Pero qué dices! Si tú .... muy .... Venga, vamos a dar un paseo.
Rafael: Bueno, vale.

3 Fill in the blanks with *es* or *está* to describe Bea. Check your answers with a partner.
Bea .... muy simpática. Cuando estamos juntos, ella .... muy divertida y siempre .... de buen humor. Esta semana .... preocupada porque tiene un examen importante. Cuando la llamo por teléfono, ... nerviosa. Me dice que .... de mal humor. ¡Pobre Bea!

4 With a partner, prepare a conversation with Bea comparing how she normally is to the way she is feeling today and give a reason why. Then, switch roles.

Modelo: El: ¿Qué te pasa, Bea? Hoy...
Bea: Es verdad, hoy... porque...

| Normalmente... tranquila y simpática. | Hoy... nerviosa. | Hoy... de mal humor. |

 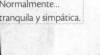 

ANSWERS

Activity 1

a. Está triste; **b.** Está contento / de buen humor; **c.** Está cansado; **d.** Está nervioso / preocupado; **e.** Está de mal humor / enfadado.

Activity 2

estás, contento, estoy, aburrido, eres, divertido.

Activity 3

es; es; está; está; está; está.

HERITAGE LANGUAGE LEARNERS

Using the text in Activity 3 as a model, have students write a similar description about someone they know, changing the adjectives as needed.

ORDERING IN A RESTAURANT

5 Read the following conversation in a restaurant between the waiter and his customers. Then match the items ordered to the correct images below.

Mesero: Hola, buenas tardes. ¿Qué les sirvo?
Cliente 1: Para mí, una hamburguesa (1) y un refresco de cola (2).
Cliente 2: Y para mí, un refresco de naranja (3).
Mesero: ¿Quiere algo de comer?
Cliente 2: Sí, yo un sándwich de jamón y queso (4), por favor.
Mesero: ¿Algo más?
Cliente 2: No, nada más, gracias.

***

Cliente 1: ¿Nos trae agua, por favor?
Mesero: Tomen, aquí tienen.

***

Cliente 1: La cuenta, por favor.
Mesero: Sí, son 17 dólares.

6 Look at the different questions and answers commonly used when ordering in a restaurant. Fill in the blanks with the missing words used in the conversation above.

Mesero	Cliente
¿Qué le/les ....? *What can I get for you?*	........, una hamburguesa. *I (will have) a hamburger.*
¿Qué quiere/n beber? *What would you like to drink?* ¿Quiere/n algo de ....? *Would you like anything to eat?*	.... un refresco de naranja. *For me, an orange soda.* ...., ... un sándwich de jamón y queso. *Yes, (I will have) a ham and cheese sandwich.*
¿Quieren tomar algo más? *Would you like to have anything else?* ¿..................................? *Anything else?*	No, ... gracias. *No, nothing, thank you.* ¿........ agua? *Would you bring us more water?* ...., por favor. *The check, please.* ¿Cuánto es? *How much do I owe you?*

7  With a partner, take turns playing the roles of waiter/waitress and customer. Use the expressions in Activity 6 and the menu as a guide. Then present your conversation to the class.

- Primeros *First course* ➡ *¿Qué quiere de primero?*
- Segundos *Second course* ➡ *¿Qué quiere de segundo?*
- Postres *Desserts* ➡ *¿Qué quiere de postre?*

Menú del día
12€

Primeros
Ensalada mixta
Paella
Sopa del día
Segundos
Pollo asado
Filete de ternera con patatas
Merluza a la romana
Postres
Fruta del tiempo
Helado
Pan y bebida

MORE IN ELETECA: EXTRA ONLINE PRACTICE

147

CULTURAL NOTES

- Point out the difference in Spain between **un sándwich** (typically served on sliced bread) and **un bocadillo** (served on a baguette or roll). In other countries, however, people may say **un bocadito** for small sandwiches made on sliced bread, while **un sándwich cubano** is a traditional grilled Cuban sandwich made of ham and cheese and served on toasted French bread.
- Tell students that a Spanish **tortilla** is a thick omelet made with eggs, onions, and potatoes and is different from a Mexican **tortilla**, which is made from flour or corn and used as bread.
- Point out that the use of **usted** is appropriate for situations in restaurants and stores as a form of courtesy.

Activity 6

- Have students complete this activity on their own.
- Then project IWB 5.1, **En el restaurante** so that students can check their answers.

Activity 7

Point out the expressions **de primero**, **de segundo**, **de postre**, and ask them if they can guess what they mean (first course, second course, and dessert). Also review menu items such as **filete de ternera** (*veal fillet*), **merluza a la romana** (*hake*) and **helado** (*ice-cream*). Encourage students to guess at the other items.

CULTURAL NOTE

Different types of lunches are eaten throughout the Spanish-speaking world. While lunches in Spain are usually heavy and long with menus of two courses and a dessert, other countries prefer something lighter served on a single plate.

ANSWERS

Activity 5

a. 3; b. 1; c. 4; d. 2.

Activity 6 and IWB 5.1: En el restaurante

Mesero: *tomar; comer; ¿Algo más?* **Cliente:** *Para mí; Yo; Me pone; nada más; ¿nos trae un poco más de...?; La cuenta.*

SLOWER-PACED LEARNERS

Before speaking freely in Activity 7, you may want to encourage students to write out the conversation first. Tell them to refer to Activity 5 as an example, adding questions about the courses and using the food from the menu.

ADVANCED LEARNERS

Building on the role play in Activity 7, have students to make a video using the language presented here. Have them post the videos to a class website or show them in class.

OBJECTIVES FOR COMUNICA

Present the communicative functions of the unit: Ordering in a restaurant

CORE RESOURCES

- Interactive Whiteboard Lesson: IWB 5.1

STANDARDS

1.1	Engage in conversation	1.3	Present information
1.2	Understand the language	4.1	Compare languages

INSTRUCTIONAL STRATEGIES

Activity 5

Ask three students to role-play the dialogue. You can bring props, such as a serving tray for the waiter.

OBJECTIVES FOR ¡ACCIÓN!

- Provide students with a structured approach to viewing the video
- Contextualize the content of the unit in a familiar scenario

CORE RESOURCES

- Unit Video 5 - Un pelo en mi cena
- Online Materials - ELEteca

STANDARDS

1.1 Interpersonal communication

1.2 Interpretive communication

2.1 Culture: Practices and perspectives

INSTRUCTIONAL STRATEGIES

Previewing: Antes del video

- Tell students to read the title of the video and look at the images. Ask: **¿Crees que las muchachas van a tener una buena experiencia en el restaurante? ¿Por qué sí o no?** Elicit ideas from the class.

Activity 1

- Have students work individually to match the images with the descriptions.
- Go over the answers as a class, explaining any new or unfamiliar vocabulary.

Activity 2

- Give students a few moments to jot down their own guesses.
- Put students in pairs or small groups to share their ideas and justify them based on the images. Call on a few groups to share their predictions with the class.

Viewing: Durante el video.

Activity 3

- 🎬 Play to video so that students can check their guesses. Encourage them to take notes as they listen.
- Go over the answers as a class, inviting students to correct or add more information to each other's responses. Note that since Activity 5 asks students to listen what the girls order in detail, you may not want to go over all of the possible answers for question **b** just yet if the students don't produce them on their own.

Activities 4 and 5 (next page)

- Before playing the video again, challenge students to complete the sentences in Activity 4 and the chart in Activity 5 based on the information that they remember. Have them work individually.
- Play the video again so they can listen for the remaining answers. Confirm the correct answers.

ANSWERS

Activities 1

1. c; 2. b; 3. a; 4. e; 5. d; 6. f.

Activities 2 and 3

a. Es un restaurante español; b. Eli pide ensalada, tortilla española y limonada. Lorena pide gazpacho, pollo con arroz y refresco de naranja; c. El cuchillo está sucio. Hay un pelo en la ensalada; d. Juanjo no es un buen mesero. No tiene experiencia. No sabe cómo servir ni retirar los platos. Grita y no resuelve bien los problemas con el cuchillo sucio y la ensalada con el pelo.

¡ACCIÓN! Un pelo en mi cena

1.   2.   3.   4.   5.   6.

ANTES DEL VIDEO

1 Match the statements to the correct image.

a. Es el dueño *(owner)* del restaurante.

b. Las muchachas no están contentas en el restaurante.

c. Juanjo habla muy alto y a Eli le molesta.

d. Las muchachas llegan al restaurante.

e. Juanjo sirve el primer plato.

f. Lorena tiene un problema con su cuchillo.

2 Look at the scenes from the episode and make your best guesses about what you think is happening.

a. ¿A qué tipo de restaurante van Eli y Lorena?

b. ¿Qué piden para cenar?

c. ¿Qué problemas crees que tienen en el restaurante?

d. ¿Crees que Juanjo es un buen mesero? Explica por qué.

DURANTE EL VIDEO

3 Watch the complete episode and check your answers to Activity 2. Did you guess correctly?

4 Select the correct option to complete each statement.

a. Lorena y Eli van a **comer/cenar** en un restaurante.

b. Es la **primera/segunda** vez que las muchachas cenan en ese restaurante.

c. El dueño del restaurante es **tío/padre** de Juanjo.

d. La tortilla española lleva huevos, cebolla y **tomates/patatas**.

e. El cuchillo de Lorena está **roto/sucio**.

f. En la ensalada de Eli hay **un pelo/una mosca**.

148

Activity 4

a. cenar; b. primera; c. tío; d. patatas; e. sucio; f. un pelo.

SLOWER-PACED LEARNERS

Consider pausing the video just before or after key information is revealed that will help students complete the sentences in Activity 4. This will help signal that they should pay attention to what's ahead or recall what they've just heard.

ADVANCED LEARNERS

After doing Activity 1, have students look at the images again to summarize and describe what they think happens in the video in their own words. Encourage them to add their own details and speculations to make it more interesting.

5 List the menu items each one orders. Use the images as a guide.

	Lorena	Eli
De primero		
De segundo		
Para beber		

6 Match the statement to the person that says it in the episode.

a. Luego pedimos el postre.
b. A mí me encanta la comida española.
c. ¿Por qué grita tan alto?
d. Uno de los camareros está enfermo hoy.
e. Sopa de jamón de primero y arroz con verdura de segundo.
f. Lo siento. Ahora te traigo uno limpio.
g. Las cosas se retiran por la izquierda.
h. Dicen que se come muy bien.

Lorena	Eli	Juanjo

DESPUÉS DEL VIDEO

7 Think about the reactions of the characters in the episode. How would you describe their mood or feelings at the particular moment described below? Vary your expressions using affirmative and negative statements and compare answers with your partner. Do you agree?

a. Juanjo: cuando sirve el primer plato.
b. El tío: cuando ve que Juanjo limpia el cuchillo en la camisa.
c. Eli: cuando encuentra el pelo en la ensalada.
d. Lorena y Eli: al final del episodio.

8 Research the following Spanish dishes and list their ingredients. Which one would you prefer?

El gazpacho	Lleva tomates...
La paella	Lleva...

9 Answer the following questions and compare answers with your classmates. Do you have similar preferences?

a. ¿Conoces algún restaurante español? ¿Cómo se llama? ¿Te gusta?
b. ¿Cuál es tu restaurante favorito? ¿Por qué? Descríbelo.
c. ¿Qué haces si vas a un restaurante y encuentras un pelo en tu plato?
d. Describe una comida cara y otra barata.

 MORE IN ELETECA: EXTRA ONLINE PRACTICE

149

INSTRUCTIONAL STRATEGIES

Activity 6

- After the second viewing, have students match the statements with the characters who said them in the video.
- Call on volunteers to read the lines aloud, and have students vote on which person from the video they think said each line. For any statements that produce a fair amount of discrepancy, find the moment in time in the video and replay it to settle the debate.

Post-viewing: Después del video

Activity 7

- Refer students back to the adjectives they learned on page 146 to help them describe the characters' moods and feelings.

Activity 8

- Have students guess the ingredients of each dish before having them do the research. You might present them with some images of the food so they can extrapolate from them.
- Alternatively, you can project a recipe for each dish and have students identify whether it's for *gazpacho* or *paella*. They can use the recipes to take note of the ingredients in each.
- Invite students who have had either food to say whether or not they like it.

Activity 9

- Circulate around the room as groups discuss the questions, taking note of any common errors that you can review later as a class.
- Call on volunteers to share any interesting information from their discussions with the class.

ANSWERS

Activity 5

	Lorena	Eli
De primero	gazpacho	ensalada
De segundo	arroz con pollo	tortilla española
Para beber	un refresco de naranja	una limonada

Activity 6

Lorena: b, h; Eli: a, c; Juanjo: d, e, f, g.

SLOWER-PACED LEARNERS

Have students find images of two different kinds of *gazpacho* or *paella*, prepare a list of the ingredients in both variations, and compare them. Encourage them to use a T-chart so they can show the information side-by-side and use it to report back to the class.

HERITAGE LANGUAGE LEARNERS

In Activity 8, encourage students to look for images and recipes of two other typical Spanish dishes others than *gazpacho* and *paella* and share them with the class. Challenge them to compare the dishes to ones they may know about from other Spanish-speaking countries.

OBJECTIVES FOR ACTIVIDADES DE OCIO Y TIEMPO LIBRE

- Present the vocabulary needed to practice the communicative and grammatical functions for the unit: Talk about what you do in your free time
- Identify words for leisure activities

CORE RESOURCES

- Audio Program: 56, 57
- Interactive Online Materials - ELEteca

STANDARDS

1.1 Engage in conversation
1.2 Understand the language
1.3 Present information
3.2 Acquire information
4.1 Compare languages

INSTRUCTIONAL STRATEGIES

🎧 56 Activity 1

- Before presenting the vocabulary, invite students to brainstorm around the idea of *tiempo libre*. If needed, they can use a dictionary to work through the vocabulary presented here.
- Check students' understanding of all the vocabulary. Tell students they will now listen to the audio with verbs to go with all these activities, such as: *ver la televisión*.
- Have students listen to the audio and repeat. If needed, play the audio twice.

Audioscript

1. jugar a los bolos / al boliche; **2.** jugar a los videojuegos; **3.** jugar al fútbol; **4.** ver una película; **5.** hacer natación; **6.** hacer esquí; **7.** hacer judo; **8.** hacer ciclismo; **9.** tomar un refresco; **10.** hacer deporte; **11.** ver la televisión; **12.** ver un concierto; **13.** ver una exposición; **14.** tomar unas tapas; **15.** navegar por Internet; **16.** navegar por el mar; **17.** hacer yoga; **18.** tomar el sol.

CULTURAL NOTE

Explain to students that *tapas* are small portions of food that are enjoyed between meals in restaurants and cafes. They can consist of such food items as *tortilla de papas*, *queso*, *chorizo* (Spanish sausage), etc. Ask students if they know of any tapas restaurants in the area as they are becoming more and more popular in the U.S.

Activity 2

- Review the **Modelo** with students and brainstorm additional activities.
- Circulate around the room to check that students are on task and responding correctly.

ANSWERS

Activity 1

a. Ver: 4, una película; 11, la televisión; 12, un concierto; 13, una exposición.
b. Hacer: 5, la natación; 6, esquí; 7, judo; 8, ciclismo; 10, deporte; 17, yoga.
c. Tomar: 9, un refresco; 14, unas tapas; 18, el sol.
d. Jugar (a): 1, los bolos; 2, los videojuegos; 3, el fútbol.
e. Navegar (por): 15, Internet; 16, el mar.

PALABRA POR PALABRA Actividades de ocio

1. los bolos / el boliche **2.** los videojuegos **3.** el fútbol **4.** una película **5.** natación **6.** esquí

7. judo **8.** ciclismo **9.** un refresco **10.** deporte **11.** la televisión **12.** un concierto

13. una exposición **14.** unas tapas **15.** Internet **16.** el mar **17.** yoga **18.** el sol

1 🎧 56 Write the number of the activity next to the verb it uses. Then listen to the verbs and activities used together to check your answers. ¡*Atención!* The first three have been done for you.

a. Ver _6_
b. Hacer _5_
c. Tomar _10_
d. Jugar (a) _____
e. Navegar (por) _____

2 👥 Make one or two recommendations for each of the following people based on their moods, personalities, and circumstances as described below. Then take turns with a partner exchanging your suggestions. Record all the suggestions provided.

¿Qué puede(n) hacer?	Puede(n)...
1. Isabel es muy tranquila. A ella no le gusta salir. Prefiere estar en casa.	
2. Violeta vive cerca de la playa (*beach*). La temperatura hoy es de 95 grados y ella tiene calor.	
3. Paco y sus amigos tienen mucha energía y son muy activos. A ellos les gusta competir.	
4. Iván está aburrido. Le gusta mucho el arte y la música. A sus amigos también.	

Modelo: E1: ¿Qué puede hacer Isabel?
E2: Isabel puede ver la televisión.

Activity 2

Answers will vary.

SLOWER-PACED LEARNERS

Poder has not been formally introduced, but it is used in Activity 2. Explain that it belongs to the *o > ue* verbs. Have some students use the verb using other forms like *puedo*, *podemos*, and *pueden*. Write the conjugations on the board.

ADVANCED LEARNERS

To continue practicing in Activity 2, have students come up with and describe the moods, personalities, and circumstances of other people (or themselves) so their partners can make suggestions.

y tiempo libre

3 👥 Select from the options you and your partner prepared in Activity 2 for each of the situations and say which one you would prefer to do in each case.

Yo prefiero...

1. ....
2. ....
3. ....
4. ....

4 🎧 57 **Look at the image of Miguel and try to guess what four activities he likes to do in his free time. Then listen to the audio to check your answers.**

☐ viajar con amigos
☐ escuchar música
☐ tomar tapas con los amigos
☐ ver conciertos en directo
☐ ver la televisión
☐ hacer deporte
☐ navegar por Internet
☐ viajar solo

5 **What can you guess about Inés and the things she likes to do in her free time based on the image of her below? Write a short description about Inés. Include the following:**

• two personality traits
• how she is feeling today
• three activities she likes to do in her free time
• one activity she doesn't like to do

> Inés es...
>
> Hoy está...
>
> A ella le gusta...
>
> A ella no le gusta...

6 **Prepare a similar description about yourself. Then share the information you wrote about yourself and Inés with the class. ¡Atención! To say what you like (and don't like) use A mí me gusta.../A mí no me gusta...**

151

Activity 3

Have students report back to the class.

🎧 57 Activity 4

Before playing the audio, ask students to look at the image and infer what this person likes by looking closely at the photo. Have students look closely at what this person is wearing and holding.

Audioscript

¿En mi tiempo libre? Pues, no sé, me gusta hacer muchas cosas. Lo que más me gusta es viajar a otros países. Prefiero viajar solo, porque así hago lo que quiero. También me encanta escuchar música, siempre llevo mi mp4 con mis canciones favoritas y cuando puedo, voy a conciertos ¡me encanta! La verdad es que no me gusta hacer deporte, prefiero navegar por Internet. Y bueno, muchas más cosas, no sé…

Activity 5

Have students brainstorm descriptions for Inés as you write them on the board. Allow students time to write their descriptions in class.

Activity 6

Assign this for homework or use as an assessment.

ANSWERS

Activity 3

Answers will vary and will reflect the expressions taught, based on the model.

Activity 4

Escuchar música, viajar solo, ver conciertos (en directo) y navegar por Internet.

Activity 5

Answers will vary. Possible answers include.

• Inés es alegre.
• Hoy está contenta.
• A ella le gusta la música.
• A ella no le gusta la televisión.

Activity 6

Answers will vary and should reflect the expressions taught.

SLOWER-PACED LEARNERS

Have students write a table with all the activities and things they like and they don't like. Decide together which ones are the most and least popular. Ask students repeatedly to ensure that they become comfortable with the verbs **gustar**, **ser**, and **estar**.

HERITAGE LANGUAGE LEARNERS

After Activity 5, have students find an image of a well-known person from the Hispanic community and complete similar sentences about him or her. Encourage students to do some research about this person so they can provide more detailed and accurate information about their likes and dislikes. Have them present the information to the class, showing the image that they've found and being sure to properly introduce who the person is.

151

OBJECTIVES FOR LOS ALIMENTOS

- Present the vocabulary needed to practice the communicative and grammatical functions for the unit: Food items
- Identify different types of food
- Express what foods we like

CORE RESOURCES

- Audio Program: 58

STANDARDS

1.1	Engage in conversation
1.2	Understand the language
1.3	Present information
3.2	Acquire information
4.1	Compare languages

INSTRUCTIONAL STRATEGIES

58 Activity 7

- Ask students to work in pairs. Have them look at the images and identify the various food items by filling in the missing letters. Do not provide corrective feedback.
- Then have them listen to the audio and repeat.
- Have students complete / check their answers against the audio.
- In order to help students remember the new vocabulary, ask questions about their likes and dislikes using the food items taught, such as: *¿Te gustan las zanahorias? ¿Comes zanahorias frecuentemente? ¿Cuál es tu plato favorito?*

CULTURAL NOTE

In some parts of Latin American, *chile* and to a certain extent *ají* and *morrón* are more frequent than *pimientos*. For more information about Spanish culinary terms throughout the Spanish-speaking world, you can consult this website: http://www.euroresidentes.com/Alimentos/diccionario_equivalencias.

Audioscript

a. frijoles; **b.** queso; **c.** zanahorias; **d.** leche; **e.** cebollas; **f.** tomates; **g.** huevos; **h.** carne; **i.** mariscos; **j.** naranjas; **k.** pimientos; **l.** pollo.

Activity 8

- Ask students to look at chef Fernando at the bottom of the page. Let them know Fernando is a very unconventional chef and he often makes bizarre dishes in which he mixes ingredients that do not usually go together. Tell them that Fernando has guests tonight and he wants to prepare the dishes with the ingredients listed.
- Have students complete the activity.
- Invite students to share which of Fernando's dishes they consider the most bizarre.

ANSWERS

Activity 7

a. frijoles; **b.** queso; **c.** zanahorias; **d.** leche; **e.** cebollas; **f.** tomates; **g.** huevos; **h.** carne; **i.** mariscos; **j.** naranjas; **k.** pimientos; **l.** pollo.

Activity 8

- **Primer plato:** tomates (f) con naranjas (j), pollo (l) y frijoles (a).
- **Segundo plato:** carne (h) con mariscos (i), pimientos (k) y queso (b).

PALABRA POR PALABRA Los alimentos

7 🎧 58 Using the list of foods below, complete the words under each image to identify the food in Spanish. Then listen to the audio recording to check your answers.

> carne o huevos o naranjas o queso o cebollas
> leche o pimientos o tomates o frijoles
> mariscos o pollo o zanahorias

> la papa = la patata (España)
> el pimiento = el chile (México)
> el tomate = el jitomate (México)

a. ☐☐[I]☐☐☐[S]

b. ☐[U]☐☐[O]

c. ☐[A]☐[H]☐☐☐[A]

d. [L]☐☐☐[E]

e. ☐[C]☐[B]☐☐☐☐☐

f. ☐[M]☐[T]☐[E]☐

g. [H]☐☐[V]☐☐☐

h. ☐[A]☐[N]☐

i. [M]☐[R]☐☐☐☐[S]

j. ☐[A]☐☐[J]☐☐

k. ☐[I]☐☐☐[N][T]☐☐

l. ☐☐[L]☐[O]

8 Read the following description of Fernando, a chef with some crazy menu ideas. Then write the letter of the image above to complete the menu he is planning to serve his dinner guests.

A Fernando le gusta cocinar, pero muchas veces hace unas mezclas un poco extrañas. Hoy vienen invitados a su casa y quiere preparar lo siguiente:

- **Primer plato:** tomates (f) con naranjas ☐ pollo ☐ y frijoles ☐.
- **Segundo plato:** carne ☐ con mariscos ☐, pimientos ☐ y queso ☐.
- **Postre:** zanahorias ☐ con leche ☐, cebollas ☐ y huevos ☐.

- **Postre:** zanahorias (c) con leche (d), cebollas (e) y huevos (g).

SLOWER-PACED LEARNERS

Put students in pairs to discuss whether or not they eat or drink each of the food items in Activity 7 and when: *¿Bebes leche? Sí, bebo leche por la mañana.*

9 Another of Fernando's problems is his bad eating habits. Select the item that answers each of the questions and which is the likely choice for Fernando.

a. ¿Qué comida no le gusta?

☐ la hamburguesa con papas fritas

☐ el helado

☐ la verdura

b. Cuando tiene dolor de estómago, ¿qué prefiere comer?

☐ pescado con arroz

☐ un yogur

☐ tarta de chocolate

c. ¿Qué no le gusta comer por la tarde?

☐ palomitas

☐ papitas fritas

☐ manzanas

10 👥 With a partner, plan out a better menu for Fernando's dinner guests using the foods in Activities 1 and 3. Present your menu to the class. ¡Atención! Use *con* (with) to combine foods that go together.

Primer plato:...
Segundo plato:...
Postre: ....

11 👥 Take turns asking your partner what foods he/she prefers.

a. ¿Qué comida no te gusta?
b. Cuando tienes mucha hambre, ¿qué prefieres comer?
c. ¿Qué te gusta comer por la tarde después de la escuela?
d. ¿Cuál es tu postre favorito?

👤💻 **MORE IN ELETECA:** EXTRA ONLINE PRACTICE

Activity 9

Make sure students understand they are to select the unhealthy food choice based on Fernando's bad eating habits.

Extension

After completing this activity, take a moment to reflect on good nutrition. Encourage them to talk about what they eat that they consider unhealthy. Ask them how often they eat sweets (*dulces*), and whether they eat fruit and vegetables every day.

CULTURAL NOTE

• Other common words for ***tarta*** is ***torta*** or ***pastel***.
• Some different words for ***palomitas*** are pororó (Uruguay), ***rosita de maíz*** (Ecuador), and ***pochoclo*** (Argentina).

Activity 10

Assign this as a mini-project and have student pairs create decorative menus to present to the class. The class then vote for the best menu in different categories such as: most healthy, most original, most decorative, etc.

Activity 11

Set up this activity as a survey and have students interview other students.

ANSWERS

Activity 9

a. la verdura; **b.** tarta de chocolate; **c.** manzanas.

Activity 10

Answers will vary and will reflect a mixture of ingredients from previous activities.

Activity 11

Answers will vary and will reflect the vocabulary and expressions taught in the unit.

SLOWER-PACED LEARNERS

Have students notice the difference between ***gustar*** and preferir in Activity 11. ***Preferir*** uses the regular conjugation pattern. ***Yo prefiero jugar a los videojuegos.***

ADVANCED LEARNERS

Have students expand on the menu mini-project in Activity 10 by asking them to include the ingredients of the specials on their menus.

HERITAGE LANGUAGE LEARNERS

Ask students to bring a copy of a menu from a restaurant that features food from a Spanish speaking country they like. Have them explain one or two dishes from the menu to their peers.

OBJECTIVES FOR GRAMÁTICA 1

- Present the grammatical structures needed to practice the communicative functions of the unit: *gustar* and similar verbs
- Expressing likes and dislikes

CORE RESOURCES

- Interactive Online Materials - ELEteca

STANDARDS

1.1	Engage in conversation
1.2	Understand the language
1.3	Present information
4.1	Compare languages

INSTRUCTIONAL STRATEGIES

1. GUSTAR and Similar Verbs

- Project the grammar chart on this page and ask students to look for the main differences between these verbs and the verb *hablar*.
- Help students realize that the verbs *gustar* and *doler* do not use subject pronouns such as *yo, tú, él*.
- Point out to students that, instead, these verbs only appear here in two forms: third person singular and plural, and they need to be preceded by indirect object pronouns: *me, te, le, nos, os, les*.
- For practice, start a wave of questions and answers, such as: *¿México?* and a student will answer *Me gusta México*. Then the wave of questions continues from one student to another, using different prompts, such as: *¿El pollo? No me gusta el pollo.*
- Point out to students that *encantar* stands alone and cannot be used with *mucho*.

Activity 1

- Make sure students understand all the words in this activity. Complete the first sentence as a model on the board.
- Stress the importance of paying attention to whether the nouns following the verb are singular or plural.
- Have students complete the activity individually and then go through their answers with the whole class and provide the correct answers.

Activity 2

The purpose of this activity is to have students practice with *nos gusta(n)*. You may want to provide the question, *¿Qué les gusta a tus amigos y a ti?*, to initiate the activity.

Activity 3

To practice *nos gusta(n)*, have students report back to the class. Call on different students to keep a tally on the board.

ANSWERS

Activity 1

a. me gusta; **b.** te encanta; **c.** no nos gustan; **d.** les encanta; **e.** le gustan.

Activity 2

Answers will vary and will reflect the expressions taught, based on the model.

Activity 3

Answers will vary and will reflect the expressions taught, based on the model.

GRAMÁTICA

1. GUSTAR AND SIMILAR VERBS

■ To express likes and dislikes, the verb **gustar** is used in Spanish. The verb endings for **gustar** always agree with what is liked. The indirect object pronouns always precede the verb forms.

Optional (Used to show emphasis)	Indirect object pronoun	Verb forms	What is liked
A mí	me		
A ti	te	gusta	la leche, cantar (singular)
A usted/él/ella	le		
A nosotros/as	nos		
A vosotros/as	os	gustan	los videojuegos (plural)
A ustedes/ellos/ellas	les		

Nos gusta salir a cenar. *We like to go out for dinner.*
No **me gusta** la carne. *I don't like meat.*

¿Te gustan las palomitas? *Do you like popcorn?*

■ The verb **encantar** is used to talk about things you really like or love.
Me encantan los conciertos en directo. *I love live concerts.*

■ The expressions **a mí, a ti, a él**... are optional. They are used to show emphasis.
¿Te gusta el helado? **A mí** me encanta. *Do you like ice cream? I love it (I really do).*

1 Complete the sentences with the correct form of the verbs in parenthesis. *¡Atención!* Remember the verb form agrees with what is liked.

a. A mí me (gusta/gustan) .... la música.
b. A ti te (encanta/encantan) .... tocar la guitarra.
c. A nosotros no nos (gusta/gustan) .... los deportes.
d. A ellos les (encanta/encantan) .... montar en bici.
e. A ella le (gusta/gustan) .... los animales.

2 Describe one thing in each of the categories below that you and your friends like and one thing you don't like. Share your preferences with a partner.

Modelo: clases ➜ A nosotros nos gusta la clase de Español. / No nos gusta la clase de Educación Física.

a. deportes   b. música   c. programas de televisión   d. clases

3 In the first column, list the activities you like to do and, in the second column, the foods you love. Then ask your partner if he likes the things you listed. Take turns asking and answering to see how many things you have in common.

Actividades	Alimentos
a. Me gusta(n)...	a. Me encanta(n)...
b.	b.
c.	c.

Modelo: E1: ¿Te gusta la natación?   E2: Sí, me gusta mucho. / No, no me gusta.

SLOWER-PACED LEARNERS

Before doing Activity 1, send students back to Activities 7 and 9 on pages 152 and 153. Have them take turns making sentences about each food item with a partner using *(No) me gusta(n)*. Circulate to monitor their progress and remind them to use the correct singular or plural form of the verb.

2. USING *TAMBIÉN* AND *TAMPOCO* TO AGREE AND DISAGREE

Agreement		Disagreement	
Me gustan los perros.	No me gusta la tarea.	Me gusta el fútbol.	No me gustan las verduras.
A mí, también.	A mí, tampoco.	A mí, no.	A mí, sí.
Me too.	*Me neither.*	*I don't.*	*I do.*
■ Use **también** when agreeing with an affirmative statement.	■ Use **tampoco** when agreeing with a negative statement.	■ To show that you don't agree with a statement, use **a mí, no**.	■ To show that you don't agree with a negative statement, use **a mí, sí**.

4 👥 Complete the conversations with *también* or *tampoco*. Use the icons to help you choose. Then practice the conversations aloud with a partner.

a. » ¿Te gusta hacer deporte?
» Me encanta. ¿Y a ti?
» A mí, ...

b. » ¿Te gustan los videojuegos?
» No. ¿Y a ti?
» A mí, ...

c. » ¿Te gusta la música?
» Sí. ¿Y a ti?
» A mí, ...

5 👥 In groups of three or four, take turns saying whether you like or don't like the following items. Then each person in the group will say if he/she agrees with the statement or not. Keep track of responses by writing the person's name in the appropriate column.

Modelo:
Me gustan los jeans.

	Agrees ✔	Disagrees ✘
	A mí, también.	A mí, no.
a. las gorras de béisbol		
b. los ojos azules		
c. el pelo muy corto		
d. hacer yoga		
e. dormir		
f. bailar		

6 Write three statements about your group based on the information you collected in Activity 5. Then report your findings to the class.

Modelo: A Dan y a Kyle les gustan los jeans.

OBJECTIVES FOR GRAMÁTICA 2

- Present the grammatical structures needed to practice the communicative functions of the unit: *también*, *tampoco*
- Express agreement or disagreement

STANDARDS

1.1 Engage in conversation
1.2 Understand the language
4.1 Compare languages

INSTRUCTIONAL STRATEGIES

2. Using *también* and *tampoco* to Agree and Disagree

- Walk students through the explanation at the top of this page.
- Make statements to the class and invite students to either agree or disagree, such as: *Me gusta el chocolate, ¿y a ti?* and *Me gusta el fútbol, ¿y a ti?*

Activity 4

Have students look at the facial expressions of the characters. A happy face represents agreement and an unhappy face represents disagreement.

Activity 5

- Provide guidance prior to the activity by proposing five topics on the board: *una comida*, *una película*, *un grupo musical*, *un deporte*, *una asignatura*.
- Model how to agree with a negative statement using *a mí, tampoco*.
- Ask students to pay close attention to what their partners will say.
- When groups have completed the activity, prompt them to report what likes and dislikes they have in common: *¿Les gustan las mismas cosas?* Have students respond using these sentence patterns: *Sí, nos gustan las mismas cosas, como...* or *No, no nos gustan las mismas cosas, como...*

ANSWERS

Activity 4

a. A mí también (agreement); **b.** A mí, sí (disagreement); **c.** A mí, también (agreement).

Activities 5 and 6

Answers will vary and should reflect the expressions taught to express agreement and disagreement.

ADVANCED LEARNERS

Have students work in a circle. On a piece of paper, each student writes a form of the verb *gustar*. Then, the paper is passed to the next student who writes something that person may like. The third student writes any additional information of his/her choice: *Nos gusta > Nos gusta jugar > Nos gusta jugar a los bolos.*

HERITAGE LANGUAGE LEARNERS

Have students write a short composition describing the likes and dislikes of the group members they worked with.

OBJECTIVES FOR GRAMÁTICA 3

- Present the grammatical structures needed to practice the communicative functions of the unit: the verb **doler**
- Express when something hurts

CORE RESOURCES

- Extension Activities: EA 5.2

STANDARDS

1.1	Engage in conversation
1.2	Understand the language
1.3	Present information
4.1	Compare languages

INSTRUCTIONAL STRATEGIES

3. The Verb DOLER and Parts of the Body

Activity 7

- After going over the grammar explanation at the top of the page, walk students through the labels for parts of the body on this page. Model how to pronounce these words several times and have students respond individually and as a group.
- Say the words for parts of the body with the book closed and have students respond by adding the article. For instance, point to your head and say **cabeza**. And students respond **la cabeza**. If needed, write the correct responses on the board for additional support.

Activity 8

Encourage students to associate other parts of the body with the articles of clothing. For example, **el pelo** for **gorra**. Provide additional vocabulary as needed: **la cara**, **las orejas**, **los hombros**, **el trasero**, and so on.

Activity 9

As a follow-up, provide additional activities for students to practice as a class.

ANSWERS

Activity 7

a. Me duele la cabeza; **b.** Les duele el brazo; **c.** Te duelen los pies; **d.** Le duele el estómago; **e.** Les duele la rodilla.

Activity 8

1. d; **2.** e; **3.** b; **4.** a; **5.** c.

Activity 9

Answers will vary and should reflect the model provided and expressions taught.

GRAMÁTICA

3. THE VERB *DOLER* AND PARTS OF THE BODY

■ The verb **doler** is an **o>ue** stem-changing verb that is used to describe aches and pains. It follows the same patterns as **gustar**.

Me duele el estómago. *My stomach hurts.*   A María **le duelen** los pies. *Maria's feet hurt.*

DOLER (o>ue) *to hurt, ache*		
A mí	me	
A ti	te	**duele** el estómago
A usted/él/ella	le	
A nosotros/as	nos	
A vosotros/as	os	**duelen** los pies
A ustedes/ellos/ellas	les	

■ Another way to describe what hurts you is with the expression **tener dolor de** + body part.
Tengo dolor de cabeza. *I have a headache.*

7 Look at the image to learn the words in Spanish for parts of the body that can hurt. Then complete the sentences with *doler* and the corresponding body part.

a. (A mí) Me duele la cabeza.
b. (A ustedes) ....
c. (A ti) ....
d. (A él) ....
e. (A ellos) ....

Las partes del cuerpo

a. la cabeza
la espalda
la mano
b. el brazo
la pierna
c. los pies
el cuello
el dedo
el pecho
d. el estómago
e. la rodilla

8 Match the following articles of clothing to the body part most closely associated with it.

1. bufanda
2. camiseta
3. calcetines
4. gorra
5. pantalón

a. la cabeza
b. los pies
c. las piernas
d. el cuello
e. el pecho y la espalda

9 👥 With a partner, practice more with the parts of the body by saying what parts you would use to do the following activities. Each of you should mention a different body part.

Modelo: E1: Para esquiar, uso las piernas.
E2: Y los brazos.
E1: Y...

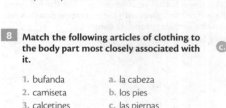

a. para bailar
b. para montar en bici
c. para tocar el piano
d. para jugar al vóleibol

156

SLOWER-PACED LEARNERS

Provide students with extra practice by asking them to list those parts of the body that are plural, such as **ojos**, **manos**, **brazos**, and **pies**. Have them practice **doler** with these nouns in both singular and plural: **Me duelen los ojos / Me duele este ojo; Me duelen las manos / Me duele esta mano.** Have them notice that **mano** is feminine.

ADVANCED LEARNERS

Based on Activity 9, have students prepare and use sentences like **Uso las piernas cuando esquí. Uso los brazos cuando bailo. Uso las manos cuando toco el piano.** Have them prepare questions as well: **¿Cuándo usas los pies? ¿Cuándo usas los ojos?**

10 Look at the patients in a doctor's waiting room. Match their symptoms to what ails them.

1. Tiene fiebre.
2. Está estresado.
3. Está cansado.
4. Tiene tos.
5. Tiene gripe.
SALAS 1 Y 2

☐ a. Le duele la cabeza y tiene 102 °F.

☐ b. Le duele el pecho cuando tose mucho.

☐ c. Tiene dolor de cabeza y está muy nervioso.

☐ d. Le duelen las piernas y no puede caminar.

☐ e. Le duele todo el cuerpo y necesita una medicina.

11 With a partner, describe how the following people are feeling. Use the verbs *estar* and *doler*, parts of the body, and expressions with *tener* to complete your description. Then present your versions to the class.

Expressions with **tener**	
• tener hambre	• tener sed
• tener calor	• tener sueño
• tener frío	• tener que + *infinitive*

Modelo: A Estela le duele todo el cuerpo. Está cansada y tiene sueño. No puede trabajar. Tiene que tomar té.

Estela   Anita   Esteban   Rosa

12 Complete the conversations with a partner and take turns role playing. ¡Atención! Remember how to agree and disagree.

a. ≫ ¿A tu padre le duele la espalda?
   ≫ Sí. ¿Y a tu padre?
   ≫ A mi padre, ...

b. ≫ ¿Te duelen los ojos?
   ≫ No. ¿Y a ti?
   ≫ A mí, ...

 MORE IN ELETECA: EXTRA ONLINE PRACTICE ◆◆ 🔲 **GRAMMAR TUTORIALS** 9 AND 10   157

• Divide the class into groups of five and provide a set of cards to each group.

• Assign one or several cards to each student. These cards will tell the students holding them "what is wrong with them" and when asked, they need to respond based on what the assigned cards say.

• Students will take turns asking each other *yes/no* questions to find out what is wrong with each group member, such as: **¿Estás resfriado/a? ¿Tienes gripe? ¿Te duele la cabeza?**

• Have students keep tallies of how many yeses they get to their questions. Whoever has more tallies wins.

• Take this opportunity to remind students of the expression **Estoy enfermo/a**. They learned this as one of the expressions with **estar** on page 75.

Activity 11

Review expressions with **tener** or call on students to act them out for the class.

Activity 12

• Clarify that in the first conversation they are agreeing with the statement and, in the second, they are disagreeing.

• Have students create similar conversations to quiz each other.

ANSWERS

Activity 10

1. a; **2.** c; **3.** d; **4.** b; **5.** e.

Activity 11

Answers will vary and should reflect the model provided and expressions taught.

Activity 12

a. también / no; **b.** tampoco / sí.

HERITAGE LANGUAGE LEARNERS

Before or after Activity 10, discuss the different ways to talk about temperature in the US versus the Spanish-speaking world, where temperature are given in Celsius. 39 °C is considered fever. Are any students in class more familiar with Celsius than Fahrenheit? Do they have any familiar members who use Celsius? What temperature signifies a hot day in Celsius? What signifies a cold day? Have students practice some conversions from °F to °C.

INSTRUCTIONAL STRATEGIES

Activity 10

Use gestures and provide context in Spanish as needed to clarify expressions.

Extension

• After students have completed this activity individually, distribute copies of EA 5.2, **¿Qué te pasa?** for students to cut up.

DESTREZAS

- Reading comprehension

1.2   Understand the language

Activities 1 and 2

Make sure students read the **Destrezas** box before proceeding to do the activity.

Activity 3

- Encourage students to infer the answer from context and not to worry too much about words they might not understand.
- After they complete the activity, go over the correct answers with the whole class.
- Go over the students' answers and ask them to provide what context clues they based their answers on.

Activity 2

Estudio: h; Navego por Internet: j; Hablo por teléfono con la familia: i; Voy al hospital: d; Hago la compra: e; Hago deporte: a; Voy a cenar fuera: g.

Activity 3

Students will read while practicing the skill individually.

Remind students that subject pronouns are frequently omitted from the sentence. This can cause problems when trying to identify what is the subject of a sentence. Also, have students realize that the pronouns **me**, **te**, **le**, **les**, **nos**, and **os** are not subject pronouns.

Have students read a text from another chapter in this book, like the one on page 216. Have them report whether it was difficult to identify and understand the most important information in that text. What strategies did they use to understand the text?

Ask students to change the text in Activity 3 as if it had been written by a) a girl or b) two brothers. What did they need to change? What information stayed the same as in the original text?

COMPRENSIÓN DE LECTURA (1)

1 Before reading the notes, review the reading strategy in Destrezas and follow the suggestion.

Destrezas

Asking yourself questions

It is helpful to ask yourself questions as you read. Skim through the notes and ask yourself if the note describes something to do or someplace to go. Mark each note accordingly to help you organize the information.

a. Montar en bici, domingo.
b. Cine. Viernes a las 20:30h.
c. Concierto de Shakira el sábado a las 22h.
d. Médico a las 12, el miércoles.
e. Comprar arroz, pan y carne.

f. Quedar con Elena para ir al cine.
g. Reservar mesa en restaurante Pepito, jueves.
h. Hacer el trabajo de Matemáticas. Miércoles por la tarde.
i. Hablar por teléfono con la tía Eva.
j. Chatear con mi amigo Michelle, lunes.

2 Read the notes again and match the activities below to the note that is most likely associated with it. ¡Atención! Not all the notes will be used.

a. Estudio. .... ☐   **e.** Hago la compra. .... ☐
b. Navego por Internet. .... ☐   **f.** Hago deporte. .... ☐
c. Hablo por teléfono con la familia. .... ☐   **g.** Voy a cenar fuera. .... ☐
d. Voy al hospital. .... ☐

COMPRENSIÓN DE LECTURA (2)

3 Before reading the selection, review the reading strategy in Destrezas and follow the suggestions.

Destrezas

Skipping words

If you are having problems understanding unfamiliar words, you may want to skip them and focus on the following:

1. Underline the subject and main verb of each sentence.
2. Find some description of the subject.
3. Identify words and phrases that refer to time and place.

Me encantan los fines de semana. Los sábados por la mañana me levanto a las 9:30 y nado en la piscina hasta las 11:00. Siempre hago algún deporte: fútbol, tenis o baloncesto. Como a las 13:00 y después duermo un poco la siesta. A las 16:30 viene mi tía Eva a visitarnos y trae siempre una tarta de chocolate. Después navego por Internet porque tengo muchos amigos para chatear. A las 20:00 salgo con mis amigos a pasear. Hay una chica que me gusta mucho. Se llama Sara, pero tiene novio. A veces me mira y me pongo rojo. Los domingos comemos todos juntos. Mamá prepara arroz con pollo. Después salimos todos a pasear y por la noche hago los deberes para el lunes.

4 Read the selection again and choose the best answer to complete each sentence.

1. La persona que escribe es…
   a. un chico.
   b. una chica.
   c. un profesor.

2. Esta persona…
   a. cena en un restaurante.
   b. va al cine.
   c. hace deporte.

3. Esta persona…
   a. duerme muchas horas por la noche.
   b. duerme la siesta.
   c. duerme en casa de sus amigos.

4. Su tía Eva viene…
   a. por la mañana.
   b. por la tarde.
   c. por la noche.

5. A esta persona…
   a. le gusta mucho Sara.
   b. no le gusta nada Sara.
   c. le gusta un poco Sara.

6. Los domingos cocina…
   a. el padre.
   b. la tía Eva.
   c. la madre.

PRONUNCIACIÓN The sounds of *r* and *rr*

■ In Spanish, the letter **r** has two sounds.

Sound /r/

Sound is equivalent to the English pronunciation of *tt* in *butter* or *dd* in *ladder*.
naranja, mariscos, ahora

Sound /rr/

Sound is equivalent to someone imitating a motor sound (*brrrrrrrr*). This is known as a trill and occurs in words:
• beginning with the letter *r*
• with an *r* after the letters *n, s, l*
• written with *rr*
repetir, Enrique, arroz, aburrido

1 🎧 59 You will hear ten words in Spanish with either the /r/ or /rr/ sounds. Listen carefully and write the number of the word in the appropriate column based on the sound of /r/ you hear in each.

Sound /r/	Sound /rr/

2 👥 Fill in the blanks with *r* o *rr* to spell out these words. Then practice saying them aloud to a partner focusing on the correct pronunciation of /r/ and /rr/.

a. favo…..ito
b. a…..oz
c. mo….eno
d. go….a
e. bo….ador
f. ma…..ón
g. abu…..ido
h. enfe….mera
i. papele…..a
j. prefe….imos

📖 **MORE IN ELETECA:** EXTRA ONLINE PRACTICE

159

Activity 4

• Have students answer the questions individually and silently.
• Go over the answers as a class, encourage students to explain how they arrived at their answers.

ANSWERS

1. a; 2. c; 3. b; 4. b; 5. a; 6. c.

OBJECTIVES FOR PRONUNCIACIÓN

• Practice correct pronunciation: /r/ and /rr/

CORE RESOURCES

• Audio Program: 59
• Interactive Online Materials - ELEteca

STANDARDS

1.2   Understand the language
4.1   Compare languages

INSTRUCTIONAL STRATEGIES

• Walk students through the explanations in the book.
• Explain that /r/ is softer and it corresponds to the sound of the single **r** between vowels, at the end of a syllable or word, or after a consonant, except **n, l, s**.
• Explain that /rr/ is stronger and corresponds to the sound of the single **r** at the beginning of a word, after **n, l, s**, and when written as a double **rr** between vowels. Add that this is also the sound of the **r** after the prefixes **sub-, ab-, post-** because the prefixes are a separate syllable.

🎧 59 Activity 1

• Introduce the sounds with sample words and books closed. For example, contrast the following minimal pairs: **pero / perro, caro / carro**.
• Ask students to sound out the words as you write them on the board.

Activity 2

Circulate and model the correct pronunciations as needed.

Audioscript

1. rana; **2.** carro; **3.** cara; **4.** brazo; **5.** amor; **6.** risa; **7.** directo; **8.** correo; **9.** arroz; **10.** caro.

ANSWERS

Activity 1

Sound /r/: cara, brazo, amor, directo, caro.
Sound /rr/: rana, carro, risa, correo, arroz.

Activity 2

a. favorito; b. arroz; c. moreno; d. gorra; e. borrador; f. marrón; g. aburrido; h. enfermera; i. papelera; j. preferimos.

ADVANCED LEARNERS

Tell students that some native speakers also have problems pronouncing the **rr**. Have them practice these two common *trabalenguas* in Spanish so they can have some fun:

– *El cielo está enladrillado,*
  quién lo desenladrillará.
  El desenladrillador que lo desenladrille,
  buen desenladrillador será.

– *El perro de San Roque no tiene rabo*
  porque Ramón Rodríguez se lo ha robado.

SABOR HISPANO CULTURE IN CONTEXT

Objectives for Sabor hispano

- Learn about countries: Panamá, Colombia and Venezuela
- Learn about currencies, products, and foods of Spanish-speaking countries
- Compare cultures of Spanish-speaking countries with culture in the U.S.

Core Resources

- Audio Program: 60

Standards

2.1 Practices and perspectives
2.2 Products and perspectives
3.2 Acquire information
5.2 Using language for personal enjoyment and enrichment

Instructional Strategies

- Introduce the topic by asking students what they know about Panamá, Colombia, and Venezuela.
- Talk about the images and the map. Elicit what they already know about these countries and places. Ask them if they have ever been to those countries or met anyone from there.
- Share what you know about these countries or the topics on this page.
- Read the captions together and ask questions to check comprehension. Explain that Simón Bolívar was the principal architect of many South American independence movements including Venezuela (1813), Colombia and Panamá (1820), Ecuador (1823), and Perú and Bolivia (1825). He also served as president of several countries during this period.
- Ask students to identify which of the points in **¿Sabes que...?** they find most surprising or interesting.
- Have students research additional information about la Gran Colombia, Salto Ángel (*Angel Falls*), and popular festivals celebrated throughout Colombia.

Cultural Note

- There are several types of cacao in the world, for example, **forastero**, **trinitario de Grenada**, and **criollo de Venezuela**. The latter is the most rare as its plant is very delicate and difficult to grow. It tastes like milk chocolate with a slight nutty flavor. This **cacao criollo** is used to make the finest chocolate varieties in the world. The other two types are more common and less expensive than the **cacao criollo**.
- The Panama hat is not from Panama but from Ecuador.
- Since 1997, the Archaeological Site of Panamá Viejo and the Historic District of Panamá are part of the UNESCO World Heritage List.

Slower-paced Learners

Ask students questions about the information on the page to check their comprehension. Then give them time to write one or two questions of their own about the information on the page. They can be either information questions or *yes/no* progress. Monitor their progress, providing support as needed. Then put the students in pairs or small groups to ask and answers the questions, further exploiting the text and developing their reading comprehension skills.

160

SABOR HISPANO

¡A COMER, BAILAR Y GOZAR!

¡Buen provecho!

Una región cálida, verde, y llena de misterios

El puerto de la ciudad de Panamá

Monumento a Simón Bolívar, en Caracas

El Salto Ángel, en Venezuela

Festival de Cartagena de Indias, en Colombia

- El nombre oficial de Venezuela es la República Bolivariana de Venezuela. Su capital es Caracas.
- Colombia tiene uno de los ecosistemas más diversos del mundo. Su capital es Bogotá.
- Panamá conecta América Central con América del Sur. Su capital es la ciudad de Panamá.
- El mar Caribe es un mar tropical muy famoso por las leyendas de piratas y tesoros escondidos (hidden).

¿Sabes que...?

- ✓ La moneda venezolana es el bolívar, en honor a Simón Bolívar, héroe político y militar.
- ✓ Panamá es el único lugar del mundo donde puedes ver la salida del sol (sunrise) en el océano Pacífico y la puesta de sol (sunset) en el océano Atlántico.
- ✓ El chocolate venezolano se hace con cacao criollo y es famoso internacionalmente.
- ✓ En Cali, Colombia, se celebra el festival de salsa más importante, con 3.000 bailarines.

Fuentes: The Economist, Café de Colombia, El País.

PANAMÁ, COLOMBIA Y VENEZUELA

60 Café de Colombia

- Colombia es el tercer productor de café mundial.
- Más de 500.000 familias colombianas trabajan en la industria del café.
- El café llega a Colombia con los españoles en el siglo XVIII.
- Los programas de cultivo (farming) respetan la biodiversidad del país.

El café colombiano es suave y delicioso

Arepas

Las arepas son un plato típico de Colombia y Venezuela. Son de origen indígena y muy ricas. La gente las come para el desayuno, el almuerzo iy hasta la cena!

Esta es una receta simple para preparar las arepas típicas de Venezuela. ¡Buen provecho! (Enjoy your meal!)

Ingredientes para 4 a 6 arepas
- 2 tazas de masarepa (refined, precooked corn flour)
- 1 cucharadita de sal (salt)
- Agua y aceite (oil)

Preparación

Pon (Put) una taza y media de agua en un bol, añade la sal y un poco de aceite. Después, mezcla la harina hasta obtener una masa (dough) suave, sin grumos. Luego, haz bolas medianas y aplástalas en forma de discos.

Cocina los discos por los dos lados en una plancha (griddle) con aceite. Después, pon las arepas en el horno a 180°C (350°F) para dorarlas. Rellena (Fill) con queso, carne o huevos. Y... ¡buen provecho!

Arepas de carne

Las compras en Panamá

¿Qué tal? Soy Cintia y vivo en la ciudad de Panamá. Me gusta mucho vivir aquí porque siempre hace calor. La temperatura media es de 29 grados centígrados (84.2ºF). Por eso, se vive mucho al aire libre... ihasta las compras son al aire libre! Me gusta comprar en los mercados porque las verduras son frescas y la fruta es dulce (sweet) y deliciosa. Las frutas tropicales son mis favoritas, como la guayaba, el mangostín, la papaya y la piña.

Además, los precios son bajos: la ciudad de Panamá es una de las ocho ciudades más baratas del mundo, según la revista The Economist.

A los panameños nos gustan mucho los turistas. ¡Visítanos!

Answer the following questions to talk about your likes and dislikes.

1. ¿Prefieres el café o el té? ¿Por qué?

2. ¿Qué tipo de chocolate prefieres? ¿Amargo (dark), con leche, con nueces (nuts), blanco...?

3. ¿Te gusta la fruta? ¿Cuál es tu fruta favorita?

4. ¿Qué plato típico es tu favorito y por qué?

5. ¿Qué tipo de comida no te gusta?

VOCES LATINAS
MI COMIDA PREFERIDA

Fill in the blank with the correct information from the readings.
Then complete the sentences to describe how it is where you live.

1. En la ciudad de Panamá, hace _____ grados todo el año. En mi ciudad

2. El plato típico de Venezuela son las _____ . El plato típico de mi país es

3. Colombia es un famoso productor de _____ . Mi país es un famoso productor de _____

161

60

- An audio recording accompanies each text on this page. Vary between silent reading, reading aloud, and playing the audio.
- Identify and explain any vocabulary from the reading students may find difficult to understand.
- Ask students questions to check comprehension.

Café de Colombia

¿Es el café original de Colombia? ¿De dónde viene?

CULTURAL NOTE

In Colombia, there are many cultural and natural properties included in the Unesco World Heritage List, such as the Coffee Cultural Landscape of Colombia (since 2011) and the Port, Fortresses and Group of Monuments, Cartagena (since 1984).

Arepas

¿Creen que son complicadas para preparar? If you have access to kitchen facilities, make **arepas** as a class project. Ask students to bring in different fillings for their **arepas**.

Las compras en Panamá

¿Por qué piensan que hay tanta fruta y verdura fresca en Panamá? Explain that the **mangostín** (mangosteen) has a dark purple skin, with a creamy white center that is segmented like an orange. The fruit is native to Southeast Asia.

- Have students complete the activities on this page and compare their answers with others in the class.

ANSWERS

Talking about your likes and dislikes

Answers will vary.

Fill in the blanks

1. 29; 2. arepas; 3. café. The second blanks in each case will vary.

ADVANCED LEARNERS

Using **Las compras en Panamá** as a model, have students write about their own food shopping and eating habits where they live. Then have them take turns reading their paragraphs aloud in pairs or small groups.

HERITAGE LANGUAGE LEARNERS

Put students in groups to discuss what they knew before the opener and what they know now about the different countries. Encourage them to add more information based on their knowledge and experience. Assign each group a country and have them prepare a short presentation about what people should do, see, or try in that country. Make sure they use visuals to support their presentations and that each person in the group presents some of the information. Have the class vote on the best presentation.

OBJECTIVES FOR RELATO

- Revisit unit themes, grammar, vocabulary, and culture in a new context
- Improve reading comprehension skills

CORE RESOURCES

- Audio Program: 61

STANDARDS

1.1	Engage in conversation
1.2	Understand the language
1.3	Present information
2.1	Practices and perspectives

INSTRUCTIONAL STRATEGIES

Activity 1

- The purpose of this activity is to review the verbs taught in this unit that go with each leisure activity.
- Students can complete this activity individually or in pairs.

🎧 61 Activity 2

- Before students read the text, tell them that the first paragraph is an introduction to the **Relato**.
- As a warm-up, ask the students if they always know what they will be doing on the weekend, and if they ever ask a friend for advice.
- After reading the text and before starting the next activity, ask them a general comprehension question about the text they have just read, such as what are the six recommendations that Monica makes to Marta: ***¿Qué seis recomendaciones le hace Mónica a Marta para hacer este fin de semana?*** The six recommendations are: ***ver una película, leer una novela, ir a un restaurante, hacer deporte, cantar en el karaoke, comer paella con su familia***.
- Encourage students to keep a word journal and write down words that are new to them in this text and their definitions.

ANSWERS

Activity 1

a. Hacer deporte; b. Ver películas; c. Navegar por el mar (Image 2); d. Jugar a los bolos (Image 1); e. Hacer judo; f. Jugar al baloncesto (Image 3).

SLOWER-PACED LEARNERS

For further practice with the vocabulary in Activity 1, put students into pairs and have them take turns acting out the different activities while their partners guess what they are. Tell them to choose activities out of order.

HERITAGE LANGUAGE LEARNERS

Have students choose one of the cultural activities mentioned in Activity 2 and find real examples or more information about it. For example, have students research comedic films in Spanish that star Penélope Cruz, Argentine dramatic films, or novels by Venezuelan authors. They might also do more research on different types of Mexican cuisine. Have them report back on their findings and be prepared to speak about the topic for about two minutes.

RELATO Las recomendaciones de Mónica

1 Match the images to the activity described.

a. .... deporte.	c. .... por el mar.	e. .... judo.
b. .... películas.	d. .... a los bolos.	f. .... al baloncesto.

2 🎧 **61** Read about the situation between Mónica and her friend Marta. Then read the suggestions for the weekend Mónica provides for her friend.

Las recomendaciones de Mónica

Todos los fines de semana Marta llama a su amiga Mónica por teléfono para hablar sobre el fin de semana. Marta nunca sabe *(never knows)* qué quiere hacer, y Mónica siempre tiene buenas ideas. Este es un resumen de las últimas recomendaciones de Mónica a su amiga.

Hola, Marta, pienso que estás contenta porque es viernes y este fin de semana hay muchísimas cosas que puedes hacer. Por ejemplo, si quieres ver una película en el cine, hay tres opciones interesantes: una comedia española con Penélope Cruz, un drama argentino y una película de animación *(animated film)*. Por cierto, tengo una novela de un escritor venezolano. Si tienes tiempo, puedes leer la novela este fin de semana, está muy bien.

Tacos

Otra opción es comer en un restaurante. Yo te recomiendo un restaurante mexicano que tiene una comida muy buena y es bastante barato *(inexpensive)*. Lo mejor son los nachos y los tacos, ¡me encantan los tacos! Además, puedes escuchar rancheras, que son las canciones típicas de México.

Si quieres hacer deporte, podemos montar juntas *(together)* en bici el domingo. Yo tengo una bici nueva. Es el regalo *(gift)* de mis abuelos por mi cumpleaños.

Rancheras

Por último, ¿te gusta cantar? Es que tengo un karaoke en casa y el domingo puedes venir a cantar con mi hermana y conmigo *(with me)*. ¿Te imaginas? Puede ser muy divertido. Además, mi padre todos los domingos hace asado, entonces puedes almorzar con nosotros también.

Un asado

3 Answer each question with *sí* or *no* according to the reading.

	Sí	No
a. ¿El padre de Mónica hace asado los sábados?	☐	☐
b. ¿A Mónica le gustan los tacos?	☐	☐
c. ¿La bici de Mónica es nueva?	☐	☐
d. ¿Mónica tiene una hermana?	☐	☐
e. La novela que tiene Mónica, ¿es de un escritor mexicano?	☐	☐
f. ¿Las rancheras son mexicanas?	☐	☐

4 Read Marta's response to Mónica's suggestions and check the ones Marta likes.

Muchas gracias por tus recomendaciones, Mónica. Me encanta el cine argentino, entonces la película argentina que me recomiendas es una buena opción. Para la novela, no tengo tiempo este fin de semana, pero gracias. Y otra cosa, no me gusta nada la comida mexicana. No puedo montar en bici porque me duele mucho la pierna; pero lo del karaoke sí, me gusta muchísimo cantar. Además, el asado es mi comida favorita.

☐ ver la película argentina   ☐ leer la novela   ☐ comer comida mexicana

☐ montar en bici   ☐ cantar con el karaoke   ☐ comer asado

5 Make some recommendations to your classmates about what to do this weekend. Then exchange papers with another classmate.

> Hola, compañeros. Estas son mis recomendaciones para el fin de semana...

6 Which of the suggestions you received do you like best? Why?

> Me gusta la recomendación de Katie. Comer una hamburguesa y después ver una película en el cine, porque...

163

INSTRUCTIONAL STRATEGIES

Activity 3

- Students do this activity in pairs.
- Remind students to go back to the text for information if they cannot remember the answer.
- Go over the correct answers with the whole class.

Activity 4

Tell students this text is Marta's response to Mónica.

Activity 5

- Ask students to write down their recommendations based on their personal preferences regarding weekend activities.
- Suggest that they review the text and carefully look at the structures and vocabulary that Mónica used to give advice to her friend.
- Students can go back to **Palabra por palabra**, if needed.
- After students complete this activity, ask for 10 volunteers to read their texts before the class.

Activity 6

Have students write about what suggestions they liked the best. Make sure they justify their choice with phrasing such as: ***Me gusta la recomendación de... que es... porque...***

ANSWERS

Activity 3

a. No; **b.** Sí; **c.** Sí; **d.** Sí; **e.** No (Es venezolano); **f.** Sí.

Activity 4

Ver la película argentina; Cantar con el karaoke; Comer asado.

Activity 5

Answers will vary and should reflect the expressions and vocabulary taught.

Activity 6

Answers will vary and should reflect the expressions and vocabulary taught.

SLOWER-PACED LEARNERS

Set a specific numbers of recommendations that you want students to write (say, three), and provide sentence stems to help get them started and to ensure that they avoid structures that would need the subjunctive.

ADVANCED LEARNERS

After reading Marta's response in Activity 4, have students use it as a model to write how they would respond to Mónica's suggestions. Have them share and compare their responses in groups to see if any of them have similar interests.

OBJECTIVES FOR EVALUACIÓN

- Review grammar, vocabulary and culture from the unit
- Complete self-assessment

CORE RESOURCES

- Interactive Online Materials - ELEteca

STANDARDS

1.2 Understand the language
1.3 Present information
2.1 Practices and perspectives
4.1 Compare cultures

INSTRUCTIONAL STRATEGIES

- Activities can be completed individually and then reviewed with the class.
- Extend by asking students if they agree with the answers given and then writing the correct answer on the board.
- Call on students at random and not in the order in which they are seated. That way, they will pay attention to what their classmates are saying.
- Provide explanations as needed.

ANSWERS

Activity 1

SER: divertido, inteligente, simpática, tímido.
ESTAR: cansada, nervioso, de mal humor, triste, contento, preocupada.

Activity 2

5, 2, 1, 8, 3, 4, 7, 6, 9.

Activity 3

Answers will vary and should include the following:

a. la carne, las papas fritas, el tomate, el huevo (and also: la lechuga).

b. la tarta de chocolate, el helado (and also: la mermelada).

c. las zanahorias, las cebollas, las papas, los pimientos, los tomates (and also: los pepinos, los ajos, el calabacín, el maíz).

d. el sándwich, la leche, la manzana, la naranja.

EVALUACIÓN

DESCRIBING MOODS AND FEELINGS

1 Categorize the following words based on whether they are used with *ser* o *estar*.

> divertido ○ cansada ○ nervioso ○ inteligente ○ de mal humor
> simpática ○ triste ○ tímido ○ contento ○ preocupada

SER	ESTAR

ORDERING IN A RESTAURANT

2 Put the following conversation in the correct order. The first one has been done for you.

☐ Mesero: ¿Quiere algo de comer?
☐ Cliente: Buenas noches.
① Mesero: Hola, buenas noches.
☐ Cliente: No, nada más, gracias. ¿Cuánto es?
☐ Mesero: ¿Qué quiere tomar?

☐ Cliente: Un refresco de limón, por favor.
☐ Mesero: ¿Algo más?
☐ Cliente: Sí, un sándwich de jamón y queso, por favor.
☐ Mesero: Son 12 dólares.

COMIDAS Y ALIMENTOS

3 Label as many food items as you can in the following images. Were you able to label all 15 words?

a.

b.

c.

d.

VERB *GUSTAR*

4 Fill in the blanks with the appropriate word from the list to complete the conversation logically.

> gusta ○ gustan ○ también ○ tampoco ○ gusta

a. **Pepe:** ¿Te .... los platos típicos españoles?
b. **Alice:** Sí, muchísimo. Me .... mucho comer.
c. **Pepe:** A mí, ..., me encanta comer. Pero no me .... cocinar.
d. **Alice:** A mí, ... Es muy complicado.

VERB *DOLER* AND THE PARTS OF BODY

5 Identify the parts of the body according to the image.

a. ....
b. ....
c. ....
d. ....
e. ....
f. ....
g. ....
h. ....

6 Answer the question: *¿Qué le duele?*

A la muchacha le duele / tiene dolor de...

CULTURE

7 Answer the following questions about Panama, Colombia, and Venezuela and compare similarities with your own country or region.

a. ¿Qué frutas son típicas de Panamá? ¿Y de tu país o región?
b. ¿Qué festivales se celebran en Colombia?
c. ¿Quién es Simón Bolivar? ¿Quién es una figura histórica de tu país o región?
d. ¿Qué ponen dentro de las arepas? ¿Qué comida es similar a las arepas en tu país o región?
e. ¿Qué país produce y exporta mucho café? ¿Qué producto produce y exporta tu país o región?

MORE IN ELETECA: EXTRA ONLINE PRACTICE

ANSWERS

Activity 4

a. gustan; b. gusta; c. también, gusta; d. tampoco.

Activity 5

a. la cabeza; b. el cuello; c. la mano; d. el brazo; e. la espalda; f. la tripa; g. la pierna; h. el pie.

Activity 6

Answers will vary and should reflect the model provided and parts of the body.

Activity 7

Answers will vary and should reflect the information provided in **Sabor hispano**.

a. La guayaba, el mangostín, la payaya, la piña; b. El festival de la salsa; c. Héroe político y militar de Latinoamérica; d. queso, carne, huevos; e. Colombia.

EN RESUMEN: Vocabulario

- Review unit vocabulary and expressions
- Practice communicative skills

STANDARDS

1.2   Understand the language

1.3   Present information

INSTRUCTIONAL STRATEGIES

- Model how to use the vocabulary list to review new words and expressions learned in this unit.
- Use simple materials, such as index cards or self-adhesive notes.
- Self-adhesive notes can be used for writing nouns from the vocabulary list on them, then using them to place the correct labels on objects in the classroom or pictures in the book.
- Index cards can be used as flash cards with the Spanish term on one side and the English term on the other, or a picture or drawing.
- Students can work in pairs or groups, using the self-adhesive notes and index cards as they would the cards of a board game to help each other practice the unit vocabulary.
- Encourage students to write labels or captions for the photos on this page. Remind them to use the vocabulary and expressions they have learned in this unit.
- If they have not done so already, have students complete all of the vocabulary practice activities in ELEteca.

EN RESUMEN: Vocabulario

Actividades de ocio y tiempo libre *Free time activities*

chatear con amigos *to chat (online) with friends*
hacer ciclismo *to bike*
hacer esquí *to ski*
hacer fotos *to take pictures*

hacer judo *to practice judo*
hacer natación *to practice swimming*
hacer yoga *to practice yoga*
ir de compras *to go shopping*
jugar a los bolos / al boliche *to bowl, go bowling*
jugar a videojuegos *to play videogames*
montar en bici *to ride a bike*
navegar por el mar *to sail*

navegar por Internet *to go on the Internet*
tomar el sol *to sunbathe*
tomar tapas *to eat tapas (small dishes of food)*
ver un concierto *to see a concert*
ver una exposición *to go to an exhibit*
ver una película *to see a movie*

Estados de ánimo *Moods and feelings*

alegre *happy*
contento/a *cheerful*
de buen humor *in a good mood*
de mal humor *in a bad mood*
nervioso/a *nervous*
preocupado/a *worried*
tranquilo/a *quiet, calm*
triste *sad*

Dolores y otros síntomas *Aches and other symptoms*

estar cansado/a *to be tired*
estar estresado/a *to be stressed*
tener dolor de cabeza (espalda) *to have a headache (backache)*
tener fiebre *to have a fever*
tener gripe *to have the flu*
tener tos *to have a cough*

Alimentos *Foods*

el arroz *rice*
la carne *meat*
las cebollas *onions*
los frijoles *beans*
la hamburguesa *hamburger*
el helado *ice cream*
los huevos *eggs*
la leche *milk*
las manzanas *apples*
los mariscos *shellfish, seafood*
las naranjas *oranges*
las palomitas *popcorn*
las papas fritas *french fries*
las papitas fritas *potato chips*
el pescado *fish*
los pimientos *peppers*
el pollo *chicken*
el postre *dessert*

el queso *cheese*
la tarta de chocolate *chocolate cake*
los tomates *tomatoes*
las verduras *vegetables*
el yogur *yogurt*
las zanahorias *carrots*

Verbos *Verbs*

doler (o>ue) *to hurt*

encantar *to love*
gustar *to like*

Partes del cuerpo *Parts of the body*

el brazo *arm*
la cabeza *head*
el cuello *neck*
el dedo *finger*
la espalda *back*
el estómago *stomach*
la mano *hand*
el pecho *chest*
el pie *foot*
la pierna *leg*
la rodilla *knee*

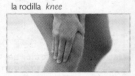

Palabras y expresiones útiles *Useful words and expressions*

A mí, también. *Me too.*
A mí, tampoco. *Me neither.*

EN RESUMEN: Gramática

USES OF *SER* AND *ESTAR*

(See page 146)

SER	ESTAR
■ Use **ser** to describe a characteristic of a person, place, or thing.	■ Use **estar** to describe a person's mood or feelings.
*María **es** una chica muy divertida.*	*Hoy **estoy** muy cansado.*
*Los leones **son** animales salvajes.*	***Estamos** nerviosos por el examen.*

INDIRECT OBJECT PRONOUNS

(See page 154)

yo	(a mí)	me
tú	(a ti)	te
usted/él/ella	(a usted/él/ella)	le
nosotros/as	(a nosotros/as)	nos
vosotros/as	(a vosotros/as)	os
ustedes/ellos/ellas	(a ustedes/ellos/ellas)	les

VERBS *GUSTAR, ENCANTAR* AND *DOLER*

(See pages 154 and 156)

A mí		me	encanta(n)	∅
A ti		te		muchísimo
A usted/él/ella	(no)	le		mucho
A nosotros/as		nos	gusta(n)	bastante
A vosotros/as		ós		un poco
A ustedes/ellos/ellas		les		nada

■ The verb **doler** (o>ue) follows the same pattern.

SHOWING AGREEMENT AND DISAGREEMENT

(See page 155)

■ Use **A mí, también** and **A mí, tampoco** to agree with what a person says.
■ Use **Yo, sí** and **Yo, no** to disagree with what a person says.

- » Yo tengo coche.
- » **Yo, también.**
- » Este año no voy a ir de vacaciones.
- » **Nosotros, tampoco.**
- » Yo tengo un carro.
- » **Yo, no.**
- » Este año no voy de vacaciones.
- » **Nosotros, sí.**

- » A mí me encanta ir a la playa por la tarde.
- » **A mí, también.**
- » No me gustan los gatos.
- » **A mí, tampoco.**
- » A mí me encanta ir a la playa por la tarde.
- » **A mí, no.**
- » No me gustan los gatos.
- » **A mí, sí.**

167

OBJECTIVES FOR UNIT OPENER

- Introduce unit theme: ***Vamos de viaje*** about traveling and getting around the city.
- Culture: Learn about cities and transportation in Hispanic countries.

STANDARDS

- 1.2   Understand the language
- 2.1   Practices and perspectives

INSTRUCTIONAL STRATEGIES

- Introduce unit theme and objectives: Talk about traveling and means of transportation and the places students would like to visit.
- Have students look at the photograph. Read the caption aloud: ***La Plaza de la Catedral***, ***La Habana***, ***Cuba***.
- Ask questions to help students recycle content from the previous unit. For instance, encourage them to use expressions from previous units, such as: **¿Quién vemos en esta foto? ¿Son jóvenes o viejos? ¿Viajan solos o en grupo? ¿Cómo es la muchacha? ¿Cómo es el muchacho? ¿Cómo están los dos? ¿Están cansados o contentos?**
- Use the photograph to preview unit vocabulary, including: **vacaciones**, **mapa**, **delante de**, **a la derecha de**, **a la izquierda de**, **detrás de**. Help students access meaning by making frequent use of gestures or visuals.
- Ask the introductory questions.
  - **– ¿Te gusta viajar a otros países?**
  - **– ¿Te gusta explorar las ciudades?**
  - **– ¿Qué ciudades quieres visitar?**
- Encourage students to talk about Spanish-speaking countries they may like to visit and why.
- Ask related questions: **¿Dónde están estos jóvenes? ¿Qué tiene el muchacho en la mano? ¿Qué llevan cuando viajan? ¿Llevan mapas cuando viajan a un lugar nuevo?**

ADVANCED LEARNERS

Use this opportunity to invite students to use what they know about the countries they have seen so far: United States, Spain, Mexico, El Salvador, Honduras, Guatemala, Nicaragua, Panama, Colombia, and Venezuela. Have them practice **ser / estar**: **¿Dónde está Caracas? ¿Cómo es Colombia? ¿Dónde está España?**

UNIDAD 6

VAMOS DE VIAJE

- ≫ ¿Te gusta viajar a otros países?
- ≫ ¿Te gusta explorar las ciudades?
- ≫ ¿Qué ciudades quieres visitar?

168

La Plaza de la Catedral, La Habana, Cuba

ADDITIONAL UNIT RESOURCES

Extension Activities (EA) (Photocopiable)	Interactive Whiteboard Lessons (IWB)	Audio	Video	Online ELEteca
EA: 6.1, 6.2	IWB: 6.1, 6.2, 6.3, 6.4	62 to 72		EXTENSIÓN DIGITAL

In this unit, you will learn to:

- Get around in a city
- Ask and give directions
- Describe where things are located
- Talk about means of transportation

Using

- Irregular verbs *ir, seguir, jugar* and *conocer*
- Prepositions of place
- *Hay* and *estar*
- Adverbs of quantity

Cultural Connections

- Share information about cities and transportation in Hispanic countries, and compare cultural similarities

SABOR HISPANO

Un viaje de aventuras

- Cuba, Puerto Rico y República Dominicana

¡ACCIÓN!

169

LEARNING OUTCOMES

- Ask and give directions in a city
- Describe where things are located
- Talk about means of transportation
- Share information about cities and transportation in Hispanic countries, and compare cultural similarities

INSTRUCTIONAL STRATEGIES

- Use the unit opener to preview the vocabulary and the cultural topics for this unit.
- Have students look at the images on this page and relate them to the objectives listed. Ask: *¿Qué buscan las muchachas en el mapa? ¿Cómo viaja la familia? ¿En tren? ¿En carro? ¿Van de vacaciones a la ciudad o a la montaña?*
- Invite students to read the topic for **Sabor hispano** and preview that section in the unit: *¿Qué deporte es popular en esta región? ¿Conocen algunos jugadores famosos?*
- Introduce the video segment in **¡Acción!** and ask students to predict what they think the episode will be about. Ask: *¿Quiénes aparecen en la foto? ¿Caminan o corren?*
- If time allows, have students work in pairs to talk about the images using the questions you have modeled. Then have volunteers present to the class what they understand this unit to be about.

SLOWER-PACED LEARNERS

Have student practice the verbs they know so far by modeling some sentences for them or asking them *yes/no* questions first. *¿Juega al béisbol el hombre de la foto? ¿Te gusta jugar al béisbol? ¿Cuándo juegas al béisbol? ¿Van de vacaciones las niñas? ¿Te gusta ir de vacaciones? ¿Cuándo tienes vacaciones?*, etc.

HERITAGE LANGUAGE LEARNERS

Ask students what sports they watch and practice their families or Latino friends. If they have been to Spanish-speaking countries, encourage them to share what they know about sports in the Spanish-speaking world with the class.

THREE MODES OF COMMUNICATION: UNIT 6			
	INTERPERSONAL	INTERPRETIVE	PRESENTATIONAL
HABLAMOS DE...	5	1, 2, 4	
COMUNICA	3, 6	1, 2, 4	5
¡ACCIÓN!	2, 5, 6	1, 3, 4	5, 6
PALABRA POR PALABRA	3, 6, 11	1, 2, 4, 7, 8, 9, 10, 11	5, 12
GRAMÁTICA	4, 6	1, 2, 3, 5, 6, 7, 8, 9	7
DESTREZAS		1, 2	
CULTURA		SABOR HISPANO	
RELATO	5	1, 2, 3, 4	5

OBJECTIVES FOR HABLAMOS DE...

- Preview vocabulary: talking about the outdoors, animals, and locations
- Preview grammatical structures: Prepositions of place, using **hay** and **está/están** to ask where something is
- Read and listen to a conversation about two friends visiting a nature reserve
- Understand language in context

CORE RESOURCES

- Audio Program: 62

STANDARDS

1.1 Engage in conversation
1.2 Understand the language
1.3 Present information
4.2 Compare cultures

INSTRUCTIONAL STRATEGIES

Activity 1

- Ask students: **¿Qué ven en la foto? ¿Dónde creen que están estos jóvenes?** Ask about other things they see in the photo, such as **mochila**, **mapa**. Recycle vocabulary already learned by asking them what these two hikers look like and what they are wearing.
- You can ask students to check their answers with a partner, and then you go over the answers with the whole class.

62 Activity 2

- Introduction to the conversation: Tell students to close their books. Explain that they will listen to a conversation between the two hikers.
- Check for prior knowledge by asking students what they think the characters will say.
- Before listening to the audio, clarify that they should focus on information that they need to answer the questions.
- Play the audio twice. During the first time, ask students to listen to the general content of the conversation. Discuss what they have understood.
- Then ask students to preview the questions. During the second time, they should pay attention to specific information they need to answer the questions.
- Finally, have students open the book and review the dialogue. Observe, provide support, and correct students as needed.

ANSWERS

Activity 1

1. c; 2. c; 3. b; 4. a.

Activity 2

a. F (Es la primera vez que va al parque); b. F (Está cerca); c. F (Osos, jirafas, etc.); d. T; e. T; f. F (Primero van al restaurante).

SLOWER-PACED LEARNERS

Focus students' attention on the visuals supporting the vocabulary in Activity 2. Have them find and circle the words in the conversations. Check their comprehension: **Es un animal pequeño que vuela y canta (pájaro).** Then put students in pairs to make their own sentences about each item.

HABLAMOS DE... Un viaje al parque natural

1 Look at the image below of two hikers finding their way around the nature reserve. Then choose the correct answer to complete the sentences.

1. La imagen representa...
   a. ◯ una foto de dos estudiantes.
   b. ◯ una foto de un grupo de amigos.
   c. ◯ una foto de dos excursionistas.

2. El muchacho tiene en la mano...
   a. ◯ una guía.
   b. ◯ un papel.
   c. ◯ un mapa.

3. Los muchachos están...
   a. ◯ en la ciudad.
   b. ◯ en el campo.
   c. ◯ dentro de una oficina.

4. La chica de la foto...
   a. ◯ está de buen humor.
   b. ◯ está triste.
   c. ◯ está preocupada.

2 🎧 62 Listen to the conversation and then decide whether the statements that follow are true (T) or false (F).

Belén: ¿Conoces este parque natural?
Jesús: No, es la primera vez que estoy aquí. ¡Es increíble!
Belén: Es verdad. A mí me gusta porque no está muy **lejos de** nuestra casa y podemos venir en carro. A mis hermanos les encanta jugar aquí. Hay árboles muy altos y muchos tipos de flores. ¡Ah! y es fácil ver animales; hay osos, jirafas y muchas especies de pájaros. También hay restaurantes para comer.
Jesús: Genial. ¿Dónde están los restaurantes? Ya tengo un poco de hambre.
Belén: Pues hay muchos, pero el más barato está **cerca de** la entrada. Nos gusta porque tiene unas mesas de madera bastante grandes.
Jesús: ¿Seguro? Creo que en la entrada no hay restaurantes, según este mapa.
Belén: Claro que sí, hay en la entrada y también **detrás del** lago. Tu mapa está mal.
Jesús: ¿Y sabes si hay una tienda donde comprar otro mapa?
Belén: Pues creo que hay una tienda **delante de** la entrada. Venga, vamos al restaurante y después de comer vamos a la tienda y seguimos con la ruta.

(árbol, entrada, oso, restaurante con mesas de madera, jirafas, lago, pájaro, tienda)

	T	F
a. Jesús conoce muy bien el parque.	◯	◯
b. Belén piensa que el parque está un poco lejos de su casa.	◯	◯
c. En el parque no hay animales.	◯	◯
d. El restaurante más barato está cerca de la entrada.	◯	◯
e. Jesús quiere comprar otro mapa.	◯	◯
f. Primero van a la tienda y después al restaurante.	◯	◯

ADVANCED LEARNERS

You may want to pose a few gist questions to the class before playing the conversation in Activity 2 for the first time with books closed: **¿De qué hablan? ¿Cuál es el problema con el mapa? ¿Cuál es su plan?**

3 🎧 **62** Listen again to the conversation and repeat after the speaker.

4 Use the expressions below and the map of the nature reserve to locate the places Belén and Jesús mention in their conversation above. Complete the sentences with the correct expression.

delante de la mesa   **detrás de** la mesa   **lejos de** la mesa   **cerca de** la mesa

1. La tienda está .... la entrada.

2. Las jirafas están .... los osos.

3. .... del lago hay un restaurante y muchos árboles.

4. Hay muchos árboles .... los osos.

5. .... del lago hay un restaurante grande y una tienda.

6. Hay una tienda grande .... la entrada.

5 👥 With a partner, take turns asking and answering the following questions about the map. Use the corresponding letters on the map as a guide.

a. ¿Qué hay delante de las jirafas?

b. ¿Dónde está la tienda grande?

c. ¿Qué hay enfrente de la entrada?

d. ¿Dónde hay muchos pájaros?

e. ¿Dónde hay árboles pequeños?

f. ¿Qué hay detrás del restaurante?

171

INSTRUCTIONAL STRATEGIES

🎧 **62** **Activity 3**

Before playing the audio, have students focus their attention on the words in bold in the conversation as they listen and repeat. Then ask students what they think the expressions describe (location).

Activity 4

- Have students read the captions for each image and use the images to decode the meaning of these prepositions.

- Use a classroom object or yourself to talk about different locations relative to your desk or table. Have students respond with each change of location, such as: *El libro está delante de la mesa. El libro está detrás de la mesa. Usted está lejos de la mesa. Usted está cerca de la mesa.*

- Have students complete the activity individually.

- Explain to students that the letters on the map correspond to the questions in the activity. This will help students locate the places referenced in the questions.

Extension

If time allows, have students work in pairs. One places an object in different locations relative to their desks or something else in the classroom and the other states where the object is, using the expressions taught. Then they change roles. Challenge them to move the object quickly and respond just as quickly.

Activity 5

As student talk to each other, make sure they are using the right form of *estar* and *hay*. The use of these two verbs to express location is explained on page 173, but some students, particularly the advanced ones, may have questions at this point.

ANSWERS

Activity 4

1. detrás de / cerca de; **2.** lejos de; **3.** Cerca / Delante; **4.** Delante; **5.** Lejos; **6.** lejos de.

Activity 5

Answers will vary. Possible answers provided.

a. Árboles grandes; **b.** Lejos de la entrada; **c.** Una tienda pequeña / Un restaurante pequeño; **d.** Delante de la tienda grande / cerca del lago; **e.** Detrás del restaurante / Cerca de la entrada; **f.** Un lago / árboles.

HERITAGE LANGUAGE LEARNERS

If students are already familiar with these structures, have them describe the school or the classroom. They can also think of a country and answer questions about it, so the other students guess the name of the country: *¿Tu país secreto está cerca de Panamá? ¿Tu país secreto está lejos de México?*, etc.

OBJECTIVES FOR COMUNICA

- Present the communicative functions of the unit:
  - Describe where things are located
  - Use **hay** and **está/están** to ask about what there is and where
- Practice stating where things are located relative to something else

CORE RESOURCES

- Interactive Whiteboard Lesson: IWB 6.1
- Audio Program: 63
- Interactive Online Materials - ELEteca

STANDARDS

1.1	Engage in conversation
1.2	Understand the language
1.3	Present information
4.1	Compare languages

INSTRUCTIONAL STRATEGIES FOR DESCRIBING WHERE THINGS ARE LOCATED

- Before going over the expressions on this page with students, present IWB 6.1, **Pedir y dar información espacial.**

- Go over each image asking students **¿Dónde está el perro?** Have students focus on the prepositional phrases to indicate place. Cover the labels for each picture and ask again: **¿Dónde está el perro?**, pointing to any image at random.

Activity 1

Preview new vocabulary with the labels shown in the picture. Have students identify other objects they already know, such as **mochila**, **silla**, **bufanda**.

🎧 63 Activity 2

See audioscript on page APP9.

Extension

Students can draw a room with objects in it. They describe it and ask a partner to draw it, providing instructions as to the location of the objects in the room using the expressions taught. Then they compare drawings to see how close they are.

Activity 3

Model this for the class first, providing clues and having students guess who you're describing. Consider giving students time to write down three clues about the secret person's location individually first. That way they'll be less likely to give away their answers later by looking overtly in that person's direction to come up with sentences on the spot.

COMUNICA

DESCRIBING WHERE THINGS ARE LOCATED

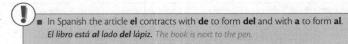

¿Dónde está el libro?

El libro está

delante de *in front of*	**cerca de** *close to, near*
detrás de *behind*	**al lado de** *next to*
encima de *on top of*	**a la izquierda de** *to the left of*
debajo de *under, below*	**a la derecha de** *to the right of*
lejos de *far from*	**dentro de** *inside*
entre... y... *between... and...*	

la mesa.

> ⓘ ■ In Spanish the article **el** contracts with **de** to form **del** and with **a** to form **al**.
> *El libro está al lado del lápiz. The book is next to the pen.*

1 Look at María's desk and select the correct expression in parenthesis that describes where the objects are located.

la pantalla
el bolso
el teclado
el ratón
el cajón
el ventilador

a. La papelera está (encima de / detrás de / debajo de) la mesa.
b. La cámara está (a la derecha de / delante de / encima de) la pantalla de la computadora.
c. La ventana está (debajo del / detrás del / al lado del) gato.
d. El cuaderno está (encima del / a la izquierda del / delante del) celular.
e. La lámpara está (al lado de / entre / dentro de) la computadora.

2 🎧 63 Listen for the one mistake María makes when describing where everything is located in the room. What did she get wrong?

3 👥 Let's play. Pick out a classmate in the class and describe where he/she is without saying who it is. Your partner will try to guess the person based on the clues you provide. Keep providing clues until your partner guesses correctly. Then switch roles.

ANSWERS

Activity 1 and 2

a. debajo de; b. encima de; c. detrás del; d. delante del; e. al lado de. The mistake she makes is this: *La mochila no está a la derecha del escritorio, está a la izquierda.*

SLOWER-PACED LEARNERS

Project the image in Activity 1. Point to the objects as María describes them in Activity 2. Pause after the first description to have students confirm whether she's described their locations correctly or not. Then call on volunteers to do as you've done –identifying the objects as María says them and confirming with the class whether or not the descriptions are correct. Pause the audio after each description.

ADVANCED LEARNERS

Challenge students to write three more sentences relating the locations of the items in the image in Activity 1.

ASKING ABOUT WHAT THERE IS AND WHERE IT IS

HAY	ESTÁ / ESTÁN
■ Use the verb **hay** to talk and ask about the existence of people or things.	■ Use **está / están** to talk or ask about where someone or something is located.
• En mi clase **hay** un pizarrón. *In my class, there is a blackboard.*	• El pizarrón **está** detrás de la mesa. *The blackboard is behind the desk.*
• También **hay** muchos libros. *There are many books too.*	• Los libros **están** en la estantería. *The books are in the bookshelf.*

Stopping someone to ask for information

	Para preguntar		Para responder
Informal	Perdona (tú), Oye (tú),	¿dónde hay un parque?	Sí, claro, mira… Pues mira…
Formal	Perdone (usted), Oiga (usted),	¿dónde está la biblioteca?	Sí, claro, mire… Pues mire…
Informal	¿Sabes (tú)	dónde hay un parque?	
Formal	¿Sabe (usted)	dónde está la biblioteca?	No lo sé, lo siento.

4 Fill in the blanks with *hay* or the correct form of *estar* as needed.

a. José: ¿Dónde .... el restaurante de Pedro?
Lola: El restaurante .... cerca de mi casa, en la calle Felicidad.

b. Jesús: Oye, ¿dónde .... una estación de policía?
Laura: No lo sé.

c. Juan: Perdona, Raquel, ¿ .... playa *(beach)* en tu ciudad?
Raquel: No, no hay playa, pero .... unos lagos muy bonitos cerca de mi casa.

5 🎧 64 Listen to the conversations above to check your answers. Then practice the conversations with a partner.

6 With a partner, take turns asking each other about the following places. Use the Modelo or any of the examples in Activity 5.

Modelo:
E1: ¿Hay carril bici en tu ciudad?
E2: Sí, claro.
E1: ¿Dónde está?
E2: Está en la calle Miraflores.

Parque de atracciones

Restaurante japonés

Parque acuático

Carril bici

MORE IN ELETECA: EXTRA ONLINE PRACTICE

173

OBJECTIVES FOR COMUNICA

• Present the communicative functions of the unit:
– Elicit information and provide information
– Use **hay** and **está/están** to ask about what there is and where something is

CORE RESOURCES

• Audio Program: 64

STANDARDS

1.1 Engage in conversation
1.2 Understand the language
1.3 Present information
4.1 Compare languages

INSTRUCTIONAL STRATEGIES FOR ASKING ABOUT WHAT THERE IS AND WHERE IT IS

• Before going over the presentation, ask students the following questions: **¿Hay un parque en esta ciudad?** Once they answer, ask and write on the board: **¿Dónde está el parque?** Follow a similar process with questions in the plural: **¿Hay tiendas en este barrio? ¿Dónde están las tiendas?**

• Invite students to notice the differences between the two sets of questions. Help them infer the rules for singular and plural. Underline the articles so they can notice and compare the use of indefinite articles **(un)** with **hay** when asking about the existence of unknown objects versus the use of definite articles **(el)** with **está** when asking about known objects. Then have them open the book and proceed to go over the grammatical explanation.

Activity 4

Have students work individually to complete the conversations. Circulate and provide assistance as needed.

🎧 **64** Activity 5

Have students work in pairs or groups to practice the conversations from the audio with a partner.

Audioscript

José: ¿Dónde está el restaurante de Pedro?
Lola: El restaurante está cerca de mi casa, en la calle Felicidad.
Jesús: Oye, ¿dónde hay una estación de policía?
Laura: No lo sé.
Juan: Perdona, Raquel, ¿hay playa en tu ciudad?
Raquel: No, no hay playa, pero hay unos lagos muy bonitos cerca de mi casa.

Activity 6

Practice role-playing the **Modelo** with students to provide sample responses: **1**. ¿Hay (un) parque de atracciones en tu ciudad? / Sí, hay uno. / ¿Dónde está el parque de atracciones? / El parque de atracciones está lejos de mi casa. **2**. ¿Hay restaurantes japoneses en tu ciudad? / Sí, hay muchos. / ¿Dónde está el más barato? / Está en el centro. **3**. ¿Hay parques acuáticos en tu ciudad? / No, en mi ciudad no hay parques acuáticos.

ANSWERS

Activity 4

a. está, está; **b.** hay; **c.** hay, hay.

HERITAGE LANGUAGE LEARNERS

Working with a partner, have students extend one of the conversations in Activity 4. They can add lines both before and after it. Then have them act out the conversations in front of the class.

¡ACCIÓN! INTEGRATED LANGUAGE VIDEO

OBJECTIVES FOR ¡ACCIÓN!

- Provide students with a structured approach to viewing the video
- Contextualize the content of the unit in a familiar scenario

CORE RESOURCES

- Unit Video 6 - Un barrio interesante
- Online Materials - ELEteca

STANDARDS

1.1	Interpersonal communication
1.2	Interpretive communication
2.1	Culture: Practices and perspectives

INSTRUCTIONAL STRATEGIES

Previewing: Antes del video

Tell students to look at the title and video stills to predict what the video is going to be about. Ask them to name the characters, locations, and objects that they see and know.

Activity 1

Have students look at the items on the list and go over any unfamiliar words as a class. Use the images on the page, glossaries in the book, drawings on the board, or bilingual dictionaries to help them discover the meanings. Note that many of these words will be presented and practiced explicitly later on in this unit in **Palabra por palabra** on p. 178.

Viewing: Durante el video

Activity 2

- Play the video for the first time. Go over the answers as a class by taking a poll as to which items were discussed in the video.
- Have students compare and contrast the items that Lorena and Eli discuss with those checked on their own lists.
- Ask some general questions to see what the students have understood: **¿Dónde están Lorena y Eli al principio del video? ¿Por qué Lorena llama a Eli? ¿Dónde están las muchachas al final del video?**

Activity 3

Now that students have watched the video once, direct their attention to Image 1 and ask them to name the items they see. Have students begin by making their own lists. Then project the image and call students up to identify and label the items.

Activity 4

- Tell students that in this activity they are going to focus on the prepositions used for different phrases related to methods of transportation. Elicit examples of prepositions. Tell them to choose between **en** or **a** to complete each phrase.
- Go over the answers as a class. Ask which ones were discussed in the video.

ANSWERS

Activity 2

restaurante, gimnasio, museo, parada de bus, biblioteca, iglesia, cine, centro comercial, estatua.

Activity 3

edificio, motocicleta, coche, estatua, fuente, árbol, autobús.

¡ACCIÓN! Un barrio interesante

ANTES DEL VIDEO

1 Think about your own neighborhood and check the places and things you can find there.

	Mi barrio	Video		Mi barrio	Video
restaurante	☐	☐	parque	☐	☐
estación de policía	☐	☐	fuente	☐	☐
farmacia	☐	☐	estación de metro	☐	☐
centro comercial	☐	☐	supermercado	☐	☐
iglesia	☐	☐	cine	☐	☐
paradas de bus	☐	☐	librería	☐	☐
museo	☐	☐	zapatería	☐	☐
banco	☐	☐	estación de tren	☐	☐
gimnasio	☐	☐	estatua	☐	☐
papelería	☐	☐	tienda de ropa	☐	☐

DURANTE EL VIDEO

2 Watch the complete episode and check the items in Activity 1 that Lorena and Eli discuss.

3 Look at Image 1 and list at least seven items you see.

4 Complete the expressions describing different ways to get around in the city with the correct preposition. Then identify the ones that appear in the episode.

a. Montar .... bicicleta.   **d.** Montar .... metro.   **g.** Ir .... avión.
b. Ir .... pie.   **e.** Viajar .... tren.   **h.** Viajar .... barco.
c. Viajar .... autobús.   **f.** Montar .... caballo.   **i.** Ir .... tranvía.

174

Activity 4

En el video aparece la bicicleta, en el metro y a pie.

a. Montar en bicicleta; **b.** Ir a pie; **c.** Viajar en autobús; **d.** Montar en metro; **e.** Viajar en tren; **f.** Montar a caballo; **g.** Ir en avión; **h.** Viajar en barco; **i.** Ir en tranvía.

SLOWER-PACED LEARNERS

Before playing the video and asking students to do Activity 2, you may want to do more vocabulary practice with the items in Activity 1 to make sure that they are understood. One way to do this might be with a quick game of Pictionary in which students take turns drawing objects that the rest of the class uses to guess the vocabulary word. Another way is to give examples of restaurants, banks, museums, shoe stores, etc. that they will know and have them name the type of place it is in Spanish.

174

5 Choose the correct option.

a. Para ir al gimnasio Lorena puede ir **a pie** / **en metro** / **en bici**.
b. Para ir a la biblioteca es mejor ir **a pie** / **en metro** / **en bici**.
c. Para llegar al centro comercial es más rápido ir **a pie** / **en metro** / **en bici**.

6 Indicate whether the following statements are true (T) or false (F).

	T	F
a. Eli lleva poco tiempo en la ciudad.	☐	☐
b. Lorena quiere encontrar un gimnasio bueno, pero no muy caro.	☐	☐
c. La biblioteca está un poco lejos de la casa de Lorena.	☐	☐
d. No es posible ir en bici en la ciudad donde viven Lorena y Eli.	☐	☐
e. El centro comercial está al sur de la ciudad.	☐	☐
f. Es posible ir a pie al centro comercial desde la casa de Lorena.	☐	☐

7 Look at Image 6 and write five sentences describing the location of the items and people from the list.

Elementos: la estatua, Lorena, Eli, la muchacha desconocida, el restaurante, la farmacia, el bazar, la farmacia…

Utiliza: delante de, a la derecha de, a la izquierda de, al lado de, en frente de, encima de…

Modelo: El bazar chino está al lado de la farmacia.

a. ....
b. ....
c. ....
d. ....
e. ....

DESPUÉS DEL VIDEO

8 Based on what you saw and heard in the video, write a brief description of the city where Eli and Lorena live. Use the images as a guide. ¡Atención! Use *hay* to describe what there is in the city.

....

MORE IN ELETECA: EXTRA ONLINE PRACTICE

175

Activity 7

- Direct students back to the Image 6 on page 174, and go over the instructions. It's difficult to see the names of the places in the photo, so you may want to replay the video from 4:50 until the end a few times. Encourage students to focus their attention on the signs on the canopies in the background and other items in the scene. Pause the video if necessary to help them identify the correct locations of the places.
- Have students work individually to write the sentences. Circulate and provide help as needed. Refer students back to **Comunica** on page 172 if they've forgotten the meanings of the prepositional phrases.
- Put students in pairs to share their sentences, encouraging them to edit each other's work as needed.

Post-viewing: Después del video
Activity 8

- Refer students back to the checklist in Activity 1 and the places called out in Activity 5 to help them remember the places discussed in the video.

ANSWERS

Activity 5
a. Para ir al gimnasio Lorena puede ir a pie.
b. Para ir a la biblioteca es mejor en bici.
c. Para llegar al centro comercial es más rápido en metro.

Activity 6
a. F; b. T; c. T; d. F; e. T; f. F.

Activity 7
Answers will vary. Possible answers:
a. Lorena está delante de la estatua.
b. Eli está a la izquierda de Lorena.
c. La chica desconocida está a la derecha de Lorena.
d. El bazar está en frente del restaurante.
e. La chica desconocida tiene la mano encima de la cabeza.

Activity 8
Answers will vary. Possible answer:
Lorena y Eli viven en una ciudad grande con muchos medios de transporte y lugares de ocio como cines, centros comerciales. En esta ciudad hay diferentes medios de transporte, como autobuses, metro y carril bici. El barrio de Lorena tiene muchas cosas y es un barrio muy interesante.

SLOWER-PACED LEARNERS

To help students develop their writing skills, work as a class to come up with possible introductory and concluding sentences for their paragraphs in Activity 8. Suggest a few ways that they can order or organize the details inside the paragraph so they can follow one of those strategies as well.

HERITAGE LANGUAGE LEARNERS

Working with a partner, have students write a conversation in which they help someone navigate an unfamiliar city, just as Eli has helped Lorena in the video. Ideally, the conversation will take place in a Spanish-speaking country that they know well or have researched, or they can imagine that a friend or family member from a Spanish-speaking country has recently moved to the US and needs some help getting around.

ADVANCED LEARNERS

To make Activity 1 more of a speaking activity, you might put students in pairs to interview their partners about what is or is not in their neighborhoods. Elicit or model how to ask these questions, and have students change the heading of the first column from **Mi barrio** to **El barrio de...**

INSTRUCTIONAL STRATEGIES

Activities 5 and 6

- Before playing the video a second time, give students a few minutes to look over the multiple choice and *true/false* items. If they're confident that they already know the answers, allow them to mark them. Otherwise, encourage them to circle or underline key words that they will want to listen / watch for.
- Play the video again, and have students complete the activities individually. Then go over the answers as a class. Have students correct the false statements in Activity 6.

OBJECTIVES FOR LOS MEDIOS DE TRANSPORTE

- Present the vocabulary needed to practice the communicative and grammatical functions for the unit: Means of transportation
- Identify words for means of transportation

CORE RESOURCES

- Audio Program: 65
- Interactive Online Materials - ELEteca

STANDARDS

- 1.1 Engage in conversation
- 1.2 Understand the language
- 1.3 Present information
- 3.2 Acquire information
- 4.1 Compare languages

INSTRUCTIONAL STRATEGIES

🎧 65 **Activity 1**

- Before listening to the audio, converse with students about means of transportation, which ones they use, which ones they prefer.
- Have students complete the activity in the book and then listen to the audio to check their answers.

  Audioscript

  1. El autobús; **2.** el taxi; **3.** el avión; **4.** el barco; **5.** la moto; **6.** el tren; **7.** el metro; **8.** ir a pie.

- After students check their answers, write a big heading on the board: *Medios de transporte*. Then write: *a pie*, *a caballo* on the line below. Tell students that all other means of transportation use the preposition *en*.

CULTURAL NOTE

Share with students that in Bolivia and Ecuador llamas serve as means of transportation through the Andes given the llamas' capacity to move through difficult terrain at high altitudes. In Spain, a ***burro taxi*** is a donkey used to transport tourists through the mountains in Granada. Compare this use of animals as a means of transportation in Spanish-speaking countries to similar uses in the US, such as the donkey rides along the Grand Canyon.

Activity 2

Use a map of Puerto Rico to review its geographical location before students complete the activity. Ask: ***¿Está cerca o lejos de Florida? ¿Qué país está a la izquierda de Puerto Rico?*** Point out the places mentioned: ***San Juan***, ***isla Culebra***, ***las cavernas de Camuy***.

Activity 3

Have students discuss their preferred modes of transportation for each circumstance with a partner.

Alternate Activity

Have students create a survey in which they provide two or three possible answer options for each scenario, leaving the last option as *otro*. Have them poll each other in small groups, or conduct the survey as a class mingling activity. Have students analyze the results and report back to the class.

ANSWERS

Activity 1

a. 6; **b.** 2; **c.** 4; **d.** 1; **e.** 5; **f.** 8; **g.** 3; **h.** 7.

PALABRA POR PALABRA Los medios de transporte

1 🎧 65 **Match the means of transportation to the correct word in Spanish. Then listen to the audio to check your answers.**

- **a.** ☐ el tren
- **b.** ☐ el taxi
- **c.** ☐ el barco
- **d.** ☐ el autobús
- **e.** ☐ la moto
- **f.** ☐ ir a pie
- **g.** ☐ el avión
- **h.** ☐ el metro

2 **Read the following blog from a travel website for Puerto Rico and fill in the blanks with an appropriate means of transportation.**

www.puertoricoisladelencanto.com

✈ *Puerto Rico*

¡Hola y bienvenidos a mi blog de Puerto Rico, la isla del encanto! Está más cerca de lo que piensas. Mira, sales de tu ciudad en (1) .... y llegas al aeropuerto de San Juan en poco tiempo. Después tomas (2) .... para ir al Hotel Paraíso. El hotel está cerca de la playa, puedes ir (3) .... todos los días, no necesitas carro. Para conocer el Viejo San Juan, tomas (4) .... que sale del hotel. En el Viejo San Juan no hay (5) ...., pero no es necesario porque el centro no es muy grande. Recomiendo visitar las cavernas de Camuy. Es muy popular alquilar (*rent*) (6) .... para ir hasta allí. Si quieres conocer la isla de Culebra, toma (7) .... pequeño desde Fajardo. El viaje es de solo 45 minutos y el mar es muy bonito. ¡Que pasen buenas vacaciones!

Calle en el viejo San Juan

3 👥 **Indicate what type of transportation you prefer to take in the following situations. Then share your answers with a partner.**

 ❗ ■ Use **ir en** with transportation to express *to go by*.

Modelo: *para ir de tu casa a casa de un amigo* → *Prefiero ir a pie.*

- **a.** para ir a la escuela
- **b.** para ir de vacaciones
- **c.** para viajar por la ciudad
- **d.** para viajar por el Caribe
- **e.** para visitar a tus abuelos (tíos...)
- **f.** para ir de Madrid a Barcelona

Activity 2

1. avión; **2.** un taxi; **3.** a pie; **4.** un autobús; **5.** metro; **6.** una moto; **7.** un barco.

Activity 3

Answers will vary and should reflect the model provided and expressions taught.

HERITAGE LANGUAGE LEARNERS

Discuss how some means of transportation, such as **carro** and **autobús**, receive different names in the different Spanish-speaking countries. Elicit any known examples from the class. For instance, **autobús** is **camión** in Mexico, **colectivo** in Colombia and Argentina, **guagua** in Puerto Rico, **ómnibus** in Argentina, and even just **bus**.

ADVANCED LEARNERS

Have students expand Activity 3 on page 176. Ask them to invent other situations: ***para ir a comprar, para visitar a un amigo, para viajar por el mar***, etc. Have them write a short paragraph with these examples using the text in Activity 2 as a model.

4 👥 Here are some adjectives you can use to describe transportation. Practice saying them aloud with a partner. Then match each adjective to its definition.

rápido/a ≠ lento/a   peligroso/a ≠ seguro/a

caro/a ≠ barato/a   incómodo/a ≠ cómodo/a

1. rápido/a
2. caro/a
3. lento/a
4. barato/a
5. seguro/a
6. práctico/a
7. peligroso/a
8. cómodo/a

a. Que cuesta mucho dinero.
b. Que tarda (takes) poco tiempo.
c. Que cuesta poco dinero.
d. Que tarda mucho tiempo.
e. Que tiene riesgo (risk).
f. Que es confortable.
g. Que no tiene riesgo.
h. Que es útil.

5 Classify each of the adjectives in Activity 4 as either positive or negative as they relate to transportation.

Positivos

Negativos

6 👥 Give your opinion about the following types of transportation using the list of adjectives you created in Activity 5. Then ask a partner for his/her opinion.

a. Para mí, el carro es…
b. Para mí, el avión es…
c. Para mí, el tren es…
d. Para mí, el metro es…
e. Para mí, el barco es…
f. Para mí, la moto es…

Asking and expressing your **opinion**
■ ¿Y para ti?
■ Para mí, también.
■ Para mí, no.

177

INSTRUCTIONAL STRATEGIES

Activity 4
Provide sample sentences and use gestures as needed to clarify vocabulary.

Activity 5
Do this as a whole class activity. Call on individual students to track responses on the board. Encourage students to come up with other adjectives.

Activity 6
Review with students the expressions for expressing opinions. Share your preferences and call on students to respond. **Para mí, ir a pie es muy práctico. ¿Y para ti?**

Extension
After students complete this activity in pairs, ask them to work in small groups to tally the results and come up with general statements about the overall results from the group. Provide these sentence stems to help students report their findings: **El transporte favorito del grupo es… / El transporte que más/menos nos gusta es…**

ANSWERS

Activity 4
1. b; 2. a; 3. d; 4. c; 5. g; 6. h; 7. e; 8. f.

Activity 5
Positivos: rápido/a, barato/a, seguro/a, práctico/a, cómodo/a.
Negativos: caro/a, lento/a, peligroso/a.

Activity 6
Answers will vary and should reflect the model provided and expressions taught.

SLOWER-PACED LEARNERS
Provide students with more opportunities to use these adjectives in the feminine form: **la bicicleta** and the plural form: **los trenes**, **los aviones**, etc.

HERITAGE LANGUAGE LEARNERS
Ask students to write a longer paragraph explaining what people use to go from one place to the other, how much it costs, how comfortable it is, etc. If appropriate, ask them to include their own experiences traveling through Spanish-speaking countries.

OBJECTIVES FOR LA CIUDAD

- Present the vocabulary needed to practice the communicative and grammatical functions for the unit: Naming places in the neighborhood and around the city

CORE RESOURCES

- Audio Program: 66
- Interactive Whiteboard Lesson: IWB 6.2

STANDARDS

1.1	Engage in conversation
1.2	Understand the language
1.3	Present information
3.2	Acquire information
4.2	Compare cultures

INSTRUCTIONAL STRATEGIES

🎧 66 Activity 7

- Use IWB 6.2, **Mi barrio**. With books closed, point to places at random on the screen and have students say the name of each place as you point.

- Explain how some of these places differ from the ones in the US. For instance, pharmacies in the US are often like supermarkets or convenience stores, but they aren't like that in many Spanish-speaking countries. **Mercados** are also very different. Bring pictures, if possible.

Activity 8

To check answers, assign numbers for each of the categories, **1** for **ir de compras**, and so on. Write the categories on the board. Call out places at random and have students hold up one, two, or three fingers to indicate the category. This way, all students participate and you can assess individual progress.

Activity 9

CULTURAL NOTE

- Ask if anyone remembers what **gazpacho** is and can describe it to the class. (Remind them that Lorena ordered it in the Unit 5 video, **Un pelo en mi cena**). Explain that **gazpacho** is an uncooked soup typically made of chopped tomatoes, cucumbers, onions, peppers and herbs and is served cold. It originated in Andalucía, a region in southern Spain that experiences very warm temperatures during the summer months. You might want to prepare **gazpacho** as a class project. Many easy-to-make recipes are available online.
- Remind students that the **tortilla** described in this activity is the Spanish version.

ANSWERS

Activity 8

Ir de compras: farmacia, librería, tienda de ropa, zapatería, supermercado; **Ocio y tiempo libre:** parque, cine, gimnasio, museo;

PALABRA POR PALABRA La ciudad

7 🎧 66 Listen to the names of places you typically find in the city. Then repeat after the speaker.

parque · cine · zapatería · estación de tren

farmacia · tienda de ropa · supermercado · gimnasio

librería · parada de autobús · estación de metro · museo

8 List each of the places in the appropriate column in the chart below.

Ir de compras	Ocio y tiempo libre	Transporte público

9 Indicate where you would buy the following items.

a. unas botas
b. unos tomates, pimientos y cebollas para hacer gazpacho
c. un diccionario de español
d. unas aspirinas para el dolor de cabeza
e. un jersey y una camisa
f. huevos, papas y cebolla para hacer una tortilla española

gazpacho

Transporte público: parada de autobús, estación de metro, estación de tren.

Activity 9

1. zapatería; **2.** supermercado; **3.** librería; **4.** farmacia; **5.** tienda de ropa, centro comercial; **6.** supermercado.

SLOWER-PACED LEARNERS

After taking note of the places to buy the items in Activity 9, put students in pairs to take turns asking and answering questions to check their answers: **¿Dónde puedes comprar unas botas? Puedo comprarlas en una zapatería; ¿Dónde puedes comprar...? Puedo comprar...**

ADVANCED LEARNERS

Have students write complete sentences in the present or past tense with the places in Activity 7 and the items in Activity 9: **Ayer, mi hermana mayor compró unas botas en una zapatería**. Then have them share their sentences with a partner.

UNIDAD 6

10 Where would you go to do the following things?

Modelo: ir al centro comercial ➡ Voy en autobús.

a. ver una exposición
b. hacer judo
c. montar en bici
d. ver una película
e. jugar al básquetbol
f. mirar un mapa del metro de la ciudad
g. hacer natación en el invierno
h. quedar con un amigo para ir al centro comercial (está lejos y no tienen carro)

El centro comercial de Miraflores en Lima, Perú

11  Look at the map of the city and fill in the blanks with the correct information. Then compare your answers with a partner.

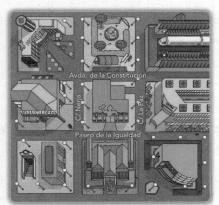

¡Tengo un barrio (*neighborhood*) genial! En mi barrio hay un centro comercial entre la .... de tren y el ....

Enfrente hay un .... muy grande, al lado del ....
Detrás del gimnasio hay un .... donde quedo con mis amigos para montar en bici. En el centro comercial hay una zapatería que me gusta mucho. El centro comercial está un poco lejos del .... , sigues todo recto por la calle La Paz y giras (*turn*) a la izquierda. El hospital está al final de la Avenida de la Constitución. ¡Ah! Yo vivo al lado del metro, en la Calle Nerja.

12 Write a similar description of your neighborhood. Include what stores there are and where they are located. Say which ones you like and what you buy there.

Modelo: En mi barrio hay...

MORE IN ELETECA: EXTRA ONLINE PRACTICE

179

INSTRUCTIONAL STRATEGIES

Activity 10

- Explain **centro comercial** in Spanish: ***Un grupo de tiendas en un edificio grande que puede tener más de una planta***. Ask students to provide examples of local malls to check comprehension.
- Clarify that the activity asks students to provide a destination and not necessarily a means of transportation.

Activity 11

After completing this activity, ask students what other stores, places, or buildings they can find in their neighborhood. Help students come up with the Spanish terms for the places they mention, such as: ***centro cultural, centro de salud, iglesia, teatro, mercado, fuente, estatua***. This will help students learn the vocabulary they will need to complete the next activity.

ANSWERS

Activity 10

Possible answers provided.

a. museo; b. gimnasio; c. parque; d. cine; e. parque, gimnasio; f. estación de metro; g. piscina cubierta; g. la parada de autobús, estación de metro.

Activity 11

estación; cine; gimnasio; supermercado; hospital; parque; hospital.

Activity 12

Answers will vary and should reflect the model provided and names of places taught.

SLOWER-PACED LEARNERS

Since most students in the US do not live in a **barrio**, writing a description in Activity 12 may be difficult for them. Ask them to draw a map similar to the one in Activity 11, and have them exchange maps when finished. Students can use the new map to explain what they can buy in those stores, etc.

ADVANCED LEARNERS

For additional speaking practice, have students ask and answer questions about the items in Activity 10 with a partner. Encourage them to ask follow-up questions to keep the conversation going.

HERITAGE LANGUAGE LEARNERS

If students have been abroad, ask them to share their experiences going to the places presented and discussed in this lesson. How were the places different? Prompt them to contrast the churches, markets, and pharmacies in particular. If they haven't been abroad, they can interview a relative who has or use representations that they have seen from movies. Have them write a paragraph summarizing this information that they can post on an online discussion forum.

OBJECTIVES FOR GRAMÁTICA 1

- Present the grammatical structures needed to practice the communicative functions of the unit: The irregular verbs *ir*, *seguir*, *jugar*, and *conocer*.

CORE RESOURCES

- Interactive Whiteboard Lesson: IWB 6.3
- Extension Activities: EA 6.1
- Interactive Online Materials - ELEteca

STANDARDS

1.1 Engage in conversation

1.2 Understand the language

4.1 Compare languages

INSTRUCTIONAL STRATEGIES

1. Irregular Verbs IR, SEGUIR, JUGAR, and CONOCER

- Use IWB 6.3, **Verbos regulares e irregulares en el presente**, to review the different types of verb conjugations students have learned so far. Start with the column on the left to review forms of regular verbs in the present. Have students fill in the blanks on the chart. Then work across to the irregular verbs. Ask questions to check comprehension.

- Remind students that verbs can be irregular in different ways: 1) a change in the stem vowel; 2) only the **yo** form is irregular; 3) verbs that have both a stem change and a different **yo** form; and 4) verbs that are completely irregular.
- However, help them realize that most irregular verbs, in spite of those differences, do have the same endings as regular verbs in most cases.
- Have students open the book and walk them through the explanations given.

Activity 1

Have students complete the activity individually, then check their answers with a partner. Go over the correct answers with the whole class.

Extension

After students complete the activity, have them close their books and do "verb ping pong" with them. Students take turns calling out a verb in the infinitive form and a pronoun, such as *ir*, *yo* and another student has to provide the correct form for that pronoun: *yo voy*. Ask students to focus first on the irregular verbs from this activity. If time allows, they can use other verbs they have learned earlier.

ANSWERS

Activity 1

a. juego; b. conocemos; c. van; d. sigues; e. voy; f. juegan; g. conozco; h. sigue; i. vas; j. conocen; k. seguimos; l. juega.

GRAMÁTICA

1. IRREGULAR VERBS *IR*, *SEGUIR*, *JUGAR*, AND *CONOCER*

■ You have already learned some irregular verbs in Spanish. Verbs such as **hacer** and **salir** that have irregular **yo** forms, verbs that stem change such as **pedir** and **poder**, and verbs that are completely irregular like **ser**. In this next group, we have examples of each of these types. Look at the forms carefully and see if you recognize the pattern.

	IR *to go*	SEGUIR *to follow, continue*	JUGAR *to play*	CONOCER *to know, be familiar with*
yo	voy	sigo	juego	conozco
tú	vas	sigues	juegas	conoces
usted/él/ella	va	sigue	juega	conoce
nosotros/as	vamos	seguimos	jugamos	conocemos
vosotros/as	vais	seguís	jugáis	conocéis
ustedes/ellos/ellas	van	siguen	juegan	conocen

■ The verb **ir** is irregular because it does not follow any pattern. It is usually followed by **a**.
Voy a la escuela en autobús. *I go to school by bus.*
Nosotros **vamos al** parque para jugar al básquetbol. *We go to the park to play basketball.*

■ The verb **seguir** has both an irregular **yo** form and a stem change, e ➔ i.
Sigo las direcciones del mapa. *I follow the directions on the map.*
Si **sigues** todo recto, llegas a la estación. *If you continue straight, you'll get to the station.*

■ The verb **jugar** is the only verb in Spanish that stem changes u ➔ ue. It is usually followed by **a**.
Jugamos a los videojuegos en casa de Rafa. *We play videogames at Rafa's house.*
Alejandro **juega** al tenis. *Alejandro plays tennis.*

■ The verb **conocer** is irregular only in the **yo** form. Use **a** after **conocer** when saying you know or are acquainted with a person.
¿**Conoces** bien la ciudad? *Do you know the city well?*
Conozco a muchas personas de Cuba. *I know (am acquainted with) many people from Cuba.*

1 **Complete the chart below with the correct form of the verbs.**

a. jugar (yo) _juego_
b. conocer (nosotros) _conocemos_
c. ir (ellos) ....
d. seguir (tú) ....
e. ir (yo) ....
f. jugar (ustedes) ....

g. conocer (yo) ....
h. seguir (ella) ....
i. ir (tú) ....
j. conocer (ellos) ....
k. seguir (nosotros) ....
l. jugar (usted) ....

SLOWER-PACED LEARNERS

Put students in pairs. Have one of the students write sentences using the first column of verbs in Activity 1, and have the other write sentences using the second column. Then have them read their sentences aloud to their partners, spelling out the conjugated verb letter by letter. Students should listen and write down their partners sentences. Finally, have them check each other's spelling.

2 Decide what places the following people are going to according to their preferences.

a. A tus amigos les gusta hacer deporte.

b. A Angelita le gusta leer.

c. A nosotros nos gusta conocer a gente nueva.

d. A ti te gusta ver exposiciones de fotografía.

e. A Ricardo le gusta preparar comida para sus amigos.

3 Complete the conversation between Graciela and Ana with the correct forms of *seguir*.

Graciela: No conozco muy bien este centro comercial. ¿Dónde está la zapatería que nos gusta?

Ana: Mira, está ahí. (Nosotras) (1) .... recto y está a la derecha.

Graciela: ¿Hay una tienda de ropa cerca también?

Ana: Creo que sí. Pero yo tengo que ir a la librería. Entonces tú (2) .... por aquí para ir a la tienda y yo (3) .... por la izquierda para ir a la librería.

Graciela: Está bien. Cada una (4) .... su camino y después quedamos en la parada de autobús delante del centro.

4 Ask your partner if he/she knows (is familiar with) any of the following sports figures and the sport they play. Use the images as clues to the sports played.

Modelo:

E1: ¿Conoces a Pau Gasol o a Marc Gasol?

E2: Sí, conozco a Pau Gasol y a Marc Gasol.

E1: ¿Qué deporte hacen?

E2: Juegan al básquetbol.

a. Rafael Nadal o David Ferrer

b. Víctor Cruz o Mark Sánchez

c. Lionel Messi o David Beckham

d. Maria Sharapova o Serena Williams

e. José Reyes o David Ortiz

f. Sergio García o Tiger Woods

181

CULTURAL NOTE

- Rafael Nadal and David Ferrer play tennis. They are originally from Spain.

- Víctor Cruz and Mark Sánchez play football. Cruz plays for the NY Giants. His mother is from Puerto Rico. Sánchez, a Mexican American, plays for the NY Jets.

- Lionel Messi and David Beckham play soccer. Messi is from Argentina but plays for FC Barcelona. Beckham at one time played for Real Madrid.

- Maria Sharapova and Serena Williams play tennis.

- José Reyes and David Ortiz play baseball. They are both Dominican. Reyes plays for the Toronto Blue Jays and Ortiz plays for the Boston Red Sox.

- Sergio García and Tiger Woods play golf. García is from Spain.

Extension

Use EA 6.1, **Trabajamos el presente**, to play tic-tac-toe using the irregular verbs presented. Save the sheets to practice prepositions after completing **Gramática 2**.

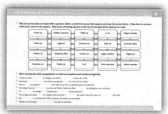

ANSWERS

Activity 2

1. Van al parque, gimnasio; 2. Va a la biblioteca o va a la librería; 3. Vamos al centro comercial; 4. Vas al museo; 5. Va al supermercado.

Activity 3

1. seguimos; 2. sigues; 3. sigo; 4. sigue.

Activity 4

Answers will vary and should reflect the models provided and the correct form of the irregular verbs taught, such as **conocer** and **jugar**.

ADVANCED LEARNERS

Using Activity 3 as a model, have students work with a partner to write a new dialogue about two people trying to find their way around a shopping center. Challenge them to try to include examples of the four verbs highlighted in this lesson: **ir**, **seguir**, **jugar**, and **conocer**.

HERITAGE LANGUAGE LEARNERS

After Activity 4, have students do research on an athlete from a Spanish-speaking country and prepare a brief presentation about him or her. Encourage them to use visuals to support their presentations.

Activity 2

- This activity combines the forms of **ir** with unit vocabulary. Have students prepare an example of their own to share with the class.

- Remind students to use the contraction **al** before masculine singular nouns.

Activity 3

- Have students work in pairs and take turns role-playing the conversation.

- Ask questions to check comprehension: **¿A qué tienda van primero? ¿Quién va a la librería?**

Activity 4

Review the **Modelo** and sports vocabulary with students before they begin.

OBJECTIVES FOR GRAMÁTICA 2

- Present the grammatical structures needed to practice the communicative functions of the unit: The prepositions *en*, *a*, *de*

CORE RESOURCES

- Extension Activities: EA 6.1

STANDARDS

1.1	Engage in conversation	1.3	Present information
1.2	Understand the language	4.1	Compare languages

INSTRUCTIONAL STRATEGIES

2. Prepositions *EN, A, DE*

- Write the sample sentences from the presentation on the board leaving a blank for the prepositions: ***Viajamos _ coche. Mis padres van _ supermercado. Salgo _ mi casa a las 9.***
- Have volunteers provide the missing prepositions and write them on the board. Then have students open the book and walk them through the explanations given.
- Point out that prepositions cannot always be translated from one language to another and that for the most part they need to learn which prepositions go with which verbs or expressions. However, certain rules do apply. Remind students of this basic rule: The preposition *en* is used for means of transportation except *a pie* and *a caballo*.
- Point out that the preposition *a* generally corresponds to the preposition *to* in English whenever you need to express destination, but that some verbs in Spanish simply require it, like ***conocer a una persona***, ***jugar al fútbol***. Compare this to the English equivalent, in which no preposition is needed: to know a person, to play soccer.
- Have students contrast ***Salgo de mi casa a las 9*** with *I leave my house at 9*. Help them realize that Spanish often uses *de* when English uses no preposition. Point out other examples of *de* on the page.

Activity 5

- Have students complete the questions individually. Then put them in pairs to ask and answer the questions.
- Encourage students to take notes so that they can report back to the class about their partners' answers. You may even want to have them switch partners so they can ask the questions in the third person and respond with their partners' information.

Activity 6

Extension

You can use the second part of EA 6.1, ***Trabajamos con el presente***, to provide additional practice with both prepositions and irregular verbs presented in this unit. Answers: **1.** tengo; hablamos; pides; voy; siguen; vengo; juega; conozco; salgo; conocen; vuelves; empiezan; como; juegan; sigues; empiezo; puedo; va; vivimos; vuelven. **2. a.** voy, vuelvo; **b.** vivimos en, en; **c.** a, sigues; **d.** juega, va; **e.** tengo, en, conozco; **f.** en, empiezan, empiezo; **g.** puedo; **h.** como, en / voy, a.

ANSWERS

Activity 5

a. a; **b.** (blank), en; **c.** del / al; **d.** al; **e.** al; **f.** (blank).

Activity 6

1. ir; **2.** a; **3.** sigues; **4.** en; **5.** en; **6.** De; **7.** Conoces; **8.** juego; **9.** vamos; **10.** vas; **11.** jugamos.

GRAMÁTICA

2. PREPOSITIONS *EN, A, DE*

- As you have seen, certain verbs of motion are often followed by prepositions **a**, **en**, or **de**. Use **en** with modes of transportation.
  *Viajamos **en** coche. We travel by car.*

- Use **a** to express destination.
  *Mis padres van **al** supermercado. My parents are going to the supermarket.*

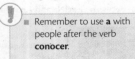

- When **a** is followed by **el** it contracts to form **al**.
  a + el = al

- Remember to use **a** with people after the verb **conocer**.

- Use **a** with sports after the verb **jugar**.

- Use **de** to express origin or point of departure.
  *Salgo **de** mi casa a las 9. I leave my house at 9.*

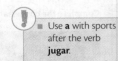

- To go on vacation ➙ ir **de** vacaciones
- To take a trip ➙ ir **de** viaje

5 🔲 **Complete the sentences with *a*, *al*, *en*, *de* or *del*. ¡Atención! Not all sentences will need a preposition. Then, with a partner, take turns asking and answering the questions.**

a. ¿Conoces .... muchos estudiantes en tu clase de español?
b. ¿Quieres jugar .... videojuegos después de la escuela o prefieres montar .... bici?
c. ¿A qué hora sale el autobús .... centro comercial?
d. ¿Te gusta jugar .... fútbol americano?
e. ¿Vas .... gimnasio?
f. ¿Conoces .... la ciudad de Nueva York?

6 🔲 **Complete the following conversations with the correct verbs and prepositions from the list. Then practice the conversations taking parts with a partner.**

> jugamos ○ en ○ ir ○ a ○ conoces ○ de ○ voy ○ sigues ○ en ○ vas ○ vamos

a. ≫ ¿Cómo puedo (1) .... a la casa de tu hermano?
   ≫ Para ir (2) .... su casa (3) .... todo recto por la calle Real, giras *(turn)* a la derecha y caminas diez minutos aproximadamente. La casa está (4) .... la calle Paz. Si *(if)* vas (5) .... autobús, es mejor.

b. ≫ ¿(6) .... dónde es Juan?
   ≫ ¿(7) .... a Juan?
   ≫ Claro, todos los domingos (8) .... con él al tenis y en verano (9) .... de vacaciones juntos.

c. ≫ ¿Dónde (10) .... ?
   ≫ Al campo de fútbol. Mis amigos y yo (11) .... al fútbol por la tarde.

ADVANCED LEARNERS

Have students write three of their own questions to add to the list in Activity 5. Each questions should use one of the prepositions highlighted here: *a*, *de*, or *en*.

HERITAGE LANGUAGE LEARNERS

Using conversation *a* in Activity 6 as a model, have students ask three Spanish speakers for detailed directions to places in town and record their responses. Then have them transcribe the responses and circle the prepositions *a*, *de*, or *en* that were used if heritage language learners are in a class with mostly non-native speakers, encourage them to ask three people for directions to the same place. Allow them to share the recorded responses with the rest of the class (or post them online) so others can practice listening to authentic speech and compare their respones.

3. ADVERBS OF QUANTITY

■ Adverbs of quantity tell how much something is done.

demasiado *too much*	*Luis trabaja* **demasiado**.
mucho *very much, a lot*	*Ana viaja* **mucho**.
bastante *enough*	*Pedro estudia* **bastante**.
poco *very little, not much*	*Rosa estudia* **poco**.

■ **Muy** can be used to intensify how an action is done (adverb) and a description (adjective).
Olivia habla **muy** *bien. Olivia speaks very well.*
Es **muy** *inteligente. She is very intelligent.*

■ **Mucho**, when used after a verb, means very much or a lot. Before a noun, **mucho** expresses quantity and functions as an adjective. Note that, as an adjective, **mucho** must agree with the noun in number and gender.

- **Adverb:**
  Juan come **mucho**. *Juan eats a lot.*
- **Adjective:**
  Juan come **muchas palomitas**. *Juan eats a lot of popcorn.*
  Creo que compras **muchos zapatos**. *I think you buy a lot of (many) shoes.*

7 Choose the correct option in parenthesis.

a. Mi hermano nunca (*never*) va al gimnasio. No le gusta **poco** / **mucho** hacer deporte.
b. Jaime come **demasiado** / **poco**. Solo una ensalada para comer y fruta para cenar.
c. Todos los días leo el periódico y una revista. Leo **poco** / **bastante**.
d. Mi padre trabaja doce horas al día. Trabaja **demasiado** / **bastante**.

8 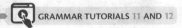 List the words on the left in the correct column based on whether they are used with *muy* or *mucho/a*. ¡Atención! Separate by adjectives and nouns. Then check your answers with a partner.

	Muy	Mucho/a
a. guapa e. sueño	....	....
b. dolor f. trabajador	....	....
c. divertido g. paciencia	....	....
d. simpática h. alegría	....	....

9 Fill in the blanks with *muy* or *mucho/a/os/as*.

a. Esta chica estudia todos los días. Es .... inteligente.
b. Mi primo siempre tiene .... calor.
c. Duermo cinco horas al día. Tengo .... sueño.
d. Mi amigo hace .... preguntas; es .... curioso.

MORE IN ELETECA: EXTRA ONLINE PRACTICE ● **GRAMMAR TUTORIALS 11 AND 12**   183

OBJECTIVES FOR GRAMÁTICA 3

- Present the grammatical structures needed to practice the communicative functions of the unit: Adverbs of quantity
- Use adverbs to express how much

CORE RESOURCES

- Interactive Whiteboard Lesson: IWB 6.4

STANDARDS

1.1   Engage in conversation
1.2   Understand the language
4.1   Compare languages

---

3. Adverbs of Quantity

- Project IWB 6.4, **Adverbios de cantidad y adjetivos indefinidos**. Use it to present and contrast adverbs of quantity vs. indefinite adjectives.

- Write **Juan come demasiado** (verb + adverb) / **Juan está demasiado cansado** (adverb + adjective) and **Juan come demasiados dulces** (adjective + noun). Ask students to reflect on the difference between this sentence and the other two: Adverbs do not change, in contrast with adjectives, which do change, and must agree in gender and number with the noun they qualify.

GRAMMAR NOTE

Traditionally, **muy** and **mucho** cannot be used together, as **muchísimo** is the common expression for very much. However, you may hear **"muy mucho"** as an idiom to express intensity among Latin American speakers, particularly speakers from Mexico.

Activity 7

Have students work individually to choose the best answers. Explain that in the case of the third sentence, it sometimes helps to think of **bastante** as meaning *quite a bit* as well as *enough*.

Activity 8

Before sorting the words, call on volunteers to write sentences on the board with each word. Then, as a class, analyze whether the word is modifying a verb or a noun. This will help them determine with the word is an adjective or adverb. Based on that information, call a new round of volunteers to the board to add **muy** or **mucho/a** to the sentence.

Activity 9

Have students complete the sentences individually. Go over the answers as a class.

ANSWERS

Activity 7

a. mucho; b. poco; c. bastante; d. demasiado.

Activity 8

Muy: guapa, divertido, simpática, trabajador. **Mucho/a:** dolor, sueño, paciencia, alegría.

Activity 9

a. muy; b. mucho; c. mucho; d. muchas, muy.

SLOWER-PACED LEARNERS

Students may need additional support regarding the parts of speech in their own language. If necessary, provide models in English so students can become more familiar with the terms. For additional grammar practice, have students rewrite the sentences in Activity 9, changing the singular subjects to plural subjects. Then have them identify what parts of the sentences changed.

OBJECTIVES FOR DESTREZAS

- Skimming for specific information to improve comprehension
- Using a map to identify and locate places mentioned in a reading

STANDARDS

1.2 Understand the language

1.3 Present information

CORE RESOURCES

- Extension Activities: EA 6.2

INSTRUCTIONAL STRATEGIES

As a motivational activity, project images from the Internet of Santo Domingo and have them guess what city it is and what country it is in (*la República Dominicana*). Depending on the images you find, you might ask them to guess what specific buildings are, too: *universidad*, *iglesia*, *teatro*, *palacio*, etc.

CULTURAL NOTE

The city of Santo Domingo is the capital of the Dominican Republic. When Christopher Colombus arrived on the island in 1492, he encountered the native people, the Tainos, whose culture is still present in the vocabulary, folklore, and traditions of the Dominican people, or *Quisqueyaños*. In 1498, the Spaniards founded the city, and it became the home of the first university, cathedral, hospital, and customs house in the New World. The design of the colonial city became a model for future town planners in the Americas. For these reasons and others, Santo Domingo has been declared a UNESCO World Heritage Site. These days, it is the most populated city in the Caribbean. .

Activity 1

Have students read the **Destrezas** box first before doing the reading.

Activity 2 (next page)

Suggested time for doing this activity is 15 minutes.

Extension

- Have students write a similar text about their own city or some other location they are familiar with and create a set of questions. Encourage students to follow the example presented substituting their own information. They can then trade their text and questions with a partner.
- Use EA 6.2, *Un día en Salamanca*, as an info gap activity for students to practice in pairs.

CULTURAL NOTE

The city of Salamanca is part of the autonomous region of Castilla y León. In 1988 it was declared a UNESCO World Heritage Center. The university, founded in 1218, is the oldest one in Spain but not the first.

DESTREZAS

COMPRENSIÓN DE LECTURA

1 Before reading, review the reading strategy in Destrezas and follow the suggestion.

> ### Destrezas
>
> **Read for locations**
> This reading mentions specific places in the city. What places are mentioned? Skim the reading to find those places and mark them on the map. Also, find out the name of the city and where it is located.
>
> A) Biblioteca Nacional
> B) Galería de Arte Moderno
> C) Museo de Historia Natural
> D) Museo de Historia y Geografía
> E) Museo del Hombre Dominicano
> F) Teatro Nacional

2 Read the selection about a famous city and answer the questions that follow.

Este es el plano del centro de Santo Domingo, la capital de República Dominicana. Muchos jóvenes estudian aquí porque su universidad, la Universidad Autónoma de Santo Domingo, es muy importante. Es la segunda universidad más antigua de las Américas y está al lado del Conservatorio Nacional de Música. Conozco Santo Domingo y me gusta pasear por la Plaza de la Cultura, que está a la derecha del conservatorio. Esta plaza es muy famosa y conocida. Aquí hay muchos turistas que visitan los museos y la Biblioteca Nacional. Por las noches, la plaza es un punto de encuentro para muchos jóvenes que van a ver conciertos y otras actuaciones en el Teatro Nacional. No es una ciudad muy grande, tiene una línea de metro, pero yo voy andando a todos los lugares. Muchos dominicanos utilizan también el autobús o la guagua, como lo llaman ellos.

184

The first university founded in Spain has not survived. Many illustrious thinkers and great authors have passed through its classrooms including a visit from Christopher Columbus who came to present and discuss his projects. Salamanca is a very cosmopolitan city, as the university attracts students from all over the world.

ANSWERS

Activity 2

1. a; **2.** c; **3.** c; **4.** a; **5.** c; **6.** c.

SLOWER-PACED LEARNERS

Before moving on to the text, allow students to spend more time with map. Tell them to take turns asking and answering questions about the locations of difference places in the city with a partner. Point out the map's key and encourage them to talk about those places as well.

UNIDAD 6

1. ¿Dónde está la Plaza de la Cultura?
   a. A la derecha del Conservatorio Nacional de Música.
   b. A la izquierda del conservatorio.
   c. Encima del conservatorio.

2. ¿Hay una estación de metro cerca de la universidad?
   a. Sí.
   b. No, no hay.
   c. No, no hay metro.

3. El Palacio Nacional está...
   a. al lado del conservatorio.
   b. a la izquierda de la universidad.
   c. cerca de la Plaza de la Cultura.

4. Es una ciudad que se puede recorrer...
   a. a pie.
   b. en tranvía.
   c. en tren.

5. En Santo Domingo hay...
   a. mucho turismo.
   b. muchos estudiantes.
   c. mucho turismo y muchos estudiantes.

6. Santo Domingo tiene...
   a. la universidad más antigua de España.
   b. el segundo conservatorio más antiguo de las Américas.
   c. una plaza muy famosa en República Dominicana.

PRONUNCIACIÓN The sounds of *g*, *gu* and *j*

1 🎧 **67** Listen to the sounds that the following letter combinations make in the words below.

ge → gente	ja → jamón	ga → gato	gui → guitarra
gi → girar	jo → joven	go → gordo	gue → Miguel
	ju → jueves	gu → guapo	

2 👥🎧 **68** Practice saying the following words aloud with a partner. Then listen to the audio recording to check your pronunciation.

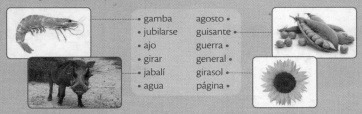

- gamba
- jubilarse
- ajo
- girar
- jabalí
- agua

- agosto
- guisante
- guerra
- general
- girasol
- página

3 Fill in the blanks with *g* or *j*. Practice saying the words aloud as you complete their spelling.

a. ca....ón   b. o....o   c. má....ico   d. ....untos   e. traba....o   f. ima....en

4 Fill in the blanks with *g* or *gu*. Practice saying the words aloud as you complete their spelling.

a. ....ato   b. ....orra   c. hambur....esa   d. ....afas   e. ....azpacho

MORE IN ELETECA: EXTRA ONLINE PRACTICE

185

OBJECTIVES FOR SABOR HISPANO

- Learn about the Caribbean: Cuba, Puerto Rico, República Dominicana
- Learn about sports and transportation in Hispanic countries

CORE RESOURCES

- Audio Program: 69

STANDARDS

2.1 Practices and perspectives

2.2 Products and perspectives

3.1 Knowledge of other disciplines

3.2 Acquire information

5.2 Using language for personal enjoyment and enrichment

INSTRUCTIONAL STRATEGIES

- Introduce the topic by asking students what they know about Cuba, Puerto Rico, or the Dominican Republic. Ask them to recall what they learned about Santo Domingo in **Destrezas** on page 184.
- Talk about the images and the map. Elicit what they already know about San Juan, Santo Domingo, or the Puerto Rican community in New York City or elsewhere in the US.
- Read the captions together and ask questions to check comprehension. Explain that el Fuerte San Felipe del Morro is more popularly known as **el Morro** which means snout and ask them why they think it got its name (the shape of the fortress resembles a snout). Ask: **¿Qué país es parte de Estados Unidos? ¿Qué países constituyen la isla Española?**
- Share what you know about these topics.
- Ask students to identify which of the points in **¿Sabes qué…?** they find most surprising.
- Ask students if they know in which conflict Spain lost these colonies along with the Philippines (Spanish-American War of 1898) and what they know of this period in US history (President McKinley, yellow journalism, sinking of the USS Maine, Theodore Roosevelt and the Rough Riders, etc.). Have students research additional information about these topics to share with the class.

CULTURAL NOTE

- Cuba is the name used for this territory by the native population before Columbus arrived on the island. La Habana is the biggest city in the Caribbean. Before the Castro revolution in 1959, many wealthy Americans used to spend time in Cuba. Even Al Capone used to spend some of his holidays there. Relations between Cuba and the US have been very difficult in the last 60 years. Little by little, restrictions for US citizens to travel to Cuba have been lifted, and more and more people and Cuban Americans have been able to visit the island where some of their relatives still live.
- Puerto Rico is a US Freely Associated State whose citizens are US citizens. It has its own governor and legislature, but Puerto Ricans can't vote in the US national presidential election. Puerto Ricans do not have a representative in congress, either. The island was handed from the Spaniards to the US after the Spanish-American War in 1898. Several plebiscites (referendums) have taken place in the last 50 years to determine what could be the best status for the island. The last plebiscite was in 2006, and the questions were so complicated that the results did not mean any change for the status of the island or its citizens.

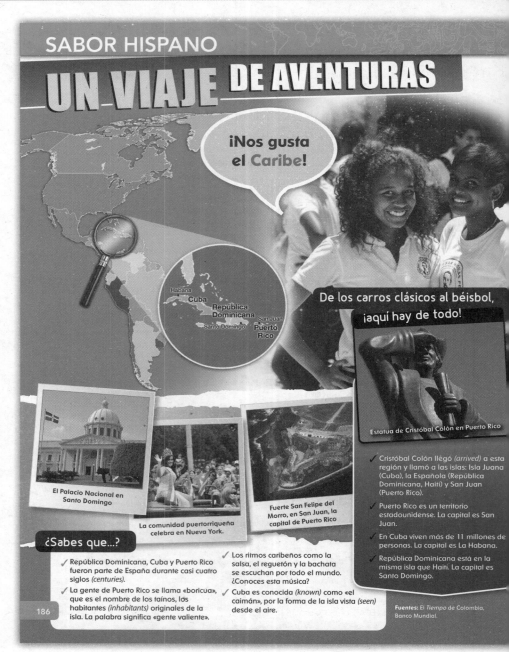

SABOR HISPANO

UN VIAJE DE AVENTURAS

¡Nos gusta el Caribe!

De los carros clásicos al béisbol, ¡aquí hay de todo!

Estatua de Cristóbal Colón en Puerto Rico

El Palacio Nacional en Santo Domingo

La comunidad puertorriqueña celebra en Nueva York.

Fuerte San Felipe del Morro, en San Juan, la capital de Puerto Rico

✓ Cristóbal Colón llegó (arrived) a esta región y llamó a las islas: Isla Juana (Cuba), la Española (República Dominicana, Haití) y San Juan (Puerto Rico).

✓ Puerto Rico es un territorio estadounidense. La capital es San Juan.

✓ En Cuba viven más de 11 millones de personas. La capital es La Habana.

✓ República Dominicana está en la misma isla que Haití. La capital es Santo Domingo.

¿Sabes que…?

✓ República Dominicana, Cuba y Puerto Rico fueron parte de España durante casi cuatro siglos (centuries).

✓ La gente de Puerto Rico se llama «boricua», que es el nombre de los taínos, los habitantes (inhabitants) originales de la isla. La palabra significa «gente valiente».

✓ Los ritmos caribeños como la salsa, el reguetón y la bachata se escuchan por todo el mundo. ¿Conoces esta música?

✓ Cuba es conocida (known) como «el caimán», por la forma de la isla vista (seen) desde el aire.

Fuentes: El Tiempo de Colombia, Banco Mundial.

SLOWER-PACED LEARNERS

Plays samples of music from the different genres mentioned in **¿Sabes que…?** After each clip, have students guess the type of music it is. Ask if they know the artist or song. Let the song play, challenging them to listen for words or phrases that are familiar to them.

CUBA, PUERTO RICO Y REPÚBLICA DOMINICANA UNIDAD 6

🎧 69 El deporte nacional

El béisbol es el deporte nacional de República Dominicana, y se practica desde 1866. El equipo más conocido se llama Tigres del Licey. En este país hay muchos jugadores famosos, como Alfonso Soriano, Alberto Pujols y David Ortiz, que juegan en Estados Unidos.

Alfonso Soriano, un famoso jugador dominicano

Los jugadores dominicanos son campeones: en 2013 ganaron (they won) el Clásico Mundial de Béisbol, una competición internacional muy importante.

Puerto Rico, isla del encanto

Puerto Rico recibe más de tres millones de turistas cada año. La isla ofrece vacaciones para todos los gustos. Si prefieres la naturaleza, visita el bosque tropical El Yunque, donde puedes admirar más de 240 tipos de árboles y hermosas cascadas (waterfalls). Si te gustan las aventuras, puedes explorar las cuevas (caves) naturales en el Parque de las Cavernas del río Camuy, al noroeste de la isla. Si tu pasión es la ciencia, visita Arecibo, en el norte de Puerto Rico, para observar las estrellas a través de un enorme radiotelescopio. ¡Y hay muchas opciones más!

El Yunque, un bosque tropical en Puerto Rico

Carros clásicos en La Habana

❖ En Cuba hay muchos carros antiguos de los años 50. Mucha gente dice que son bonitos, otra gente dice que son demasiado viejos.

❖ Hay pocos carros nuevos porque la ley no permite la importación.

❖ En general, los carros están bastante cuidados (cared for).

❖ Hay muchos taxis que son carros clásicos de colores alegres.

❖ Hay una competición anual de estos carros en las calles de La Habana. Se llama «Rally de Automóviles Clásicos Cubanos».

TAXI

Un taxi Chevrolet en la capital cubana

Indicate whether these statements are true or false.

Correct the statements that are false.

1. La gente de Puerto Rico se llama «boricua». T ○ F ○
2. República Dominicana está en la misma isla que Haití. T ○ F ○
   _____
3. En Cuba es fácil comprar un carro nuevo. T ○ F ○
   _____
4. Arecibo es una zona famosa por sus cuevas naturales. T ○ F ○
5. Alfonso Soriano es un jugador desconocido. T ○ F ○

VOCES LATINAS ▶ TURISMO DE AVENTURA

Join the two parts of the sentence.

1. La música del Caribe
2. Isla Juana
3. Santo Domingo
4. El Yunque

a. es la capital de República Dominicana.
b. es un bosque tropical puertorriqueño.
c. es famosa en el mundo.
d. es el antiguo nombre de Cuba.

187

INSTRUCTIONAL STRATEGIES

🎧 69

- An audio recording accompanies each text on this page. Vary between silent reading, reading aloud, and playing the audio.
- Elicit what students know about baseball in the Dominican Republic, the natural beauty of Puerto Rico, or classic American cars in Havana. Have students who have visited the region share information about their experiences or impressions.
- Ask: *¿Qué otros jugadores dominicanos conocen? ¿Qué tipo de vacaciones prefieren hacer en Puerto Rico? ¿Por qué creen que no hay carros americanos más modernos en Cuba?* (*el bloqueo* or *embargo* placed on U.S. exports to Cuba in 1962). *¿Quién es el presidente actual de Cuba?* Expand on the topic as much as you feel comfortable doing.
- Encourage students to do additional research on any of the topics that interest them.
- Have students complete the activities on this page and compare their answers with others.

CULTURAL NOTE

In the Dominican Republic, baseball is known as **la pelota** and baseball player as **pelotero**. The first baseball club was funded in 1898 in Santo Domingo. Baseball and history, particularly the relations between the US and the Dominican Republic have been always connected. For instance, the first no hitter game in the history of creole baseball was in 1914, during a game between Nuevo Club and the US Marines from the USS Washington battleship. Source: http://www.dominicanaonline.org/portal/espanol/cpo_beisbol_his.asp

ANSWERS

True or false
1. T; 2. T; 3. F; 4. F; 5. F.

Join the two parts of the sentence
1. c; 2. d; 3. a; 4. b.

ADVANCED LEARNERS

Have students pick one of the topics presented here and find out more information about it. Challenge them to learn three new and interesting facts that they can present to the class along with visual support.

HERITAGE LANGUAGE LEARNERS

Have students discuss stereotypes of Puerto Ricans, Dominicans, and Cubans. Where do all these stereotypes come from? Do people actually visit these countries? For what purposes? Is that enough to get to know a country and its culture?

OBJECTIVES FOR RELATO

- Revisit unit themes, grammar, vocabulary, and culture in a new context
- Improve reading comprehension skills

CORE RESOURCES

- Audio Program: 70

STANDARDS

- 1.1   Engage in conversation
- 1.2   Understand the language
- 1.3   Present information
- 2.1   Practices and perspectives

INSTRUCTIONAL STRATEGIES

Activity 1

- The purpose of this activity is to review proper use of prepositions taught in this unit.
- Students complete this activity individually or in pairs.

🎧 70 Activity 2

- Before students read the text, have them look at the photographs on this page. Ask them what these photographs suggest to them: **¿Qué les sugieren estas fotos?** Possible answers are: **vacaciones**, **México**, **la naturaleza**, etc. Review the words for *butterfly* and *whale*.
- Tell students that they are going to read a text about Lucía's vacation, and they will be able to check their answers from Activity 1. Let students know that they are allowed to look up words they might not know.

CULTURAL NOTE

For more information about the **Santuario de las mariposas monarca**, visit http://mariposamonarca.semarnat.gob.mx. The website includes fotos and a two-minute video that you can show to the class.

ANSWERS

Activity 1

1. b; **2.** c; **3.** a.

ADVANCED LEARNERS

Using Lucía's diary entry as a model, have students write a diary entry about their own upcoming vacation plans. If they don't have plans, they can make them up. Tell them to include two or three things they are going to do and explain why they are excited to do them.

HERITAGE LANGUAGE LEARNERS

Have students investigate and learn more whale-watching in Mexico. They can find several helpful articles here: http://www.mexicodesconocido.com.mx/especial-ballenas-a-la-vista.html. Tell them make recommendations, give suggestions, or provide information to Lucía that might be helpful or interesting to know before her trip. Have them share the information in the form of a friendly email.

RELATO El día a día

1 Match the words to complete the expressions.

1. ir de	a. bote
2. ir a	b. vacaciones
3. ir en	c. México

2 🎧 70 Read about Lucía's vacation plans.

Las vacaciones de Lucía

Me gusta ir de vacaciones con mis padres. Siempre organizan viajes muy interesantes y diferentes. Este año vamos a ir a México. ¡Me encanta!

¿Y qué voy a hacer? Pues no voy a visitar monumentos ni nada por el estilo. Voy a disfrutar *(enjoy)* de la naturaleza. ¡Voy a ver ballenas y mariposas monarca! ¿Sabes, querido diario, que todos los años, entre octubre y marzo, 300 millones de mariposas monarca viajan desde Canadá hasta México para hibernar? Estas mariposas viajan 4.000 kilómetros (durante más de 25 días) en busca de *(to search of)* una temperatura más cálida. Dicen que es fantástico poder verlas a todas juntas volando *(flying)*. Su destino es lo que se llama el "Santuario de las mariposas monarca", un bosque *(forest)* donde se quedan hasta primavera. A medida que entras en este bosque hay más y más mariposas que cubren las ramas de los árboles, y con la luz *(light)* del sol empiezan a volar *(to fly)*, y todo se vuelve de color naranja. ¿Cómo algo tan pequeño como una mariposa puede volar tantos kilómetros? ¡Es increíble!

También vamos a ver las ballenas grises. En la misma época, muchas de estas ballenas se juntan en las aguas de Baja California para tener sus crías *(young)*. Además, cuando ven gente en un bote, se acercan y muestran la cola *(tail)*. ¡Voy a hacer un montón de fotos!

mariposa

ballena

188

3 **Check the boxes for the sentences that are correct.**

a. ◯ Lucía está en México.

b. ◯ Todos los años viaja con sus padres a México.

c. ◯ El final de la migración de la mariposa monarca es un bosque.

d. ◯ Las ballenas grises van a las aguas de Baja California para tener sus crías.

e. ◯ Las mariposas viajan en primavera.

f. ◯ Lucía escribe a una amiga sobre sus planes.

4 **Read about the following people and then match the people to the best destination below based on their preferences.**

Elena y Diego
"Nos encanta la aventura y la naturaleza. Siempre vamos de vacaciones a lugares con muchos árboles, flores, ríos y lagos".

Macarena
"Prefiero visitar ciudades y lugares donde puedo aprender sobre la historia y la cultura de esa región".

Daniela
"A mí me encanta tomar el sol y descansar".

Enrique y Marta
"Estamos muy enamorados y queremos un lugar especial y romántico".

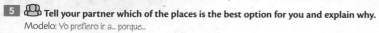
Para las vacaciones... ¡elige tu destino favorito!

a. Teotihuacán es una zona arqueológica a 40 kilómetros de la capital. Tiene muchos restos arqueológicos y puedes aprender mucho sobre la antigua historia de México. Hay edificios estupendos como las pirámides del Sol y la Luna.

b. Guanajuato es un lugar romántico, donde las leyendas y la tradición son los ingredientes principales. Tiene calles tranquilas para caminar durante horas y restaurantes muy íntimos.

c. En Playa de Carmen hay hermosas playas, con aguas de color turquesa del mar Caribe. Puedes descansar y tomar el sol mientras escuchas el relajante sonido del mar.

d. En Chihuahua, las Barrancas del Cobre son un gran espectáculo. Hay grandes montañas y puedes admirar paisajes fantásticos además de observar la naturaleza. Es posible viajar en tren, a caballo, en bicicleta, a pie o en kayak. En la ciudad, la catedral es una de las más importantes del norte de México.

5 👥 **Tell your partner which of the places is the best option for you and explain why.**

Modelo: Yo prefiero ir a... porque...

189

Activity 3

Students can do this activity individually, then compare answers with a partner. Review answers with the whole class.

Activity 4

- Students will choose the ideal destination for each person or couple. This activity can be done individually or in pairs.
- Pre-teach the following terms: ***restos arqueológicos***, ***pirámides***, ***color turquesa***, ***leyendas***, ***barrancas***. Help students, realize that some of these terms are cognates or near cognates and their meaning can be deduced based on their similarity to English. The word ***barrancas*** is not a cognate and it means *gullies*, *ravines*, or *gorges*.

CULTURAL NOTE

- **Teotihuacan** is an ancient city and ceremonial center outside Mexico City. Teotihuacan was founded over 2,000 years ago, at the beginning of the Common Era. It quickly became the largest city with the largest population in what we know today as the Americas. Today, it is a tourist attraction thanks to pyramids of the Sun and the Moon, as well as a major archeological research center on early cultures in the Americas. For additional information, visit the official website.

- **Guanajuato** is a city in central Mexico. It was declared a UNESCO World Heritage Site. One of its major attractions is its colonial architecture, particularly its baroque buildings such as the Iglesia de la Compañía and the Teatro Juárez. During the 18th Century Guanajuato was the world's largest silver-extraction center. It has underground tunnels connecting opposite ends of the city. For additional information, visit the official UNESCO site.

- **Playa del Carmen** is a town on the Mayan Riviera, along the Yucatan Peninsula. Originally founded as a fishing village around 1900, it became a popular destination for tourists in the 1990s because of its beautiful beaches. For additional information, visit the Playa del Carmen official website.

- **Chihuahua** is the largest state in Mexico, located in the northeast of the country. It is slightly bigger than the United Kingdom. Chihuahua is the richest state in Mexico due to its livestock production and silver mining. Ciudad de Chihuahua is the capital of the state, founded in 1709, and offers a mixture of colonial architecture and modern industrial buildings. The Chihuahua dog originated in the state of Chihuahua in pre-Columbian times. The Olmec, original settlers in the region, kept and bred Chihuahuas.

ANSWERS

Activity 3

True: c and d.

Activity 4

Elena y Diego: d; Macarena: a; Daniela: c; Enrique y Marta: b.

SLOWER-PACED LEARNERS

Working with a partner, have students make a poster advertising one of the places in Activity 4 to travelers. Suggest that they target a particular group of travelers by including pictures, slogans, and information that will appeal to them and their interests. Display the finished posters around the room.

EVALUACIÓN SELF-ASSESSMENT

- Review grammar, vocabulary and culture from the unit
- Complete self-assessment

CORE RESOURCES

- Interactive Online Materials - ELEteca

STANDARDS

- 1.2   Understand the language
- 2.1   Practices and perspectives
- 4.1   Compare cultures

INSTRUCTIONAL STRATEGIES

- Activities can be completed individually and then reviewed with the class.
- Expand by asking students if they agree with the answers given and then writing the correct answer on the board.
- You may wish to assign point values to each activity as a way for students to monitor their progress.
- If students achieve less than 80% on each activity, direct them to **En resumen** for page numbers to review.

ANSWERS

Activity 1

a. encima de / en; **b.** dentro de / en; **c.** detrás del; **d.** al lado de / debajo de; **e.** debajo de; **f.** al lado de / delante de.

Activity 2

a. ir, giras; **b.** izquierda, recto; **c.** hay, Sigues.

Activity 3

a and c.

EVALUACIÓN

DESCRIBING WHERE THINGS ARE LOCATED

1   **Complete the sentences to describe where these animals are located.**

a. El pájaro está .... la rama.   **b.** El gato está .... la cesta.   **c.** La jirafa está .... el árbol.

d. El elefante está .... su madre.   **e.** El perro está .... la mesa.   **f.** El caballo está .... los árboles.

ASKING AND GIVING DIRECTIONS

2   **Complete the conversations with the correct word from the list.**

> hay ○ recto ○ giras ○ sigues ○ ir ○ izquierda

a. Alicia: ¿Cómo puedo .... a la plaza de España?
    Enrique: Sigues todo recto, ... a la derecha y allí está la plaza de España.

b. Beatriz: ¿Me puedes indicar cómo llegar a Callao?
    Samuel: En la primera calle giras a la .... y después todo ....

c. Liliana: ¿Dónde .... una farmacia por aquí cerca?
    Nicolás: .... todo recto y luego giras a la derecha.

3   **Check the boxes for the questions you would use to ask where something is located.**

a. ☐ Perdone, ¿para ir a la biblioteca?
b. ☐ Oye, ¿sabes si hay un parque por aquí cerca?
c. ☐ Perdona, ¿sabes dónde está el museo?
d. ☐ Oiga, ¿hay un restaurante cubano en este pueblo?

LOS MEDIOS DE TRANSPORTE Y LA CIUDAD

4 **Use the images below to complete the sentences.**

a. Mi tío va en .... a la oficina porque es más rápido.

b. Raquel va en .... todos los días para ir a trabajar.

c. Estudio mejor en la .... que en casa.

d. Compro toda la fruta y la verdura en el ....

IRREGULAR VERBS

5 **Complete the sentences with *hay, está* or *están*.**

a. ¿Dónde .... Javier?

b. En mi calle .... una biblioteca.

c. El cuaderno .... encima de la mesa.

d. Los platos .... en mi casa.

e. No .... farmacia en está calle.

f. En la calle Marina .... otras paradas de autobús.

g. ¿Dónde .... mis zapatillas favoritas?

h. ¿Dónde .... el supermercado?

6 **Complete the sentences with the correct forms of the verb in parenthesis.**

a. » ¿Cómo (ir, yo) .... al centro comercial?

» Sí, mira, (seguir) .... por la calle Ocho y giras a la derecha en la avenida Juárez.

b. » ¿(Conocer) .... ustedes la tienda Zara?

» Lo siento, no (conocer) .... esa tienda. No somos de aquí.

c. » ¿En qué equipo de básquetbol (jugar) .... LeBron James?

» Creo que él y Dwayne Wade (jugar) .... juntos para los Miami Heat.

d. » ¿Te gusta (seguir) .... los resultados deportivos?

» Sí, (seguir) .... los resultados de la NBA y del tenis.

CULTURA

7 **Answer the following questions about Cuba, Puerto Rico, and the Dominican Republic and compare similarities with your own country or region.**

a. ¿Cómo son los taxis en Cuba? ¿Por qué? ¿Cómo son los taxis en tu ciudad o región?

b. ¿Cuál es el deporte más popular de República Dominicana? ¿Qué otros jugadores dominicanos conoces que juegan en Estados Unidos?

c. ¿De quién reciben estas islas su nombre? ¿Siguen con el mismo *(same)* nombre o tienen uno diferente? ¿De quién recibe tu país su nombre?

d. ¿Qué tipo de música es popular en el Caribe? ¿Es popular en tu ciudad o región también?

 **MORE IN ELETECA:** EXTRA ONLINE PRACTICE

ANSWERS

Activity 4

a. taxi; **b.** autobús; **c.** biblioteca; **d.** supermercado.

Activity 5

a. está; **b.** hay; **c.** está; **d.** están; **e.** hay; **f.** hay; **g.** están; **h.** está.

Activity 6

a. voy, sigues; **b.** Conocen, conocemos; **c.** juega, juegan; **d.** seguir, sigo.

Activity 7

a. Son coches clásicos de muchos colores. La razón es que no hay coches modernos en Cuba; **b.** El béisbol; **c.** De Cristóbal Colón. Isla Juana es actualmente Cuba, la Española es ahora República Dominicana y Haití, San Juan de Puerto conserva su nombre original; **d.** Los ritmos caribeños: salsa, reguetón y bachata son los más populares y conocidos en el mundo entero.

OBJECTIVES FOR EN RESUMEN: VOCABULARIO

- Review unit vocabulary and expressions
- Practice communicative skills

STANDARDS

1.2 Understand the language
1.3 Present information

INSTRUCTIONAL STRATEGIES

- Model how to use the vocabulary list to review new words and expressions learned in this unit.
- Use simple materials, such as index cards or self-adhesive notes.
- Self-adhesive notes can be used for writing nouns from the vocabulary list on them, then using them to place the correct labels on objects in the classroom or pictures in the book.
- Index cards can be used as flash cards with the Spanish term on one side and the English term on the other, or a picture or drawing.
- Students can work in pairs or groups, using the self-adhesive notes and index cards as they would the cards of a board game to help each other practice the unit vocabulary.
- Encourage students to write labels or captions for the photos on this page. Remind them to use the vocabulary and expressions they have learned in this unit.
- Challenge students to write conversations using as many of the vocabulary words as possible. Create a competition by saying that they'll earn one point for each word or expression from the page that they use correctly and logically in context. Pose some scenarios to help get them started, such as a foreigner or visitor in town who needs help getting around.

EN RESUMEN: Vocabulario

Expresiones de lugar
Adverbs of place

a la derecha de *to the right of*
a la izquierda de *to the left of*
al lado de *next to*
cerca de *close to, near*
debajo de *under, below*
delante de *in front of*
dentro de *inside*
detrás de *behind*
encima de *on top of*

entre *between*
lejos de *far from*

Verbos *Verbs*

conocer *to know, to be familiar
  with*
girar *to turn*
hay *there is, there are*
ir *to go*
ir a pie *to go on foot*

ir de vacaciones *to go on
  vacation*
ir de viaje *to go on a trip*
jugar *to play*
seguir *to follow*

Medios de transporte
Means of transportation

el autobús *bus*
el avión *airplane*
el barco *ship*
el metro *subway*
la moto *motorcycle*

el taxi *taxi*
el tren *train*

Descripciones *Descriptions*

barato/a *inexpensive*
caro/a *expensive*
cómodo/a *comfortable*
incómodo/a *uncomfortable*
lento/a *slow*
peligroso/a *dangerous*
rápido/a *fast*
seguro/a *safe, certain*

En la ciudad *In the city*

centro comercial *shopping
  center, mall*
cine *movie theater*
estación de metro *subway
  station*
estación de tren *train station*
farmacia *pharmacy*
librería *bookstore*
museo *museum*
parada de autobús *bus stop*

supermercado *supermarket*
tienda de ropa *clothing store*
zapatería *shoe store*

Preposiciones *Prepositions*

a, al *to, to the (masculine)*
de, del *from, from the
  (masculine)*
en *on*

Adverbios de cantidad
Adverbs of quantity

bastante *enough*
demasiado *too much*

mucho *very much, a lot*
muy *very*
poco *very little, not much*

Animales y plantas
Animals and plants

árbol *tree*
flor *flower*
jirafa *giraffe*
lago *lake*
oso *bear*

pájaro *bird*

EN RESUMEN: Gramática

UNIDAD 6

HAY / ESTÁ(N)

(See page 173)

Existence	Location
hay + un, una, unos, unas + noun	el, la, los, las + noun + está(n)

IRREGULAR VERBS

(See page 180)

	IR	SEGUIR	JUGAR	CONOCER
yo	voy	sigo	juego	conozco
tú	vas	sigues	juegas	conoces
usted/él/ella	va	sigue	juega	conoce
nosotros/as	vamos	seguimos	jugamos	conocemos
vosotros/as	vais	seguís	jugáis	conocéis
ustedes/ellos/ellas	van	siguen	juegan	conocen

PREPOSITIONS EN, A, DE

(See page 182)

Preposition	Use...	
en	with modes of **transportation**	*Viajamos **en** tren.* We travel by train.
a	to express **destination**	*Voy **a** Florida.* I'm going to Florida.
de	to express **origin** or point of **departure**	*Salgo **de** Miami.* I'm leaving from Miami.

ADVERBS OF QUANTITY

(See page 183)

To express how much	
Action Verbs	**demasiado**
	*Luis trabaja **demasiado**.* Luis works too much.
	mucho
	*Ana viaja **mucho**.* Ana travels a lot.
	bastante
	*Pedro estudia **bastante**.* Pedro studies enough.
	poco
	*Luis estudia **poco**.* Luis doesn't study much.

MUY / MUCHO

(See page 183)

- *Él/ella es **muy** inteligente.*
- *Él/ella habla **muy** despacio.*

- *Ellos/ellas son **muy** inteligentes.*
- *Ellos/ellas hablan **muy** despacio.*

- *Hace **mucho** calor.*
- *Hay **mucha** gente.*

- *Juan lee **muchos** libros.*
- *María tiene **muchos** amigos.*

193

OBJECTIVES FOR AHORA COMPRUEBA

- Review grammar, vocabulary and culture from the last two units
- Complete self-assessment

CORE RESOURCES

- Interactive Whiteboard Lesson: IWB 6.5
- Audio Program: 71, 72

STANDARDS

1.2	Understand the language
1.3	Present information
2.1	Practices and perspectives
4.1	Compare cultures

INSTRUCTIONAL STRATEGIES

- Activities can be completed individually or in pairs and then reviewed with the class.
- When reviewing answers in class, expand by asking students if they agree with the answers given and then writing the correct answer on the board.
- You may wish to assign point values to each activity as a way for students to monitor their progress. If students achieve less than 80% on each activity, direct them to **En resumen** in the previous two units for page numbers to review.

Activity 1

Have students sort the foods into the different categories on the plate. Project IWB Material 6.5, **Los alimentos**. Invite students to identify what food items are healthier and which are less healthy.

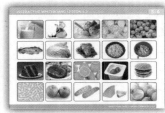

🎧 71 **Activity 2**

See audioscript on page APP9.

Activity 3

If needed, guide students by suggesting they first determine what kind of restaurant this is, and focus on just two items for each category on the menu. Students will write down the dialogue prior to presenting it to the class.

ANSWERS

Activity 1

Frutas: manzana; **Vegetales:** pimientos; **Granos:** arroz, cereales, pan, pasta; **Proteína:** carne, huevos, marisco, pescado, pollo; **Productos Lácteos:** leche, queso, yogur; **Otro:** aceite, dulces.

Activity 2

Menú del día. 1.ᵉʳ plato: ensalada de zanahorias, tomates y pasta; **2.º plato:** pescado con arroz o ensalada con pollo; **Postre:** manzanas, plátano o naranjas.

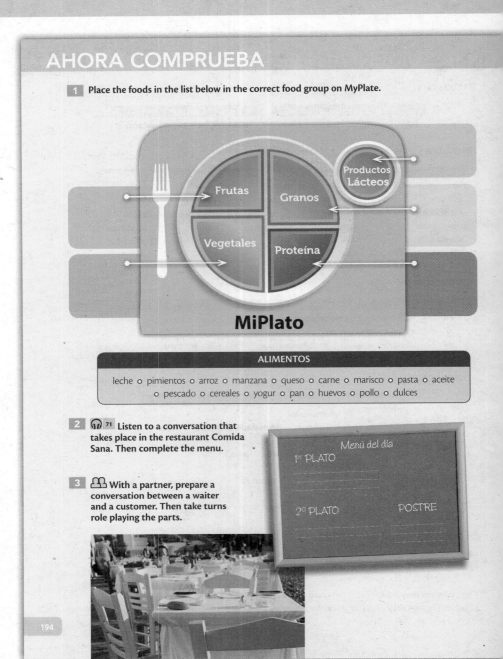

AHORA COMPRUEBA

1 Place the foods in the list below in the correct food group on MyPlate.

MiPlato

ALIMENTOS

leche ○ pimientos ○ arroz ○ manzana ○ queso ○ carne ○ marisco ○ pasta ○ aceite ○ pescado ○ cereales ○ yogur ○ pan ○ huevos ○ pollo ○ dulces

2 🎧 71 **Listen to a conversation that takes place in the restaurant Comida Sana. Then complete the menu.**

Menú del día
1ᵉʳ PLATO
2º PLATO   POSTRE

3 👥 **With a partner, prepare a conversation between a waiter and a customer. Then take turns role playing the parts.**

194

Activity 3

Students' dialogues should reflect the food items and communication skills learned in the unit for ordering at a restaurant.

SLOWER-PACED LEARNERS

Have students make a list of the learning objectives noted in the opening spreads of the two previous units. Tell them to ask themselves: *How well can I do this: very well, well, or not well?* Then pair students who can't do an objective well with another student who can; that way, they can teach each other what they know and help each other review.

REPASO UNIDADES 5 Y 6

REPASO
5-6

4 🎧 **72** **Carlos and Julián are going on a trip to Patagonia. Listen to the description of this region and answer the questions. You may have to listen more than once.**

a. ¿Dónde está la Patagonia?
b. ¿Qué hay en la Patagonia?
c. ¿Qué se puede visitar?
d. ¿Cómo es el invierno (winter)?
e. ¿Qué animales se pueden ver?
f. ¿Dónde pueden dormir?
g. ¿Hay metro, autobuses o trenes?
h. ¿Necesitan tener buena condición física para este viaje?
i. ¿Qué pueden comer?
j. ¿Qué documentos necesitan para hacer el viaje?

a. _____
b. _____
c. _____
d. _____
e. _____
f. _____
g. _____
h. _____
i. _____
j. _____

5 **Read the conversation between Carlos and Julián and fill in the blanks with the words from the list.**

muchos ○ hay ○ visitamos ○ viven ○ tomamos ○ glaciar
estamos ○ muchas ○ hay ○ viaje ○ vamos

Carlos: Me encanta este viaje. ¿Cómo vamos?
Julián: .... en avión hasta Buenos Aires. Allí .... tres días, ... la ciudad y luego .... otro avión hasta la Patagonia. Seguimos el .... en barco, vemos las ballenas y visitamos el .... Perito Moreno.
Carlos: ¿ .... muchas ballenas en la Patagonia?
Julián: Sí, hay .... ballenas y también .... animales que .... en el agua.

6 👥 **Check the boxes of the things Julián and Carlos will need to take on their trip. Work with a partner and decide what they will take and what five items they should leave behind.**

- ☐ una mochila
- ☐ zapatillas
- ☐ camisetas
- ☐ pantalones cortos
- ☐ pantalones largos
- ☐ abrigo
- ☐ protector solar
- ☐ impermeable
- ☐ gafas de sol
- ☐ cámara de fotos
- ☐ gorra
- ☐ champú

195

🎧 **72** Activity 4

It is recommended that students listen to the audio several times. They can do selective listening where each group of students listens for the purpose of answering two or three questions only. Then the groups gather at the end and share their findings.

Audioscript

La Patagonia está en Argentina y hay montañas y muchos animales marinos. En nuestro viaje a la Patagonia podemos ver y hacer lo siguiente: ver el glaciar más famoso del mundo, el Glaciar Perito Moreno, explorar los parques nacionales y ver ballenas. La Patagonia tiene inviernos muy fríos. Allí, de junio a agosto es invierno y el verano, de diciembre a marzo. En primavera durante el día hace sol, pero puede llover por la noche. Puedes dormir en pequeños hoteles. En este viaje, que es de aventura, hay que tomar autobuses o caminar para estar más en contacto con la naturaleza y la gente del lugar. No hay que tener un estado físico especial pero tenemos que caminar mucho y hay que saber soportar el calor y

el frío, el sol y la lluvia. En la Patagonia puedes comer asados, pescado y una gran variedad de pizzas. Para viajar, solo es necesario llevar el pasaporte.

Activity 6

This activity is intended to develop oral expression and interaction. Ask students to explain why they made those choices, as a way to encourage the imagination and oral expression.

ANSWERS

Activity 4

a. La Patagonia está en Argentina; **b.** Hay montañas y muchos animales marinos; **c.** Se puede visitar el glaciar más famoso del mundo, el Glaciar Perito Moreno, explorar los parques nacionales y ver ballenas; **d.** La Patagonia tiene inviernos muy fríos; **e.** Ballenas; **f.** Se puede dormir en pequeños hoteles; **g.** Hay autobuses; **h.** No hay que tener un estado físico especial, pero hay que caminar mucho y hay que saber soportar el calor y el frío, el sol y la lluvia; **i.** Se puede comer asados, pescado y una gran variedad de pizzas; **j.** Necesitan el pasaporte.

Activity 5

Vamos, estamos, visitamos, tomamos, viaje, glaciar, Hay, muchas, hay, muchos, viven.

Activity 6

Answers will vary.

ADVANCED LEARNERS

For those students who have a good handle on the vocabulary, grammar, and cultural content of the units, encourage them to focus on the development of their listening, speaking, reading, and writing skills prior to quizzes and tests. Challenge them to spend thirty minutes a night for four nights before the assessment focusing on one of each of the four skills each night. In addition to redoing the skills-based activities within the units, encourage them to seek new, related (and fun) material online to help them practice.

HERITAGE LANGUAGE LEARNERS

For students who already have a base of the language, challenge them to put themselves in the position of the teacher prior to assessments. How would they teach a non-native speaker the content of the previous two units? Have them develop worksheets, activities, games, presentations, and lesson plans that could be used to teach other students the material. By putting students in this new role, they will enhance their own knowledge and become masters of the content.

OBJECTIVES FOR UNIT OPENER

- Introduce unit theme: **¡Cuántas cosas!** about objects and their uses
- Culture: Learn about **Carnaval** in Hispanic countries

STANDARDS

- 1.2 Understand the language
- 2.1 Practices and perspectives

INSTRUCTIONAL STRATEGIES

- Introduce unit theme and objectives: Talk about objects and their uses.
- Have students look at the photograph. Read the caption aloud: **Le encantan la música y la tecnología.**
- Ask questions to help students recycle content from the previous unit. **¿Cómo es el muchacho? ¿Es muy ordenado, bastante ordenado o poco ordenado? ¿Qué hay a la derecha del muchacho? ¿Qué ven a la izquierda? ¿Qué ven detrás del muchacho? ¿Le gusta mucho la música? ¿Cómo lo saben?**
- Use the photograph to preview unit vocabulary, including: **el escritorio**, **los muebles**, **la portátil**, **la pantalla / el monitor**, **el teclado**. Help students access meaning by making frequent use of gestures or visuals.
- Ask the introductory questions.
  - **– ¿Cómo es tu habitación?**
  - **– ¿Qué cosas tienes en tu habitación?**
  - **– ¿Te gusta tener una habitación ordenada o no es importante para ti?**
- Ask related questions: **¿Tienes tantas cosas en tu habitación como este muchacho? ¿Pasas mucho tiempo en tu habitación?**

SLOWER-PACED LEARNERS

Encourage students to recycle and retrieve vocabulary, including verbs, and structures (mainly, the present tense) from previous units. Ask them to describe the pictures using colors, adjectives, **ser / estar**, and regular and irregular verbs. Begin with *yes/no* questions first and then progress to open-ended questions.

UNIDAD

7 ¡CUÁNTAS COSAS!

⧓ ¿Cómo es tu habitación?

⧓ ¿Qué cosas tienes en tu habitación?

⧓ ¿Te gusta tener una habitación ordenada o no es importante para ti?

Le encantan la música y la tecnología

196

ADDITIONAL UNIT RESOURCES

Extension Activities (EA) (Photocopiable)	**Interactive Whiteboard Lessons (IWB)**	**Audio**	**Video**	**Online ELEteca**
EA: 7.1, 7.2, 7.3, 7.4, 7.5	IWB: 7.1	🎧 73 to 79		EXTENSIÓN DIGITAL

LEARNING OUTCOMES

- Describe objects and their uses
- Make comparisons
- Point out things
- Talk about larger quantities (100–999)
- Avoid repetition
- Share information about gift-giving and holidays in Hispanic countries, and compare cultural similarities

INSTRUCTIONAL STRATEGIES

- Use the unit opener to preview the vocabulary and the cultural topics for this unit.
- Have students look at the images on this page and relate them to the objectives listed. Ask: *¿Qué relación creen que tienen la señora y la niña? ¿Qué miran? ¿Qué ven en la segunda foto? Y este señor, ¿trabaja aquí o quiere comprar estas plantas?*
- Introduce the video segment in **¡Acción!** and ask students to predict what they think the episode will be about given the theme of the unit.
- Invite students to read the topic for **Sabor hispano** and preview that section in the unit. Ask if they have ever heard of *Carnaval* and what they know about it. *¿Dónde están estos países? ¿Están en la costa este u oeste de América del Sur?* Use hand gestures to indicate directions.
- Have students work in pairs to talk about the images using the questions you have modeled. Then have volunteers present to the class what they understand this unit to be about.

ADVANCED LEARNERS

Ask students to prepare questions about the pictures using question words seen in previous units. Invite them to ask these questions to the class.

HERITAGE LANGUAGE LEARNERS

Have students share what they know about the countries in this chapter: Bolivia, Ecuador and Perú. What are Los Andes? How do you think the geography of a country influences its culture? What other countries with a Pacific coast have they already covered in this book? What do they remember about those countries?

In this unit, you will learn to:

- Describe objects and their uses
- Make comparisons
- Point out things
- Talk about larger quantities (100–999)
- Avoid repetition

Using

- *Para qué* and *para*
- Comparatives
- Demonstrative pronouns
- Direct object pronouns

Cultural Connections

- Share information about gift-giving and holidays in Hispanic countries, and compare cultural similarities

SABOR HISPANO

¡Viva el Carnaval!
- Bolivia, Ecuador y Perú

¡ACCIÓN!

197

THREE MODES OF COMMUNICATION: UNIT 7			
	INTERPERSONAL	INTERPRETIVE	PRESENTATIONAL
HABLAMOS DE...	5	1, 2, 3, 4	5
COMUNICA	2, 3, 5	1, 2, 4	5
¡ACCIÓN!	1	2, 3, 4, 5	6
PALABRA POR PALABRA	6, 7, 11, 12, 13	1, 2, 3, 4, 5, 9, 10	7
GRAMÁTICA	3, 5, 6, 7	1, 2, 4, 7	3
DESTREZAS		1, 2	
CULTURA		SABOR HISPANO	
RELATO	5	1, 2, 3, 4	5

OBJECTIVES FOR HABLAMOS DE...

- Preview vocabulary: household furniture and objects
- Preview grammatical structures: demonstrative pronouns, direct object pronouns
- Read and listen to a conversation describing Manuela's room and personal items
- Understand language in context

CORE RESOURCES

- Audio Program: 73

STANDARDS

1.1 Engage in conversation
1.2 Understand the language
1.3 Present information
4.2 Compare cultures

INSTRUCTIONAL STRATEGIES

Activity 1

- Explain that they will listen to a conversation between Manuela and Sara talking about how Manuela has arranged her room.
- Check for prior knowledge by asking students to name all the items and furniture they see in the image. Pre-teach *pared* (wall): *La habitación tiene cuatro paredes, pero nosotros solo vemos tres paredes.*
- Then have students examine the photo carefully and answer the questions that follow.

🎧 73 Activity 2

- Before listening to the audio, clarify that they should focus on information that they need to answer the *true/false* questions.
- Play the audio twice. During the first time, ask students to listen to get the gist of the conversation. Ask students to share what they've understood: *¿De qué cosas hablan?*
- During the second time, they should listen for the information they will need to complete the activity.
- Use the audio to focus students' attention on rhythm, intonation, and pronunciation. Have students respond chorally as needed.

ANSWERS

Activity 1

a. En la habitación de Manuela, encima de la cama de Manuela; **b.** Está en la pared, encima de la cama; **c.** Hay ropa y una mochila; **d.** Hay una televisión; **e.** Detrás de la cama; **f.** Hay libros, una estantería, una cámara digital, unos bolígrafos, una raqueta de tenis, etc.

Activity 2

a. F; **b.** F; **c.** T; **d.** T; **e.** F; **f.** T.

HABLAMOS DE... La habitación de Manuela

1 Look at the image below of Manuela and Sara hanging out in Manuela's new room. Then answer the following questions about the things she has in her room.

a. ¿Dónde están Manuela y Sara? ....
b. ¿Dónde está el póster del concierto? ....
c. ¿Qué hay debajo de la cama? ....
d. ¿Qué hay encima del mueble a la derecha? ....
e. ¿Dónde está la ventana *(window)*? ....
f. ¿Qué más hay en su habitación? ....

2 🎧 73 Listen to the conversation between Manuela and Sara. Then decide whether the sentences below are true (T) or false (F).

	T	F
a. Manuela no puede guardar su ropa en los cajones.	☐	☐
b. La habitación de Manuela está muy ordenada.	☐	☐
c. La computadora nueva de Manuela es portátil.	☐	☐
d. El nuevo mp4 de Manuela es más grande.	☐	☐
e. El póster es de la hermana de Manuela.	☐	☐
f. Sara tiene muchas cosas en su habitación.	☐	☐

198

SLOWER-PACED LEARNERS

Encourage students to label the objects in the photo for additional reinforcement. Challenge them to write a caption for the scene as well.

ADVANCED LEARNERS

Before playing the audio, ask some additional discussion questions for them to discuss in pairs or as a class: *¿Invitas amigos a tu casa? ¿Para qué? ¿Pasan tiempo en tu habitación? ¿Qué hacen allí? ¿De qué hablan?*

3 Read the conversation and check your answers for Activity 2.

Manuela: Mira, Sara, esta es mi nueva habitación.
Sara: ¡Qué bonita!, tienes muchas cosas y todo está bastante ordenado, ¿dónde guardas la ropa?
Manuela: La guardo allí, en aquel mueble. Tiene cajones muy grandes y caben muchas cosas. Y bueno, también la pongo debajo de la cama. Shhh…. Mi madre se enfada y dice que me va a quitar *(take away)* mi nuevo portátil si no soy más ordenada.
Sara: ¿Tienes portátil? ¿Dónde?
Manuela: Ahí, debajo del escritorio. Todavía está en la caja *(box)*. Es más moderno que la computadora de mesa. Ahora es de mi hermana. La tiene en su habitación.
Sara: ¿Qué es esto? ¿Un regalo para mí?
Manuela: No, es mi nuevo mp4. Este tiene más espacio para mi música.
Sara: ¿Y ese póster? ¿De qué concierto es?
Manuela: Es de uno de los conciertos de Pitbull, ¡mi cantante favorito! Pero tengo uno nuevo que me ha regalado mi padre. No es tan grande como ese, pero es mejor, porque es de este año.
Sara: ¡Cuántas cosas tienes!

4 Write the word in Spanish for the objects in the images. Then match them to what they are used for.

1. ....   3. ....   5. ....
2. ....   4. ....   6. ....

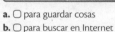

a. ○ para guardar cosas   **c.** ○ para mirarse en él   **e.** ○ para estudiar o escribir
b. ○ para buscar en Internet   **d.** ○ para dormir   **f.** ○ para leer

5 With a partner, talk about your own room. Mention at least three items and where they are located. Say what you like about your room and what you don't like.

Modelo: En mi habitación hay/tengo…

```
■ Prepositions of place
  • delante de      • dentro de           • detrás de      • al lado de
  • encima de       • a la izquierda de   • debajo de      • a la derecha de

  ■ Hay There is/there are      ■ Me gusta (singular)      ■ Me gustan (plural)
```

INSTRUCTIONAL STRATEGIES

Activity 3
Finally, students open the book and review the dialogue. Observe, provide support, and correct students as needed.

Activity 4
Students match objects to their purpose. They can also add other uses for the objects. For example, the laptop can be used for studying or writing, but also for playing videogames, listening to music, etc.

Activity 5
• Have students work in pairs for this activity. Encourage them to use the vocabulary and sentence patterns from the dialogue. Review the expressions in the recycling box as necessary.
• Call on individual students to share their description with the class.

ANSWERS

Activity 3
Students will read the dialogue and check their answers. Provide support as needed.

Activity 4
1. escritorio; **2.** computadora portátil; **3.** libro; **4.** armario; **5.** cama; **6.** espejo.

a. 4; **b.** 2; **c.** 6; **d.** 5; **e.** 1; **f.** 3.

Activity 5
Answers will vary and should reflect the model provided and expressions taught about household articles.

SLOWER-PACED LEARNERS
After Activity 4, ask additional questions to give students more practice with *estar / hay*. For instance, ask them: *¿Tienes un espejo en tu habitación? ¿Dónde está el espejo? ¿Tienes una computadora en tu habitación? ¿Dónde está la computadora exactamente?*

ADVANCED LEARNERS
Have students expand on their rooms' descriptions in Activity 5 by adding adjectives introduced in previous chapters, such as *caro/a, práctico/a, barato/a*, etc.

HERITAGE LANGUAGE LEARNERS
What is missing? As a follow-up to Activity 5, ask students to write a description of their rooms with some blanks. Then have them ask a partner to fill in the description. Encourage them to write interesting descriptions and leave a few challenging gaps. After they complete their partners' paragraphs, have them swap their papers back and discuss the real answers.

OBJECTIVES FOR COMUNICA

- Present the communicative functions of the unit:
  - Describing objects

CORE RESOURCES

- Extension Activities: EA 7.1
- Audio Program: 74
- Interactive Online Materials - ELEteca

STANDARDS

1.1 Engage in conversation
1.2 Understand the language
1.3 Present information
4.1 Compare languages

INSTRUCTIONAL STRATEGIES FOR DESCRIBING OBJECTS

- Before reviewing the information in the chart, write the following words in three columns on the board: (1) **forma y dimension**, (2) **material**, (3) **uso**.
- Cut up the words ahead of time from EA 7.1, **Describir un objeto**, and distribute a set to student pairs. Have students classify the words into one of the three categories on the board. Provide sample sentences in Spanish or point to examples to clarify new vocabulary.

- Then ask students to name objects that fit the following descriptions: **¿Qué objeto puede ser nuevo / viejo / cómodo / moderno?**
- Review the chart using a question-and-answer format and some classroom objects to demonstrate.

Activity 1

Have students work individually to complete the sentences. Point out that they will need to use **sirven** and **se usan** to describe the use of plural items / subjects.

🎧 74 Activity 2

- Have students fill in as many blanks as possible before playing the audio, depending on the level of your group.
- Ask student pairs to present in class. Encourage students to role-play the characters of *Abuelita* and *Adriana* for fun.

Activity 3

Model how they can ask *yes/no* questions about an object's functionality, too: **¿Se usa para...? ¿Sirve para...?**

ANSWERS

Activity 1

a. es, es, se usa / sirve para; **b.** es, es de, se usa / sirve para; **c.** son, se usan / sirven para; **d.** son, se usan / sirven para.

Activity 2

1. sirven; **2.** sirve para; **3.** para; **4.** para que; **5.** se usa; **6.** cosas.

COMUNICA

DESCRIBING OBJECTS

■ To describe **shape, dimension, texture,** etc.:
¿Cómo es? *What's it like?*
Es... *It's...*

grande *big*	ligero/a *light*
pequeño/a *little*	pesado/a *heavy*
cuadrado/a *square*	útil *useful*
redondo/a *round*	sencillo/a *simple, easy*
rectangular *rectangular*	moderno/a *modern*

■ To describe its **function** or use:
¿Para qué sirve? / ¿Para qué se usa?
What's it used for?
Sirve para... / Se usa para... *It's used for...*

leer *(for) reading*	escribir *(for) writing*
escuchar música *(for) listening to music*	
guardar ropa *(for) storing clothes*	
poner libros *(for) putting books*	

■ To describe the **material** something is made of:
¿De qué es? *What's it made of?* **Es de...** *It's...*

plástico *plastic*	metal *metal*	cristal *glass*	cuero *leather*	madera *wood*

1 Fill in the blanks with an appropriate expression to describe the items below and what they are used for.

¿Cómo es y para qué se usa?	¿Cómo son y para qué sirven?

a. El balón .... redondo, ... cuero y .... jugar al fútbol.

b. El portátil .... rectangular, ... metal y plástico y .... trabajar, leer, escribir y conectarse a Internet.

c. Los DVD .... redondos, de plástico y .... reproducir sonido e imágenes.

d. Los estuches .... cuadrados y .... guardar los DVD.

2 🎧 74 👥 Adriana is showing her grandmother what she knows about using a computer. Listen to their conversation and fill in the blanks with the missing words. Then take turns role playing the parts with a partner.

Adriana: Mira, abuelita, la nueva computadora de Javi.
Abuelita: ¡Qué moderna! ¿Me explicas para qué (1) .... esas cosas?
Adriana: Claro. Mira, esto es el monitor y (2) .... ver las imágenes. Esto se llama "teclado" y se usa (3) .... escribir.
Abuelita: ¿Y eso que mueves con la mano? ¿(4) .... se usa?
Adriana: Esto es el ratón y (5) .... para mover el cursor.
Abuelita: ¡Cuántas (6) .... aprendes de tu hermano!

3 👥 Let's play. Think of an object in your room or classroom and your partner will try to guess what it is by asking yes or no questions about it.

Modelo: *¿Es grande? ¿Es redondo?*

Activity 3

1. son; **2.** sirve para; **3.** para; **4.** Para qué; **5.** se usa; **6.** cosas.

Activity 4

Answers will vary and should reflect the model provided and expressions taught to describe objects.

SLOWER-PACED LEARNERS

As an alternate activity or extension of Activity 3, give each student two index cards. Have them write an object from inside the class on one card. On the other, they should write three sentences: one describing its shape, one describing the materials it's made of, and one describing its function or use. Collect the index cards. Put students in small groups, and give each group a portion of the cards to sort and match.

COMPARING PEOPLE AND THINGS

La silla es **más** moderna **que** el sofá. *The chair is more modern than the sofa.*
El sofá es **menos** nuevo **que** la silla. *The sofa is less new than the chair.*
La silla es **tan** cómoda **como** el sofá. *The chair is as comfortable as the couch.*

| **más** + adjective / adverb + **que** *more than* |
| **menos** + adjective / adverb + **que** *less than* |
| **tan** + adjective / adverb + **como** *equal to* |

 ■ Irregular comparatives
• *better* → **mejor** *El portátil es* **mejor que** *la computadora de mesa.*
• *worse* → **peor** *El equipo del F.C. Barcelona es* **peor que** *el equipo del Real Madrid.*
• *older* → **mayor** *La abuela de Adriana es* **mayor que** *Adriana.* (with people)

4 Match the image to its corresponding word in Spanish. Then match the word to its appropriate description.

a. b. c. d. e. f.

1. el teléfono celular.
2. el teléfono fijo.
3. el mapa.
4. el GPS.
5. el portátil.
6. la computadora de mesa.

a. Clásico, grande, pesado, sencillo. 40 dólares.
b. Pesada, grande, resistente. 900 dólares.
c. Moderno, útil, ligero, pequeño. 200 dólares.
d. Viejo, pequeño, complicado. 10 dólares.
e. Moderno, útil, frágil, cómodo. 500 dólares.
f. Ligero, cómodo, fácil de seguir. 100 dólares.

 ■ teléfono celular = teléfono móvil (España)

5  With a partner, take turns comparing the objects in Activity 4 using the information in the descriptions provided.

caro/a ≠ barato/a

Modelo: *El mapa es más barato que el GPS.*

 MORE IN ELETECA: EXTRA ONLINE PRACTICE

GRAMMAR NOTE

Remind students as needed that it is incorrect to use **más bueno**, **más malo** and to use **mayor** and **menor** when comparing people's ages. Point out that **más grande**, **pequeño/a** and **viejo/a** can be used to compare size and age of objects. For example, **Mi computadora es más vieja / grande / pequeña que tu portátil.** Finally, point out that sports teams are usually referred to without **el equipo de...** in front of them. It was add in the sample sentence for clarity.

Activity 4

• Have students match the objects listed to the correct image. Then have them match each object to its characteristics. Encourage students to guess at the meaning of unfamiliar words by looking at context and familiar patterns.

• Call on students to describe the objects in complete sentences. Point out that the verb **ser** is used with these adjectives, while **costar** is used with prices, such as: **Es moderno, práctico y frágil y cuesta $50.**

Activity 5

• Have students practice oral communication making comparisons among the objects from Activity 4. They can prepare comparisons before they practice with a partner.

• Have a class debate, with the following questions:

1. ¿Es mejor la computadora portátil o la de mesa?; 2. ¿Es mejor la radio o el mp4?; 3. ¿Es mejor el teléfono celular o el fijo?

Organize students into two groups to debate their opinions.

ANSWERS

Activity 4

Images: **a.** 5; **b.** 3; **c.** 1; **d.** 2; **e.** 6; **f.** 4. Descriptions: **1.** c; **2.** a; **3.** d; **4.** f; **5.** e; **6.** b.

Activity 5

Answers will vary and should reflect the model provided and expressions taught to compare objects.

ADVANCED LEARNERS

Working with a partner, have students write and role play a conversation about one of the objects in Activity 4. Have them imagine that they are in a store deciding whether or not to buy the item.

HERITAGE LANGUAGE LEARNERS

Have students pick an aspect of Hispanic culture to compare and debate. For example, they might compare two different cities in Spanish-speaking countries, two different traditional dishes, two Hispanic writers / directors / actors, two pre-Hispanic civilizations, etc. Allow them to do research to prepare for the debate.

OBJECTIVES FOR COMUNICA

• Present the communicative functions of the unit:
– Comparing people and things

STANDARDS

1.1 Engage in conversation
1.2 Understand the language
1.3 Present information
4.1 Compare languages

INSTRUCTIONAL STRATEGIES FOR COMPARING PEOPLE AND THINGS

• Project chart with functional explanations.
• Explain that we use these adverbs in front of an adjective to compare qualities of objects or people.

OBJECTIVES FOR ¡ACCIÓN!

- Provide students with a structured approach to viewing the video
- Contextualize the content of the unit in a familiar scenario

CORE RESOURCES

- Unit Video 7 - Un bolso para mi hermana
- Online Materials - ELEteca

STANDARDS

1.1   Interpersonal communication
1.2   Interpretive communication
2.1   Culture: Practices and perspectives

INSTRUCTIONAL STRATEGIES

Previewing: Antes del video

Activity 1

- Focus students' attention on the title and stills from the video. Have them predict what the video is going to be about and who is going to be in it.
- Working with a partner, have students look more closely at the images to identify the different objects and clothing in them.

Activity 2

Point out that each sentence will only be matched with one image. A few different images may seem like possible matches for the first sentence, but as they do the other sentences, the answer will be become clearer by process of elimination.

Viewing: Durante el video

Activity 3

- Before playing the video, have students read the statements.
- Pause the video at 1:12 so students can complete their answers. Review them as a class, prompting students to correct the false statements.

ANSWERS

Activity 1

camisa, camiseta, bolsos, vestidos, pantalones, bufandas, cinturones, zapatillas de deporte, pantalones cortos, blusa, jeans.

Activity 2

a. muchas (Imagen 3); **b.** muy (Imagen 4); **c.** más (Imagen 1); **d.** muy (Imagen 5); **e.** ese, este (Imagen 2); **f.** aquí, allí (Imagen 6).

Activity 3

a. F; **b.** F; **c.** T; **d.** F; **e.** T; **f.** T.

¡ACCIÓN! Un bolso para mi hermana

ANTES DEL VIDEO

1 Look at the scenes from the episode and then together with your partner, list the names for the different clothes and items you see.

....

....

2 Choose the correct option and then match each sentence with the correct image.

	Imagen
a. En esta tienda hay **muy / muchas** cosas para regalar.	
b. Es **muy / mucho** caro.	
c. Ahora la ropa es **más / menos** barata.	
d. Es **muy / más** bromista.	
e. Me gusta **este / ese** bolso blanco, pero prefiero **este / ese** azul.	
f. Lorena está **aquí / ahí / allí** y Felipe está **aquí / ahí / allí**, al lado de la puerta.	

DURANTE EL VIDEO

3 00:00 - 01:50 Watch the following scene from the episode and decide if the statements are true (T) or false (F).

	T	F
a. Lorena no recuerda quién es Sebas.	☐	☐
b. Sebas quiere pedir una cita a Lorena.	☐	☐
c. Lorena no tiene novio.	☐	☐
d. Sebas es el novio de Lorena.	☐	☐
e. A Lorena le gusta hacer bromas *(to joke)*.	☐	☐
f. Sebas quiere comprar un regalo.	☐	☐

202

ADVANCED LEARNERS

Before watching the video, have a discussion about buying gifts for siblings: **¿Compras regalos para tus hermanos? ¿Cuándo? ¿Cuánto gastas? ¿Qué cosas compras para ellos?**

HERITAGE LANGUAGE LEARNERS

Looking at the images, discuss whether or not they think the video will involve bargaining. Have a discussion about shopping and bargaining in different cultures: **¿Crees que van a regatear (o negociar) el precio de las cosas en la tienda? ¿Por qué sí o por qué no? ¿Regateas cuando vas de compras? ¿Dónde? ¿Es común regatear en otros lugares o países? ¿Cuáles?**

UNIDAD 7

4 🔲 Watch the rest of the episode. List the features (material, price, etc.) for each of the handbags Lorena shows Sebas.
01:50 - 04:28

Bolso blanco	Bolso beige	Bolso azul

5 🔲 Listen again as Lorena talks about the handbags. Write some sentences comparing the beige handbag and the blue one.
01:50 - 03:30

....

....

....

....

6 Answer the questions.

a. ¿Cuánto dinero tiene Sebas para comprar el regalo?

b. ¿Puede comprar el bolso blanco? ¿Por qué?

c. ¿Puede comprar el bolso azul? ¿Por qué?

d. ¿Qué objetos dice Lorena que se pueden guardar en el bolso?

e. ¿Por qué se ríe (laughs) Felipe cuando entra en la tienda?

DESPUÉS DEL VIDEO

7 👥 With your partner, take an object or garment that you both have (jacket, backpack, glasses, cell phone) and write a few sentences comparing them.

8 👥 Look at the images from the video and select a handbag or another object in the shop. With your partner, prepare a conversation between the customer and the sales assistant asking and comparing the different materials, sizes, prices, etc., and present it to the class. Use the following expressions as a guide:

Dependiente/a	Cliente
• ¿En qué puedo ayudarle?	• Mire, quería un/una… Este/esta me gusta, ¿cuánto cuesta?
• Son/Cuesta… dólares.	• ¿Cuánto cuesta este/esta…?
• ¿Cómo va a pagar? ¿Efectivo o tarjeta?	• En efectivo/Con tarjeta, por favor.
• Aquí tiene.	• ¿Puedo cambiarlo?
• Sí, con el recibo de compra.	

 MORE IN ELETECA: EXTRA ONLINE PRACTICE

203

INSTRUCTIONAL STRATEGIES

Activity 4

• Go over the instructions. Elicit examples of some terms they think they might hear as Lorena and Sebas discuss the three different bags. Remind students that they don't need to write complete sentences here. Tell them to focus on the key words.

• Continue to play the rest of the video.

• Draw the chart on the board. Call on volunteers to come up and add details from their notes into it.

Activity 5

• Go over the instructions. Looking at the their notes and the chart on the board, have students make some comparative sentences of their own before checking them against the video.

• Play the clip suggested, pausing at 2:57 to give students time to write what Lorena has said.

Activity 6

• Allow students to read the questions before continuing the clip from 2:57 through to the end of the clip suggested in Activity 5 or to the end of the video.

Post-viewing: Después del video

Activity 7

• Suggest that students compare two of the same kind of object as opposed to two completely different objects.

• Circulate and provide assistance as needed. Refer them back to the structures presented in **Comunica** if they need additional support. If you hear common or recurring mistakes, go over them with the class.

Activity 8

Remind them to begin and end the conversation appropriately. They should also include information about the who they're buying the item for and why.

ANSWERS

Activity 4

Bolso blanco: Es blanco, de cuero y cuesta $580. Es bonito y espectacular pero demasiado caro.

Bolso beige: Es demasiado grande y muy pesado. No es práctico.

Bolso azul: Es moderno, cómodo, sencillo y elegante. Es de plástico. Cuesta $48.

Activity 5

Es menos caro que el bolso blanco. Es más pequeño que el bolso beige.

Activity 6

a. Tiene $50; b. No. Es demasiado caro; c. Sí. Es más barato. Es menos de $50; d. Se pueden guardar el celular, los lentes de sol y las llaves; e. Se ríe porque Sebas lleva el bolso en el hombro y está caminando como Eli. Parece que quiere comprar el bolso para sí mismo.

SLOWER-PACED LEARNERS

You may want to provide students with portions of the transcript from the video that they can use as a base for their conversations in Activity 8.

HERITAGE LANGUAGE LEARNERS

Have students make a video acting act the conversations they've written in Activity 8. Encourage them to invite other Spanish-speaking friends or family members to appear in the video and write small additional parts for them. Have them present the videos in class.

OBJECTIVES FOR OBJETOS DE LA CASA Y DE LA CLASE

- Present the vocabulary needed to practice the communicative and grammatical functions for the unit: Identify words for common household and classroom objects
- Talk about items found at school or at home and describe their functions

CORE RESOURCES

- Audio Program: 75
- Extension Activities: EA 7.2, 7.3
- Interactive Online Materials - ELEteca

STANDARDS

1.1	Engage in conversation
1.2	Understand the language
1.3	Present information
3.2	Acquire information
4.1	Compare languages

INSTRUCTIONAL STRATEGIES

🎧 75 Activity 1

- Before listening to the audio, distribute EA 7.2 and 7.3, **Objetos de casa y de la clase**. Use these cutouts to pre-teach vocabulary, repeating to help with memorization.

- Divide the board in half: **casa** and **escuela**. With books closed, have students sort the cutouts by sticking them under the appropriate heading.
- Play the audio with books open to check that cutouts were correctly sorted.
- Have volunteers write the name of each object they represent next to the image. Review the work with the class and provide corrective feedback as needed.

Activity 2

Ask students for additional vocabulary under these categories.

ANSWERS

Activity 1

Cognates: planta, lámpara, póster, calculadora; **False cognate:** carpeta.

PALABRA POR PALABRA Objetos de casa

1 🎧 75 👥 Listen to the words in Spanish for items typically found at home and at school. Then make a list of the words that are cognates. ¡Atención! One of the words is a false cognate.

- Remember **cognates** are words that look and mean the same thing in Spanish and in English.
  estudiante = student
- **False cognates** may look similar but will have different meanings.
  dinero ≠ dinner

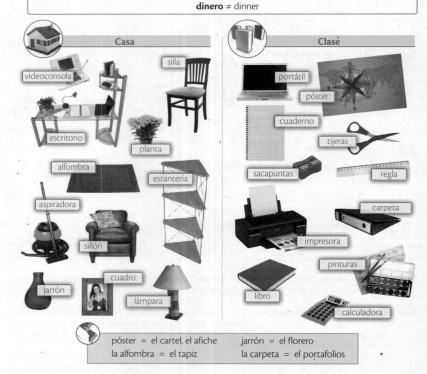

póster = el cartel, el afiche   jarrón = el florero
la alfombra = el tapiz   la carpeta = el portafolios

2 Complete the chart by placing each of the words above in the appropriate category.

Material escolar	Muebles	Objetos de decoración	Aparatos

Activity 2

Students will sort the items under new categories. Sample answers provided.
Aparatos: portátil, impresora, videoconsola, aspiradora, calculadora; **Material escolar:** cuaderno, libro, regla, carpeta, pinturas, calculadora, tijeras, sacapuntas; **Muebles:** escritorio, estantería, silla, sillón; **Objetos de decoración:** planta, jarrón, cuadro, alfombra, póster, lámpara.

HERITAGE LANGUAGE LEARNERS

Put students in pairs to discuss the items in Activity 1 in detail. Do they own or have examples of them at home? Prompt them to talk about describe what they look like, where they are from, how much they cost, where they are located, how often they are used, by whom, etc. Who do they associate each item with? Why?

3 Fill in the blanks with the correct word.

a. Manuela tiene un .... de un concierto en su habitación.

b. Usa .... para escribir los ejercicios.

c. Este .... de español es muy interesante.

d. En la exposición hay un .... de Picasso.

e. Estas .... no cortan bien.

Pablo Picasso

4 Select the adjective in each set below that does not relate to the item.

1. aspiradora...
a. ruidosa
b. pesada
c. frágil

3. planta...
a. natural
b. divertida
c. artificial

5. silla...
a. alta
b. abierta
c. baja

7. mesa...
a. cuadrada
b. redonda
c. blanda

2. computadora...
a. de mesa
b. de cristal
c. portátil

4. estanterías...
a. de madera
b. de metal
c. eléctricas

6. celular...
a. pequeño
b. triangular
c. práctico

8. jarrón...
a. antiguo
b. clásico
c. simpático

5 Identify the items above described below according to their uses.

a. Sirve para limpiar la alfombra.

b. Se usa para hacer cálculos en las clases de Álgebra y de Física.

c. Se usan para pintar cuadros.

d. Sirve para guardar libros.

e. Se usa para jugar.

f. Se usa para imprimir fotos, tareas y artículos de Internet.

6 With a partner, take turns describing to each other the words your teacher gives you.

Modelo: tijeras

E1: Sirven para cortar papel.
E2: ¿Son las tijeras?
E1: Sí.

7 Think about your desk at home or about one you would like to have. What things are on it? What are they like? What about on your bookshelf? Be specific and use as many words from the new vocabulary as possible. Then exchange information with a partner.

Modelo: En mi escritorio tengo...
En mi estantería tengo...

205

---

with six statements. Then have volunteers share their sentences with the class and take a vote to determine who gets the award for the funniest sentences.

Activity 5

CULTURAL NOTE

Point out that words that begin with "al" like **álgebra** come from Arabic.

Activity 6

- Call out a noun and have students provide the verb that should go with it. Write these pairs on the board, such as: **tijeras / cortar**, **carpeta / archivar**, **póster / decorar**.

- Ask students to write down phrases in their notebooks using these noun / verb pairs. For example: **Las tijeras sirven / se usan para cortar**.

- Finally, have them practice related questions and answers in pairs: **¿Para qué sirven las tijeras? Las tijeras sirven para cortar**.

- Give each student pair the following list of words to describe to each other. Allow students some time to prepare. Remind students to use the plural forms **se usan** and **sirven** as needed. Students may also work in groups of four with two students giving the clues and two students guessing. Add additional words from previous unit to vary and expand. Estudiante 1: *armario, póster, libro, ojos*; Estudiante 2: *carpeta, jarrón, pies, lápiz*.

Activity 7

To focus students' listening and reinforce their comprehension of the new vocabulary, have students draw the desks that their partners' describe. For an additional challenge, prompt students to provide the precise locations of the items as well.

ANSWERS

Activity 3

a. póster; **b.** cuadernos / bolígrafos; **c.** libro; **d.** cuadro; **e.** tijeras.

Activity 4

1. c; **2.** b; **3.** b; **4.** c; **5.** b; **6.** b; **7.** c; **8.** c.

Activity 5

a. aspiradora; **b.** calculadora o computadora; **c.** pinturas; **d.** estanterías; **e.** computadora; **f.** impresora.

INSTRUCTIONAL STRATEGIES

Activity 3

- Have students complete the activity.

Activity 4

- Pre-teach the new adjectives by providing definitions and having the class identify the adjective. For example, say: **Es algo que se rompe fácilmente** and students will guess **frágil**. Use gestures and other strategies as needed, for example, **Hace mucho ruido** (then imitate the sound of a vacuum cleaner). Encourage students to guess at unfamiliar words by using cognates: **natural**, **artificial**, **eléctricas**, and so on.

- Have them complete this activity individually.

Extension

Use this list of nouns and adjectives to review comparatives learned in the unit, such as: **La aspiradora es más ruidosa que la planta**. Invite students to work in pairs and come up

---

SLOWER-PACED LEARNERS

Rather than giving the students the words, you may choose to pass out cutouts from EA 7.2 and 7.3 to assign students different items to talk about in Activity 6. This provides the added step of having students recall or find the words for themselves. Swap the cutouts between pairs for continued practice with different items.

ADVANCED LEARNERS

Challenge students to write three more gapped sentences that could be added to Activity 3. Have them exchange sentences with a partner and complete their partners' sentences.

OBJECTIVES FOR LOS NÚMEROS DEL 100 AL 999

- Present the vocabulary needed to practice the communicative and grammatical functions for the unit: Talk about larger quantities (100–999)
- Ask and state how much something costs

CORE RESOURCES

- Audio Program: 76, 77

STANDARDS

- 1.1 Engage in conversation
- 1.2 Understand the language
- 1.3 Present information
- 4.2 Compare cultures

INSTRUCTIONAL STRATEGIES

🎧 76 Activity 8

- Project the number chart from the book on the board to teach numbers 100 through 999.
- Students can help each other by working in pairs: Student A says a number and Student B writes it down using digits. If correct, then Student B calls out a different number to Student A, who will write it down using digits. If incorrect, Student A will rewrite it correctly with the help of Student B, using a different color. Those with the least errors are declared winners.

🎧 77 Activity 9

Students write down the number they hear using digits, then in words. See audioscript on page APP10.

CULTURAL NOTE

Point out to students that in many countries the speed limit on highways is 110 km, which is about 68 mph.

Activity 10

Extension

Students may enjoy a competition with numbers. Write the following numbers on index cards or pieces of paper and put them in a box: 324, 565, 329, 743, 621, 104, 299, 963, 321, 645, 349, 439. Divide the class into three teams. Each team will take turns drawing a number and reading it out to his or her group. A team member will write the number out on the board. The team member who drew the number will then show it to the whole class to see if the answer is correct. The team with the most correct numbers written on the board wins.

Activity 11

As a follow-up, you can tell students to use each number on their card in a logical sentence. For additional practice, you can circulate and give students more numbers.

ANSWERS

Activity 10

a. ciento ochenta y cinco; b. doscientos dos; c. cuatrocientos cincuenta; d. setecientos cincuenta y tres; e. quinientos sesenta; f. novecientos cuarenta y uno.

PALABRA POR PALABRA Los números del 100 al 999

8 🎧 **76 Follow along as you listen to the numbers.**

100	cien	400	cuatrocientos	700	setecientos
101	ciento uno	415	cuatrocientos quince	720	setecientos veinte
200	doscientos	500	quinientos	800	ochocientos
202	doscientos dos	526	quinientos veintiséis	897	ochocientos noventa y siete
300	trescientos	600	seiscientos	899	ochocientos noventa y nueve
303	trescientos tres	669	seiscientos sesenta y nueve	900	novecientos

9 🎧 **77 Write the number you hear in the boxes. Then write out the word(s) in Spanish next to the number.**

a. ☐ ....
b. ☐ ....
c ☐ ....
d. ☐ ....
e. ☐ ....
f. ☐ ....
g. ☐ ....
h. ☐ ....

110

¿Cuál es el límite de velocidad según la señal?

10 **Write out the following numbers.**

a. 185 — ciento ochenta y cinco
b. 202 — ....
c. 450 — ....
d. 753 — ....
e. 560 — ....
f. 941 — ....

> ❗ Remember to use **y** only between the tens and ones, not after the hundreds.
> - 180 = ciento ochenta
> - 183 = ciento ochenta y tres

11 👥 **With a partner, take turns saying the numbers on your card to your partner in Spanish. He/she will write out the numbers you say. Then switch roles.**

Estudiante 1

| 349 | 788 | 455 | 519 |

Los números de tu compañero:
a. ☐
b. ☐
c ☐
d. ☐

Estudiante 2

| 746 | 590 | 623 | 168 |

Los números de tu compañero:
a. ☐
b. ☐
c. ☐
d. ☐

Activity 11

Alumno A: a. trescientos cuarenta y nueve; **b.** setecientos ochenta y ocho; **c.** cuatrocientos cincuenta y cinco; **d.** quinientos diecinueve. **Alumno B: a.** setecientos cuarenta y seis; **b.** quinientos noventa; **c.** seiscientos veintitrés; **d.** ciento sesenta y ocho.

SLOWER-PACED LEARNERS

Have write down a number from100 to 999 (or any other range you decide –you can do this in rounds) and hide it from their partners. Students have to guess their partners' numbers. After each guess, students respond to indicate whether the target number is lower (**más bajo**) or higher (**más alto**) under they arrive at the correct number. Create a competition by seeing who's can figure out the secret number the fastest.

12 Look at the paper currency from different Spanish-speaking countries. With a partner, take turns counting out the bills and totaling the amount shown.

Modelo: *Cien y cien son doscientos nuevos soles.*

Nuevos soles de Perú

a.
Pesos de México

b.
Euros de España

c.
Bolivianos de Bolivia

d.
Pesos de Argentina

e.
Dólares de Estados Unidos

f.
Nuevos soles de Perú

g.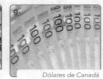
Dólares de Canadá

h.
Bolívares de Venezuela

13 Take turns asking and answering the following questions about how much these things cost. Use your best guess. Then tell your partner if you think it costs more or less and give the price you think it is.

Modelo: E1: *¿Cuánto cuesta un portátil sencillo?*
E2: *Cuesta quinientos cincuenta dólares.*
E1: *Creo que cuesta más, como seiscientos dólares. /*
Creo que cuesta menos, como quinientos dólares.

a. una videoconsola de Nintendo
b. unas botas UGG
c. una tableta de Apple
d. un mp4
e. unas zapatillas de deporte
f. una cena en el restaurante más caro de la ciudad

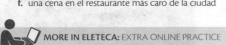
MORE IN ELETECA: EXTRA ONLINE PRACTICE

INSTRUCTIONAL STRATEGIES

Activity 12

- As a warm-up for Activity 12, have students read out the dollar amounts for the items in **Comunica**, Activity 4.
- Review the names of the different currencies with students.

Activity 13

- Encourage students to make their best guess at how much these items cost.
- Model the sample conversation with a couple of students to practice.
- Allow students time to prepare prices for each item before starting the activity.

ANSWERS

Activity 12

a. ochocientos cincuenta pesos; b. ochocientos euros; c. trescientos bolivianos; d. cuatrocientos pesos argentinos; e. ciento sesenta dólares; f. trescientos nuevos soles; g. novecientos dólares canadienses; h. ciento setenta y siete bolívares.

Activity 13

Answers will vary and should reflect the model provided and numbers taught.

ADVANCED LEARNERS

As a follow-up to Activity 12, have students look for other currencies from Spanish-speaking countries. Have them research how much a dollar converts into it. Remind students about Bolívar, and have them notice the name of the Venezuelan currency.

HERITAGE LANGUAGE LEARNERS

Ask students to bring a store catalogue, preferably in Spanish, that sells some of the items presented and discussed in this unit. Put students in pairs, and give them a budget. Have them work together to decide what to buy from the store on that budget.

OBJECTIVES FOR GRAMÁTICA 1

- Present the grammatical structures needed to practice the communicative functions of the unit: Demonstrative pronouns
- Indicate which item you want

CORE RESOURCES

- Interactive Online Materials - ELEteca

STANDARDS

1.1 Engage in conversation
1.2 Understand the language
1.3 Present information
4.1 Compare languages

INSTRUCTIONAL STRATEGIES

1. Demonstrative Pronouns

Walk students through the presentation. Then create the following chart on the board and ask students to help you complete it with their books closed. When done, ask students to check their answers against the book.

Location of speaker	Singular		Plural	
	Masculine	Feminine	Masculine	Feminine
aquí *here*				
ahí *there*				
allí *over there*				

Activity 1

Write **Demonstratives** on the board. Call on volunteers to come and write the demonstrative adjectives and pronouns as they find them. For the adjectives, they should include the noun it modifies after it. For the pronouns, they should put the noun in parentheses after it.

ANSWERS

Activity 1

Mira, Sara, esta es mi nueva habitación. (DP- replaces *habitación*); en aquel mueble (DA); ¿Qué es esto? (DP - replaces an unknown); Este tiene más espacio para mi música. (DP- replaces *mp4*); ¿Y ese póster? (DA); No es tan grande como ese, (DP- replaces *póster*); pero es mejor, porque es de este año. (DA).

SLOWER-PACED LEARNERS

Remind students that **este**, **esto**, and **esta** also refer to things that are close in time: **Esta noche, esta tarde, esta mañana,** etc. To refer to the night before, use **anoche**.

ADVANCED LEARNERS

Ask students to write sentences describing facts that are not easy to believe, so they can practice with **esto**. Follow this model:

¿Te puedes creer esto?: La Habana es la ciudad más grande de El Caribe. ¿Qué piensas de esto?: Los peloteros de la República Dominicana son famosísimos en todo el mundo.

GRAMÁTICA

1. DEMONSTRATIVE PRONOUNS

■ You learned that demonstrative adjectives point out people and things relative to where the speaker is located. Demonstrative pronouns function in much the same way, except that they replace the noun and stand alone. In Spanish, demonstrative adjectives and pronouns share the same forms.

Location of speaker	Singular		Plural		
	Masculine	Feminine	Masculine	Feminine	
aquí *here*	este	esta	estos	estas	*this, these*
ahí *there*	ese	esa	esos	esas	*that, those*
allí *over there*	aquel	aquella	aquellos	aquellas	*that (over there), those (over there)*

Quiero esa carpeta.

¿Quieres esta o aquella?

■ Demonstrative adjective	■ Demonstrative pronouns
*Quiero **esa** carpeta.* *I want that binder.*	*¿Quieres **esta** o **aquella**?* *Do you want this one or that one over there?*
Modifies and agrees with the noun **carpeta**.	Replaces the noun **carpeta**. Must agree in number and gender with the noun it replaces.

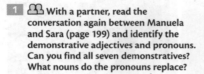

≫ *¿Te gustan **estos zapatos**? Do you like these shoes?*
≫ *No, prefiero **esos**. No, I prefer those.*

■ The neuter pronouns **esto**, **eso** and **aquello** are used when referring to unknown objects (nouns). These pronouns are invariable and can never be used to replace people.

≫ *¿Qué es **esto**? What's this?*
≫ ***Esto** es un libro de español. This is a Spanish book.*

≫ *¿Qué es **aquello**? What's that over there?*
≫ ***Aquello** es mi escritorio. That's my desk.*

1 👥 **With a partner, read the conversation again between Manuela and Sara (page 199) and identify the demonstrative adjectives and pronouns. Can you find all seven demonstratives? What nouns do the pronouns replace?**

2 Fill in the blanks with the correct demonstrative or neuter pronoun. *¡Atención!* Use the clues in the sentence that point out location to help you select the correct pronoun.

a. Esta computadora es muy lenta. .... de ahí es más rápida.
b. ¿Qué es .... de allí? No lo veo bien.
c. Aquella pizarra está muy lejos. .... (de aquí) está más cerca.
d. Aquellos sillones son más modernos que .... (de ahí).
e. Mira, esos DVD de ahí son tan baratos como .... (de aquí).
f. Quiero ese bolígrafo, ... que estoy usando no escribe.

3 👥 You are doing some shopping for yourself and also buying gifts for others. Take turns with a partner recreating the conversations in the following scenarios. Use the correct demonstrative adjectives and pronouns as needed.

Modelo:

Necesito unas pinturas para mi clase de arte.

Tenemos ..estas.. detrás de mí o ..esas.. en la estantería.

a. Es el cumpleaños de mi abuela. ¿Tienes unas plantas bonitas?

¿Te gustan .... o prefieres .... más grandes?

b. Necesito unas gafas nuevas.

¿Quieres ver .... o ....?

c. Perdone, ¿qué es .... que tiene usted en la mano?

.... es lechuga, para hacer ensalada.

d. ¿Te gustan .... jeans?

Sí, pero, ¿por qué no miras ....?

e. Me encanta .... vestido blanco. ¿Cuánto cuesta?

¿........? Cuesta 120 dólares.

209

INSTRUCTIONAL STRATEGIES

Activity 2

Students complete the activity individually or with a partner.

Activity 3

- Introduce the activity by reviewing the conversation in the bookstore on the previous page. Point out that demonstratives are commonly used to distinguish between the same or similar objects, often in store settings.
- Remind students to create the conversations as if they are talking directly with the person in the image. The location of the items is highlighted in the squares.
- Model the sample conversation to clarify.
- Have students present to the class. Use index cards with pictures or words of the items as props to demonstrate location.

ANSWERS

Activity 2

a. Esa; **b.** aquello; **c.** Este; **d.** esos; **e.** estos; **f.** este.

Activity 3

a. estas, aquellas; **b.** estas, esas / aquellas; **c.** eso, Esto; **d.** estos, aquellos / esos; **e.** ese, Este.

SLOWER-PACED LEARNERS

For additional practice, have students rewrite the sentences in Activity 2 with new items that you give to them. Remind them to make sure the demonstratives and other adjectives agree in gender and number with the new nouns and that the verbs are conjugated correctly.

HERITAGE LANGUAGE LEARNERS

Ask students to prepare a short skit in a market or store. One student is the salesperson and the others, the customers. Have them discuss prices and use demonstrative adjectives.

GRAMÁTICA

OBJECTIVES FOR GRAMÁTICA 2

- Present the grammatical structures needed to practice the communicative functions of the unit: Direct object pronouns
- Answering questions using direct object pronouns in place of nouns

CORE RESOURCES

- Extension Activity: EA 7.4

STANDARDS

1.1 Engage in conversation
1.2 Understand the language
1.3 Present information
4.1 Compare languages

INSTRUCTIONAL STRATEGIES

2. Direct Object Pronouns

- Start off with the following riddles. Tell students you have recently bought two items and they are to guess what they are based on your cues: **1. *Lo peino todos los días, lo llamo y viene, lo saco a pasear (un perro). 2. La pongo en el escritorio, la uso para leer, la necesito por la noche, la pongo y la apago. (una lámpara).***
- Then write the two cues on the board and circle the pronouns. Explain that we use direct object pronouns to refer to a noun, in this case **perro** and **lámpara**.
- Walk students through the explanations in the chart.

Activity 4

Have students complete the activity individually and then take turns with a partner saying and responding to the cues.

ANSWERS

Activity 4

1. f; **2.** d; **3.** c; **4.** a; **5.** e; **6.** b.

SLOWER-PACED LEARNERS

Have students practice the direct objects with their daily activities, for instance:

– *leer / el periódico: No lo leo todos los días.*

– *tomar / el bus escolar. Lo tomo por la mañana y por la tarde.*

– *hacer / la tarea: La hago por la tarde.*

– *ver / la televisión: La veo por la noche.*

– *escribir / un reporte: Lo escribo por la mañana.*

HERITAGE LANGUAGE LEARNERS

Explain that many speakers from Spain substitute **lo** with **le** when talking about people. This is not the case in Latin American countries, and most probably they will not be exposed to this use, so encourage them to use **lo**. You can use this opportunity to discuss language variation and how this affects not only vocabulary, but also grammar constructions.

GRAMÁTICA

2. DIRECT OBJECT PRONOUNS

■ Just as we use subject pronouns to avoid repetition of names, we use direct object pronouns to refer to someone or something already mentioned.

» ¿Dónde guardas **los zapatos**? *Where do you keep **your shoes**?*	Direct object of the sentence.
» **Los** pongo en el armario. *I put **them** in the closet.*	Direct object pronoun replaces the noun.
» ¿Conoces **a Pedro**? *Do you know **Pedro**?*	Direct objects can be people or things. Remember to use **a** before direct objects that are people.
» Sí, **lo** conozco de la escuela. *Yes, I know **him** from school.*	Direct object pronouns must agree with the noun they replace.

■ Here are the direct object pronouns in Spanish with their English equivalents.

me	replaces *me*
te	replaces *you (informal)*
lo/la	replaces *you (formal), him, her, it*
nos	replaces *us*
os	replaces *you (plural, Spain)*
los/las	replaces *you (plural), them*

■ In Spanish, direct object pronouns are placed before the conjugated verbs.

*Uso **el portátil** todos los días.* ⇒ **Lo** *uso todos los días.*

*Guardo **la carpeta** en la mochila.* ⇒ **La** *guardo en la mochila.*

*Llamo **a mis amigas** por teléfono.* ⇒ **Las** *llamo por teléfono.*

4 👥 Match the description to the correct item on the right. *¡Atención!* Be sure the direct object pronoun in the sentence agrees with the item it replaces. Then, with a partner, take turns asking each other about the items.

1. La ponemos encima del escritorio.	a. el portátil
2. Las ponemos en el garaje.	b. la ropa
3. Los guardamos en los estuches.	c. los DVD
4. Lo usamos para hacer la tarea.	d. las bicicletas
5. Los vemos en el museo.	e. los cuadros
6. La compramos en el centro comercial.	f. la impresora

Modelo: E1: La tenemos encima de la mesilla para leer por la noche. ¿Qué es?
E2: La lámpara.

5 👥 With a partner, take turns asking each other where you can buy the following items. Remember to use a direct object pronoun in your answers to avoid repeating the noun.

Modelo: un cuaderno
E1: ¿Dónde puedo comprar **un cuaderno**?
E2: **Lo** puedes comprar en una librería.

> ■ In Spanish some stores have set names such as:
> *una librería*
> *una zapatería*
>
> ■ A store can also be identified by what it sells:
> *una tienda de libros*
> *una tienda de zapatos*

a. unas naranjas y manzanas
b. un regalo para mi madre
c. unas aspirinas para el dolor de cabeza
d. un póster para mi hermano
e. una lámpara
f. un cinturón para mi padre

6 👥 Using the vocabulary you have learned for clothes, furniture, and school supplies, take turns asking each other about the things you have in the following places. Use the chart to list the items you want to ask your partner about.

En la habitación	En el armario de la habitación	En el escritorio

Modelo: E1: ¿Tienes **un espejo** en tu habitación?
E2: Sí, **lo** tengo. / No, no **lo** tengo.

7 👥 Write out the answers to the following questions. Then practice asking and answering the questions with your partner.

Modelo: E1: ¿Llamas **a tu abuelo** por teléfono?
E2: Sí, **lo** llamo. / No, no **lo** llamo.

a. ¿Entiendes **a la profesora** de español? ....
b. ¿**Me** entiendes cuando hablo español? ....
c. ¿Quién cuida **a los enfermos** en el hospital? ....
d. ¿**Te** cuida tu madre cuando estás enfermo/a? ....
e. ¿Visitas **a tus tíos y primos** mucho? ....
f. ¿Quién **te** visita en casa? ....

👤💻 MORE IN ELETECA: EXTRA ONLINE PRACTICE ◀ 📷 GRAMMAR TUTORIALS 13 AND 14   211

Alternative Activity

• You can also do a concentration memory game. Place the cutouts facedown to form three rows and four columns. Students take turns picking a card and matching it with its partner from memory.
• Review other names for stores in the box. Encourage students to provide other examples.
• Go over the **Modelo**. Point out that some students may have seen constructions with the pronoun attached to the infinitive (**Puedes comprarlo...**), which has the same meaning.

Activity 6

• Give students about 5 minutes to list items in the chart.
• Model the sample with two or more students.

Activity 7

Model the sample with two or more students. Remind students to use the correct form of the verb when responding.

ANSWERS

Activity 5

Answers will vary. Sample answers provided.

a. Las puedes comprar en el supermercado / la frutería; **b.** Lo puedes comprar en un centro comercial; **c.** Las puedes comprar en una farmacia; **d.** Lo puedes comprar en una tienda de música; **e.** La puedes comprar en una tienda de muebles; **f.** Lo puedes comprar en una tienda de ropa de hombres.

Activity 6

Answers will vary and should reflect the model to include the household items taught in this unit.

Activity 7

Answers will vary. Sample answers provided.
a. Sí, la entiendo; **b.** Sí, te entiendo; **c.** Los cuidan las enfermeras; **d.** Sí, mi madre me cuida; **e.** No, no los visito mucho; **f.** Me visitan en mi casa mis amigos / abuelos / primos / vecinos.

SLOWER-PACED LEARNERS

You may want to generate lists of items as a class for each category in Activity 6 to ensure that students are getting a sufficient amount of practice with multiple items.

ADVANCED LEARNERS

As an extension to Activity 7, have students ask and answer the questions again, but this time changing the boldface words from singular to plural or vice versa. **¿Entiendes a las profesoras de español? ¿Nos entiendes cuando hablamos español?**

INSTRUCTIONAL STRATEGIES

Activity 5

• Before starting this activity, review the vocabulary for the different types of stores with EA 7.4, **Las tiendas.** Organize the students into small groups and have them match the labels with the picture.

OBJECTIVES FOR DESTREZAS

- Reading comprehension
- Scanning for specific information

STANDARDS

1.2   Understand the language

INSTRUCTIONAL STRATEGIES

Activity 1

- To activate schema, pose questions about public swimming pools in the US. For example: **¿Vas a las piscinas públicas? ¿Hay piscinas públicas en tu barrio? ¿Cuánto pagan los niños? ¿Cuánto pagan los adultos? ¿En qué mes abren? ¿A qué hora abren? ¿A qué hora cierran? ¿Qué actividades hay? ¿Qué te gusta hacer en la piscina?**
- Make sure students read the **Destrezas** box before proceeding to do the activity.

CULTURAL NOTE

Explain students that in big cities like Madrid some apartment buildings, particularly those built since the 90s, have private swimming pools. For people who do not have access to such facilities, public swimming pools are a great choice, as temperatures are high in the summer in Madrid, and kids have July and August off from school.

Activity 2

Remind students to go back to the text and review the information carefully before selecting their responses. They will have to use context clues and infer meaning in some cases.

ANSWERS

Activity 1

Students will read the text applying the strategy "Scanning for specific information".

Activity 2

1. b; 2. a; 3. b; 4. b; 5. a.

SLOWER-PACED LEARNERS

When going over the answers for Activity 2, consider projecting the text and having students identify the words, phrases, or sentences in the text related to each item. Help them determine the correct answers with more pointed questions if they're still unsure about the answers.

HERITAGE LANGUAGE LEARNERS

Have students research public swimming pools / areas in other Spanish-speaking countries and compare them to those in Madrid. Have them write a paragraph similar to the sample text here. Consider assigning them different countries so they can learn about and compare more places.

DESTREZAS

COMPRENSIÓN DE LECTURA

1 Before reading, review the reading strategy in Destrezas and follow the suggestion.

Destrezas

Scanning for specific information

Use the comprehension questions at the end of a reading to help you decide what information to search for as you read.

List some key words or phrases you should focus your attention on.

_____

_____

Sesenta piscinas abren sus puertas en Madrid

En Madrid, como en muchas otras ciudades grandes, las piscinas de verano están preparadas para abrir al público. El primer día, el 29 de mayo, se celebra con una jornada de puertas abiertas en la que los usuarios no pagan la entrada. El resto de la temporada los precios serán los mismos que el ayuntamiento de Madrid aprobó el año pasado. La entrada incluye el uso de las instalaciones deportivas. El precio es de 4,35 euros para adultos, 2,65 euros la entrada infantil, 3,50 euros los jóvenes y 1,35 euros los mayores de 65 años. Las personas con discapacidad tienen la entrada gratuita, si presentan el carné de deporte especial. El horario de las piscinas es de 11:00h a 21:00h durante los tres meses de verano, hasta el 5 de septiembre. Además, hay cursos de natación, y otras actividades deportivas durante los meses de julio y agosto. Por otra parte, el ayuntamiento de Madrid asegura que hay socorristas en todas las piscinas.

Fuente: adaptado de www.20minutos.es

2 Read the article again and complete the sentences with the correct information.

1. Las piscinas públicas abren...
   a. a principios de mayo.
   b. a finales de mayo.
   c. a mediados de mayo.

2. El primer día de piscina...
   a. es gratuito para todo el mundo.
   b. es la mitad del precio.
   c. cuesta 4,35€ para los adultos.

3. Las personas con discapacidad...
   a. entran gratis los días de fiesta.
   b. no pagan si presentan un carné.
   c. no entran gratis, tienen un descuento.

4. Si tienes 9 años pagas...
   a. 4,35€.
   b. 2,65€.
   c. 3,50€.

5. Todas las piscinas tienen...

a.  b.  c.

PRONUNCIACIÓN Word stress and the written accent

■ All words in Spanish have a syllable that is pronounced with more stress than the other syllables in the word. For most words, the stressed syllable is the second to the last syllable.

■ In some cases, a written accent is needed to identify the stressed syllable. You will learn more about these later. For now, you should know to pronounce the syllable marked with an accent more strongly.

pe-rro   ca-sa   ar-ma-rio   as-pi-ra-do-ra

árbol   jarrón   bolígrafo

1 🗣 **Practice saying the following words aloud with a partner. Mark the syllable with the most stress in its pronunciation.**

a. JARRÓN
b. CUADERNO
c. ESTANTERÍA
d. ESPAÑOL
e. PLANTA
f. SILLA
g. HERMANO
h. MALETA
i. RATÓN
j. NÚMEROS
k. LÁMPARA
l. PORTÁTIL

2 🗣 **What other words have you learned that have written accents? List them here and then compare your list with your partner.**

 **MORE IN ELETECA:** EXTRA ONLINE PRACTICE

213

Mojave *desert (DE-sert)*" vs "a chocolate *dessert (des-SERT)*". Help them realize that *dessert* is stressed in the last syllable while *desert* is stressed in the syllable before last.

· Tell students that most words in Spanish are stressed in the syllable before last. Provide examples: *lápiz*, *árbol*, *casa*, *muchacho*, *libro*, *escuela.*

· Walk them through the explanation and samples in the book.

Alternative Activity

To understand syllable stress, students will need to first understand how words are broken into syllables in Spanish, which is different from English. To help students develop a better sense of how words are broken into syllables in Spanish, use IWB 7.1, *Sopa de letras silábica*: Project the grid and ask students to put syllables together to come up with vocabulary words from this unit, such as *jarrón*, *hermano, planta*, *español*, *cuaderno*, *cuadro*, *silla*, *maleta*, *estantería*. Answers:

Activity 2

Create a competition in which students only get points for those items on their lists that no one else has.

ANSWERS

Activity 1

a. ja**rrón**; b. cua**der**no; c. estante**rí**a; d. espa**ñol**; e. **plan**ta; f. **si**lla; g. her**ma**no; h. ma**le**ta; i. ra**tón**; j. **nú**meros; k. **lám**para; l. por**tá**til.

Activity 2

Answers will vary.

ADVANCED LEARNERS

Have students create more *sopas de letras silábicas* and play with each other.

OBJECTIVES FOR PRONUNCIACIÓN

· Practice correct pronunciation: word stress and the written accent

CORE RESOURCES

· Interactive Whiteboard Lesson: IWB 7.1
· Interactive Online Materials - ELEteca

STANDARDS

1.2 Understand the language
4.1 Compare languages

INSTRUCTIONAL STRATEGIES

Activity 1

· Help students realize that both English and Spanish words with more than one syllable always have one of the syllables carrying the main stress. For example, compare English "the

OBJECTIVES FOR SABOR HISPANO

- Learn about Bolivia, Ecuador, and Peru
- Learn about *carnaval* and other celebrations in Hispanic countries
- Compare celebrations in Hispanic countries with celebrations in the U.S.

CORE RESOURCES

- Audio Program: 78

STANDARDS

1.2	Understand the language
2.1	Practices and perspectives
2.2	Products and perspectives
3.2	Acquire information
4.1	Compare cultures
5.2	Using language for personal enjoyment and enrichment

INSTRUCTIONAL STRATEGIES

- Introduce the topic by asking students what they know about Ecuador, Peru, or Bolivia.
- Talk about the images and the map. Elicit what they already know about carnival and other celebrations in Hispanic countries.
- Read the captions together and ask questions to check comprehension. Ask students if they can guess what *desfile* means (parade) by looking at the images.
- Ask students to identify which of the points in **¿Sabes que...?** they find most surprising and if there were any already familiar to them. Encourage students to research and read more about these topics:
- **Lago Titicaca:** Explain students that the Uros, a pre-Incan people, build floating islands and canoes from reeds *(totoras)* and live on the lake. There are about 80 floating islands.
- Bolivia has the largest salt deposits in the world. Salar de Uyuni, located south of Oruro, is the largest salt flat underneath which lie rich deposits of lithium used in the production of batteries.
- **La Mitad del Mundo** is the symbolic although not the accurate location of the imaginary line of the Equator.
- Share with students what you know about these topics.

CULTURAL NOTE

Bolivia

- This country is officially known as the Plurinational State of Bolivia. It has six official languages: Spanish, Aymara, Guaraní, Leco, Chiquitano, Puquina. It is, with Paraguay, one of the two South American countries with no coast. It is the fifth biggest country in South America has many natural resources, including minerals such as zinc, silver, tin, lead, antimony, wolfram and gold. It also has a rich biodiversity.
- Lago Titicaca is also the highest lake navigable to large boats. The quechua spelling is Titiqaqa.

Perú

- Perú means "land of abundance" in quechua. Perú was the heart of the Inca empire from the 12th to 16th centuries. Its capital was Cusco. The Inca empire was destroyed by the Spaniards, who founded Lima and made it the capital.
- Perú is one of the world's top producers of silver, copper, lead, and zinc. Perú also exports fish and fish products. Spanish is the official language and in the zones where they are predominant, Quechua, Aymara, and other native languages are also official.

¡VIVA EL CARNAVAL!

¡Me encanta el carnaval! ¿Y a ti?

El carnaval de Oruro

El carnaval de Oruro, Bolivia

- En la ciudad de Oruro se celebra un carnaval muy famoso: el carnaval de Oruro.
- En 2001 la UNESCO declaró esta celebración Obra Maestra del Patrimonio Oral e Intangible de la Humanidad.
- Se celebra durante la semana antes de la Cuaresma *(Lent)* y dura ocho días.
- Durante los desfiles *(parades)* del carnaval, se baila la Diablada. La gente baila con máscaras y un traje de diablo.

Bailarines en el carnaval de Cartagena de Indias, Colombia

Desfile del carnaval de Gran Canaria, islas Canarias, España

Desfile de carnaval en Pisac, Perú

¿Sabes que...?

✓ A unos 24 km al norte de Quito está el monumento La Mitad del Mundo, que marca la línea imaginaria del ecuador.

✓ La papa es original de Perú. Más de 3.000 clases de papas se cultivan hoy día en Perú. De allí viene el dicho *(saying)* popular: "Soy más peruano que la papa".

✓ Machu Picchu, la ciudad perdida de los incas, y las islas de los Uros en el Lago Titicaca son dos de los lugares más populares y famosos de Perú.

✓ Entre Perú y Bolivia se encuentra el Lago Titicaca, el lago más grande de América del Sur.

214

Ecuador

- Spanish is the official language of Ecuador, which is spoken by 94% of the population. Indigenous languages are also recognized, such as Quichua and Shuar.
- Because its location at the equator, both sunrise and sunset occur each day at the two six o'clock hours.
- Islas Galápagos are an archipelago of volcanic islands located in the Pacific Ocean. They belong to Ecuador and are considered one of the places with the most biodiversity in the world. UNESCO recognized the islands in 1978 as a World Heritage Site.

BOLIVIA, ECUADOR Y PERÚ

78 ¡Mi celebración favorita!

Julia es una chica de 17 años. Vive en San Luis de Otavalo, Ecuador. Ella habla de su celebración favorita.

Festival de Inti Raymi en Otavalo, Ecuador

¿Dónde está San Luis de Otavalo?

Julia: Está en el norte de mi país, Ecuador, en la provincia de Imbabura.

¿Cómo es tu ciudad?

Julia: Es muy bonita. Está entre montañas y al lado de un volcán. Otavalo es una zona turística. ¡Mucha gente visita mi ciudad!

¿Cuál es el evento más especial?

Julia: Inti Raymi. También se llama el Festival del Sol. Es el evento más importante en mi comunidad. Comienza con el solsticio de verano, el 22 de junio. Esta celebración es una explosión de colores, música y tradiciones indígenas. ¡Es mi fiesta favorita!

El carnaval de Barranquilla

«¡Hola! Soy Manuel y vivo en Barranquilla, Colombia. Mi ciudad es caribeña y está al norte de Colombia. Es un lugar muy importante porque allí celebramos el carnaval de Barranquilla. Los personajes más famosos del carnaval son la reina (queen) del carnaval y el diablo (devil) Arlequín. La reina es el personaje más querido y el diablo es el personaje menos popular. ¡Todos temen al diablo! A mí me gusta esta celebración porque me encantan los disfraces (costumes). ¡Me gusta pintarme de verde! ¿Te gusta disfrazarte? ¿Qué disfraz te gusta?».

Participante en el carnaval de Barranquilla.

El carnaval de las islas Canarias

- Cada mes de febrero, Santa Cruz de Tenerife, una de las dos capitales de las islas Canarias, celebra su carnaval.
- Este carnaval es el segundo más grande del mundo. El primero es el de Río de Janeiro, Brasil.
- El carnaval tiene dos partes: el carnaval oficial y el carnaval de la calle. En el carnaval oficial participan más de 100 grupos. El carnaval de la calle está abierto a todo el mundo y participan miles de personas.
- Este carnaval se celebra desde el siglo XVII.

Los ingredientes más importantes del carnaval son: los disfraces, el maquillaje (make-up), la música y la danza.

Esta fiesta es un evento enorme y se necesita un año para organizarlo.

La reina del carnaval, protagonista de la fiesta.

True or false?

		T	F
1	Oruro está en Bolivia.	○	○
2	Barranquilla es una ciudad colombiana.	○	○
3	El carnaval de Oruro es uno de los más importantes del mundo.	○	○
4	En las islas Canarias el carnaval se celebra desde el siglo XV.	○	○
5	El personaje más querido del carnaval de Barranquilla es el diablo.	○	○

Complete this e-mail with the following words.

¡Atención! Not all the words will be used.

Ecuador	*	este	*	oeste	*	Otavalo	*	Perú
las islas Canarias	*		Barranquilla	*		Estados Unidos		

«¡Hola! Hoy visito el carnaval de Oruro en Bolivia. ¿Sabes que Bolivia está en el _____, cerca del océano Pacífico? El carnaval de Oruro es importante. Otros carnavales importantes son el de _____ y el de _____. Podemos verlos otro año. Ahora en junio, viajo hasta _____ para ver el Festival del Sol, Inti Raymi, en _____. ¡Hasta pronto!».

VOCES LATINAS
CARNAVAL Y VIDA

215

INSTRUCTIONAL STRATEGIES

78

- An audio recording accompanies each text on this page. Vary between silent reading, reading aloud, and playing the audio.
- Identify and explain any vocabulary words from the readings students may find difficult to understand.
- Remind students that the Canary Islands are located off the coast of northern Africa in the Atlantic and are one of Spain's autonomous regions. Point them out on a map. Their name comes from the Latin *canes* and refers to the large dogs found living on the islands. The name has no connection to the bird.
- Encourage students to describe the photos in these pages and comment on what they find interesting. You can also project other colorful images of these celebrations from the Internet.
- Have students complete the activities on this page and compare their answers with others.

ANSWERS

True or False

1. T; 2. T; 3. T; 4. F; 5. F.

Complete an email with the words provided

oeste, Barranquilla, las islas Canarias, Ecuador, San Luis de Otavalo.

SLOWER-PACED LEARNERS

Have students find video footage of one of the carnivals presented here. Have them choose a one-minute clip to show to the class. They should introduce the clip, play it, and then describe some of what was seen and provide some general background information about it.

HERITAGE LANGUAGE LEARNERS

Have students discuss the importance of keeping one's language, as it is the case with the indigenous people of Ecuador, Bolivia and Perú. What might be the advantages and disadvantages of a multilingual state? If any of the students know a native language of Latin America, invite them to share some words and knowledge with the class. Students can find out more about the languages spoken in Latin America by checking http://www.ethnologue.com/region/Americas. Note that there are different ways to write the names of Quechuan languages spoken in this area.

ADVANCED LEARNERS

Have students create a fact file of five interesting facts of Bolivia, Perú, or Ecuador. Encourage them to look for information in Spanish, but they may also find information in English that they reword and translate on their own in Spanish. One website you might recommend that they visit is the CIA's World Factbook: https://www.cia.gov/library/publications/the-world-factbook/. Encourage them to find visuals to support their facts and create a poster with them. Have them present their posters to the class

OBJECTIVES FOR RELATO

- Revisit unit themes, grammar, vocabulary, and culture in a new context
- Improve reading comprehension skills

CORE RESOURCES

- Audio Program: 79
- Extension Activities: EA 7.5

STANDARDS

1.1 Engage in conversation
1.2 Understand the language
1.3 Present information
2.1 Practices and perspectives

INSTRUCTIONAL STRATEGIES

🎧 79 Activity 1

- The purpose of this activity is to review vocabulary for household objects and introduce students to how Mother's Day is celebrated in Hispanic countries.
- Students can read the selection silently to themselves or aloud to a partner taking turns.
- After students have finished reading, ask the following questions to check comprehension:
  - *¿En qué mes se celebra el Día de la Madre en muchos países de Hispanoamérica?*
  - *¿Qué le regala el padre?*
  - *¿Qué le regala la hermana mayor?*
  - *¿Le gustan a la madre los perfumes que le regala la hermana mayor?*
  - *¿Qué le regalan los abuelos?*
  - *¿Qué le compra la tía Rosa?*
  - *El protagonista del relato, ¿es un niño o es un adulto?*
  - *¿Le compra algo a su madre?*

Alternative Activity

Use **EA 7.5, *Un día solo para mamá***, to introduce the reading. Distribute a set of cutouts to groups of three students and have them arrange the information in the correct order with books closed.

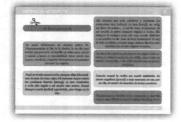

SLOWER-PACED LEARNERS

To avoid confusion between direct and indirect object pronouns, as a follow-up to Activity 1, you might ask comprehension questions that avoid indirect object pronouns: **¿Quién compra las rosas? ¿Quién compra el perfume? ¿Qué compra el protagonista del relato?**, etc. To keep students on task, have them write captions under each image to identify who gave them as a gift.

---

1 🎧 79 Read the description about a special day celebrated in many parts of the world.

Un día solo para mamá

En mayo celebramos en muchos países de Hispanoamérica el Día de la Madre. Es un día muy bonito porque toda mi familia se reúne para comer y mamá prepara su especialidad: carne asada con papas y ensalada. Después del postre es el momento de sacar los regalos.

Papá es el más conservador, siempre elige (*chooses*) una docena de rosas rojas. Mi hermana mayor adora los perfumes fuertes (*strong*), es una romántica y cada año regala a mi madre uno nuevo. Mamá siempre sonríe (*smiles*) agradecida, pero luego no lo usa. Mis abuelos son más prácticos y prefieren los accesorios: una bufanda de lana (*wool*), un reloj, un libro de cocina… A mi tía Rosa, la hermana de mi madre, le gusta comprar regalos a todos. Ella siempre le compra cada año una novela histórica a mi madre. La tía Rosa es muy intelectual. Yo soy el más modesto, porque tengo menos dinero, pero también soy el más original de todos. En clase de Arte siempre preparo un regalo hecho a mano. A veces es un jarrón de arcilla, otras veces un cuadro de madera, o un collar (*necklace*) con piezas de ámbar. Cuando mamá lo recibe me sonríe satisfecha. Se siente orgullosa (*proud*) y muy contenta de ser, por un día, el centro de atención de todos nosotros. Terminamos la comida todos contentos y después vemos una película: mi madre siempre la elige, claro.

2 List the presents mentioned in the reading with a brief description.

3 Match the members of the family with their personality traits.

1. El padre es...   a. intelectual.
2. La hermana es...   b. modesto y original.
3. La tía Rosa es...   c. romántica.
4. Los abuelos son...   d. conservador.
5. El autor del relato es...   e. prácticos.

4 Each of the mother's gifts serves a purpose. Use the expressions from the list to describe the purpose of each gift.

> decorar un lugar o preparar diferentes tipos de comida o entretenerse o leer o estar más guapa o vestirse o saber la hora o poner flores o no tener frío o poner fotos

a. Una docena de rosas sirve para decorar un lugar.
b. _____
c. _____
d. _____
e. _____
f. _____
g. _____
h. _____
i. _____

5 👥 With a partner, discuss the types of presents you typically receive from your family and how they relate to your particular personality.

Modelo: *Mi madre me regala... porque soy... y me gusta(n)...*

217

---

una tarjeta regalo porque me gusta ir de compras.

Extension

After completing this activity, students write a description about what their family is like and the personality of each family member, and exchange with a partner. The partner can make a recommendation as to what gift to get for each family member based on the description.

ANSWERS

Activity 2

Una docena de rosas, un perfume nuevo, una bufanda de lana, un reloj o un libro de cocina; una novela histórica; algo hecho a mano, como un jarrón de arcilla, un cuadro de madera o un collar.

Activity 3

1. d; 2. c; 3. a; 4. e; 5. b.

Activity 4

Answers will vary. Sample answers provided.

a. Una docena de rosas sirve para decorar un lugar.
b. Un perfume nuevo sirve para estar más guapa.
c. Una bufanda de lana sirve para no tener frío.
d. Un libro de cocina sirve para preparar diferentes tipos de comida.
e. Una novela histórica sirve para entretenerse o para leer.
f. Un cuadro de madera sirve para poner fotos.
g. Un jarrón sirve para poner flores.
i. Algo hecho a mano sirve para decorar un lugar.

Activity 5

Answers will vary and should reflect the model provided and expressions taught.

SLOWER-PACED LEARNERS

In Activity 5, give students time to write down some of their ideas first. Make sure that their nouns and adjectives agree in gender and number and they're using singular / plural verbs correctly, including ***gustar***. Monitor their conversations as speak, taking note of any errors but not interrupting them at this stage. Then have an error-correction session afterward as a class.

ADVANCED LEARNERS

Have students write the sentences in Activity 4 leaving the name of the gift out. Working in pairs or as a class, have other students guess what the missing words are.

HERITAGE LANGUAGE LEARNERS

Ask students to name and describe the best present they've ever gotten: what it looks like, what it's used for, and why they like it. Then have them discuss how they find out what a person likes or not to determine what gifts to get for others.

INSTRUCTIONAL STRATEGIES

Activity 2

After students have written down the presents, ask them to circle the stressed syllable to review stressed syllables in Spanish.

Activity 3

To confirm their understanding of the adjectives, ask students to give examples from their own lives of people whom they would describe with those words and why.

Activity 4

Review the expressions in the list as needed. Encourage students to use context clues to guess at unfamiliar words.

Activity 5

Provide students with sample sentences using the **Modelo**. For example, *Mi madre me regala figuritas de cristal porque me gusta coleccionar cristal. Mi padre me regala*

OBJECTIVES FOR EVALUACIÓN

- Review grammar, vocabulary and culture from the unit
- Complete self-assessment

CORE RESOURCES

- Interactive Online Materials - ELEteca

STANDARDS

1.2	Understand the language
1.3	Present information
2.1	Practices and perspectives
4.1	Compare cultures

INSTRUCTIONAL STRATEGIES

- Activities can be completed individually and then reviewed with the class.
- Extend by asking students if they agree with the answers given and then writing the correct answer on the board.
- You may wish to assign point values to each activity as a way for student to monitor their progress.
- If students achieve less than 80% on each activity, direct them to **En resumen** for page numbers to review.

ANSWERS

Activity 1

a. un autobús; **b.** una televisión; **c.** un periódico; **d.** una regla; **e.** un libro.

Activity 2

a. más… que; **b.** tan… como; **c.** menor; **d.** más…que; **e.** menos… que; **f.** mayor.

Activity 3

a. aquella; **b.** Ese; **c.** estos; **d.** Estas; **e.** Esa.

EVALUACIÓN

DESCRIBING OBJECTS AND THEIR USES

1 **Write the word from the list that matches the description given.**

> un cuaderno ○ unas gafas ○ un periódico ○ un libro ○ una televisión
> un autobús ○ una computadora ○ una planta ○ una regla

a. Es rectangular, de metal y cristal, y sirve para ir de un lugar a otro. ⟶ ....

b. Es grande, cuadrada, de cristal y plástico, y sirve para ver noticias. ⟶ ....

c. Es mediano, de papel y sirve para leer noticias. ⟶ ....

d. Es pequeña, de plástico y sirve para dibujar líneas rectas. ⟶ ....

e. Es pequeño, de papel y sirve para leer historias. ⟶ ....

MAKING COMPARISONS

2 **Using the prices indicated, fill in the blanks to compare the items.**

a. La cámara es .... cara .... los libros.

b. El balón es .... caro .... la cámara.

c. El precio del rotulador es .... que el de la cámara.

d. La planta es .... barata .... el balón.

e. Comprar unos libros es .... barato .... comprar una planta y un balón.

f. El precio de la cámara es .... que el de la planta.

DEMONSTRATIVE PRONOUNS

3 **Fill in the blanks with the correct demonstrative pronoun.**

a. Esa botella, no. Quiero .... que está allí.

b. .... de ahí es mi hermano.

c. Busco un libro. ¿Cuánto cuestan .... que están aquí en la mesa?

d. .... que tienes aquí son revistas de la semana pasada.

e. .... de ahí es la profesora de español.

218

DIRECT OBJECT PRONOUNS

4 Fill in the blanks with the correct direct object pronoun.

a. » ¿Dónde compras el periódico?
» .... compro siempre en el quiosco cerca de casa.

b. » ¿Dónde nos llevas?
» .... llevo a mi habitación.

c. » ¿Cuándo ves a Carlos?
» .... veo esta tarde, después de clase.

d. » ¿Dónde tienes las plantas?
» .... tengo en la cocina, al lado de la ventana.

e. » ¿Me ves mucho en Facebook?
» No, solo .... veo en Twitter.

f. » ¿Usas mucho la computadora?
» Bueno, ... uso dos horas al día.

5 Answer the questions using a direct object pronoun in your response.

a. ¿Quieres el lápiz?
No, gracias, no ....

b. ¿Tienes flores para mí?
No, no ....

c. ¿Ves a Pedro en el gimnasio?
No, no ....

d. ¿Me llamas esta noche?
No, no ....

e. ¿Invitas a tus amigos a la fiesta?
No, no ....

f. ¿Conoces a María y Ana?
No, no ....

NÚMEROS DEL 100 AL 999

6 Write out the numbers in Spanish.

a. 475 ....
b. 823 ....
c. 914 ....
d. 561 ....

CULTURA

7 Answer the following questions about Bolivia, Ecuador, and Peru, and compare similarities with your own country or region.

a. ¿En qué países de América del Sur celebran el carnaval? ¿Hay una celebración similar en tu región? ¿Cómo es? ¿Llevan disfraces?
b. ¿Cómo se llama la danza más popular durante los desfiles de carnaval? ¿Qué representa?
c. ¿Qué elementos tienen en común todas las celebraciones de carnaval en el mundo hispano?
d. ¿Dónde está el Lago Titicaca? ¿Por qué es interesante?
e. ¿Qué recursos (*resources*) naturales tiene Bolivia? ¿Cuál crees que es más importante?
f. ¿Qué alimento cultivan en Perú? ¿En qué parte de Estados Unidos se cultiva también?

 **MORE IN ELETECA:** EXTRA ONLINE PRACTICE

ANSWERS

Activity 4
a. Lo; b. Los; c. Lo; d. Las; e. te; f. la.

Activity 5
a. No, gracias, no lo quiero; b. No, no las tengo; c. No, no lo veo; d. No, no te llamo; e. No, no los invito; f. No, no las conozco.

Activity 6
a. cuatrocientos setenta y cinco; b. ochocientos veintitrés; c. novecientos catorce; d. quinientos sesenta y uno.

Activity 7
a. En Perú, Bolivia, Ecuador y Colombia; b. La Diablada, representa el diablo; c. Desfiles, disfraces, música, baile, etc.; d. Entre Perú y Bolivia. Es uno de los lugares más populares y famosos de Perú, es el lago más grande de América del Sur; e. Depósitos de sal y de litio; f. Papas, en Idaho y Maine.

OBJECTIVES FOR EN RESUMEN: VOCABULARIO

- Review unit vocabulary and expressions
- Practice communicative skills

STANDARDS

1.2 Understand the language

1.3 Present information

INSTRUCTIONAL STRATEGIES

- Model how to use the vocabulary list to review new words and expressions learned in this unit.
- Use simple materials, such as index cards or self-adhesive notes.
- Self-adhesive notes can be used for writing nouns from the vocabulary list on them, then using them to place the correct labels on objects in the classroom or pictures in the book.
- Index cards can be used as flash cards with the Spanish term on one side and the English term on the other, or a picture or drawing.
- Students can work in pairs or groups, using the self-adhesive notes and index cards as they would the cards of a board game to help each other practice the unit vocabulary.
- Encourage students to write labels or captions for the photos on this page. Remind them to use the vocabulary and expressions they have learned in this unit.
- Working with a partner, have students make sentences with the words in **Descripciones** and **Comparativos**. Remind them to pay attach to gender-number agreement with the nouns they modify.
- Have students make word webs with each of the words in **Materiales**. At the center of each word web should be the material. Around it, students add words for items that are made of that material.
- Have students write and act out mini dialogues with the words in **Objetos y cosas** and **Demostrativos**.

EN RESUMEN: Vocabulario

Descripciones *Descriptions*

abierto/a *open*
cuadrado/a *square*
frágil *fragile*
ligero/a *light*
moderno/a *modern*
pesado/a *heavy*

práctico/a *practical*
rectangular *rectangular*
redondo/a *round*
ruidoso/a *noisy*

sencillo/a *simple, plain*
útil *useful*
viejo/a *old*

Materiales *Materials*

el cristal *glass*
el cuero *leather*

la madera *wood*
el metal *metal*
el plástico *plastic*

Comparativos *Comparatives*

más... que *more... than*
mayor *older*

mejor *better*
menos... que *less... than*
peor *worse*
tan... como *as... as*

Verbos *Verbs*

guardar *to put away*
llamar *to call*
poner *to put, to place*

usar *to use*

Objetos y cosas *Objects and things*

la aspiradora *vacuum cleaner*
la calculadora *calculator*
la carpeta *binder, folder*

el cuadro *frame, painting*
el escritorio *desk*
el estuche *case*
la impresora *printer*
el jarrón *vase*
la lámpara *lamp*
el monitor *monitor*

las pinturas *paints*
la planta *plant*
el portátil *laptop*
el póster *poster*
el ratón *mouse*

la regla *ruler*
el sacapuntas *pencil sharpener*
el sillón *armchair*
el teclado *keyboard*
el teléfono celular (móvil) *cell phone*
las tijeras *scissors*

la videoconsola *video game console*

Demostrativos *Demonstratives*

aquel/aquella, aquellos/as *that one (over there), those ones (over there)*

aquello *that (over there)*
ese/esa, esos/as *that one, those ones*
eso *that*
este/esta, estos/as *this one, these ones*
esto *this*

220

EN RESUMEN: Gramática

COMPARATIVES (WITH ADJECTIVES AND ADVERBS)   (See page 201)

■ **más... que** → Julián es **más** rápido **que** Pedro.	*more... than*
■ **menos... que** → Pedro camina **menos** lento **que** Julián.	*less... than*
■ **tan... como** → Julián es **tan** divertido **como** Pedro.	*as... as*

NUMBERS (100-999)   (See page 206)

100	cien	400	cuatrocientos	700	setecientos
101	ciento uno	415	cuatrocientos quince	720	setecientos veinte
200	doscientos	500	quinientos	800	ochocientos
202	doscientos dos	526	quinientos veintiséis	897	ochocientos noventa y siete
300	trescientos	600	seiscientos	899	ochocientos noventa y nueve
303	trescientos tres	669	seiscientos sesenta y nueve	900	novecientos

DEMONSTRATIVE PRONOUNS   (See page 208)

	Singular		Plural		
	Masculine	Feminine	Masculine	Feminine	Neuter
Aquí (cerca)	este	esta	estos	estas	esto
Ahí (intermedio)	ese	esa	esos	esas	eso
Allí (lejos)	aquel	aquella	aquellos	aquellas	aquello

■ Demonstrative pronouns
» ¡Hola, Encarna! ¿Cómo estás?
» Muy bien, gracias. Mira, **esta** es Manuela, mi hermana.

Aquella (bicicleta) es de mi primo.

» ¿Te gustan estos plátanos?
» No, me gustan **aquellos**.

Esas (botas) son de Luis.

■ Neuter pronouns
» ¿Qué es **esto**?
» Es una lámpara.

Este es mi celular.

» ¿Qué es **eso**?
» Es un celular.

» ¿Qué es **aquello**?
» Son unas zapatillas.

DIRECT OBJECT PRONOUNS   (See page 210)

me
te
lo/la
nos
os
los/las

» ¿Tienes el libro de Matemáticas?
» Sí, **lo** tengo en mi casa.

» ¿Quién compra la tarta de cumpleaños?
» **La** compramos nosotros.

221

OBJECTIVES FOR UNIT OPENER

- Introduce unit theme: *¿Qué tiempo va a hacer?* about the weather and seasons
- Culture: Learn about weather and climate in Hispanic countries

STANDARDS

1.2 Understand the language
2.1 Practices and perspectives

INSTRUCTIONAL STRATEGIES

- Introduce unit theme and objective: Talk about the weather and the seasons, and the fact that the seasons are opposite each other in the Northern and Southern Hemispheres. Have students look at the photograph. Read the caption aloud: *Paseando por la playa en enero en Valparaíso, Chile.*
- Ask questions to help students recycle content from the previous unit, such as: *¿Está de vacaciones esta muchacha? ¿Adónde crees que va? ¿Cómo está? ¿Preocupada o tranquila?*
- Use the photograph to preview unit vocabulary, including: *el verano, hace buen tiempo, hace sol, hace calor, gafas de sol*. Help students access meaning by making frequent use of gestures or visuals.
- Ask the introductory questions.
  - *¿Te gusta pasear por la playa?*
  - *¿Vas a la playa o a la piscina en enero o en agosto?*
  - *¿Qué otras actividades haces en enero? ¿Y en agosto?*
- Ask related questions: *¿Hay alguna playa cerca? ¿Vas mucho a la playa? ¿Prefieres ir a la montaña o a la playa?*

SLOWER-PACED LEARNERS

Encourage students to recycle and retrieve vocabulary, including verbs, and structures (mainly, the present tense) from previous units. Ask them to describe the pictures using colors, adjectives, *ser / estar*, and regular / irregular verbs, and *gustar*. Begin by prompting them with *yes/no* questions and then progress to open-ended questions.

ADVANCED LEARNERS

Have students imagine what the girl in the photo is thinking and write a speech bubble or monologue for her. Have them share their ideas with a partner or in small groups.

UNIDAD 8 ¿QUÉ TIEMPO VA A HACER?

≫ ¿Te gusta pasear por la playa?
≫ ¿Vas a la playa o a la piscina en enero o en agosto?
≫ ¿Qué otras actividades haces en enero? ¿Y en agosto?

Paseando por la playa en enero en Valparaíso, Chile.

222

ADDITIONAL UNIT RESOURCES

Extension Activities (EA) (Photocopiable)	Interactive Whiteboard Lessons (IWB)	Audio	Video	Online ELEteca
EA: 8.1, 8.2,	IWB: 8.1, 8.2	80 to 88		

In this unit, you will learn to:

- Express obligation, needs, and give advice
- Make plans about what you are going to do and when
- Talk about the weather and the seasons

Using

- *Hay que, tener que* and *deber* + infinitive
- *Ir a* + infinitive
- Weather expressions with *hace, hay,* and *está*

Cultural Connections

- Share information about weather and climate in Hispanic countries, and compare cultural similarities

SABOR HISPANO

Paisajes y climas extremos
- Paraguay, Uruguay, Argentina y Chile

¡ACCIÓN!

223

LEARNING OUTCOMES

- Express obligation, needs, and give advice
- Make plans about what you are going to do and when
- Talk about the weather and the seasons

INSTRUCTIONAL STRATEGIES

- Use the unit opener to introduce a preview of the vocabulary and the cultural topics for this unit.
- Have students look at the images on this page and relate them to the objectives listed. Ask: **¿Qué hace el muchacho? ¿Adónde creen que va la muchacha?**
- Introduce the video segment in **¡Acción!** and ask students to predict what they think the episode will be about. Ask: **¿Quiénes son? ¿Dónde están? ¿Qué hacen?**
- Invite students to read the topic for **Sabor hispano** and preview that section in the unit. Ask students if the images reflect extreme climates and in what way. **¿Son climas extremos? ¿Qué hay en la foto de la derecha que no hay en la foto de la izquierda? ¿Qué colores predominan en cada imagen?**
- Encourage students to use the images to practice interpersonal and interpretive communication skills. Ask questions such as: **¿Qué ven en estas fotos? ¿Qué les gusta de estas fotos? ¿Qué fotos son interesantes?**
- Have students work in pairs to talk about the images using the questions you have modeled. Then have volunteers present to the class what they understand this unit to be about.

HERITAGE LANGUAGE LEARNERS

Ask students to write a list of all the Spanish countries seen so far. Which ones are missing? Where are they located? Why do they think these countries are called **Cono Sur**? Draw a picture of a cone to help them. Then ask them whether they know where these cities are located: Asunción, Santiago, Montevideo, Buenos Aires, Mendoza, and Valparaíso. Point out that many cities in the Spanish-speaking world are called Santiago, after a famous Catholic saint. Ask students what they know about these countries: soccer, politics, language particularities, etc.

THREE MODES OF COMMUNICATION: UNIT 8

	INTERPERSONAL	INTERPRETIVE	PRESENTATIONAL
HABLAMOS DE...	5	1, 2, 3, 4	5
COMUNICA	2, 4	1, 3	
¡ACCIÓN!	1	2, 3, 4, 5, 6	
PALABRA POR PALABRA	4, 6	1, 2, 3, 5	4, 6
GRAMÁTICA	3, 4, 5, 8, 11	1, 2, 6	3, 4, 7, 9, 10
DESTREZAS		1	2
CULTURA		SABOR HISPANO	
RELATO	1, 6	2, 3, 5	4, 6

OBJECTIVES FOR HABLAMOS DE...

- Preview vocabulary: **Las excursiones**
- Preview grammatical structures: **ir a**, **tener que**, **deber**, **hay que**
- Read and listen to a conversation about an outing in Patagonia
- Understand language in context

CORE RESOURCES

- Audio Program: 80
- Extension Activity: EA 8.1

STANDARDS

1.1   Engage in conversation
1.2   Understand the language
1.3   Present information
4.2   Compare cultures

INSTRUCTIONAL STRATEGIES

Activity 1

Have students look at the photo and connect the visual information to the questions. Encourage students to make educated guesses about what they don't actually see but can infer given the context of the image.

🎧 80 Activity 2

- Introduction to the conversation: Tell students to close their books. Explain that they will listen to a conversation between Javi and his mother and have them listen.
- Have students open books and review the dialogue. Play the audio a second time for students to fill in the missing words.
- Observe, provide support, and correct students as needed. (Note: An **anorak** is a ski jacket or a warm, hooded parka.)

ANSWERS

Activity 1

Answers will vary. Possible answers provided.

a. seis; **b.** Son amigos; **c.** Están en las montañas; **d.** Llevan abrigos, bufandas, botas, etc.; **e.** Llevan agua y comida en las mochilas; **f.** Están de vacaciones. Les gusta ir de excursión.

Activity 2

1. excursión; **2.** visitar; **3.** profesor; **4.** bocadillos; **5.** frío; **6.** gorro; **7.** cámara; **8.** 128 pesos; **9.** ocho; **10.** pronto.

SLOWER-PACED LEARNERS

Have students practice the conversation in Activity 2 with a partner for additional oral practice.

ADVANCED LEARNERS

Challenge students to provide explanations for their answers in Activity 1.

HERITAGE LANGUAGE LEARNERS

Before playing the audio in Activity 2, have students read the conversation and try to complete the gaps using contextual clues come up with logical answers. Then play the audio so they can compare their guesses with the recording and correct them.

HABLAMOS DE... Las excursiones

1 Look at the image below of people on an outing in Patagonia, Chile. Then answer the questions based on what you see or can infer from the image.

a. ¿Cuántas personas hay en la foto?
b. ¿Crees que son amigos o es una familia?
c. ¿Están en las montañas o en la costa?
d. ¿Qué ropa crees que llevan?
e. ¿Qué crees que llevan en las mochilas?
f. ¿Por qué están allí?

2 🎧 80 Listen to the conversation between Javi and his mother and fill in the blanks with the missing words.

Javi: ¡Hola, mamá!
Mamá: Hola, Javi, ¿qué tal la escuela?
Javi: Pues, bien, como siempre.
Mamá: Y ese papel, ¿qué es?
Javi: Ah, es para la (1) .... de este fin de semana. Vamos toda la clase.
Mamá: ¿Y a dónde van, Javi?
Javi: Pues, vamos a (2) .... el Parque Nacional La Campana.
Mamá: Muy bien. Y, ¿qué necesitas?
Javi: El (3) .... dice que **tenemos que llevar** unos (4) .... y unas bebidas.
Mamá: Pero en la montaña normalmente hace (5) .... Yo creo que **debes llevar** un anorak, los guantes y el (6) ....
Javi: Está bien, mamá. También quiero hacer fotos.
Mamá: Bueno, puedes usar mi (7) ....
Javi: ¡Fenomenal! Muchas gracias.
Mamá: ¿Cuánto **hay que pagar** por la excursión?
Javi: Muy poco, solo (8) .... ¡Ah! Vamos a salir el sábado a las (9) .... de la mañana.
Mamá: Entonces, esa noche tienes que acostarte (10) ....

3 Indicate whether the following sentences are true (T) or false (F).

	T	F
a. Javi va de excursión a la montaña.	○	○
b. No tiene que llevar comida.	○	○
c. Su madre le aconseja llevar ropa para el frío.	○	○
d. La excursión cuesta 128 pesos.	○	○
e. Javi lleva la cámara de fotos de su madre.	○	○

4 Match the two columns to make complete sentences. Then read the sentences aloud with a partner.

1. Para hacer la excursión...

2. La madre dice que en la montaña hace frío y que Javi...

3. El profesor dice que todos los estudiantes...

4. La excursión es a las ocho de la mañana y Javi...

a. tienen que llevar unos y unas ___.

b. tiene que  pronto el viernes.

c. debe llevar un ___, unos ___ y un gorro.

d. hay que pagar ___.

5 The Aconcagua Provincial Park in the Andes mountains of Argentina draws hikers to its popular trails. Use the image to plan an outing to this park. First, fill in the information in the chart. Then, with a partner, discuss what each of you are going to bring.

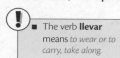

■ The verb **llevar** means *to wear or to carry, take along*.

Modelo: E1: ¿Qué ropa vas a llevar?
E2: Voy a llevar... ¿Y tú?

Ropa:
Comida:
Equipo *(equipment)*:
¿Algo más?

Parque provincial Aconcagua

225

INSTRUCTIONAL STRATEGIES

Activity 3

Remind students that while listening they should focus on information that they need to answer the *true/false* questions.

Activity 4

- Have students work in pairs for this activity. Encourage them to use the vocabulary and sentence patterns from the conversation.
- Direct students to the expressions in bold and remind them that they already learned the expression **tener que + infinitive** in **Unidad 4.**
- Once students have completed the activity and have read the sentences aloud to their partner or to the class, distribute copies of EA 8.1, **La excursión de Javi** to preview the grammar in the unit. Walk students through the questions in the chart before they

---

complete the chart with a partner. Offer options for **¿A quién va dirigido?** such as: **Javi, los estudiantes, o todos**.

- At this point, it is not necessary to provide additional grammar explanations beyond what is presented in the chart. Ask students to hold on to this sheet for use later in the unit.

Activity 5

Give students 3 or 4 minutes to prepare their answers for the clothes, food, equipment and other things they are planning to take before they ask each other. Make sure they follow the sentence patterns from the **Modelo** and are taking turns asking each other.

ANSWERS

Activity 3

a. T; b. F; c. T; d. T; e. T.

Activity 4

1. d; 2. c; 3. a; 4. b.

Activity 5

Answers will vary and should reflect the model provided and expressions taught.

SLOWER-PACED LEARNERS

After Activity 4, have students work in small groups to make posters related to Aconcagua Provincial Park in Argentina. The posters should include a map locating the park in the country, a hiking trail, and images of the park.

ADVANCED LEARNERS

Encourage students to use adjectives when preparing their lists in Activity 5. For instance, **unas botas amarillas, una mochila grande, un gorro caliente, unos bocadillos de queso**, etc.

HERITAGE LANGUAGE LEARNERS

As a follow-up to Activity 5, have students do more research the Aconcagua Provincial Park in the Argentina. Tell them to compare their lists with any information or recommendations they can find online for hikers visiting there. Have them revise or update their lists, if necessary.

OBJECTIVES FOR COMUNICA

- Present the communicative functions of the unit:
  - Describing the weather
  - Talking about the weather

CORE RESOURCES

- Extension Activities: EA 8.2
- Audio Program: 81
- Interactive Online Materials - ELEteca

STANDARDS

1.1 Engage in conversation
1.2 Understand the language
1.3 Present information
4.1 Compare languages

INSTRUCTIONAL STRATEGIES FOR DESCRIBING THE WEATHER

- To introduce weather expressions, have students go back to page 224 and identify any words or expressions referring to the weather (*hace frío*).
- Walk students through the explanations and expressions on this page of the student book using complete sentences to describe the weather: Ask: *¿Qué tiempo hace? Hace calor. Hace frío*, and so on, so students become accustomed to hearing the correct usage with *hace*, *hay*, and *está*.
- Distribute the cutouts from EA 8.2, *El tiempo atmosférico*, and call out one of the nouns from EA 8.2, such as *sol*. The student who has the card that says *sol* will answer: *Hace sol*. Continue to call out the other nouns. As an alternative, ask volunteers to show their cards and say the expression that would go with them, such as *hace calor, hace frío...*

- Help students realize that many of these expressions are similar to English in structure: *Está nublado* (It is cloudy), while others are not. Point out that the verbs in Spanish for raining and snowing, *llover* and *nevar*, are impersonal verbs and are only used in the *llueve* or *nieva* forms in the present tense.

Activity 1

Have students complete the sentences with the correct verbs.

Activity 2

- Review the **Modelo** with students to make sure they understand to use *Hace...* and *Hay que...* Remind students that *hay que* is used when referring to everyone in general.
- Go over the new vocabulary in the box and have students refer to **Unidad 3** for more clothes vocabulary.

ANSWERS

Activity 1

a. hace; b. hay; c. está; d. llueve; e. hace.

COMUNICA

DESCRIBING THE WEATHER

¿Qué tiempo hace? *What's the weather like?*

Hace

calor / frío	sol / viento	buen tiempo	mal tiempo
It's hot. / It's cold.	*It's sunny. / It's windy.*	*The weather is good.*	*The weather is bad.*

Hay

nieve *There's snow. (It's snowy).*   niebla *There's fog. (It's foggy).*   tormenta *There's a storm. (It's stormy).*

Está	Llueve	Nieva

nublado *It's cloudy.* | En el sur de Chile **llueve** mucho. *In southern Chile, it rains a lot.* | **Nieva** mucho en las montañas de los Andes. *It snows a lot in the Andes mountains.*

1 Fill in the blanks with the correct word to complete the sentences.

a. Mañana voy a la playa porque .... calor.
b. En esta época .... nieve en la montaña.
c. Cerca de la costa .... nublado.
d. Hoy necesito el paraguas (*umbrella*) porque ....
e. Es difícil jugar al tenis cuando .... viento.

2 With a partner, take turns describing the weather in your area today and during different months of the year. Talk about what clothes you typically need to wear.

 La ropa ➡ Unidad 3

Modelo:
E1: En agosto hace mucho calor.
E2: Hay que llevar pantalones cortos y una camiseta.

a. hoy
b. julio
c. noviembre
d. abril
e. febrero
f. mayo

! Otras palabras útiles:	■ gorro *knitted hat*
■ anorak *ski jacket*	■ guantes *gloves*
■ chanclas *flip-flops*	■ impermeable *raincoat*
■ gafas de sol *sunglasses*	■ paraguas *umbrella*

226

ADVANCED LEARNERS

Have students thinking of new sentences for each weather condition in Activity 1: *hace calor*, *hay nieve*, *está nublado*, *llueve*, and *hace viento*. For example: *No necesito una chaqueta hoy porque hace calor.*

TALKING ABOUT THE WEATHER

¡Qué frío / calor (hace)!	It's so cold / hot!
¡Qué frío / calor tengo!	I'm so cold / hot! .
¿Tienes frío / calor?	Are you cold / hot?
Hace mucho (muchísimo) frío / calor.	It's very (really) cold / hot.
¡Cuánto llueve!	It's really raining!
¿Qué día / tiempo hace?	What's the day / weather like?
Hace un día muy bueno / malo.	It's a nice / bad day.
Estamos a 20 grados.	It's 20 degrees.
No hace nada de frío / calor.	It's not at all cold / hot.

!

- To convert degrees Celsius to Fahrenheit:
1. Multiply Celsius temperature by 1.8.
2. Add 32.
20ºC x 1.8 = 36 + 32 = 68 ºF

3 🎧 **81** **Listen to the weather report for Argentina. Then write the letter of the correct weather symbol missing on the weather map according to the report. ¡Atención!** Not all boxes nor all symbols will be used.

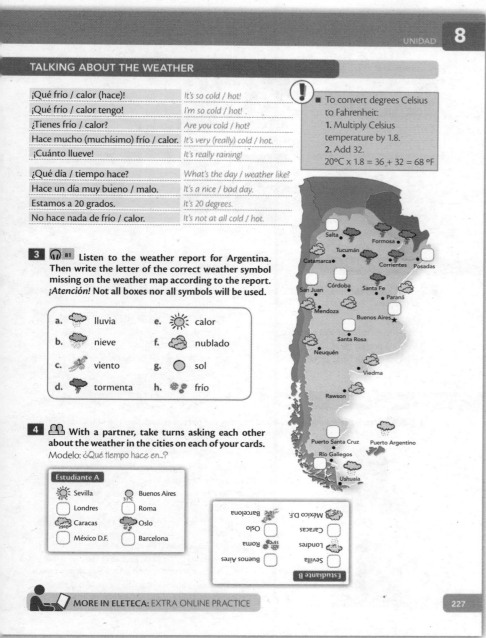

- a. lluvia
- b. nieve
- c. viento
- d. tormenta
- e. calor
- f. nublado
- g. sol
- h. frío

4 👥 **With a partner, take turns asking each other about the weather in the cities on each of your cards.**
Modelo: ¿Qué tiempo hace en…?

Estudiante A
- Sevilla
- Londres
- Caracas 29ºC
- México D.F.
- Buenos Aires 31ºC
- Roma
- Oslo
- Barcelona

Estudiante B
- Barcelona -1ºC
- Oslo
- Roma 15ºC
- Buenos Aires
- México D.F. 13ºC
- Caracas
- Londres
- Sevilla

👤💻 **MORE IN ELETECA:** EXTRA ONLINE PRACTICE

227

---

temperatures. The formula for converting Fahrenheit to Celsius: Subtract 32 from temperature and divide by 1.8. Example: 74 °F - 32 = 42 ÷ 1.8 = 23 °C.

🎧 **81** Activity 3

- Tell students they will now listen to a weather report from Argentina.
- Review the weather symbols to make sure they are clear to students: **a. lluvia; b. nieve; c. viento; d. tormenta; e. calor; f. nublado; g. sol; h. frío.** Project the map of Argentina for students to become familiar with the places mentioned. Ask about weather in other cities. For example, **¿Qué tiempo hace en Viedma? ¿Y en Corrientes?** and so on. Also, use *either/or* questions, such as: **¿Está nublado o hace sol en Mendoza?**
- Play the audio and ask students to pay attention to the report. Ask them to match the letters of the weather icons to the appropriate location on the map.

See audioscript on page APP11.

Activity 4

Students work in pairs. This is an information gap activity. Student Card A has the information missing from Student Card B and vice versa. Students ask questions such as: **¿Qué tiempo hace en…? ¿Qué temperatura hay en…? ¿Qué temperatura tienen en…? ¿A qué temperatura están en…?** Read out the model provided to help students understand the activity. Once the activity is completed, students check their answers by looking at their partner's card.

ANSWERS

Activity 3

Cities on map with letters: Salta, b; Córdoba, d; Buenos Aires, f; San Juan, a; Posadas, g; Puerto Santa Cruz, h; Río Gallego,s c; Letter and symbol not used: e. hace calor. City not mentioned: Santa Rosa.

SLOWER-PACED LEARNERS

After doing Activity 4, have students switch roles and do it again. This time, have them add a sentence to react to the information or keep the conversation going.

HERITAGE LANGUAGE LEARNERS

Have students go online and find out what the weather is like today in at least five of the Argentine cities labeled on the map. Encourage them to choose cities from different parts of the country and to use Spanish-language sources to find the information.

OBJECTIVES FOR COMUNICA

- Present the communicative functions of the unit:
  - Ask and respond to questions about the weather
  - Listen to weather information for understanding

INSTRUCTIONAL STRATEGIES FOR TALKING ABOUT THE WEATHER

- Walk students through the expressions provided.
- With books closed, have students repeat the expressions after you. Use gestures and facial expressions to help students understand meaning.
- Point out that, in addition to **Estamos a 20 grados**, we can also say: **Tenemos una temperatura de 20 grados** or: **Hay una temperatura de 20 grados.**
- Ask students: **Si estamos a 20 grados centígrados, ¿hace frío, calor, o buen tiempo? (Hace buen tiempo, ni frío ni calor).** Review the note and practice converting

OBJECTIVES FOR ¡ACCIÓN!

- Provide students with a structured approach to viewing the video
- Contextualize the content of the unit in a familiar scenario

CORE RESOURCES

- Unit Video 8 - 30 grados
- Online Materials - ELEteca

STANDARDS

1.1. Interpersonal communication

1.2 Interpretive communication

2.1 Culture: Practices and perspectives

INSTRUCTIONAL STRATEGIES

Previewing: Antes del video

- Have students look at the images and speculate why the characters are indoors in most of them. Direct their attention to the title and discuss what the temperature would be in degrees Fahrenheit (86).
- Ask: *¿Te gusta jugar al básquetbol? ¿Con quién juegas? ¿Dónde juegas, en un gimnasio, un parque u otro lugar?*

Activity 1

Tell students to produce logical responses to the questions. Encourage them to speculate and share ideas.

Viewing: Durante el video

Activity 2

- Before playing the video, give students time to read the sentences and familiarize themselves with the content to come. Clarify which character is Felipe and which is Sebas by referring to the photos.
- Play the video. Stop it at 3:24 before Eli and Lorena enter so students can focus on what they've just heard and correctly identify the speakers of each sentence. Replay the clip if necessary.

ANSWERS

Activity 1

- Image 1: **a.** Primavera o verano; **b.** Hace un buen tiempo. Hace sol y calor; **c.** Puedes pasear por el parque, salir con amigos, montar en bici y jugar al fútbol.
- Image 2: **a.** Están en un gimnasio; **b.** Van a jugar al baloncesto; **c.** Hablan de sus amigos, del instituto, de las clases, etc.

Activity 2

a. Felipe; **b.** Sebas; **c.** Felipe; **d.** Felipe; **e.** Sebas; **f.** Felipe; **g.** Felipe; **h.** Felipe.

SLOWER-PACED LEARNERS

To facilitate Activity 2 and keep students focused while trying to listen and write down the characters' names, consider pausing the video very briefly after each line or exchange in the dialogue to help them to keep up.

ADVANCED LEARNERS

Using some of the sentences from Activity 2 as inspiration, have students work in pairs to write a conversation in which someone talks about the weather in an exaggerated way and the other person disagrees. Have students act out their conversations in class.

¡ACCIÓN! 30 grados

1.   2.   3.

4.   5.   6.

ANTES DEL VIDEO

1 Look at the Images 1 and 2, and answer the following questions. Compare answers with a partner.

Image 1
a. ¿Qué estación del año crees que es?
b. ¿Qué tiempo hace?
c. ¿Qué puedes hacer un día así?

Image 2
a. ¿Dónde están?
b. ¿Qué van a hacer?
c. ¿De qué crees que hablan?

DURANTE EL VIDEO

2 Watch the following scene and identify the person that makes the following claims.
00:40 - 03:22

¿Felipe o Sebas?

a. .... Hoy parece que estamos en verano.
b. .... Sí, y es otoño... ¿Qué temperatura tenemos?
c. .... Estamos a 30 grados centígrados.
d. .... En mi país hace mucho más calor. No podemos comparar este calor con el que hay en mi país.
e. .... En tu país no hace más calor que aquí en verano, seguro. A veces llegamos a los 40 grados...
f. .... Pues en mi país una vez llegamos en verano a los ¡60 grados!
g. .... ¿Imposible? Pues es verdad. ¡El clima de mi país es muy extremo! En verano hace mucho calor y, en invierno, siempre hay viento y nieve.
h. .... ¡Que sí! ¡Que sí! Durante el invierno cae mucha nieve, hay terribles tormentas, hace mucho viento y el cielo siempre está nublado.

228

HERITAGE LANGUAGE LEARNERS

Invite students to share their experience with extreme weather. Do they know of any places with weather conditions similar to those that Felipe describes? Where?

UNIDAD 8

3 Match the character to his behavior or attitude portrayed in the episode.

1. Sebas   **a.** exagera mucho.

2. Felipe   **b.** no cree a su amigo.

4 03:22 - 03:55 Watch the following scene and put the conversation between Eli and her brother Sebas in the correct order.

a. ◯ Yo ayudo a mamá. Papá dice que debes ayudarle tú…

b. ◯ Sebas, papá dice que tienes que ir luego a casa para ayudar a organizar el garaje.

c. ◯ Yo no sé nada, yo solo te digo que tienes que ir.

d. ◯ ¿Por qué no vas tú a ayudarle?

e. ◯ ¿Yo? ¡Yo ya le ayudo a lavar el carro! ¿También debo ir a organizar el garaje?

5 Watch the rest of the episode. Put the Images 4, 5 and 6 in the order they occurred and describe what is happening in each. Share your descriptions with a partner.

DESPUÉS DEL VIDEO

6 Complete the sentences for you and your family. Share your answers with a partner. What do you have in common?

a. Tus responsabilidades en casa:

> Tengo que...
> Debo...

b. Responsabilidades de tu familia:

> Mi padre...
> Mi madre...
> Mis hermanos...

7 Take turns with a partner asking and answering the questions on each of your cards.

Estudiante 1

a. ¿Cómo es el tiempo en primavera y verano en tu ciudad?

b. ¿Qué planes tienes para el próximo verano?

Estudiante 2

a. ¿Cómo es el tiempo en otoño e invierno en tu ciudad?

b. ¿Qué planes tienes para el próximo verano?

8 With which side do you agree more? Choose a side to defend and prepare your thoughts. Your teacher will set up the debate groups.

Pro	Con
Los hijos mayores tienen más responsabilidades en casa, pero tienen más libertad.	Los padres no son tan estrictos con los hijos menores como son con los mayores.

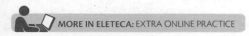

MORE IN ELETECA: EXTRA ONLINE PRACTICE

229

- Play the reminder of the video for them to confirm or adjust their answers.
- Put students in pairs to describe the images and recall the content of the video related to each scene.

Post-viewing: Después del video

Activity 6

- Have students brainstorm different responsibilities at home and household chores. Make a list on the board. Then have them complete the boxes with the information that is true for them and their families.
- Put students in pairs to share their information. Have students report back on their partners' information.

Activity 7

- The purpose of this activity is to continue to practice vocabulary and structures around weather as well as activities and plans associated with different seasons.
- Circulate and observe students conversations. After their discussions, go over any common errors you heard them make.

Activity 8

- Divide the class in half, assigning each half one side of the debate. Have each student write down one idea in support or defense of the point of view. Encourage them to use examples from their personal lives to articulate their ideas.
- Then have students share their ideas and examples with their groups. They should choose three to five of the strongest arguments in defense of their point of view. Have each group elect members to deliver the arguments in front of the class. Decide which group makes the best case for their point of view.

Answers

Activity 3

1. b; **2.** a.

Activity 4

a. 5; **b.** 1; **c.** 3; **d.** 4; **e.** 2.

Activity 5

Answers will vary. Possible answer:

Las muchachas quieren jugar al básquetbol con los muchachos, pero ellos no quieren porque dicen que ellas juegan muy mal. Ellos juegan y ellas miran, pero los muchachos no juegan bien. Ellas se ríen y deciden darles una lección. Ellos se sorprenden y se van un poco tristes. Ellas están muy contentas.

INSTRUCTIONAL STRATEGIES

Activity 3

Have students match the characters with the descriptions before continuing with the video.

Activity 4

- Ask students to anticipate what will happen in the next scene. Have them look at the introductory video stills to help them make educated guesses.
- Go over the instructions and let students read the lines of dialogue. Then continue playing the video until end of the conversation between Eli and Sebas at around 3:55. Check students' comprehension: **¿Sebas quiere ayudar a su papá? ¿Por qué sí o no? ¿Qué tiene que hacer? ¿Tienes conversaciones como esas con tus hermanos?**

Activity 5

- Go over the instructions. Encourage students to guess the correct order of the images.

SLOWER-PACED LEARNERS

Help students along with the target grammar structures needed to complete the sentences in Activity 6, which preempts the presentation in **Gramática**. Elicit how to conjugate the expressions to use them in part **b**.

HERITAGE LANGUAGE LEARNERS

Have students write and act out a conversation that Sebas might have with his father later on based on the information in Activity 4.

OBJECTIVES FOR EL TIEMPO ATMOSFÉRICO Y LAS ESTACIONES DEL AÑO

- Present the vocabulary needed to practice the communicative and grammatical functions for the unit: Talking about the weather
- Identify the seasons

CORE RESOURCES

- Audio Program: 82
- Interactive Online Materials - ELEteca

STANDARDS

1.1	Engage in conversation
1.2	Understand the language
1.3	Present information

INSTRUCTIONAL STRATEGIES

🎧 82 Activity 1

- Before playing the audio, let students know that they will listen to four recordings describing the seasons of the year.
- Have students listen to the audio twice. Students fill in the blanks during the first listening and then determine what season is being described during the second listening.

See audioscript on page APP11.

Activity 2

Ask students to work in pairs to complete this activity. Encourage them to use the context from the previous activity to determine the correct answer. Point out that some words are Spanish / English cognates, such as **estable**, **inestable**, **cero**. Remind them they can also look up words or ask their partners.

Activity 3

Have students complete this activity with the new words they learned in Activity 2.

Extension

Encourage students to write the new words on index cards with a definition. They can use these cards as a word file that will grow as they learn more words. Encourage students to include drawings whenever possible.

ANSWERS

Activity 1

a. norte, nieve, viento, niebla: invierno, 4; **b.** calor, llueve, nieva, grados: primavera, 1; **c.** buen tiempo, tormentas: verano, 2; **d.** frío, Llueve, norte: otoño, 3.

Activity 2

1. d; **2.** a; **3.** f; **4.** b; **5.** c; **6.** e.

Activity 3

a. caluroso; **b.** bajo cero; **c.** relámpagos; **d.** truenos; **e.** inestable.

ADVANCED LEARNERS

Have students write three sentences explaining what activities they do or what routines they have during each season in Activity 1. Then have them sharing their sentences with a partner without explicitly naming the seasons. Their partners guess which seasons match each set of sentences.

PALABRA POR PALABRA El tiempo atmosférico

1 🎧 82 Listen to the following audio recordings about average weather patterns in the northern hemisphere. Fill in the blanks with the missing words and then match the season to its description.

La primavera

El verano

El otoño

El invierno

a. Es especialmente duro en la zona .... e interior, con temperaturas bajo cero y .... frecuente. También son habituales otros fenómenos como el ...., la .... o el hielo. En el sur es más suave.

b. Es bastante inestable. Hace ...., frío, viento, pero también .... mucho y a veces .... Es una época perfecta para ver el campo verde y lleno de flores. Las temperaturas varían entre los 15 y los 25 ....

c. Es un periodo muy caluroso, especialmente en el sur y el interior. Hace muy .... con temperaturas entre los 35 y los 40 grados. También son frecuentes las ...., con rayos y truenos.

d. Normalmente hace ...., pero no demasiado. .... bastante y también nieva, especialmente en el .... Además, son frecuentes las nieblas. Las temperaturas están entre los 5 y los 20 grados.

2 👥 Match the weather phenomenon to its definition. Use the context above to help you with the meaning. Then check your answers with a partner.

1. inestable	**a.**	Temperatura menos de cero grados.
2. bajo cero	**b.**	El ruido que se escucha durante una tormenta.
3. el relámpago	**c.**	Mucho calor.
4. el trueno	**d.**	No es estable.
5. caluroso/a	**e.**	Agua helada (*frozen*).
6. el hielo	**f.**	El rayo de luz (*light*) que sale durante una tormenta.

3 Fill in the blanks with a word from the list in Activity 2.

a. En verano el tiempo es ....

b. En Tierra del Fuego están .... porque está cerca de Antártica.

c. ¿Los ves? Hay muchos .... con esta tormenta.

d. No puedo dormir con todos estos ....

e. En esta época el tiempo es muy .... Hoy llueve y mañana hace sol.

y las estaciones del año

4 👥 With a partner, form logical sentences by combining elements from the columns below.

When or Where		Verb	Intensity of Weather	Weather Condition
En invierno				frío
En verano				calor
En la costa		hace	demasiado/a/s	nieve
En el interior		hay	mucho/a/s	lluvia
En el norte	no	está	bastante/s	hielo
En el sur		llueve	un poco (de)	sol
En el este		nieva	nada (de)	viento
En el oeste				niebla
				nubes
				nublado

Modelo: En el norte hace bastante frío.

Norte
Oeste · Este
Sur

5 Arrange the following words to form logical sentences about the weather.

a. bastante / frío / hace / montaña / En / la ➡ ....

b. todo / el / hace / sur / tiempo / En / el / buen / año ➡ ....

c. pero / también / la / hace / mucho / calor / hace / En / playa / viento ➡ ....

d. En / norte / en / el / hay / y / niebla / invierno / lluvia ➡ ....

e. mal / llueve / tiempo / y / En / hace / interior / el ➡ ....

6 👥 Complete the following sentences to explain what you and others do or don't do in different weather conditions. Then take turns exchanging information with a partner.

a. Cuando llueve yo...

b. Cuando hace mal tiempo, mis amigos y yo...

c. En verano, mi familia...

d. Cuando hace mucho calor, los estudiantes...

e. Cuando hay niebla, no puedo...

f. Cuando hace mucho sol, me gusta...

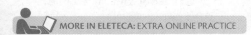 MORE IN ELETECA: EXTRA ONLINE PRACTICE

INSTRUCTIONAL STRATEGIES

Activity 4

- Project the chart to model how to put a sentence together using the elements from the chart: **En invierno hace demasiado frío**. Review the directions on the compass.

- Have students work in pairs to construct sentences from the elements provided, following your model. Encourage students to use the general weather patterns in the United States to help them create logical sentences.

Activity 5

Have students work individually to arrange the words to form logical sentences. Remind students to use the word beginning with a capital letter as the starting point.

Activity 6

- For this activity, encourage students to bring photos of what they do in different weather conditions or at different times of the year and talk about them.

- Allow students time to prepare their answers to the questions individually.

  Extension

  For additional practice, have students write 4-5 sentences about their favorite type of climate, the region that has this climate, and the activities they can do there. Then they present their preference to the class. Use the following sentence stems: *Para mí,... tiene un clima ideal. Hace / hay... Me gusta porque...*

ANSWERS

Activity 4

Answers will vary and should reflect the expressions taught. Possible answers provided.

– En invierno hace mucho frío.

– En verano hace mucho calor.

– En el interior hace mucho sol.

– En la costa hay mucha niebla.

– En el norte no hace mucho calor.

– En el sur no hace mucho frío.

– En el este nieva mucho.

– En el oeste no llueve mucho.

Activity 5

a. En la montaña hace bastante frío; **b.** En el sur hace buen tiempo todo el año; **c.** En la playa hace calor pero también hace mucho viento; **d.** En invierno, en el norte, hay lluvia y niebla; **e.** En el interior hace mal tiempo y llueve.

Activity 6

Answers will vary and should reflect the expressions taught.

SLOWER-PACED LEARNERS

Before putting students in pairs in Activity 6, elicit a possible ending for each sentence from the class so they'll have something to model when speaking with their partners.

HERITAGE LANGUAGE LEARNERS

Have students interview someone they know who lives or has lived in a Spanish-speaking country and ask them about the weather and seasons there. Encourage students to ask follow-up questions about people's habits, routines, and activities during each season in that country. (You may want to come up with a list of target questions as a class first). If possible, have students record the interviews and play them back for the class. Alternatively, have them write a paragraph summarizing the information that they've learned. They should be prepared to point out the location discussed on a map. If it's an unfamiliar town or region, they should bring in additional visual support to educate the class about it.

OBJECTIVES FOR GRAMÁTICA 1

- Present the grammatical structures needed to practice the communicative functions of the unit: Talk about future plans
- Use **ir a + infinitive**

CORE RESOURCES

- Interactive Whiteboard Lessons: IWB 8.1, 8.2
- Interactive Online Materials - ELEteca

STANDARDS

1.1	Engage in conversation
1.2	Understand the language
1.3	Present information
4.1	Compare languages

INSTRUCTIONAL STRATEGIES

1. IR A + Infinitive

- Refer back to Javi's excursion as a way to connect the grammar to the unit theme. Project IWB 8.1, **ir a + infinitive**. Have students work in pairs to come up with the answers, then share with the whole class. Invite volunteers to write their answers directly on the Interactive Whiteboard.

Alternative Activity

Project IWB Lesson 8.2, to check for correct answers.

- Have students open books and walk them through the explanations given and the various expressions. Point out that **ir a + infinitive** corresponds to the English *going to + infinitive*. Invite students to compare and contrast these structures in both languages to better understand similarities and differences.
- Review time expressions used to talk about the future.

Activity 1

Make sure students understand that, in this exercise, they need to focus on the various verb forms for **ir a + infinitive** and meaning.

ANSWERS

Activity 1

1. e; **2.** a; **3.** d; **4.** f; **5.** b; **6.** c.

GRAMÁTICA

1. IR A + INFINITIVE

- The construction **ir a + infinitive** is used to talk about future plans and what you are going to do.
  Esta tarde voy a ver una película. This afternoon, I am going to see a movie.
  Hace mucho frío. Creo que va a nevar. It's very cold. I think it's going to snow.

yo	**voy**	
tú	**vas**	
usted/él/ella	**va**	+ a + infinitive
nosotros/as	**vamos**	
vosotros/as	**vais**	
ustedes/ellos/ellas	**van**	

- Use the following time expressions to talk about the future.

hoy *today*
mañana *tomorrow*
ahora *now*
esta mañana / tarde / noche / semana *this morning / afternoon / night / week*
este lunes / mes / año *this Monday / month / year*
la semana / el mes / el año **que viene** *the upcoming week / month / year*
la próxima semana *next week*
el próximo jueves / invierno / año *next Thursday / Winter / year*

El mes que viene voy a correr en un maratón. This month coming up, I'm going to run in a marathon.
Esta tarde voy a jugar al tenis. This afternoon, I'm going to play tennis.
El próximo año voy a estudiar francés. Next year, I'm going to study French.
Son las doce, ahora voy a comer. It's twelve o'clock. I'm going to eat.

1 Match the sentences to describe what people are going to do in each situation.

Modelo: *Mañana es domingo.* → *Mi familia y yo vamos a visitar a mis abuelos.*

1. La próxima semana no tenemos clase.
2. Este viernes es el cumpleaños de Dani.
3. A mi padre le encanta cocinar.
4. Estoy de mal humor.
5. Julia tiene dolor de cabeza.
6. Va a hacer buen tiempo este fin de semana.

a. Voy a invitar a unos amigos a casa para celebrarlo.
b. Va a tomar una aspirina.
c. Pero el lunes va a llover.
d. Esta noche va a preparar arepas de carne.
e. Vamos a ir de excursión de martes a jueves.
f. No voy a salir con mis amigos.

SLOWER-PACED LEARNERS

After doing Activity 1, elicit how to form *yes/no* questions, information questions, and negative statements with **ir a + infinitive** as well. Then have students write two questions (one *yes/no* question and one information question) to ask a partner about his or her future plans using the time expressions presented. Then put them in pairs to ask and answer the questions.

2 Read the e-mail Inés writes to her friend Elena about all the plans she has for next year. Fill in the blanks with the correct form of *ir a + infinitive*.

> ● ● ● Asunto: ¡Qué día he tenido!
>
> De: Inesbv@gmail.com   Para: Elemo@hotmail.com
>
> ¡Hola, Elena!
>
> ¿Cómo estás? Yo estoy muy bien y muy contenta porque el próximo año 1. (yo, hacer) .... muchas cosas nuevas. Primero, 2. (nosotros, vivir) .... en Montevideo. Es que mi padre 3. (empezar) .... un nuevo trabajo allí. Mi hermana Celia y yo 4. (estudiar) .... en una nueva escuela. Seguro que 5. (nosotras, conocer) .... a mucha gente interesante. También 6. (nosotras, jugar) .... mucho al tenis, porque tenemos una pista cerca de casa. ¡Qué bien! Como ves, 7. (yo, estar) .... muy ocupada *(busy)* pero siempre 8. (yo, tener) .... tiempo para ti. Me tienes que visitar el verano que viene. ¿Está bien? Ahora me 9. (dormir) ....
>
> Muchos besos y escribe pronto.
>
> Inés.

3 👥 Describe how the following people are feeling based on what they are going to do or not do. Combine elements from each column to form six logical sentences. Then create one of your own (¿...?). Share your sentences with the class.

Modelo: *Tú estás nervioso porque vas a hablar en público.*

A	B	C	D
yo tú el profesor la profesora mis padres ustedes/ellos/ellas ¿...?	contento/a nervioso/a de mal humor preocupado/a enfadado/a de buen humor	(no) ir a	llamar a los padres salir con los amigos cantar en el concurso *(contest)* La Voz de la televisión hacer deporte y llover mucho conocer al presidente de Estados Unidos hacer sol y calor para ir a la playa hablar en público ¿...?

4 👥 With a partner, take turns saying where the people on the following page are going and what they are going to do there. Use the image and your imagination to include as much information as possible.

Modelo:

El muchacho va al parque. Va a jugar fútbol. Después...

233

Activity 2

This cloze activity allows students to practice with *ir a + infinitive*. Make sure students understand that they are not conjugating the infinitive provided, but using the correct form of *ir* with *a* in front of it, based on the subject pronoun provided.

Activity 3

- Do this as a timed activity or class competition. Give students about 5 minutes to create as many logical sentences as they can.
- Encourage students to vary sentences by including what people are not going to do.

Activity 4 (continued on the next page)

- Pre-teach the vocabulary for this activity if you feel it is necessary. This can also be assigned as a written activity in class.
- Review the **Modelo** with students and brainstorm other possible activities the boy in the image is going to do.
- As additional practice, have students write about their own plans for the upcoming weekend, or next vacation, or next year. Collect the papers, have volunteers read a paper by someone else and have the class guess who wrote it.

ANSWERS

Activity 2

1. voy a hacer; 2. vamos a vivir; 3. va a empezar; 4. vamos a estudiar; 5. vamos a conocer; 6. vamos a jugar; 7. voy a estar; 8. voy a tener; 9. voy a dormir.

Activity 3

Answers will vary and should reflect the model provided and sentence structures taught using *ir a + infinitive*.

SLOWER-PACED LEARNERS

Students may need some extra help retrieving the verbs they need for Activity 4. Allow extra time for them to check the vocabulary lists at the end of each unit to locate the action verbs they may want to use here.

ADVANCED LEARNERS

Have students use new ideas to come up with two of their own sentences following the same structure as those in Activity 3. You may want to elicit examples of varied emotions as a class first to help get them started.

HERITAGE LANGUAGE LEARNERS

As a follow-up to Activity 4, have students prepare a list of activities that a celebrity or well-known person (preferably from the Hispanic community) will be likely doing in the future and present it to the class. Classmates will have to guess who the celebrity is: *Va a ponerse un pantalón blanco y una camiseta azul. Va a agarrar su raqueta y una pelota pequeña. Va a jugar un partido de tenis. Va a ganar un campeonato. Va a sonreír. ¿Quién es?*

GRAMÁTICA GRAMMAR IN CONTEXT

INSTRUCTIONAL STRATEGIES

Activity 4 (continued from previous page)

Project the images and have students present their ideas to the class.

Activity 5

- Make sure students understand that they have to take turns inviting each other to do something next week by asking a question, then answering it.
- Point out that they need to follow the model and use a form of *ir a + infinitive* in their answers.
- Call on different students to practice the **Modelo** with you. Brainstorm different activities to help students get started.

ANSWERS

Activity 4

- Answers will vary and should reflect the model provided and vocabulary taught, along with sentence structures using *ir a + infinitive*. Possible answers provided.
  - Alicia va a la tienda. Después va a ir de excursión.
  - Los amigos van al restaurante. Van a tomar refrescos.
  - El cocinero va a entrar. Va a trabajar.
  - Esteban va al parque. Va a jugar vóleibol.
  - Raúl va a una fiesta. Va a comer pizza con sus amigos.
  - Los estudiantes van en autobús. Van a ir a la escuela.

Activity 5

Answers will vary and should reflect the model provided and expressions taught with *ir a + infinitive*.

SLOWER-PACED LEARNERS

Have students prepare a list of activities first, and check it before they begin to use the verbs for Activity 5.

ADVANCED LEARNERS

Have students expand on Activity 5 by adding in their answers: ***No puedo el lunes porque voy a ir con mi familia, pero puedo el martes. ¿Y tú?***

HERITAGE LANGUAGE LEARNERS

Ask students to complete the schedule in Activity 5 by also adding the time of day for each activity, for instance: ***El lunes a las 10 de la mañana, voy a ir a la biblioteca. El martes a las 5 voy a ir a un partido de béisbol***, etc.

GRAMÁTICA

Alicia — los amigos — el cocinero

Esteban — Raúl — los estudiantes

5 Create a schedule for the activities you are planning to do next week and list them under the correct day. Then, with a partner, take turns inviting each other to join you that day for that activity. ¡Atención! If you have other plans, be sure to tell your partner what you are going to do instead.

Modelo: E1: ¿Quieres estudiar para el examen conmigo el lunes?
E2: No puedo. El lunes voy a cenar con mi familia.

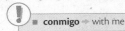 ■ **conmigo** ➞ with me

L	M	X	J	V
E1: Estudiar para el examen. E2: Cenar con mi familia.				

2. HAY QUE, TENER QUE AND DEBER + INFINITIVE

■ To express obligation or what is necessary for all, use **hay que** + infinitive.
*En la clase de español **hay que hablar** español.*
In Spanish class, everyone needs to speak Spanish.
*Cuando hace calor **hay que llevar** ropa ligera.*
When it's hot, it's necessary to wear light clothing.

■ To express obligation or what is necessary for a particular person, use **tener que** + infinitive.
*Para mis exámenes **tengo que** estudiar mucho. I have to study a lot for my tests.*
***Tienes que ser** más paciente. You need to be more patient.*

■ To express obligation in terms of making a recommendation or giving someone advice, use **deber** + infinitive.
*Si estás muy cansado, **debes dormir** más. If you are very tired, you should sleep more.*
*Los estudiantes **deben hacer** la tarea. Students should do homework.*

6 **Fill in the blanks with the correct verb. ¡Atención! There may be more than one possibility.**
   a. Estoy muy ocupado, ... que estudiar mucho.
   b. Si vienes al cumpleaños, ... traer *(bring)* un regalo para Ana.
   c. Me encanta la piscina. Pero, ¿cuánto .... que pagar?
   d. Lo siento, ahora no puedo hablar. .... que ir a casa.

7 **Read the following situations and decide what the people involved have to do and what they shouldn't do. Share your answers with the class. Who made the best recommendations?**

Modelo: Tu hermana necesita un teléfono celular nuevo.
       Tiene que ir a una tienda especializada.
       No debe comprar un teléfono caro.

   a. Tu amigo tiene un examen difícil mañana.
      Él .... No ....
   b. No hay comida en casa.
      Tú .... No ....
   c. Tus abuelos vienen a visitar y la casa está completamente desordenada.
      Todos .... No ....
   d. Vamos de excursión al Gran Cañón del Colorado.
      Nosotros .... No ....

OBJECTIVES FOR GRAMÁTICA 2

• *Hay que, tener que* and *deber* + *infinitive*
  – Express obligation for all or for a particular person
  – Make recommendations

STANDARDS

  1.1 Engage in conversation
  1.2 Understand the language
  1.3 Present information
  4.1 Compare languages

CORE RESOURCES

• Interactive Whiteboard Lesson: IWB 8.1

INSTRUCTIONAL STRATEGIES

HAY QUE, TENER QUE AND DEBER + INFINITIVE

• Remind students of Javi's conversation with his mother and ask them to pull out the sheet they completed. Project IWB 8.1, **Expresar obligación o necesidad y aconsejar** to review and reinforce this concept. Then walk students through the explanations in the book.
• Help them compare these expressions in Spanish with equivalent expressions in English. How are they alike? How are they different?

Activity 6

Students work individually or in pairs.

Activity 7

Review sample sentences with students and ask for other options for the situation. Allow students 10 to 12 minutes to work on these and then present to the class.

ANSWERS

Activity 6

a. tengo; **b.** debes; **c.** tengo / hay; **d.** Tengo.

Activity 7

Answers will vary and should reflect the model provided and expressions taught with **hay que + infinitive, tener que + infinitive**, and **deber + infinitive.**

SLOWER-PACED LEARNERS

Provide extra help with Activity 7 if necessary. Review students' answers or have them work with more advanced learners so they can receive appropriate feedback and support.

ADVANCED LEARNERS

Have students invent new situations for Activity 7. Then collect the papers and redistribute them to different students so they discuss new scenarios.

HERITAGE LANGUAGE LEARNERS

Have students prepare a skit of a situation in which two friends want to do something together, but they have so many things to do that they can't find a time that is convenient for both of them.

GRAMÁTICA GRAMMAR IN CONTEXT

INSTRUCTIONAL STRATEGIES

Activity 8

- Make sure students understand the model and that the answer requires use of **tengo que + infinitive**.
- Observe, provide support, and correct students as needed.

Activity 9

Remind students that the seasons in the northern and southern hemispheres are inverted. They need to take this into consideration when they make their recommendations.

> **Extension**
>
> Ask students to write the season for the following months as it applies to the United States (northern hemisphere) and then how it applies to Chile, Argentina, and Uruguay (southern hemisphere): **1. enero; 2. octubre; 3. agosto; 4. mayo; 5. diciembre.** Model possible answers using the following patterns: **En enero, en Estados Unidos es..., pero en Chile, Argentina y Uruguay es...**

Activity 10

- Make sure students understand that they need to use the grammatical structures taught, namely: **hay que, tener que** and **deber + infinitive**.
- Point out that they are not limited to just eating habits but to think of activities and other aspects that contribute to a healthy lifestyle in young children.
- Provide additional vocabulary as needed.

ANSWERS

Activity 8

Answers will vary and should reflect the model provided and proper use of **tengo que + infinitive**.

Activity 9

Answers will vary and should reflect the model provided and proper use of **deber + infinitive**.

Activity 10

Answers will vary and should reflect the model provided and proper use of **hay que, tener que** and **deber + infinitive**.

SLOWER-PACED LEARNERS

Activities 8, 9 and 10 are open-ended, so students may need extra supervision while working on these exercises. You may want to pair them with more advanced students.

ADVANCED LEARNERS

Have students expand on Activity 10 by adding what will happen if students do not follow the advice on the posters:

– **Si no comen muchas verduras, no van a ser buenos deportistas.**

– **Si beben muchos refrescos, no van a poder correr mucho.**

– **Si no hacen ejercicio, van a tener poca energía.**

GRAMÁTICA

8 🙎🙎 **Indicate the tasks below that you regularly have to do. Then exchange information with a partner and add when you normally do these things.**

- ☐ pasear al perro
- ☐ hacer deporte
- ☐ preparar la comida
- ☐ trabajar
- ☐ hacer la cama

- ☐ ir al supermercado
- ☐ pasar la aspiradora a la habitación
- ☐ lavar (wash) la ropa
- ☐ poner los platos en el lavaplatos
- ☐ ir a clase de…

Modelo:
E1: Tengo que poner los platos en el lavaplatos todos los días. ¿Y tú?
E2: Yo no tengo que poner los platos en el lavaplatos pero tengo que pasar la aspiradora a mi habitación los sábados.

9 🙎🙎 **What recommendations would you make to a group of exchange students from Argentina visiting your region (state, city, etc.)? With a partner, list four or five recommendations of places to visit and things to do. Then share them with the class and vote on the five best ideas.**

Modelo: Ustedes deben ir al museo de arte. Hay cuadros muy famosos.

Lugares	Actividades

10 🙎🙎 As a community service project, you have been asked to prepare a poster for healthy habits to present to elementary school students. With a partner, prepare a list of five or six healthy habits that would apply to everyone. Then share your ideas with the class.

Hay que comer muchas verduras.

11 🐣 **Choose either option A or B and ask your partner for his/her recommendations. Use the expressions below as a guide.**

Modelo:
a. Para ir a la montaña
   El: ¿Qué necesito para ir a la montaña?
   E2: Para ir a la montaña debes llevar botas.

b. Para ir a la playa
   El: ¿Qué necesito para ir a la playa?
   E3: Para ir a la playa tienes que usar protector solar.

| usar protector solar | tomar el sol con precaución | ir en chanclas |

(No) debes...
(No) tienes que...
(No) hay que...

| llevar botas | ponerse gafas de sol | llevar dinero |

| llevar unos bocadillos | llevar una mochila | usar vasos de cristal |

 MORE IN ELETECA: EXTRA ONLINE PRACTICE  GRAMMAR TUTORIALS 15 AND 16   237

INSTRUCTIONAL STRATEGIES

Activity 11

- For this activity, students can choose to use any of the grammatical structures taught. Remind them to pay attention to the correct verb forms. Encourage them to talk about what *not* to do or *not* to take with them.
- Review vocabulary using gestures to make sure students understand.

Extension

Students work in groups to create a class poster titled ***Para hablar bien el español***. Each poster should have three sections labeled ***Obligaciones***, ***Necesidades***, and ***Consejos***. Alternatively, different groups can create posters on different topics, such as: ***Para viajar al extranjero***, ***Para aprobar un examen***, ***Para divertirse***, ***Para conocer a nuevos amigos***, ***Para usar Internet***, ***Para estudiar***. Once posters are completed, students present them to the class, supporting the items they have chosen to include. Students vote for the most original poster.

ANSWERS

Activity 11

Answers will vary and should reflect the model provided and expressions taught. Students should pay special attention to correct verb forms.

SLOWER-PACED LEARNERS

Have students work with more advanced students for the extension project described in Activity 11. Alternatively, have them work on a recipe. You can use the Arepas recipe on page 161. Model the activity as follows: ***Para hacer arepas, tienes que poner una taza y media...***

HERITAGE LANGUAGE LEARNERS

For the extension of Activity 11, have students choose which set of recommendations, suggestions, and needs is the best. Students can decide who will be the winner, those who write the most pieces of advice or those whose ideas are most creative.

OBJECTIVES FOR DESTREZAS

- Written and oral expression
- Organize key ideas before writing

STANDARDS

1.2 · Understand the language

1.3 Present information

INSTRUCTIONAL STRATEGIES

Activity 1

- Make sure students review the **Destrezas** box before they start the activity.
- Remind students that they are to use the images to compose their writing sample and not necessarily their own vacation experiences.
- Encourage students to use vocabulary and expressions from the unit.

Extension

Students can exchange their texts with a partner. They can imagine that the text is something they have read on a travel website and they can then write questions or add comments as you would on a blog. Each partner can then respond to those questions and comments.

ANSWERS

Activity 1

Answers will vary and should reflect the vocabulary and structures about the weather taught in this unit, as well as grammatical structures used to express obligation or suggestions.

Activity 2 (next page)

Answers will vary and should reflect the vocabulary and structures about the weather taught in this unit, as well as grammatical structures used to express obligation or suggestions.

SLOWER-PACED LEARNERS

Have students write each noun with the article so they can use the appropriate agreement with the adjectives. Also, ask students to identify regular and irregular verbs so they keep that in mind when writing their paragraphs.

ADVANCED LEARNERS

Have students exchange their paragraphs after they finish Activity 2 on page 239. Ask them to compare their vacations and write a new paragraph with the similarities and differences they found.

DESTREZAS

EXPRESIÓN E INTERACCIÓN ESCRITAS

1 Below are a series of photos from the place you vacation each summer and where you are going to go again this summer. Before writing about your plans, review the writing strategy in Destrezas and follow the suggestion.

Destrezas

Organize key ideas before writing

List the words and phrases that you will need to write your description. Once you see your ideas laid out, you can start to organize them for your writing. Jot down some of these ideas under each of the photos.

238

2 Using the information you prepared, write a paragraph about your vacation destination. Use the suggestions below as a guide.

- Cómo es el tiempo normalmente en ese lugar.
- Cómo es la ciudad.
- Con quién vas.
- Qué haces allí normalmente.
- Qué vas a hacer este verano allí.

PRONUNCIACIÓN The sounds *n* and *ñ*

- The letter **n** in Spanish generally sounds like the *n* in the English word *nice*.
  - **n**atación • **n**aranja • ca**n**sado • exame**n** • **n**unca

- The letter **ñ** does not exist in English. Its sound in Spanish is similar to *ny* in the English word *canyon*.
  - ca**ñ**ón • se**ñ**ora • ni**ñ**o • ba**ñ**o • a**ñ**o

El cañón de Cotahuasi en Perú

1 🎧 83 Number the words below in the order you hear them. Listen to the difference in pronunciation between *n* and *ñ*.

- ☐ peña
- ☐ mano
- ☐ maño
- ☐ caña
- ☐ cana
- ☐ Miño
- ☐ mino
- ☐ pena

2 🎧 84 Listen to each pair of words and write in the missing consonant. ¡Atención! Listen carefully as one of the words in the pair will contain *ñ* and the other can be any consonant.

- **a.** ni...o / ni...o
- **b.** Espa...a / espa...a
- **c.** ca...o / ca...o
- **d.** mo...o / mo...o
- **e.** u...a / hu...a
- **f.** ba...a / ba...a

MORE IN ELETECA: EXTRA ONLINE PRACTICE

239

OBJECTIVES FOR PRONUNCIACIÓN

- Practice correct pronunciation: /n/ and /ñ/

CORE RESOURCES

- Audio Program: 83, 84
- Interactive Online Materials - ELEteca

STANDARDS

1.2 Understand the language
4.1 Compare languages

INSTRUCTIONAL STRATEGIES

Walk students through the explanations on this page for proper pronunciation of /n/ and /ñ/ in Spanish.

🎧 83 Activity 1

- Walk students through the explanation and samples in the book.
- Encourage students to compare the words with **n** and those with **ñ**. Can they draw any conclusions or general rules about these two sounds? Help students realize that **n** can occur anywhere in the word: beginning, middle, or end. However, in all the examples provided, **ñ** occurs only in the medial position and between vowels. Point out that only a few words in Spanish start with **ñ**, such as: **ñandú**, **ñoño**, **ñame** and that this sound never appears in the final position in Spanish. Tell students not to worry about the meaning of these words; although they are all words in Spanish, they are infrequent and are only used in this activity to distinguish between the sounds of /n/ and /ñ/.

Audioscript

Miño; caña; mano; pena; maño; mino; peña; cana.

🎧 84 Activity 2

You may want to point out to students that this activity compares and contrasts /n/ and /ñ/ in the medial position, that is, in the middle of a word, and between vowels, since this is the only environment that is shared by these two sounds in Spanish, where either sound can occur. After correcting the activity, explain the meaning of the words.

Audioscript

a. niño / nicho; **b.** España / espada; **c.** callo / caño; **c.** moño / mocho; **d.** uña / hucha; **e.** baña / baya.

ANSWERS

Activity 1

1. Miño; **2.** caña; **3.** mano; **4.** pena; **5.** maño; **6.** mino; **7.** peña; **8.** cana.

Activity 2

a. niño / nicho; **b.** España / espada; **c.** callo / caño; **c.** moño / mocho; **d.** uña / hucha; **e.** baña / baya.

HERITAGE LANGUAGE LEARNERS

Have students read this article about the **ñ** and report back on what they understood and any new or interesting information that they learned: http://www.donquijote.org/cultura/espana/lenguajes/la-letra-n-en-espanol.

OBJECTIVES FOR SABOR HISPANO

- Learn about Paraguay, Uruguay, Argentina, Chile
- Learn about extreme climates in South America
- Compare climate in South America with climate in the U.S.

CORE RESOURCES

- Audio Program: 85

STANDARDS

1.2	Understand the language
2.1	Practices and perspectives
2.2	Products and perspectives
3.2	Acquire information
4.1	Compare cultures
5.2	Using language for personal enjoyment and enrichment

INSTRUCTIONAL STRATEGIES

- Introduce the topic by asking students what they know about these South American countries: Paraguay, Uruguay, Argentina, and Chile.
- Talk about the images and the map. Elicit what students already know about the southern tip of South America and its climate.
- Read the captions together and ask questions to check comprehension. Explain that Punta del Este in Uruguay, in addition to being a popular tourist destination, is also a cultural center, boasting the Universidad de Verano in Pueblo Blanco and the house of artist Carlos Páez Vilaró, which includes a museum, an art gallery, and the Hotel Casapueblo. Las cataratas del Iguazú, while predominantly between Brazil and Argentina, at the junction of the Paraná and Iguazú rivers, mark the border between Brazil, Argentina, and Paraguay. Another popular tourist destination is the Perito Moreno glacier located in Los Glaciares National Park, due to its size and accessibility. It includes a walking circuit that allows views of both faces and surface views of the glacier. Its icefield is the worlds' third largest reserve of fresh water.
- Share with students what you know about this topic.

CULTURAL NOTE

Argentina

- Argentina is the second biggest country in South America and the eighth in the world. The highest mountain in Los Andes and in all America (6959 meters) is the Aconcagua, which is in the province of Mendoza.
- Most of the population in Argentina is concentrated in big cities, such as Buenos Aires, Córdoba, Rosario, and Mendoza. The national dance, el Tango, was declared Intangible Cultural Heritage by the UNESCO.

Chile

- There are many different theories about the origin of the country's name. Some claim that it was the name of the Aconcagua Valley; others refer to the Mapuche word **chilli**, which may mean "where the land ends". Chile was colonized by the Spaniards, but they were never able to conquer a vast land ruled by the Mapuche.
- Chile has many natural resources, including copper, coal, iron, and nitrates. One of the most intriguing places in Chile is Easter Island (**Isla de Pascua**), which is located 3760 km away from Santiago, the capital of Chile.

Paraguay

- Paraguay achieved its independence from Spain in 1811. In the disastrous War of the Triple Alliance (1865-70) –between Paraguay and Argentina, Brazil, and Uruguay– Paraguay lost two-thirds of its

adult males and much of its territory. The country stagnated economically for the next half century. Following the Chaco War of 1932-35 with Bolivia, Paraguay gained a large part of the Chaco lowland region.
- Paraguay has a stable democracy nowadays and is a land of harsh contrasts. It has two official languages Spanish and guaraní.

Uruguay

- The Eastern Republic of Uruguay is, after Suriname, the smallest country in South America. Its capital, Montevideo, is separated from Buenos Aires by the **Río de la Plata** estuary. By ferry, it takes 2 and a half hours to go from one capital to the other.
- Uruguay is an important global exporter of wool, rice, soybeans, beef, malt, and milk. Its beaches attract many tourists from Argentina. The Historic Quarter of the City of Colonia de Sacramento is a UNESCO World Heritage Site.

Image content (Sabor Hispano feature)

SABOR HISPANO

PAISAJES Y CLIMAS EXTREMOS

¡Descubre conmigo el Cono Sur!

Paraguay • Asunción
Chile
Santiago de Chile
Uruguay
Buenos Aires • Montevideo
Argentina

El Cono Sur

Las Catedrales de Roca, en Salar de Tara, Chile

✓ Los países hispanohablantes que forman el Cono Sur (Southern Cone) son: Paraguay, Argentina, Chile y Uruguay.

✓ Estos países ofrecen una naturaleza increíble, desde el desierto más árido del mundo, hasta la cordillera (mountain range) más alta del hemisferio sur, pasando por los glaciares más activos del planeta.

✓ El idioma oficial es el español, pero también se hablan dialectos o lenguas indígenas como el guaraní (en Paraguay y Argentina), el español rioplatense (en Uruguay y Argentina), el quichua (en Argentina) o la lengua mapuche (en Chile).

Glaciar Perito Moreno en Patagonia, Argentina

Pueblo Blanco en Punta del Este, Uruguay

Las cataratas del Iguazú, entre Paraguay, Brasil y Argentina

¿Sabes que...?

✓ El Cono Sur experimenta todos los climas posibles, desde el tropical hasta el frío más extremo y la nieve.

✓ Los paisajes del Cono Sur son los más diversos del mundo. Aquí hay glaciares, desiertos, selvas (jungles), montañas, cordilleras y playas.

✓ Paraguay tiene unas de las más altas temperaturas del planeta 45 °C (113 °F). Algunos puntos de Chile alcanzan (reach) los -37 °C (-35 °F).

240

PARAGUAY, URUGUAY, ARGENTINA Y CHILE

🎧 85 Estaciones del sur

El Cono Sur tiene estaciones muy marcadas. Sin embargo (however), en diciembre, enero y febrero hace calor y en junio, julio y agosto hace frío. ¿Por qué? Porque los países que forman el Cono Sur pertenecen al hemisferio sur. Esto significa que mientras en la mayor parte de EE.UU. las temperaturas son bajas en diciembre, enero y febrero, en Argentina, por ejemplo, son altas. Por eso en este territorio geográfico... ¡hay que celebrar la Navidad en la playa y hay que llevar abrigos (coats) en agosto!

Árbol de Navidad en la Casa Rosada, Buenos Aires, Argentina

¡Sandboarding en el desierto de Atacama!

«¡Hola! Me llamo Luca y soy de Buenos Aires, Argentina. La semana próxima voy a ir de viaje con mis amigos Suso, Chico y David. Vamos a ir al desierto de Atacama, en Chile. Este desierto es el lugar más seco (dry) del planeta. ¿Qué vamos a hacer allí? ¡Vamos a vivir una aventura extraordinaria! Vamos a practicar el deporte de moda en ese país: el sandboarding. Es como el snowboarding pero se practica en la arena (sand), no en la nieve».

Un chico practica el sandboarding en el desierto de Atacama, Chile.

Fuentes: Oficina de Turismo de Ushuaia, Oficina de Turismo de Argentina, The Lonely Planet, Turismo Paraguay, Españoles en el Mundo (RTVE).

Ushuaia: el fin del mundo

❖ Ushuaia, en Tierra del Fuego, Argentina, es la ciudad más al sur del mundo.
❖ Esta ciudad es conocida como el fin del mundo, por su localización, en el extremo sur del continente americano.
❖ En Ushuaia hay ríos, lagos y glaciares.
❖ Aquí nieva mucho y las temperaturas son frías durante todo el año, con una temperatura media de 5,7 °C (42 °F).
❖ Cuando visitas este lugar, recibes un sello en tu pasaporte donde pone... ¡fin del mundo!

Un letrero anunciador de Ushuaia

USHUAIA fin del mundo

Link the two parts of the sentence.

1 En el Cono Sur — a muy extremas.
2 El idioma oficial de esta región — b hay cuatro países.
3 Hay temperaturas — c deportes extremos.
4 En el Cono Sur se practican — d es el español.
5 Los paisajes del Cono Sur — e son muy variados.

VOCES LATINAS ▶ NATURALEZA EXTREMA EN EL CONO SUR

Fill in the blank with the correct information from the readings. Then complete the sentences to describe how it is where you live.

1 En Ushuaia, las temperaturas son _____ durante todo el año.
En mi ciudad _____
2 En el desierto de Atacama hace mucho _____. En mi país _____
3 En Argentina, durante el verano hace _____. En mi país _____

241

INSTRUCTIONAL STRATEGIES

🎧 85

- Vary between silent reading, reading aloud, and playing the audio.
- Identify and explain any vocabulary from the reading students may find difficult to understand.
- **Estaciones del sur**

Elicit what they know about the landscape and climate in the southern tip of South America. Before reading, ask: *¿En qué meses tienen los estudiantes argentinos sus vacaciones de verano? (diciembre, enero). ¿En qué meses debes usar anorak y gorro en Buenos Aires, Argentina? (julio y agosto). Si quieres celebrar el año nuevo allí, ¿qué ropa tienes que llevar? (camisetas, pantalón corto, chanclas, etc.).*
- **Ushuaia**

Help students pronounce this word as follows: /Oos-"why"-a/. Point out to students that Ushuaia is the capital of the province of Tierra del Fuego, Antártida, and Islas del Antártico Sur.
- **El desierto de Atacama**

Explain to students that this desert extends from Peru's southern border into northern Chile and is the driest place on earth. Some parts have never seen any rain according to records.
- Encourage students to describe what they see in the photographs.
- Have students complete the activities on this page and compare their answers with others.

ANSWERS

Link the two parts of the sentence.
1. b; **2.** d; **3.** a; **4.** c; **5.** e.

Fill in the blanks
1. frías; **2.** calor; **3.** frío.

SLOWER-PACED LEARNERS

Find and show video clips of people sandboarding in the Atacama desert. (There are several available on YouTube). After watching the video(s), have students discuss or write responses to these questions: *¿Qué opinas de sandboarding? ¿Cómo es? ¿Quieres hacerlo? ¿Por qué sí o no? ¿Cómo es el desierto de Atacama? ¿Quieres visitarlo? ¿Por qué sí o no?*

ADVANCED LEARNERS

Have students choose one of the images and use its caption to help them find more information online about it. They should find two more pictures and three more facts about it to present to the class

HERITAGE LANGUAGE LEARNERS

Have students pick one of the cultural topics presented here or another topic that interests them and is related to one of these four countries. Have them use a software presentation tool to prepare and give a presentation about it to the class. Challenge them to include at least five slides in their presentations and be able to talk about their topic for five minutes. Remind them to use visuals and encourage them to embed audio or video clips that might make their presentations more dynamic.

OBJECTIVES FOR RELATO

- Revisit unit themes, grammar, vocabulary, and culture in a new context
- Improve reading comprehension skills

CORE RESOURCES

- Audio Program: 86

STANDARDS

1.1   Engage in conversation
1.2   Understand the language
1.3   Present information
2.1   Practices and perspectives

INSTRUCTIONAL STRATEGIES

Activity 1

As a warm-up, ask students what types of activities they do over the weekend and what types of obligations they have throughout the week. They can express and organize their ideas using the following prompts, which you can write on the board: *Este fin de semana voy a _____, _____ y _____, pero también tengo que _____, _____ y _____.* Encourage students to complete these statements on their own, then share answers with the rest of the class. A possible answer is: *Este fin de semana voy a escuchar música, ir al cine y practicar deporte, pero también tengo que ir a la biblioteca, ir a clases particulares y estudiar.*

🎧 86 Activity 2

- As a motivational activity before students read the text, ask them if they believe the question *¿Quedamos para estudiar?* is used by some speakers of Spanish to refer to a plan, an obligation or both. Explain that the expression *quedar para + infinitive* has been introduced in previous units.
- Help them understand that a common variant to this expression is *Quedamos en vernos para...* or *Quedamos en reunirnos para...* Explain also the meaning of the verb *quedar* to mean "remain" or "stay", as in: *No voy a la escuela hoy. Me quedo en casa.*
- If necessary, write the following on the board to clarify how these various expressions are taught in this unit:

  Quedar(se) en un lugar = To remain at or stay in a place.

  Quedar con alguien = To agree to meet someone.

  Quedar para + infinitive = To agree to do something.

- Prior to reading the text, suggest that students read the statements in Activity 3 to help them read with a purpose.

ANSWERS

Activity 1

Answers will vary and should reflect the model provided and expressions taught about daily and weekly activities.

Activity 2

Students will read the text and listen to the audio.

ADVANCED LEARNERS

As a follow-up to Activity 1, conduct a class mingling activity in which students go around the room asking and answering questions of each other to find people who have the same weekend plans as them. Set a time limit and create a competition to see who can find the most people with similar plans during that time.

RELATO ¿Quedamos para estudiar?

1 👥 In groups of three, take turns talking about which of the following activities do you normally do on weekends.

Modelo:
E1: Normalmente escucho música los fines de semana, ¿y tú?
E2: Yo, también.
E3: Yo, no. Normalmente practico deporte.

> Use **también** and **tampoco** to agree with what a person says.
> Use **sí** and **no** to disagree with what a person says.

a. escuchar música   d. ir a la biblioteca
b. practicar deporte   e. ir a clase
c. ir al cine   f. estudiar

2 🎧 86 Read about Marta, Luisa and Cristina and what they typically do on weekends.

¿Quedamos para estudiar?

Son las cinco de la tarde y, como todos los viernes, Marta, Luisa y Cristina quedan en el parque para planear el finde. Pero esta vez va a ser diferente. Las muchachas no tienen mucho tiempo para salir a divertirse, porque la próxima semana tienen que hacer tres exámenes. La idea es reunirse para estudiar. Sin embargo, las jóvenes no se ponen de acuerdo, porque Cristina y Luisa tienen algunas cosas que hacer. La madre de Cristina trabaja este sábado y la muchacha tiene que cuidar a su hermano pequeño, porque la guardería está cerrada. Por su parte, Luisa va a ir al dentista y después va a acompañar a sus padres al supermercado. Marta es la única que tiene la mañana libre, pero quiere esperar a sus amigas porque le gusta estudiar mucho en equipo. Además, a Marta le encantan las Matemáticas y prefiere ayudar a sus compañeras. Así que las tres muchachas van a intentar verse el sábado por la tarde en la biblioteca del barrio. Si todo va bien, el domingo van a tener tiempo para salir, después de una tarde de trabajo en equipo. ¡La unión hace la fuerza!

242

3 Decide if the following sentences are true (T) or false (F) based on the reading.

	T	F
a. Las muchachas van a estudiar el sábado por la mañana.	☐	☐
b. Marta va a ir al dentista con Luisa.	☐	☐
c. Marta tiene más tiempo libre que Luisa y Cristina.	☐	☐
d. Cristina tiene que llevar a su hermano a la guardería.	☐	☐
e. A Marta no le gustan las Matemáticas.	☐	☐
f. Las muchachas van a estudiar juntas.	☐	☐

4 Complete the chart with the things Marta, Luisa and Cristina have to do.

	Marta	Luisa	Cristina
El sábado por la mañana.	No tiene nada que hacer.		
El sábado por la tarde.			

5 Select the correct completion.

a. Las muchachas son muy...
   ○ responsables.　○ vagas.

b. Las muchachas tienen muchas...
   ○ tareas.　○ obligaciones.

c. A Marta le gustan mucho...
   ○ las Matemáticas.　○ los estudios.

d. La madre de Cristina tiene que...
   ○ trabajar.　○ cuidar al hermano pequeño.

e. Las muchachas van a tener tiempo para salir...
   ○ el domingo.　○ el sábado.

f. Ahora ellas están en...
   ○ el parque.　○ la biblioteca.

6 Write about your own weekend. Make a list of your plans and another list of the things you have to do. Share your lists with the class to see who has the most free time.

Planes

Obligaciones

INSTRUCTIONAL STRATEGIES

Activity 3
Students complete individually or in pairs.

Activity 4
Remind students to use full sentences and employ the target structures to express plans and obligations from the unit.

Activity 5
Ask students to explain their answers. Provide the following sentence stems to help students make statements that will explain their answers: **Las muchachas son muy responsables porque...**, **Las muchachas tienen muchas obligaciones como...**, and **A Marta le gustan mucho las Matemáticas y por eso...**

Activity 6
· Ask students to complete the chart individually, thinking about their own plans and obligations.
· Then, in order to encourage oral interaction, have students work in pairs to share what they have written. As a next step, have pairs of students talk to other pairs of students and share what they have learned from each other. At the end, invite students to draw conclusions about who has the most free time, who has the least plans and obligations.

ANSWERS

Activity 3
a. F (El sábado por la tarde); **b.** F (Es Luisa la que tiene que ir al dentista); **c.** T; **d.** F (La guardería está cerrada); **e.** F (Le encantan); **f.** T.

Activity 4
El sábado por la mañana: Marta. No tiene nada que hacer; **Luisa.** Tiene que ir al dentista. Tiene que acompañar a sus padres al supermercado; **Cristina.** Tiene que cuidar de su hermano.
El sábado por la tarde: Las tres. Tienen que estudiar y tienen que quedar con sus amiga.

Activity 5
a. responsables; **b.** obligaciones; **c.** las Matemáticas; **d.** trabajar; **e.** el domingo; **f.** el parque.

Activity 6
Answers will vary and should reflect the expressions and vocabulary about activities and obligations taught in this unit.

SLOWER-PACED LEARNERS
Ask students to correct the false statements in Activity 3 in writing before going over the answers with the class. Tell them to use full sentences.

HERITAGE LANGUAGE LEARNERS
Have students volunteer to ask their classmates questions based on Activity 6. For instance, **¿Quién tiene que hacer tarea el sábado? ¿Quién va a ir al cine el domingo? ¿Quién tiene que ayudar a su mamá el fin de semana?** You can model first by asking a few students a series of *yes/no* questions: **¿Tienes que lavar el carro de tu papá el domingo? ¿Tienes que estudiar español? ¿Vas a salir con tus amigos? ¿Vas a ir al cine?**

OBJECTIVES FOR EVALUACIÓN

- Review grammar, vocabulary and culture from the unit
- Complete self-assessment

CORE RESOURCES

- Interactive Online Materials - ELEteca

STANDARDS

1.2	Understand the language
2.1	Practices and perspectives
4.1	Compare cultures

INSTRUCTIONAL STRATEGIES

- Activities can be completed individually and then reviewed with the class.
- Expand by asking students if they agree with the answers given and then writing the correct answer on the board.
- You may wish to assign point values to each activity as a way for student to monitor their progress.
- If students achieve less than 80% on each activity, direct them to **En resumen** for page numbers to review.

ANSWERS

Activity 1

a. Hace; **b.** hace / tengo; **c.** hay; **d.** Está; **e.** Estamos.

Activity 2

a. hay nieve, hace frío; **b.** llueve; **c.** hace, hace viento; **d.** está nublado; **e.** hace calor; **f.** hacer, viento.

Activity 3

a. tiene; **b.** tiene; **c.** debe; **d.** debe; **e.** tiene; **f.** tiene.

EVALUACIÓN

TALKING ABOUT THE WEATHER

1 Fill in the blanks with the missing words.

a. ¿ .... calor en esta ciudad?
b. ¿Y mi jersey? ¡Qué frío .... !
c. En verano a veces .... tormentas.
d. .... nublado y no se ve nada.
e. .... a 25 grados.

2 Look at the weather map of Spain and describe the weather in each of the regions.

🌧	lluvia
🌨	nieve
💨	viento
⛈	tormenta
☁	nublado
☀	calor
❄	frío

a. En Galicia 🌧 .... y también ❄ ....
b. En el País Vasco hoy ☁ ....
c. En Cataluña .... buen tiempo pero 💨 ....
d. En Castilla y León el cielo ☁ ....
e. En Extremadura y Andalucía ☀ ....
f. En Murcia hoy va a .... un poco de 💨 ....

HAY QUE, TENER QUE, DEBER + INFINITIVE

3 Enrique needs to clean up his act. Look at the list of things he currently does that he needs to improve. Complete the sentences with what Enrique should do and has to do.

a. No estudia mucho. ➡ Enrique .... que estudiar más.
b. Llega siempre tarde al colegio. ➡ Al colegio .... que llegar puntual.
c. Nunca ordena su habitación. ➡ Enrique .... ordenar su habitación.
d. Nunca hace la tarea. ➡ Enrique .... hacer la tarea.
e. Habla mal a su hermana. ➡ No .... que hablar mal a su hermana.
f. No hace deporte. ➡ .... que hacer deporte.

IR A + INFINITIVE

4 **Answer the questions with the correct form of *ir a* + infinitive.**

Modelo:

¿Qué vas a hacer el próximo mes? Voy a ir a la ciudad con mis padres.

a. ¿Qué vas a hacer esta tarde?
➡ .... estudiar con Andrés.

b. ¿Qué va a hacer la madre de Javi mañana?
➡ .... ir al dentista.

c. ¿Qué película van a ver ustedes esta noche?
➡ .... ver una película en casa.

d. ¿Qué vamos a hacer ahora?
➡ .... leer un texto.

e. ¿Dónde vas a comer el sábado?
➡ .... comer en un restaurante mexicano.

5 **Write sentences about what you are going to do this weekend. Use the cues in parenthesis.**

a. (correr / parque) ➡ ....

b. (jugar / fútbol) ➡ ....

c. (visitar / abuelos) ➡ ....

d. (hacer / tarea) ➡ ....

e. (ir de excursión / con la clase) ➡ ....

f. (lavar el carro / padre) ➡ ....

CULTURA

6 **Answer the following questions about Chile, Paraguay, Argentina and Uruguay and compare similarities with your own country or region.**

a. ¿Qué tipo de paisajes *(landscapes)* hay en el Cono Sur? ¿Y en tu región?

b. ¿Qué país tiene una de las más altas temperaturas? ¿Cuál es la temperatura en Fahrenheit? ¿Cuál es la temperatura más alta en tu ciudad?

c. ¿Qué deporte está de moda *(is in)* y dónde lo practican? ¿Existe este deporte en Estados Unidos?

d. ¿Por qué ponen "el fin del mundo" en los pasaportes de los turistas que visitan Ushuaia?

e. ¿Qué tiempo hace en el Cono Sur los meses de enero y febrero? ¿Y en tu región?

f. ¿Qué cataratas famosas hay en esta zona? ¿Qué cataratas hay en tu país?

 **MORE IN ELETECA:** EXTRA ONLINE PRACTICE

245

ANSWERS

Activity 4

   a. Van a / Vamos a; **b.** Va a; **c.** Vamos a; **d.** Vamos a / Van a; **e.** Voy a.

Activity 5

   a. Voy a correr por el parque; **b.** Voy a jugar fútbol; **c.** Voy a visitar a mis abuelos; **d.** Voy a hacer la tarea; **e.** Voy a ir de excursión con la clase; **f.** Voy a lavar el carro de mi padre. / Voy a lavar el carro con mi padre.

Activity 6

   a. Hay glaciares, desiertos, selvas, montañas, playas, etc; **b.** Chile, 113° F; **c.** el *sandboarding* en el desierto de Atacama en Chile; **d.** Porque está en el extremo sur del continente americano; **e.** Hace calor; **f.** Las cataratas de Iguazú.

OBJECTIVES FOR EN RESUMEN: VOCABULARIO

- Review unit vocabulary and expressions
- Practice communicative skills

STANDARDS

- 1.2 Understand the language
- 1.3 Present information

INSTRUCTIONAL STRATEGIES

- Model how to use the vocabulary list to review new words and expressions learned in this unit.
- Use simple materials, such as index cards or self-adhesive notes.
- Self-adhesive notes can be used for writing nouns from the vocabulary list on them, then using them to place the correct labels on objects in the classroom or pictures in the book.
- Index cards can be used as flash cards with the Spanish term on one side and the English term on the other, or a picture or drawing.
- Students can work in pairs or groups, using the self-adhesive notes and index cards as they would the cards of a board game to help each other practice the unit vocabulary.
- Encourage students to write labels or captions for the photos on this page. Remind them to use the vocabulary and expressions they have learned in this unit.
- Working with a partner, have students write a weather report in which a meteorologist talks about the upcoming weather in three very different places. Tell them add recommendations or suggestions that the meteorologist might make to people at home watching / listening to the report. If possible, have students make videos of their weather reports using maps and other props, and allow them to share their videos with the class.

EN RESUMEN: Vocabulario

Verbos *Verbs*
deber *should / must*
decir *to say*

ir de excursión *to go on an excursion or an outing*
lavar *to wash*

llevar *to take, to carry, to wear*
pagar *to pay*
traer *to bring*
venir *to come*

El tiempo atmosférico
The weather
bajo cero *below zero*
está nublado *it is cloudy*

los grados *degrees*
hace buen tiempo *the weather is nice*
hace calor *it is hot*
hace frío *it is cold*
hace mal tiempo *the weather is bad*
hace sol *it is sunny*
hace viento *it is windy*
el hielo *ice*

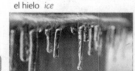

llueve (llover o>ue) *it is raining*
la lluvia *rain*
la niebla *fog*
nieva *it is snowing*
la nieve *snow*
el relámpago *lightning*
la temperatura *temperature*

la tormenta *storm*
el trueno *thunder*

Las estaciones del año
Seasons of the year

el invierno *winter*
el otoño *autumn or fall*
la primavera *spring*
el verano *summer*

Descripciones *Descriptions*
caluroso/a *hot*
inestable *unstable*
ocupado/a *busy*

Expresiones temporales
Expressions of time
ahora *now*
hoy *today*
mañana *tomorrow, morning*
próximo/a *next*
que viene *upcoming, next*

La ropa *Clothes*
el anorak *ski jacket*
las chanclas *flip flops*
las gafas de sol *sunglasses*

el gorro *knitted hat*
los guantes *gloves*
el impermeable *raincoat*
el paraguas *umbrella*

Palabras y expresiones útiles
Useful words and expressions
¡Cuánto llueve! *It's really raining!*
Hace mucho frío / calor. *It's very cold / hot.*

Estamos a 20 grados. *It's 20 degrees.*
Hace muchísimo frío / calor. *It's really very cold / hot.*
Hace un día muy bueno / malo. *It's a nice / bad day.*
No hace nada de frío / calor. *It's not at all cold / hot.*
¡Qué frío hace! *It's so cold!*
¡Qué calor! *It's so hot!*
¡Qué frío / calor tengo! *I'm so cold / hot!*
¿Qué día / tiempo hace? *What's the day / weather like?*
¿Tienes frío / calor? *Are you cold / hot?*

246

EN RESUMEN: Gramática

TALKING ABOUT FUTURE PLANS AND HAPPENINGS

(See page 232)

ir a + infinitive	Saying what you and others are going to do	**Voy a ir** al cine con mis amigos.
	Describing what is going to happen	Hay nubes en el cielo, **va a llover.**
	With time expressions	Esta tarde **voy a jugar** al tenis.

EXPRESSING OBLIGATION

(See page 235)

hay que + infinitive	**tener que** + infinitive	**deber que** + infinitive
To express obligation or what is necessary for all	To express obligation or a need for a particular person	To express obligation in terms of making a recommendation or giving advice
Hay que hacer la tarea.	**Tengo que** estudiar mucho para ciencias.	Si tienes hambre, **debes comer** algo.

Irregular verbs: *decir, traer, venir*

DECIR *(to say)*	TRAER *(to bring)*	VENIR *(to come)*
digo	**traigo**	**vengo**
dices	traes	vienes
dice	trae	viene
decimos	traemos	venimos
decís	traéis	venís
dicen	traen	vienen

La mamá de Olga **dice** que va a llover. *Olga's mom says it's going to rain.*

¿**Traes** un regalo para Ana? *Are you bringing a present for Ana?*

Mis amigos **vienen** a mi casa para estudiar. *My friends are coming to my house to study.*

El verano que **viene** vamos a ir a Madrid. *This summer coming up (next summer), we are going to go to Madrid.*

247

OBJECTIVES FOR EN RESUMEN: GRAMÁTICA

- Review unit grammar
- Practice communicative skills

STANDARDS

1.2 Understand the language

1.3 Present information

INSTRUCTIONAL STRATEGIES

- Model how to review grammar.
- Ask them if they can remember additional examples for each grammar topic.
- Model how to find and go back to the appropriate page in the unit to review any grammar topic they may need help with.
- Invite students to review the grammar activities they completed in this unit.
- Ask them what grammar activities they found easy and which they found challenging. Encourage them to repeat any activities they found particularly challenging.
- Create groups of students with mixed abilities (some who have mastered the unit grammar, and some who have not), and have them review and practice the grammar activities with each other.
- Encourage students to take the online test in ELEteca to determine which aspects of the unit they need to study and review the most.

OBJECTIVES FOR AHORA COMPRUEBA

- Review grammar, vocabulary and culture from the last two units
- Complete self-assessment

CORE RESOURCES

- Audio Program: 87

STANDARDS

1.2	Understand the language
1.3	Present information
2.1	Practices and perspectives
4.1	Compare cultures

INSTRUCTIONAL STRATEGIES

- Activities can be completed individually or in pairs and then reviewed with the class.
- When reviewing answers in class, expand by asking students if they agree with the answers given and then writing the correct answer on the board.
- You may wish to assign point values to each activity as a way for student to monitor their progress. If students achieve less than 80% on each activity, direct them to **En resumen** in the previous two units for page numbers to review.

🎧 87 Activity 1

- Prior to the activity, review orally the rooms of a house and the furniture for each room. Point out that **habitación** is used both as a general term for room, as well as a specific term for bedroom, similar to the uses of English *room*.
- Tell students that they will hear three people talk about their homes. Then have them read all the questions and compare answers with a partner.

Extension

To review direct object pronouns, project the transcript for the audio and ask students to underline them and state what noun they refer to. See the Audioscript on page APP2.

Activity 2

Start with a description of the images. Ask students to look closely at the characteristics of all the objects in them.

Activity 3

Before comparing the rooms, encourage students to reflect on the use of the comparative forms in the various grammatical structures. Write on the board what those structures are or simply project page 201 of the student book, "Comparing People and Things."

ANSWERS (next page)

Activity 1

Isabel: a. De su dormitorio; **b.** Porque allí están todas sus cosas; **c.** Porque es muy pequeño y no sirve para poner su computadora.
Sara: a. En el salón de la casa de su abuela; **b.** Porque tiene muchos muebles antiguos y muchos objetos de decoración muy delicados; **c.** Para comer en verano.

---

1 🎧 87 Listen to the following people talk about their homes. Then answer the following questions.

Isabel
a. ¿De qué parte de la casa habla Isabel?
b. ¿Por qué le gusta mucho?
c. ¿Por qué quiere cambiar su escritorio?

Sara
a. ¿Dónde está Sara?
b. ¿Por qué le encanta ese lugar?
c. ¿Para qué usan la mesa de la terraza?

Javi
a. ¿Qué piensan los padres del escritorio de Javi?
b. ¿Qué hace Javi todas las mañanas?
c. ¿Qué va a hacer Javi para tener más espacio?

2 Look at Sara's and Javier's living rooms and label in Spanish all the items you recognize.

Salón de Sara

Salón de Javier

3 Compare Sara's and Javier's living rooms by completing the sentences. Use the cues in parenthesis.
a. El salón de Sara es (grande)..
b. El salón de Javier es (moderno)..
c. Las plantas de Sara son (pequeñas) ....
d. En el salón de Javier hay (cuadros)..................................
e. El teléfono de Javier es (antiguo)......................................
f. El sofá de Sara es (cómodo) ....

SLOWER-PACED LEARNERS

Have students make a list of the learning objectives noted in the opening spreads of the two previous units. Tell them to ask themselves: *How well can I do this: very well, well, or not well?* Then pair students who can't do an objective well with another student who can; that way, they can teach each other what they know and help each other review.

4 Fill in the blanks with *ir a* + infinitive.

a. Mi madre (ir) .... a Londres la próxima semana.
b. Mi hermana y yo la (llamar) .... todos los días.
c. Mis padres (comprar) .... una televisión nueva.
d. Juan, ¿qué (hacer) .... este fin de semana?
e. Ustedes viajan mucho. ¿Dónde (viajar) .... este verano?
f. Este sábado Lucía y Marta (estudiar) .... a la biblioteca.

5 Fill in the blanks with the number of the correct expression.

1. tienes que	2. hay que	3. debes

a. Si quieres estar sano, ...3...... tener una dieta equilibrada.
b. Para aprobar todas las asignaturas .... estudiar día a día.
c. Para escribir bien .... leer mucho.
d. .... ver poco la televisión.
e. En los viajes, ... comer lo que come la gente del país al que vas.
f. Si no quieres resfriarte, ... llevar ropa de abrigo.

6 🎧 **88** Listen to the following description and select the appropriate recommendation.

Cantabria

Ávila

Andalucía

• a. Si vas a viajar al norte de España, tienes que llevar un paraguas. Si visitas esa zona, debes visitar sus montañas; son preciosas.

• b. Si vas a viajar al sur de España, tienes que usar un protector solar y llevar ropa de verano.

• c. Si vas a viajar allí este fin de semana, tienes que conducir con precaución y debes llevar ropa para el frío.

7 Write the advice you would give the following people based on what they tell you.

a. Mi habitación está muy desordenada. ....

c. Voy a esquiar. ....

b. No hago mi tarea. ....

d. Esta semana tengo cuatro exámenes. ....

249

Javi: a. Que siempre está muy desordenado; **b.** Ordena su escritorio; **c.** Le va a regalar a su hermana los videojuegos y va a guardar todos los CD en una caja de plástico.

Activity 2

Answers will vary and should reflect the vocabulary and grammatical structures similar to what they heard in the audio.

Activity 3

a. El salón de Sara es más grande que el (salón) de Javi; **b.** El salón de Javi es menos moderno que el (salón) de Sara; **c.** Las plantas de Sara son más pequeñas que las (plantas) de Javi; **d.** En el salón de Javi hay menos cuadros que en el (salón) de Sara; **e.** El teléfono de Javi es más antiguo que el (teléfono) de Sara; **f.** El sofá de Sara es más cómodo que el (sofá) de Javi.

INSTRUCTIONAL STRATEGIES

Activity 4

Write *ir a* + *infinitive* on the board and remind students of when it is used. Have students do this activity individually, then go over the answers with the whole class.

Activity 5

Remind students of the differences between **hay que**, **tener que** and **deber**. Refer them to the grammar explanations on page 235 of the Student's book. Point out that some questions may take any of the three expressions, depending on context and our intended emphasis.

🎧 **88** Activity 6

Students can go back to page 230 and review how seasons are different. Use some of the places mentioned in the audio.
See audioscript on page APP11.

Activity 7

After writing the questions, use this as an exercise for oral interaction, where students can ask each other and give each other advice.

ANSWERS

Activity 4

a. va a ir; **b.** vamos a llamar; **c.** van a comprar; **d.** vas a hacer; **e.** van a viajar; **f.** van a estudiar.

Activity 5

a. 3; **b.** 1, 2, 3; **c.** 1, 3; **d.** 2; **e.** 2, 3; **f.** 3.

Activity 6

a. Cantabria; **b.** Andalucía; **c.** Ávila.

Activity 7

Answers will vary.

ADVANCED LEARNERS

For those students who have a good handle on the vocabulary, grammar, and cultural content of the units, encourage them to focus on the development of their listening, speaking, reading, and writing skills prior to quizzes and tests. Challenge them to spend thirty minutes a night for four nights before the assessment focusing on one of each of the four skills each night. In addition to redoing the skills-based activities within the units, encourage them to seek new, related (and fun) material online to help them practice.

HERITAGE LANGUAGE LEARNERS

For students who already have a base of the language, challenge them to put themselves in the position of the teacher prior to assessments. How would they teach a non-native speaker the content of the previous two units? Have them develop worksheets, activities, games, presentations, and lesson plans that could be used to teach other students the material. By putting students in this new role, they will enhance their own knowledge and become masters of the content.

APÉNDICES

■ Resumen y expansión gramatical

■ Tabla de verbos

RESUMEN GRAMATICAL

UNIDAD 1

ARTICLES

	Indefinite articles		Definite articles	
	Masculine	Feminine	Masculine	Feminine
Singular	un	una	el	la
Plural	unos	unas	los	las

SUBJECT PRONOUNS

Singular	Plural
yo	nosotros/nosotras
tú	vosotros/vosotras
usted/él/ella	ustedes/ellos/ellas

PRESENT TENSE

	LLAMAR(SE)	SER	TENER
yo	me llamo	soy	tengo
tú	te llamas	eres	tienes
usted/él/ella	se llama	es	tiene
nosotros/as	nos llamamos	somos	tenemos
vosotros/as	os llamáis	sois	tenéis
ustedes/ellos/ellas	se llaman	son	tienen

NUMBERS 0-31

0	cero	8	ocho	16	dieciséis	24	veinticuatro
1	uno	9	nueve	17	diecisiete	25	veinticinco
2	dos	10	diez	18	dieciocho	26	veintiséis
3	tres	11	once	19	diecinueve	27	veintisiete
4	cuatro	12	doce	20	veinte	28	veintiocho
5	cinco	13	trece	21	veintiuno	29	veintinueve
6	seis	14	catorce	22	veintidós	30	treinta
7	siete	15	quince	23	veintitrés	31	treinta y uno

EXPANSIÓN GRAMATICAL

Interrogative words:

- ¿**Cuánto**, **cuánta**, **cuántos**, **cuántas** + noun? *How much? How many?*
  ¿Cuántos años tienes? *How (many years) old are you?*

- ¿**Cuál**, **cuáles** + verb? *What?*
  ¿Cuál es tu comida favorita? *What is your favorite food?*

- **¿Qué** + verb/noun? *What?*
  ¿Qué haces? What do you do?
  ¿Qué hora es? What time is it?

- **¿Dónde** + verb? *Where?*
  ¿Dónde vives? Where do you live?

- **¿Cómo** + verb? *How?*
  ¿Cómo estás? How are you?

- **¿Quién** + verb? *Who?*
  ¿Quién es esa muchacha? Who is that girl?

UNIDAD 2

GENDER, NUMBER, AND AGREEMENT OF NOUNS AND ADJECTIVES

Singular	
Masculine	Feminine
–o	**–a**
el bolígraf**o**	**la** cámar**a**

Plural		
Masculine/Feminine		
Termina en vocal: **+s**	Termina en consonante: **+es**	Termina en z: **–ces**
Ends in a vowel: +s	*Ends in a consonant: +es*	*End in a z: -ces*
mesa / mesa**s**	actor / actor**es**	lápiz / lápi**ces**

Feminine forms of adjectives

Adjectives that end in **–o** change to **–a**: *blanc**o** / blanc**a***.

Adjectives that end in **–e**, no change: *elegante*.

Adjectives that end in a consonant, no change: *fácil*.

Nationalites that end in a consonant, add **–a**: *franc**és** / franc**esa***.

Plural forms of nouns and adjectives

Words that end in a vowel, add **–s**: *moren**o** / moren**os***.

Words that end in consonant, add **–es**: *jove**n** / jóve**nes***.

AGREEMENT

Singular			
Masculine	Feminine	Masculine/ Feminine	
–o	**–a**	**–e**	**–consonante**
el carro bonit**o**	**la silla** bonit**a**	**el carro** grande	**el carro** azul
		la silla grande	**la silla** azul
los carros bonit**os**	**las sillas** bonit**as**	**los carros** grande**s**	**los carros** azul**es**
		las sillas grande**s**	**las sillas** azul**es**

EXPANSIÓN GRAMATICAL

- Generally, nouns with the following endings are masculine:

  –o: *el libro, el dedo, el dinero, el vaso, el bolígrafo...*

  –aje: *el paisaje, el viaje, el garaje, el equipaje, el peaje...*

  –an: *el plan, el pan...*

  –or: *el pintor, el amor, el dolor, el error, el señor, el televisor, el ordenador*

- Generally, nouns with the following endings are feminine:

  –a: *la mesa, la casa, la caja, la crema, la niña, la chaqueta, la sopa...*

  –dad, –tad, –ción, –sión: *la edad, la ciudad, la verdad, la amistad, la canción, la traducción, la televisión, la decisión, la expresión...*

- **Exceptions**

  El problema, *el* día, *el* mapa, *el* diploma.

  La mano, *la* radio.

PRESENT TENSE OF –AR VERBS AND ESTAR

	HABLAR	ESTAR (irregular)
yo	hablo	estoy
tú	hablas	estás
usted/él/ella	habla	está
nosotros/as	hablamos	estamos
vosotros/as	habláis	estáis
ustedes/ellos/ellas	hablan	están

EXPANSIÓN GRAMATICAL

Uses of the present tense:

- To talk about habitual actions that you and others generally do (or don't do).
  *Todos los días **me levanto** a las 7:30. Every day, I get up at 7:30.*

- To express an ongoing action.
  *Andy y Carmen **viven** en Cartagena. Andy and Carmen live (are living) in Cartagena.*

- To describe or define.
  *"Casa" es el lugar donde **vivimos**. Home is the place where we live.*
  ***Tiene** dormitorios, cocina, baño y salón. It has bedrooms, a kitchen, bath and living room.*

UNIDAD 3

PRESENT TENSE OF –ER AND –IR VERBS

	COMER	VIVIR
yo	como	vivo
tú	comes	vives
usted/él/ella	come	vive
nosotros/as	comemos	vivimos
vosotros/as	coméis	vivís
ustedes/ellos/ellas	comen	viven

POSSESSIVE ADJECTIVES

	Singular		Plural	
	Masculine	Feminine	Masculine	Feminine
my	**mi** carro	**mi** casa	**mis** carros	**mis** casas
your	**tu** carro	**tu** casa	**tus** carros	**tus** casas
his/her/your (for.)	**su** carro	**su** casa	**sus** carros	**sus** casas
our	**nuestro** carro	**nuestra** casa	**nuestros** carros	**nuestras** casas
your (pl., Spain)	**vuestro** carro	**vuestra** casa	**vuestros** carros	**vuestras** casas
their/your (pl.)	**su** carro	**su** casa	**sus** carros	**sus** casas

DEMONSTRATIVE ADJECTIVES

Location of speaker	Singular		Plural		
	Masculine	Feminine	Masculine	Feminine	
aquí *here*	**este**	**esta**	**estos**	**estas**	*this, these*
ahí *there*	**ese**	**esa**	**esos**	**esas**	*that, those*
allí *over there*	**aquel**	**aquella**	**aquellos**	**aquellas**	*that (over there), those (over there)*

UNIDAD 4

STEM-CHANGING VERBS

	ENTENDER	VOLVER	PEDIR
	e ➡ ie	o ➡ ue	e ➡ i
yo	ent**ie**ndo	v**ue**lvo	p**i**do
tú	ent**ie**ndes	v**ue**lves	p**i**des
usted/él/ella	ent**ie**nde	v**ue**lve	p**i**de
nosotros/as	entendemos	volvemos	pedimos
vosotros/as	entendéis	volvéis	pedís
ustedes/ellos/ellas	ent**ie**nden	v**ue**lven	p**i**den

EXPANSIÓN GRAMATICAL

Other stem-changing verbs in Spanish:

■ e ➡ ie:

cerrar *(to close) cierro, cierras... / cerramos*

comenzar *(to begin, start) comienzo, comienzas... / comenzamos*

despertarse *(to wake up) me despierto, te despiertas... / nos despertamos*

divertirse *(to have fun) me divierto, te diviertes... / nos divertimos*

empezar *(to begin, start) empiezo, empiezas... / empezamos* encender *(to turn on)* enciendo, enciendes... / encendemos

mentir *(to lie)* miento, mientes... / mentimos

querer *(to want)* quiero, quieres... / queremos

recomendar *(to recommend)* recomiendo, recomiendas... / recomendamos

sentarse *(to sit down)* me siento, te sientas... / nos sentamos

sentirse *(to feel emotion)* me siento, te sientes... / nos sentimos

- **o → ue:**

  acordarse *(to remember)* me acuerdo, te acuerdas... / nos acordamos

  acostarse *(to go to bed)* me acuesto, te acuestas... / nos acostamos

  contar *(to count)* cuento, cuentas... / contamos

  resolver *(to resolve)* resuelvo, resuelves... / resolvemos

  soñar *(to dream)* sueño, sueñas... / soñamos

  volar *(to fly)* vuelo, vuelas... / volamos

  llover *(to rain)* llueve

  morir *(to die)* muero, mueres... / morimos

  probar *(to try, to taste)* pruebo, pruebas... / probamos

- **e → i:**

  despedirse *(to say good-bye)* me despido, te despides... / nos despedimos

  repetir *(to repeat)* repito, repites... / repetimos

  vestirse *(to get dressed)* me visto, te vistes... / nos vestimos

THE VERBS *HACER* AND *SALIR*

	HACER	SALIR
yo	**hago**	**salgo**
tú	haces	sales
usted/él/ella	hace	sale
nosotros/as	hacemos	salimos
vosotros/as	hacéis	salís
ustedes/ellos/ellas	hacen	salen

EXPANSIÓN GRAMATICAL

- Other verbs with irregular **yo** forms:

  caer *(to fall)* caigo

  estar *(to be)* estoy

  tener *(to come)* tengo

  venir *(to have)* vengo

  traer *(to bring)* traigo

  poner *(to put, to place)* pongo

REFLEXIVE VERBS

	LEVANTARSE
yo	**me** levanto
tú	**te** levantas
usted/él/ella	**se** levanta
nosotros/as	**nos** levantamos
vosotros/as	**os** levantáis
ustedes/ellos/ellas	**se** levantan

INDIRECT OBJECT PRONOUNS

yo	(a mí)	**me**	*(to me, for me)*
tú	(a ti)	**te**	*(to you, for you)*
usted/él/ella	(a usted/él/ella)	**le**	*(to you/him/her, for you, him, her)*
nosotros/as	(a nosotros/as)	**nos**	*(to us, for us)*
vosotros/as	(a vosotros/as)	**os**	*(to you, for you, Spain)*
ustedes/ellos/ellas	(a ustedes/ellos/ellas)	**les**	*(to you pl./them, for you pl./them)*

VERBS *GUSTAR*, *ENCANTAR* AND *DOLER*

A mí		me	**encanta(n)**	∅
A ti		te		muchísimo
A usted/él/ella		le		mucho
A nosotros/as	(no)	nos	**gusta(n)**	bastante
A vosotros/as		os		un poco
A ustedes/ellos/ellas		les		nada

- The verb **doler** (o ➡ ue) follows the same pattern.

SHOWING AGREEMENT AND DISAGREEMENT

- Use **también** and **tampoco** to agree with what a person says.
- Use **sí** and **no** to disagree with what a person says.

≫ Yo tengo carro.
≫ **Yo, también.**

≫ Yo tengo carro.
≫ **Yo, no.**

≫ Este año no voy a ir de vacaciones.
≫ **Nosotros, tampoco.**

≫ Este año no voy de vacaciones.
≫ **Nosotros, sí.**

>> A mí me encanta ir a la playa por la tarde.

>> **A mí, también.**

>> No me gustan los gatos.

>> **A mí, tampoco.**

>> A mí me encanta ir a la playa por la tarde.

>> **A mí, no.**

>> No me gustan los gatos.

>> **A mí, sí.**

USES OF *SER* AND *ESTAR*

SER	ESTAR

- Use **ser** to describe a characteristic of a person, place, or thing.

    *María **es** una chica muy divertida.*

    *Los leones **son** animales salvajes.*

- Use **estar** to describe a person's mood or feelings.

    *Hoy **estoy** muy cansado.*

    ***Estamos** nerviosos por el examen.*

EXPANSIÓN GRAMATICAL

- To identify a person or thing.

    *La chica a la derecha **es** María.* The girl on the right is Maria.

- To express an opinion or judgment.

    ***Es** bueno estudiar.* It's good to study.

- To indicate where an event takes place.

    *¿Dónde **es** la fiesta de fin de curso?* Where is the end of year party?

- To express origin.

    *Señores, ¿ustedes **son** de Zaragoza?* Gentlemen, are you from Zaragoza?

- To indicate possession.

    ***Es** de mi madre.* It's my mother's. (It belongs to my mother.)

- To express time.

    ***Son** las tres y cuarto de la tarde.* It's quarter past three in the afternoon.

- To express location.

    ***Estoy** aquí.* I'm here.

    *Mi casa **está** cerca del centro.* My house is close to downtown.

- To express an opinion.

    *No **estoy** de acuerdo contigo.* I don't agree with you.

- To say how you and others are feeling.

    *Mi abuela **está** bien.* My grandmother is fine (well).

UNIDAD 6

HAY / ESTÁ(N)

Existence	Location
Use **hay** to talk or ask about what there is/are. Hay is invariable. *En mi clase **hay** muchos libros.* In my class, there are many books.	Use **estar** to talk or ask about where people or things are located. *Los libros **están** en la estantería.* The books are in the bookcase.
hay + un, una, unos, unas + noun	**el, la, los, las** + noun + **está(n)**

IRREGULAR VERBS

	IR	SEGUIR	JUGAR	CONOCER
yo	**voy**	**sigo**	**jue**go	cono**zco**
tú	**vas**	sigues	**jue**gas	conoces
usted/él/ella	**va**	sigue	**jue**ga	conoce
nosotros/as	**vamos**	seguimos	jugamos	conocemos
vosotros/as	**vais**	seguís	jugáis	conocéis
ustedes/ellos/ellas	**van**	siguen	**jue**gan	conocen

EXPANSIÓN GRAMATICAL

■ Other verbs with **–zc** in the **yo** form:

agradecer *(to be grateful)* *agradezco*

conducir *(to drive)* *conduzco*

producir *(to produce)* *produzco*

traducir *(to translate)* *traduzco*

■ Other verbs with **–gu** ➡ **g** in the **yo** form:

conseguir *(to attain, to get)* *consigo*

distinguir *(to distinguish)* *distingo*

PREPOSITIONS *A, EN, DE*

Preposition	Use...	
en	with modes of **transportation**	*Viajamos **en** tren. We travel by train.*
a	to express **destination**	*Voy **a** Florida. I'm going to Florida.*
de	to express **origin** or point of **departure**	*Salgo **de** Miami. I'm leaving from Miami.*

ADVERBS OF QUANTITY

To express how much		
Action Verbs	**demasiado**	
	*Luis trabaja **demasiado**. Luis works too much.*	
	mucho	
	*Ana viaja **mucho**. Ana travels a lot.*	
	bastante	
	*Pedro estudia **bastante**. Pedro studies enough.*	
	poco	
	*Luis estudia **poco**. Luis doesn't study much.*	

MUY/MUCHO

MUY	MUCHO

- **Muy** is invariable and can be used before adjectives to express *very*.

  *Él/ella es **muy** inteligente.*
  He/she is very intelligent.

  *Ellos/ellas son **muy** inteligentes.*
  They are very intelligent.

- And before adverbs to express *how*.

  *Él/ella habla **muy** despacio.* He/She speaks slowly.

  *Ellos/ellas hablan **muy** despacio.*
  They speak slowly.

- Use **mucho** after a verb to express *how much*. As an adverb, it does not change form.

  *Juan come **mucho**. Juan eats a lot.*

- Use **mucho** before a noun to express *how many*. Here it functions as an adjective and must agree with the noun in number and gender.

  *Juan lee **muchos** libros. Juan reads many books.*

  *Hay **mucha** gente. There are many people.*

  *María tiene **muchos** amigos.*
  Maria has many friends.

UNIDAD 7

COMPARATIVES (WITH ADJECTIVES AND ADVERBS)

■ **más... que**	→ Julián es **más** rápido **que** Pedro.	more... than...
■ **menos... que**	→ Pedro camina **menos** lento **que** Julián.	less... than...
■ **tan... como**	→ Julián es **tan** divertido **como** Pedro.	as... as...

EXPANSIÓN GRAMATICAL

To compare quantities (with nouns):

■ **más... que**	→ Julián tiene **más** tiempo libre **que** Pedro. Julián has more free time than Pedro.
■ **menos... que**	→ Julián tiene **menos** tiempo libre **que** Pedro. Julián has less free time than Pedro.
■ **tanto/a/os/as... como**	→ Julián tiene **tanto** tiempo libre **como** Pedro. Julián has as much free time as Pedro.

To compare actions (with verbs)

■ ... **más que**	→ Julián estudia **más que** Pedro. Julián studies more than Pedro.
■ ... **menos que**	→ Julián habla **menos que** Pedro. Julián talks less than Pedro.
■ ... **tanto como**	→ Julián come **tanto como** Pedro. Julián eats as much as Pedro.

DEMONSTRATIVE PRONOUNS

	Singular		Plural		
	Masculine	Feminine	Masculine	Feminine	Neuter
Aquí (cerca)	este	esta	estos	estas	esto
Ahí (intermedio)	ese	esa	esos	esas	eso
Allí (lejos)	aquel	aquella	aquellos	aquellas	aquello

- **Este**, **esta**, **estos**, **estas**, and **esto** refer to a person or thing that is next to the speaker. They correspond to the adverb, **aquí**.
  Este es mi celular. This is my cell phone.

- **Ese**, **esa**, **esos**, **esas**, and **eso** refer to a person or thing that is near the speaker. They correspond to the adverb **ahí**.
  Esas son las botas de Luis. Those are Luis's boots.

- **Aquel**, **aquella**, **aquellos**, **aquellas** and **aquello** refer to a person or thing that is farther away from the speaker. They correspond to the adverb, **allí**.
  Aquella es la bicicleta de mi primo.
  That over there is my cousin's bicycle.

Aquella bicicleta es de mi primo.

Esas botas son de Luis.

Este es mi celular.

■ Demonstrative pronouns

» ¡Hola, Encarna! ¿Cómo estás?
  Hi, Encarna! How are you?
» Muy bien, gracias. Mira, **esta** es Manuela, mi hermana.
  Fine, thanks. This is Manuela, my sister.

» ¿Te gustan estos tomates?
  Do you like these tomatoes?
» No, me gustan **aquellos**.
  No, I like those (over there).

■ Neuter pronouns

» ¿Qué es **esto**? *What is this?*
» Es una lámpara. *It's a lamp.*

» ¿Qué es **eso**? *What is that?*
» Es un celular. *It's a cell phone.*

» ¿Qué es **aquello**? *What is that (over there)?*
» Son unas zapatillas. *They're sneakers.*

DIRECT OBJECT PRONOUNS

me
te
lo/la
nos
os
los/las

» ¿Tienes el libro de Matemáticas? *Do you have the math book?*
» Sí, **lo** tengo en mi casa. *Yes, I have it at home.*

» ¿Quién compra la tarta de cumpleaños? *Who is buying the birthday cake?*
» **La** compramos nosotros. *We are buying it.*

NUMBERS (100-999)

100	cien	400	cuatrocientos	700	setecientos
101	ciento uno	415	cuatrocientos quince	720	setecientos veinte
200	doscientos	500	quinientos	800	ochocientos
202	doscientos dos	526	quinientos veintiséis	897	ochocientos noventa y siete
300	trescientos	600	seiscientos	899	ochocientos noventa y nueve
303	trescientos tres	669	seiscientos sesenta y nueve	900	novecientos

261

EXPRESSING OBLIGATION

hay que + infinitive	To express obligation or what is necessary for all	**Hay que hacer** la tarea.
tener que + infinitive	To express obligation or a need for a particular person	**Tengo que estudiar** mucho para Ciencias.
deber que + infinitive	To express obligation in terms of making a recommendation or giving advice	Si tienes hambre, **debes comer** algo.

TALKING ABOUT FUTURE PLANS AND HAPPENINGS

ir + infinitive	Saying what you and others are going to do	**Voy a ir** al cine con mis amigos.
	Describing what is going to happen	Hay nubes en el cielo, **va a llover**.
	With time expressions	Esta tarde **voy a jugar al tenis**.

IRREGULAR VERBS: *DECIR, TRAER, VENIR*

DECIR	TRAER	VENIR
digo	**traigo**	**vengo**
dices	traes	vienes
dice	trae	viene
decimos	traemos	venimos
decís	traéis	venís
dicen	traen	vienen

TABLA DE VERBOS

Present indicative of regular verbs

−AR CANTAR	−ER COMER	−IR VIVIR
canto	como	vivo
cantas	comes	vives
canta	come	vive
cantamos	comemos	vivimos
cantáis	coméis	vivís
cantan	comen	viven

Present tense of regular reflexive verbs

BAÑARSE	DUCHARSE	LAVARSE	LEVANTARSE	PEINARSE
me baño	me ducho	me lavo	me levanto	me peino
te bañas	te duchas	te lavas	te levantas	te peinas
se baña	se ducha	se lava	se levanta	se peina
nos bañamos	nos duchamos	nos lavamos	nos levantamos	nos peinamos
os bañáis	os ducháis	os laváis	os levantáis	os peináis
se bañan	se duchan	se lavan	se levantan	se peinan

Present tense of irregular reflexive verbs

ACORDARSE	ACOSTARSE	DESPERTARSE	REÍRSE	VESTIRSE
me acuerdo	me acuesto	me despierto	me río	me visto
te acuerdas	te acuestas	te despiertas	te ríes	te vistes
se acuerda	se acuesta	se despierta	se ríe	se viste
nos acordamos	nos acostamos	nos despertamos	nos reímos	nos vestimos
os acordáis	os acostáis	os despertáis	os reís	os vestís
se acuerdan	se acuestan	se despiertan	se ríen	se visten

Verbs like *gustar*

DOLER	ENCANTAR	MOLESTAR	PARECER
me duele/duelen	me encanta/encantan	me molesta/molestan	me parece/parecen
te duele/duelen	te encanta/encantan	te molesta/molestan	te parece/parecen
le duele/duelen	le encanta/encantan	le molesta/molesta	le parece/parecen
nos duele/duelen	nos encanta/encantan	nos molesta/molestan	nos parece/parecen
os duele/duelen	os encanta/encantan	os molesta/molestan	os parece/parecen
les duele/duelen	les encanta/encantan	les molesta/molestan	les parece/parecen

Irregular verbs in the present indicative

CERRAR	PROTEGER	COMENZAR	CONCLUIR
cierro	protejo	comienzo	concluyo
cierras	proteges	comienzas	concluyes
cierra	protege	comienza	concluye
cerramos	protegemos	comenzamos	concluimos
cerráis	protegéis	comenzáis	concluís
cierran	protegen	comienzan	concluyen

CONDUCIR	CONOCER	CONSTRUIR	CONTRIBUIR
conduzco	conozco	construyo	contribuyo
conduces	conoces	construyes	contribuyes
conduce	conoce	construye	contribuye
conducimos	conocemos	construimos	contribuimos
conducís	conocéis	construís	contribuís
conducen	conocen	construyen	contribuyen

DAR	DECIR	DESTRUIR	DORMIR
doy	digo	destruyo	duermo
das	dices	destruyes	duermes
da	dice	destruye	duerme
damos	decimos	destruimos	dormimos
dais	decís	destruís	dormís
dan	dicen	destruyen	duermen

EMPEZAR	ENCONTRAR	ENTENDER	ESTAR
empiezo	encuentro	entiendo	estoy
empiezas	encuentras	entiendes	estás
empieza	encuentra	entiende	está
empezamos	encontramos	entendemos	estamos
empezáis	encontráis	entendéis	estáis
empiezan	encuentran	entienden	están

HACER	HUIR	IR	JUGAR
hago	huyo	voy	juego
haces	huyes	vas	juegas
hace	huye	va	juega
hacemos	huimos	vamos	jugamos
hacéis	huis	vais	jugáis
hacen	huyen	van	juegan

MERENDAR	OÍR	PEDIR	PENSAR
mer**ie**ndo	**oigo**	p**i**do	p**ie**nso
mer**ie**ndas	o**y**es	p**i**des	p**ie**nsas
mer**ie**nda	o**y**e	p**i**de	p**ie**nsa
merendamos	oímos	pedimos	pensamos
merendáis	oís	pedís	pensáis
mer**ie**ndan	o**y**en	p**i**den	p**ie**nsan

PERDER	PODER	PONER	QUERER
p**ie**rdo	p**ue**do	**pongo**	qu**ie**ro
p**ie**rdes	p**ue**des	pones	qu**ie**res
p**ie**rde	p**ue**de	pone	qu**ie**re
perdemos	podemos	ponemos	queremos
perdéis	podéis	ponéis	queréis
p**ie**rden	p**ue**den	ponen	qu**ie**re

RECORDAR	SABER	SALIR	SER
rec**ue**rdo	**sé**	**salgo**	**soy**
rec**ue**rdas	sabes	sales	**eres**
rec**ue**rda	sabe	sale	**es**
recordamos	sabemos	salimos	**somos**
recordáis	sabéis	salís	**sois**
rec**ue**rdan	saben	salen	**son**

SERVIR	SOÑAR	TENER	TRADUCIR
s**i**rvo	s**ue**ño	**tengo**	tradu**zco**
s**i**rves	s**ue**ñas	t**ie**nes	traduces
s**i**rve	s**ue**ña	t**ie**ne	traduce
servimos	soñamos	tenemos	traducimos
servís	soñáis	tenéis	traducís
s**i**rven	s**ue**ñan	t**ie**nen	traducen

TRAER	VENIR	VER	VOLVER
traigo	**vengo**	**veo**	v**ue**lvo
traes	v**ie**nes	ves	v**ue**lves
trae	v**ie**ne	ve	v**ue**lve
traemos	venimos	vemos	volvemos
traéis	venís	veis	volvéis
traen	v**ie**nen	ven	v**ue**lven

APÉNDICES

- Audioscripts
- Lesson plans

AUDIOSCRIPTS Student book

UNIT 0: ASÍ SOMOS

TRACK 1

¡Hola! Bienvenidos todos a la clase español. Soy la señora Blanco. Soy de Madrid, la capital de España. El español es una lengua importante. Muchas personas en el mundo hablan español. ¿En qué países hablan español? Miren el mapa. Hablan español en México, Guatemala, El Salvador, Honduras, Costa Rica, Nicaragua, Panamá, Colombia, Ecuador, Perú, Bolivia, Chile, Argentina, Uruguay, Paraguay, Venezuela, Puerto Rico, República Dominicana, Cuba y España. ¿Hablan español en Estados Unidos?

TRACK 2

1. cafetería; **2.** música; **3.** clase; **4.** teléfono; **5.** familia; **6.** mapa; **7.** alfabeto; **8.** computadora.

TRACK 3

A, be, ce, de, e, efe, ge, hache, i, jota, ka, ele, eme, ene, eñe, o, pe, cu, erre, ese, te, u, ve/uve, doble ve/doble uve, equis, i griega/ye, zeta.

TRACK 4

1. b; **2.** g; **3.** j; **4.** r; **5.** j; **6.** x; **7.** c; **8.** p.

TRACK 5

ge, hache, efe / eme, eñe, pe / ka, uve doble, c / be, de, e / i griega, i, te.

TRACK 6

Escucha, lee, escribe, marca, completa, relaciona, habla, pregunta, fíjate.

TRACK 7

1. la profesora; **2.** el estudiante; **3.** la papelera; **4.** la mesa; **5.** la silla; **6.** el lápiz; **7.** el marcador; **8.** el borrador; **9.** el libro; **10.** el pizarrón; **11.** el cuaderno; **12.** el diccionario; **13.** la goma de borrar; **14.** la tableta; **15.** el bolígrafo; **16.** la mochila; **17.** la carpeta; **18.** el mp4; **19.** el tablero de anuncios; **20.** la puerta..

TRACK 8

≫ ¿Cómo se dice *blackboard* en español?
≫ Pizarrón.

≫ Estos son mis amigos, Luis y Pablo.
≫ No entiendo. ¿Puede repetir, por favor?
≫ Estos son mis amigos, Luis y Pablo.

≫ ¿Qué significa "pizarrón"?
≫ *Blackboard.*

≫ ¿Cómo se escribe "cuaderno" en español?
≫ Ce-u-a-de-e-erre-ene-o.

≫ ¿Puede escribirlo en el pizarrón?
≫ Sí, claro.

≫ ¿Está bien así?
≫ Sí, está bien.

TRACK 9

marca, carpeta, habla
mesa, estudiante, clase
sí, escribe, amigo
nombre, profesora, goma
anuncio, pregunta, escucha.

TRACK 10

1. banana; **2.** dividir; **3.** tú; **4.** color; **5.** insistir; **6.** depender; **7.** planta; **8.** foto; **9.** mapa; **10.** excelente; **11.** lente; **12.** un; **13.** honor; **14.** sí; **15.** bus.

TRACK 11

«Hola, mi nombre es Sofía y soy estudiante. Estudio inglés en la escuela. Mi escuela es grande y tengo muchos amigos. Mis amigos son de Ecuador, México, y Perú. Uso la computadora para comunicarme con mis amigos. También uso la computadora para estudiar y escuchar música. Y tú, ¿estudias español en clase?».

UNIT 1: HOLA, ¿QUÉ TAL?

TRACK 12

Nélida: Hola, ¿qué tal? Me llamo Nélida. Y ustedes, ¿cómo se llaman?
Alberto: Hola, yo soy Alberto y él es Miguel.
Miguel: ¿Qué tal? Ella es Cecilia. Es colombiana, de Bogotá.
Cecilia: Hola a todos, ¿qué tal? ¿De dónde eres Alberto? ¿Eres americano?
Alberto: No, soy argentino, de Buenos Aires, pero vivo aquí en Estados Unidos.
Nélida: Cecilia, ¿cuántos años tienes?
Cecilia: Tengo 14 años. ¿Y tú?
Nélida: Tengo 15 años.
Miguel: Bueno, muchachos, vamos a clase. ¡Hasta luego!
Alberto: Sí, es verdad, ¡hasta luego!
Nélida y Cecilia: ¡Adiós!

TRACK 13

a. Hola, soy Miguel. Soy americano, de Los Ángeles.
b. Hola, yo soy Alberto. Soy de Buenos Aires, argentino.
c. Hola, me llamo Nélida. Soy española, de Madrid.
d. Hola, yo soy Cecilia. Soy colombiana, de Bogotá.

TRACK 14

Víctor: ¡Hola, Susana! ¿Qué tal estás?
Susana: Bien. Mira, este es Antonio, un amigo de clase.
Víctor: Hola, Antonio.
Antonio: ¡Hola! ¿Qué tal?

Jesús: Buenos días, Leonor. ¿Cómo está usted?
Leonor: Muy bien, gracias. Mire, le presento al señor Fernández.
Sr. Fernández: Encantado.
Jesús: Encantado.

TRACK 15

1. En el médico
   Médica: ¿Cómo te llamas?
   Carlos: Me llamo Carlos.
   Médica: ¿Cuántos años tienes?
   Carlos: Tengo 5 años.

2. En la biblioteca
   Sra. Díaz: ¿Cómo te llamas?
   Rosalía: Me llamo Rosalía Castro Gómez.
   Sra. Díaz: ¿Dónde vives?
   Rosalía: Vivo en la calle Molina.

3. En la calle
   Miguel: ¿De dónde eres?
   Beatriz: Soy puertorriqueña.
   Miguel: ¿Y qué haces?
   Beatriz: Soy profesora.

TRACK 16

Cero, uno, dos, tres, cuatro, cinco, seis, siete, ocho, nueve, diez, once, doce, trece, catorce, quince, dieciséis, diecisiete, dieciocho, diecinueve, veinte, veintiuno, veintidós, veintitrés, veinticuatro, veinticinco, veintiséis, veintisiete, veintiocho, veintinueve, treinta, treinta y uno.

TRACK 17

Veintiocho, catorce, once, veinticinco, quince, trece, nueve.

TRACK 18

enero, febrero, marzo, abril, mayo, junio, julio, agosto, septiembre, octubre, noviembre, diciembre.

TRACK 19

Olga: Hola, Susie.
Susie: Hola, ¿qué tal?
Olga: Muy bien. Mira, este es Daniel, mi amigo de Francia.
Susie: ¡Hola Daniel! Yo soy china. ¿Qué tal en la clase de español?
Daniel: Muy bien. Mi amiga cubana, Olga, es mi guía…

TRACK 20

1. muchacho, muchacha, coche, dieciocho, escuchar.
2. niño, español, enseñar, mañana, compañero.

TRACK 21

¡Famosos y en español!
Muchos famosos que viven en EE. UU. son hispanos o de origen hispano. También hay muchos famosos que hablan español: Will Smith, Gwyneth Paltrow, Viggo Mortensen y otros. ¿Sabes qué famosos son hispanos o de origen hispano? ¡Marca las casillas!

Univisión, ¿la cadena más popular?
Univisión es la cadena de televisión más grande de EE. UU. Univisión emite desde 1962. Los programas más populares son las telenovelas. Muchos programas y telenovelas son producciones de canales mexicanos como Televisa y El Canal de las Estrellas. Univisión tiene una media de 1,81 millones de espectadores de entre 18 y 49 años, más que las cadenas en inglés. Fusión es una nueva cadena de Univisión. Es para jóvenes latinos educados en español e inglés.

Un día sin hispanos
Juan Martínez trabaja en una fábrica de conservas. Él habla de un día importante en su vida. «Son las seis de la mañana. Camino al centro de mi ciudad. Hoy es un día importante. Las personas ilegales de origen hispano protestamos: trabajamos aquí y somos parte de la comunidad. Hay mucha gente. Todos queremos vivir aquí legalmente. Los hispanos sí somos importantes».

TRACK 22

El club del español en la escuela
Hola, Michael:
¿Qué tal? Mira, esta es una foto del club de español en la escuela. El Sr. Pérez es el consejero del club y también es profesor de español. Es colombiano y habla perfectamente inglés y español. En el comité ejecutivo somos cuatro estudiantes: Bo, Óscar, Asmita y yo.
Bo tiene quince años y es chino. Habla un poco de español pero comprende mucho. Todos los días habla con sus amigos por teléfono. Quiere ser médico y trabajar en un hospital.
Óscar es estudiante. Es dominicano y tiene diecisiete años. Habla mucho en clase y siempre escucha música en su mp4. Tiene un perro, se llama Chato. Tiene muchas fotos de Chato en su teléfono.
Asmita es india. Tiene catorce años y es estudiante. Asmita habla muy bien español, pero a veces dice palabras en inglés.
En el club solo hablamos en español y es un poco difícil comprendernos, pero es muy divertido.
Hasta luego,
Guillermo

UNIT 2: ESTÁS EN TU CASA

TRACK 23

María: Hola, Juan. ¿Tienes las fotos de Barcelona?
Juan: Sí, aquí tienes mis fotos.
María: En esta foto, estás en la Sagrada Familia, ¿verdad?
Juan: Sí, es un lugar muy bonito y conocido.
María: Para mí, esta foto es bellísima. ¿Dónde es?
Juan: Es en el Parque Güell, otro lugar importante de la ciudad.
María: ¿Y cuál es tu foto favorita?
Juan: Esta. Estoy con dos amigos en la Casa Milà, otro edificio conocido de Gaudí.
María: ¿Quiénes son estos chicos?
Juan: Se llaman Karen y Mateo, son mexicanos, pero viven en Barcelona.

María: Para ti, ¿cómo es la gente en Barcelona?
Juan: Es muy simpática y amable.
María: Para mí, también.
Juan: Aquí tienes más fotos.

TRACK 24

a. **Mateo:** Para mí, Colombia es un país muy bonito. ¿Y para ti?
   Belén: Para mí, también.

b. **Jesús:** Para mí, el fútbol americano es fantástico. ¿Y para ustedes?
   María y Daniel: Para nosotros, no.

c. **Pedro:** Para ti, el español es un idioma muy fácil, ¿verdad?
   Jorge: Sí, es verdad

TRACK 25

Entrevistador: Oye, chicos, para vosotros, ¿cómo es la gente de Barcelona?
María: Para mí, la gente en Barcelona es muy abierta.
Juan: Sí, sí. Para mí, también.
Entrevistador: ¿Cuál es vuestro deporte favorito?
Juan: Ah, eso es fácil. Mi deporte favorito es el fútbol. Para mí el fútbol es muy divertido.
María: Pufff, para mí, no. Creo que el fútbol es aburrido. Mi deporte favorito es el tenis.
Entrevistador: ¿Y el inglés? ¿Es un idioma fácil?
Juan: Yo creo que sí.
María: Para mí, es muy difícil.
Entrevistador: Las ciudades pequeñas, ¿son aburridas o divertidas?
María: En mi opinión, son aburridas.
Juan: Sí, es verdad. Son aburridas.
Entrevistador: Y, por último, chicos. ¿Para vosotros leer es interesante?
María: Sí, pienso que leer todos los días es muy interesante.
Juan: Para mí, leer es aburrido.

TRACK 26

rojo, blanco, amarillo, marrón, anaranjado, azul, negro, verde, gris.

TRACK 27

Para mí, la cocina es mi lugar favorito de la casa. Mi cocina es muy grande y de color anaranjado. Es un color que no me gusta mucho. Yo prefiero el color blanco, como mi salón, porque es un color más tranquilo y relajado. Aunque el amarillo es un color que da mala suerte en España, mi dormitorio es de este color. No tengo problemas. Un color que no me gusta es el verde, como el color de mi clase.

TRACK 28

la cama, la mesilla, el armario, la estufa, la ducha, el horno, el lavabo, la mesa, la bañera, el sofá, el espejo y la cómoda, la estantería.

TRACK 29

treinta y dos; cuarenta; cuarenta y tres; cincuenta; cincuenta y cuatro; sesenta; sesenta y cinco; setenta; setenta y seis; ochenta; ochenta y siete; noventa; noventa y ocho; noventa y nueve; cien; ciento uno.

TRACK 30

Noventa y siete; treinta y ocho; cuarenta y cinco; ciento uno; sesenta y cuatro; setenta y nueve.

TRACK 31

1. hablamos; **2.** caminan; **3.** escuchas; **4.** bailo; **5.** hablo; **6.** camina; **7.** bailamos; **8.** escuchan.

TRACK 32

Una casa famosa

«¡Hola! Mi nombre es Lidia y soy de Barcelona. Me encanta vivir en mi ciudad: es bonita, cosmopolita y moderna. Yo vivo en un piso en el centro: es viejo, pero la decoración y los muebles son modernos.
Mi edificio favorito en Barcelona es la Casa Milà, o La Pedrera. Está en el Paseo de Gracia, número 92. Es un famoso edificio del arquitecto Antonio Gaudí, inspirado en la naturaleza. Me gustan mucho los balcones de la casa porque son originales. También me encanta la azotea: allí hay muchas columnas y una vista bonita de la ciudad. En La Pedrera viven varias familias… ¡Qué suerte tienen!».

Vivir en familia

En España, muchos jóvenes españoles menores de 30 años viven con sus padres.
Solo el 20% es independiente.
Los motivos son una combinación de tradición y economía. La familia es muy importante en la cultura española, pero, además, muchos jóvenes no tienen trabajo y no pueden alquilar una casa.
Los jóvenes españoles dicen que la familia y los amigos son las cosas más importantes en su vida.
Vivir con los padres hasta los 30 años también es normal en muchos países latinoamericanos.

El pueblo más bonito

El pueblo de Priego de Córdoba está en Andalucía, una región en el sur de España. Según una encuesta del periódico ABC, es el pueblo más bonito de España.
Es un lugar con mucha historia y sitios interesantes. Por ejemplo, la Calle Real es una calle pequeña, de piedra, con casas de color blanco. En primavera, la gente decora sus casas con plantas y flores.

TRACK 33

Los problemas de Raquel

Para mí, la música es lo más importante. Yo escucho música todos los días en mi casa. En mi opinión, Shakira es la mejor cantante y me gusta bailar con su música. Compro todas las canciones nuevas de mis cantantes favoritos y bailo y canto en mi dormitorio. Vivo en un edificio de apartamentos en Barcelona y mi vecino habla con mi madre: "¡Señora, Raquel hace mucho ruido! ¡Baila por las noches y es imposible descansar!". Mi madre escucha atentamente y luego habla conmigo: "¡Raquel, prohibido bailar en tu dormitorio!". Pienso que mi vecino es horrible. Seguro que el color preferido de mi vecino es el negro.
¡Pero tengo 14 años! ¡Solo estoy contenta cuando bailo y canto con la música!
En la escuela, la profesora me pregunta: "Raquel, ¿de dónde es Cristobal Colón?", pero yo escucho mi mp4 y no respondo a la pregunta. La profesora habla con mi madre: "Raquel escucha todo el día el mp4 en clase". Seguro que el color preferido de mi profesora es el negro también.
No puedo escuchar el mp4 en clase porque la profesora habla con mi madre.
No puedo bailar en el salón porque mi vecino es antipático y habla con mi madre.
No puedo bailar en la cocina porque es pequeña y mi madre está ahí.
¡Tengo muchos problemas!

TRACK 34

Entrevistador: Tenemos con nosotros al cantante José Sol. Buenos días, José.
José Sol: Hola, buenos días.
Entrevistador: Encantado de conocerte, es un placer para mí.
José Sol: Igualmente.
Entrevistador: De todas tus canciones, ¿cuál es tu canción favorita?
José Sol: Mi canción favorita es La canción de los colores. Es mi nueva canción.
Entrevistador: Has cantado en muchas ciudades. Pero, ¿cuál es tu ciudad favorita?
José Sol: Pienso que Madrid es genial, pero, para mí, Toledo es mi ciudad favorita. Yo soy de Toledo y me gusta cantar allí.
Entrevistador: ¿Dónde vives? ¿En Toledo?
José Sol: No, no, ahora vivo en Madrid, en una casa muy grande, con cuatro dormitorios, dos cocinas, tres cuartos de baño y un salón.
Entrevistador: Increíble. ¿Cuál es tu habitación favorita?
José Sol: Creo que el salón. En el salón escribo mis canciones.
Entrevistador: Muchas gracias por la entrevista y hasta pronto.
José Sol: Gracias a vosotros, adiós.

TRACK 35

Nicolás: Mira, María, mi familia.
María: ¿Quién es ese hombre?
Nicolás: Es mi padre. Y ella es mi madre. Es morena, igual que todos nosotros.
María: Sí, es verdad. Tu padre es muy alto, ¿no?
Nicolás: Sí y es calvo…
María: ¿Tu hermano es este que lleva pantalón marrón? Es muy guapo.
Nicolás: Sí, y también es muy simpático.
María: ¿Cuántos años tiene?
Nicolás: Es mi hermano pequeño. Tiene 8 años.
María: Tiene el pelo rizado como tú. Ustedes son muy parecidos.
Nicolás: Sí, es cierto. Y tú, ¿cuántos hermanos tienes?
María: No tengo hermanos. Soy hija única.

TRACK 36

Mi hermano pequeño se llama Pedro y tiene siete años. Es delgado, es moreno con el pelo rizado y tiene los ojos oscuros. Lleva unos jeans y una camiseta verde. Mi padre se llama Ricardo. Es alto, mayor y fuerte. Tiene el pelo gris. Lleva traje, corbata y camisa. Mi abuelo José es alto, gordo y tiene el pelo blanco. Lleva una camiseta verde y un pantalón gris. Mi profesora de Matemáticas se llama Ana. Es alta, delgada, joven y guapa. Es morena y lleva un vestido rojo.

TRACK 37

a. **Nuria:** Mi amiga Marta tiene frío.
   Luis: ¿Por qué?
   Nuria: Porque no lleva abrigo.

b. **Alberto:** El profesor de lengua es muy amable.
   Luis: Sí, es verdad, y también es muy divertido en clase.

c. **Juanjo:** Mi novia es divertida, trabajadora, inteligente…
   Carlos: ¿No tiene defectos?
   Juanjo: Bueno, sí, es un poco habladora.

TRACK 38

La familia de Jaime no es muy grande. Su papá se llama Francisco Arnal y su mamá, Rosa Sabater. Francisco y Rosa son esposo y esposa. Tienen tres hijos: la mayor es Carmen que tiene 16 años, Jaime, su hermano, tiene 12 años, y Daniela, la hermana pequeña, tiene 8 años. El padre de Francisco se llama Juan, y su madre, Ester. Juan y Ester son los abuelos de Carmen, Jaime y Daniela. Jaime y sus hermanos son los nietos de Juan y Ester y los sobrinos de Pilar, su tía, la hermana de Francisco. Pilar está casada con Pablo y tienen dos hijos: María y Luis. María y Luis son los primos de Jaime y de sus hermanas.

TRACK 39

Hola, me llamo Paula y tengo doce años. Vivo en Valencia con mis padres y mis hermanos. Tengo dos hermanos: Julia, mi hermana mayor y Carlos, mi hermano pequeño. Mis padres se llaman Manuel y Sara. El hermano de mi padre, mi tío Antonio, vive también cerca de nuestra casa y es muy divertido. Mis abuelos, Pepe y Carmen, viven en Madrid, pero en verano vienen a vernos a Valencia.

TRACK 40

gorra, suéter, pantalones, jeans, chaqueta, zapato de tacón, bufanda, abrigo, camisa, cinturón, bota, corbata, falda, vestido, traje, tenis, camiseta, sandalias, calcetín.

TRACK 41

calvo, corto, curso, pequeño, tranquilo, cero, cinco, rizado, zorro, zurdo.

TRACK 42

Cielo, zapatos, rizado, boca, querer, cine.

TRACK 43

Un domingo en el bosque Chapultepec

El bosque Chapultepec es un parque muy grande. Está en México D.F. En él hay muchas fuentes, árboles y lagos. Muchas familias visitan el parque los domingos. Allí comen, pasean, practican deporte o hablan. «¡Me fascina el parque. Mi actividad favorita es ir allí con mi familia», dice Camila, una chica de 15 años que vive en la capital.

El Día de los Muertos

«¡Hola! ¿Qué onda? Me llamo René y soy del D. F. Mi fiesta favorita es el Día de Muertos. El Día de Muertos es un día muy importante en mi país. Se celebra el 2 de noviembre. Es una celebración de origen prehispano. La fiesta recuerda a los muertos. La familia se reúne y se disfraza, prepara un altar con fotografías de antepasados, visita los cementerios y toma comida especial… ¡como las calaveritas de azúcar!
Este día también se celebra en otras partes de América Latina como Guatemala, Venezuela, Perú y Nicaragua. Y tú, ¿cuál es tu celebración favorita?».

La Quinceañera

La Quinceañera es un evento importante en México. En el resto de América Latina también se celebra: en algunos países, como Argentina, se llama la Fiesta de Quince. Se celebra cuando una joven cumple quince años. Es una fiesta enorme: las familias ahorran dinero durante muchos años. Las cosas más importantes en una fiesta de Quinceañera son: la familia, el vestido, la misa y el pastel. Según la tradición, solo las chicas celebran la Quinceañera. Pero hoy en día, muchos chicos tienen una fiesta especial cuando cumplen quince años… ¡con muchos regalos especiales!

TRACK 44

La cena de Nochebuena

Todos los años el mismo problema. Mi madre no sabe cómo organizar a la familia en la mesa. En total, somos nueve. Siempre es un desastre porque todos somos muy diferentes.
La abuela Julia, muy nerviosa y habladora, lleva siempre una falda y una camisa amarillas. Odia los teléfonos móviles, los vaqueros y el pelo largo en los hombres.
El tío Pepe, con corbata y traje negros, es muy pesimista y habla muy poco. Su mujer, Carmen, siempre habla por el móvil.
La prima Maribel es muy alegre pero bastante supersticiosa. Es actriz y no soporta el color amarillo. Lleva pantalones y vestidos de colores excepto el amarillo, claro…
Mi hermana Sara es muy tranquila e inteligente pero un poco tímida, siempre con sus vaqueros viejos y una camiseta donde está escrito: "Prohibido hablar por el móvil, gracias". Óscar, el novio de Sara, lleva el pelo largo y rizado. No habla mucho.
Mi padre es muy hablador, optimista y sociable, pero sus ojos no soportan los colores claros ni los muy oscuros.
La pobre mamá que es muy buena, no sabe qué hacer ni dónde sentarnos para evitar conflictos.

TRACK 45

Daniel: ¿Qué les parece si hacemos un poco de deporte?
Lucía: Yo tengo mucho sueño. Me levanto todos los días a las 7 de la mañana.
Andrés: Yo no puedo ir. Los miércoles salgo a cenar con mis padres y me acuesto muy tarde.
Candela: ¿Y a qué hora estudias?
Andrés: Por las mañanas, me visto muy rápido y estudio un poco.
Daniel: Yo, en cambio, me despierto a las 9 y llego siempre tarde a la escuela.
Lucía: Chicos… Parecemos cuatro abuelos. Mi padre, que es médico, trabaja todo el día y siempre hace alguna actividad con nosotros.
Candela: Es verdad. Mi madre es profesora y siempre hace mucho deporte.
Daniel: Entonces, ¿por qué no quedamos mañana?
Lucía: Perfecto. ¿Quedamos a las 4?
Daniel: Vale. ¿Dónde quedamos?
Candela: Podemos quedar en la puerta de la escuela.
Andrés: Estupendo. Entonces… quedamos a las 4 en la puerta.

TRACK 46

a. Sara: ¿A qué hora te levantas?
Javier: Me levanto a las siete y cuarto.
Sara: Es muy pronto, ¿no?

b. Jesús: ¿Quieres ir al cine Patio esta noche?
Marta: Sí, genial. ¿A qué hora quedamos?
Jorge: Quedamos a las ocho y media en la puerta del cine.

c. Cristina: ¿A qué hora quedamos?
Begoña: A la una menos veinte.
Cristina: Vale.

TRACK 47

lunes, martes, miércoles, jueves, viernes, sábado, domingo.

TRACK 48

1. Hola, me llamo Adela. Soy profesora y trabajo en una escuela; **2.** Buenos días. Yo soy Antonio. Trabajo en un taller, porque soy mecánico; **3.** Me llamo Elisa, soy enfermera y trabajo en un hospital; **4.** Hola a todos. Mi nombre es David. Soy bombero y trabajo en Barcelona; **5.** Me encantan los animales. Soy veterinaria y trabajo en la Clínica Mascotas; **6.** Hola, ¿qué tal? Soy Carlos. El cocinero de los famosos y me encanta mi trabajo.

TRACK 49

1. Hola, me llamo Juan. Soy estudiante de 1.º de la ESO. Mis clases empiezan a las nueve, por eso yo me levanto todos los días a las ocho; **2.** En esta fotografía estamos mi madre, mi hermana y yo. Mi madre lleva unos zapatos rosas y mi hermana rojos; **3.** Hola, me llamo Marta y soy profesora de este instituto. Los estudiantes estudian inglés por la tarde y español por la mañana; **4.** Yo también soy profesor. Normalmente quedo con mis estudiantes para practicar español. El mejor día es el domingo, pero no puedo. Así que voy a quedar con ellos el martes.

TRACK 50

1. Barcelona, saber, biblioteca, bolígrafo, bueno.
2. Valencia, veinte, vivir, vosotros, vuestro.

TRACK 51

Un día «pura vida»

Mi nombre es Ana y soy de Costa Rica. Es el país más feliz del mundo, según el *Happy Planet Index*, porque la gente está contenta, vive una larga vida y respeta la naturaleza.

Aquí tenemos una frase típica: «pura vida». Significa que es importante disfrutar cada día.

Normalmente, me levanto temprano y desayuno un café. Después, voy a la escuela. Las clases son interesantes y me gusta charlar con mis amigos.
Por la tarde, voy a la playa y hago surf. Dos veces por semana, voy a un santuario de animales, donde soy voluntaria. Vivir en Costa Rica es increíble. ¡Pura vida!

Las maras y la educación

Las maras son pandillas de jóvenes violentos. Son un problema en varios países de América Central.
La violencia de las maras afecta a la educación, porque los profesores y los alumnos tienen miedo de ir a clase.
En El Salvador, el gobierno tiene desde 2012 un pacto con las maras para terminar con la violencia. Honduras, donde 5.000 jóvenes son parte de alguna mara, quiere un pacto similar.

El mundo maya y la tecnología

En América Central se hablan varias lenguas indígenas. Guatemala es el país con más diversidad: ¡hay 21 idiomas, además del español!
Más de 3 millones de personas hablan maya.
Hay muchos proyectos que combinan la lengua maya y la tecnología. Por ejemplo, un traductor de Microsoft y una versión del navegador Firefox están en este idioma.
El maya también se habla en México. Una nueva telenovela, *Baktún*, se emite en Internet en 2013. Es en maya, con subtítulos en español.

TRACK 52

El día a día de muchos hispanos

La gente que visita nuestros países siempre dice que los horarios son diferentes al resto del mundo y que todo se hace más tarde.
Durante la semana no desayunamos mucho, solo café con leche o jugo de naranja, y salimos corriendo, mis padres al trabajo y mi hermana y yo a la escuela. Comemos normalmente de dos a tres de la tarde: papá en un restaurante cerca de la oficina, mamá en la cafetería de la empresa y yo en la escuela. No dormimos la siesta, porque también hacemos cosas por la tarde: ellos trabajan y yo voy a clases de guitarra. La cena en mi familia es a las ocho de la noche. Nos acostamos tarde, a las doce.
Los fines de semana son más relajados. El sábado por la mañana hacemos la compra y limpiamos la casa; por la tarde, quedamos con amigos, cenamos fuera o tomamos algo en una terraza. Los domingos nos levantamos mucho más tarde, desayunamos chocolate con pan dulce o tostadas con mantequilla y mermelada. Visitamos a la familia y comemos juntos. Ese día mis padres preparan una buena comida, como arroz con pollo o carne asada. Por la tarde, paseamos por el parque o vemos una película en el cine. Y descansamos para empezar la semana con energía. Este es el día a día de mi familia, ¿y el de la tuya?

TRACK 53

Hola, me llamo Elena, y os presento a mis amigos de la escuela: Julián es el muchacho de pelo corto, liso y rubio que lleva una camiseta a rayas. Está detrás del sofá. Santiago tiene pelo corto también, pero es moreno, lleva jeans y una camiseta azul, es muy alto. Beatriz es muy guapa y simpática, tiene el pelo largo, liso y es morena; tiene los ojos azules. Es hermana de Santiago. Javier es el más hablador de todos, tiene el pelo rizado y es muy moreno, sus ojos son marrones. Marta es su novia y mi mejor amiga, tiene un pelo precioso, largo y rojo; sus ojos son verdes. Y yo estoy sentada en el centro. Soy rubia, tengo el pelo rizado y muy largo, mis ojos son azules, llevo gafas pero solo para estudiar.

TRACK 54

Quique: ¿Qué tal, muchachos? ¿Qué tal llevan el examen?
Germán: Yo no muy bien, estoy un poco preocupado.
Carmen: Pero si tú estudias mucho, ¡seguro que te sale bien! ¿A que sí, Noelia?
Noelia: Pues claro. Yo creo que va a ser bastante fácil. Además, esta tarde ya no tenemos que estudiar.
Quique: Es verdad. ¿Qué quieren hacer? ¡Ah!, podemos jugar a videojuegos. Me encantan los videojuegos.
Germán: Es que estoy cansado de jugar siempre con los videojuegos.
Carmen: Vale, ¿y qué tal si hacemos deporte?
Germán: No sé, es que me duele la pierna por el partido de fútbol del domingo.
Noelia: Podemos ir a comer algo. Germán, tú siempre tienes hambre, ¿no?
Germán: Vale, pero no quiero ir a un restaurante con mucha gente, que seguro que tenemos que esperar mucho para sentarnos y estoy de mal humor.
Quique: ¿Qué? ¡Pero si siempre estás contento!
Carmen: Chévere, pues más tarde decidimos. Después del examen seguro que estás más contento.
Germán: Es verdad, chicos. ¿Vemos una película? Me gusta la nueva de ciencia ficción.
Quique: A mí también.
Carmen: Sí, de acuerdo.

TRACK 55

Carlos: ¿Qué te pasa, Rafael? Hoy no estás muy contento.
Rafael: Bueno, es que estoy un poco aburrido.
Carlos: ¡Pero qué dices! Si tú eres muy divertido. Venga, vamos a dar un paseo.
Rafael: Bueno, vale.

TRACK 56

1. jugar a los bolos o al boliche; **2.** jugar a los videojuegos; **3.** jugar al fútbol; **4.** ver una película; **5.** hacer natación; **6.** hacer esquí; **7.** hacer judo; **8.** hacer ciclismo; **9.** tomar un refresco; **10.** hacer deporte; **11.** ver la televisión; **12.** ver un concierto; **13.** ver una exposición; **14.** tomar unas tapas; **15.** navegar por Internet; **16.** navegar por el mar; **17.** hacer yoga; **18.** tomar el sol.

TRACK 57

¿En mi tiempo libre? Pues, no sé, me gusta hacer muchas cosas. Lo que más me gusta es viajar a otros países. Prefiero viajar solo, porque así hago lo que quiero. También me encanta escuchar música, siempre llevo mi mp4 con mis canciones favoritas y cuando puedo, voy a conciertos ¡me encanta! La verdad es que no me gusta hacer deporte, prefiero navegar por Internet. Y bueno, muchas más cosas, no sé…

TRACK 58

a. frijoles; **b.** queso; **c.** zanahorias; **d.** leche; **e.** cebollas; **f.** tomates; **g.** huevos; **h.** carne; **i.** mariscos; **j.** naranjas; **k.** pimientos; **l.** pollo.

TRACK 59

1. rana; **2.** carro; **3.** cara; **4.** brazo; **5.** amor; **6.** risa; **7.** directo; **8.** correo; **9.** arroz; **10.** caro.

TRACK 60

Café de Colombia

Colombia es el tercer productor de café mundial.
Más de 500.000 familias colombianas trabajan en la industria del café.

El café llega a Colombia con los españoles en el siglo XVIII.
Los programas de cultivo respetan la biodiversidad del país.

Arepas

Las arepas son un plato típico de Colombia y Venezuela. Son de origen indígena y muy ricas. La gente las come para el desayuno, el almuerzo ¡y hasta la cena! Esta es una receta simple para preparar las arepas típicas de Venezuela. ¡Buen provecho!

Ingredientes para 4 a 6 arepas
2 tazas de masarepa
1 cucharadita de sal
agua y aceite
Preparación
Pon una taza y media de agua en un bol, añade la sal y un poco de aceite. Después, mezcla la harina hasta obtener una masa suave, sin grumos. Luego, haz bolas medianas y aplástalas en forma de discos.
Cocina los discos por los dos lados en una plancha con aceite. Después, pon las arepas en el horno a 180ºC para dorarlas. Rellena con queso, carne o huevos. Y… ¡Buen provecho!

Las compras en Panamá

¿Qué tal? Soy Cintia y vivo en la ciudad de Panamá. Me gusta mucho vivir aquí porque siempre hace calor. La temperatura media es de 29 grados centígrados. Por eso, se vive mucho al aire libre… ¡hasta las compras son al aire libre! Me gusta comprar en los mercados porque las verduras son frescas y la fruta es dulce y deliciosa. Las frutas tropicales son mis favoritas, como la guayaba, el mangostín, la papaya y la piña.
Además, los precios son bajos: la ciudad de Panamá es una de las ocho ciudades más baratas del mundo, según la revista *The Economist*.
A los panameños nos gustan mucho los turistas. ¡Visítanos!

TRACK 61

Las recomendaciones de Mónica
Todos los fines de semana Marta llama a su amiga Mónica por teléfono para hablar sobre el fin de semana. Marta nunca sabe qué quiere hacer, y Mónica siempre tiene buenas ideas. Este es un resumen de las últimas recomendaciones de Mónica a su amiga.

Hola, Marta, pienso que estás contenta porque es viernes y este fin de semana hay muchísimas cosas que puedes hacer. Por ejemplo, si quieres ver una película en el cine, hay tres opciones interesantes: una comedia española con Penélope Cruz, un drama argentino y una película de animación. Por cierto, tengo una novela de un escritor venezolano. Si tienes tiempo, puedes leer la novela este fin de semana, está muy bien.
Otra opción es comer en un restaurante. Yo te recomiendo un restaurante mexicano que tiene una comida muy buena y es bastante barato. Lo mejor son los nachos y los tacos, ¡me encantan los tacos! Además, puedes escuchar rancheras, que son las canciones típicas de México.
Si quieres hacer deporte, podemos montar juntas en bici el domingo. Yo tengo una bici nueva. Es el regalo de mis abuelos por mi cumpleaños.
Por último, ¿te gusta cantar? Es que tengo un karaoke en casa y el domingo puedes venir a cantar con mi hermana y conmigo. ¿Te imaginas? Puede ser muy divertido. Además, mi padre todos los domingos hace asado, entonces puedes almorzar con nosotros también.

TRACK 62

Belén: ¿Conoces este parque natural?

Jesús: No, es la primera vez que estoy aquí. ¡Es increíble!

Belén: Es verdad. A mí me gusta porque no está muy lejos de nuestra casa y podemos venir en carro. A mis hermanos les encanta jugar aquí. Hay árboles muy altos y muchos tipos de flores. ¡Ah! y es fácil ver animales; hay osos, jirafas y muchas especies de pájaros. También hay restaurantes para comer.

Jesús: Genial. ¿Dónde están los restaurantes? Ya tengo un poco de hambre.

Belén: Pues hay muchos, pero el más barato está cerca de la entrada. Nos gusta porque tiene unas mesas de madera bastante grandes.

Jesús: ¿Seguro? Creo que en la entrada no hay restaurantes, según este mapa.

Belén: Claro que sí, hay en la entrada y también detrás del lago. Tu mapa está mal.

Jesús: ¿Y sabes si hay una tienda donde comprar otro mapa?

Belén: Pues creo que hay una tienda delante de la entrada. Venga, vamos al restaurante y después de comer vamos a la tienda y seguimos con la ruta.

TRACK 63

Mi habitación es muy bonita y grande, la zona que más me gusta es la de la mesa, pero hoy no está muy ordenada: por ejemplo, las zapatillas están encima de la silla, el ventilador está entre los cajones y la silla, la papelera está debajo de la mesa, las gafas están delante del bolso, el gato está a la izquierda de la pelota y lejos del póster, los papeles están dentro de la papelera, la mochila está a la derecha de la mesa, el calendario está detrás de la computadora, el teclado está al lado del ratón y cerca del calendario está mi jirafa.

TRACK 64

a. José: ¿Dónde está el restaurante de Pedro?

Lola: El restaurante está cerca de mi casa, en la calle Felicidad.

b. Jesús: Oye, ¿dónde hay una estación de policía?

Laura: No lo sé.

c. Juan: Perdona, Raquel, ¿hay playa en tu ciudad?

Raquel: No, no hay playa, pero hay unos lagos muy bonitos cerca de mi casa.

TRACK 65

1. el autobús; **2.** el taxi; **3.** el avión; **4.** el barco; **5.** la moto; **6.** el tren; **7.** el metro; **8.** ir a pie.

TRACK 66

parque, cine, zapatería, estación de tren, farmacia, tienda de ropa, supermercado, gimnasio, librería, parada de autobús, estación de metro, museo.

TRACK 67

gente, girar / jamón, joven, jueves / gato, gordo, guapo / guitarra, Miguel.

TRACK 68

Gamba, jubilarse, ajo, girar, jabalí, agua, agosto, guisante, guerra, general, girasol, página.

TRACK 69

El deporte nacional

El béisbol es el deporte nacional de República Dominicana, y se practica desde 1866. El equipo más conocido se llama Tigres del Licey. En este país hay muchos jugadores famosos, como Alfonso Soriano, Alberto Pujols y David Ortiz, que juegan en Estados Unidos. Los jugadores dominicanos son campeones: en 2013 ganaron el Clásico Mundial de Béisbol, una competición internacional muy importante.

Puerto Rico, isla del encanto

Puerto Rico recibe más de tres millones de turistas cada año. La isla ofrece vacaciones para todos los gustos. Si prefieres la naturaleza, visita el bosque tropical El Yunque, donde puedes admirar más de 240 tipos de árboles y hermosas cascadas. Si te gustan las aventuras, puedes explorar las cuevas naturales en el Parque de las Cavernas del río Camuy, al noroeste de la isla. Si tu pasión es la ciencia, visita Arecibo, en el norte de Puerto Rico, para observar las estrellas a través de un enorme radiotelescopio. ¡Y hay muchas opciones más!

Carros clásicos en La Habana

En Cuba hay muchos carros antiguos de los años 50. Mucha gente dice que son bonitos, otra gente dice que son demasiado viejos.

Hay pocos carros nuevos porque la ley no permite la importación.

En general, los carros están bastante cuidados.

Hay muchos taxis que son coches clásicos de colores alegres.

Hay una competición anual de estos carros en las calles de La Habana. Se llama «Rally de Automóviles Clásicos Cubanos».

TRACK 70

Las vacaciones de Lucía

Me gusta ir de vacaciones con mis padres. Siempre organizan viajes muy interesantes y diferentes. Este año vamos a ir a México. ¡Me encanta!

¿Y qué voy a hacer? Pues no voy a visitar monumentos ni nada por el estilo. Voy a disfrutar de la naturaleza. ¡Voy a ver ballenas y mariposas monarca! ¿Sabes, querido diario, que todos los años, entre octubre y marzo, 300 millones de mariposas monarca viajan desde Canadá hasta México para hibernar?

Estas mariposas viajan 4.000 kilómetros (durante más de 25 días) en busca de una temperatura más cálida. Dicen que es fantástico poder verlas a todas juntas volando. Su destino es lo que se llama el "Santuario de las mariposas monarca", un bosque donde se quedan hasta primavera. A medida que entras en este bosque hay más y más mariposas que cubren las ramas de los árboles, y con la luz del sol empiezan a volar, y todo se vuelve de color naranja. ¿Cómo algo tan pequeño como una mariposa puede volar tantos kilómetros? ¡Es increíble! También vamos a ver las ballenas grises. En la misma época, muchas de estas ballenas se juntan en las aguas de Baja California para tener sus crías. Además, cuando ven gente en un bote, se acercan y muestran la cola. ¡Voy a hacer un montón de fotos!

TRACK 71

⟫ Buenas noches señorita. Bienvenida al restaurante de Comida Sana. ¿Le gusta la comida sana?

⟫ Sí, por eso estoy aquí. Me encantan las verduras y las frutas.

⟫ Perfecto. Tengo ensalada de zanahorias, tomates y pasta de primero. De segundo, tengo pescado con arroz, o ensalada con pollo.

⟫ ¿Y de postre?

⟫ De postre tengo manzanas, plátano o naranjas.

TRACK 72

La Patagonia está en Argentina y hay montañas y muchos animales marinos. En nuestro viaje a la Patagonia podemos ver y hacer lo siguiente: ver el glaciar más famoso del mundo, el Glaciar Perito Moreno, explorar los parques nacionales y ver ballenas. La Patagonia tiene inviernos muy fríos. Allí, de junio a agosto es invierno, y el verano, de diciembre a marzo. En primavera durante el día hace sol, pero puede llover por la noche. Puedes dormir en pequeños hoteles. En este viaje, que es de aventura, hay que tomar autobuses o caminar para estar más en contacto con la naturaleza y la gente del lugar. No hay que tener un estado físico especial pero tenemos que caminar mucho y hay que saber soportar el calor y el frío, el sol y la lluvia. En la Patagonia puedes comer asados, pescado y una gran variedad de pizzas. Para viajar, solo es necesario llevar el pasaporte.

UNIT 7: ¡CUÁNTAS COSAS!

TRACK 73

Manuela: Mira, Sara, esta es mi nueva habitación.

Sara: ¡Qué bonita!, tienes muchas cosas y todo está bastante ordenado, ¿dónde guardas la ropa?

Manuela: La guardo allí, en aquel mueble. Tiene cajones muy grandes y caben muchas cosas. Y bueno, también la pongo debajo de la cama. Shhh… Mi madre se enfada y dice que me va a quitar mi nuevo portátil si no soy más ordenada.

Sara: ¿Tienes portátil? ¿Dónde?

Manuela: Ahí, debajo del escritorio. Todavía está en la caja. Es más moderno que la computadora de mesa. Ahora es de mi hermana. La tiene en su habitación.

Sara: ¿Qué es esto? ¿Un regalo para mí?

Manuela: No, es mi nuevo mp4. Este tiene más espacio para mi música.

Sara: ¿Y ese póster? ¿De qué concierto es?

Manuela: Es de uno de los conciertos de Pitbull, ¡mi cantante favorito! Pero tengo uno nuevo que me ha regalado mi padre. No es tan grande como ese, pero es mejor, porque es de este año.

Sara: ¡Cuántas cosas tienes!

TRACK 74

Adriana: Mira, abuelita, la nueva computadora de Javi.

Abuelita: ¡Qué moderna! ¿Me explicas para qué sirven esas cosas?

Adriana: Claro. Mira, esto es el monitor y sirve para ver las imágenes. Esto se llama "teclado" y se usa para escribir.

Abuelita: ¿Y eso que mueves con la mano? ¿Para qué se usa?

Adriana: Esto es el ratón y se usa para mover el cursor.

Abuelita: ¡Cuántas cosas aprendes de tu hermano!

TRACK 75

Casa: videoconsola, silla, escritorio, planta, alfombra, estantería, aspiradora, sillón, jarrón, cuadro, lámpara.

Clase: portátil, póster, cuaderno, tijeras, sacapuntas, regla, carpeta, impresora, pinturas, libro, calculadora.

TRACK 76

Cien, ciento uno, doscientos, doscientos dos, trescientos, trescientos tres, cuatrocientos, cuatrocientos quince, quinientos, quinientos veintiséis, seiscientos, seiscientos sesenta y nueve, setecientos, setecientos veinte, ochocientos, ochocientos noventa y siete, ochocientos noventa y nueve, novecientos.

TRACK 77

(303) trescientos treinta y tres; (679) seiscientos setenta y nueve; (510) quinientos diez; (967) novecientos sesenta y siete; (701) setecientos uno; (480) (cuatrocientos ochenta; (992) novecientos noventa y dos; (216) doscientos dieciséis.

TRACK 78

¡Mi celebración favorita!

Julia es una chica de 17 años. Vive en San Luis de Otavalo, Ecuador. Ella habla de su celebración favorita.

¿Dónde está San Luis de Otavalo?

Julia: Está en el norte de mi país, Ecuador, en la provincia de Imbabura.

¿Cómo es tu ciudad?

Julia: Es muy bonita. Está entre montañas y al lado de un volcán. Otavalo es una zona turística. ¡Mucha gente visita mi ciudad!

¿Cuál es el evento más especial?

Julia: Inti Raymi. También se llama el Festival del Sol. Es el evento más importante en mi comunidad. Comienza con el solsticio de verano, el 22 de junio. Esta celebración es una explosión de colores, música y tradiciones indígenas. ¡Es mi fiesta favorita!

El carnaval de Barranquilla

«¡Hola! Soy Manuel y vivo en Barranquilla, Colombia. Mi ciudad es caribeña y está al norte de Colombia. Es un lugar muy importante porque allí celebramos el carnaval de Barranquilla. Los personajes más famosos del carnaval son la reina del carnaval y el diablo Arlequín. La reina es el personaje más querido y el diablo es el personaje menos popular. ¡Todos temen al diablo! A mí me gusta esta celebración porque me encantan los disfraces. ¡Me gusta pintarme de verde! ¿Te gusta disfrazarte? ¿Qué disfraz te gusta?».

El carnaval de las islas Canarias

Cada mes de febrero, Santa Cruz de Tenerife, una de las dos capitales de las Islas Canarias, celebra su carnaval.

Este carnaval es el segundo más grande del mundo. El primero es el de Río de Janeiro, Brasil.

El carnaval tiene dos partes: el carnaval oficial y el carnaval de la calle. En el carnaval oficial participan más de 100 grupos. El carnaval de la calle está abierto a todo el mundo y participan miles de personas.

Este carnaval se celebra desde el siglo XVII.

Los ingredientes más importantes del carnaval son: los disfraces, el maquillaje, la música y la danza.

Esta fiesta es un evento enorme y se necesita un año para organizarlo.

TRACK 79

Un día solo para mamá

En mayo celebramos en muchos países de Hispanoamérica el Día de la Madre. Es un día muy bonito porque toda mi familia se reúne para comer y mamá prepara su especialidad: carne asada con papas y ensalada. Después del postre es el momento de sacar los regalos.

Papá es el más conservador, siempre elige una docena de rosas rojas. Mi hermana mayor adora los perfumes fuertes, es una romántica y cada año regala a mi madre uno nuevo. Mamá siempre sonríe agradecida, pero luego no lo usa. Mis abuelos son más prácticos y prefieren los accesorios: una bufanda de lana, un reloj, un libro de cocina… A mi tía Rosa, la hermana de mi madre, le gusta comprar regalos a todos. Ella siempre le compra cada año una novela histórica a mi madre. La tía Rosa es muy intelectual. Yo soy el más modesto, porque tengo menos dinero, pero también soy el más original de todos. En clase de Arte siempre preparo un regalo hecho a mano. A veces es un jarrón de arcilla, otras veces un cuadro de madera, o un collar con piezas de ámbar. Cuando mamá lo recibe me sonríe satisfecha. Se siente orgullosa y muy contenta de ser, por un día, el centro de atención de todos nosotros. Terminamos la comida todos contentos y después vemos una película: mi madre siempre la elige, claro.

UNIT 8: ¿QUÉ TIEMPO VA A HACER?

TRACK 80

Javi: ¡Hola, mamá!

Madre: Hola, Javi, ¿qué tal la escuela?

Javi: Pues, bien, como siempre.

Madre: Y ese papel, ¿qué es?

Javi: Ah, es para la excursión de este fin de semana. Vamos toda la clase.

Madre: ¿Y a dónde van, Javi?

Javi: Pues, vamos a visitar el Parque Nacional La Campana.

Madre: Muy bien. Y, ¿qué necesitas?

Javi: El profesor dice que tenemos que llevar unos bocadillos y unas bebidas.

Madre: Pero en la montaña normalmente hace frío. Yo creo que debes llevar un anorak, los guantes y el gorro.

Javi: Está bien, mamá. También quiero hacer fotos.

Madre: Bueno, puedes usar mi cámara.

Javi: ¡Fenomenal! Muchas gracias.

Madre: ¿Cuánto hay que pagar por la excursión?

Javi: Muy poco, solo 128 pesos. ¡Ah! Vamos a salir el sábado a las ocho de la mañana.

Madre: Entonces, esa noche tienes que acostarte pronto.

TRACK 81

Muy buenos días. Este es el tiempo que tenemos hoy en Argentina. En la zona norte hace mal tiempo. Nieva en Salta y hay tormentas en Córdoba. En el este de Argentina, en Buenos Aires está nublado, llueve mucho en San Juan y las tormentas van a continuar todo el día. Sin embargo, en el noreste de Argentina, hace sol, y en Posadas, tenemos una temperatura de 30 grados. En el sur, hace frío, especialmente en Puerto Santa Cruz, con temperaturas que van a llegar a solo a los 7 grados. En Río Gallegos, como siempre, hay fuertes vientos. Es todo. Muchas gracias por su atención. Buenos días.

TRACK 82

a. Es especialmente duro en la zona norte e interior, con temperaturas bajo cero y nieve frecuente. También son habituales otros fenómenos como el viento, la niebla o el hielo. En el sur es más suave.

b. Es bastante inestable. Hace calor, frío, viento, pero también llueve mucho y a veces nieva. Es una época perfecta para ver el campo verde y lleno de flores. Las temperaturas varían entre los 15 y los 25 grados.

c. Es un periodo muy caluroso, especialmente en el sur y el interior. Hace muy buen tiempo con temperaturas entre los 35 y los 40 grados. También son frecuentes las tormentas, con rayos y truenos.

d. Normalmente hace frío, pero no demasiado. Llueve bastante y también nieva, especialmente en el norte. Además son frecuentes las nieblas. Las temperaturas están entre los 5 y los 20 grados.

TRACK 83

1. Miño; 2. caña; 3. mano; 4. pena; 5. maño; 6. mino; 7. peña; 8. cana.

TRACK 84

a. niño/nicho; **b.** España/espada; **c.** callo/caño; **d.** moño/mocho; **e.** uña/hucha; **f.** baña/baya.

TRACK 85

Estaciones del sur

El Cono Sur tiene estaciones muy marcadas. Sin embargo, en diciembre, enero y febrero hace calor y en junio, julio y agosto hace frío. ¿Por qué? Porque los países que forman el Cono Sur pertenecen al Hemisferio Sur. Esto significa que mientras en la mayor parte de EE.UU. las temperaturas son bajas en diciembre, enero y febrero, en Argentina, por ejemplo, son altas. Por eso en este territorio geográfico… ¡hay que celebrar la Navidad en la playa y hay que llevar abrigos en agosto!

¡Sandboarding en el desierto de Atacama!

«¡Hola! Me llamo Luca y soy de Buenos Aires, Argentina. La semana próxima voy a ir de viaje con mis amigos Suso, Chico y David. Vamos a ir al desierto de Atacama, en Chile. Este desierto es el lugar más seco del planeta. ¿Qué vamos a hacer allí? ¡Vamos a vivir una aventura extraordinaria! Vamos a practicar el deporte de moda en ese país: el *sandboarding*. Es como el *snowboarding* pero se practica en la arena, no en la nieve».

Ushuaia: el fin del mundo

Ushuaia, en Tierra del Fuego, Argentina, es la ciudad más al sur del mundo. Esta ciudad es conocida como el fin del mundo, por su localización, en el extremo sur del continente americano.

En Ushuaia hay ríos, lagos y glaciares.

Aquí nieva mucho y las temperaturas son frías durante todo el año, con una temperatura media de 5,7 °C (42 °F).

Cuando visitas este lugar, recibes un sello en tu pasaporte donde pone… ¡fin del mundo!

TRACK 86

¿Quedamos para estudiar?

Son las cinco de la tarde y, como todos los viernes, Marta, Luisa y Cristina quedan en el parque para planear el finde. Pero esta vez va a ser diferente. Las muchachas no tienen mucho tiempo para salir a divertirse, porque la próxima semana tienen que hacer tres exámenes. La idea es reunirse para estudiar. Sin embargo, las jóvenes no se ponen de acuerdo, porque Cristina y Luisa tienen algunas cosas que hacer. La madre de Cristina trabaja este sábado y la muchacha tiene que cuidar a su hermano pequeño, porque la guardería está cerrada.

Por su parte, Luisa va a ir al dentista y después va a acompañar a sus padres al supermercado. Marta es la única que tiene la mañana libre, pero quiere esperar a sus amigas porque le gusta estudiar mucho en equipo. Además, a Marta le encantan las Matemáticas y prefiere ayudar a sus compañeras. Así que las tres muchachas van a intentar verse el sábado por la tarde en la biblioteca del barrio. Si todo va bien, el domingo van a tener tiempo para salir, después de una tarde de trabajo en equipo. ¡La unión hace la fuerza!

TRACK 87

Isabel: Este es mi dormitorio. Me gusta mucho, porque aquí están todas mis cosas: mis libros, mis cómics, mi música… ¿Ven esa cama? Es nueva. Esta es más grande y cómoda que la vieja. La cama vieja ahora la utilizamos para las visitas y está en la habitación de invitados. El escritorio no me gusta y lo quiero cambiar, porque este es muy pequeño y no sirve para poner la computadora.

Sara: Este es el salón de la casa de mi abuela. Me encanta, porque tiene muchos muebles antiguos y muchos objetos de decoración muy delicados, como aquel jarrón de cristal y ese sofá de cuero. Yo la ayudo a limpiar y les paso la aspiradora a estas alfombras una vez a la semana. Lo mejor es la terraza. ¿Ven aquella mesa de metal? La utilizamos en verano para almorzar.

Javi: Pues, este es mi escritorio. Mis padres me dicen que siempre está desordenado. Yo les digo que lo ordeno todas las mañanas, pero por las noches vuelve a estar igual. Creo que no tengo mucho espacio para mis cosas, por eso le voy a regalar a mi hermana estos videojuegos. Yo no los uso ya y los cedés los voy a guardar en esa caja de plástico.

TRACK 88

≫ En Cantabria llueve mucho y normalmente está nublado. Por eso tiene un paisaje muy verde. Uno de los lugares más interesantes para visitar son los Picos de Europa.

≫ Andalucía es la región más seca de España. En verano hace mucho calor y en invierno casi no llueve. En Sevilla a veces tienen 40 grados en verano.

≫ Ávila está en Castilla y León, una de las regiones más frías de España. En invierno hace mucho frío y normalmente nieva en diciembre y enero.

AUDIOSCRIPTS Workbook

UNIT 1: HOLA, ¿QUÉ TAL?

TRACK 1

Ana: Hola, buenos días. Me llamo Ana González y soy la nueva profesora de Español. ¿Cómo estás?

Diego: Encantado, Ana. Bienvenida a nuestra escuela.

Ana: Muchas gracias. ¿Cómo te llamas?

Diego: Me llamo Diego.

Ana: ¿Y qué haces?

Diego: Soy profesor de Matemáticas.

Ana: ¿Cuántos años tienes?

Diego: Tengo 25 años.

Ana: Ah, yo también tengo 25 años.

Diego: Entonces tenemos la misma edad.

Ana: ¿Y dónde vives?

Diego: Vivo en la avenida de la Paz, cerca de la escuela. Vivo en una residencia con otros profesores.

Ana: ¡Ah!, ¿sí? ¿Y cuántos sois?

Diego: Somos seis en total. ¡Ah! Y también tenemos un perro y un gato.

Ana: ¡Qué bien! Yo también tengo un perro.

Diego: ¡Magnífico! Podemos salir todos juntos a pasear.

Ana: ¡Sí!

Diego: Bueno, Ana, tengo que irme, adiós, encantado de conocerte.

Ana: Igualmente.

TRACK 2

Presentador: Y aquí estamos con la concursante Lola. Lola, ¿estás nerviosa?

Concursante: Sí, un poco.

Presentador: ¡Puedes ganar un maravilloso viaje a Europa! ¿Preparada?

Concursante: Sí.

Presentador: El tema es: "Los hispanos en Estados Unidos".

Concursante: ¡Uf!, difícil.

Presentador: Mucha suerte, Lola. Primera pregunta. El porcentaje de hispanos que vive en Estados Unidos es del… ¿a) 16,9 por ciento, b) 18% o c) 59 por ciento?

Concursante: Opción a.

Presentador: Lola dice *a) 16.9 por ciento,* y la respuesta es… ¡Correcta! Efectivamente, casi 17 por ciento de hispanos. Segunda pregunta: Rodríguez, Méndez, López, Alba, García, Lovato… son apellidos de origen hispano. Di tres nombres de famosos con estos apellidos y su profesión.

Concursante: ¡Uf!… eh… las actrices Demi Lovato y Jennifer López y el escritor Gabriel García Márquez.

Presentador: ¡Correcto! Pregunta número 3. Monterrey, San Francisco, Los Ángeles, Florida… son ciudades con nombres españoles. Di el nombre de dos estados que también tienen nombre español.

Concursante: Colorado y Las Vegas.

Presentador: ¡Correcto! Pregunta 4. ¿Verdadero o Falso? El español es el segundo idioma más hablado en Estados Unidos.

Concursante: ¡Verdadero!

Presentador: ¡Correcto!

Presentador: Pregunta 5. Ben Affleck, Gwyneth Paltrow y Matt Damon no son hispanos pero hablan español. ¿Verdadero o falso?

Concursante: Ehhhh… Verdadero. Es verdadero.

Presentador: ¡Pues sí! ¡Todos saben hablar español! ¡Perfecto, Lola! La última pregunta y ¡un viaje a Europa! Atención. Pregunta número 6. Este es un mapa de California. En el mapa hay varias ciudades con nombre español y que tienen algo en común. ¿Sabes qué es?

Concursante: ¡Uf!, a ver… ¿Tienen playa?

Presentador: ¡Noooooooooooo! La respuesta correcta es que muchas ciudades tienen nombres de santos: Santa Mónica, San Francisco, Santa Cruz… ¡Qué pena! ¡Qué mala suerte! Bueno, Lola…

UNIT 2: ESTÁS EN TU CASA

TRACK 3

Texto 1: Hola, me llamo Eliana. Para mí, el lugar preferido de mi casa es mi dormitorio.
Allí hablo con mis amigos, escucho música y hablo por teléfono. Mi dormitorio es amarillo y tiene una cama, un armario, una lámpara y una mesa para estudiar. En la mesa está la computadora para hacer trabajos para la escuela, pero yo la utilizo mucho para chatear con mis amigos.

Texto 2: Hola, me llamo Marisa. Yo pienso que el salón es el lugar más interesante de la casa. Allí hablamos mis amigas y yo sobre nuestros hijos y nuestras profesiones. Mi salón es blanco y tiene dos sofás negros. También hay una estantería, una mesa y una lámpara amarilla. En el salón está el televisor. Cuando no tengo mucho trabajo veo documentales o las noticias.

Texto 3: Hola, me llamo Enrique. En mi opinión, la cocina es el lugar más divertido de la casa. Para mí, cocinar es fantástico. Tomo un refresco, escucho música y preparo platos deliciosos para mi familia. Es un lugar muy relajante. Es azul, tiene horno y estufa.

UNIT 3: MI FAMILIA ES MUY SIMPÁTICA

TRACK 4

Miguel tiene una familia pequeña, solo tiene dos hermanas, Teresa y Bárbara, y son más mayores que él. Sus padres se llaman Patricia y Enrique, ahora viven en Sevilla y Miguel no los ve con mucha frecuencia. Miguel está casado con Julia y se conocen hace 22 años. Tiene solo dos primos y cuatro sobrinos: Alejandra, la mayor, María, Julia y Diego, el más pequeño.

UNIT 4: TODOS LOS DÍAS LO MISMO

TRACK 5

De lunes a viernes me levanto a las 8 porque tengo escuela y empiezo a las 9. Me ducho rápido, desayuno leche con cereales y corro a la escuela para no llegar tarde. Como a las 2 con mi familia. Mi madre es profesora de Matemáticas en Secundaria y llega a casa para comer con mi hermano y conmigo. Mi padre llega más tarde porque es médico y su día es más largo. Por la tarde quedo con Marta y estudiamos juntas, después hacemos deporte los martes y jueves. Los lunes y miércoles toco el piano. Me acuesto a las 11 y leo un poco hasta las 12. ¡El fin de semana es mucho mejor! Quedo con mis amigos y jugamos a los videojuegos y vemos una película en el cine.

UNIT 5: ¿TE GUSTA?

TRACK 6

Padre: ¿Qué prefieren hacer este fin de semana?
Hijo: Yo quiero ir de compras.
Hija: Pues yo prefiero ver una película. No me gusta ir de compras.
Madre: ¿Por qué no vamos a visitar a la tía Margarita?
Los dos hijos: ¡¡¡¡Noooo!!! ¡¡¡¡Otra vez a casa de la tía Margarita noooo!!!
Padre: A mí tampoco me gusta esa idea. ¿Y si montamos en bici por el parque?
Madre: Bueeeno, vale, está bien.

Hijo: ¡Genial!, ¡un paseo en bici!, ¡me encanta montar en bici!
Hija: ¡Puf!… Bueno, pero por la tarde vamos al cine, ¿vale?
Padre: De acuerdo, por la mañana, bici, por la tarde, cine.
Madre: Y el domingo, visitar a la tía Margarita…
Hijo: ¡Mamá…!
Hija: ¡Que noooo!
Padre: Bueno, el domingo lo decidimos…

UNIT 6: VAMOS DE VIAJE

TRACK 7

1. No me gusta viajar en autobús, prefiero ir en tren.
2. ¿Conoces a Iker? Es mi primo, vive en Colombia.
3. ¿De dónde vienes?
4. Esta noche voy a una fiesta.
5. Estela es de México.
6. María siempre va a pie. No le gusta el metro.

TRACK 8

Amaya: Ven, que quiero enseñarte mis fotos del viaje por el Caribe. Mira qué foto más bonita. La foto está hecha en la selva de Matagalpa.
Estela: ¡Ay, qué simpática! Es una rana muy bonita.
Amaya: Esta rana es uno de los animales más característicos de Nicaragua y Costa Rica.
Estela: ¿Y en esta foto dónde estás?

Amaya: A ver, aquí estoy en el Parque Natural del volcán Arenal. En un puente colgante.
Estela: ¡Qué miedo pasar por ahí!
Amaya: Sí, la verdad es que sí. Es un puente bastante alto.
Estela: ¿Y este monumento? Es una pirámide, ¿no?
Amaya: Sí, es Chichén Itzá. Es una pirámide maya que está en la Península del Yucatán. Tiene unas escaleras y puedes subir hasta arriba.
Estela: ¿Y estos muchachos quiénes son?
Amaya: ¡Ah! Esta foto es de La Habana, bailando en la playa con unos amigos.
Estela: Allí todo el mundo baila muy bien, ¿verdad?
Amaya: Sí. La salsa es el baile más popular, pero también hay otros bailes.
Estela: Ya. Oye y esta foto, ¡guau!
Amaya: ¿Te gusta? La foto está tomada desde un barco. Esto es en Samaná. Entre diciembre y marzo, las ballenas están en el Caribe y puedes tomar un barco para ver cómo saltan. ¡Es impresionante!

UNIT 7: ¡CUÁNTAS COSAS!

TRACK 9

1. Llamo mucho a mis amigas por teléfono, no me gusta enviar mensajes, prefiero hablar. Creo que mantener una conversación es más personal que chatear. Además prefiero el teléfono fijo, es más económico.

2. Yo nunca uso Internet. Todas mis fotos las tengo en papel y las pongo en un álbum. Las fotos digitales son menos bonitas.

3. Pues yo para comunicarme con mis amigas uso What's App. Me encanta poner emoticonos, son más divertidos que las palabras. También podemos compartir fotos, es más rápido así.

4. Me conecto a Internet desde la computadora, desde el celular y desde la tableta para cosas de trabajo… estoy siempre *online*. Internet es la mejor forma de estar en contacto.

UNIT 8: ¿QUÉ TIEMPO VA A HACER?

TRACK 10

Periodista: ¿Raúl, duermes mucho?

Raúl: Sí, para estar en forma necesito dormir nueve horas como mínimo.

Periodista: ¿Y haces algún tipo de dieta?

Raúl: No, yo creo que hay que comer de todo, especialmente, frutas, verduras, pollo y pescado. No debemos comer mucha carne ni dulces como pasteles o helado.

Periodista: ¿Y cuando estás enfermo…?

Raúl: Casi nunca estoy enfermo, solo algún resfriado o tos, cuando hace frío. Me cuido mucho.

Periodista: Entonces, ¿qué aconsejas a nuestros oyentes para una vida sana?

Raúl: Yo creo que la gente tiene que comer bien, salir a la calle cuando hace buen tiempo, necesitamos tener amigos, hacer un poco de deporte, dormir bastante y en general yo creo que hay que disfrutar simplemente de las cosas sencillas de la vida… ¡¡¡Eso es!!!

Periodista: Bueno, parece sencillo, vamos a ver si todos tomamos nota.

VIDEOSCRIPTS

EPISODIO 1: SALUDOS Y MOCHILAS

Alfonso: En esta tienda no hay, seguro…
Juanjo: Sí, aquí venden mochilas, seguro que sí, vamos…
Alfonso: Esta es una tienda de ropa…
Juanjo: Sí, sí, pero también venden mochilas…
Alfonso: No creo…
Juanjo: ¡Uf!, sí.
Eli: Mochilas, no sé… Pero tienen ropa muy bonita.
Lorena: ¿Hola, puedo ayudarles en algo?
Alfonso: Hola. Buscamos mochilas.
Juanjo: Sí,… eh… mochilas pequeñas.
Lorena: ¿Mochilas?
Juanjo: Sí, para ir a clase.
Alfonso: Para llevar los libros.
Juanjo: Y las carpetas.
Alfonso: Y los bolígrafos.
Juanjo: Y el diccionario.
Lorena: Sí, sí, ya sé. Allí hay varias mochilas.
Alfonso: Muy bien. Vamos a mirar.
Juanjo: Sí, vamos.
Lorena: ¿Tú también buscas mochilas?
Eli: Sí, pero también quiero comprar ropa.
Lorena: Pues aquí tienes mucha ropa.
Eli: Sí. Es agosto. Pronto comienzo las clases en la universidad. ¡Necesito ropa!
Lorena: ¿Eres estudiante?
Eli: Sí. Voy a la Universidad. Ellos también. Somos compañeros.
Lorena: Por cierto, mi nombre es Lorena.
Eli: Hola, Lorena. ¡Encantada! Yo me llamo Eli.

Lorena: ¡Encantada, Eli!
Eli: ¿De dónde eres, Lorena?
Lorena: Soy de Venezuela. Estoy aquí por trabajo. Es mi primera semana en la ciudad. ¡Y mi primer día de trabajo en esta tienda!
Eli: ¡Bienvenida a la ciudad!
Lorena: ¡Gracias! ¿Ustedes son de aquí?
Eli: Yo soy colombiana. Vivo aquí con mis padres desde agosto de 2010.
Lorena: ¡Qué bien!
Eli: Muchachos, les presento a Lorena, es venezolana. Él es Alfonso y es mexicano.
Alfonso: Encantado, Lorena.
Lorena: Encantada.
Juanjo: Yo me llamo Juanjo.
Lorena: Encantada. ¿De dónde eres? Tu acento no es de aquí…
Juanjo: Yo soy español. De Madrid.
Eli: Lorena es nueva en la ciudad. Es su primera semana aquí. ¿Quieres conocer la ciudad? Puedo enseñarte la ciudad un poco.
Lorena: ¡Genial! No conozco a nadie aquí.
Juanjo: Pues ya nos conoces a nosotros tres.
Eli: ¿Cuál es tu número de teléfono? Te llamo otro día y quedamos.
Lorena: ¡Estupendo! Apunta…
Lorena: Uno – cuatro – ocho – diecisiete – veintidós – treinta.
Eli: Muy bien, ya lo tengo. ¿Te llamo el fin de semana?
Lorena: Sí, el fin de semana no trabajo.
Eli: Muy bien. Pues… ¡estupendo! ¿Nos vamos, muchachos?
Alfonso: Chao, Lorena.
Juanjo: Sí, hasta luego…
Lorena: ¡No compraron nada!

EPISODIO 2: UNOS MUEBLES HO-RRI-BLES

Alfonso: 67.
Juanjo: La mesa mide… 57 centímetros. Y aquí… 78 centímetros. Tenemos un problema, Alfonso. Esta mesa mide 78 centímetros. No entra ahí.
Alfonso: ¿78? No es un problema: cambiamos la cama y ponemos ahí la mesilla blanca. ¿Dónde está la estantería?
Juanjo: En la puerta del armario grande.
Alfonso: ¿Cuál ponemos?, ¿la verde?
Juanjo: No. Esa, la azul. ¡Es mi estantería favorita!, ¿eh?
Alfonso: ¿En serio? Está bien, entonces la ponemos aquí. Pero para mí, el azul con el marrón es feo. ¿Qué piensas?
Juanjo: Mira, Alfonso: sinceramente, yo creo que estos muebles no son para esta habitación.
Alfonso: Pues hay espacio para todos.
Juanjo: Pero yo no hablo del tamaño. En mi opinión, estos muebles son feos. ¡Muy feos! No me gustan nada.
Alfonso: ¿Feos? ¡Pero qué dices, güey! Para mí, son unos muebles muy elegantes.
Juanjo: ¿Elegantes? Sí, claro. Muy modernos. Última moda.
Alfonso: No, modernos no son, es verdad. Son muebles de estilo antiguo. Pero lo más importante para nosotros es que… ¡estos muebles son muy baratos! ¡Solo 99 dólares! Son de segunda mano…
Juanjo: ¿Pero quién compra muebles así? ¿Drácula?
Alfonso: ¡Muy gracioso! Para mí son perfectos. Y creo que a Eli le va a gustar esta decoración.
Juanjo: Pues yo no sé qué piensa Eli, pero para mí, ¡estos muebles son realmente HO-RRI-BLES!

Alfonso: ¡Bah!
Juanjo: En serio, yo pienso que… ¡son realmente HO-RRI-BLES!
Alfonso: Ni modo, tú no sabes nada de decoración. Voy a poner la estantería encima de la mesa, es el lugar perfecto, verás…
Eli: Hola, chicos, ¿qué tal?… ¿Qué hacen? ¿Jugar a los vaqueros?
Alfonso: Hola, Eli… Pues aquí estamos, decorando la habitación.
Juanjo: Sí… ¡La habitación de Drácula!
Eli: Aquí tienes el libro que me pediste en clase. Chicos, ¿y todos estos muebles? ¿Cómo van ustedes a ordenar todo esto? ¿Dónde ponen ese sofá grande? Para mí, esta habitación es demasiado pequeña y no hay espacio para todo…
Alfonso: Pues yo pienso que sí.
Eli: ¿Y de dónde son estos muebles?
Alfonso: De una tienda de muebles de estilo "retro".
Juanjo: Sí, sí, son de diseño. Son muy caros…
Alfonso: ¿Te gustan?
Eli: Pues no sé, chicos, para mí son un poco… no sé… antiguos.
Alfonso: ¡Ese es el secreto! Son de estilo clásico y elegante. Para nosotros estos muebles son perfectos, ¿verdad, Juanjo?
Juanjo: Sí, sí, claro. ¡Perfectos! ¡Mi estilo favorito!
Alfonso: ¿Qué opinas tú?
Eli: ¿La verdad?
Alfonso y Juanjo: ¡Sí!, ¡sí!
Eli: Pues yo pienso que estos muebles son realmente HO-RRI-BLES. Eh… bueno, voy a la biblioteca. ¡Hasta luego, chicos!
Alfonso: Oh, Dios mío, ¡es verdad! ¡Estos muebles son realmente HO-RRI-BLES!

Lorena: ¡Qué casa más bonita tienes, Eli!

Eli: ¡Gracias! Vivo aquí con mis padres y mi hermano. Hay días en los que me gustaría vivir en un apartamento, como tú.

Lorena: Sí, pero mi apartamento es muy pequeño.

Eli: Es muy bonito, seguro. En fin, vamos a mi dormitorio y miramos la ropa. Necesito tu consejo, Lorena, ¡muchas gracias por venir a ayudarme a elegir la ropa para mi cita!

Lorena: De nada, para eso estamos las amigas. ¿Es esta tu familia?

Eli: Sí, mi mamá siempre toma fotos de todo. Mira… Aquí estoy yo de pequeña.

Lorena: Qué bonita. En esa foto tienes el pelo muy rizado.

Eli: Sí, pero en esta otra lo tengo liso.

Lorena: ¿Y esta es tu mamá de joven?

Eli: Sí, y la muchacha que está al lado con el pelo largo es mi tía. Aquí estamos en la graduación de mi tía.

Lorena: ¡Qué jóvenes y guapas! Tu tía es muy alta y delgada. ¿Este es tu padre?

Eli: Sí, está aquí con mi hermano Sebas de pequeño. Pero ahora está casi calvo y tiene el pelo blanco.

Lorena: ¿Y esta es tu madre ahora? Se conserva muy bien.

Eli: Sí, solo que ahora usa lentes y lleva el pelo más largo.

Lorena: Y este niño con cara de simpático es tu hermano, ¿verdad?

Eli: Sí, es mi hermano Sebastián, aunque todos lo llamamos Sebas. En esta foto tiene 6 años. Es simpático pero un poco tímido… Bueno, vamos a mirar la ropa. Primera pregunta, ¿falda o pantalones?

Lorena: Para la primera cita con un chico, falda, siempre falda.

Eli: Perfecto, a ver… ¿Te gusta esta?

Lorena: Sí, un poco corta, quizás, ¿qué blusa tienes para llevar con la falda?

Eli: Tengo por aquí una blusa que es perfecta. ¿Esta te gusta?

Lorena: Mm… ¿Qué tal si llevas un vestido?

Eli: Sí, tengo varios… ¿Este te gusta?

Lorena: No sé… ¿Llevas zapatos o sandalias?

Eli: Este vestido queda muy bonito con… estos zapatos.

Sebas: ¡Dios mío! ¡No puedes imaginar lo que estoy viendo ahora mismo aquí, en casa, Felipe!

Felipe: ¿Qué?

Sebas: Mi hermana está en casa con una amiga nueva, ¡y qué linda!

Felipe: ¡Pero todas las amigas de tu hermana son guapas, Sebas!

Sebas: Esta es totalmente diferente.

Felipe: ¿En serio? ¿Cómo es?

Sebas: Tiene el pelo liso y castaño. Es delgada, es alta. Un momento… Ah, sí. Tiene los ojos grandes y marrones.

Felipe: ¡Uf! ¿Qué lleva?

Sebas: Lleva pantalones cortos de color blanco y una blusa de flores de color azul. ¡Felipe, esta es la chica más linda de todas las amigas de mi hermana!

Felipe: Pregúntale si tiene novio…

Sebas: Sí, claro, ¿y le pregunto también si esta noche quiere salir con mi amigo Felipe?

Felipe: Tú pregúntale si tiene novio… ¿O eres tímido?

Sebas: ¿Yo tímido? Ahora verás… Hola, me llamo Sebas, soy el hermano de Eli. ¿Tienes novio?

Eli: ¡Pero qué maleducado que eres! Perdona, Lorena, mi hermano… Tiene 16 años y solo piensa en chicas.

Lorena: Sí, es verdad. Y no es nada tímido. Bueno, ¿qué opinas de este vestido para mí?

Eli: ¿Para ti?

Lorena: Sí, ¡para mi primera cita con tu hermano pequeño!

Alfonso: ¡Estos horarios de clase son horribles!

Juanjo: Mis horarios sí que son horribles.

Alfonso: Todas las mañanas mis clases empiezan a las 8:30. Desde el lunes hasta el viernes. ¡Todos los días entre semana! ¡Todos!

Juanjo: ¡Y yo no tengo ni una sola tarde libre! ¡Eso sí es un problema!

Alfonso: ¿A qué hora empiezan tus clases por las mañanas?

Juanjo: Lunes, martes y jueves a las 10.

Alfonso: ¡Qué suerte! Al menos no tienes que levantarte muy temprano.

Juanjo: No es verdad. Mira, los miércoles y los viernes… ¡me levanto a las 7 de la mañana!

Alfonso: Pues esa es la hora a la que yo me levanto todos los días, excepto los fines de semana. ¡No puede ser!

Juanjo: Pero así tú tienes mucho tiempo libre por las tardes. ¡Yo tengo clases todas las tardes!

Alfonso: Pues yo prefiero tener clases por las tardes. Me acuesto tarde y es difícil levantarme temprano como mi padre. Es mecánico y se despierta todos los días a las 6 de la mañana.

Juanjo: Pues, mi madre es enfermera y trabaja en un hospital en otra parte de la ciudad. Se levanta a las 5:30. ¡Es de noche cuando toma el autobús!

Alfonso: Comprendo, pero es algo que hacen todos los días y ya es parte de su rutina. ¿Crees que vamos a sobrevivir a estos horarios de clase?

Juanjo: ¡No es tan terrible, hombre! Por lo menos tienes tiempo libre todas las tardes para hacer lo que quieres.

Alfonso: ¡Bah! A mí no me importa mucho tener las tardes libres. Las tardes solo son para estudiar o para hacer la tarea.

Juanjo: Pues a mí sí que me importan las tardes. Me importan mucho. Todos los martes y los jueves voy al gimnasio.

Alfonso: ¡Pero si hace mucho que tú no vas al gimnasio!

Juanjo: Sí, es verdad. Pero durante este curso yo quiero ir para hacer ejercicio regularmente. Además, todos los lunes, por las tardes, quedo con unos amigos para jugar al Mario Kart.

Alfonso: ¿Al Mario Kart?

Juanjo: Sí. Soy miembro del "Club de Amigos del Mario Kart". Y todos los lunes quedamos para jugar.

Alfonso: ¡Qué emocionante!

Juanjo: Y con estos horarios, ¿cuándo vamos a ir juntos a jugar al fútbol? Por las mañanas no puede ser.

Alfonso: Sí, por la mañana juntos, imposible. Tú entras en clase muy temprano.

Juanjo: ¿Y las noches? ¿Qué tienes por las noches? Estamos libres los dos, y las instalaciones deportivas están abiertas hasta tarde.

Alfonso: No me gusta jugar al fútbol por la noche, Juanjo, lo sabes. A mí por las noches me gusta estar en casa y leer, o ver una película, o navegar por Internet.

Juanjo: Bueno, si quieres yo voy al gimnasio solo los martes, así tengo las tardes de los jueves libres y podemos jugar. ¿Qué tienes las tardes de los jueves?

Alfonso: ¡Libres! De acuerdo. Los jueves, fútbol. Oye, ¿sabes que voy a levantarme muy temprano todos los días mientras tú duermes? ¡Voy a sentir envidia al verte dormir!

Juanjo: Pues yo, en realidad, prefiero levantarme temprano todos los días para ir a clase. Sí, vale, lo sé: voy a clase como un zombi, pero… ¡prefiero tener las tardes libres!

Alfonso: Tú vas como un zombi a todas las horas del día.

Juanjo: ¡Muy gracioso! Y tú despierto de noche y durmiendo de día, ¿no? ¡Como un vampiro!

Alfonso: Un zombi y un vampiro viviendo juntos en la misma habitación. ¡Perfecto!

Juanjo: Pues hablando de compartir habitación. Con estos horarios de clase y con todas las tardes ocupadas, yo no voy a poder hacer las tareas de casa.

Alfonso: ¿Qué quieres decir?

Juanjo: Que a partir de ahora eres tú quien tiene las tardes libres…

Alfonso: ¿Y?

Juanjo: Que ya tienes cosas que hacer por las tardes: limpiar la casa, ordenar de una vez estos muebles, lavar la ropa, hacer la compra…

Alfonso: Pues aquí no veo nada de eso.

Juanjo: Pues toma, escríbelo y ¡nunca lo olvides!

EPISODIO 5: UN PELO EN MI CENA

Eli: Bonito restaurante. Es la primera vez que vengo a cenar aquí.
Lorena: Yo también. Dicen que se come muy bien. A mí me encanta la comida española.
Eli: ¿Pero no será muy caro?
Lorena: No, dicen que además está muy bien de precio. Todo el mundo habla maravillosamente de este lugar.
Juanjo: Buenas noches, señoritas...
Eli y Lorena: ¡JUANJO!
Juanjo: ¡Uy! Hola, chicas... ¿Qué hacen aquí?
Eli: ¿Nosotras? Mejor dicho, ¿qué haces tú aquí?
Juanjo: Bueno, este es el restaurante de mi tío. Yo, a veces, le ayudo. Normalmente, estoy en la cocina pero uno de los camareros está enfermo hoy y tengo que servir las mesas esta noche.
Lorena: Estás muy guapo vestido así... Pareces un chico serio y todo...
Juanjo: Gracias... bueno, ¿qué quieren para cenar, señoritas?
Eli: No sé. ¿Qué recomiendas?
Juanjo: Pues no sé... ¿Os gusta la comida española?
Lorena: ¡Me gusta mucho! Pero no conozco todo... A ver... ¿Qué es "gazpacho"?
Juanjo: Es una sopa fría de tomate. Una buena elección para el primer plato.
Eli: Yo, de primero, quiero una ensalada. Y de segundo, quiero tortilla española.
Lorena: ¿Qué es tortilla española?
Juanjo: Es una tortilla pero con huevos, cebolla y patatas, o papas como decís vosotras. Está deliciosa. Seguro que te gusta.
Lorena: Ah, no. Yo quiero pollo con arroz. Me encanta el pollo.

Juanjo: Muy bien, ¿y de beber?
Eli: Yo quiero una limonada.
Lorena: Para mí, refresco de naranja, por favor.
Juanjo: ¡Marchando!
Eli: ¡Ay! ¿Por qué grita tan alto?
Lorena: No sé, seguramente... ¡porque es español!
Juanjo: Chicas, perdonad, estoy confundido... ¿Era sopa de jamón de primero y arroz con verdura de segundo, verdad?
Eli: ¡No! Ensalada y tortilla para mí, y gazpacho y pollo con arroz para Lorena...
Juanjo: Será mejor que tome nota... Ensalada y tortilla para ti..., y... gazpacho y arroz con verdura para ti...
Lorena: ¡No! ¡Arroz con verdura, no! ¡Arroz con pollo!
Juanjo: Sí, sí, eso... con pollo. Bien. ¿Algo más, señoritas?
Eli: No. Luego pedimos el postre.
Lorena: Por cierto, Juanjo, este cuchillo está un poco sucio.
Juanjo: Tome, señorita, ya está perfecto... Lo siento, ahora te traigo uno limpio.
Lorena: Parece que Juanjo no tiene mucha experiencia como mesero.
Eli: No. Se ve que es su primer día. Oye, ¡realmente tengo hambre!
Lorena: Sí, yo también estoy hambrienta.
Juanjo: ¡Aquí tenéis! A ver... ¿Cómo es?... Los platos se sirven por la izquierda y se retiran por la derecha... ¿O era al revés? Ahora sí que está todo correcto. Los platos servidos por la derecha. ¡Buen provecho, señoritas!
Eli: Perdona, Juanjo, pero... hay un pelo en mi ensalada.
Juanjo: ¡Ay, perdón, perdón, perdón!, las cosas se retiran por la izquierda.

EPISODIO 6: UN BARRIO INTERESANTE

Eli: ¿Sí?
Lorena: Hola, Eli, ¿qué tal?
Eli: Hola, Lorena, justamente estaba pensando en ti. Muchas gracias por la cena de anoche. ¡Qué divertido todo!
Lorena: Sí, sí, muy divertido. Y la comida, muy rica. Es un buen restaurante. ¡Pobre Juanjo, tiene mucho que aprender!
Eli: Sí, es verdad... Oye, ¿para qué me llamas?
Lorena: Necesito tu ayuda. Ya sabes, llevo poco tiempo en la ciudad y necesito localizar algunos lugares.
Eli: No te preocupes, ¿qué es lo que necesitas saber?
Lorena: Ahora lo más importante es encontrar un gimnasio bueno, pero no muy caro.
Eli: Déjame pensar... Sí... Tú vives en el barrio de Los Arenales, ¿verdad?
Lorena: Sí, cerca del museo.
Eli: ¿Sabes dónde está la parada de bus de la línea 12?
Lorena: Claro que sí, está delante de mi calle.
Eli: Pues justo detrás de la parada de bus hay una calle pequeña.
Lorena: Sí, me parece que sé cuál es.
Eli: Pues ahí hay un gimnasio. Es muy bueno y está bastante cerca de tu calle.
Lorena: ¡Perfecto! Mañana mismo voy a visitarlo.
Eli: Sí, en la zona en la que vives hay muchas cosas. Es un barrio muy interesante.
Lorena: Bueno, yo todavía no lo conozco bien. ¿Y sabes dónde hay una biblioteca cerca de casa?
Eli: Pues creo que sí, pero está un poco lejos de tu casa.
Lorena: ¿Puedo ir a pie?
Eli: Sí, pero... oye, ¿tienes bicicleta? Hay muchos carriles de bici por la ciudad que pasan por las zonas con más tráfico. Hay un carril de esos que te lleva directamente a la biblioteca.
Lorena: Chévere, me encanta andar en bicicleta. ¿Dónde está la biblioteca?

Eli: Está detrás de la iglesia de San Luis.
Lorena: No sé dónde está eso. Espera, voy a mirar el Google Maps... Sí, aquí está la iglesia. La veo.
Eli: Pues detrás, no sé exactamente el nombre de la calle.
Lorena: Calle Acacia. Sí, aquí está. También hay un cine, ¿verdad?
Eli: ¿Un cine? No lo sé...
Lorena: Pues sí. Chévere. Un cine cerca de mi casa... Y una última pregunta, ¿dónde puedo comprar algunas cosas para decorar mi casa?
Eli: Precisamente estoy de compras en el centro comercial y aquí hay una tienda de decoración muy bonita. ¡Ven aquí y compramos juntas!
Lorena: ¡Genial! ¡Ay, perfecto! ¿Y dónde está el centro comercial?
Eli: Al sur de la ciudad. Está un poco lejos.
Lorena: ¿Puedo ir en la bici?
Eli: No. Mejor en el metro, es más rápido. Sube a la a línea seis. La parada es Plaza Sur.
Lorena: Estupendo. Voy para allá ahora mismo. ¡Chao!... Disculpe, ¿puede usted decirme dónde está el centro comercial?
Señor: Sí, claro. Sigue todo recto y la segunda calle a tu izquierda, gira y lo vas a encontrar de frente.
Lorena: Gracias, muy amable... ¿Eli? ¿Aló! Ya estoy aquí, delante de la puerta del centro comercial.
Eli: Yo también, pero no te veo.
Lorena: Sí, aquí, al lado de la estatua.
Eli: ¿La estatua? ¿Pero qué dices? ¿En qué lado estás?
Lorena: Pues en el de... Ah, espera, ahora te veo...
Muchacha: ¿Sí?
Lorena: Perdona, busco a otra persona...
Eli: Creo que me buscas a mí, ¿verdad?

EPISODIO 7: UN BOLSO PARA MI HERMANA

Sebas: Hola.

Lorena: Hola, ¿puedo ayudarte en algo?

Sebas: Sí... esto... yo..., ¿no me recuerdas?

Lorena: Bueno... ¡Ah, sí! ¡Tú eres el hermano de Eli!

Sebas: Sí, tú te llamas Lorena, ¿verdad?

Lorena: Sí, y tu nombre es Sebas, ¿no?

Sebas: Sí. Qué chévere que lo recuerdes.

Lorena: Tú eres el que quieres saber si tengo novio, ¿verdad?

Sebas: Bueno... yo... mi amigo Felipe es muy bromista y...

Lorena: No te preocupes, Sebas. No pasa nada. Me gustan las bromas...

Sebas: Perdón...

Lorena: Bueno, ¿y en qué puedo ayudarte? ¿Vienes para pedirme una cita? Porque yo no tengo novio...

Sebas: Pues no, no... yo...

Lorena: ¡Vamos, Sebas! Es una broma, chico. A mí también me gusta hacer bromas...

Sebas: En realidad vengo para comprar un regalo.

Lorena: ¿Para una chica?

Sebas: Sí, sí... pero... es para mi hermana. Muy pronto es su cumpleaños.

Lorena: ¿Para Eli! ¡Perfecto! Aquí hay muchas cosas interesantes para ella. ¿Qué quieres regalarle? ¿Lo sabes ya?

Sebas: Quiero comprarle un bolso. Pero necesito tu ayuda.

Lorena: ¿Un bolso? Es una gran idea. Aquí hay mucha variedad de bolsos... ¿Cuál te gusta?

Sebas: Este de cuero me parece bonito. ¿Tú qué piensas?

Lorena: Pues sí, pero no te va a gustar el precio. ¿Sabes cuánto cuesta? Ahí está el precio, puedes mirarlo.

Sebas: ¿580 dólares?

Lorena: Sí, es un bolso espectacular, pero es muy caro.

Sebas: ¿Y este? ¿Mejor?

Lorena: Demasiado grande para Eli. La conozco y no es el bolso apropiado.

Sebas: Pues a mí creo que me gusta.

Lorena: Mira, Sebas, yo soy chica y entiendo de bolsos, y ese bolso no es práctico y es muy pesado... Mira, este me gusta más para ella. Es moderno y muy alegre.

Sebas: ¡Pero... es de plástico!

Lorena: Eso no es un problema. Además es menos caro que el otro y es más pequeño que el que te gusta a ti. ¿Cuánto dinero tienes para gastar en el regalo?

Sebas: Pues... no puedo gastar más de 50 dólares.

Lorena: Perfecto, este tiene muy buen precio. Cuesta 48 dólares.

Sebas: ¿Y piensas que va a gustarle a mi hermana?

Lorena: Claro que sí. Es muy cómodo, puedes guardar aquí el celular..., aquí, los lentes de sol, tiene un bolsillo para las llaves. Es sencillo y a la vez elegante. Es perfecto para Eli.

Sebas: ¿Tú crees?

Lorena: Claro que sí. A ver, póntelo aquí en el hombro...

Sebas: ¿Yo? ¿En mi hombro?

Lorena: Sí, claro. Tienes que probarlo para asegurarte. Mm... A ver... ¿Puedes caminar un poco como tu hermana?

Sebas: ¿Como mi hermana?

Lorena: Sí, claro. Es para imaginar cómo le queda el bolso a ella.

Sebas: Pero...

Lorena: Vamos, chico, camina, no seas tímido... Muy bien, así, a ver un poco más de movimiento de caderas...

Felipe: ¡Hey, amigo!, perdona el retraso, ¿ya tienes elegido el regalo para tu her...?

Sebas: ¡No, no! ¡No es lo que parece!

EPISODIO 8: 30 GRADOS

Sebas: ¡Qué calor! ¡No es normal este calor en esta época del año!

Felipe: No, no es normal. Hoy parece que estamos en verano.

Sebas: Sí, y es otoño... ¿Qué temperatura tenemos?

Felipe: Estamos a 30 grados centígrados. Lo vi antes, en el termómetro de la guagua... Digo, el termómetro del autobús.

Sebas: ¿30 grados? Eso es demasiado calor. ¡No llevo la ropa adecuada para este calor!

Felipe: Bueno, son solo 30 grados, no es mucho calor.

Sebas: ¿Que no? Pues yo estoy sudando horriblemente.

Felipe: En mi país hace mucho más calor. No podemos comparar este calor con el que hay en mi país.

Sebas: En tu país no hace más calor que aquí en verano, seguro. A veces llegamos a los 40 grados...

Felipe: ¡Bah! ¡Eso no es calor! En mi país, durante el verano, la gente no puede salir a la calle. Si sales a la calle, ¡te mueres!

Sebas: Pues a nosotros, en verano, nos sale humo por las orejas.

Felipe: Pues, en mi país, una vez en verano, llegamos a los ¡60 grados!

Sebas: ¿60? Vamos, Felipe, eso es imposible... ¡Eso es demasiado calor!

Felipe: ¿Imposible? Pues es verdad. ¡El clima de mi país es muy extremo! En verano hace mucho calor y, en invierno, siempre hay viento y nieve.

Sebas: ¿Qué dices, Felipe? Pero si tú eres dominicano, el clima es tropical. ¡Siempre hace buen tiempo!

Felipe: Pues te equivocas. Yo nací en la provincia de La Vega, en las montañas. Allá, en invierno, la temperatura es de ¡15 grados bajo cero!

Sebas: No. ¡Qué barbaridad!

Felipe: ¡Que sí! ¡Que sí! Durante el invierno cae mucha nieve, hay terribles tormentas, hace mucho viento y el cielo siempre está nublado.

Sebas: ¡Eso no puede ser!

Felipe: Pues lo es. ¡Y ni te hablo del frío! ¡No puedes quitarte el abrigo, el gorro de lana ni los guantes en todo el día!

Sebas: No te creo...

Felipe: ¿Que no? Pues luego lo vamos a ver en Internet, y vas a ver que es totalmente cierto.

Lorena: Hola, chicos.

Sebas y Felipe: ¡Qué onda!

Eli: Sebas, papá dice que tienes que ir luego a casa para ayudar a organizar el garaje.

Sebas: ¿Yo? ¡Yo ya le ayudo a lavar el carro! ¿También debo ir a organizar el garaje?

Eli: Yo no sé nada, yo solo te digo que tienes que ir.

Sebas: ¿Por qué no vas tú a ayudarle?

Eli: Yo ayudo a mamá. Papá dice que debes ayudarle tú...

Sebas: ¡No es justo!

Lorena: Chicos, ¿están ustedes jugando al básquetbol?

Sebas y Felipe: ¡Sí!

Lorena: ¡Me encanta el básquetbol! ¿Puedo jugar?

Sebas: ¿Tú? ¿Una chica?

Lorena: ¿Qué pasa? ¿Nunca viste a una chica jugar al básquetbol?

Sebas: Sí, claro, pero...

Felipe: Las chicas no saben jugar bien.

Lorena: ¿Estás seguro de eso?

Felipe: Yo no juego al básquetbol con chicas. Mejor se quedan acá sentadas y nos ven jugar a nosotros.

Eli: ¡A ver cómo juegan ustedes! ¡Qué tontos son los chicos! ¡Y seguro que creen que nos están impresionando!

Lorena: ¡Hombres! Siempre igual... Voy a darles una pequeña lección...

Eli: ¡Y no te olvides de ir luego a casa a ayudar a papá.

UNIDAD 0: ASÍ SOMOS

	OBJECTIVES / TOPIC	PRESENT/PRACTICE/COMMUNICATE	ADDITIONAL TEACHER RESOURCES	HOMEWORK	ELETECA ONLINE PRACTICE

DAY 1	• Introduce unit theme **Así somos**: people and objects in the classroom
	• Culture: learn about Spanish and its presence around the world
	• Preview vocabulary: names of Spanish-speaking countries
	• Preview grammatical structures: the verbs **ser**, **estar**, **hablar**
		• **Unit Opener** (15 minutes)
		• *Los países del mundo hispano* (30 minutes)
		  – Activity 1
		  – Activity 2 (Audio 1)
		  – Activity 3
		• **Wrap-up/Assess** (5 minutes)
			• IWB 0.1		

DAY 2	• Present common cognates
	• Provide practice to recognize and identify cognates in Spanish
	• Use vocabulary to refer to everyday objects
		• **Warm-up** (10 minutes)
		• *En español* (35 minutes)
		  – Activity 1 (Audio 2)
		  – Activity 2
		  – Activity 3
		  – Activity 4
		• **Wrap-up/Assess** (5 minutes)			

DAY 3	• Recognize letters in Spanish	• **Warm-up** (10 minutes)
		• *El alfabeto español* (35 minutes)
		  – Activity 1 (Audio 3)
		  – Activity 2 (Audio 4)
		  – Activity 3 (Audio 5)
		  – Activity 4
		  – Activity 5
		  – Activity 6
		• **Wrap-up/Assess** (5 minutes)			

DAY 4	• Learn classroom expressions
	• Learn names for common classroom objects
		• **Warm-up** (10 minutes)
		• *En la clase de español* (35 minutes)
		  – Activity 1 (Audio 6)
		  – Activity 2
		  – Activity 3 (Audio 7)
		  – Activity 4
		  – Activity 5 (Audio 8)
		  – Activity 6
		  – Activity 7
		• **Wrap-up/Assess** (5 minutes)			

DAY 5	• Strategies for learning new vocabulary
	• Practice correct pronunciation of Spanish vowels
		• **Warm-up** (10 minutes)
		• **Destrezas** (35 minutes)
		  – Presentation
		  – Activity 1
		  – Activity 2
		• **Pronunciación** (30 minutes)
		  – Presentation
		  – Activity 1 (Audio 9)
		  – Activity 2 (Audio 10)
		• **Wrap-up/Assess** (5 minutes)			

	OBJECTIVES / TOPIC	PRESENT/PRACTICE/COMMUNICATE	ADDITIONAL TEACHER RESOURCES	HOMEWORK	ELETECA ONLINE PRACTICE
DAY 6	· Learn about Spanish-speaking countries in Latin America and Spain · Learn how many people speak Spanish around the world · Learn more about Spanish speakers in the U.S.	· **Warm-up** (10 minutes) · **Sabor Hispano** (35 minutes) *Yo hablo español, ¿y tú?* · **Wrap-up/Assess** (5 minutes)			

DAY 7	· Review unit vocabulary and expressions
	· Practice communicative skills
	· Review unit grammar
		· **Wrap-up/Assess** (5 minutes)
		· **En resumen** (30 minutes)
		  – Vocabulario
		  – Gramática
		· **Wrap-up/Assess** (10 minutes)			

UNIDAD 1: HOLA, ¿QUÉ TAL?

	OBJECTIVES / TOPIC	PRESENT/PRACTICE/COMMUNICATE	ADDITIONAL TEACHER RESOURCES	HOMEWORK	ELETECA ONLINE PRACTICE

DAY 1	· Introduce unit theme **Hola, ¿qué tal?**: greetings, introductions, and responding to basic questions
	· Culture: learn about Spanish-speakers in the U.S.
	· Preview vocabulary: greetings, introductions, and adjectives
		· **Unit Opener** (15 minutes)
		· **Hablamos de...** (30 minutes)
		Los compañeros de clase
		  – Activity 1
		  – Activity 2 (Audio 12)
		  – Activity 3 (Audio 12)
		· **Wrap-up/Assess** (5 minutes)
				· Vocabulario: 1.1 - 1.10	· Hablamos de...
					  – Activity 1 (10 minutes)
					  – Activity 2 (10 minutes)
					  – Activity 3 (10 minutes)

DAY 2	· Preview grammatical structures: the verbs **ser**, **tener**, **llamarse**	· **Warm-up** (10 minutes)
		· **Hablamos de...** (35 minutes)
		Los compañeros de clase
		  – Activity 4 (Audio 13)
		  – Activity 5 (Audio 14)
		  – Activity 6
		  – Activity 7
		· **Wrap-up/Assess** (5 minutes)			

DAY 3	· Present the communicative functions of the unit:
	  – Greetings, introductions, and saying good-bye
	  – Asking and giving information about yourself
	· Practice formal and informal ways of introducing oneself
		· **Warm-up** (10 minutes)
		· **Comunica** (35 minutes)
		· Greetings, introductions, and saying good-bye
		  – Presentation
		  – Activity 1
		  – Activity 2
		· **Wrap-up/Assess** (5 minutes)
			· EA 1.1		· Comunica
					  – Activity 1 (10 minutes)
					  – Activity 2 (10 minutes)
					  – Activity 3 (10 minutes)

DAY 4	· Present the communicative functions of the unit:
	  – Asking and giving information about yourself and others
	  – Learn common professions in Spanish
		· **Warm-up** (10 minutes)
		· **Comunica** (35 minutes)
		· Asking and giving information about yourself
		  – Presentation
		  – Activity 3 (Audio 15)
		  – Activity 4
		· **Wrap-up/Assess** (5 minutes)
			· EA 1.2		

	OBJECTIVES / TOPIC	PRESENT/PRACTICE/COMMUNICATE	ADDITIONAL TEACHER RESOURCES	HOMEWORK	ELETECA ONLINE PRACTICE

DAY 5	• Contextualize the content of the unit: *¡Acción!* Video
	• Provide students with a structured approach to viewing the video
		¡Acción! (50 minutes)
		Saludos y mochilas
		Antes del video
		  – Activities 1, 2, 3
		Durante el video
		  – Activities 4, 5 , 6, 7
		Después del video
		  – Activities 8, 9
			• DVD Episodio 1: *Saludos y mochilas*		• Vídeo 1: *Saludos y mochilas* (10 minutes)
					• Extra activity (16 minutes)

DAY 6	• Present the vocabulary needed to practice the communicative and grammatical functions for the unit: numbers 0 through 31
	• Communicate numbers 0–31 in Spanish
	• Use numbers to share personal information, such as age and phone number
		Warm-up (10 minutes)
		Palabra por palabra (35 minutes)
		Los números del 0 al 31
		  – Activity 1 (Audio 16)
		  – Activity 2 (Audio 17)
		  – Activity 3
		  – Activity 4
		  – Activity 5
		  – Activity 6
		  – Activity 7
		  – Activity 8
		Wrap-up/Assess (5 minutes)
			• IWB 1.1	• WB Online practice: Vocabulario 1.1 - 1.10	• Palabra por palabra
					  – Activity 1 (10 minutes)
					  – Activity 2 (10 minutes)
					  – Activity 3 (10 minutes)

DAY 7	• Present the vocabulary needed to practice the communicative and grammatical functions for the unit: months of the year
	• Ask and provide dates in Spanish
	• Identify common dates in a year
		Warm-up (10 minutes)
		Palabra por palabra (35 min)
		Los meses del año y la fecha
		  – Activity 9 (Audio 18)
		  – Activity 10
		  – Activity 11
		  – Activity 12
		Wrap-up/Assess (5 minutes)			

DAY 8	• Present the communicative functions of the unit: Countries and nationalities	**Warm-up** (10 minutes)
		Palabra por palabra (35 minutes)
		Los países y las nacionalidades
		  – Activity 13
		  – Activity 14
		  – Activity 15 (Audio 19)
		Wrap-up/Assess (5 minutes)
			• IWB 1.2		

DAY 9	• Present the grammatical structures needed to practice the communicative functions of the unit: definite and indefinite articles
	• Use articles to identify specific people, places, and things
		Warm-up (10 minutes)
		Gramática (35 minutes)
		1. Definite and indefinite articles
		  – Presentation
		  – Activity 1
		  – Activity 2
		Wrap-up/Assess (5 minutes)
				• WB Online practice: Gramática 1.11 - 1.24	• Grammar tutorials
					  – Tutorial 1 (8 minutes)
					  – Extra activity (14 minutes)
					  – Tutorial 2 (8 minutes)

DAY 10	• Present the grammatical structures needed to practice the communicative functions of the unit: subject pronouns and the verb *ser*
	• Talk about where people are from
		Warm-up (10 minutes)
		Gramática (35 minutes)
		2. Subject pronouns and the verb *ser*
		  – Presentation
		  – Activity 3
		  – Activity 4
		  – Activity 5
		  – Activity 6
		  – Activity 7
		Wrap-up/Assess (5 minutes)
					• Extra activity (14 minutes)

	OBJECTIVES / TOPIC	PRESENT/PRACTICE/COMMUNICATE	ADDITIONAL TEACHER RESOURCES	HOMEWORK	ELETECA ONLINE PRACTICE

DAY 11	· Present the grammatical structures needed to practice the communicative functions of the unit: the verbs **llamar(se)** and **tener**
	· Ask someone's age and give one's name
		· **Warm-up** (10 minutes)
		· **Gramática** (35 minutes)
		3. Present tense of **llamar(se)** and **tener**
		  – Presentation
		  – Activity 8
		  – Activity 9
		  – Activity 10
		· **Wrap-up/Assess** (5 minutes)			

DAY 12	· Use information within images to aid comprehension of text
	· Look for clues in images to understand unfamiliar words
	· Practice correct pronunciation: **ch** and **ñ**
		· **Destrezas** (45 minutes)
		· **Comprensión de lectura**
		  – Activity 1
		  – Activity 2
		· **Pronunciación**
		  – Presentation
		  – Activity 1 (Audio 20)
		  – Activity 2
		· **Wrap-up/Assess** (5 minutes)
				· WB Online practice: Destrezas 1.25 - 1.28	· Destreza lectora (15 minutes)
					· Destreza escrita (15 minutes)
					· Destreza oral (15 minutes)
					· Pronunciación
					  – Activity 1 (10 minutes)
					  – Activity 2 (10 minutes)
					  – Activity 3 (10 minutes)

DAY 13	· Learn about people of Hispanic origin in the U.S.
	· Learn about Spanish and its influences on U.S. culture and in U.S. communities
	· Connect new information to what you already know about Spanish
		· **Warm-up** (10 minutes)
		· **Sabor Hispano** (35 minutes)
		Hispanos en EE.UU.
		  – ¡Famosos y en español! (Audio 21)
		  – Univisión, ¿la cadena más popular?
		  – Un día sin hispanos
		· **Wrap-up/Assess** (5 minutes)
			· Voces latinas video: *Hispanos influyentes en EE.UU.*	· WB Online practice: Cultura 1.29	· Voces latinas video: *Hispanos influyentes en EE.UU.* *Extra activity* (10 minutes)

DAY 14	· Revisit unit themes, grammar, vocabulary, and culture in a new context
	· Improve reading comprehension skills
		· **Warm-up** (5 minutes)
		· **Relato** (40 minutes)
		El club de español de la escuela
		  – Activity 1
		  – Activity 2 (Audio 22)
		  – Activity 3
		  – Activity 4
		  – Activity 5
		· **Wrap-up/Assess** (5 minutes)			

DAY 15	· Review grammar, vocabulary, and culture from the unit
	· Monitor student's progress
		· **Warm-up** (5 minutes)
		[Option 1]
		· **Evaluación** (35 minutes)
		  – Activities 1-9
		[Option 2]
		· **Casa del español-videos** (35 minutes)
		  – Videos 1 and 2
		  – Extra activities
		· **En resumen** (10 minutes)
		  – Vocabulario
		  – Gramática
					· Evaluación
					· Casa del español vídeos
					  – Video 1 (5 minutes)
					  – Extra activity (10 minutes)
					  – Video 2 (5 minutes)
					· Extra activity (10 minutes)

	OBJECTIVES / TOPIC	PRESENT/PRACTICE/COMMUNICATE	ADDITIONAL TEACHER RESOURCES	HOMEWORK	ELETECA ONLINE PRACTICE
DAY 16	• Assessment	• **Warm-up** (5 minutes) • **Online test Unit 1** (30 minutes)	• Unit 1 assessment		
DAY 17	• Gamification project				

UNIDAD 2: ESTÁS EN TU CASA

	OBJECTIVES / TOPIC	PRESENT/PRACTICE/COMMUNICATE	ADDITIONAL TEACHER RESOURCES	HOMEWORK	ELETECA ONLINE PRACTICE

DAY 1	• Introduce unit theme ***Estás en tu casa***: home, people, and things
	• Culture: learn about homes in Hispanic countries
	• Preview vocabulary: words to describe and express liking something
		• **Unit Opener** (15 minutes)
		• **Hablamos de...** (30 minutes)
		Una ciudad española
		  – Activity 1
		  – Activity 2
		  – Activity 3 (Audio 23)
		• **Wrap-up/Assess** (5 minutes)
			• EA 2.1		• Hablamos de...
					  – Activity 1 (10 minutes)
					  – Activity 2 (10 minutes)
					  – Activity 3 (10 minutes)

DAY 2	• Preview grammatical structures: descriptive adjectives, ***-ar*** verbs, verb ***estar***	• **Warm-up** (10 minutes)
		• **Hablamos de...** (30 minutes)
		Una ciudad española
		  – Activity 4 (Audio 23)
		  – Activity 5
		• **Wrap-up/Assess** (5 minutes)
			• EA 2.2		

DAY 3	• Present communicative functions of the unit:
	  – Talking about preferences
	  – Talking about school subjects and sports
	• Practice using adjectives that describe a preference, such as ***favorito/a***
		• **Warm-up** (10 minutes)
		• **Comunica** (35 minutes)
		Talking about preferences
		  – Presentation
		  – Activity 1
		  – Activity 2
		• **Wrap-up/Assess** (5 minutes)
					• Comunica
					  – Activity 1 (10 minutes)
					  – Activity 2 (10 minutes)
					  – Activity 3 (10 minutes)

DAY 4	• Present the communicative functions of the unit:
	  – Expressing opinions
	  – Practice using adjectives to express an opinion
		• **Warm-up** (10 minutes)
		• **Comunica** (35 minutes)
		Expressing opinions
		  – Presentation
		  – Activity 3 (Audio 24)
		  – Activity 4 (Audio 25)
		  – Activity 5
		• **Wrap-up/Assess** (5 minutes)
			• EA 2.3		

DAY 5	• Contextualize the content of the unit: ***¡Acción!*** Video
	• Provide students with a structured approach to viewing the video
		• **¡Acción!** (50 minutes)
		Unos muebles ho-rri-bles
		Antes del video
		  – Activities 1, 2, 3
		Durante el video
		  – Activities 4, 5, 6, 7, 8, 9
		Después del video
		  – Activities 10, 11, 12, 13
			• DVD Episodio 2: *Unos muebles ho-rri-bles*		• Vídeo 1: *Unos muebles ho-rri-bles* (10 minutes)
					• Extra activity (16 minutes)

	OBJECTIVES / TOPIC	PRESENT/PRACTICE/COMMUNICATE	ADDITIONAL TEACHER RESOURCES	HOMEWORK	ELETECA ONLINE PRACTICE
DAY 6	• Present the vocabulary needed to practice the communicative and grammatical functions for the unit: colors • Identify the main colors in Spanish • Talk about objects of different colors • Present the vocabulary needed to practice the communicative and grammatical functions for the unit: rooms in the house • Identify the main rooms in a house • Talk about rooms in a house	**Warm-up** (10 minutes) **Palabra por palabra** (35 minutes) *Los colores* – Activity 1 (Audio 26) – Activity 2 – Activity 3 *La casa* – Activity 4 – Activity 5 (Audio 27) – Activity 6 **Wrap-up/Assess** (5 minutes)		• WB Online practice: Vocabulario 2.1 - 2.7	• Palabra por palabra – Activity 1 (10 minutes) – Activity 2 (10 minutes) – Activity 3 (10 minutes)
DAY 7	• Present the vocabulary needed to practice the communicative and grammatical functions for the unit: furniture and household items • Identify pieces of furniture and household items • Describe the furniture in a room	**Warm-up** (10 minutes) **Palabra por palabra** (35 minutes) *Los muebles* – Activity 7 – Activity 8 (Audio 28) – Activity 9 – Activity 10 **Wrap-up/Assess** (5 minutes)	• IWB 2.1		
DAY 8	• Present the vocabulary needed to practice the communicative and grammatical functions for the unit: numbers 32 to 101 • Talk about prices and furniture	**Warm-up** (10 minutes) **Palabra por palabra** (35 minutes) *Los números del 32 al 101* – Activity 11 (Audio 29) – Activity 12 (Audio 30) – Activity 13 – Activity 14 **Wrap-up/Assess** (5 minutes)			
DAY 9	• Present the grammatical structures needed to practice the communicative functions of the unit: gender, number, and agreement of nouns and adjectives • Describe how things are using adjectives that agree in gender and number with the noun they modify	**Warm-up** (10 minutes) **Gramática** (35 minutes) 1. Gender, number, and agreement of nouns and adjectives – Presentation – Activity 1 – Activity 2 – Activity 4 **Wrap-up/Assess** (5 minutes)		• WB Online practice: Gramática 2.8 - 2.19	• Grammar tutorials • Tutorial 3 (8 minutes) • Extra activity (14 minutes) • Tutorial 4 (8 minutes) • Extra activity (14 minutes)
DAY 10	• Present the grammatical structures needed to practice the communicative functions of the unit: present tense of verbs ending in **–ar** • Talk about actions in the present	**Warm-up** (10 minutes) **Gramática** (35 minutes) 2. Present tense of **–ar** verbs – Presentation – Activity 5 (Audio 31) – Activity 6 – Activity 7 – Activity 8 **Wrap-up/Assess** (5 minutes)			
DAY 11	• Present the grammatical structures needed to practice the communicative functions of the unit: present tense of **estar** • Talk about where	**Warm-up** (10 minutes) **Gramática** (35 minutes) 3. The verb **estar** – Presentation – Activity 9 – Activity 10 **Wrap-up/Assess** (5 minutes)			

	OBJECTIVES / TOPIC	PRESENT/PRACTICE/COMMUNICATE	ADDITIONAL TEACHER RESOURCES	HOMEWORK	ELETECA ONLINE PRACTICE

DAY 12	• Listing furniture and household objects to improve vocabulary
	• Labeling as a learning strategy to remember vocabulary
	• Practice correct pronunciation: silent **h** and **y**
		• **Destrezas** (45 minutes)
		• **Comprensión de vocabulario**
		  – Activity 1
		  – Activity 2
		  – Activity 3
		• **Pronunciación**
		  – Activity 1
		• **Wrap-up/Assess** (5 minutes)
				• WB Online practice: Destrezas 2.20 - 2.23	• Destreza lectora (15 minutes)
					• Destreza escrita (15 minutes)
					• Destreza oral (15 minutes)
					• Pronunciación
					  – Activity 1 (10 minutes)
					  – Activity 2 (10 minutes)
					  – Activity 3 (10 minutes)

DAY 13	• Learn about Spain
	• Learn about different types of housing in Hispanic Countries
	• Compare housing in Hispanic countries with housing in the U.S.
		• **Warm-up** (10 minutes)
		• **Sabor Hispano** (35 minutes)
		Vivir en España
		  – Una casa famosa (Audio 32)
		  – Vivir en familia
		  – El pueblo más bonito
		• **Wrap-up/Assess** (5 minutes)
			• Voces latinas video: *Vivir en España*	• WB Online practice: Cultura 2.24	• Voces latinas video: *Vivir en España*
					• Extra activity (10 minutes)

DAY 14	• Revisit unit themes, grammar, vocabulary, and culture in a new context
	• Improve reading comprehension skills
		• **Warm-up** (5 minutes)
		• **Relato** (40 minutes)
		Los problemas de Raquel
		  – Activity 1
		  – Activity 2 (Audio 33)
		  – Activity 3
		  – Activity 4
		  – Activity 5
		  – Activity 6
		• **Wrap-up/Assess** (5 minutes)			

DAY 15	• Review grammar, vocabulary, and culture from the unit
	• Review unit vocabulary and expressions
	• Practice communicative skills
		• **Warm-up** (5 minutes)
		[Option 1]
		• **Evaluación** (35 minutes)
		  – Activities 1-9
		[Option 2]
		• **Casa del español-videos** (35 minutes)
		  – Videos 1 and 2
		  – Extra activities
		• **En resumen** (10 minutes)
		  – Vocabulario
		  – Gramática			

DAY 16	• Assessment	• **Warm-up** (5 minutes) • **Online test Unit 2** (30 minutes)	• Unit 2 assessment		
DAY 17	• Gamification project				

	OBJECTIVES / TOPIC	PRESENT/PRACTICE/COMMUNICATE	ADDITIONAL TEACHER RESOURCES	HOMEWORK	ELETECA ONLINE PRACTICE
DAY 18	· Review grammar, vocabulary, and culture from the last two units · Complete self-assessment	**Ahora comprueba** (50 minutes) – Activity 1 – Activity 2 (Audio 34) – Activity 3 – Activity 4 – Activity 5 – Activity 6			

UNIDAD 3: ¡MI FAMILIA ES MUY SIMPÁTICA!

	OBJECTIVES / TOPIC	PRESENT/PRACTICE/COMMUNICATE	ADDITIONAL TEACHER RESOURCES	HOMEWORK	ELETECA ONLINE PRACTICE
DAY 1	· Introduce unit theme **Mi familia**: people, clothing, and family activities · Culture: learn about Hispanic families and celebrations · Preview vocabulary: family, physical characteristics, and personality traits	**Unit Opener** (15 minutes) **Hablamos de...** (30 minutes) *La familia de Nicolás* – Activity 1 – Activity 2 (Audio 35) **Wrap-up/Assess** (5 minutes)	· IWB 3.1		· Hablamos de... – Activity 1 (10 minutes) – Activity 2 (10 minutes) – Activity 3 (10 minutes)
DAY 2	· Preview grammatical structures: possessive adjectives and demonstrative adjectives	**Warm-up** (10 minutes) **Hablamos de...** (35 minutes) *La familia de Nicolás* – Activity 3 (Audio 35) – Activity 4 – Activity 5 **Wrap-up/Assess** (5 minutes)			
DAY 3	· Present the communicative functions of the unit: describing physical characteristics · Practice adjectives with **ser**, **tener**, and **llevar**	**Warm-up** (10 minutes) **Comunica** (35 minutes) Describing physical characteristics – Presentation – Activity 1 – Activity 2 (Audio 36) – Activity 3 **Wrap-up/Assess** (5 minutes)	· EA 3.1		· Comunica – Activity 1 (10 minutes) – Activity 2 (10 minutes) – Activity 3 (10 minutes)
DAY 4	· Present the communicative functions of the unit: describing personality traits and physical states · Practice adjectives with **ser** and expressions with **tener** · Recycle the forms of **ser** and **tener**	**Warm-up** (10 minutes) **Comunica** (35 minutes) Describing personality traits and physical conditions – Presentation – Activity 4 (Audio 37) – Activity 5 **Wrap-up/Assess** (5 minutes)			
DAY 5	· Contextualize the content of the unit: **¡Acción!** Video · Provide students with a structured approach to viewing the video	**¡Acción!** (50 minutes) *La chica más guapa del mundo* Antes del video – Activity 1 Durante el video – Activities 2, 3 Después del video – Activities 4, 5, 6	· DVD Episodio 3: *La chica más guapa del mundo*		· Vídeo 3: *La chica más guapa del mundo* (10 minutes) · Extra activity (16 minutes)

	OBJECTIVES / TOPIC	PRESENT/PRACTICE/COMMUNICATE	ADDITIONAL TEACHER RESOURCES	HOMEWORK	ELETECA ONLINE PRACTICE

DAY 6	• Present the vocabulary needed to practice the communicative and grammatical functions of the unit: family and family relationships
	• Identify family members
		Warm-up (10 minutes)
		
		• **Palabra por palabra** (35 minutes)
		La familia
		   – Activity 1 (Audio 38)
		   – Activity 2
		   – Activity 3 (Audio 39)
		   – Activity 4
		   – Activity 5
		   – Activity 6
		
		• **Wrap-up/Assess** (5 minutes)
			• EA 3.2	• WB Online practice: Vocabulario 3.1 - 3.10	• Palabra por palabra
					   – Activity 1 (10 minutes)
					   – Activity 2 (10 minutes)
					   – Activity 3 (10 minutes)

DAY 7	• Present the vocabulary needed to practice the communicative and grammatical functions for the unit: articles of clothing
	• Talk about what people are wearing
		• **Warm-up** (10 minutes)
		
		• **Palabra por palabra** (35 minutes)
		La ropa
		   – Activity 7 (Audio 40)
		   – Activity 8
		   – Activity 9
		   – Activity 10
		   – Activity 11
		
		• **Wrap-up/Assess** (5 minutes)
			• IWB 3.2		

DAY 8	• Present the grammatical structures needed to practice the communicative functions of the unit: present tense of regular –*er* and –*ir* verbs
	• Describe what your family does
		• **Warm-up** (10 minutes)
		
		• **Palabra por palabra** (35 minutes)
		1. Present tense of regular –*er* and –*ir* verbs
		   – Presentation
		   – Activity 1
		   – Activity 2
		   – Activity 3
		
		• **Wrap-up/Assess** (5 minutes)
			• EA 3.3	• WB Online practice: Gramática 3.12 - 3.21	• Grammar tutorials
					• Tutorial 5 (8 minutes)
					• Extra activity (14 minutes)

DAY 9	• Present grammatical structures needed to practice the communicative functions of the chapter: possessive adjectives
	• Talk about your family and friends
		•• **Warm-up** (10 minutes)
		
		• **Gramática** (35 minutes)
		2. Possessive adjectives
		   – Presentation
		   – Activity 4
		   – Activity 5
		   – Activity 6
		
		• **Wrap-up/Assess** (5 minutes)
			• EA 3.4		• Tutorial 6 (8 minutes)
					• Extra activity (14 minutes)

DAY 10	• Present the grammatical structures needed to practice the communicative functions of the unit: demonstrative adjectives
	• Pointing out people and things
		• **Warm-up** (10 minutes)
		
		• **Gramática** (35 minutes)
		3. Demonstrative adjectives
		   – Presentation
		   – Activity 7
		   – Activity 8
		   – Activity 9
		
		• **Wrap-up/Assess** (5 minutes)			

	OBJECTIVES / TOPIC	PRESENT/PRACTICE/COMMUNICATE	ADDITIONAL TEACHER RESOURCES	HOMEWORK	ELETECA ONLINE PRACTICE

DAY 11	• Listing and identifying descriptive words to improve reading comprehension
	• Making a chart to organize and improve writing skills
		Warm-up (10 minutes)
		Destrezas (45 minutes)
		Comprensión de lectura
		  – Activity 1
		  – Activity 2
		Wrap-up/Assess (5 minutes)
				• WB Online practice: Destrezas 3.22 - 3.25	• Destreza lectora (15 minutes)
					• Destreza escrita (15 minutes)
					• Destreza oral (15 minutes)

DAY 12	• Review the strategy with students to make sure they understand
	• Practice correct pronunciation: **k** and **s**
		Destrezas (45 minutes)
		Comprensión e interacción escritas
		  – Activity 3
		  – Activity 4
		Pronunciación
		  – Activity 1 (Audio 41)
		  – Activity 2
		  – Activity 3 (Audio 42)
		Wrap-up/Assess (5 minutes)
					• Pronunciación
					  – Activity 1 (10 minutes)
					  – Activity 2 (10 minutes)
					  – Activity 3 (10 minutes)

DAY 13	• Learn about Mexico
	• Learn about Mexican families, celebrations, and traditions
	• Compare celebrations with those in the United States
		Warm-up (10 minutes)
		Sabor Hispano (35 minutes)
		La familia mexicana
		  – Un domingo en el bosque Chapultepec (Audio 43)
		  – La quinceañera
		  – El día de los Muertos
		Wrap-up/Assess (5 minutes)
			• Voces latinas video: *Mi fiesta favorita*	• WB Online practice: Cultura 3.26	• Voces latinas video: *Mi fiesta favorita*
					• Extra activity (10 minutes)

DAY 14	• Revisit unit themes, grammar, vocabulary, and culture in a new context
	• Improve reading comprehension skills
		Warm-up (5 minutes)
		Relato (40 minutes)
		La cena de Nochebuena
		  – Activity 1
		  – Activity 2 (Audio 44)
		  – Activity 3
		  – Activity 4
		  – Activity 5
		  – Activity 6
		  – Activity 7
		Wrap-up/Assess (5 minutes)			

DAY 15	• Review grammar, vocabulary, and culture from the unit
	• Complete self-assessment
	• Review unit vocabulary and expressions
	• Practice communicative skills
		Warm-up (5 minutes)
		[Option 1]
		Evaluación (35 minutes)
		  – Activities 1-7
		[Option 2]
		Casa del español-videos (35 minutes)
		  – Videos 1 and 2
		  – Extra activities
		En resumen (10 minutes)
		  – Vocabulario
		  – Gramática
					• Evaluación
					• Casa del español vídeos
					  – Video 5 (5 minutes)
					  – Extra activity (10 minutes)
					  – Video 6 (5 minutes)
					• Extra activity (10 minutes)

DAY 16	• Assessment	**Warm-up** (5 minutes) **Online test Unit 3** (30 minutes)	• Unit 3 assessment		
DAY 17	• Gamification project				

UNIDAD 4: TODOS LOS DÍAS LO MISMO

	OBJECTIVES / TOPIC	PRESENT/PRACTICE/COMMUNICATE	ADDITIONAL TEACHER RESOURCES	HOMEWORK	ELETECA ONLINE PRACTICE

DAY 1	• Introduce unit theme **Todos los días lo mismo**: daily routines and everyday activities
	• Culture: learn about daily life in Hispanic countries
	• Preview vocabulary: making plans, expressions of time, days of the week, and professions
		• **Unit Opener** (15 minutes)
		• **Hablamos de...** (30 minutes)
		Los planes
		  – Activity 1
		  – Activity 2 (Audio 45)
		  – Activity 3 (Audio 45)
		• **Wrap-up/Assess** (5 minutes)
			• IWB 4.1		• Hablamos de...
					  – Activity 1
					  (10 minutes)
					  – Activity 2
					  (10 minutes)
					  – Activity 3
					  (10 minutes)

DAY 2	• Preview grammatical structures: irregular verbs; present tense of **hacer**, **venir**, **salir**	• **Warm-up** (10 minutes)
		• **Hablamos de...** (35 minutes)
		Los planes
		  – Activity 4
		  – Activity 5
		  – Activity 6
		• **Wrap-up/Assess** (5 minutes)
			• IWB 4.2		

DAY 3	• Present the communicative function: talking about everyday activities and different times of the day
	• Practice using numbers to tell time
		• **Warm-up** (10 minutes)
		• **Comunica** (35 minutes)
		Talking about everyday activities
		  – Presentation
		  – Activity 1
		  – Activity 2
		• **Wrap-up/Assess** (5 minutes)
					• Comunica
					  – Activity 1
					  (10 minutes)
					  – Activity 2
					  (10 minutes)
					  – Activity 3
					  (10 minutes)

DAY 4	• Present the communicative function: asking and giving the time
	• Talking about activities done at different times of the day
		• **Warm-up** (10 minutes)
		• **Comunica** (35 minutes)
		Asking and giving the time
		  – Presentation
		  – Activity 3
		  – Activity 4 (Audio 46)
		  – Activity 5
		• **Wrap-up/Assess** (5 minutes)
			• IWB 4.3		

DAY 5	• Contextualize the content of the unit: ¡Acción! video
	• Provide students with a structured approach to viewing the video
		• **¡Acción!** (50 minutes)
		Problemas de horarios
		Antes del video
		  – Activities 1, 2, 3, 4
		Durante el video
		  – Activities 5, 6, 7
		Después del video
		  – Activities 8, 9
			• DVD Episodio 4: *Problemas de horarios*		• Vídeo 4: *Problemas de horarios* (10 minutes)
					• Extra activity (16 minutes)

DAY 6	• Present the vocabulary for days of the week and schedules
	• Identify days of the week in Spanish
	• Talk about events during the week
		• **Warm-up** (10 minutes)
		• **Palabra por palabra** (35 minutes)
		Los días de la semana
		  – Activity 1 (Audio 47)
		  – Activity 2
		  – Activity 3
		  – Activity 4
		  – Activity 5
		  – Activity 6
		• **Wrap-up/Assess** (5 minutes)
				• WB Online practice: Vocabulario 4.1 - 4.7	• Palabra por palabra
					  – Activity 1
					  (10 minutes)
					  – Activity 2
					  (10 minutes)
					  – Activity 3
					  (10 minutes)

	OBJECTIVES / TOPIC	PRESENT/PRACTICE/COMMUNICATE	ADDITIONAL TEACHER RESOURCES	HOMEWORK	ELETECA ONLINE PRACTICE

DAY 7	• Present the vocabulary needed to practice the communicative and grammatical functions for the unit: jobs and occupations
	• Talk about what people do
		Warm-up (10 minutes)
		Palabra por palabra (35 minutes)
		Las profesiones
		  – Activitiy 7 (Audio 48)
		  – Activity 8
		  – Activity 9
		  – Activity 10
		  – Activity 11
		Wrap-up/Assess (5 minutes)
			• EA 4.1		• Palabra por palabra
					  – Activity 1 (10 minutes)
					  – Activity 2 (10 minutes)
					  – Activity 3 (10 minutes)

DAY 8	• Present the grammatical structures needed to practice the communicative functions of the unit: stem-changing verbs *e>ie*, *o>ue*, *e>i*	**Warm-up** (10 minutes)
		Gramática (35 minutes)
		1. Stem-changing verbs *e>ie*, *o>ue*, *e>i*
		  – Presentation
		  – Activity 1
		  – Activity 2
		  – Activity 3
		Wrap-up/Assess (5 minutes)
				• WB Online practice: Gramática 4.8 - 4.17	• Grammar tutorials
					• Tutorial 7 (8 minutes)
					• Extra activity (14 minutes)
					• Tutorial 8 (8 minutes)
					• Extra activity (14 minutes)

DAY 9	• Present the grammatical structures needed to practice the communicative functions of the unit: the verbs *hacer* and *salir*	**Warm-up** (10 minutes)
		Gramática (35 minutes)
		2. Verbs *hacer* and *salir*
		  – Presentation
		  – Activity 4
		  – Activity 5
		Wrap-up/Assess (5 minutes)			

DAY 10	• Present the grammatical structures needed to practice the communicative functions of the unit: reflexive verbs	**Warm-up** (10 minutes)
		Gramática (35 minutes)
		3. Reflexive verbs
		  – Presentation
		  – Activity 6
		  – Activity 7
		  – Activity 8
		  – Activity 9
		Wrap-up/Assess (5 minutes)			

DAY 11	• Listen to specific information about daily activities to improve listening comprehension	**Destrezas** (45 minutes)
		Comprensión auditiva
		  – Activity 1
		  – Activity 2 (Audio 49)
		Wrap-up/Assess (5 minutes)
				• WB Online practice: Destrezas 4.18 - 4.23	• Destreza lectora (15 minutes)
					• Destreza escrita (15 minutes)
					• Destreza oral (15 minutes)

DAY 12	• Making a chart to organize and improve writing skills
	• Practice correct pronunciation of *b* and *v*
		Destrezas (45 minutes)
		Comprensión e interacción escritas
		  – Activity 1
		  – Activity 2
		Pronunciación
		  – Activity 1 (Audio 50)
		  – Activity 2
		  – Activity 3
		Wrap-up/Assess (5 minutes)
					• Pronunciación
					  – Activity 1 (10 minutes)
					  – Activity 2 (10 minutes)
					  – Activity 3 (10 minutes)

	OBJECTIVES / TOPIC	PRESENT/PRACTICE/COMMUNICATE	ADDITIONAL TEACHER RESOURCES	HOMEWORK	ELETECA ONLINE PRACTICE
DAY 13	• Learn about Central America • Learn about Central America's cultural heritage and ecological diversity • Compare the landscape and cultural heritage of Central America with that of the U.S.	**Warm-up** (10 minutes) **Sabor Hispano** (35 minutes) *El Puente entre las Américas* – Un día "pura vida" (Audio 51) – El mundo maya y la tecnología – Las maras y la educación **Wrap-up/Assess** (5 minutes)	• Voces latinas video: *Vivir en Buenos Aires*	WB Online practice: Cultura 4.24	• Voces latinas video: *Vivir en Buenos Aires* • Extra activity (10 minutes)
DAY 14	• Revisit unit themes, grammar, vocabulary, and culture in a new context • Improve reading comprehension skills	**Warm-up** (5 minutes) **Relato** (40 minutes) *El día a día* – Activity 1 – Activity 2 (Audio 52) – Activity 3 – Activity 4 – Activity 5 **Wrap-up/Assess** (5 minutes)			
DAY 15	• Review unit vocabulary, expressions, and grammar • Practice communicative skills	**Warm-up** (5 minutes) [Option 1] **Evaluación** (35 minutes) – Activities 1-6 [Option 2] **Casa del español-videos** (35 minutes) – Videos 1 and 2 – Extra activities **En resumen** (10 minutes) – Vocabulario – Gramática			• Evaluación • Casa del español vídeos – Video 7 (5 minutes) – Extra activity (10 minutes) – Video 8 (5 minutes) • Extra activity (10 minutes)
DAY 16	• Assessment	**Warm-up** (5 minutes) **Online test Unit 4** (30 minutes)	• Unit 4 assessment		
DAY 17	• Gamification project				
DAY 18	• Review and recycle grammar, vocabulary, and culture from the last two units • Complete self-assessment	**Ahora comprueba** (50 minutes) – Activity 1 – Activity 2 (Audio 53) – Activity 3 – Activity 4 – Activity 5 – Activity 6			

UNIDAD 5: ¿TE GUSTA?

	OBJECTIVES / TOPIC	PRESENT/PRACTICE/COMMUNICATE	ADDITIONAL TEACHER RESOURCES	HOMEWORK	ELETECA ONLINE PRACTICE
DAY 1	• Introduce unit theme *¿Te gusta?*: foods we like and leisure activities • Culture: learn about traditional foods in Hispanic countries • Preview vocabulary: after-school and free time activities	**Unit Opener** (15 minutes) **Hablamos de...** (30 minutes) *El tiempo libre* – Activity 1 – Activity 2 (Audio 54) **Wrap-up/Assess** (5 minutes)			• Hablamos de... – Activity 1 (10 minutes) – Activity 2 (10 minutes) – Activity 3 (10 minutes)

	OBJECTIVES / TOPIC	PRESENT/PRACTICE/COMMUNICATE	ADDITIONAL TEACHER RESOURCES	HOMEWORK	ELETECA ONLINE PRACTICE

DAY 2	• Preview grammatical structures: *estar, gustar, doler*	• **Warm-up** (10 minutes)
		• **Hablamos de...** (35 minutes)
		El tiempo libre
		  – Activity 3
		  – Activity 4
		  – Activity 5
		• **Wrap-up/Assess** (5 minutes)
					• Hablamos de...
					  – Activity 1
					  (10 minutes)
					  – Activity 2
					  (10 minutes)
					  – Activity 3
					  (10 minutes)

DAY 3	• Present the communicative functions of the unit:
	  – Using the verb *ser* to describe personality traits and characteristics
	  – Using the verb *estar* to describe moods
	• Practice describing personality traits and moods
		• **Warm-up** (10 minutes)
		• **Comunica** (35 minutes)
		Estar
		  – Presentation
		  – Activity 1
		  – Activity 2 (Audio 55)
		  – Activity 3
		  – Activity 4
		• **Wrap-up/Assess** (5 minutes)
			• EA 5.1		• Comunica
					  – Activity 1
					  (10 minutes)
					  – Activity 2
					  (10 minutes)
					  – Activity 3
					  (10 minutes)

DAY 4	• Present the communicative function: ordering in a restaurant	• **Warm-up** (10 minutes)
		• **Comunica** (35 minutes)
		Ordering in a restaurant
		  – Presentation
		  – Activity 5
		  – Activity 6
		  – Activity 7
		• **Wrap-up/Assess** (5 minutes)
			• IWB 5.1		

DAY 5	• Contextualize the content of the unit: *¡Acción!* Video
	• Provide students with a structured approach to viewing the video
		• **¡Acción!** (50 minutes)
		Un pelo en mi cena
		  Antes del video
		  – Activities 1, 2
		  Durante el video
		  – Activities 3, 4, 5, 6
		  Después del video
		  – Activities 7, 8, 9
			• DVD Episodio 5: *Un pelo en mi cena*		• Vídeo 3: *Un pelo en mi cena* (10 minutes)
					• Extra activity (16 minutes)

DAY 6	• Present the vocabulary needed to practice the communicative and grammatical functions for the unit: talk about what you do in your free time
	• Identify words for leisure activities
		• **Warm-up** (10 minutes)
		• **Palabra por palabra** (35 minutes)
		Actividades de ocio
		  – Activity 1 (Audio 56)
		  – Activity 2
		Y tiempo libre
		  – Activity 3
		  – Activity 4 (Audio 57)
		  – Activity 5
		  – Activity 6
		• **Wrap-up/Assess** (5 minutes)
				• WB Online practice: Vocabulario 5.1 - 5.6	• Palabra por palabra
					  – Activity 1
					  (10 minutes)
					  – Activity 2
					  (10 minutes)
					  – Activity 3
					  (10 minutes)

DAY 7	• Present the vocabulary needed to practice the communicative and grammatical functions for the unit: food items
	• Identify different types of food
	• Express what foods we like
		• **Warm-up** (10 minutes)
		• **Palabra por palabra** (35 minutes)
		Los alimentos
		  – Activitiy 7 (Audio 58)
		  – Activity 8
		  – Activity 9
		  – Activity 10
		  – Activity 11
		• **Wrap-up/Assess** (5 minutes)
			• EA 4.1		

	OBJECTIVES / TOPIC	PRESENT/PRACTICE/COMMUNICATE	ADDITIONAL TEACHER RESOURCES	HOMEWORK	ELETECA ONLINE PRACTICE
DAY 8	• Present the grammatical structures needed to practice communicative functions of the unit: *gustar* and similar verbs to express likes and dislikes	**Warm-up** (10 minutes) **Gramática** (35 minutes) 1. *Gustar* and similar verbs – Presentation – Activity 1 – Activity 2 – Activity 3 **Wrap-up/Assess** (5 minutes)		• WB Online practice: Gramática 5.7 - 5.17	• Grammar tutorials • Tutorial 9 (8 minutes) • Extra activity (14 minutes) • Tutorial 10 (8 minutes) • Extra activity (14 minutes)
DAY 9	• Present the grammatical structures needed to practice the communicative functions of the unit: *también* and *tampoco* • Express agreement and disagreement	**Warm-up** (10 minutes) **Gramática** (35 minutes) 2. Using *también* and *tampoco* to agree and disagree – Presentation – Activity 4 – Activity 5 – Activity 6 **Wrap-up/Assess** (5 minutes)			
DAY 10	• Present the grammatical structures needed to practice communicative functions of the unit: the verb *doler* and parts of the body to express when something hurts	**Warm-up** (10 minutes) **Gramática** (35 minutes) 3. The verb *doler* and parts of the body – Presentation – Activities 7-12 **Wrap-up/Assess** (5 minutes)	• EA 5.2		
DAY 11	• Improve reading comprehension	**Destrezas** (45 minutes) **Comprensión de lectura I** – Activity 1 – Activity 2 **Wrap-up/Assess** (5 minutes)		• WB Online practice: Destrezas 5.18 - 5.21	• Destreza lectora (15 minutes) • Destreza escrita (15 minutes)
DAY 12	• Practice the correct pronunciation of *r* and *rr*	**Destrezas** (45 minutes) **Comprensión de lectura II** – Activity 3 – Activity 4 **Pronunciación** – Presentation – Activity 1 (Audio 59) – Activity 2 **Wrap-up/Assess** (5 minutes)			• Destreza oral (15 minutes) • Pronunciación – Activity 1 (10 minutes) – Activity 2 (10 minutes) – Activity 3 (10 minutes)
DAY 13	• Learn about Panamá, Colombia, and Venezuela • Learn about currencies, products, and foods of Spanish-speaking countries • Compare cultures of Spanish-speaking countries with culture in the U.S.	**Warm-up** (10 minutes) **Sabor Hispano** (35 minutes) ¡A comer, bailar y gozar! – Café de Colombia (Audio 60) – Las compras en Panamá – Arepas **Wrap-up/Assess** (5 minutes)	• Voces latinas video: *Mi comida preferida*	• WB Online practice: Cultura 5.22	• Voces latinas video: *Mi comida preferida* • Extra activity (10 minutes)

	OBJECTIVES / TOPIC	PRESENT/PRACTICE/COMMUNICATE	ADDITIONAL TEACHER RESOURCES	HOMEWORK	ELETECA ONLINE PRACTICE
DAY 14	• Revisit unit themes, grammar, vocabulary, and culture in a new context • Improve reading comprehension skills	• **Warm-up** (5 minutes) • **Relato** (40 minutes) *Las recomendaciones de Mónica* – Activity 1 – Activity 2 (Audio 61) – Activity 3 – Activity 4 – Activity 5 – Activity 6 • **Wrap-up/Assess** (5 minutes)			
DAY 15	• Review grammar, vocabulary, and culture from the unit • Complete self-assessment	• **Warm-up** (5 minutes) [Option 1] • **Evaluación** (35 minutes) – Activities 1-7 [Option 2] • **Casa del español-videos** (35 minutes) – Videos 1 and 2 – Extra activities • **En resumen** (10 minutes) – Vocabulario – Gramática			• Evaluación • Casa del español vídeos – Video 9 (5 minutes) – Extra activity (10 minutes) – Video 10 (5 minutes) • Extra activity (10 minutes)
DAY 16	• Assessment	• **Warm-up** (5 minutes) • **Online test Unit 5** (30 minutes)	• Unit 5 assessment		
DAY 17	• Gamification project				

UNIDAD 6: VAMOS DE VIAJE

	OBJECTIVES / TOPIC	PRESENT/PRACTICE/COMMUNICATE	ADDITIONAL TEACHER RESOURCES	HOMEWORK	ELETECA ONLINE PRACTICE
DAY 1	• Introduce unit theme **Vamos de viaje**: traveling and getting around the city • Introduce culture for the unit: learn about cities and transportation in Hispanic countries	• **Unit Opener** (15 minutes) • **Hablamos de...** (30 minutes) *Un viaje al parque natural* – Activity 1 – Activity 2 (Audio 62) • **Wrap-up/Assess** (5 minutes)			• Hablamos de... – Activity 1 (10 minutes) – Activity 2 (10 minutes) – Activity 3 (10 minutes)
DAY 2	• Preview vocabulary: talking about the outdoors, animals, and locations • Preview grammatical structures: prepositions of place, using **hay** and **está**/**están** to ask where something is	• **Warm-up** (10 minutes) • **Hablamos de...** (35 minutes) *Un viaje al parque natural* – Activity 3 (Audio 62) – Activity 4 – Activity 5 • **Wrap-up/Assess** (5 minutes)			

	OBJECTIVES / TOPIC	PRESENT/PRACTICE/COMMUNICATE	ADDITIONAL TEACHER RESOURCES	HOMEWORK	ELETECA ONLINE PRACTICE
DAY 3	• Present the communicative function: – Describe where things are located – Use **hay** and **está/están** to ask about what there is and where • Practice stating where things are located relative to something else	• **Warm-up** (10 minutes) • **Comunica** (35 minutes) Describing where things are located – Presentation – Activity 1 – Activity 2 (Audio 63) – Activity 3 • **Wrap-up/Assess** (5 minutes)	• IWB 6.1		• Comunica – Activity 1 (10 minutes) – Activity 2 (10 minutes) – Activity 3 (10 minutes)
DAY 4	• Present the communicative functions of the unit: – Elicit information and provide information – Use **hay** and **está/están** to ask about what there is and where something is	• **Warm-up** (10 minutes) • **Comunica** (35 minutes) Asking about what there is and where it is – Presentation – Activity 4 – Activity 5 (Audio 64) – Activity 6 • **Wrap-up/Assess** (5 minutes)			
DAY 5	• Contextualize the content of the unit: **¡Acción!** Video • Provide students with a structured approach to viewing the video	• **¡Acción!** (50 minutes) *Un barrio interesante* Antes del video – Activity 1 Durante el video – Activities 2- 7 Después del video – Activities 8, 9 • **Wrap-up/Assess** (5 minutes)	• DVD Episodio 6: *Un barrio interesante*		• Vídeo 6: *Un barrio interesante* (10 minutes) • Extra activity (16 minutes)
DAY 6	• Present the vocabulary needed to practice the communicative and grammatical functions for the unit: means of transportation • Identify words for means of transportation	• **Warm-up** (10 minutes) • **Palabra por palabra** (35 minutes) *Los medios de transporte* – Activity 1 (Audio 65) – Activity 2 – Activity 3 – Activity 4 – Activity 5 – Activity 6 • **Wrap-up/Assess** (5 minutes)		• WB Online practice: Vocabulario 6.1 - 6.14	• Palabra por palabra – Activity 1 (10 minutes) – Activity 2 (10 minutes) – Activity 3 (10 minutes)
DAY 7	• Present the vocabulary needed to practice the communicative and grammatical functions for the unit: naming places in the neighborhood and around the city	• **Warm-up** (10 minutes) • **Palabra por palabra** (35 minutes) *La ciudad* – Activity 7 (Audio 66) – Activity 8 – Activity 9 – Activity 10 – Activity 11 – Activity 12 • **Wrap-up/Assess** (5 minutes)	• IWB 6.2		
DAY 8	• Present the grammatical structures needed to practice communicative functions of the unit: the irregular verbs **ir**, **seguir**, **jugar**, and **conocer**	• **Warm-up** (10 minutes) • **Gramática** (35 minutes) 1. Irregular verbs **ir**, **seguir**, **jugar**, and **conocer** – Presentation – Activity 1 – Activity 2 – Activity 3 – Activity 4 • **Wrap-up/Assess** (5 minutes)	• IWB 6.3	• WB Online practice: Gramática 6.15 - 6.26	• Grammar tutorials • Tutorial 11 (8 minutes) • Extra activity (14 minutes) • Tutorial 12 (8 minutes) • Extra activity (14 minutes)

	OBJECTIVES / TOPIC	PRESENT/PRACTICE/COMMUNICATE	ADDITIONAL TEACHER RESOURCES	HOMEWORK	ELETECA ONLINE PRACTICE
DAY 9	• Present the grammatical structures needed to practice the communicative functions of the unit: the prepositions *en*, *a*, *de*	**Warm-up** (10 minutes) **Gramática** (35 minutes) 2. Prepositions *en*, *a*, *de* – Presentation – Activity 5 – Activity 6 **Wrap-up/Assess** (5 minutes)	• EA 6.1		
DAY 10	• Present the grammatical structures needed to practice communicative functions of the unit: the adverbs of quantity to express how much	**Warm-up** (10 minutes) **Gramática** (35 minutes) 3. Adverbs of quantity – Presentation – Activity 7 – Activity 8 – Activity 9 **Wrap-up/Assess** (5 minutes)	• IWB 6.4		
DAY 11	• Skimming for specific information to improve comprehension • Using a map to identify and locate places mentioned in a reading	**Destrezas** (45 minutes) *Comprensión de lectura* – Activity 1 – Activity 2 **Wrap-up/Assess** (5 minutes)	• EA 6.2	• WB Online practice:: Destrezas 6.27 - 6.30	• Destreza lectora (15 minutes) • Destreza escrita (15 minutes) • Destreza oral (15 minutes)
DAY 12	• Practice correct pronunciation: *g* and *gu* and *j*	**Warm-up** (10 minutes) **Pronunciación** – Activity 1 (Audio 67) – Activity 2 (Audio 68) – Activity 3 – Activity 4 **Wrap-up/Assess** (5 minutes)			• Pronunciación – Activity 1 (10 minutes) – Activity 2 (10 minutes) – Activity 3 (10 minutes)
DAY 13	• Learn about the Caribbean, Cuba, Puerto Rico, and República Dominicana • Learn about sports and transportation in Hispanic countries	**Warm-up** (10 minutes) **Sabor Hispano** (35 minutes) *Un viaje de aventuras* – El deporte nacional (audio 69) – Carros clásicos en la Habana – Puerto Rico, isla del encanto **Wrap-up/Assess** (5 minutes)	• Voces latinas video: *Turismo de aventuras*	• WB Online practice: Cultura 6.31	• Voces latinas video: *Turismo de aventuras* Extra activity (10 minutes)
DAY 14	• Revisit unit themes, grammar, vocabulary, and culture in a new context • Improve reading comprehension skills	**Warm-up** (5 minutes) **Relato** (40 minutes) *Las vacaciones de Lucía* – Activity 1 – Activity 2 (Audio 70) – Activity 3 – Activity 4 – Activity 5 **Wrap-up/Assess** (5 minutes)			
DAY 15	• Review unit vocabulary, grammar, and culture from the unit • Practice communicative skills	**Warm-up** (5 minutes) [Option 1] **Evaluación** (35 minutes) – Activities 1-7 [Option 2] **Casa del español-videos** (35 minutes) – Videos 1 and 2 – Extra activities **En resumen** (10 minutes) – Vocabulario – Gramática			• Evaluación • Casa del español vídeos – Video 11 (5 minutes) – Extra activity (10 minutes) – Video 12 (5 minutes) • Extra activity (10 minutes)

	OBJECTIVES / TOPIC	PRESENT/PRACTICE/COMMUNICATE	ADDITIONAL TEACHER RESOURCES	HOMEWORK	ELETECA ONLINE PRACTICE
DAY 16	• Assessment	**Warm-up** (5 minutes) **Online test Unit 6** (30 minutes)	• Unit 6 assessment		
DAY 17	• Gamification project				
DAY 18	• Review grammar, vocabulary, and culture from the last two units • Complete self-assessment	**Ahora comprueba** (50 minutes) – Activity 1 – Activity 2 (Audio 71) – Activity 3 – Activity 4 (Audio 72) – Activity 5 – Activity 6	• IWB 6.5		

UNIDAD 7: ¡CUÁNTAS COSAS!

	OBJECTIVES / TOPIC	PRESENT/PRACTICE/COMMUNICATE	ADDITIONAL TEACHER RESOURCES	HOMEWORK	ELETECA ONLINE PRACTICE
DAY 1	• Introduce unit theme *¡Cuántas cosas!*: objects and their uses • Culture: learn about carnaval in Hispanic countries • Preview vocabulary: household furniture and objects	**Unit Opener** (15 minutes) **Hablamos de…** (30 minutes) *La habitación de Manuela* – Activity 1 – Activity 2 (Audio 73) **Wrap-up/Assess** (5 minutes)			• Hablamos de… – Activity 1 (10 minutes) – Activity 2 (10 minutes) – Activity 3 (10 minutes)
DAY 2	• Preview grammatical structures: demonstrative pronouns and direct object pronouns	**Warm-up** (10 minutes) **Hablamos de…** (35 minutes) *La habitación de Manuelas* – Activity 3 – Activity 4 – Activity 5 **Wrap-up/Assess** (5 minutes)			
DAY 3	• Present the communicative function: describing objects	**Warm-up** (10 minutes) **Comunica** (35 minutes) Describing objects – Presentation – Activity 1 – Activity 2 (Audio 74) – Activity 3 **Wrap-up/Assess** (5 minutes)	• IEA 7.1		
DAY 4	• Present the communicative function: comparing people and things	**Warm-up** (10 minutes) **Comunica** (35 minutes) Comparing people and things – Presentation – Activity 4 – Activity 5 **Wrap-up/Assess** (5 minutes)			

	OBJECTIVES / TOPIC	PRESENT/PRACTICE/COMMUNICATE	ADDITIONAL TEACHER RESOURCES	HOMEWORK	ELETECA ONLINE PRACTICE
DAY 5	• Contextualize the content of the unit: **¡Acción!** Video • Provide students with a structured approach to viewing the video	**¡Acción!** (45 minutes) *Un bolso para mi hermana* Antes del video – Activities 1,2 Durante el video – Activities 3, 4, 5, 6 Después del video – Activities 7, 8 • **Wrap-up/Assess** (5 minutes)	• DVD Episodio 7: *Un bolso para mi hermana*		• Vídeo 7: *Un bolso para mi hermanas* (10 minutes) • Extra activity (16 minutes)
DAY 6	• Present the vocabulary needed to practice the communicative and grammatical functions for the unit: identify words for common household and classroom objects • Talk about items found at school or at home and describe their functions	**Warm-up** (10 minutes) **Palabra por palabra** (35 minutes) *Objetos de casa* – Activity 1 (Audio 75) – Activity 2 *Y de la clase* – Activities 3-7 • **Wrap-up/Assess** (5 minutes)	• EA 7.2 • EA 7.3	• WB Online practice: Vocabulario 7.1 - 7.7	• Palabra por palabra – Activity 1 (10 minutes) – Activity 2 (10 minutes) – Activity 3 (10 minutes)
DAY 7	• Present the vocabulary needed to practice the communicative and grammatical functions for the unit: talk about larger quantities (100–999) • Ask and state how much something costs	**Warm-up** (10 minutes) **Palabra por palabra** (35 minutes) *Los números de 100 al 999* – Activity 8 (Audio 76) – Activity 9 (Audio 77) – Activity 10 – Activity 11 – Activity 12 • **Wrap-up/Assess** (5 minutes)			
DAY 8	• Present the grammatical structures needed to practice communicative functions of the unit: demonstrative pronouns • Indicate which item you want	**Warm-up** (10 minutes) **Gramática** (35 minutes) 1. Demonstrative pronouns – Presentation – Activity 1 – Activity 2 – Activity 3 • **Wrap-up/Assess** (5 minutes)		• WB Online practice: Gramática 7.8 - 7.19	• Grammar tutorials • Tutorial 13 (8 minutes) • Extra activity (14 minutes) • Tutorial 14 (8 minutes)
DAY 9	• Present the grammatical structures needed to practice the communicative functions of the unit: direct object pronouns • Answering questions using direct object pronouns in place of nouns	**Warm-up** (10 minutes) **Gramática** (35 minutes) 2. Direct object pronouns – Presentation – Activity 4 – Activity 5 – Activity 6 – Activity 7 • **Wrap-up/Assess** (5 minutes)	• EA 7.4		• Extra activity (14 minutes)
DAY 10	• Reading comprehension • Scanning for specific information	**Warm-up** (10 minutes) **Destrezas** (40 minutes) *Comprensión de lectura* – Activity 1 – Activity 2 • **Wrap-up/Assess** (5 minutes)		• WB Online practice: Destrezas 7.20 - 7.23	• Destreza lectora (15 minutes) • Destreza escrita (15 minutes) • Destreza oral (15 minutes) • Pronunciación – Activity 1 (10 minutes)

	OBJECTIVES / TOPIC	PRESENT/PRACTICE/COMMUNICATE	ADDITIONAL TEACHER RESOURCES	HOMEWORK	ELETECA ONLINE PRACTICE

DAY 11	· Practice word stress and the written accent	· **Warm-up** (10 minutes)
		· **Pronunciación**
		  – Presentation
		  – Activity 1
		  – Activity 2
		· **Wrap-up/Assess** (5 minutes)
					· Destreza lectora (15 minutes)
					· Destreza escrita (15 minutes)
					· Destreza oral (15 minutes)
					· Pronunciación
					  – Activity 1 (10 minutes)

DAY 12	· Learn about Bolivia, Ecuador, and Peru
	· Learn about **carnaval** and other celebrations in Hispanic countries
	· Compare celebrations in Hispanic countries with celebrations in the U.S.
		· **Warm-up** (10 minutes)
		· **Sabor Hispano** (35 minutes)
		¡Viva el carnaval!
		  – ¡Mi celebración favorita! (audio 78)
		  – El Carnaval de las islas Canarias
		  – El Carnaval de Barranquilla
		· **Wrap-up/Assess** (5 minutes)
			· Voces latinas video: *Bolivia, Ecuador y Perú: carnaval y vida*	· WB Online practice: Cultura 7.24	· Voces latinas video: *Bolivia, Ecuador y Perú: carnaval y vida*
					· Extra activity (10 minutes)

DAY 13	· Revisit unit themes, grammar, vocabulary, and culture in a new context	· **Warm-up** (10 minutes)
		· **Relato** (35 minutes)
		Un día solo para mamá
		  – Activity 1 (Audio 79)
		  – Activity 2
		· **Wrap-up/Assess** (5 minutes)
			· EA 7.5		

DAY 14	· Improve reading comprehension skills	· **Warm-up** (10 minutes)
		· **Relato** (35 minutes)
		Un día solo para mamá
		  – Activity 3
		  – Activity 4
		  – Activity 5
		· **Wrap-up/Assess** (5 minutes)			

DAY 15	· Review unit vocabulary, expressions, and grammar
	· Practice communicative skills
		· **Warm-up** (5 minutes)
		[Option 1]
		· **Evaluación** (35 minutes)
		  – Activities 1-7
		[Option 2]
		· **Casa del español-videos** (35 minutes)
		  – Videos 1 and 2
		  – Extra activities
		· **En resumen** (10 minutes)
		  – Vocabulario
		  – Gramática
					· Evaluación
					· Casa del español vídeos
					  – Video 13 (5 minutes)
					  – Extra activity (10 minutes)
					  – Video 14 (5 minutes)
					· Extra activity (10 minutes)

DAY 16	· Assessment	· **Warm-up** (5 minutes) · **Online test Unit 7** (30 minutes)	· Unit 7 assessment		
DAY 17	· Gamification project				

	OBJECTIVES / TOPIC	PRESENT/PRACTICE/COMMUNICATE	ADDITIONAL TEACHER RESOURCES	HOMEWORK	ELETECA ONLINE PRACTICE
DAY 1	• Introduce unit theme ¿Qué tiempo va a hacer?: weather and seasons • Culture: learn about weather and climate in Hispanic countries • Preview vocabulary: las excursiones	• **Unit Opener** (15 minutes) • **Hablamos de...** (30 minutes) *Las excursiones* – Activity 1 – Activity 2 (Audio 80) • **Wrap-up/Assess** (5 minutes)	• EA 8.1		• Hablamos de... – Activity 1 (10 minutes) – Activity 2 (10 minutes) – Activity 3 (10 minutes) – Activity 4 (10 minutes)
DAY 2	• Preview grammatical structures: ir a, tener que, deber, hay que	• **Warm-up** (10 minutes) • **Hablamos de...** (35 minutes) *Las excursiones* – Activity 3 – Activity 4 – Activity 5 • **Wrap-up/Assess** (5 minutes)			
DAY 3	• Present the communicative functions of the unit: – Describing the weather – Talking about weather	• **Warm-up** (10 minutes) • **Comunica** (35 minutes) Describing the weather – Presentation – Activity 1 – Activity 2 • **Wrap-up/Assess** (5 minutes)	• EA 8.2		• Comunica – Activity 1 (10 minutes) – Activity 2 (10 minutes) – Activity 3 (10 minutes)
DAY 4	• Present the communicative function: – Ask and respond to questions about the weather – Listen to weather information for understanding	• **Warm-up** (10 minutes) • **Comunica** (35 minutes) Talking about the weathers – Presentation – Activity 3 (Audio 81) – Activity 4 • **Wrap-up/Assess** (5 minutes)			
DAY 5	• Contextualize the content of the unit: ¡Acción! Video • Provide students with a structured approach to viewing the video	• **¡Acción!** (50 minutes) *30 grados* Antes del video – Activity 1 Durante el video – Activities 2, 3, 4, 5 Después del video – Activities 6, 7, 8	• DVD Episodio 8: *30 grados*		• Vídeo 8: 30 grados (10 minutes) • Extra activity (16 minutes)
DAY 6	• Present the vocabulary needed to practice the communicative and grammatical function for the unit: talking about the weather	• **Warm-up** (10 minutes) • **Palabra por palabra** (35 minutes) *El tiempo* – Activity 1 (Audio 82) – Activity 2 – Activity 3 • **Wrap-up/Assess** (5 minutes)		• WB Online practice Vocabulario 8.1 - 8.9	• Palabra por palabra – Activity 1 (10 minutes) – Activity 2 (10 minutes) – Activity 3 (10 minutes)
DAY 7	• Present the vocabulary needed to practice the communicative and grammatical functions for the unit: identify the seasons	• **Warm-up** (10 minutes) • **Palabra por palabra** (35 minutes) *Y las estaciones del año* – Activity 4 – Activity 5 – Activity 6 • **Wrap-up/Assess** (5 minutes)			

	OBJECTIVES / TOPIC	PRESENT/PRACTICE/COMMUNICATE	ADDITIONAL TEACHER RESOURCES	HOMEWORK	ELETECA ONLINE PRACTICE

DAY 8	• Present the grammatical structures needed to practice communicative function of the unit: talk about future plans
	• Use *ir a* + infinitive
		Warm-up (10 minutes)
		
		• **Gramática** (40 minutes)
		1. *Ir a* + infinitive
		  – Presentation
		  – Activity 1
		  – Activity 2
		  – Activity 3
		  – Activity 4
		  – Activity 5
		
		• **Wrap-up/Assess** (5 minutes)
			• IWB 8.1, 8.2	• WB Online practice: Gramática 8.10 - 8.18	• Grammar tutorials
					• Tutorial 15 (8 minutes)
					• Extra activity (14 minutes)
					• Tutorial 16 (8 minutes)
					• Extra activity 14 minutes)

DAY 9	• Present the communication function: *hay que*, *tener que* and *deber* + infinitive	**Warm-up** (10 minutes)
		
		• **Gramática** (35 minutes)
		2. *Hay que*, *tener que* and *deber* + infinitive
		  – Presentation
		  – Activity 6
		  – Activity 7
		  – Activity 8
		  – Activity 9
		  – Activity 10
		  – Activity 11
		
		• **Wrap-up/Assess** (5 minutes)			

DAY 10	• Written and oral expression
	• Organize key ideas before writing
		• **Warm-up** (10 minutes)
		
		• **Destrezas** (40 minutes)
		Expresión e interacción escritas
		  – Activity 1
		  – Activity 2
		
		• **Wrap-up/Assess** (5 minutes)
				• WB Online practice: Destrezas 8.19 - 8.22	• Destreza lectora (15 minutes)
					• Destreza escrita (15 minutes)
					• Destreza oral (15 minutes)
					• Pronunciación – Activity 1 (10 minutes)

DAY 11	• Practice correct pronunciation: *n* and *ñ*	• **Warm-up** (10 minutes)
		
		• **Pronunciación** (35 minutes)
		  – Presentation
		  – Activity 1 (Audio 83)
		  – Activity 2 (Audio 84)
		
		• **Wrap-up/Assess** (5 minutes)			

DAY 12	• Learn about Paraguay, Uruguay, Argentina, and Chile
	• Learn about extreme climates in South America
	• Compare climate in South America with climate in the U.S.
		• **Warm-up** (5 minutes)
		
		• **Sabor Hispano** (40 minutes)
		Paisajes y climas extremos
		  – Estaciones del sur (audio 85)
		  – Ushuaia: el fin del mundo
		  – ¡*Sandboarding!* en el desierto de Atacama
		
		• **Wrap-up/Assess** (5 minutes)
			• Voces latinas video: *Naturaleza extrema en el Cono Sur*	• WB Online practice: Cultura 8.23 - 8.25	• Voces latinas video: *Naturaleza extrema en el Cono Sur*
					• Extra activity (10 minutes)

DAY 13	• Revisit unit themes, grammar, vocabulary, and culture in a new context	• **Warm-up** (10 minutes)
		
		• **Relato** (35 minutes)
		¿*Quedamos para estudiar?*
		  – Activity 1
		  – Activity 2 (Audio 86)
		
		• **Wrap-up/Assess** (5 minutes)			

	OBJECTIVES / TOPIC	PRESENT/PRACTICE/COMMUNICATE	ADDITIONAL TEACHER RESOURCES	HOMEWORK	ELETECA ONLINE PRACTICE

DAY 14	• Improve reading comprehension skills	• **Warm-up** (10 minutes)
		• **Relato** (35 minutes)
		¿Quedamos para estudiar?
		  – Activity 3
		  – Activity 4
		  – Activity 5
		  – Activity 6
		• **Wrap-up/Assess** (5 minutes)			

DAY 15	• Review unit vocabulary, expressions, and grammar
	• Practice communicative skills
		• **Warm-up** (5 minutes)
		[Option 1]
		• **Evaluación** (35 minutes)
		  – Activities 1-6
		[Option 2]
		• **Casa del español-videos** (35 minutes)
		  – Videos 1 and 2
		  – Extra activities
		• **En resumen** (10 minutes)
		  – Vocabulario
		  – Gramática
					• Evaluación
					• Casa del español vídeos
					  – Video 15
					   (5 minutes)
					  – Extra activity
					   (10 minutes)
					  – Video 16
					   (5 minutes)
					• Extra activity
					  (10 minutes)

DAY 16	• Assessment	• **Warm-up** (5 minutes) • **Online test Unit 8** (30 minutes)	• Unit 8 assessment		
DAY 17	• Gamification project				

DAY 18	• Review grammar, vocabulary, and culture from the last two units
	• Complete self-assessment
		• **Ahora comprueba** (50 minutes)
		  – Activity 1 (Audio 87)
		  – Activity 2
		  – Activity 3
		  – Activity 4
		  – Activity 5
		  – Activity 6 (Audio 88)
		  – Activity 7			